HUMAN MOTIVATION

BERNARD WEINER
University of California, Los Angeles

HOLT, RINEHART AND WINSTON   NEW YORK   CHICAGO   SAN FRANCISCO
ATLANTA   DALLAS   MONTREAL
TORONTO   LONDON   SYDNEY

Copyright © 1980 by Holt, Rinehart and Winston

Library of Congress Catalog Card Number: 78-20731

ISBN: 0-03-055226-5

Printed in the United States of America

Press of W. B. Saunders Company

0123   006   98765432

To my father and in memory of my mother

PREFACE

This book represents a major revision of my earlier work, *Theories of Motivation: From Mechanism to Cognition.* A number of shortcomings in the previous book became increasingly evident to me. First of all, there were serious omissions. Second, there has been much new knowledge since the inception of the prior book, so that it was becoming outdated. And finally, I was dissatisfied with some of the writing, feeling that parts of the book were needlessly complex and that certain topics did not deserve the space that they were allotted.

A revision, therefore, was initiated. I attempted to fill some of the gaps by including chapters on psychoanalytic, social learning, and humanistic theory. Furthermore, other topics that could have been discussed within the outline of *Theories of Motivation* but were neglected are incorporated into the present volume. These topics include, for example, social facilitation, arousal, emotions, personal responsibility, and the irrationality of attributions. In addition to this new material, I updated the ideas examined in *Theories of Motivation.* Little could be altered in the sections on Hullian and Lewinian theory, for these conceptions are no longer undergoing modification. The discussion of these theories was merely shortened and simplified, bringing them more in line with their current influence in psychology. But achievement and attribution theories have changed in the past years—or at least our understanding in these areas has changed—and discussion of these topics was greatly altered.

To document the extent of the alterations that were made, I compared references in this book with those in *Theories of Motivation.* *Theories of Motivation* has about 400 references, while *Human Motivation* has more than 600 references. Of these 600, fewer than 33 per cent were included in the prior book.

The audience for *Human Motivation* is advanced undergraduates and graduate students enrolled in a motivation course. I have assumed some psychological knowledge on the part of the reader. In addition, there is much discussion of material relevant to personality. Hence, the book can be used as either the main or supplementary text in a personality course. The reader will find that although the chapters of *Human Motivation* have traditional titles, the material covered is rather unique.

There are some biases that I do want to acknowledge, lest the reader feel that some pertinent material inadvertently has been omitted. The approach to human motivation taken in this book is aphysiological. That means little mention has been made of the vast physiological literature that considers, for example, hunger, thirst, and sexual motivation. There simply is not room within a single volume to deal with the breadth of this field, and my own approach is to consider more molar (personality and social psychological) aspects of the area. Furthermore, because of my molar orientation, little attention has been paid to infrahuman research and the learning-associationistic approaches to motivation, as exemplified in the writings of Dollard, Miller, Skinner, and others.

This book was written while I was supported by Grant MH25687 from the Public Health Service, National Institute of Mental Health. I am greatly appreciative of its support for the many past years. Many publishers permitted reproduction or quotation of pertinent material. I am especially thankful to those publishers releasing figures and tables without cost, for monetary demands made by some companies are making reproductions virtually impossible. The companies and sources permitting free reproduction were: Holt, Rinehart and Winston, McGraw-Hill, New England Journal of Medicine, Stanford University Press, University of California Press, Van Nostrand, and Wiley.

Finally, Natalia Hamlin and Jane Sugerman aided in many ways, for which I am grateful.

BERNARD WEINER

June, 1979

CONTENTS

Section III
MASTERY AND GROWTH THEORIES

Section IV
CONCLUSION

Chapter One

INTRODUCTION

There are two distinct approaches to the study of motivation. One stratagem is a product of academic, experimental procedures, while the second is an outgrowth of clinical, non-experimental methods. Each of the approaches has unique advantages and disadvantages. But all investigators in this field are guided by a single basic question, namely, *Why do organisms think and behave as they do?*

The Experimental Stratagem

To answer the above question, the dominant experimental stratagem has been to identify the immediate determinants of behavior and then specify the mathematical relations between the variables. In this manner a "model" of behavior is developed. This *ahistorical* approach is guided by the laws of motion developed in the physical sciences. For example, assume that you want to predict the force of attraction of one object toward another. To predict this accurately, you need to know the masses of the objects. These might be considered their "personalities" or stable dispositions. In addition, to predict the force of attraction, you must know some other facts, such as the distance between the two objects. It could then be ascertained through empirical tests that the force of attraction between the objects is, in part, directly related to their masses and inversely related to the square of their separation distance:

$$\text{Force} = \frac{\text{Mass of Object 1} \times \text{Mass of Object 2}}{(\text{Distance between Object 1 and Object 2})^2}$$

Now consider a problem concerned with human attraction. Children are playing in the family room and their parents call them to the kitchen for dinner. A psychologist might want to predict how long it takes the children to leave their ongoing play activities (the *latency* of the response) or how swiftly they come to the dinner table once the approach response has been initiated (the *intensity* of the response).

TABLE 1–1 ADDITIVE RELATION OF DEPRIVATION AND BOREDOM

		Deprivation Level	
		1	2
Boredom	1	2	3
	2	3	4

To do this, the psychologist must identify the determinants of the approach to food and discover their mathematical relations.

Introspection on the part of the reader will readily reveal some of the factors that influence the latency and the intensity of the food-related approach response. For example, it is likely that the longer the time since the children last ate (deprivation level) and the more gluttonous they are (motive for food), the faster will be the speed of approach and the shorter the latency of going to the kitchen. In addition, serving hot dogs rather than spinach (incentive value), being engaged in a boring play activity, fear of parental punishment, and the absence of fatigue are also likely to increase the measured index of motivation.

Ideally, the psychologist would like to develop a model for hunger motivation. This model might take the following form:

$$\text{Hunger motivation} = (\text{Deprivation level} \times \text{Motive for food} \times \text{Incentive value} \times \text{Fear}) + \text{Boredom with current activity} - \text{Fatigue}$$

In sum, the answer to the question of why people behave as they do is given by a mathematical equation that includes all the determinants of an action. Note that the particular history of the children is not needed to predict their response latency or intensity. That is, why they have come to love hot dogs or what has caused their boredom or

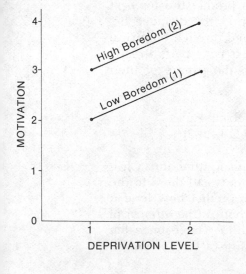

Figure 1–1. Additive relation of deprivation and boredom.

TABLE 1–2   MULTIPLICATIVE RELATION OF DEPRIVATION AND BOREDOM

		Deprivation Level	
		1	2
Boredom	1	1	2
	2	2	4

fatigue is not relevant. What is essential is that the present values of these constructs be known.

Of course, listing all the determinants of a particular action is exceedingly difficult, and specifying their mathematical relations is even more difficult. The problems are especially complex because the units of measurement of the various determinants of behavior are not equivalent. For example, is eight hours of food deprivation equivalent to the incentive value of a steak? This may sound like a facetious question, but it highlights the complications of developing standard units of comparison for factors that are much more disparate than apples and pears.

It is possible, however, to discover whether the components in a motivational model are related additively or multiplicatively. Assume, for example, it is hypothesized that deprivation and boredom are related in an additive manner, as indicated in the previous equation. In Table 1–1 deprivation and boredom are assigned the arbitrary values of one and two. The body of the table shows the total of these values. These totals are plotted in Figure 1–1. Note that the lines in Figure 1–1 are parallel.

On the other hand, if deprivation and boredom are hypothesized to relate multiplicatively, the values are changed, as shown in Table 1–2. When plotted in Figure 1–2, it can be seen that the lines diverge.

Figure 1–2. Multiplicative relation of deprivation and boredom.

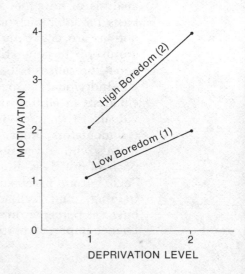

Thus, parallel lines reveal additive relations, while diverging lines indicate a multiplicative relationship between the variables.

To ascertain the relations between components in models, psychologists typically manipulate the strengths of the variables in an experimental setting, and graphs similar to those in Figures 1–1 and 1–2 are generated. Thus, for example, bored and not bored subjects may be deprived of food for four or eight hours and then called to a "food break." The speed or latency of their response is then assessed, and the mathematical relation between boredom and hunger is ascertained.

In sum, the experimental approach to motivation attempts to develop mathematical formulas or models that account for behavior. The models are tested in experimental settings where there is control over the variables under consideration. The observed behaviors provide evidence for the validity of the model. This ahistorical approach typically is used to explain a limited range of phenomena with accuracy.

The Clinical Stratagem

To answer the question of why people behave as they do, psychologists studying motivation from a clinical orientation assert or presume that there are one or more basic principles of behavior, such as "people strive to fulfill their potential" or "people strive to satisfy their aggressive and sexual urges." Then a broad range of clinical, historical, anecdotal, literary, and experimental evidence is marshaled to support this contention. In contrast to the experimental approach, there is little attempt to develop a formal or mathematical model. But there is an endeavor to encompass a wide breadth of phenomena. For example, in the Freudian system, the striving to satisfy sexual and aggressive urges is presumed to be manifested in slips of the tongue, dreams, neurotic behavior, and artistic creativity. Often an historical analysis of how the person has become what he or she is provides a basis for inferences about underlying motivational tendencies. These notions are not really subject to definitive proof or disproof, but they are useful in generating ideas and research and in providing insights about the causes of behavior.

Individuals associated with the clinical stratagem often are psychiatrists or clinical psychologists interested in the adaptation of individuals to their environment. Thus, they also frequently are social commentators about "quality of life" and can become visible public figures who add to our vocabularies and indirectly alter numerous aspects of our lives. For example, concepts such as "id," "defense," and "ego," from psychoanalytic theory, or "self-disclosure," "sensitivity training," and "self-actualization" from humanistic psychology change how we perceive ourselves, how we perceive others, and perhaps influence important portions of our lives.

Plan of the Book

In this book, seven approaches to the problem of motivation are presented, along with related conceptions or ideas. The grouping of the theories is arbitrary. The initial two conceptions presented are Freudian psychoanalytic theory and Hullian drive theory. Although these theories differ greatly because of their respective allegiances to the clinical and experimental stratagems, they are paired because both assume that tension or need reduction is the basic principle of action. In addition, these two theories have dominated the study of motivation and thus are given more space than most of the remaining conceptions.

The second group of three theories includes Lewin's field theory, Atkinson's theory of achievement motivation, and Rotter's theory of social learning. These three are joined because all are expectancy-value theories. That is, behavior is assumed to be a function of the expectancy of goal attainment and the incentive value of the goal. All also adhere to the experimental, model-building stratagem.

Attribution theory and humanistic psychology are the last conceptions to be presented. These approaches differ in a number of fundamental ways, but both assume that humans strive to understand themselves and their environment and that growth processes are inherent to human motivation. Thus, these theories most contrast with the Freudian and Hullian approaches.

Within this list of seven theoretical approaches, the first and last (Freudian and humanistic psychology) most closely follow the clinical stratagem. But the theories can be compared and contrasted in a number of other important respects. For example, Hull and, at times, Freud accepted a mechanical or a materialistic view of humans. Behavior often is interpreted without invoking mental processes or thoughts as explanatory concepts. Rather, humans are considered machines with input (antecedent) and output (consequent) connections that need a source of energy to be "driven." On the other hand, expectancy-value theorists such as Lewin, Atkinson, and Rotter, attribution theorists such as Heider and H. H. Kelley, and humanists such as Maslow, Rogers, and Allport accept a cognitive view of humans. It is contended by these theorists that mental events intervene between input-output relations and that thought influences action. Furthermore, many of these theorists assume that individuals are always active and are not in need of any "motor" to get behavior started. The relation between the mind and the body, or what is known as the Mind-Body Problem, and the necessity of energy concepts to explain human motivation are examined in greater detail in the subsequent chapters.

The research focus of each theory also differs. For example, Freudian theory led to an examination of defense mechanisms, aggression, dreams, and sexual behavior; Hullian drive theory is empirically supported by observations of hungry animals running down a maze for food, or humans receiving an aversive puff of air in the eye; and At-kinson's theory of achievement motivation has most thoroughly exam-ined the choice between achievement-related activities that differ in difficulty level. Thus, each theoretical approach appeals to a particular *reference experiment* or observation to demonstrate its validity. The theories are not *commensurate;* that is, there is not a domain or a behavior at which they all can be compared so that one theory can be judged as "better" or more accurate than the others. Rather, the theories focus upon disparate phenomena and stand side by side with their unique ability to account for certain observations. There is not a hierarchical ordering of "Truth," although there are occasions when two or three of the theories can be compared with respect to a certain observation.

The theories presented in this book were, for the most part, for-mulated by clinical psychologists and psychiatrists. Individuals such as Freud, Rotter, Maslow, Rogers, Allport, and G. Kelly form the heart of many textbooks in the field of personality. These theories, in vary-ing degrees, focus upon the person and intra-psychic influences on action. This does not imply that the environment or the social context of behavior is neglected, for such a neglect would make predictions of human action impossible. Rather, situational and social factors are rec-ognized, but they frequently are not the center of attention.

It is increasingly evident, however, that we are social animals and that the study of motivation must be broadened to include social con-cerns. Thus, this book examines topics related to social behavior, such as altruism, cognitive balance, competition and cooperation, group for-mation, and social facilitation, to name just a few topics of concern.

Summary

There are two basic approaches to the study of motivation: experimental and clinical. The former attempts to develop mathematical models that account for limited aspects of behavior, while the latter posits psychologi-cal axioms that are pertinent to a diverse range of action. But even within these stratagems, the theories that have been developed differ in the phenomena that they examine. Thus, conceptions of motivation typically are not commensurate and one cannot be judged as "better" than the others. Nevertheless, all the theories are guided by the same underlying question, namely, *Why do organisms behave as they do?*

Section I

Need Reduction Theories

Chapter Two

THE PSYCHOANALYTIC THEORY OF MOTIVATION

Introduction

Freud's psychoanalytic theory offers the most general and well-known conception of the dynamics of motivation. This conception is so vast that it is meaningless to ask whether it is "correct" or "incorrect." Rather, some aspects of the theory have been shown to have reasonable validity, other facets have no empirical support at all, and still other propositions are beyond empirical test. In this chapter Freud's theory of motivation and subsequent modifications introduced by "ego psychologists" are presented. Conceptions devised by other theorists such as Adler, Jung, and Rank are ignored inasmuch as these have had less impact than Freud's ideas and the motivational aspects of these theories are not as clearly formulated.

Following a description of the psychoanalytic approach, seven areas of research pertinent to Freud's conception are briefly exam ned. The research topics are instincts, aggression and catharsis, sexual behavior, dreams, defense mechanisms, delay of gratification, and cognitive styles. The first four of these areas (instincts, aggression, sex, and dreams) primarily pertain to id functioning, while the next grouping (defense, delay of gratification, and cognitive styles) concerns ego-mediated states and processes.

BASIC PRINCIPLES OF FREUD'S THEORY

Homeostasis and Hedonism

It is useful to consider Freud's theory within the context of a biological and survival model. Given this viewpoint, which borrows much from Darwin, individuals are conceived as striving to satisfy personal needs within a world of limited and restricted resources. To satisfy these needs, behaviors must be undertaken that will lead to the desired goals. Virtually all such goals are located in the external

SIGMUND FREUD

(Culver Pictures, Inc., New York)

Sigmund Freud was born in Frieberg, Moravia, on May 6, 1856, and died in London on September 23, 1939. The vast majority of his life was spent in Vienna; he left that city only when the Nazis invaded Austria in 1938. Freud started his scientific career as a neurologist and quickly established a reputation for his neurological research and medical investigations. This work was conducted despite grave financial difficulties that even forced a temporary postponement of his marriage.

During 1885 Freud traveled to Paris to study hypnosis and the alleviation of hysteria with Jean Charcot. However, he found hypnosis an unsatisfactory method and began to use a treatment technique developed by Joseph Breuer in which patients were cured by talking about their symptoms. In 1895 Freud and Breuer published *Studies in Hysteria,* which contained Freud's first ideas about the unconscious.

The self-report and introspective data that Freud collected led him to concentrate increasingly on sexual conflicts as the cause of hysteria. Thereafter, Freud and Breuer parted ways, and Freud worked alone to develop startling and original ideas about psychosexual development, the Oedipus complex, dreams, the unconscious, and a wealth of other psychological processes and phenomena.

Freud surrounded himself with a group of disciples, including Jung from Switzerland and Adler from Austria. But often his interpersonal relationships were stormy and friendships were aborted. His fascinating life included his own psychoanalysis, years of addiction to cocaine, cancer of the jaw, and an invitation to Clark University in 1909 that paved the way for his acceptance after a long period of scientific ostracism.

There are a number of reasons why Freud was not accepted by the scientific community. He did not communicate with other scientists, having virtually no academic

world. Thus, the individual must adapt to, and function within, the world at hand.

For example, consider a psychological analysis of how behavior is governed by the need for food. All organisms have a biological need to ingest food. This need makes itself known to the organism by causing discomfort. There is a limited supply of food in the external world, and organisms must compete for these resources. After the individual engages in the appropriate activities and eats, the internal stimulation and pain (e.g., hunger cramps) that accompany food deprivation cease. The organism then feels satisfied and remains in an unmotivated state or at rest until the onset of new hunger pains. These follow a cyclical pattern, again generating food-relevant behavior.

Two central concepts guided the above analysis: *homeostasis* and

(Courtesy of National Library of Medicine)

(The Bettmann Archive, Inc.)

correspondence. Furthermore, he did not present carefully accumulated evidence to support his ideas and gathered his "data" in a mysterious and secret atmosphere that was closed to all but his patients. And finally, Freud came from an unknown, Jewish family at a time of religious discrimination. Thus, his theory initially met with a very negative reception from other scientists. For a fuller discussion of Freud's life and his difficulties in gaining acceptance, see Jones (1953–1957) and Shakow and Rapaport (1964).

It is of interest to note that Freud is part of a continuing trend of thought that relegates humans to a lower status level. First, Copernicus took the Earth and its inhabitants from the center of the universe; then Darwin argued that humans are not unique; finally, Freud contended that individuals are irrational and not even aware of their own motivations. Perhaps the next step, which is already taking place, will be to find that inanimate objects can be made that are more intelligent than their makers.

hedonism. Homeostasis refers to the "tendency toward the maintenance of a relatively stable internal environment." That is, there is a propensity for the organism to remain in a state of internal equilibrium. If, for example, there is a condition of deprivation because food is absent, then a state of disequilibrium exists. Food-related actions, therefore, are initiated to return the organism to equilibrium, or balance. This conception is most closely linked with ideas of Walter Cannon (1932), the English physiologist who worked in the early and mid 1900's. *Hedonism,* a utilitarian doctrine associated with the philosopher Jeremy Bentham (1779), asserts that pleasure and happiness are the chief goals in life. If homeostasis is the governing principle of behavior, then pleasure is the result or the by-product of being in a state of equilibrium, where all one's goals are gratified.

Freud accepted the doctrine of hedonism and the principle of homeostasis. For Freud, the satisfied individual typically is not in pursuit of any stimulation, for activity indicates dissatisfaction. On the contrary, nirvana is the absence of tension or need and is accompanied by quiescence. One logical extension of this position is Freud's postulation of a "death instinct" or "death wish," for in death there are no unsatisfied desires. This is similar to the alleged wish to "return to the womb," where all needs are fulfilled and we are completely under the benevolent care of another.

Psychological Energy

It was indicated above that Walter Cannon (homeostasis), Jeremy Bentham (hedonism), and Charles Darwin (survival model) are associated with Freud's thinking. In addition, Freud was influenced by Hermann von Helmholz, the German physicist who argued that physiological events could be explained with mechanical principles from physics and chemistry. Freud contended that all psychological work (e.g., both attaining food and just thinking about it) requires the use of energy. Three energy-related concepts are especially pertinent to his explanation of human behavior: conservation of energy, entropy, and a distinction between kinetic and potential energy.

Freud conceived of humans as closed energy systems. That is, there is a constant amount of energy for any given individual. This idea was derived from the principle of the conservation of energy proposed by Helmholz in 1847, which states that energy is neither created nor destroyed. One corollary of this law is that if energy is spent performing one function, then it is unavailable for other functions.

Entropy refers to the amount of energy that is not available for doing work. According to Freud, some energy is kinetic, or bound. Such bound energy is referred to as "cathected." A cathexis (from the Greek "kathexo," meaning "to occupy") involves an attachment to some object that is desired but has not been attained. The attachment, or cathexis, does not mean that energy literally leaves the person. Rather, there is a feeling of longing for the object and there are repeated thoughts, images, and fantasies about him or her. A cathexis may be only temporary, for if the desired goal is attained, then there is a freeing of the energy. As a result, the bound energy is transformed into free (potential) energy that is now available for use in other functions. If all one's desires are fulfilled, then all energy is free. Thus, energy distribution is related to happiness.

Consider how Freud might analyze the situation in which a loved one must go away for a period of time. Because that person is no longer available as a need satisfier, he or she becomes an object of cathexis. Energy is now bound and the unsatisfied individual might fantasize about being with the loved one, daydream of their reunion, and so forth. The binding of energy is unpleasant, indicating that needs have not been fulfilled. In addition, the energy is not available for other activities. The individual might therefore experience a lack of interest in other friends and hobbies. When the longed-for person returns, then (ideally) needs are again satisfied, the cathected energy is freed to do other work, and there is a state of subjective pleasure. Note how closely the concepts of homeostasis, hedonism, and energy are linked in Freud's theory.

Psychological Determinism

Psychological or psychic determinism refers to the axiom that thoughts and actions have causes. Freud carried this principle to its extreme, stating that *all* psychological events are caused and therefore can be explained. This is an optimistic position and provides the foundation needed for scientific prediction, for if events are caused, then they can be predicted. Yet Freud did not predict events; he *postdicted* behavior. That is, instead of prophesying the future, he interpreted the past. He began his scientific quest with an already neurotic person and then attempted to discover what caused this situation.

Having a postdictive theory is not necessarily a shortcoming, for it often is considered just as important to be able to explain the past as it is to be able to predict the future. Darwin's theory is not criticized for being postdictive, i.e., explaining how humans evolved. But postdiction carries built-in dangers: One must be wary of explanations that are just "made up" to fit the known facts, and have little bearing on the overall formal theory.

HUMOR, SLIPS OF THE TONGUE, AND DREAMS. Freud applied the principle of determinism to pathological phenomena, such as hysteria and obsessions, and to normal actions that had not been subject to systematic psychological analysis before his conception. Three *apparently* different aspects of normal behavior—humor, slips of the tongue, and dreams—were singled out by Freud for special attention. According to Freud, all three behaviors serve the same function — vicariously gratifying a forbidden impulse or an unfulfilled wish. That is, they are hidden methods of tension reduction.

Consider, for example, the following joke:

> Standing on a golf course green, one golfer is vigorously choking another to death. A third party arrives on the scene and casually says to the aggressor: "Excuse me, but your grip's all wrong."

Freud believed that such a joke evokes laughter because unconscious aggressive urges are being satisfied. Expression of these desires is typically prevented. However, they can find an outlet through the socially acceptable form of a joke. In addition, "a good joke needs a listener; its aim is not only to bypass a prohibition, but also to implicate the listener via laughter, to make the laughing listener an accomplice and, thereby, as it were, *socialize* the transgression" (Volosinov, 1976, pp. 58–9).

In a similar manner, mental lapses, such as slips of the tongue and forgetting, also have psychological determinants.

An error of this sort is said once to have crept into a Social-Democratic newspaper, where, in the account of a festivity, the following words were printed: "Amongst those present was His Highness, the Clown Prince." The next day a correction was attempted. The paper apologized and said: "The sentence should of course have read, the Crow Prince." Again, in a war-correspondent's account of meeting a famous general whose infirmities were pretty well-known, a reference to the general was printed as "this battle-scared veteran." Next day an apology appeared which read "the words of course should have been, the bottle-scarred veteran"! (Freud, 1915, p. 35)

Dreams also are wish fulfillments, or at least attempts at wish fulfillment, having their origin in sexual and aggressive impulses. Freud argued that the true meaning of the dream, or its *latent* content, often is masked. The *manifest* content of the dream, or what the dreamer reports, typically is a distortion of the "real" dream contents. However, Freud believed that with proper analyses the latent meaning of the dream could be uncovered. He therefore thought that the dream provided the "royal road" to the unconscious. Freud also stated that the vicarious satisfaction provided by the dream has the function of preserving sleep. He thought that in the absence of dreams, unpleasant impulses would disturb and waken the sleeper (see pp. 60–63 for research related to the dream state).

The Structure of Personality

According to Freud, there are three components or parts of personality: the id, the ego, and the super-ego. These structures have specific and unique functions as well as distinct processes by which they operate. The id, ego, and super-ego are not parts of the person to be found somewhere in the brain or in the body. Rather, they are constructs that represent interacting, hypothetical structures. They were proposed by Freud to explain the observation that behaviors typically result from compromises involving desires, the restrictions placed by the environment, and internalized moral values. In other words, behaviors are governed by needs, rationality, and ideals.

The Id

The id is conceived by Freud to be the first system within the person. It is most intimately related to the biological inheritance of sexual and aggressive drives. The individual is unaware of the existence of many of these inborn drive states. Hence, the contents of the id are primarily unconscious (see Figure 2–1).

The id is the reservoir of all psychological energy (also termed "libido," the Latin for "lust"). The availability of this energy allows the id to be directly responsive to bodily needs. Internal bodily tension cannot be tolerated by the id, which functions to discharge it immediately. Thus, the id operates according to the pleasure principle, or the doctrine of hedonism. Immediate pleasure is sought, and this is accomplished through homeostatic processes and tension reduction.

Now, how can the id accomplish its goals? First of all, it has the command of reflexive processes. For example, consider the infant with hunger pains. The reflexive response to this need is sucking. Given appropriate environmental stimulation, such as a breast or bottle, this reflexive behavior. discharges hunger needs, producing a pleasurable state and sleep.

The id has another process to aid in the service of the pleasure principle, one that is less immediately evident. Id functioning is characterized by "primary process" thinking. This mode of thought is perhaps best known to us through our personal dream experiences. Primary process thought is illogical and timeless, and reality is not distinguished from irreality. Hallucinations, for example, are not distinguished from actual occurrences. Thus, in the absence of external goal gratification, the id can call upon internal mental acts, such as hallucinations, to fulfill its wishes. The infant, according to Freud, can imagine that it is ingesting milk to reduce tension. In a similar manner, extensions of this theory suggest we might dream about great accomplishments and temporarily fulfill some of our achievement desires.

The Ego

It is evident that for survival organisms must learn to differentiate between milk and the idea or image of milk. That is, fantasy must be distinguished from reality. The id, inasmuch as it follows the rules of primary process thinking, is unable to make this distinction. In addition, at times immediate goal gratification will lead to more pain than pleasure, as in the case of a sexual or aggressive action that later is punished by society. Because the id seeks immediate satisfaction, gratification is not delayed. To meet the problems of discrimination and the necessity of delay, a new structure is created out of the id that can come to terms with the objective world. This structure is the ego.

The ego is governed by the "reality principle" rather than the pleasure principle. But this does not mean that hedonism is given up. Rather, the ego serves the id in its pursuit of pleasure and tension

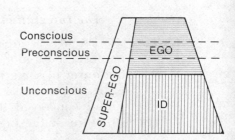

Figure 2–1. The relationship of the personality structures to the levels of awareness.

reduction, taking into account the demands of reality. The ego follows the rules of "secondary process" thought. This is adult thinking characterized by logic, time orientation, and a distinction between reality and irreality. The ego also has the tools of memory and attention and the control of motor activity. Thus, its existence provides a means for delay of gratification, long-term goal planning, and so on.

The contents of the ego are primarily conscious (see Figure 2–1). However, the person is not aware of all aspects of ego functioning. The ego includes the mechanisms of defense, such as repression, which protect the individual from psychic pain. The defenses, which generally are not part of the conscious experience of the person, are examined more fully later in this chapter. Furthermore, most prior experience is preconscious, i.e., not in consciousness but readily available to us from memory storage.

The Super-Ego

According to Freud, the last of the three structures to develop is the super-ego. The super-ego has two main functions, both based on built-in reinforcement processes: 1) to reward individuals for acceptable moral behavior and 2) to punish actions that are not socially sanctioned by creating guilt. The super-ego thus represents the internalization of moral codes and is often called one's "conscience." The super-ego opposes the expression of unacceptable impulses rather than merely postponing them as does the ego.

Freud contended that the development of the super-ego occurs when the child identifies with the same-sex parent. In so doing, moral values become internalized, appropriate sex-role behaviors are undertaken, and the conflict with the same-sex parent for the affection of the opposite-sex parent (the Oedipal situation) is resolved. The analysis of the resolution of the Oedipal conflict led to the detection of the universality of the incest taboo, which is considered to be one of the major discoveries in the social sciences. (More will be said about this topic later in the chapter). Because the id and the super-ego are represented in the unconscious, "a normal human being is far more immoral than he himself believes ... and far more moral than he knows" (Volosinov, 1976, p. 46).

The Integration of the Structures

Freud was greatly influenced by his training in neurology, where he observed a hierarchical ordering of neural structures. For example, the onset of some neural firings can inhibit the onset of other neural firings. In a similar manner, the ego can inhibit the strivings of the id. Freud conceived the ego to be the executive agency or "highest" structure of the person, responsible for final behavioral decisions. In

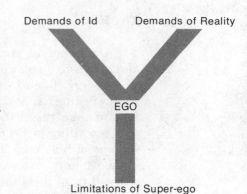

Figure 2–2.   The ego as the mediator of behavior.

this capacity it must satisfy the constant demands of the id and pacify the ideals of the super-ego, while being bound by the constraints of reality (see Figure 2–2).

As Freud said:

> The ego, driven by the id, confined by the super-ego, repulsed by reality, struggles to master its economic task of bringing about harmony among the forces and influences working in and upon it; we can understand how it is that so often we cannot suppress a cry: "Life is not easy." (Freud, 1933, p. 78)

The Role of Personality Structures in the Dynamics of Behavior

Freud directly related homeostasis and hedonism to the structure of personality. First of all, the energy needed for behavior resides within the id, which is directly responsive to bodily needs. The ego, however, as the "higher" structure, has the power to prevent immediate gratification. If goal attainment will lead to more pain than pleasure, the ego establishes a "counter-cathexis." The counter-cathexis, the force opposing goal satisfaction, takes the form of a psychological defense or a defense mechanism. The defense might be, for example, repression, which banishes the threatening wish from consciousness so that the wish is not directly acted upon by the individual. The defense might be manifested as a neurotic symptom such as hysterical blindness, which also prevents the person from reaching the desired goal. The existence of a conflict between an id cathexis and a counter-cathexis established by the ego is the heart of Freud's model of motivated behavior. Freud viewed the person as in a state of continuous conflict between personal desires and the demands of society. Such conflicts, according to Freud, provide the foundation for the development of neurosis.

The Instincts

A number of concepts essential to Freud's theory of motivation already have been introduced, including hedonism and homeostasis; free energy, bound energy, and a closed energy system; cathexis and counter-cathexis; and id, ego, and super-ego. But one of his most important concepts, *instinct*, remains to be discussed.

According to Freud, the instincts, or drives, are appetitive internal sources of behavior. They are appetitive because they are directed toward, rather than away from, objects; internal because they are derived from metabolic and somatic processes; and sources of behavior because the instincts propel behavior or drive the organism. Furthermore, instincts have an aim (i.e., to be satisfied) and are linked with an object that functions as a satisfier.

An instinct corresponds to a bodily need. However, instincts do not instigate a merely mechanical process. Rather, instincts are represented mentally as wishes or desires. Thus, Freud contended that an instinct is a "measure of demand made upon the mind for work."

Freud did not attempt to derive a definitive list of instincts, and he vacillated in his position, at times postulating one, and at other times two, basic instincts. Initially he suggested that there were two classes of instincts: those in service of the preservation of life (hunger) and those directed toward the attainment of pleasure (sex). After puberty sexual pleasure becomes centered in the genital organs. Thus, the sexual instincts also are related to the preservation of the species.

Subsequently, Freud revised this scheme and postulated that the internally directed libidinal energy (hunger) and its external counterpart (love) should not be separate. The reason for this change was his belief that when libido is withdrawn from the external world, as in schizophrenia, it becomes more focused on the self (narcissism). Because of the reciprocal relationship between external and internal object cathexis, Freud concluded that there is only one primary source of instincts, and this leads to both the preservation of the self and the preservation of the species.

Later, Freud again returned to a dualistic position regarding the instincts. Dichotomies or dualisms are more in keeping with Freud's general theory because of his conflict-ridden conception of human nature. Freud suggested that in addition to libidinal or life energy, there is a death instinct. This notion has been accepted by very few psychoanalysts, and thus it is of interest to trace Freud's thinking and discover what led him to this rather startling idea (see Monte, 1977).

In Freud's observations of children he noted a tendency for them to repeat disappearance-return games such as peek-a-boo. This apparently involves the repetition of an unpleasant event (the disappearance of a desired object). Freud felt that by reworking or reliving painful events, and attempting to control them, individuals eventually come to master their environments.

In a similar manner, many repetitions of traumatic events in dreams have been reported. Likewise, according to Freud, when a patient reacts to a therapist as though the therapist were his or her parent (transference), a prior significant and unpleasant experience is being relived.

Because of the apparent compulsion to repeat unpleasant experiences, Freud contended that there is something "beyond the pleasure principle" — something that is in direct opposition to it. In addition, Freud also believed that the instincts operate to return the organism to an earlier state, one that was free of stimulation. This would revert the organism to a state of equilibrium, which is the goal being sought. Hence, Freud concluded that "the aim of all life is death" (Freud, 1920, p. 38).

Guided by these ideas, Freud postulated the existence of two instincts: Eros (love), which includes the preservation tendencies, and Thanatos (the name of the Greek goddess of death). He contended that aggressiveness is one manifestation of the death instinct and that it is self-destructiveness turned outward rather than upon oneself. Thus, aggression is an inherited, although displaced, urge. This point will be examined in detail later in this chapter.

The idea of instincts seems far removed from any discussion of observable behavior. But Freud believed that there are certain phenomena that cannot be explained without invoking a concept akin to an instinct or an internal driving state. He wanted to account for irrational ideas and pathological behavior; activities that individuals experience as beyond their personal control, such as compulsions and obsessions; and phenomena such as dreams that "spontaneously" emerge without any external instigating stimulus. The instincts or driving forces can account for these behaviors because of their special properties and characteristics. According to Freud, instincts are preemptory. That is, they do not have a "take-it-or-leave-it" quality. Furthermore, instincts are cyclical, falling in intensity after goal attainment and progressively rising again with the passage of time. And although instincts are selective and directed toward the attainment of certain objects, they also are displaceable, and there are many potential substitutes for a desired object that is absent or unavailable because of social restrictions.

Formal Models of Thought and Action

With this background in mind we are now ready to examine more closely Freud's formal models of behavior. Recall that all behavior is instigated by, and derived from, instinctual (id) wishes. These wishes are represented in the mind as demands made on the body, and they instigate actions that reduce the instinctual urges. As already intimated, a wish is conceptualized as cathected or bound energy; this energy, or libido, is freed when the desired goal is attained.

The empirical or observational base of this theory is the restlessness that is displayed by hungry infants, and their subsequent quiescence when the breast or bottle is reached:

restlessness $\longrightarrow$ sucking at breast $\longrightarrow$ quiescence

On the theoretical level, this behavioral sequence is conceptualized as:

cathexis $\longrightarrow$ action on object $\longrightarrow$ discharged cathexis; or
drive $\longrightarrow$ drive action $\longrightarrow$ gratification; or
pain $\longrightarrow$ behavior $\longrightarrow$ pleasure

The observational and theoretical analyses depicted above pertain to what is known as Freud's "primary model of action" and are based on the pleasure-pain, or hedonic, principle. This motivational model does not account for thought processes and represents "actions motivated by basic drives without the intervention of psychic structures" (Rapaport, 1959, p. 71). It is therefore a "reflex arc" model, or a model of a driven machine with input-output or antecedent-consequent relations.

Freud posits three other simple models of motivated behavior in addition to the primary model of action. One is called the primary model of thought. Thoughts, as overt behavior, are initiated by an instinctual desire or a wish. However, in this case, the object that will satisfy the wish is absent or unavailable. Gratification can then occur by remembering past experiences with the satisfying object and hallucinating that such experiences again are occurring:

cathexis $\longrightarrow$ absence of drive object $\longrightarrow$ hallucinatory idea

A hallucinatory idea is an example of primary process thinking. As previously discussed, primary process thoughts do not distinguish reality from irreality. Thus, internal mental processes may serve as a means of gratification. All thoughts governed by primary processes, such as dreams, are therefore wish-fulfillments, and *all* cognitive processes are derived from basic needs. This means that thoughts serve to satisfy aggressive or sexual urges.

Freud's primary models of thought and action coordinate drives, or instinctual wishes, with immediate expression. There are no intervening processes (ego functions) that aid the organism in its adaptation to the environment. However, Freud noted that at times immediate gratification may result in more pain than pleasure. Therefore, the ego intervenes between the driving instinctual stimuli and the behavior, imposing delays and altering the direction of behavior. The ego serves the id by attaining the maximum resultant pleasure for the person. The so-called "secondary model of action" includes these delay mechanisms:

TABLE 2-1   FREUD'S MODELS OF MOTIVATION

	Action	Thought
Primary	id — activity — satisfaction	id — object absent — hallucination — satisfaction
	"reflex arc"	fantasy behavior as a wish fulfillment
Secondary	id — ego — delay behavior — satisfaction	id — ego — plans — satisfaction
	ego prevents immediate expression	cognitions aid goal attainment

cathexis $\longrightarrow$ delay of gratification $\longrightarrow$ detour activity $\longrightarrow$ gratification

In a similar manner, Freud also has outlined a secondary model of thought:

cathexis $\longrightarrow$ drive object absent $\longrightarrow$ delay, with thoughts given to anticipation and plans for reaching the goal objective.

The four motivational models proposed by Freud are outlined in Table 2-1. The difference between the primary and secondary models is that only in the secondary models does the ego intervene between the onset of the wish and expression. The differentiating feature between action and thought models, as the labels indicate, is that action models deal with overt behavior, while the thought models consider mental events or cognitions directed toward attainment of the goal.

Summary: Freud's Theory

A specific example will help clarify Freud's view of motivation as well as review some of the complex material presented in the preceding pages. Assume that an individual has 40 units of id energy, or libido. Freud did not discuss this issue in detail, but it can be presumed that the amount of libidinal energy one has remains constant throughout life and that persons differ in their supply of libido. The individual is completely satisfied, with no unfulfilled needs or wishes. But because of the cyclical nature of the instincts, after a certain period of time aggressive or sexual urges make demands on the individual for satisfaction.

Let us also assume that there exist objects in the external environment, such as father and mother, that can satisfy these urges. The appropriate external object then becomes "cathected." If the cathected object binds five units of energy, reflecting the strength or intensity of the instinctual wish, then 35 units of energy remain unbound and free for use. The subsequent attainment of the goal object through reflex action or other overt behavior (i.e., a manifestation of the primary action model) dissipates the cathexis so that again there are 40 units of free energy available; the individual is thus returned to a satisfied state.

It may be, however, that attainment of the desired object will result in greater overall pain than pleasure. If this is the case, then the ego establishes a counter-cathexis that prevents immediate goal attainment. The counter-cathexis takes the form of a defense, such as repression or denial, that inhibits the undesirable wish from entering consciousness. As with any psychic reaction, the counter-cathexis also requires energy to maintain itself. Let us assume that the counter-cathexis binds five units of energy so that it is equal in force but opposite in direction to the cathexis. Now the individual is in a state of conflict (cathexis versus counter-cathexis) with ten of its 40 units of energy bound and unavailable for use. This leaves less energy available for action upon other goals and for plans and thoughts.

If the ego is doing an effective job, then alternative goals are selected, plans are made, and so on to aid the id in its goal of reducing the internal need state. Attaining partial satisfaction via a substitute goal object or a modulated response (e.g., hiding the newspaper instead of hitting father), which represents the secondary model of action, will release some of the cathected and counter-cathected energy. But if the ego is "weak," then a potentiality for neurotic-type behavior is established, for an inadequate method of coping with stress and fulfilling wishes is likely to be selected. An inappropriate method, for example, could be the development of a neurotic symptom such as an arm paralysis. This symptom might gain attention and affection from a loved one or even serve as a miniature aggressive response (these benefits are called the "secondary gains" of a symptom). But in the long run symptom formation is an ineffective and inadequate means of tension reduction.

This example highlights some of the basic principles and assumptions of Freud's theory of the dynamics of behavior:
1. The subject matter of psychoanalytic theory is thought and behavior, both normal and pathological.
2. The foundation for the explanation of overt and covert action is a belief in psychological determinism.
3. Behavior is "overdetermined." That is, behavior has conscious and unconscious components, and id, ego, and super-ego determinants.
4. All behavior is ultimately drive determined, with the crucial determinants of behavior being unconscious.
5. All behavior disposes of psychological energy and is regulated by it. There is a basic tendency toward drive reduction, which is pleasurable.

6. The ego prevents immediate goal gratification, is responsible for the inhibition of action, and can control the id.

7. Behavior is socially determined and governed by reality, for both the social norms that inhibit action and the objects of the instincts typically exist in the external environment.

Scientific Method

The scientific procedure followed by Freud is certainly a far cry from the conditioning laboratory of Pavlov or the Skinner box. Nonetheless, Freud was well acquainted with the scientific method, having previously been trained in neurology and medicine. Indeed, he believed that his methods paralleled those of other experimentalists. He would set forth a hypothesis, collect relevant data by observation of his therapeutic patients, and then alter his ideas to fit the new data. Therapeutic sessions were the "microscope" that enabled Freud to uncover the pertinent evidence. Freud believed that proper tests of his theory could be conducted only during psychoanalytic treatment; no other validation was needed. His method therefore can be described as primarily *dialectic*, i.e., he arrived at "Truth" through a critical and logical examination of the arguments and issues.

Freud was unimpressed by the demonstrative or experimental procedures used by psychologists in their search to understand the dynamics of behavior. When an American experimental psychologist (Saul Rosenzweig) apparently demonstrated the existence of repression in a laboratory study, Freud wrote:

> I have examined your experimental studies for the verification of the psychoanalytic assertions with interest. I cannot put much value on these confirmations because the wealth of reliable observations on which these assertions rest make them independent of experimental verification. Still, it [experimental verification] can do no harm. [Figure 2–3]

In spite of this statement, it was an *experimental* demonstration that perhaps first convinced Freud of the existence of the unconscious. When still early in his career Freud observed an hypnosis experiment conducted by Bernheim. A woman patient was given the posthypnotic suggestion that, after waking, she should walk to the corner of the room and open an umbrella. Upon awakening, and after the designated time had elapsed, she did exactly that. When questioned about the reason for her action, she stated that she wanted to determine whether the umbrella was hers. On the basis of this demonstration, Freud reached two essential conclusions: First, "for all its subjective sincerity, the conscious does not always supply a motivation corresponding to the real reasons for an act," and second, "an act can

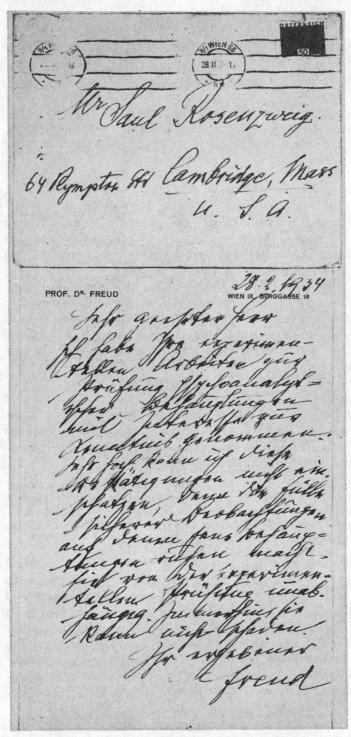

Figure 2–3. (Sigmund Freud Copyrights Ltd., London.)

sometimes be determined by forces that operate in the psyche but do not reach the conscious" (Volosinov, 1976, pp. 32–3).

In addition, Freud examined other diverse sources of evidence to test his theory and his belief in unconscious determinants of behavior. Hogan (1976) identified eight behaviors that Freud considered valid indicators of unconscious motivations:

1. Free associations. These are the products of typical psychoanalytic techniques that require the person to say whatever comes into his or her mind.
2. Resistances. Areas of resistance in part encompass topics that the individual is unwilling to discuss. Frequently, however, resistance is inferred from an obvious interpretation of a behavior that an individual is unwilling to accept.
3. Patterns of dislikes. Freud noted that people often object to attitudes or characteristics that they themselves possess. This behavior is captured by the defense mechanism of "reaction formation," which theoretically can reverse an affect, such as love, into its opposite, hate. It is often suggested, for example, that individuals who lead crusades against pornography and spend a great deal of time reading and viewing pornographic material have strong unconscious approach motivations toward such literature.
4. Life patterns. Recurring themes in a person's life may reveal unconscious desires. For example, repeated school or marriage failures, alcoholism, drug addiction, and similar experiences may indicate underlying urges of which the individual is unaware.
5. Jokes and errors, as previously discussed.
6. Dreams, as also previously discussed.
7. Neurotic symptoms. Freud contended that such behaviors are expressions of unconscious forces that have been denied fulfillment.
8. Works of art. Artistic creations are also supposed to reveal the artist's unconscious desires.

The Formation of Culture

It is evident from the prior discussion that Freud conceived of the person as basically antisocial. Individuals are considered egocentric and naturally selfish, striving to satisfy sexual and aggressive urges to reduce biological tensions. Why, Freud asked, should one love thy neighbor, when this is unnatural and an unreasonable demand? Thus, civilization is an intrusion, preventing the free expression of the instincts. For organized society to exist, the individual must transform sexual and aggressive urges into expressions that do not harm, or actually benefit, society. For example, Freud believed that great artists such as da Vinci and Michelangelo had unfulfilled sexual urges toward their mothers. Their id desires were sublimated and expressed in artistic achievements. But the psychic costs of such transformations are great. Neurosis, Freud claimed, is the result of inhibited instinctive expression and is the price that one must pay for the benefit of living in society.

Ego Psychology

One of the most prominent features of Freud's theory was that it was always in flux. Throughout his 40 years of active work, Freud's conceptual scheme underwent continual modification. Following his death in 1939, his adherents pursued further changes. Today, the importance of sexual and aggressive drives is still stressed by psychoanalysts. But there is now greater emphasis upon how one copes with these needs or adapts to stressful situations. This change is very evident in psychotherapeutic procedures. In earlier years the focus of psychotherapy was upon dreams and free associations, phenomena that occurred when the ego was "less vigilant," allowing the basic drives to be uncovered and come into consciousness. But now many therapists examine the choices that individuals are making and their strategies for dealing with anxiety and stress. That is, the ego and learning processes, rather than the id and instinctual impulses, are focal.

The transition point at which the ego and cognitive factors began to play a more central role in Freud's theory came in 1926 with the publication of *The Problem of Anxiety*. There Freud proposed that his "repression produces anxiety" sequence be reversed to the now famous "anxiety produces repression." Originally Freud argued that anxiety is the result of undischarged libidinal energy. The absence of wished-for objects or a lack of gratification because of repression was believed to result in an accumulation of drive energy. The binding of this energy resulted in an affective (anxiety) discharge. Anxiety therefore was considered a product of the id. However, in reversing this sequence to "anxiety produces repression," Freud converted anxiety to an ego, rather than an id, derivative. Freud contended that when drive expression may lead to more pain than pleasure, the ego "inoculates itself" with anxiety. This anxiety serves as a cue or warning that, if the organism engages in the expected activity, the ego will experience a greater, and perhaps uncontrollable, amount of the anxiety it has just felt in mitigated form. Hence, action is initiated (defenses are activated) that interfere with and delay drive expression. Freud thus reconceptualized anxiety as a cognitive signal rather than an affective id discharge.

Subsequent theoretical analysis also suggested that the ego be given its own source of energy, rather than developing out of energy "borrowed" from the id (see Hartmann, Kris, & Lowenstein, 1946). The reason for this change was to overcome an apparent flaw in the logic of psychoanalytic theory. Recall that the id operates according to the principle of primary process thought and cannot distinguish reality from irreality. Furthermore, the ego is supposedly created by the id to advance its aims. But if the id cannot distinguish reality from irreality, and if hallucinations have the same wish-fulfilling characteristics as real actions, then how does the id "know" that it needs a structure that will have greater contact with reality and will better serve its desires? There is a contradiction between the irrationality of the id and the development of the ego. For this reason, so-called "ego" psychologists contend that the ego should have its own source of energy. This permits psychoanalytic theorists to accept the idea that there are thoughts and actions that do not serve id drives or reduce stimulation. That is, we can be curious, read, think, and ride roller coasters for reasons other than sexual or aggressive fulfillment.

General Evaluation

What, then, can we conclude about Freud's theory of motivation? As was stated at the beginning of the chapter, it is useless to ask if the theory is "correct" or "incorrect." Some of the ideas and concepts, such as defense mechanisms, have led to a great deal of research and have gained general acceptance. Other concepts, such as the death instinct or the postulation of a closed energy system, have generated no research and have few adherents. In general, the theory provides a new language with which to examine human action. It is therefore a most important first step toward the development of a theory of motivation, a step that provides the foundation for further work. But it also is only a first step, with many shortcomings. The theory is often vague and without empirical support; it overemphasizes various facets of human behavior while neglecting others; it often leads to false interpretations and unwarranted generalizations.

There is a tendency to ask too much of this theory, to expect it to explain why we engage in sports, why we are doing poorly in our interpersonal relationships, and why war has occurred. At this time, it is not possible for any theory to account for such a diversity of phenomena with any degree of accuracy. Thus, rather than being too critical or too skeptical, we should accept Freud's theory for what it is and was: a monumental attempt by a genius to account for a great diversity of human behavior with a few basic concepts and ideas. It has provided an abundance of insights and will influence psychology for many, many years.

SELECTED RESEARCH TOPICS

Turning from Freud's general theory, I will now examine specific research topics and empirical investigations. Some of the research to be described provides direct evidence for the acceptance or rejection of aspects of Freud's theory. Other investigations have little bearing upon psychoanalytic theory, but do relate to concepts that were employed by Freud. For example, current research concerning instinctive behavior and dreams often does not permit one to have either more or less confidence in Freud's theory. However, these topics are of great importance in the field of motivation and clearly are pertinent to Freud's interests. As previously indicated, the research areas to be presented can be broadly subsumed within the headings of id functions (instincts, aggression, sex, dreams) and ego functions (defense mechanisms, delay of gratificaion, cognitive styles). Thus, the research topics consider the biologically rooted drives of sex and aggression and the renunciation or prevention of action upon such desires. Detailed examination of super-ego functions (morality and guilt) is not undertaken here because of space limitations.

Instincts

There is a saying that can be paraphrased as follows: A human is like all other humans, like some other humans, like no other humans. The similarity of *all* humans leads to the search for the universal laws of behavior. For example, it might be proposed that certain principles of learning or perception hold for all living organisms. The homogeneity of *some* humans focuses attention on intra-group or intra-species similarities and inter-group or inter-species dissimilarities. Members of a certain social group or culture may behave in a way that distinguishes them from the members of other social groups and cultures. The study of instinctive patterns of behavior is based on the premise of similarities in behavior within a species and is the focus of this section of the book. The *dissimilarity* of *all* humans, the third possible area of study, results in an examination of individual differences and genetic variability within a species.

Definition and Characteristics of Instincts

There are two basic meanings of the term "instinct" and they are often confused (Valle, 1975). On the one hand, instinct or, more appropriately, instinctive behavior, refers to an unlearned, fixed, stereotyped pattern of activity. Such behavior is diplayed by all members of a species when in a given environment, assuming that the members within the species are of like sex and at the same level of development. Responses of birds to particular mating calls, the web spinning of spiders, and the hoarding of food by squirrels are examples of such unlearned patterns of responses. These behaviors primarily are caused by genetically transmitted physiological states and functions; they are akin to the built-in behaviors that are exhibited by plants, such as a tropism toward light. Instinctive behaviors frequently are not single responses, but action sequences that follow a predetermined and predictable course (e.g., nest building and hoarding).

The second meaning of instinct refers to a specific motivational tendency that is *inferred* from overt behavior. Instincts in this sense are potentialities for action and are considered unlearned "wants" or "urges," which are built into the structure of the organism. They are imperatives that "must" find expression, although they do not have to be recognized or labelled by the organism. Although the ends or goals of the instincts are presumed to be fixed, the means of expression can be quite diverse. For example, Freud suggested that aggressive instincts can be satisfied through war, antisocial behavior, or self-destructive acts. Because an urge can be gratified in a variety of manners, the existence of instinctive desires is believed to be antithetical to a mechanical model of humans that equates humans with machines. The urge definition is related to the Freudian conception of instinct; identification of internal commands, particularly of an aggressive or sexual nature, would provide positive evidence for the validity of the psychoanalytic theory of motivation.

Instinctive Urges

The concept of an instinctive urge has been part of our intellectual heritage since antiquity (see Beach, 1955). Infrahumans were often described as base and instinctive, acting irrationally without any control over their behavior, guided by internal urges that were acted upon directly. The postulation of an infrahuman-human continuity by Darwin paved the way for using this conception of instinct to explain human actions.

Freud was certainly influenced by Darwin and, as already indicated, adopted the notion of instinct. Some version of the instinct doctrine was accepted not only by Freud, but by many other prominent psychologists as well. Perhaps the most elaborate instinct theory was proposed by McDougall (1923). McDougall postulated that instincts, or propensities, propel the organism toward certain end states. Each instinct was believed to have a cognitive, affective, and conative component. For example, the instinct of escape causes the animal to attend to aversive stimuli, exhibit the emotion of fear, and initiate avoidance behavior or flight. Instincts were believed to be directed toward particular end states; the means to attain these ends could be modified. But in the early 1930's the concept of instinctive urges fell into disfavor among behavioral scientists (see Chapter III for further discussion).

Recently, ethologists have promoted the scientific study of instinctive behavior, and the idea of instincts has re-emerged. Their investigations may have provided evidence for the notion of internal urges that are striving for expression.

Vacuum Behavior and Displacement Activity

Ethologists have demonstrated that the probability of the appearance of some responses increases as a function of the time since the response was previously made. The increasing response readiness is most dramatically displayed in what has been labelled *vacuum behavior,* or behavior patterns that appear when the stimulus is not identifiable. For example, if a captive starling is raised in a cage, at times the bird may engage in complex sequences of hunting, killing, and eating a prey, even though there is no prey in the cage. In a similar manner, caged female birds have been seen taking hold of some of their own feathers and going through the motions of building a nest.

Another interesting observation that is pertinent to the idea of an instinctive urge is *displacement activity*. Displacement activity occurs when two incompatible response tendencies are simultaneously aroused. For example, a bird might be faced with a rival that elicits both attack and flight. In this situation, behaviors are displayed that appear to be irrelevant to the situation, such as grooming. At times the activity differs from normal grooming behavior in that it seems hurried and is discontinued before it is completed. But on other occasions the behavior is not distinguishable from normal grooming activity. Certain species of fish, such as the stickleback, also exhibit such out-of-context displacement activity. When at the boundary between its own territory and that of another stickleback, where both attack and escape behaviors are elicited, inappropriate nest-building behavior is often displayed (Tinbergen and Van Iersel, 1947).

An Energy Model of Action

To account for vacuum behavior and displacement activity, Lorenz (1950) and Tinbergen (1952) postulated that every action pattern has its own energy source. When a fixed action pattern does not occur, the energy accumulates. When the action is expressed, the energy is discharged. Hinde (1960) summarizes this conception as follows:

> Lorenz's "reaction specific energy" . . . [can be thought of] as a liquid in a reservoir. [It] is supposed that the reservoir can discharge through a spring-loaded valve at the bottom. The valve is opened in part by the hydrostatic pressure in the reservoir, and in part by . . . the external stimulus. As the reservoir discharges, the hydrostatic pressure . . . decreases, and thus a great weight is necessary to open the valve again. (p. 200)

This theoretical analysis can account for the variation in the probability of occurrence of an action as a function of the recent history of the organism.

A fixed-action pattern can therefore be considered internal agitation (pressure) that continues as long as certain responses are not made. This is very similar to the notion of internal, instinctive stimuli that was proposed by Freud. Note that it is the separation of the behavior from the normal releaser, as in vacuum behavior, that provides the crucial evidence concerning the internal, instinctive urges. In a similar manner, the unavailability of gratifying objects provided Freud with the evidence to infer the dynamic principles of behavior.

While the above conception can readily account for vacuum behavior, it is less appropriate for explaining displacement activity. Tinbergen (1952) therefore suggested that action-specific energy is arranged in a hierarchical, inter-dependent organization so that specific energy can motivate a number of different responses. Thus, during a conflict state, the thwarting of the prepotent responses is presumed to activate other behaviors because the undischarged energy "spills over" into those systems. Inasmuch as the nature of the displaced activity is inappropriate and does not aid in problem solution, it bears some conceptual resemblance to neurotic activities among humans. Neurotic symptoms are assumed to arise in situations of strong unresolved conflict and are not adaptive responses.

Criticism of the Energy Model and an Alternate Explanation

The energy models proposed by Lorenz and Tinbergen have not met with widespread acceptance (see Lehrman, 1953; Hinde, 1960). The main criticism has been that the so-called "accumulated energy" is nowhere to be found! Inasmuch as ethologists have operated at a molecular level, with detailed analysis of the hormonal and physiological substrates that influence action, this criticism is especially embarrassing.

There has been another interpretation of displacement activity and vacuum behavior that appears less mysterious and does not invoke the notion of accumulated energy (see Zeigler, 1964). It has been suggested that displacement activity emerges because the dominant habits or responses are not being made, thus allowing the next most dominant response or habit in the organism's hierarchy to be expressed. There is some empirical data that supports this "response repertoire" explanation. For example, it has been demonstrated that the nature of the displaced activity is influenced by environmental conditions. Specifically, the type of grooming behavior displayed during a conflict can be varied by altering the stimulus situation. If water is placed on a bird's feathers just prior to the conflict, preening is the displacement activity; but placing sticky material on the bird's bill results in bill-wiping behavior during the conflict (Rowell, 1961). However, it has not been demonstrated that these forms of grooming behavior are indeed the next most dominant responses in the bird's hierarchy. It seems necessary for investigators to determine *a priori* the exact habit structure of the organism in a particular situation before the associative or habit explanation of displacement can be accepted.

In a similar manner, it has been argued that vacuum behavior is a result of "stimulus generalization." That is, stimuli that are related to the sign stimulus acquire the capacity to elicit the response when that response has not been expressed. Again this explanation appears plausible, but it does not explain *why* a lack of responding increases stimulus generalization.

Ethologists have been sensitive to criticisms of their theoretical analysis and now confine their work primarily to a search for the mechanisms that control action. There has been less defense of the concept of instinct as an internal urge or energy system. Thus, instincts have been stripped of many of the surplus meanings that made their study directly applicable to some of the ideas expressed by Freud. However, there remain some puzzles that could be very relevant to the study of human motivation.

Aggression

It is natural to turn our attention now to aggression, for Lorenz (1966) and others contend that aggression is instinctive and genetically built into the structure of human beings. One empirical observation that might be considered as supporting this argument is the universal presence of aggressive actions in humans. It has been estimated that more than 130 million humans have been killed in wars. Furthermore, war plays a dominant role in the lives of many primitive cultures, which are also characterized by hunting and killing. Finally, humans are among the very few organisms that kill members of their own species without direct provocation, and are the only species that commits mass murders (although attacks by infrahuman adults on their own infants frequently have been reported; see Marler, 1975).

In an exchange between Freud and Einstein in 1932 on the topic of "Why War?," Freud stated:

> . . . You express astonishment at the fact that it is so easy to make men enthusiastic about a war and add your suspicion that there is something at work in them — an instinct for hatred and destruction — which goes half-way to meet the effects of the warmongers. Once again, I can only express my entire agreement. . . .
>
> According to our hypothesis human instincts are of only two kinds: those which seek to preserve and unite—which we call "erotic". . .—and those which seek to destroy and kill and which we class together as the aggressive or destructive instinct. . . .
>
> In any case, as you yourself have remarked, there is no question of getting rid entirely of human aggressive impulses; it is enough to try to divert them to such an extent that they need not find expression in war. . . .
>
> If willingness to engage in war is an effect of the destructive instinct, the most obvious plan will be to bring Eros, its antagonist, into play against it. Anything that encourages the growth of emotional ties between men must operate against war. . . .

Of course, the prevalence of acts of hostility such as war or crime does not necessarily provide evidence that aggression is inborn or instinctive. For example, the following facts about violent crime in the United States between 1960 and 1970 point out some social determinants of aggression (from Johnson, 1972):

1. Violent crime is concentrated in large cities. The 26 largest cities in the United States contain only 17 per cent of the total population, but contribute 45 per cent of the major crimes of violence. . . .
2. Violent crime is overwhelmingly committed by males. The ratio of males to females arrested in connection with murder is five to one.
3. Most crime in the cities is concentrated among youths between 15 and 24 years of age. . . .
4. Violent crime is committed primarily by those in the lower occupational brackets. . . .

5. Violent crime in cities is disproportionately more frequent in slums and ghettos.
6. Victims and offenders usually share similar characteristics. With the exception of robbery, most violent crime is not inter-racial. The victims of most black offenders are other blacks, while whites attack whites. Most robbery carried out against poor people is initiated by other poor people.
7. Most homicides and assaults take place between relatives, friends, or acquaintances. . . .

Johnson therefore concludes that:

> In general, violent crime feeds and perpetuates itself on social and environmental adversity, including poor housing and schools, lack of jobs, social disorganization, and racial prejudice. (p. 166)

Whatever the cause, whether an instinctive urge, social adversity, or both, there has been an alarming increase in crime in the United States (see Figure 2–4). It is therefore evident that aggressive expressions will remain a topic of great concern to social scientists for years to come.

The study of aggression is so extensive that only a few relevant programs of research can be examined in this context. Investigations pertinent to the psychoanalytic conception of aggression will first be discussed. This includes the ethological view of aggression as an instinctive urge, the authoritarian personality, aggressive inhibition, and catharsis. Some social determinants of aggression will then be presented, including contagion, mass media effects, obedience to authority, and de-individuation. Later in this book, other conceptions of aggression, including the frustration-aggression hypothesis, are analyzed.

An Ethological View of Aggression

Ethologists view aggression within the broad framework of evolution. Thus, they ask, what are the functions or the significance of aggressive actions and why are these potentialities built into the structure of the organism?

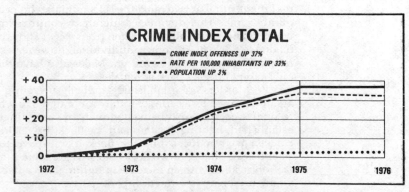

Figure 2–4. Change in crime and population between 1972 and 1976. (From FBI Uniform Crime Reports, 1977.)

It is evident that aggression has great value for survival. Aggressive displays enable organisms to protect their territory and young. In addition, aggression promotes intra-species dominance, which brings rewards of food and shelter. And finally, it is crucial for survival to be able to hunt and kill. Thus, ethologists consider aggression an adaptive instinct rather than the "destructive urge" championed by Freud. Since aggression promotes survival, and hostile displays intimidate sexual rivals, the most aggressive organisms have the greatest likelihood of propagating the species. This, in turn, leads to the perpetuation of aggressive dispositions among organisms.

AGGRESSION AS AN INTERNAL AGITATION. Two conceptions of aggressive instincts have been proposed by ethologists. One view is that aggressive instincts correspond to a state of internal agitation. This internal urge persists as long as an appropriate stimulus or object of attack is *absent*. Non-expression of the instinct results in an accumulation of action-specific aggressive energy. As already indicated, this conception is very similar to Freud's notion of aggression as a biologically rooted drive that constantly seeks an outlet.

Given an "internal urge" view of aggression, it is reasonable to wonder why organisms within a species typically are not killing one another, which could eventually lead to extinction of the entire species. According to Lorenz (1966) and other ethologists, species survival is in part protected because dominance hierarchies (also called pecking or ranking orders) are established. Once a hierarchical ranking is fixed, fighting is avoided through displays of threat. Johnson (1972) describes the process of establishing a ranking order:

> Social rank may be established in many ways, but usually relationships are established through force or threats of force. A good example is the well-known peck order found among chickens (Guhl, 1956). In any flock of hens there is usually one (sometimes referred to as the *alpha* animal) which is dominant and pecks freely at any of the other hens. They accept this insult and rarely fight back. The alpha hen struts about with her head erect and feathers fluffed, which serves to indicate her high status. Subordinate hens communicate their submission by meekly lowering their heads whenever there is an encounter with a higher ranking hen. Following the highest ranking is number two rank (the *beta* animal) who pecks at all the hens except number one. This dominance hierarchy continues down the line with the weakest and most submissive hen (the *omega*) at the bottom of the order with no one to peck at. The omega individual, however, is usually simply ignored rather than constantly picked on. Males also have their own peck order and only rarely do they peck at females.
>
> Peck orders are established gradually in young chickens, and rankings are determined by a series of round-robin fights in which individuals come to recognize each other as being dominant or subordinate. Once the hierarchy is established, fighting declines and the flock thrives in relative peace. If a new chicken is introduced into the flock it will have to fight each member to establish its status. If two flocks of birds are joined together, social disorganization results, with an increase in fighting and a decrease in egg laying until a new hierarchy is formed. (pp. 52–53)

In addition to the establishment of a ranking order, the presentation of particular stimuli or complex patterns of stimulation inhibits hostile responses and aggression. These stimuli frequently are displayed within a ritualistic pattern of interaction. Lorenz (1966) describes one such ritual fighting sequence among fallow deer:

> . . . In these animals, the highly ritualized antler fight, in which the crowns are swung into collision, locked together, and then swung to and fro in a special manner, is preceded by a broadside display in which both animals goose-step beside each other, at the same time nodding their heads to make the great antlers wave up and down. Suddenly, as if in obedience to an order, both stand still, swing at right angles toward each other, and lower their heads so that their antlers collide with a crash and entangle near the ground. A harmless wrestling match follows, in which. . .the victor is the one with the longest endurance span. Among fallow deer, too, one of the fighters sometimes wants to proceed, in advance of the other, to the second stage of the fight and thus finds his weapon aimed at the unprotected flank of his rival — a highly alarming spectacle, considering the formidable thrust of the heavy, jagged antlers. But quickly. . .the deer stops the movement, raises his head, and now, seeing that his unwitting, still goose-stepping enemy is already several yards ahead, breaks into a trot till he has caught up with him and walks calmly, antlers nodding, in goose-step beside him, till the next thrust of the antlers leads, in better synchronization, to the ring fight. (p. 110)

Frequently the stimuli that inhibit aggression are signals of submission, or appeasement gestures.

> . . .The wolf turns his head away from his opponent, offering him the vulnerable, arched side of his neck; the jackdaw holds under the beak of the aggressor the unprotected base of the skull, the very place which these birds attack when they intend to kill. . . . In the wolf and the dog, it really looks as if the suppliant is offering his neck veins to the victor. . . .
> It would indeed be suicidal if an animal presented to an opponent still at the height of aggressiveness a very vulnerable part of its body, acting on the supposition that the simultaneous switching-off of fight-eliciting stimuli would suffice to prevent attack. We all know too well how slowly the balance changes from the predominance of one drive to that of another, and we can safely assert that a simple removal of fight-eliciting stimuli would effect only a very gradual ebbing of the aggressive mood. When a *sudden* presentation of the submissive attitude inhibits the threatened attack, we can safely assume that an active inhibition was elicited by a specific stimulus situation.
> This is certainly the case in the dog, in which I have repeatedly seen that when the loser of a fight suddenly adopted the submissive attitude, and presented his unprotected neck, the winner performed the movement of shaking to death, in the air, close to the neck of the morally vanquished dog, but with closed mouth. (Lorenz, 1966, p. 127)

Lorenz (1966) argues that among humans slaughter occurs at such great distances that inhibitory mechanisms are ineffective. That is, the slow course of evolution has not kept pace with the increased sophistication of our weapons.

AGGRESSION AS AN AVERSIVE REACTION. A second conception of instinctive aggression accepted by some ethologists is that aggression is an aversive reaction, or a state of agitation that persists as long as a particular stimulus is *present*. Thus, organisms have a capacity for violent expression, but it is exhibited only when certain environmental events occur. Aggression, therefore, is not "spontaneously" expressed.

Tinbergen (1968) argues that the crucial determinant of aggression is territorialism. It is known that many infrahumans defend specific territories and, in so doing, control population density. Of course, this is survival relevant in that it enhances the likelihood of finding food. Tinbergen states that humans carry the animal heritage of group territorialism. However, among humans there is not appropriate flight behavior for any of the parties in a territorial disagreement or contention. According to Tinbergen (1968),

> . . .warriors are both brainwashed and bullied into all-out fighting. They are brainwashed into believing that fleeing — originally, as we have seen, an adaptive type of behavior — is despicable, "cowardly." (p. 1415)

Furthermore, in a manner similar to Lorenz, Tinbergen contends:

> [One] cultural excess is our ability to make and use killing tools, especially long-range weapons. These make killing easy, not only because a spear or a club inflicts, with the same effort, so much more damage than a fist, but also, and mainly, because the use of long-range weapons prevents the victim from reaching his attacker with his appeasement, reassurance, and distress signals. Very few aircrews who are willing, indeed eager, to drop their bombs "on target" would be willing to strangle, stab, or burn children (or, for that matter, adults) with their own hands; they would stop short of killing, in response to the appeasement and distress signals of their opponents. (p. 1415)

Criminologists are now making use of some of these principles. In the event of a kidnapping, they first allow a long "waiting" period prior to acting directly upon a threat. During this time interval, they hope that the victim and the abductor will establish a positive interpersonal relationship. This makes it more difficult for the kidnapper to harm the previously "faceless" victim.

Both Lorenz and Tinbergen believe that we must live with our aggressive instincts. But actions that mitigate the likelihood of aggressive outbreaks are possible. Lorenz (1966) suggests that we should engage in sports and other activities to "drain off" our aggressive urges. In the same spirit, Tinbergen (1968) argues for sublimation activities and a deeper study of our roots to overcome our instinctual aggressive dispositions.

CRITICISM AND EVALUATION.   The conception of instinctive aggression has met with numerous criticisms. Instinctive behaviors are supposedly expressed by all members of a species, given similar age and gender groupings. But it is clear that not all humans within age and sex groups engage in similar hostile or aggressive actions. In addition, there is no evidence to support the idea of an accumulation of aggressive energy. Engaging in sports activity or a recent aggressive action does not decrease the likelihood of future aggressions. Furthermore, the complex symbolic and linguistic capacities of humans do not necessitate face-to-face communication to elicit inhibitory processes. And finally, as previously indicated, it is evident that aggression among humans is greatly influenced by social factors such as poverty, deindividuation, and obedience to authority. It is reasonable to conclude that humans have a capacity for aggressive behavior, but it does not necessarily follow that aggression is an urge striving for expression. Rather, hostility typically requires an aversive event prior to its manifestation. Even among lower animals it has been documented that a variety of external situations can influence aggression. The situational determinants of aggressive reactions include:

1. Proximity of an animal
2. Of one's own kind
3. A stranger
4. Behaving aggressively
5. Inflicting pain
6. Or otherwise creating frustration (Marler, 1975, p. 242)

Nevertheless, the ethologists have made important contributions in pointing out the apparent similarity of human and infrahuman aggression; in the discovery of rituals, inhibitory stimuli, dominance hierarchies, and territoriality; and in their careful analysis of the survival value of aggressive actions.

The Overcontrol of Aggression

Both Freud and Lorenz have postulated that aggression is an inborn, biologically based drive that seeks expression. On the other hand, to be an effective member of society, aggression must be inhibited or modified. A large number of psychological factors have been identified as determinants of aggressive inhibition. Specific external cues, such as postures, have been discussed as means of preventing aggressive responses. In addition, fear of retaliatory punishment can obviously decrease the immediate expression of aggression. And finally, intra-psychic structures such as the super-ego have been thought to produce aggressive inhibition.

Individuals who are overly inhibited in their expression of aggression are labelled as "overcontrolled" (Megargee, 1966). There are data suggesting that persons who unexpectedly exhibit extreme acts of violence have a life history of overcontrolling their aggressive tendencies. Megargee (1966) reports:

> In case after case the extremely assaultive offender proves to be a rather passive person with no previous history of aggression. In Phoenix an 11-year-old boy who stabbed his brother 34 times with a steak knife was described by all who know him as being extremely polite and soft spoken with no history of assaultive behavior. In New York an 18-year-old youth who confessed he had assaulted and strangled a 7-year-old girl in a Queens church and later tried to burn her body in the furnace was described in the press as an unemotional person who planned to be a minister. A 21-year-old man from Colorado who was accused of the rape and murder of two little girls had never been a discipline problem and, in fact, his stepfather reported, "When he was in school the other kids would run all over him and he'd never fight back. There is just no violence in him." In these cases the homicide was not just one more aggressive offense in a person who had always displayed inadequate controls, but rather a completely uncharacteristic act in a persn who had always displayed extraordinarily high levels of control. (p. 2)

In addition, a large proportion of persons convicted of homicide have no prior history of assaultive behavior, are better behaved when incarcerated, and have a lower recidivism rate than most prisoners (see Megargee, 1966).

The finding that extreme violence is associated with aggressive inhibition can be considered as supporting the ideas of Freud and Lorenz. Both these theorists believe that aggression can be "stored up"; an accumulation of this energy can then lead to inappropriate expression.

There are two general principles that enable one to infer that intrapsychic factors are important determinants of a reaction:

1. If the reaction changes although the external circumstances remain constant; and
2. If the intensity of the reaction is inappropriate to the external stimulus (e.g., great fear when a door is slammed).

Both these principles characterize the violent acts of overcontrolled individuals. Clearly, detailed analysis of these particular individuals could shed important light on the psychodynamics of aggression, provide evidence for some of the ideas forwarded by Freud and Lorenz, and perhaps aid in the development of a general theory of behavior.

The Catharsis of Aggression

In the event that physical or psychological barriers to goal attainment are encountered, psychological processes and mechanisms are thought to be elicited that aid the individual in coping with the persisting, unsatisfied wish. These coping processes enable the individual to attain partial goal satisfaction even though the original goal is not obtainable. One process that presumably alleviates the individual involves a change of goal objects, or the establishment of substitute goals. A second method of partial goal fulfillment may be through identification with others, as in the resolution of the Oedipal situation. Finally, fantasy activity such as hallucinations or dreaming has been conceived as a method of gratification.

There has been a long-standing belief that fantasy activity can have substitute value or serve to satisfy unfulfilled needs. Aristotle, for example, stated that one function of witnessing tragedy in the theater is that the observer is "purged of passions." This is labelled a *catharsis* of emotions. The research most resembling this Aristotelian conception examines the general hypothesis that observing motivational expression in others reduces one's own motivation. Stated more concretely, the so-called "catharsis hypothesis" leads to the prediction that watching one's hero hit a home run reduces achievement strivings; that sexual desires are reduced after reading or viewing erotic material; and that watching a powerful leader reduces one's desires for power.

The experimental study of catharsis has been virtually restricted to the area of aggression. The specific hypothesis examined is that observation of an aggressive act reduces the viewer's aggressive tendencies. The practical implications of this question are far-reaching. For example, a great amount of violence is depicted on television. A content analysis of television programs in 1968 revealed that more than one-half of the main characters in the programs sampled used violence. Furthermore, the violence generally resulted in a positive outcome. Children in particular are exposed to the frequent hostilities that are shown in cartoons; it has been estimated that between the ages of 5 and 15, children watch 13,400 persons being killed on television (Liebert, Neale & Davidson, 1973). An important current debate concerns the possible effects of such television programming on the personalities of the children. Parents fear that their children will become more aggressive because of exposure to the fantasy aggressions. On the other hand, the notion of catharsis suggests that current television programming might reduce personal aggressive tendencies.

Unfortunately, the question of whether viewing aggression increases or decreases aggressive tendencies and aggressive expression is exceedingly difficult to answer. One reason for this difficulty is that the observation of violence can have contrasting effects upon a variety of psychological processes and mechanisms (see Feshbach, 1964). For example, new aggressive strategies or instrumental behaviors might be learned from viewing television violence. The hijacking of airplanes did not emerge as a threat until this form of kidnapping was portrayed in a television program, thus planting a new idea for a potential aggressor. Viewing also can lead to imitation and thus increase expressed violence. Hence, the depiction of violence on television might be teaching aggressive behaviors. At the same time, avoidance tendencies generated by fear and guilt may be reduced when one witnesses successful violations of social rules. And finally, perhaps there also is a catharsis, or a decrease in persisting tension, that accompanies the viewing of violence. But because so many processes and structures may be affected by the same external input, it is difficult to provide a definitive test of the catharsis notion. It also is clear that there will not be a simple "yes" or "no" answer to the question of whether viewing violent programs increases or decreases subsequent tendencies toward violence. Rather, the answer is likely to be dependent upon a variety of factors. The reader, however, should be aware that most psychological investigations report an *increase* rather than a decrease in aggressive expression following the viewing of hostile actions. The catharsis hypothesis is not accepted by the majority of psychologists.

Perhaps the most extensive real-life testing of the motivational effects of viewing violence on television was conducted by Feshbach and Singer (1971). These investigators controlled the television "diet" of boys in private boarding schools. Some of the boys were from predominantly middle-class backgrounds, while other children were of lower-class parentage. Feshbach and Singer had one-half of the boys view primarily aggressive programs, while the others were generally restricted to nonaggressive shows. (Needless to say, such intervention and control created many problems, and one restricted aggressive program was so popular that the experimenters had to allow all the boys to view it!)

Feshbach and Singer then assessed the effects of these viewing patterns on subsequent aggressive behavior over a six-week period. They report that the aggressiveness of the boys was not greatly affected by the experimental viewing manipulation. However, the boys from the lower-class backgrounds exhibited *less* aggressive behavior when allowed to view the aggressive programs. This reduction in aggression was particularly evident in boys rated high in aggressive tendencies. Thus, the catharsis hypothesis was confirmed in a portion of the sample in this investigation. Needless to say, the results reported by Feshbach and Singer are controversial and have generated much discussion and debate.

It appears from this study and from other research that when the catharsis hypothesis does receive confirmation, the individuals viewing the aggressive fantasy content have been aroused to aggress or are predisposed to act aggressively. Thus, the state of the organism must be taken into account when attempting to predict whether observations of aggression will increase or decrease subsequent aggressive expression.

The Authoritarian Personality

Following the atrocities committed during the period of Nazi Germany, the American Jewish Committee established a Department of Scientific Research to study prejudice and racial hatred. The ultimate goal of this organization was to aid in preventing the reoccurrence of a Nazi-like regime.

The social scientists connected with the Department of Scientific Research were strongly influenced by the psychoanalytic formulations of Freud. Their intuitions and clinical observations suggested that prejudiced individuals could be characterized as possessing nine interrelated personality traits (Sanford, 1956):

1. *Conventionalism* — rigid adherence to conventional middle-class values.
2. *Authoritarian Submission* — submissive, uncritical attitude toward idealized moral authorities of the in-group.
3. *Authoritarian Aggression* — tendency to be on the lookout for, and to condemn, reject, and punish people who violate conventional values.
4. *Anti-Intraception* — opposition to the subjective, the imaginative, the tender-minded.
5. *Superstition and Stereotype* — the belief in mystical determinants of the individual's fate and the disposition to think in rigid categories.
6. *Power and Toughness* — identification with power figures and exaggerated assertion of strength and toughness.
7. *Destructiveness and Cynicism* — generalized hostility and vilification of the human.
8. *Projectivity* — the disposition to believe that wild and dangerous things go on in the world and the projection outward of unconscious emotional impulses.
9. *Ego-Alien Sexuality* — an exaggerated concern with sexual goings-on, and punitiveness toward violators of sex mores.

Prejudice, therefore, was part of a more general syndrome that included anti-democratic attitudes, conservatism, and a rejection of the unconventional. Furthermore, the anti-Semitic person also was believed to be anti-minorities in general and against any deviation from the norm. An individual with these characteristics was labelled as having an *authoritarian* personality (Adorno, Frenkel-Brunswick, Levinson, & Sanford, 1950).

Using psychoanalytic terminology, researchers described authoritarian individuals as having strong, unfulfilled id drives. A dominant super-ego prevents drive expression, and the ego uses defenses such as repression to control direct gratification. The built-up tension is then released through displacement activities against figures who are acceptable targets of hostility. Furthermore, sexual and aggressive needs are projected onto others so that personal aggressive expression is justified (see also the discussion of the frustration–aggression hypothesis in Chapter III).

Adorno et al. (1950) contend that this mode of functioning results from harsh child-rearing practices and the stressing of conventional values by the socializing agents. Furthermore, hostile expressions against the socializing agents are strongly forbidden. This produces the cycle depicted in Figure 2–5. Figure 2–5 also contrasts authoritarian and equalitarian socialization experiences.

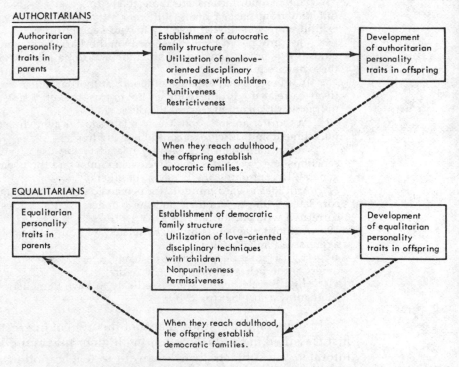

Figure 2–5. The antecedents and perpetuation of authoritarian and equalitarian personalities. (From Byrne, 1974, p. 99.)

EMPIRICAL EVIDENCE.   To aid in testing these theoretical ideas, as well as to further the theoretical scheme, a scale was constructed to identify authoritarian individuals. Subjects respond to various statements on the so-called "F-scale" (F stands for fascism), some of which are:

Sex crimes, such as rape and attacks on children, deserve more than mere imprisonment; such criminals ought to be publicly whipped, or worse.

What the youth needs most is strict discipline, rugged determination, and the will to work and fight for family and country.

There is harldy anything lower than a person who does not feel a great love, gratitude, and respect for his parents.

Every person should have complete faith in some supernatural power whose decisions he obeys without question.

Young people sometimes get rebellious ideas, but as they grow up they ought to get over them and settle down.

Agreement with the above items indicates authoritarianism. Hence, this scale neglects the left-wing authoritarian personality.

This scale has been used in literally hundreds of research investigations. Many of the research findings support the ideas of Adorno et al. (1950). Korman (1974) summarized some of the basic findings:

1.   Authoritarianism is negatively correlated with attitudes toward the blind and the deaf.
2.   Authoritarianism is positively correlated with the tendency to keep social distance from others in Germany, Japan, and the United States.
3.   High authoritarians are more likely to be aggressive toward groups different from oneself across different situations; they are more likely to exhibit more generalized hostility toward such groups.
4.   Task groups led by leaders low in authoritarianism were more likely to adjust to changing demands of situation and to be more flexible in meeting these new requirements.
5.   In an experimental game situation, authoritarianism scores were positively correlated with the tendency not to trust the other side and to act in an untrustworthy manner toward the other side.
6.   Authoritarianism is positively related to the tendency to use physical punishment and ridicule in controlling children.
7.   Authoritarianism is positively related to the use of negative (hostile) sanctions (e.g., penalties, negative evaluations) and the use of sanctions, in general, in controlling the behavior of others.
8.   Attitudes toward minority (or perceived different) groups are all highly correlated with one another, and these generalized attitudes are negatively correlated with authoritarianism.
9.   Authoritarianism is highly correlated with militaristic attitudes and an aggressive foreign policy.
10.   High F-scale people are more likely to act in a hostile fashion toward others at the behest of an authority figure.
11.   High F-scale people were less likely to have demonstrated against the Vietnam war in 1969. (p. 229)

In one empirical study that is of theoretical interest, Epstein (1965) first classified individuals as scoring high or low in the F-scale. He then informed the subjects that they were to teach another subject (really a confederate) a memory task. To facilitate learning, the subjects were allowed to shock the confederate for incorrect answers. The confederate was portrayed as either a low or a high status individual on the basis of physical appearance and the background information made known to the subject.

Epstein then measured the amount and the duration of the shock that was supposedly administered. He reports that the high F-scale individuals gave more shock to the low status confederate and less shock to the high status confederate than individuals scoring low in the F-scale. These findings are in general accord with the theory of aggressive inhibition and displacement put forth by Adorno et al. (1950).

CRITICISMS AND CURRENT STATUS. Investigations of authoritarianism have been subject to criticisms that remain to be definitively substantiated or resolved. One critical issue concerns the structure of the F-scale. Agreement with the items on the scale is taken to be an indicator of authoritarianism. But some psychologists have argued that this confounds authoritarianism with a personality disposition labelled an "acquiescent response set," or the tendency to agree with test items regardless of their content. The existence of this confounding element is a moot point (see Rorer, 1965), but as a consequence of this criticism, investigators became reluctant to use the scale.

It also has been found that scores on the F-scale consistently correlate negatively with IQ; that is, high authoritarians score relatively low in intelligence. This relationship could indicate that less intelligent individuals are willing to accept any extreme ideologies, that less intelligent individuals face more frustrations in life and therefore develop authoritarian personalities, or that authoritarian personalities have rigid outlooks that interfere with intellectual growth. Regardless of the meaning of the correlation, it is possible that some of the reported correlates of the F-scale are dynamically related to low intelligence rather than to authoritarianism.

Finally, there is a paradox in citing authoritarianism research as supporting Freud's theory. Buck-Morss (1977) points out that Adorno, the main contributor to this development, was a deeply committed Marxist who contended that the true determinants of behavior are to be found in social conditions. Thus, he was critical of Freud and biological theories of motivation. Adorno believed that authoritarian responses ultimately could be traced back to the capitalistic society, which kept its members in "ignorance and confusion" (Buck-Morss, 1977).

It is generally accepted that the research on the authoritarian personality beautifully combined the talents of psychiatrists, clinical psychologists, psychometrists, and social psychologists. The study of authoritarianism surely left a permanent mark in the fields of personality and motivation. However, this field of investigation seemed to fade away because of criticisms of the scale and a general shift in research interests by other investigators. Why a research area fades before the problems are solved is a problem for the sociology of science. In the field of motivation, such bursts of activity and subsequent disappearance are the rule rather than the exception.

Social and Situational Determinants of Aggression

In the previous section of this chapter, some of the research and thought directly bearing upon Freud's conception of aggression was reviewed. The research examined the instinctive nature of aggression, aggressive inhibition, catharsis, and the authoritarian personality. Perhaps the most telling criticism leveled against these research areas (excluding, in part, the ethological work) is that the situation or the environment in which the organism is placed is almost totally disregarded by the investigator. That is, intra-psychic influences on behavior, particularly the building up of tension, are believed to be the dominant determinants of action. Hence, some of the facts mentioned before, such as the differential expression of aggression as a function of social class and place of residence, cannot be explained. To correct this imbalance, this section of the book will examine briefly some of the environmental factors that influence hostile expression.

AGGRESSION AND EXPOSURE TO AGGRESSIVE STIMULI. Leonard Berkowitz, a social psychologist who has made important contributions to our understanding of aggressive behavior, contends that stimuli having aggressive implications or meanings are capable of automatically eliciting aggressive responses, particularly when the individual is primed and ready to aggress. Aggressive actions, therefore, are similar to conditioned responses in that aggression is impulsively expressed, given the presence of certain external cues.

In one experiment supporting this position (Berkowitz & LaPage, 1967), subjects were given an opportunity to administer shocks to another subject. In fact, the other "subject" was a stooge, although this was unknown by the person administering the shocks. (A shock delivered by a subject to a "victim" is a frequently used dependent variable in aggression research, for the amount of shock delivered and the duration of the shock are readily measurable.) As in the experiment by Epstein (1965) discussed previously, the shock in this experiment was given following the stooge's performance at an assigned task and supposedly was feedback indicating the subject's evaluation of the performance. One-half of the subjects were angry at the stooge because they previously had received seven shocks from him for their own performance. The other half of the subjects received only one prior shock.

To demonstrate the importance of situational cues as elicitors of aggression, in one experimental condition a gun and a rifle were lying near the shock apparatus. These weapons purportedly were being used in another experiment and were described as belonging either to the stooge or to a different experimenter. In two other experimental conditions, either non-aggressive objects (badminton racquets) or nothing was next to the shock apparatus.

The results of this experiment are given in Table 2–2, which shows the number of shocks administered by the subject to the stooge. (The stooge was in a different room with the connecting wires removed!)

TABLE 2–2 MEAN NUMBER OF SHOCKS
GIVEN IN EACH CONDITION

| Condition | Shocks Received | |
	1	7
Associated weapons	2.60	6.07
Unassociated weapons	2.20	5.67
No object	3.07	4.67
Badminton racquets	–	4.60

(Adapted from Berkowitz & LaPage, 1967, p. 205.)

Table 2–2 reveals that angered subjects (seven shocks) gave more shocks than non-angered subjects (one shock). Among the non-angered subjects the presence of weapons did not significantly alter aggressive expression. But, given prior provocation, greater punishment was elicited in the weapons condition than in the no-weapons situation. Thus, *given an aroused state of aggressiveness*, the presence of guns facilitated aggressive behavior. The increase in hostile expression presumably was due to the prior association, or contiguity, between guns and violence. The facilitation of aggression by the weapons apparently occurred without any intervening cognitive awareness on the part of the subjects. This finding is known as the "weapons effect." It should be noted that, in this teacher-learner paradigm, subjects believe delivering shock is beneficial to the learner. Thus, they consider their own motives to be altruistic, not aggressive (see Baron & Eggleston, 1972).

Of course, it is difficult to determine whether some of the violence in our society is due to the eliciting effects of guns. Weapons clearly serve an instrumental function, but do they actually *instigate* aggression? Our gun control laws are very lax; there are between 100 million and 200 million privately owned guns in the United States. In addition, about 20,000 Americans are killed and 200,000 injured each year with guns. Therefore, the question of whether the presence of guns elicits, as well as serves, aggressive motivations is indeed very critical.

AGGRESSION, CONTAGION, AND THE MASS MEDIA. We may not frequently find guns in our immediate presence, but we are inundated by the violence depicted in television, in comic books, and in our daily newspapers. There is suggestive evidence that exposure to media violence also may increase hostile expression.

In one study examining the effects of aggressive stimuli in the mass media, Berkowitz and his colleagues first had children in the third to fifth grades read comic books. The books varied in their aggressive content. One group of children read a war story, while another group was exposed to a non-aggressive comic book ("Gidget"). Both before and after the reading the children were asked to select words to complete a sentence (e.g., I want to _____ the book.) The choice was between an aggressive and a non-aggressive alternative (e.g., "read" or "tear"). Table 2–3 shows the change in the amount of aggressive responses between the pre- and the post-reading periods in the aggressive and

TABLE 2–3   NUMBER OF AGGRESSIVE RESPONSES
TO FIVE INCOMPLETE SENTENCES

	Before Reading	After Reading
War Comics	0.87	1.73
"Gidget"	1.20	1.27

(Adapted from Berkowitz, 1970, p. 111.)

non-aggressive conditions. The table clearly reveals that reading the war-related comic book promoted hostile ideation.

The weapon and the comic book experiments differ in at least one important respect. In the latter investigation the *prior* reading, rather than the *immediate* presence, of aggression-related stimuli increased aggressive responses. Thus, exposure to hostility can have long-term as well as immediate consequences. Berkowitz (1970) therefore suggested that there is a "contagion of violence." That is, violent events stimulate later violence. Lending support to this view, crimes of violence increased greatly in our country after the assassination of President Kennedy and following a widely publicized mass murder by an individual named Richard Speck (see Figure 2–6).

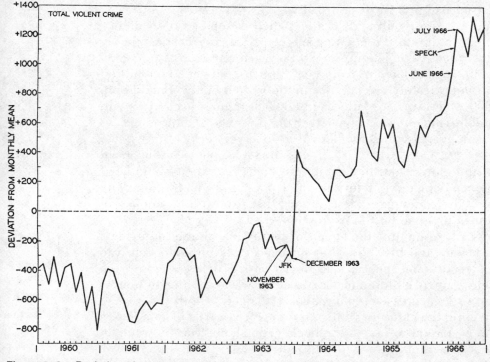

Figure 2–6.   Deviations from monthly mean for sum of violent crimes, 1960–1966. (From Berkowitz, 1970, p. 101.)

In sum, the data support the notion that the presence of violence or stimuli associated with violence, as well as prior exposure to violence, promotes hostile expression. These environmental occurrences are, therefore, important determinants of aggression. This research can be considered evidence against the "catharsis" view of aggression.

OBEDIENT AGGRESSION.   It is known that social influence is an important determinant of behavior. For example, many aspects of our lives are guided by the tendency to conform, that is, to act in accordance with social norms. This was dramatically illustrated in a series of investigations by Asch (1956). Asch found that individuals judged the shorter of two lines as being longer when aware that a group of others (confederates of the experimenter) had made this judgment.

It also has been demonstrated that individuals will obediently perform aggressive acts when "expected to" by others. The many atrocities committed during war, including the Nazi extermination of the Jews and the massacres in Viet Nam, attest to the overpowering influence of peer and authority figures, even in situations in which the requested or expected act is morally wrong.

In a series of oft-cited experiments, Milgram (1963, 1964, 1965) demonstrated that when individuals are subject to peer or authority pressure, violent acts are more readily undertaken. Again, use was made of the shock paradigm described in later studies conducted by Berkowitz and LaPage (1967) and Epstein (1965). Milgram first noted that the vast majority of individuals assert that they would refuse to participate in an experiment that required them to shock others. But when actually confronted with this experiment and the presence of an authority figure (the experimenter), they readily participate. Thus, the power of situational determinants of behavior is greatly underestimated.

In the investigations by Milgram, subjects operated a shock generator with controls labelled from "slight shock" to "danger, severe shock." They were told to shock a "victim" to facilitate performance in a learning task. The "learner" purposely made errors so that the willingness of the subjects to administer various levels of shock could be examined. When supposedly receiving the shock, the victim protested, and as the subject increased the level of shock in response to demands made by the experimenter, the screams of pain grew. Despite the severe objections and indications of pain, close to 66 per cent of the subjects obediently administered the highest amount of shock (see review by Milgram, 1974). However, in accordance with the notions of inhibition advanced by Lorenz and Tinbergen, there was increasing resistance to comply with the shock commands when the subjects were placed closer and closer to the victim (see Figure 2–7).

In sum, the general conclusion from this body of research is that aggression can be easily instigated by situational (social) demands. Hence, intra-psychic factors such as the "amount" of accumulated aggressive energy or the degree of authoritarianism clearly are not the only determinants of action.

DE-INDIVIDUATION.   Individuation refers to the "process by which

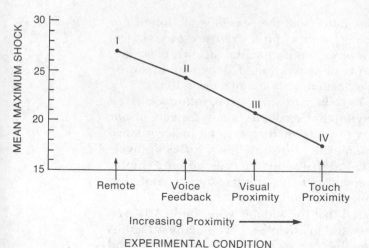

Figure 2–7. Severity of shock inflicted by subjects as a function of their proximity to the victim. In Condition I the subject neither sees nor hears his victim; in II he hears his victim's protests; in III he also sees his victim close up; in IV he must touch his victim, placing the victim's hand on the shock apparatus. (Adapted from Milgram, 1965.)

individuals in society become differentiated from one another." Thus, de-individuation connotes a breakdown of the distinctions between individuals, or the process of losing the belief that one is perceived as a separate entity. De-individuation often occurs as a consequence of being a member of a group, particularly when the group is large and confined to an institution such as prison, or when a person is subject to constant control from others, as exemplified by the Army or some boarding schools (see Goffman, 1961). Festinger, Pepitone, and Newcomb (1952) state:

> Anyone who observes persons in groups and the same persons individually is forced to conclude that they often behave differently in these two general kinds of situations. Casual observation would seem to indicate that one kind of behavior difference stems from the fact that people obtain release in groups, that is, are sometimes more free from restraints, less inhibited, and able to indulge in forms of behavior in which, when alone, they would not indulge.
>
>   The most often noted instance of such freedom from restraint is the behavior of persons in crowds. In a crowd, persons will frequently do things which they would not allow themselves to do under other circumstances. In fact, they may even feel very much ashamed later on. Such behavior is not, however, limited to crowds. It occurs regularly in groups of all sizes and of many different types. For example, a group of boys walking down the street wili often be wilder and less restrained than any of them individually would be; at an evening party persons who are usually very self-conscious and formal will sometimes behave quite freely; the delegates to an American Legion convention, all dressed in the same uniform manner, will sometimes exhibit an almost alarming lack of restraint. (p. 382)

Zimbardo (1969a) also contends that de-individuation involves a weakening of personal controls. Furthermore, in a manner similar to Freud, he suggests that individuals have instinctive drives that are striving for expression. These irrational and impulsive drives typically are blocked from expression by ego structures. But when the ego controls are weakened during the process of de-individuation, inhibitions dissipate and there is impulsive expression.

Table 2–4 shows the de-individuation process as conceived by Zimbardo (1969a). De-individuation occurs when self- and social-evaluations are minimized, thus weakening ego control. A number of antecedent conditions, such as anonymity, giving up of personal responsibility, and being a part of a large group, can lead to decreases in self-evaluation, perception of social evaluation, and ego control. Weakening of control, in turn, may eventuate in impulsive and irrational behavior that is difficult to terminate. These impulsive actions can be socially positive, such as a deep and meaningful interpersonal exchange, but they also may be antisocial and manifested in aggressive actions.

In one study demonstrating the effects of anonymity on aggressive behavior, Zimbardo (1969a) told female subjects that he was studying empathy and requested that they shock another female subject. One-half of the subjects administering the shock were not introduced by name, wore a mask because "facial expression had to be concealed," and were tested in darkness. The other half of the subjects were introduced by name, wore no mask, and were tested in dim lighting. Zimbardo reports that in the former "anonymity" condition there was greater duration of the administered shocks. In a similar manner, Watson (1973) contends that primitive societies exhibiting highly aggressive acts during battle, such as torture, tend to alter their appearance (e.g., wear masks or war-paint) prior to the battle.

In a field study, Diener, Fraser, Beaman, and Kelem (1976) examined the antisocial behavior of trick-or-treaters on Halloween. Some of these children were alone, while others were in groups. On some

TABLE 2–4   REPRESENTATION OF THE DE-INDIVIDUATION PROCESS

Input Variables →	Inferred Subjective Changes →	Output Behaviors
Anonymity	Minimization of:	Behavior emitted is emotional, impulsive, irrational, regressive, with high intensity
	1. Self-observation-evaluation	
Responsibility: shared, diffused, given up	2. Concern for social evaluation	
	↓	Not under the controlling influence of usual external discriminative stimuli
Group size	Weakening of controls based upon guilt, shame, fear, and commitment	
Physical involvement in the act		
		Behavior is self-reinforcing and is intensified, amplified with repeated expressions of it
Novel or unstructured situation	↓	
	Lowered threshold for expressing inhibited behaviors	Difficult to terminate
Altered states of consciousness, drugs, alcohol, sleep, etc.		Possible memory impairments; some amnesia for act
		Greater liking for group or situation associated with "released" behavior
		Destruction of traditional forms and structures

(Adapted from Zimbardo, 1969a, p. 253.)

TABLE 2-5 PERCENTAGE OF CHILDREN TRANSGRESSING

Condition	Total Number of Children	Per Cent Transgressing
Nonanonymous		
Alone	40	7.5
Group	384	20.8
Anonymous		
Alone	42	21.4
Group	297	57.2

(Adapted from Diener, Fraser, Beaman, & Kelem, 1976, p. 181.)

of the house calls the experimenter asked the children to introduce themselves, while on the rest no such request was made (the "anonymous" condition). The experimenter then told the children that they could take one, and only one, candy from a bowl, but he walked away and remained out of sight while the children took their treat. Unknown to the children, they were secretly observed. The observations revealed that anonymous children transgressed more than children who identified themselves, particularly when in a group setting (see Table 2–5). In sum, it is again evident that social factors exert an important influence on aggressive expression.

It should be mentioned here, however, that there is an entirely distinct approach to the effects of de-individuation. Some psychologists posit that "man seeks a separate and a unique identity" (Dipboye, 1977). A loss of this identity arouses negative affect and strivings for a sense of self. This position is often associated with the humanist movement. Thus, some of the observed effects of de-individuation are subject to an alternate interpretation, one which does not asume a release of ego restraints. Identity aggression, for example, is believed to be the source of motivation at times for riots or even graffiti (see Dipboye, 1977).

Summary: The Study of Aggression

According to Freud, aggression is a biologically rooted instinctive urge that promotes preservation of the self. In the absence of aggressive expression, aggressive energy accumulates and exerts increasing pressure on the organism for satisfaction. The evidence supporting this view of aggression derives from a variety of sources:

1. There is an enormous amount of fighting and overt hostility between humans. The expression of aggression in infrahumans typically is prevented by rituals and pre-established dominance hierarchies (Lorenz, 1966; Tinbergen, 1968).
2. Individuals who exhibit extreme acts of violence often have a life history of the overcontrol of aggression (Megargee, 1966).

3. At times, a catharsis of emotions has been demonstrated; i.e., engaging in fantasy aggression reduces the likelihood of subsequent hostile behaviors (Feshbach and Singer, 1971).
4. Individuals identified as authoritarian personalities are characterized as having repressed aggressive wishes against their parents. These unfulfilled desires are then expressed against minority groups (Adorno et al., 1950).
5. In situations of de-individuation, where ego controls are weakened and social sactions are less possible, there is enhanced aggressive responding (Zimbardo, 1969a).

On the other hand, there is an abundance of evidence that aggression is a reaction to an aversive situation and that there is not a constant pressure on the organism to engage in hostile behaviors. Support for this position includes the following facts:

1. Accumulated aggressive energy cannot be "found" or identified.
2. Aggression among infrahumans is influenced by a variety of situational factors, such as the proximity of a stranger.
3. Social factors such as poverty and place of residence greatly influence criminal activity and other forms of overt aggression.
4. There is little empirical support for the belief that hostile expression, as in certain contact sports, reduces subsequent aggression. The catharsis hypothesis is not accepted by most psychologists.
5. Reports in the mass media of aggression and the presence of cues associated with aggression increase hostile expression (Berkowitz, 1970).
6. Obedience to authority can cause aggressive responding (Milgram, 1974).
7. Anonymity and group action promote hostile expression (Zimbardo, 1969a).

In sum, there is empirical evidence that both inborn characteristics and situational factors determine aggression. Again it can be stated that behavior is a function of both the person and the environment. Of course, it is optimistic to believe that the genetic determinants of aggression are weak in comparison with the influence of the situation, for environmental factors perhaps can be more readily controlled or modified. We all hope that the Freudian position is incorrect; the empirical evidence demonstrates that it at least gives insufficient attention to external determinants of behavior. Furthermore, most investigators in this field contend that environmental factors are much more important influences on aggressive responding than genetically inherited urges.

Sexual Motivation

Recall that according to Freud there are two primary instincts: sex and aggression. To provide evidence concerning the importance of sexual motivation, Freud pointed to the following propositions:

1. Neurotic symptoms are caused by unfulfilled sexual urges;
2. Psychological traumas are products of sexual encounters during infancy;
3. Infants and children exhibit great interest in sexual matters; and
4. The incest taboo is universal, intimating that very powerful drives for sexual expression must be operative. (Klein, 1969)

Sexual motivation was incorporated within Freud's drive-cathexis-discharge model of motivation. Sexual drives were conceived as persistent, biologically rooted stimuli demanding satisfaction. The strength of the motivational force toward gratification was postulated to be a direct function of the quantity of undischarged libido. Gratification of sexual desires leads to pleasure and a state of quiescence, while lack of gratification, usually because of a defensive counter-cathexis, could result in maladaptive behaviors such as neurotic symptoms.

It often is contended that Freud's concentration on sexual motivation was a result of his own particular circumstances — living in repressive Vienna in the late 1800's. But this argument is not acceptable. The fact that sexual behavior is now more freely discussed and practiced does not minimize the importance of sexual dilemmas and conflict. Laing (1965) has pointed out that:

> . . . A good deal of effort in all societies is given to deciding which bodies may be joined with which on which occasion and at what age. Persons in all cultures are governed in their actions by an intricate web of injunctions about whose bodies of what sex their own bodies should come into contact with.

In his textbook on personality, Byrne (1974) offers the following fantasy to highlight the social inhibitions and conflict associated with sexual expression, even in contemporary American culture:

> . . . Of the various other psychological needs of mankind, sex holds a unique position. There is a short story which points out some of the absurdities of our sexual attitudes by presenting a society in which eating is treated in the way that we treat sexual activity. That is, sex is freely expressed and openly and publicly encouraged while eating is regarded as shameful and private and limited to a single dish which must be chosen by late adolescence. In that fictional society there were, of course, places where one could go illegally to obtain sumptuous meals cooked by women willing to sell their services. Also, cook books could be surreptitiously obtained from book dealers who specialized in such material. If we lived in such a society, the present text might well contain a chapter on eating behavior but leave sexual behavior to the physiological psychologists. (p. 411)

The Evolution of Sexual Inhibition

Why should there be such great control and inhibitions in our sexual behaviors and motivations? Given an evolutionary or Darwinian perspective, the social taboos and inhibitions regarding sexual expression must have the function of aiding the survival of the organism and the species.

Sexual behaviors, in contrast to actions that satisfy other motivations, exhibit great plasticity. The most satisfying sexual agents are thought to be those closest to us, or, in contemporary American culture, our mother and father. But the ultimate "goal" of sexual behavior is propogation of the species. Thus, for the male of the species, sexual desires toward the father must be given up. Furthermore, as will be discussed, there are functional reasons why the male's desires toward the mother also must be abandoned. Thus, sexual behavior is characterized by a desire-conflict-renunciation sequence (Breger, 1974).

THE INCEST TABOO.   The incest taboo refers to a restriction of sexual choice. In our culture the restriction primarily includes parents and siblings, but also extends to close cousins. One function of these restrictions is to avoid intra-family rivalry, which could cause jealousy and a disruption of the family. In addition, marriage outside the family often strengthens the involved families. The alliance of two countries, for example, frequently has been secured by marriage between members of the ruling families. In earlier cultures, intergroup marriage frequently was forced. Service (1966) states:

> . . . there is but one means of keeping up permanent alliance, and that means is intermarriage. . . . Again and again in the world's history, savage tribes must have had plainly before their minds the simple practical alternative between marrying-out and being killed-out. Even far on in culture, the political value of intermarriage remains. . . . "Then we will give our daughters unto you, and we will take your daughters to us, and we will dwell with you and we will become one people," is a well-known passage of Israelite history. (p. 36)

Finally, and perhaps of greatest importance, research in genetics reveals that inbreeding leads to weakness, whereas outbreeding counteracts deficiencies and produces "hybrid vigor" (Lindzey, 1967).

For these many reasons, inhibitions were erected not only against particular sexual actions, but even against the arousal of certain desires. That is, anticipatory controls over sexual wishes were developed. Freud (1930) suggests that society as we know it first came into existence when family members banded together to prohibit sexual behavior between the mother and her sons. Over many years of time, then, sexual barriers became erected, and sexual behavior become governed by rules and customs.

Determinants of Sexual Expression

Among lower animals, sexual expression is bound by hormonal and physiological conditions following the cyclical pattern that Freud stated is characteristic of the instincts. However, among humans, sexual behavior reflects the total impact of biological, psychological, and social factors. Because sexual expression among humans is not bound by specific time (hormonal) periods, we might be considered more "animal-like" in our pursuit of sexual pleasure than infrahumans (Breger, 1974).

The freeing of sexual expression from hormonal conditions in humans may have had evolutionary significance. The long period of immaturity and great demands that infants make place increasing pressure on humans for stable family relationships. Stability in part requires pair-binding to be very rewarding. The freeing of sexual expression from dependence upon physiological conditions so that sexual motivation could be constantly reinforced could have been one factor that led to more permanent family linkages (Wiggins, Renner, Clore, & Rose, 1971). This position has been questioned, however, for there are stable relations among infrahumans whose sexual behaviors are relatively infrequent (Washburn, 1978).

Given a Freudian position, one would anticipate some cyclical variation in sexual behavior, with expression followed by a period of quiescence, a subsequent build-up of libido, and a repetition of sexual behavior. However, empirical evidence contradicts this notion. Sexual activity among females shows little decrement as a function of orgasm, and sexual responsiveness after sexual satisfaction often increases (Masters & Johnson, 1966). These findings are in contrast with the aggression data cited by ethologists, which allegedly support the notion of a building up of unexpressed instinctive energy, with decreased responsiveness following an aggressive action.

Laboratory Research

Compared with aggression, there is great paucity of research in the area of sexual activity. The first researchers concentrated on animal sexuality, characterizing some of the determinants of sexual approach behavior (such as hormonal conditions) and describing sexual activity. (This research often involved the viewing of what humorously are known as "fur-flicks" rather than "skin-flicks.") Direct study of human sexuality during this early period was limited to abnormalities in behavior and some cross-cultural observations. Research concerning normal human sexuality first began with sociological surveys, such as the famous "Kinsey Report." Now, however, there also is research that directly investigates sexual behavior in an experimental setting, such as the studies conducted by Masters and Johnson (1966, 1970), who monitored the physiological responses of humans as they engaged in sexual intercourse. (For a more complete history of research on sexual activity, see Byrne, 1977).

As indicated above, much of the laboratory research has used infrahuman subjects and focused on the identification of factors that influence sexual behavior. Such factors are legion. For example, social status clearly affects sexual activity. One of the most unusual relationships between status and sexual activity is displayed by a species of coral fish (Robertson, 1972). Valle (1975) reports:

> Males of the species control the process of *sex reversal*. That is to say, each group of fish consists of a male and a harem of females, with the larger females dominating the smaller females (they compete for favored territories within the male's territory). The presence of the dominant male in each group suppresses the tendency of the females to change sex. If the male dies,

however, the dominant female of the group undergoes a sex change. Within one to two hours after the death of the male, the dominant female begins to perform aggressive displays that are characteristic of males, and within a few days the old female completely changes into the new male and performs courtship displays and exhibits its spawning behavior. Thus, in this species, dominance not only determines the probability of sexual responses, it also determines the nature of sexual responses. (p. 254)

Of course, whereas dominance hierarchies among infrahumans are determined by size, strength, and biochemical factors, such rankings among humans are affected by factors such as economic wealth, social skills, and so on.

Homosexuality

Freud maintained that events prior to puberty have an effect on how sexuality is expressed at puberty. Particular socialization practices and frustrations encountered during early childhood were expected to produce aberrant sexual behavior at adulthood.

Freud also contended that, at birth, individuals do not have a clear sexual preference. That is, sexual preferences are learned rather than genetically endowed. Sexual attraction becomes stabilized only after the resolution of the Oedipal conflict, which leads to appropriate sex-role behavior. Freud, therefore, was not sure whether homosexual behavior should be considered an "illness." On the one hand, attraction for the same-sex partner is a normal and inborn tendency. However, homosexual preferences at adulthood indicate "a certain arrest of sexual development." The following letter from Freud (1935) to a concerned American parent reveals his compassion toward homosexuals as well as his ambivalence about the normal-versus-abnormal diagnosis of homosexual behavior:

Dear Mrs. X

I gather from your letter that your son is a homosexual. I am most impressed by the fact that you do not mention this term yourself in your information about him. May I question you, why do you avoid it? Homosexuality is assuredly no advantage, but it is nothing to be ashamed of, no vice, no degradation, it cannot be classified as an illness; we consider it to be a variation of the sexual function produced by a certain arrest of sexual development. Many highly respectable individuals of ancient and modern times have been homosexuals, several of the greatest men among them (Plato, Michelangelo, Leonardo da Vinci, etc.). It is a great injustice to persecute homosexuality as a crime, and cruelty too. If you do not believe me, read the books of Havelock Ellis.

By asking me if I can help, you mean, I suppose, if I can abolish homosexuality and make normal heterosexuality take its place. The answer is, in a general way, we cannot promise to achieve it. In a certain number of cases we succeed in developing the blighted germs of heterosexual tendencies which are present in every homosexual, in the majority of cases it is no more possible. It is a question of the quality and the age of the individual. The result of the treatment cannot be predicted.

What analysis can do for your son runs in a different line. If he is unhappy, neurotic, torn by conflicts, inhibited in his social life, analysis may bring him harmony, peace of mind, full efficiency, whether he remains a homosexual or gets changed. If you make up your mind he should have analysis with me (I don't expect you will!!!) he has to come over to Vienna. I have no intention of leaving here. However, don't neglect to give me your answer.

Sincerely yours with kind wishes,
Freud

P.S. I did not find it difficult to read your handwriting. Hope you will not find my writing and my English a harder task.

HOMOSEXUALITY AND PARANOIA.   Freud believed that homosexuality, in part, is the cause of paranoia. Paranoia refers to the tendency of individuals to believe that others are against them. The association between homosexuality and paranoia starts, according to Freud, with the self-perception that "I (a male) love him." This is an unacceptable state and is opposed by a defense called "reaction formation." This defense converts an affect into its opposite. Thus, "I love him" gives way to "I hate him." However, the admission of hate toward a significant other also provokes anxiety. Thus, another defense mechanism, projection, is elicited, resulting in one's own affect becoming attributed to others — "He hates me." The belief that others hate oneself is the sign of paranoia.

Although the sequence of events sketched above seems to stretch credulity, there is a reasonable amount of empirical evidence supporting Freud's insight concerning an association between homosexuality and paranoia. In one experimental investigation, Zamansky (1958) showed paranoid and non-paranoid patients pairs of pictures in a tachistoscope. Some pictures portrayed males and females engaged in common activities, while others showed males engaging in homosexual (e.g., two men kissing) and heterosexual activities. Zamansky was able to monitor secretly which pictures the patients were viewing. In addition, he asked the patients to state their preferences among the pictures. The data revealed that the verbalized preferences of the paranoids contradicted their viewing behavior. Although they indicated a preference for the pictures that included females, they spent more time viewing the pictures of the males, but only when those pictures were not too threatening. Thus, it appears that the paranoids were defending against their sexual preferences.

A very different approach to the study of paranoia and its relation to sexuality was undertaken by John Whiting (1959), a well known anthropologist and psychologist. Whiting reasoned that cultures can be classified according to their degree of paranoia. One index of paranoia in primitive cultures could be the belief in sorcery — a magical power that others can use for harm.

What, Whiting asked, might lead individuals in a culture to believe in sorcery? Guided by Freud, Whiting hypothesized that one antecedent could be sexual anxiety during the early, formative years. But this leads to another puzzle: What conditions in a society could produce such anxiety? Whiting noted that societies vary in their degree of post-partum sexual taboos, or rules that determine when the husband and wife may again have sexual intercourse after the birth of a child. In some societies, such as ours, there are no restrictions, save those generated by medical concerns. But in other societies, taboos may last until the mother stops nursing the child or even until the child is five years old. These societies often are nomadic, making it difficult to carry and feed more than one infant in the endless travels and search for food. Furthermore, in this situation the mother typically sleeps with her infant child, while the husband has his own tent or remains in a shelter with other males.

Whiting suggests that given this sleeping arrangement, the mother may consciously or unconsciously engage in sexual, or at least in overly sensual, interactions with the child. Such contact, he argues, produces childhood anxiety and paranoia (fear of sorcery) during later years.

To put these ideas to empirical test, Whiting (1959) gathered information on post-partum sexual taboos and beliefs about sorcery from a variety of societies. These data are available from extensive cross-cultural files. Whiting's hypothesis was confirmed (see Table 2–6). Table

TABLE 2–6 RELATIONSHIP BETWEEN THE DURATION OF THE POST-PARTUM SEX TABOO AND THE STRENGTH OF THE BELIEF THAT SORCERERS CAN CAUSE ILLNESS

| Duration of Post-Partum Sex Taboo | Belief in Sorcery | |
	Low	High
Long		12* Arapesh
		18 Azande
		36 Chagga
		21 Chiricahua
		24 Kurtachi
		18 Kwakiutl
		24 Kwoma
	22 Bena	30 Lesu
	24 Dahomeans	18 Tiv
	18 Masai	18 Trobrianders
	48 Teton	42 Venda
	21 Thonga	30 Wogeo
Short	9 Alorese	0 Baiga
	3 Ashanti	0 Maori
	1 Balinese	1 Sanpoil
	2 Chamorro	9 Yagua
	1 Chewa	
	1 Hopi	
	0 Lakher	
	1 Lamba	
	1 Lepcha	
	2 Navaho	
	2 Ontong Java	
	0 Papago	
	1 Siriono	
	6 Tanala	
	1 Yukaghir	

*The numbers represent the duration in months of the post-partum sex taboo.
(Adapted from Whiting, 1959, p. 178.)

2–6 shows the societies that were examined, their classification as to high or low beliefs in sorcery, and the lengths of the post-partum sexual taboo.

Of course, the existence of an association between fear of sorcery and post-partum sexual taboos does not prove that this relationship is mediated by sexual anxiety and unconscious seduction by the mother. Perhaps a more parsimonious or intuitively reasonable explanation is available. However, the Freudian sequence of "I love him — I hate him — He hates me" was responsible for uncovering this association and, therefore, must be seriously considered.

It should be pointed out that studies demonstrating the aberrant qualities of homosexuals have become increasingly questioned by individuals active in attaining acceptance and civil rights for homosexuals. These persons point out that there is a research bias to demonstrate that homosexuality *per se* is indicative of psychopathology. They contend that the focus of research should be altered to include

> the dynamics of gay relationships; the development of positive gay identity; the ... variables associated with self-disclosure; ... specific problems of gay children and adolescents; aspects of aging in the gay subculture; and conflict involving gay civil liberties. (Morin, 1977, p. 636)

Sex and Aggression

As previously indicated, Freud vacillated in his thinking about the instincts. Near the end of his career he postulated two instincts: Eros (life) and Thanatos (death). But at other times he concluded that there is one basic instinct, Eros, which includes sexual (preservation of the species) and aggressive (preservation of the self) components.

The belief that sex and aggression are related is held by many laymen. For example, it is often contended that exposure to pornography increases crime, particularly rape and other sexual attacks. Empirical evidence, however, suggests an opposite linkage. In what is known as "The Danish Experiment," Denmark legalized all forms of "hard-core" pornographic material. After the passage of this controversial law, sexual violence decreased. Furthermore, the decrease in sexual crime appeared to be caused by the relaxation of sexual censorship.

In recent years academic psychologists have been discovering that sexual and aggressive motivations are linked in a complex manner. In one experiment, Jaffe, Malamuth, Feingold, and Feshbach (1974) had subjects read erotic or neutral material prior to an opportunity to shock a confederate during a learning task. The data clearly revealed that shock administration increased both among male and female subjects following the reading of erotic material, regardless of whether the recipient of the shock was a male or a female (see Table 2–7).

However, other research studies (e.g., Baron, 1974) have reported just the opposite: reduction of aggression following exposure to erotic material. It appears that the effects of sexual excitement on aggressive behavior, in part, depend upon whether the viewer is aroused to aggress

TABLE 2–7 MEAN SHOCK LEVEL AS A FUNCTION OF SEXUAL AROUSAL, SEX OF AGGRESSOR, AND SEX OF RECIPIENT OF AGGRESSION

Aggressor	Recipient of Aggression			
	Male		Female	
	Sexual arousal	Control	Sexual arousal	Control
Male	3.10	2.41	3.51	2.81
Female	2.94	2.32	2.53	1.72

(Adapted from Jaffe, Malamuth, Feingold & Feshbach, 1974, p. 762.)

prior to the reading of erotic passages and whether inhibitions and approach motivations are affected by the stimuli. Clearly, reconciliation of the disparate findings awaits additional experimentation. However, one agreed-upon fact that emerges from these research investigations is that sexual and aggressive motivation are not independent.

Sociobiology and Sexual Behavior

In recent years a new scientific discipline, labelled sociobiology, has developed. Sociobiologists seek to establish that social behavior has a biological or a genetic basis. It has even been suggested that genes transmit social behaviors such as conformity and altruism (and cheating on exams!).

Sociobiologists have been guided by the ideas of Darwin. They accept that behavior that promotes survival is passed on between generations. But they contend that it is the genes themselves, rather than entire organisms, which are struggling to survive. Thus, for example, a bird may risk its life to warn the rest of the flock of impending danger because, in this manner, the survival of the entire gene pool is aided. Altruistic behavior, therefore, is really in the self-interest of the genes. Sociobiologists contend that evolution produces organisms that follow this logic and "calculate" genetic gains and losses.

These ideas have been invoked to explain some puzzling facts. For example, why is it that female ants devote their lives to aiding the queen ant to breed rather than breeding themselves? Sociobiologists have answered this question by pointing out that female ants share more genes in common with their sisters than they would with their offspring. Hence, it is in the self-interest of their gene pool to assist the queen in producing more daughters rather than breeding themselves!

Sociobiological concepts also led to a reinterpretation of various facets of sexual behavior. The sociobiologists contend that male aggression and displays are a reproductive strategy to impress females. Since this strategy "works," females are responsible for male machismo!

The male, sociobiologists argue, has one prime goal — to transmit as many personal genes as possible into the next generation. On the other hand, the female must invest a great deal of time into each birth and can have a very limited number of offspring. Thus, only male promiscuity has great pay-off, and males are, in general, more promiscuous than females. Furthermore, because females must invest more of themselves in each pregnancy, they are important resources that males must "purchase." Hence, in most cultures older males (who have the necessary resources) marry younger women (who have many years of childbearing left).

Sociobiologists also point out that males have one great disadvantage in breeding — they cannot be certain that the offspring is their own. Thus, sexual jealousy is aroused, and courtship rituals have emerged in which the female's time is totally monopolized. During this extended courtship the male also can determine whether the female is already pregnant.

Needless to say, these are controversial ideas that have made many individuals and groups quite angry. The hypotheses also are supported by relatively few human data. In addition, it is obvious that cultural factors greatly influence sexual behavior. How, for example, could sociobiologists account for the fact that today so many males are undergoing voluntary sterilization? Furthermore, one wonders why species have evolved beyond mere self-reproduction, if reproduction of one's genes is the guiding principle of evolution. Nonetheless, this extreme biological view, which also was present, in part, in Freudian psychology, has proven exceedingly provocative and has paved the way for the interpretation (and reinterpretation) of a variety of phenomena.

Dreams

Freud's primary model of thought (see Table 2–1) specifies that in the absence of gratifying goal objects, the individual can hallucinate the desired goal to gain satisfaction. Thus, fantasy serves a wish-fulfillment function. As already discussed, there is weak but suggestive evidence that a catharsis of emotions does occur when viewing aggressive-related imagery (Feshbach and Singer, 1971). Of course, if all instinctual wishes are satisfied, then theoretically the person will not engage in fantasy activity. Thus, the antecedent of fantasy behavior is drive deprivation; the consequence of such behavior is drive reduction.

Dreams are one form of fantasy activity that apparently is universal, spanning all cultures and age groups. Indeed, they fit the characteristics of an instinctive behavior. Because of this universality, there has been much concern with the dream process. But psychology's interest in dreams is best ascribed to the influence of Freud. As previously indicated, Freud believed that the dream is the "royal road" to the unconscious. Through dream analysis, he contended, we can learn about unconscious wishes and desires and the symbolic manifestations of needs.

According to Freud, the purpose of dreams is to preserve sleep. By serving as a goal substitute, the dream allows the release of some of the internal tension that is associated with unfulfilled desires. Without this release the dreamer would be awakened by excessive internal stimulation. A simple illustration can clarify this idea. Assume that you go to bed without dinner. After some period of time, hunger cramps are felt that might cause awakening. During sleep, however, you dream about the ingestion of food. The content of the dream might be disguised, with the food appearing in symbolic form. The wish-fulfilling dream produces a diminution in subjective hunger, thereby reducing the stomach cramps and preserving sleep.

As the reader might anticipate, it is extremely difficult to gather scientific evidence that dreams are wish fulfillments and that they preserve sleep by reducing internal stimulation. But recent advances in dream research have generated data that are pertinent to some of Freud's presumptions.

For many years, useful scientific research on dreaming was not conducted. One reason for this shortcoming was that only the dreamer had direct access to the dream. Therefore, it was not possible to assess the reliability of dream reports. There was a need to have a witness to the dream in addition to the dreamer.

An objective technique for the detection of dreams was discovered in the early 1950's (see Dement and Kleitman, 1957). During sleep, rapid eye movements (REM) under the lid were discovered. Individuals awakened during these REM periods reported dreams with a high frequency, while persons awakened at other times did not report having dreams. Some mental and cognitive activities do occur during the non-REM periods, but reports of visual-like experiences occur only during REM sleep.

Subsequent research also revealed that during the course of sleep there are cyclical patterns of brain activity (see Dement, 1965). This activity can be monitored with an electroencephalogram (EEG) or polygraph. Four different patterns of brain waves have been detected during sleep (see Figure 2–8). "Stage 1 sleep," in which there is a lack of

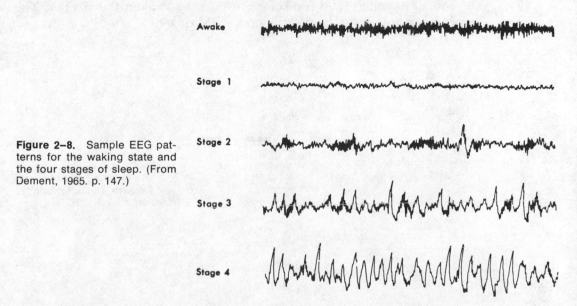

Figure 2–8. Sample EEG patterns for the waking state and the four stages of sleep. (From Dement, 1965. p. 147.)

spindle activity and no "Delta" or large waves, is highly associated with REM periods and dream reports. It is now quite clear that the REM observations and particular patterns of brain waves provide reliable outward criteria for identifying the internal dream process.

Figure 2–9 depicts a typical night's sleep for a young adult. During the course of an eight-hour sleep period, the individual has about five dream episodes, or an average of about one dream every 90 minutes. In general, the longer one sleeps, the greater the total dream activity. The average dream lasts approximately fourteen minutes, with the length of the dream increasing as the night progresses. In addition, the time between dream episodes decreases as the waking state is approached.

Given an objective dream index, one would expect that the "royal road" to the unconscious would become a superhighway and that the speculations of Freud would be either confirmed or discarded. This has not been the case. However, inferential data have been gathered that do bear upon some of the issues raised by Freud.

First, it appears that all individuals dream. The universality of the dream was anticipated by Freud and apparently lends support to his conception. But the universality even exceeds the boundaries suggested by Freud. Many species in addition to humans exhibit dream-state sleep (see Table 2–8). If it is inferred from REM observations that lower organisms also dream, then it is difficult to contend that the function of dreams is to drain internal stimulation. It is generally assumed that infrahumans have few social inhibitions and that their basic sexual and aggressive needs are satisfied. It seems, therefore, that dreams do not preserve sleep, but rather the presence of sleep ensures dreams.

Another finding that may be considered evidence in support of the Freudian conception of dreams is that there appears to be a "need" to dream (Dement, 1960). If the sleeper is awakened every time a REM period is entered, then the REM periods are more frequent on subsequent evenings, and it takes more vigor to awaken the sleeper. The organism appears to be making up a REM deficit.

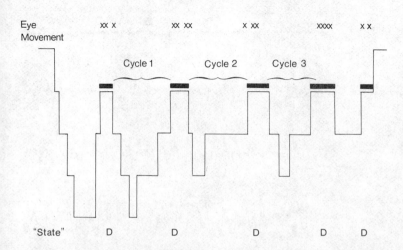

Figure 2–9. Typical night's sleep in a young adult. D indicates dream. (Adapted from E. Hartmann, 1965, p. 30.)

TABLE 2–8   DREAM STATE IN VARIOUS MAMMALIAN SPECIES (YOUNG ADULT ANIMALS)

Species	Average Length of Dream Period (min.)	Average Cycle Length (min.)	Dream-Time as Percentage of Total Sleep
Man	14	80–90	20–24
Monkey	4–10	40–60	11–20
Cat	10	20–40	20–60
Sheep	–	–	2–3
Rabbit	–	24	1–3
Rat	4–7	7–13	15–20
Mouse	–	3–4	–
Opossum	5	17	22–40

(From E. Hartmann, 1965, p. 32.)

But if there is a need to dream, then dream deprivation should affect psychological functioning. At present, it is uncertain whether REM deprivation causes psychological dysfunctioning. Some investigators do report that individuals become more emotional and less psychologically balanced following the loss of REM sleep. But other investigators do not find any disturbing psychological effects from the prevention of dream sleep. Furthermore, there are perfectly adjusted individuals who sleep less than one hour per night!

Recall Freud stated that dreams preserve sleep by "draining off" internal stimulation. It is evident that what Freud labelled as "day residues," or memory traces of experiences during the day, do influence the content of dreams. In addition, stimulation during sleep, such as the onset of a light or tactile input, often is incorporated into dreams. But such stimulation does not *instigate* dreams. That is, the onset of stimulation that might awaken the sleeper does not initiate a REM episode, although the stimulation may be incorporated into an ongoing dream. Further, emotional upsets during the day, or reported frustrations or unfulfilled desires, are unrelated to the amount of time spent in dream activity.

In sum, it appears that dreaming is primarily a function of biological factors. There is a cyclical course of sleep during the night that is relatively uniform across individuals. The question of the dream's function remains moot. Perhaps not every psychological process must contribute to the survival and the well-being of the organism. If this is so, then the search for the function of dreams will be fruitless. At present, no clear function has been uncovered, and one must question the notion of the dream as having substitute value and reducing internal stimulation. It seems more probable that dreams aid in thinking through problems and in providing creative solutions that have escaped individuals during normal waking thought (see Singer, 1974). That is, dreams may have a cognitive, rather than an affective (stimulation-reducing), function. But at this time further evidence is needed before the Freudian conception of the dream as a wish-fulfillment can be entirely discarded.

Defense Mechanisms

In the previous pages of this book, various products of the id—instincts, aggressive and sexual motivation, and dreams—were examined. These are the basic biologically rooted motivations and processes. The discussion will now turn from the id to the ego. Recall that the ego forms to distinguish reality from irreality and to protect the organism from the pain that might be experienced as a consequence of direct sexual or aggressive expression. Thus, the ego inhibits and redirects goal-oriented activities, acting in service of the id. Because the mechanisms used by the ego have a protective function, they frequently are called *defense mechanisms,* or just *defenses.* Hence, this section of the chapter deals with how one copes with desires that often are not permitted fulfillment by social rules.

The psychological defenses that protect an individual from anxiety, punishment, or other unpleasant experience are at times quite manifest. For example, one mechanism that prevents continued exposure to aversive sensations (e.g., the sight of blood or the feelings that accompany the death of a significant other) is fainting. Psychologists believe that most defenses operate on an unconscious level (see Figure 2–2). In other words, individuals generally are not conscious of either the defenses or their functional significance. In addition, it is not self-evident to an observer that defenses are inhibiting goal attainment. Of course, not all defenses are unconscious. Individuals also may consciously and rationally implement strategies that enable them to cope with the stresses and problems in life.

In the following discussion, only the unconscious mechanisms stressed by psychologists are examined. These mechanisms are particularly likely to be evoked in situations of great emotion and personal involvement. Four defenses that have received attention from both clinical and experimental psychologists—repression, perceptual defense, denial, and intellectualization—have been selected for discussion. Freud and others identified additional defenses, including sublimation, reaction formation, projection, regression, and displacement. Some of these defenses are examined elsewhere in this book, while others have been neglected because of space limitations and because they are not central to Freud's thinking.

Repression

Freud believed that repression is the most significant defense mechanism. He poetically described repression as follows:

> . . . Every mental process . . . first exists in an unconscious state or phase, and only develops out of this into a conscious phase, much as a photograph is first a negative and then becomes a picture through the printing of the positive. But not every negative is made into a positive, and it is just as little necessary that every unconscious mental process should convert itself into a conscious one. It may be best expressed as follows: Each single process

belongs in the first place to the unconscious psychical system; from this system it can under certain conditions proceed further into the conscious system.

The crudest conception of these systems is the one we shall find most convenient, a spatial one. The unconscious system may therefore be compared to a large ante-room, in which the various mental excitations are crowding upon one another, like individual beings. Adjoining this is a second, smaller apartment, a sort of reception-room, in which consciousness resides. But on the threshold between the two there stands a personage with the office of door-keeper, who examines the various mental excitations, censors them, and denies them admittance to the reception-room when he disapproves of them. You will see at once that it does not make much difference whether the door-keeper turns any one impulse back at the threshold, or drives it out again once it has entered the reception-room; that is merely a matter of the degree of his vigilance and promptness in recognition. Now this metaphor may be employed to widen our terminology. The excitations in the unconscious, in the ante-chamber, are not visible to consciousness, which is of course in the other room, so to begin with they remain unconscious. When they have pressed forward to the threshold and been turned back by the door-keeper, they are "incapable of becoming conscious;" we call them then repressed. (Freud, 1934, pp. 305–6)

Freud's conception of repression grew from hypnotic experimentation and from his observations as a therapist. Freud noted that his patients had amnesia for important memories. But these memories were not truly forgotten; they could be retrieved. Bringing the memories back into consciousness required special methodologies, such as free association and dream interpretation, during the therapy hour. Because the memories could be retrieved, Freud concluded that their emergence into consciousness was opposed by an active force (the "door-keeper"). When the active inhibitory force was weakened, the memories could be displayed.

THE EXPERIMENTAL STUDY OF REPRESSION.   Many different experimental procedures have been used to demonstrate repression in the laboratory. However, none has been entirely satisfactory (see Rapaport, 1942; Weiner, 1966). But because some of the experimental evidence is promising, and because many clinical observations of repression have been reported, the belief in inhibited memories remains strongly entrenched among most psychologists.

One early technique employed to demonstrate repression was merely to ask subjects to recall past events. If more pleasant than unpleasant experiences were remembered, then it was inferred that repression was operating to interfere with the memory of the unpleasant occurrences. However, this approach is weak because we may indeed have more pleasant than unpleasant experiences. That is, the recall may be accurate and does not necessarily demonstrate repression.

A second frequently used procedure is to pair distinctive stimuli, such as digits or words, with pleasant and unpleasant sensations, such as various smells or the receipt of money versus shock. Subjects are later asked to recall the stimuli. When the stimuli paired with the aversive consequences are recalled less often than the stimuli paired with the positive consequences, repression is inferred. Note that this procedure is better than merely asking subjects to recall life events because the positive and negative experiences are controlled and equalized.

But these studies also are weak. First, consistent data are not reported. At times there is greater recall of stimuli associated with pleasant experiences, and at times the reverse is found. Further, when "repression" is demonstrated, it is difficult to argue that the retrieval of the "forgotten" stimuli is opposed by an *active restraining force*. The experimental stimuli are far removed from the dangerous sexual and aggressive urges discussed by Freud.

A third research procedure examines the recall of successful and failed achievement activities. It is reasoned that it is "ego-protective" to forget failures. Thus, repressive forces should impede the retention of prior poor performances. Subjects in these experiments typically are given a number of tasks to solve. Half of the tasks are too long to solve within the time allotted, while the remaining one-half are easily soluble. Thus, the subjects experience success on one-half of the tasks and failure on the other half. They then are asked to name the tasks on which they worked. Again, however, the findings are inconsistent. At times there is greater recall of the incompleted tasks; at other times the opposite is true. (For a fuller discussion of this phenomenon, see Chapter Four.)

Finally, a fourth experimental procedure for studying repression involves the recall of "complex-related" words. The notion of a "complex-related" word was first advanced by Jung. Jung would read subjects a list of words and ask them to respond with the first word that came into mind. This was called the "word-association" technique. Jung noted that some responses were preceded by unusually long pauses. He inferred that in those instances the stimulus words were related to a particular "personality complex," or an area of emotional disturbance and personal difficulty. He believed that the stimulus words therefore were associated with repressed and conflictive material. Because of this association, the immediate responses were likely to meet with censorship, resulting in a longer latency, or time period, prior to the verbalized response.

Some convincing experimental demonstrations of repression make use of complex-related words. In a study conducted by Clemes (1964), association reaction times were first ascertained for a series of words.

TABLE 2–9   OUTLINE OF EXPERIMENT USING COMPLEX-RELATED WORDS AND HYPNOSIS TO DEMONSTRATE REPRESSION

	Control Condition	Experimental Condition
Stage 1	Determine conflict-related and neutral words	
Stage 2	Nothing	Hypnosis
Stage 3	Learn selected conflict-related and neutral words	
Stage 4	Nothing	Instructions to later recall only ten words
Stage 5	First recall, waking state	First recall, waking state
Stage 6	Nothing	Lift post-hypnotic suggestion
Stage 7	Second recall	Second recall

TABLE 2–10   COMPARISON OF RETRIEVED
COMPLEX-RELATED VERSUS NEUTRAL WORDS

Group	Complex-Related > Neutral	Complex-Related = Neutral	Neutral > Complex-Related
Control	6*	15	6
Hypnotic	15	7	4

*Indicates number of subjects
(Adapted from Clemes, 1964, p. 66.)

Some days later the subjects were given a list of words to learn that contained nine normal-latency (neutral) and nine long-latency (complex-related) words.

There were two experimental conditions. Subjects in one of the conditions learned the list while in a hypnotic state. Further, while in the hypnotic trance, each subject was told that later, when asked to recall the words in a waking state, "he would be able to remember only ten words, no matter how hard he tried." After being asked to recall the words in the waking state, the post-hypnotic trance was lifted and a second recall was obtained. Thus, the first recall, but not the second, took place under conditions of active interference. Subjects in a second experimental condition merely learned the list and recalled the words on two occasions, without the post-hypnotic interference. This rather complex experimental design is outlined in Table 2–9.

The words forgotten on the first recall but remembered on the second were then analyzed. For each subject, the number of "reappearing" (first forgotten but later recalled) neutral and complex-related words were compared. Table 2–10 shows the number of subjects recalling more complex-related words than neutral ones, the same amount of each, or more neutral than complex-related. The table shows that among the control subjects there is no difference in the memory return of complex-related versus neutral words on the second recall (6 subjects each). But among the hypnotic subjects, a significantly larger number (15 to 4) recall more complex-related words between the second and first recall periods.

This is a reasonable demonstration of what Freud meant by repression because:

1. The experimental stimuli were relevant to each subject's areas of emotional disturbance. This contrasts with investigations using smells or shock, or successes and failures in certain tasks.
2. An active inhibiting force was introduced, in this case via an experimental instruction during hypnosis. This force interfered with the emergence of some thoughts into consciousness.
3. When the active inhibiting force subsided with the removal of the post-hypnotic suggestion, more of the emotionally related words were retrieved back into consciousness by most subjects. Selective

amnesia was demonstrated because the active inhibitory force had little effect upon neutral words. Thus, there is an analogue to the therapeutic process, in which repressed material supposedly becomes available following the weakening of the repressive force.

In sum, there is a great deal of clinical and anecdotal evidence supporting the notion of repression. On the other hand, the vast majority of laboratory studies have failed to support the concept. Yet, a few well conducted experimental investigations have demonstrated the phenomenon of repression. Among these is the study by Clemes (1964), which made use of complex-related words as the emotional material.

Perceptual Defense

Perceptual defense also refers to a resistance against threatening material. It is conceptually similar to repression, but repression prevents selected memories from becoming conscious, while perceptual defense keeps selected perceptions from the awareness of the perceiver.

Perceptual defense has received a vast amount of attention from personality psychologists. This appeal is in part due to the relationship between perceptual defense and subliminal perception. At one time, claims were made that behavior could be controlled by television and movie advertisements processed without the knowledge of the viewer. That is, the ads were to be flashed on the screen and perceived at a "subliminal" level, below conscious awareness. The claims, thankfully, were unfounded.

There is a great deal of anecdotal and clinical evidence to support the notion of perceptual defense. However, as is true for the concept of repression and many other defense mechanisms, the experimental evidence in support of these claims has not been conclusive. Nevertheless, there have been some experimental demonstrations that appear convincing, and new ways of thinking about perceptual defense are adding to the validity of the concept.

AN EXPERIMENTAL CONTROVERSY.   An investigation conducted by McGinnies (1949) first aroused interest in the experimental study of perceptual defense and best illustrates the goals of research in this area. Subjects were shown words on a tachistoscope. This instrument allows the exposure of material for extremely short durations, such as 1/1000 of a second. It is therefore possible to flash stimuli so quickly that they cannot be identified.

In the McGinnies study, some of the flashed words were neutral, or nonaffective, such as "house" and "flower," while others were "taboo" words, such as "whore" and "bitch." The subjects' task was to identify the words. The speed of exposure was gradually decreased until the word shown was correctly identified. In addition to word recognition, galvanic skin responses (GSRs) to the words were recorded. The GSR is a measure of electrical conductance. It is generally recorded from the palm, and is accepted as an index of emotionality. It is one measure taken during a lie detection test.

Two interesting findings were reported. First, taboo words were recognized later than the neutral words. That is, the duration of the flash needed for the perceiver to be able to identify taboo words was greater than that required to recognize neutral words. A second provocative finding was that heightened GSRs were exhibited on trials in which the subjects did not correctly report the flashed taboo word. That is, emotion was exhibited without conscious word recognition.

These findings posed somewhat of a paradox, for how can a perceiver defend against a stimulus unless that stimulus is first perceived? That is, the material must be sufficiently processed to realize that it produces anxiety, but blocked so that the perceiver is not made anxious!

In part because of this apparent logical inconsistency, investigators attempted to discredit the findings of McGinnies and other reports of perceptual defense. Many of the opponents argued that perceptual defense is nothing more than a response bias. For example, subjects could be reluctant to say the taboo words, particularly if they are somewhat unsure of the correctness of their guesses. Thus, the results could be attributed to simple response suppression. Further, there is evidence that the frequency of prior exposure to words influences both recognition and what the subject is likely to guess (Howes and Solomon, 1951). It was argued by some experimentalists that the neutral words in the McGinnies experiment were much more frequently heard or read by the subjects than the taboo words (recall that the experiment took place in the 1940's). Thus, although the neutral words were more quickly recognized, the results could merely be due to different exposure frequencies. And finally, it was pointed out that the verbal response was dichotomous; that is, it was scored as either correct or incorrect. On the other hand, the GSR was a continuous response that allowed for a full range of magnitude. Thus, for example, an individual might be unsure whether the word exposed was "bitch" or "bite." If the subject decided on "bite," which was incorrect, there was likely to be some GSR deflection. It would not be reasonable to label the discrepancy between the incorrect score and the GSR deflection as perceptual defense (see Eriksen, 1958, 1960).

Some writers have posited that there are different response systems (e.g., verbal and physiological); this has enabled them to reinterpret apparently "unconscious" phenomena. Bandura (1971) suggests that thinking taboo words is not punished, but that overtly repeating such words is. Hence, the phenomenon of perceptual defense merely indicates that there are differential reinforcement contingencies in the world, and that reinforcement controls behavior. One may respond at one level (internally) but not at another (verbally). The observation of a phenomenon labelled perceptual defense, Bandura argues, is not proof that unconscious perceptions exist.

However, other investigators have come to the defense of perceptual defense, and it appears that none of the counter-arguments attempting to do away with the defense concept has been completely adequate (see Dixon, 1971; Erdelyi, 1974). For example, experimenters controlling for frequency of word exposure report perceptual defense (e.g., Dulany,

1957). Defense is also exhibited when methods are used to eliminate a response suppression explanation (e.g., subjects are required to respond with a taboo word to indicate the perception of a neutral word, and vice versa; see Zigler and Yospe, 1960).

AN EXPERIMENTAL DEMONSTRATION.   To demonstrate perceptual defense, it is necessary that the stimuli used in an experiment elicit anxiety among most of the subjects. Employing a stimulus such as "bitch" is not likely to arouse anxiety among many college students. Further, to demonstrate this defense, it is also necessary that the subjects respond to anxiety with avoidance and inhibition. The problem of using rather emotionally bland material and not ensuring that subjects will respond with avoidance plagues the laboratory study of virtually all the defense mechanisms. Therefore, the relative weakness of the experimental findings, in the face of strong clinical and case-report evidence, suggests shortcomings in the experimental methodology rather than the nonexistence of the phenomenon.

One dramatic clinical example of perceptual defense is observed in the case of hysterical blindness. In this condition, patients report an inability to see, although they avoid bumping into objects and react quite differently from a congenitally blind person. Gerald Blum (1961), a personality psychologist trained in the use of hypnotic techniques, attempted to induce "hysterical blindness" in a laboratory experiment. His experiment perhaps best illustrates the concept of perceptual defense.

Blum linked anxiety to a particular stimulus by hypnotic suggestion. The subjects were told that any time they perceived three dots on a tachistoscopic presentation they would feel anxious. GSR measures confirmed that this induction was effective. Thus, Blum was able to employ stimuli that aroused anxiety for each subject.

Blum then trained the subjects "not to see" the three-dot stimulus when it was flashed. But, of course, for the "not seeing" to occur, there must first be a registration of the stimulus! That is, the stimulus must first be perceived at an unconscious level and then kept from conscious recognition. After extensive training of subjects, Blum was able to demonstrate that they did not exhibit GSR responses on the trials in which they were told "not to see" the anxiety-provoking material. Various control conditions ensured that the subjects were still emotionally aroused by the stimulus and that they were not "blind" to all the material being flashed.

This dramatic demonstration made use of hypnosis to increase the affective importance of the stimuli and to induce the subjects to respond with avoidance. Many psychologists are reluctant to accept data from hypnotic subjects, for there is little understanding of hypnotic states. Nevertheless, Blum's demonstration is fascinating and may be the best experimental illustration of the meaning of perceptual inhibition.

INFORMATION PROCESSING AND PERCEPTUAL DEFENSE.   Perceptual defense becomes logically more acceptable when considered within the framework of contemporary conceptions of information processing. It is now evident that many processes are involved between the perception of a stimulus and a final response, or conscious awareness. These processes include stimulus reception, analysis, transfer into short-term and then long-term memory storage, and so on.

A process akin to perceptual defense can occur at any stage of this multiprocess system. For example, common observation shows that people frequently avoid traumatic input (as during a horror movie) by fixating away from the stimulus, or closing their eyes. In this instance, control over stimulus input is voluntary and conscious. But in other circumstances the avoidance may be neither voluntary nor conscious. For example, it has been documented that pupils expand and contract in different situations as a function of the needs of the person (see Hess, 1965). This alteration influences the perceiver's sensitivity.

In addition, one can scan incoming information and, on the basis of a partial analysis, decide whether to encode or reject this material for additional processing. For example, at a party one might receive different messages in each ear. The contents of one "channel" can then be rejected, although this rejected information is "heard." However, the message content may not be transferred into memory. In a similar manner, we can perceive without remembering; many more stimuli are apprehended than are put into memory storage. This "selectivity" analysis can readily account for the more esoteric notion of perceptual defense (see Erdelyi, 1974) and the demonstration by Blum that there can be stimulus registration and screening without the conscious awareness of the perceiver.

Individual Differences in Defensive Preferences

As might be anticipated, individuals differ in their defensive reactions to threatening stimuli. Defensive preferences can be distinguished in many ways, such as their complexity, generality, effectiveness, and the degree to which they distort reality. One differentiating dimension receiving much attention from psychologists is labelled repression-sensitization (see Byrne, 1964). It is reasoned that some individuals respond to particular kinds of threat with defenses such as repression and perceptual defense. In so doing, they avoid anxiety-laden information. Hysterical reactions, including symptoms such as blindness and limb paralysis, are generally associated with the use of repressive defenses. Conversely, it appears that one may cope with a particular threat by using sensitizing defenses. In such cases the person becomes more vigilant to threat and remains in close contact with the stressful material. The individual may then be better able to monitor and control the threat. The constant worrier and the obsessive-compulsive neurotic are typically linked with the use of sensitizing defensive orientations.

Individual differences in the repression-sensitization dimension are generally assessed with a true-false, self-report inventory called the R-S scale (Byrne, 1961). Some typical items on the scale (scored here in the direction of repression) are:

Most of the time I feel blue. (True)
I don't seem to care what happens to me. (True)
Often I feel as if there were a tight band about my head. (True)

The items on this measure were taken from the Minnesota Multiphasic Personality Inventory (MMPI), and many of the items are also included in popular measures of general anxiety, such as the Manifest Anxiety Scale (MAS). Precisely what the scale measures is, therefore, not entirely clear.

Many investigations have examined the behavioral correlates of responses to the scale items. It has been found, for example, that repressors (as compared with persons labelled sensitizors) require a longer tachistoscopic exposure before recognizing threatening words, remember more successful than failed tasks, and are slower at learning a list of affective arousing words. Thus, the scale has some empirical validity (see Byrne, 1964).

There is a paucity of knowledge about why individuals use one particular defense rather than another or how various defensive strategies come to be used. A research investigation by Dulany (1957) has nicely demonstrated the influence of prior learning histories on defensive preferences. Dulany simultaneously presented four geometric figures on a tachistoscope below the level of recognition, or below what is termed the "threshold level." The subjects responded by indicating the figure that most stood out. One-half of the subjects were given an electric shock whenever they designated one particular "critical" figure as most visible or salient. The other subjects were shocked when they *did not* select this critical figure as the stimulus that most stood out. Thus, the subjects in the two groups had experiences designed to promote avoidance (repression) or approach (sensitization) behavior.

After the training period, the shock apparatus was disconnected, and the subjects were made aware that the shock was no longer contingent upon their response. Then the four figures were again presented simultaneously for recognition. Dulany found that stated recognition of the critical geometric figure was far greater in the sensitization than the

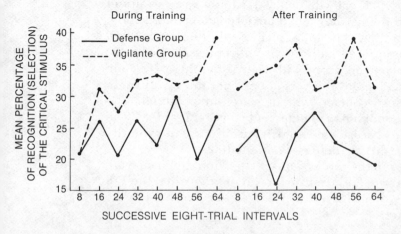

Figure 2–10. Effects of defense and vigilance training on perceptual recognition. During training, in the defense group recognition of the critical stimulus produces shock and nonrecognition avoids it; in the vigilance group, conversely, nonrecognition produces shock and recognition avoids it. As a result, subjects became either defensive or vigilant toward the critical stimulus, even after training ended. (Adapted from Dulany, 1957.)

repression condition both during and after training (see Figure 2–10). In sum, it appears that prior learning experiences that have instrumental or functional significance are one antecedent that may produce different defensive preferences and contrasting coping strategies.

Denial and Intellectualization

Two additional mechanisms of defense that have been the subjects of experimental investigation are denial and intellectualization. Denial refers to a refusal to accept consciously the existence of a threatening situation. Intellectualization, or isolation, occurs when an idea and its emotional accompaniment become detached. That is, an emotional event is dealt with in an overly intellectual manner, thus neutralizing its affective significance. The doctor who must concentrate upon the medical features of an illness and ignore its emotional meaning often may be adapting to continual stress with the defense of intellectualization (see Lazarus, 1975).

The existence of these defenses has been best demonstrated by examining their controlling effects on stress reactions. In the field of physics, stress connotes a force that acts upon a body, producing some sort of strain. Psychologists use the word "stress" to connote that an individual is undergoing "strain," i.e., emotional difficulty or disturbance. This occurs when environmental demands extend or exceed one's coping abilities.

Stress: Reactions and Causes

The first stage of a stress response includes alarm and shock (Selye, 1956). There is autonomic excitability, an increased heart rate, a decrease in body temperature, and a number of other hormonal and physiological changes. These physiological changes are accompanied by emotional reactions, such as feelings of threat and distress. Following the initial reactions, defense mechanisms are activated. The individual searches for methods of coping and dealing with the subjectively harmful and aversive situation. If the individual is able to adapt and deal effectively with the environment, then the alarm reaction and anxiety state subside. But if the mechanisms fail and the stressor continues to control behavior, then a state of "exhaustion" sets in. The failure of coping can give rise to any number of psychological reactions, including depression, withdrawal, physical illness, and even suicide.

Stress reactions are caused by many factors, including the death of a significant figure, marriage or divorce, and the changing of jobs or retirement. Table 2–11 includes a scale that quantifies situations giving rise to stress reactions (see Holmes & Rahe, 1967). Some investigations have suggested that a score near 150 on this scale is associated with a 37 per cent chance of developing a physical illness, a score between 150 and 300 indicates a 50 per cent chance of poor health, and a score above 300 signifies that the chance of developing a physical illness is as high as 80

TABLE 2–11 A STRESS INDEX

Event	Value	Your Score	Event	Value	Your Score
Death of spouse	100	_____	Trouble with in-laws	29	_____
Divorce	73	_____	Outstanding personal achievement	28	_____
Marital separation	65	_____	Spouse begins or stops work	26	_____
Jail term	63	_____	Starting or finishing school	26	_____
Death of close family member	63	_____	Change in living conditions	25	_____
Personal injury or illness	53	_____	Revision of personal habits	24	_____
Marriage	50	_____	Trouble with boss	23	_____
Fired from work	47	_____	Change in work hours, conditions	20	_____
Marital reconciliation	45	_____	Change in residence	20	_____
Retirement	45	_____	Change in schools	20	_____
Change in family member's health	44	_____	Change in recreational habits	19	_____
Pregnancy	40	_____	Change in church activities	19	_____
Sex difficulties	39	_____	Change in social activities	18	_____
Addition to family	39	_____	Mortgage or loan under $10,000	17	_____
Business readjustment	39	_____	Change in sleeping habits	16	_____
Change in financial status	38	_____	Change in number of family gatherings	15	_____
Death of close friend	37	_____	Change in eating habits	15	_____
Change to different line of work	36	_____	Vacation	13	_____
Change in number of marital arguments	35	_____	Christmas season	12	_____
Mortgage or loan over $10,000	31	_____	Minor violation of the law	11	_____
Foreclosure of mortgage or loan	30	_____	Total		_____
Change in work responsibilities	29	_____			
Son or daughter leaving home	29	_____			

(From Holmes & Rahe, 1967.)

per cent. However, the scale does not differentiate between positive and negative events, or between chosen events (e.g., marriage) and unwilled occurrences (e.g., death of a spouse).

Figure 2–11 shows the self-reported feelings of stress among males and females as a function of marriage, age of children, and subsequent widowhood or separation. One very significant aspect of Figure 2–11 is the differential stress reactions of males and females to divorce or separation.

METHODS OF DEALING WITH STRESS. As already indicated, the consequences of failing to cope adequately with stress are grave. Thus, it is essential that the organism develop means of adapting to and dealing with the environment. Of course, experience with stressful situations aids in coping behavior. In one experiment nicely demonstrating this point, sport parachutists were interviewed before and after a jump. Half of the subjects had previously made more than 100 jumps; the rest were inexperienced jumpers. The interview included self-ratings of fear. The fears reported by the parachutists as a function of temporal proximity to the jump are shown in Figure 2–12.

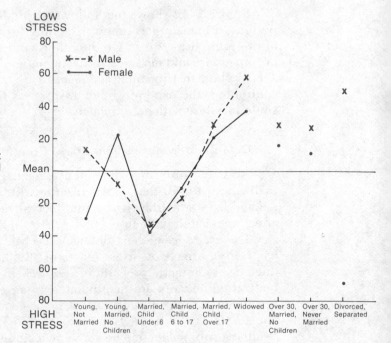

Figure 2–11. Reported stress at various life phases. (Adapted from Campbell, 1976, p. 122.)

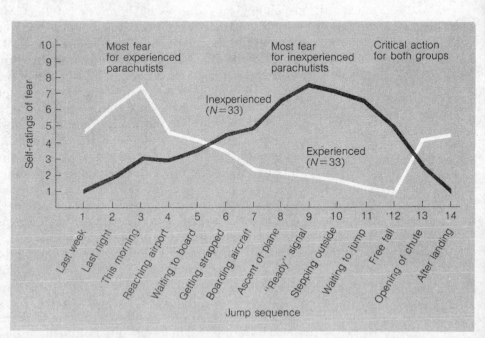

Figure 2–12. Parachutists' self-ratings of fear experienced before, during, and after a jump. (Adapted from Epstein & Fenz, 1965, p. 2.)

Figure 2–12 shows that following the decision to make a jump, experienced parachutists report becoming less and less fearful as the time of the jump draws near. On the other hand, the inexperienced jumpers become more and more fearful as the impending jump becomes a reality. Thus, when instrumental action must be taken and danger is directly confronted, the experienced chutist is less likely to feel anxiety, which could interfere with performance.

Defense Mechanisms and Stress Reactions

Now let us return to the defense mechanisms of denial and intellectualization. Recall that denial reactions literally reject the existence of danger in a situation, while intellectualization processes divorce the affect associated with an event.

The existence of these defenses has been best demonstrated by their controlling effects on stress reactions. Richard Lazarus (1966) has conducted a systematic program of research in which denial and intellectualization actually are manipulated in an experimental situation. The general experimental procedure is to have subjects view a film that gives rise to stress reactions. Lazarus has used two films that yield similar results: a subincision movie showing a stone-age ritual in which adolescent boys have their penises deeply cut and a safety film depicting workshop accidents. While subjects view the movie, various measures of autonomic arousal, such as heart rate and galvanic skin response, are continuously recorded.

The sound track that precedes or accompanies the film presentation evokes the psychological defenses of denial or intellectualization. The denial theme indicates that the subincision operation is not harmful or that the participants in the safety film merely are actors. The intellectualization sound track offers a detached view of the situations. The subincision film apparently is narrated by an objective anthropologist simply observing strange customs, while during the safety film, the viewer is asked to take an objective look at the dynamics of the situation. Lazarus then ascertains whether the manipulations of these defensive processes, or modes of thought, influence the manner in which the individual copes with the film. More specifically, he examines whether the emotional reactivity to the film is lowered when the defenses are introduced.

Figure 2–13 shows the results of one study that induced the defensive orientation of denial (Lazarus and Alfert, 1964). In this experiment the subincision film was used, and the denial set was introduced either before the film as orientation or during as commentary. Skin conductance was used to measure emotional reactivity. The results show that the denial message reduced the degree of reactivity to the stressor, relative to a control group not receiving the defensive sound track. As is evident in Figure 2–13, the reduction of the emotional reactivity is most efficient when the defense is introduced in its entirety before the subjects view the film.

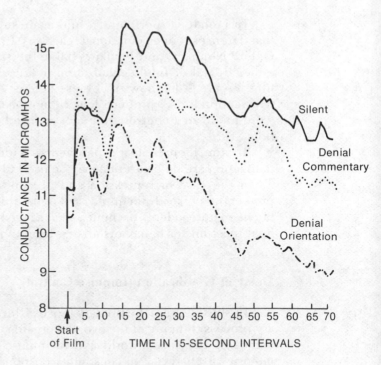

Figure 2–13. Skin conductance curves during orientation and film periods under three experimental conditions. Denial orientation indicates that the sound track was presented in its entirety prior to the film onset. Denial commentary indicates that the denial sound track accompanied, rather than preceded, the film. The control condition is designated as "silent," that is, there is no accompanying sound track. (Adapted from Lazarus & Alfert, 1964, p. 199.)

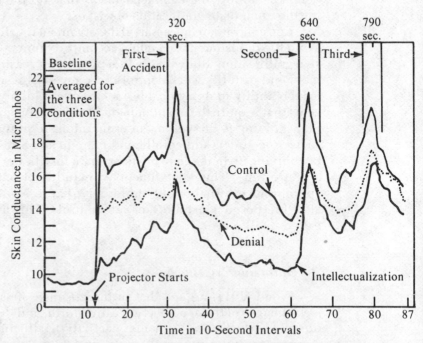

Figure 2–14. Effects of experimental conditions on skin conductance, given the defensive orientations of denial or intellectualization. (Adapted from Lazarus, Opton, Nomikos, & Rankin, 1965, p. 628.)

In a related experiment, results again supported the basic hypothesis that defenses reduce emotional reactions. In this experiment by Lazarus, Opton, Nomikos, and Ramkin (1965), the safety movie was shown, and either denial or intellectualization defenses were aroused prior to the film. Figure 2–14 shows that these defensive interpretations, or "cognitive reappraisals," produce lower emotional responses to the film than were found in a control group not exposed to the defensive indoctrination.

In sum, there is clear experimental evidence that denial and intellectualization are defenses that may be used to reduce noxious stimulation. As in the case of repression and perceptual defense, these defenses protect the person from unpleasant or painful sensations. They intervene between antecedents or inputs, such as wishes and perceptions, and the final reactions or behaviors arising from those inputs.

Delay of Gratification (Impulse Control)

In shifting from the primary process thinking of the id to the secondary process thinking of the ego, the organism is able to recognize the demands of the social world and to impose restraints on behavior and motoric discharge. Ego constraints posmone goal-directed actions until external conditions that are suitable for the expression of one's drives have been identified. Defense mechanisms such as repression and denial exemplify the ego mechanisms that aid the organism in preventing the immediate gratification of wishes.

Ego controls are necessary if the organism is to function in society and avoid the punishment that might accompany immediate sexual or aggressive gratification. But with the individual's increasing cognitive development and maturity, such controls become a virtue as well as a necessity, for the ability to delay enables one to attain highly desirable long-term goals that require the abandonment of immediate gratification. For example, studying to do well on an exam might require foregoing a pleasant social encounter, and enrollment in graduate or medical school necessitates giving up immediate monetary gain for a better position or income at a future time. Thus, ego functions include not only the recognition of appropriate external conditions for drive expression, but also more general self-imposed constraints, or self-controls. This latter capacity often is called "will power."

Hallucinatory Images

Freud (1911) argued that in the absence of satisfying external objects, images of these objects are called forth, and there is partial satisfaction via hallucinations or fantasy activity. Hallucinations, therefore, are one way to cope temporarily with a lack of gratification; they bridge the delay between one's desires and motoric expression. This bridging function frequently is referred to as "time binding."

The effects of mental representations of rewards on the ability to delay gratification have been examined experimentally (see Mischel, 1974a, 1974b). In studies using the experimental procedure developed by Mischel, children are given a choice dilemma in which they may receive either a smaller, immediate reward (e.g., a candy bar) or a larger reward (e.g., two candy bars) at a later time. A variety of factors can then be manipulated to assess their effects on the gratification choices.

To examine the influence of the visual presence of the reward on delay of gratification, Mischel and Ebbesen (1970) created situations in which the delayed reward, the immediate reward, both rewards, or neither reward occupied the visual field of the subjects during the delay period. In this study the child could wait for the experimenter to return with the larger reward, or could signal for him to return and immediately receive the smaller reward. The results of this investigation are shown in Figure 2–15. The graph clearly reveals that waiting time is maximal with no rewards visible and is minimal when both rewards can be seen.

In a subsequent investigation of the effects of the mental representation of the reward, researchers devised two experimental conditions in which the rewards were not visible and the subjects were instructed either to think about the rewards or to think "fun" (Mischel, Ebbesen, & Zeiss, 1972). Figure 2–16 shows that thinking about the reward decreases the ability to delay gratification, based on the delay times exhibited by the two experimental groups and a third given no fantasy instructions.

On the basis of these and other data, Mischel (1974a, 1974b) contends that one consequence of the mental representation of a reward

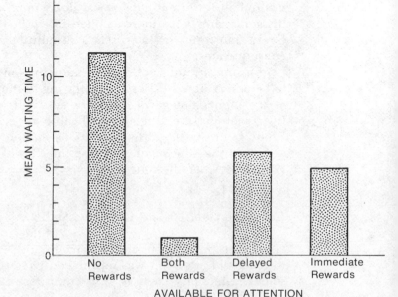

Figure 2–15. Mean minutes of voluntary waiting time for the delayed reward in each attention condition. (From Mischel & Ebbesen, 1970.)

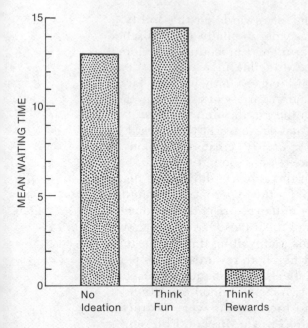

Figure 2–16. Mean minutes of voluntary waiting time for treatment conditions and controls. (Adapted from Mischel, Ebbesen, & Zeiss, 1972.)

object during the delay interval is an increase in frustration. The additional frustration decreases the ability to delay gratification. Hence, any activity that distracts the person from thinking about the reward, such as instructions to think "fun," lessens frustration and increases delay behavior. Furthermore, even given the visual appearance of the desired reward, the individual may engage in coping activities that aid in the delay of gratification. For example, thinking about a reward of pretzels as large logs or construing marshmallows as clouds increases delay, whereas thinking about the taste or consummatory properties of the desired objects greatly decreases delay behavior. As Lazarus (1966) and his colleagues have demonstrated in studies of stress, how one cognitively transforms or interprets a stimulus has important psychological consequences.

In sum, Freud's notion that hallucinations are time binding appears to be contradicted if Freud is referring to the consummatory properties of the mental image of a reward and if it is accepted that Mischel's investigations are directly applicable to Freud's ideas. However, if Freud's conception of hallucinations includes distracting thoughts that are about the nonconsummatory properties of a reward, then such fantasy activities may be time binding.

Cognitive Controls and Cognitive Styles

In the prior discussion of primary and secondary process thinking, the focus of attention was on the *content* of our unconscious and conscious reflections, such as unfulfilled desires and the plans that might lead to a gratification of these desires. How (rather than what) an individual thinks, or the *structure* of thought, is completely neglected by psychoanalytic theorists. In addition, within psychoanalytic theory, defense mechanisms such as repression and denial are conceived as dynamic forces, arising in situations of danger and dissipating when the danger is over or when the forbidden, instinctive impulses have been "drained off." Defenses, however, also may be considered as relatively enduring ways of thinking that are independent of the driving instincts.

Cognitive controls, or cognitive styles, are structures that influence how individuals perceive, process, and retrieve information. As intimated by the label "control," these information processing strategies, or biases, affect both the gratification and the inhibition of drives. Cognitive "style" has a broader connotation and typically is not considered in relation to drive cathexis and counter-cathexis. However, psychologists often do not distinguish between cognitive controls and cognitive styles.

Ego psychologists (e.g., Gardner, Holzman, Klein, Linton, & Spence, 1959), have identified a variety of dimensions of thought that characterize or differentiate individuals. They include leveling-sharpening, which pertains to the articulation of memories, and constricted-flexible, which relates to the manner of coping with distracting stimuli.

The *leveling-sharpening* dimension of control is believed to influence the formation of memory schemata. Levelers assimilate incoming percepts with prior memory traces. Thus, new percepts do not stand out as "figures" and readily lose their distinct label. Individuals with this mode of cognitive functioning are believed prone to use repression as a psychological defense, for it is relatively easy to "forget" threatening thoughts when their traces are not distinguished. Conversely, sharpeners are believed to organize their memories into distinctive elements. Highly differentiated memories should render it more difficult to employ repression as a defense. Thus, sharpeners may be prone to employ other defenses when protecting themselves from unacceptable drive wishes.

To ascertain the disposition to assimilate new percepts with prior memories, researches ask subjects to estimate the size of a series of squares. After every fifth trial, the smallest of the squares shown drops out. Four of the previously viewed squares, along with one that is slightly larger, are presented in the next series of five trials. Leveling is inferred when the judgment of the square size lags behind the progressive incremental sequence. It is believed that this lag is caused by the assimilation of the new percept with the prior memory traces.

Note that in this assessment procedure the subject is asked to give an accurate size estimate. Virtually all of the devices for cognitive control assessment make use of perceptual tests in which there is a "correct" response. Individual differences in personality structure are then inferred from performance inaccuracies.

Two studies reported by Holzman and Gardner (1959, 1960) suggest that the proposed leveling-sharpening personality dimension is related to the use of repression and to the accuracy of memory. Holzman and Gardner argue that a leveler may not be a repressor, but one who represses must function cognitively as a leveler. These investigators therefore conclude that in the study of psychological defenses one must also examine general cognitive functioning.

The concept of *constricted versus flexible thinking* pertains to information registration rather than to information retrieval. This dimension of thought is assessed with a color-word interference test, frequently referred to as the "Stroop test" (J. Stroop, 1935, first used this technique in America). In this procedure, the name of a color is written (e.g., r-e-d) in blue ink, for example. The subject must respond with the name of the perceived color (blue) and ignore the written word (red). Klein (1954) contends that individuals characterized as constricted in their thought-processes are unable to perform this task well, whereas flexible control subjects ignore the irrelevant written word.

In one demonstration of the influence of constricted-flexible control on need-related behavior, Klein (1954) examined the thoughts and behaviors of thirsty and non-thirsty subjects in a variety of situations. He found that on a word-association test in which the subject responds with the first word that comes into mind, the thirsty constricted subjects were preoccupied with thirst-related words. This was not true for the thirsty but flexible subjects. In addition, only the thirsty constricted subjects found perception obstructed when a thirst-satisfying object also was in their visual field. That is, given a constricted mode of control, one's field of perception or information registration is restricted by unsatisfied needs. In sum, the research on cognitive controls integrates normal cognitive functioning with behavioral dynamics (need inhibition and satisfaction).

Summary

In this chapter some of the basic concepts of psychoanalytic theory, and research bearing upon this theory, were presented. The concepts that were examined pertain to the structure of personality (id, ego, super-ego), energy dynamics (conservation of energy, bound energy, free energy, instinctive urges), the content and the structure of thought (primary and secondary thought processes, cognitive styles), indirect or vicarious methods of need gratification (hallucinations, catharsis, dreams), the inhibition of action (counter-cathexis, defense mechanisms, cognitive controls), and the underlying principles of behavior (homeostatis, hedonism, psychic determinism). Freudian theory conceives of individuals as caught in a never-ending conflict between instinctual and aggressive drives on the one hand, and the restraints demanded by the social world and by internalized ideals on the other. The laws of motivation emerge from the analysis of this dilemma between expression and inhibition.

The research areas that were reviewed relate to the expression (instincts, aggression, sex, dreams) versus the inhibition (defense mechanisms, delay of gratification, cognitive controls) of action. Analysis of instinctive behavior revealed that the concept of an instinctive "urge" is supported by the observation of vacuum and displacement behavior among infrahumans. The existence of instinctive urges among humans has not been convincingly documented, although the prevalence of aggressive expressions, the identification of authoritarian personalities, dramatic aggressive acts by overly controlled persons, the possible catharsis of needs, and the enhancement of aggression in situations of de-individuation intimate that the idea of drives striving for expression cannot be discarded. But the many social and situational determinants of aggression—including sociological factors such as poverty level and place of residence, the presence of stimuli associated with violence, mass media effects, obedience to authority, and a general contagion of violence—amply document the importance of environmental determinants of hostility.

In a similar manner, sexual expression is influenced by a variety of social factors, including social dominance. In addition, the notion of the damming up of sexual energy is contradicted by the absence of a negative relationship between sexual expression and subsequent sexual desires. Dreams also appear to be uninfluenced by unfulfilled desires, although external stimuli and memories of day activities are incorporated into dreams. Dreams are universal and follow a fixed temporal sequence that can be traced by observing eye movements or brain wave patterns.

Behavioral restraint in service of the id is a function of the ego. Defenses such as repression, perceptual defense, denial, and intellectualization act as dynamic forces that inhibit the expression of harmful impulses and protect the organism from anxiety and threat. The research evidence bearing on the existence of these defenses is not strong. However, some convincing experimental demonstrations have been reported.

The defenses are believed to aid in the delay of gratification. "Time binding" can also be enhanced by cognitive distractions that direct attention away from unfulfilled wishes. Contrary to Freudian thinking, mental images of desired objects appear to create frustration and decrease the ability to delay gratification.

Finally, ego functions include cognitive controls and cognitive styles, which are conceptualized as enduring ways of processing and retrieving information. They relate to normal functioning as well as to the gratification and the inhibition of desires. The empirical evidence in the cognitive control area is rather limited.

In sum, a rich array of research has been generated by, or is related to, the Freudian notions of instinctual urges, primary process thought, and the workings of the ego. Some of the findings support Freud's notions, while other data contradict psychoanalytic ideas. At this time, however, the main contribution of the theory does not lie in the confirmation of hypotheses. Rather, the theoretical networks proposed by Freud and other psycho-analytic theorists have been heuristic, and new knowledge has been, and is being, gathered. It is this *generative* aspect of psychoanalytic theory that is most important†.

Chapter Three

DRIVE THEORY

Introduction

In Chapter One it was indicated that there are two major approaches that address the question, Why do people behave as they do? One plan is to postulate a basic principle of action and then account for a wide array of behaviors by appealing to that principle. Freudian psychology, which assumes that individuals are striving to reduce sexual and aggressive urges, is the example *par excellence* of this theoretical strategy. Dreams, slips of the tongue, war, neurosis, art, and humor are just some of the phenomena that were systematically incorporated into Freudian theory because they allegedly gratify sexual or aggressive needs.

The second approach to understanding motivated behavior involves an identification of the determinants of action and then a specification of the mathematical relations between the motivational factors. Food-getting behavior, for example, might be determined by the time since last eating, the amount of expected food, the number of prior reinforcements in the stimulus setting, and so on. Further, these terms could combine additively, or multiplicatively, with one another. The theory of motivation formulated by Clark L. Hull, referred to as drive theory, is the most ambitious example of this "model building" theoretical strategy.

In this chapter Hull's theory is presented along with some of its precursors and subsequent elaborations. I will not document the shortcomings of this conception in any detail; criticisms already have been voiced in numerous sources (Atkinson, 1964; Bolles, 1975b; Weiner, 1972). Rather, I will portray this theory primarily from the point of view of its adherents, although I will discuss the main reason for the demise of this conception. Various phenomena that have been analyzed in the Hullian framework, including anxiety, conflict, frustration, and social facilitation, will also be examined.

CLARK L. HULL

Clark Hull was born in 1884 in New York, but he was reared on a farm in Michigan and attended a one-room rural school. Early in life he contracted polio, and one leg remained permanently paralyzed. Hull was completely dedicated to his work, completing his fifth book just prior to his death in 1952.

Hull played a dominant role within academic psychology, although he is little known among the lay public. He is second only to Freud in the number of literature citations from other psychologists; between 1940 and 1960, more than 30 per cent of the articles published in the two main journals covering the fields of learning and motivation cited his work. Furthermore, in a recent poll, psychologists voted him the most important contributor to psychology during the period 1930 to 1950.

Hull had three relatively independent careers in psychology. He first studied aptitude testing and statistical procedures. Then he turned to hypnosis and conducted classic experiments on suggestibility. It is interesting that both Freud and Hull were involved in the study of hypnosis and both moved away from it — Freud because it was not a reliable therapeutic method, and Hull because the technique was opposed by medical authorities and because he believed it nothing more than a form of normal, waking suggestibility. During this period, Hull also was concerned with robots (he majored in engineering as an undergraduate); his postulation of a mechanical model of humans may have grown from this interest. But Hull's main contributions to psychology came during the next phase of his work and involved the study of learning and motivation, the latter being the focus of the present chapter.

Hull spent the major portion of his academic life at Yale University, where he provided the leadership for the Institute of Human Relations. This institute embraced people from all fields and, under Hull's influence, gave rise to one of the most fruitful periods of collaborative research in the history of the social sciences.

Comparison of Hull and Freud

Freud and Hull had dissimilar backgrounds and training: Contrast the culture of Vienna with a log cabin in Michigan and the study of medicine with mining engineering. In spite of these historical differences, there are great similarities in their conclusions about motivated behavior (see McClelland, 1957). First of all, both were determinists. That is, they assumed that acts are caused and that the causes could be identified. Second, both believed that physiological and psychological laws would complement one another. In addition, they accepted tension (need) reduction as the basic goal of behavior, with organisms striving to maintain a state of internal equilibrium. And finally, both were greatly influenced by Darwin and searched for the functional significance of actions.

There also are, of course, some fundamental disparities in the methods they employed and in the theoretical systems that they espoused. As indicated in Chapter Two, Freud did not place much faith in laboratory experiments; his data were free associations drawn from therapy, his personal dreams, or the reported dreams of his patients. On the other hand, Hull's data were generated in carefully controlled experimental studies, primarily of rats running down a maze for a reward of food. Second, Hull was explicitly quantitative in his approach, formulating behavioral postulates from which exact hypotheses could be derived. The majority of his concepts were anchored to operational definitions. For example, hunger was defined in terms of hours of deprivation or percentage loss of body weight; attractiveness of food was defined, in part, as the number of pellets available for consumption. Freud was little concerned with the preciseness of his concepts and their measurement. Finally, and perhaps of greatest importance, Hull formulated a mechanical model of behavior. Hull conceived of humans as mere machines; he denied that mental processes were determinants of action. Thus, for example, the idea of "purposive" behavior, or action "in order to get something," was accounted for entirely by bodily reactions, without appealing to mental capacities and processes such as "foresight" and "anticipation." Freud also used many mechanical or physicalistic concepts in his discussion of human behavior. However, he believed that thoughts do influence action. For example, the ego can inhibit overt action by invoking a defense such as repression to prevent a wish from entering consciousness. Even instincts were regarded by Freud as "demands made on the mind." The characterization of a theory as mechanistic or cognitive and the relation between mental and bodily processes are fundamental issues in the psychology of motivation and, therefore, deserve additional attention here.

The Mind-Body Problem

The contrasting orientations of Freud and Hull concerning the influence of thought on action lead directly into what is known as the "Mind-Body Problem." Many hypotheses or presumptions relating central (Mind) and peripheral (Body) processes have been entertained. Here I will consider only the views accepting the existence of both the mind and the body ("dualistic" positions). One dualistic supposition is that the Mind and the Body are completely independent, with distinct and parallel functions that do not interact (see Diagram 3–1). The processes of the Mind and the Body may, however, be correlated. For example, deprivation may lead one to think about food, to experience an "intention" to obtain food, and to produce approach behavior towards food. But the thoughts and the intention do not *affect* the action; the central representations are *epi-phenomena* ("epi" indicates "upon"). Mechanists frequently accept this dualist formulation and, among the dualistic conceptions, it best characterizes the position advocated by Hull.

DIAGRAM 3–1

The Mind and the Body as Independent Organizations

Thought: A .... B C

Action: A′ .... B′ .... C′

In contrast to the independence depicted in Diagram 3–1, it has been proposed that the Mind and the Body interact. There are various interactionist positions. One group of interactionists contends that thoughts are the product of action (see Diagram 3–2). Sequences of events illustrating this position are: "I am eating a great deal; I must be hungry," or "I just argued for the passage of this controversial bill; I must be in favor of it," or "I am running; I must be afraid." In these examples thoughts are not causes; they are behavioral by-products. Once more, they might be considered epiphenomena, for they do not influence action. Therefore, this conception also is consistent with a mechanistic view of motivation. William James frequently is associated with this position, for he explained emotions as products of bodily states. James's theory is examined in detail later in this book.

DIAGRAM 3–2

The Mind and the Body as Interacting Organizations: Thought Follows Action

Thought: A .... B C
                ↗   ↗   ↗
Action: A′ .... B′ .... C′

Diagram 3–3 depicts a contrasting interactionist position. In Diagram 3–3 thoughts are causes; in part, they determine action (e.g., "I am in favor of this bill; I will argue for it"). This is the belief espoused by the vast majority of cognitive motivational theorists. Although thoughts are presumed to influence action, it is generally accepted by cognitivists that not all behaviors must be mediated by thoughts (e.g., reflex action, such as the sucking behavior of infants, which is central to Freud's primary action model). In addition, cognitivists also accept that not all of the determinants of behavior need to have a conscious or a cognitive representation (e.g., hormonal influences). They also hold that behaviors may have informational value and may influence thought processes (as shown in Diagram 3–2 and in the A′→B and B′→C linkages in Diagram 3–3). Freud is best described by the interactionist position shown in Diagram 3–3.

DIAGRAM 3–3

The Mind and the Body as Interacting Organizations: Action Influenced by Thought

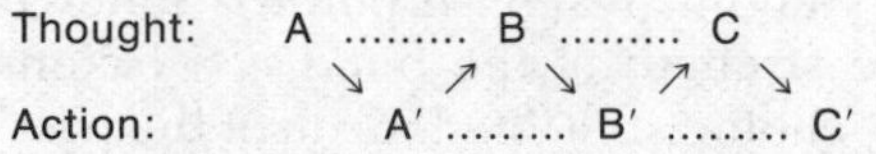

Thought: A .... B C

Action: A' .... B' .... C'

Mechanistic Theory Prior to Hull

The mechanistic analysis of behavior shows in Diagram 3–1 was accepted by many American psychologists. Their beliefs about the determinants of behavior were built upon the principles of association and the laws of learning. Two types of learning were identified in the early 1900's, and in both cases theorists adopted the principle of association as the cause of action.

One category of learning, initially studied by Ivan Pavlov, is called classical conditioning, or respondent learning. Pavlov's central quest was to determine how an inborn reflex could become modified as a result of experience. For example, he observed that a dog responds with salivation at the sight of bread. Yet this clearly must be a learned reflex, for the sight of bread without prior commerce with it does not evoke salivation. Pavlov called such salivation a *conditional* reflex, because its occurrence was conditional upon a prior association between the food and tasting it.

To study conditional reflexes systematically, Pavlov tested dogs in a severely restricted environment. He paired a conditional stimulus (a bell) with food (the unconditional stimulus) by sounding the bell immediately before the food was placed in the animal's mouth. Eventually the sound of the bell would elicit salivation (the conditional response) before the food was placed in the animal's mouth.

It is evident that, for Pavlov, the appearance of the stimulus provided the cause of the behavior (response). Pavlov noted that salivation would not occur when the organism was not hungry, but he did not incorporate motivational principles into his analysis of action.

The second type of learning identified in the early 1900's is called operant or instrumental learning, and was first systematically examined by Edward Thorndike (1911). Thorndike began his investigations in the basement of William James's home in the mid-1870's. His general procedure was to place animals, frequently cats or chicks, in an enclosed box. Outside of the box, food was placed. If the animal made the "correct" response — the one the experimenter had designated as the response that would release it from the box — the animal received the food. Thorndike observed that initially the animal engages in relatively random (trial and error) behavior until it accidentally emits the response resulting in its release. When returned to the box, the animal makes that response sooner and sooner. Ultimately, the correct response becomes the most immediate in the animal's hierarchy.

To explain this change in response hierarchies, or learning, Thorndike postulated his well known Law of Effect. The law states that when a particular stimulus-response bond is followed by a satisfying state of affairs, the strength of that bond increases. Conversely, when a particular stimulus-response bond is followed by an annoying state of affairs, the strength of the bond is weakened. This has been called by many psychologists a "hedonism of the past" and is contrasted with Freud's formulation, which is considered a "hedonism of the future." Thorndike believed that reward or punishment strengthens or weakens the preceding response, while Freud contended that anticipated pleasure or pain determines future responses.

Thorndike's conception is indeed mechanistic. No mention is made of higher mental processes. Rather, the contiguous association of a stimulus and a response, along with the presence of a reinforcer (satisfier), produces a mechanically rigid coupling, or an adhesion; the satisfier provides the "glue" for the stimulus-response association. Thorndike, as did Pavlov, knew that if an animal was not hungry, it would not engage in the associated action. However, he likewise did not incorporate motivational rules into his behavioral system.

In sum, before Hull the laws of learning were synonymous with the laws of behavior. Behavior was determined by rigid couplings and not mediated or caused by thoughts. Hull was especially influenced by Thorndike and accepted that reinforcement provided the necessary cement for the establishment of stimulus-response connections.

THE DRIVE CONCEPT

Prior to the advent of Hull, motivational concepts were used to explain a different set of phenomena than those focused on by learning theorists. The behaviors set aside for motivation were grouped under the term "instinctive" the so-called "inner urges" that were striving for expression.

The use of instinct as an explanatory motivational construct reached its peak near the 1920's. Psychologists employed the term to account for a broad array of human and infrahuman behavior. Holt (1931) satirized the overuse of the concept of instinct as follows:

> If he goes with his fellows, it is the "herd instinct" which activates him; if he walks alone, it is the "anti-social instinct"; . . . if he twiddles his thumbs, it is the "thumb-twiddling instinct"; if he does not twiddle his thumbs, it is the "thumb-not-twiddling instinct." Thus everything is explained with the facility of magic — word magic. (p. 428)

Some even contended that there must be an instinct to believe in instincts.

In the face of such criticisms the use of instinct as an explanatory principle began to wane (see Beach, 1955). But, as is so often true in science, a theory or concept does not die — it is replaced. The concept of instinct was replaced by the concept of drive.

The introduction of the drive concept to experimental psychology is attributed to Woodworth (1918), although the concept of "driving force" was introduced in the eighteenth century as part of the study of ethics and also was employed by Freud. Drive was in many respects a "better" motivational construct than was instinct. First, it provided mechanists with a principle of mechanical causation. Second, drives, unlike instincts, promised to be empirically tied to some physiological base. Finally, drives could be investigated in the laboratory. Drive antecedents, such as hours of deprivation, could be manipulated systematically and their behavioral effects could be observed under controlled conditions.

Early Experimental Investigations Guided by the Concept of Drive

Various experimental procedures were established in the 1920's to assess the strength and the consequences of deprivation (drive) on behavior. A number of studies, particularly those by Richter (1927), demonstrated that deprivation is related to general level of activity. That is, the greater the level of deprivation, the more active the organism becomes until enervation from lack of food sets in. Of course, if an animal is active when deprived, it is more likely to find the needed goal object. Thus, the relationship between deprivation and activity has survival value.

In addition, Richter observed cyclical variations in behavior, with a period of relative activity followed by a period of quiescence. In one investigation of the linkage between periods of activity and hunger, Richter allowed rats to eat whenever they desired. Activity level and consumption were measured. It was found that the period of maximum food intake corresponded to the time of maximum activity. Thus, it was again concluded that activity is related to specific physiological (tissue) deficits.

A second general experimental procedure for studying drive effects made use of what is known as the Columbia Obstruction Box (see Figure 3–1). In investigations using this apparatus, animals were first deprived of a commodity necessary for survival, such as food or water. Then an incentive relevant to the drive (for example, food for a hungry organism) was placed in the goal chamber. Between the organism and the goal object was an electric grid. The animal had to cross the grid and receive shock to obtain the goal.

Investigators making use of the obstruction box varied the strength of the "drive to action," which was considered to be a function of the number of hours of deprivation, and the strength of "resistance," which, in turn, was a function of the magnitude of shock. The general

Figure 3–1. The Columbia Obstruction Box.

| Start Box | Electric Grid | Goal Object |

findings were that there is a monotonic relationship between deprivation and the likelihood of crossing the goal and that with greater deprivation the animals were willing to endure higher levels of shock to reach the food. The broad implication of this work was that investigators believed drive could be measured with some precision.

Hull's Conception of Drive

Guided by the empirical evidence reviewed above, Hull (1943) suggested that physiological deficits, or needs, instigate the organism to undertake behaviors that result in the offset of those needs. Drives, therefore, are a motivational characteristic or property of need states. They result from physiological disequilibrium and instigate behaviors that return the organism to a state of equilibrium. In sum, needs generate the energy that is required for survival. Hull (1943) summarized his position as follows:

> ... Since a need, either actual or potential, usually precedes and accompanies the action of an organism, the need is often said to motivate or drive the associated activity. Because of this motivational characteristic of needs they are regarded as producing primary animal *drives*. ... The major primary needs ... include the need for foods of various sorts (hunger), the need for water (thirst), the need for air, the need to avoid tissue injury (pain), the need to maintain an optimal temperature, the need to defecate, the need to micturate, the need for rest (after protracted exertion), the need for sleep (after protracted wakefulness), and the need for activity (after protracted inaction). (pp. 57, 59–60)

Hull's conception of the relationship between need and drive was:

$$\text{antecedent operation} \longrightarrow \text{need} \longrightarrow \text{drive (energizer)}$$
(e.g., deprivation,
shock)

In adopting this position, Hull was greatly influenced by Darwin's notion of the survival relevance of action. Just as it is survival relevant to become active when in a state of need, it also is debilitating for an organism to search for food if satiated. That is, it is adaptive for behavior to occur if, and only if, a need exists that is not satisfied.

In addition, Hull specified that drive is a *nonspecific* energizer of behavior. All drives pool into one, and this aggregate drive energizes the organism. Hull (1943) contended:

> ... The drive concept, for example, is proposed as a common denominator of all primary motivations, whether due to food privation, water privation, thermal deviations from the optimum, tissue injury, the action of sex hormones, or other causes. ... This implies to a certain extent the undifferentiated nature of drive in general contained in Freud's concept of the "libido." However, it definitely does not presuppose the special dominance of any one drive, such as sex, over the other drives. (pp. 239, 241)

The Integration of Drive and Habit

Recall that according to the learning theories of Pavlov and Thorndike, stimuli were the causes of behavior, and a prior linked response was repeated when the appropriate stimulus reappeared. However, it also was known that when the organism was sated, it often would not exhibit a response to the previously paired stimulus.

Hull therefore asserted that the associative or stimulus-response linkages provided the direction, but not the energy, for action. In order for prior associations to be displayed, there must be some unsatisfied need. Furthermore, because drive is a nondirectional energizer of behavior, any extant need would activate whatever associative linkage was most probable of evocation, or highest in the organism's habit structure. Note, therefore, that a drive does not have to result in overt behavioral activation. If the dominant habit in a fear-inducing situation is to "freeze," then augmentation of drive merely intensifies or energizes the freezing response.

In addition, Hull specified a mathematical relationship between the drive (energy) and habit (direction) determinants of behavior:

$$\text{Behavior} = \text{Drive} \times \text{Habit}$$

In sum, Hull's conception of motivation can be portrayed as follows:

$$\left.\begin{array}{l}\text{Drive Operation} \text{------} \text{Need} \text{------} \text{Drive} \\ \qquad\qquad\qquad\qquad\qquad\qquad\qquad \times \\ \text{Learning Operation} \text{------} \text{Habit} \text{------} \text{Direction}\end{array}\right\} = \text{Behavior}$$

Of course, Hull realized the complexity of behavior and included many other terms in his final theory of motivation. But his best known statement is simply that Behavior = Drive × Habit. This simplicity does not mean that the conception is not rich. Quite the contrary, it will be seen that a great diversity of behavior could be accounted for with this formula.

Freud and Hull: Some Conceptual Comparisons

There are many similarities between the above equation and the conception of behavior outlined by Freud:

1. According to both Freud and Hull, behavior is determined by psychological energy (id, drive) and psychological structures (ego organizations, habits).
2. According to both Freud and Hull, actions are undertaken that satisfy unfulfilled needs (the principle of homeostasis).
3. According to both Freud and Hull, the fulfillment of needs is satisfying and results in quiescence (the doctrine of hedonism).

However, Hull did not conceive of the organism as a closed energy system. Rather, prolonging deprivation, or needs originating from multiple sources such as hunger and thirst, increases the total energy available for "work." In addition, for Freud, the energy of the instincts exerts influence on the mind. On the other hand, the mechanistic principles of a driven machine, with the direction of behavior determined by prior "switchboard" connections, account for motivated behavior in Hull's theory.

Empirical Support for Drive Theory

The statement Behavior = Drive × Habit generated a vast amount of research. Many of the empirical studies were undertaken to support one or more of the following assertions:

1. Drive energizes behavior;
2. Drive and habit relate multiplicatively; and
3. Drive is a pooled energy source.

A brief review of some of that research will more concretely show the kind of data generated by the Hullian conception.

Perhaps the studies most often cited as models of the research generated by drive theory are those of Perin (1942) and Williams (1938). These investigators trained rats to make a simple bar-press response to receive food. The animals learned this response while under 23 hours of food deprivation and received from 5 to 90 reinforced trials. The groups were then subdivided, and extinction (nonrewarded) trials were administered when the animals had been deprived for either 3 or 22 hours. Figure 3–2 shows the results of these experiments. The figure shows that both the number of reinforced trials (learning or habit strength) and the amount of deprivation (drive) influence resistance to extinction. As anticipated, the greater the magnitude of drive during the extinction trials, and the greater the number of reinforced trials during original learning, the stronger the tendency to emit the previously learned response. The curves representing the two deprivation groups also diverge. This reveals that the

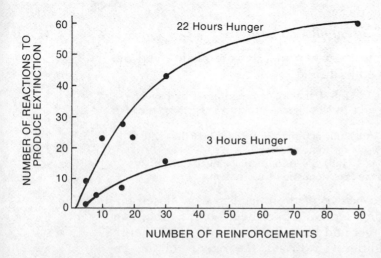

Figure 3–2. Graphic representation showing the combined effects of two levels of drive (hours of deprivation) and habit (number of reinforced trials) on resistance to extinction. (Adapted from Perin, 1942, p. 101.)

relationship between habit and drive is multiplicative. As indicated in Chapter One, if the two determinants were related additively, then the curves would be parallel rather than divergent. The general pattern of results found by Perin and Williams has been replicated many times with somewhat different experimental procedures and various dependent variables (see reviews in Bolles, 1975b; Brown, 1961).

Consider now a more subtle hypothesis and experiment from research conducted by Newman (1955). Newman trained rats to run toward a circle for food when under 23½ hours of food deprivation. After training, one-half of the animals were shifted toward a higher level of deprivation (48 hours), while the rest were shifted downward (12 hours' deprivation). This manipulation created a high- and a low-drive group at the time of testing. In addition, within each of the groups, some of the animals were tested with a circle of the same diameter as the one used in training, while for other animals the diameter was changed. The question raised is, What are the effects of varying deprivation level (drive) and the similarity of the training and testing stimulus (associative or habit strength) on performance level?

Some simple mathematical procedures supply the answer to this question and elucidate Hull's theory. For the group high in drive (D_h), the strength of motivation is represented as:

$$\text{Motivation} = D_h \times H$$

The strength of motivation for the low drive (D_1) group is:

$$\text{Motivation} = D_1 \times H$$

Thus, the difference in motivation between the two groups is:

$$(D_h \times H) - (D_1 \times H) \text{ or } H\,(D_h - D_1)$$

It therefore follows that as H (habit) decreases, the motivational differences between the high- and the low-drive groups also will decrease. Substituting a few numbers will clarify this point. Assume that $D_h = 5$, $D_1 = 2$, $H_h = 4$, and $H_1 = 1$. Given a high habit strength ($H_h = 4$), the motivations of the drive groups are:

$$\text{Motivation (High Drive)} = 5 \times 4 = 20$$
$$\text{Motivation (Low Drive)} = 2 \times 4 = 8$$

But for the low-habit ($H_1 = 1$) condition, the strengths of motivation are:

$$\text{Motivation (High Drive)} = 5 \times 1 = 5$$
$$\text{Motivation (Low Drive)} = 2 \times 1 = 2$$

Note that the difference in motivation between the high- and low-drive groups decreases as habit strength decreases from 4 to 1. It

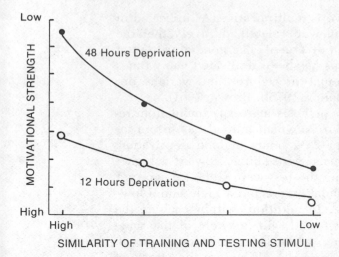

Figure 3-3. Data from Newman (1955) showing the joint effects of hours of deprivation and habit strength on motivation (response latency). Habit strength was varied by manipulating the similarity of the stimuli during the training and testing periods. (Adapted from Spence, 1958b, p. 84.)

follows that, in the experiment by Newman, as the diameter of the training circle increasingly differs between the periods of training and testing (thus decreasing habit strength), the differences in performance between the high- and low-drive groups will decrease. However, in all cases the groups with high deprivation will exhibit greater motivation than the groups low in deprivation if habit strength is equal for both groups.

The data from Newman's study are shown in Figure 3-3. As drive theory predicted, the curves tend to converge as habit or associative strength, which in this situation is a function of the similarity of the training and testing circles, decreases. In sum, Hullian theory is able to make simple yet precise predictions that are derived from basic motivational postulates.

Evidence for Drive as a Pooled Energy Source

The conception of drive as a pooled energy source has been tested with a variety of experimental procedures. In one paradigm, attempts are made to demonstrate that responses acquired under one deprivation condition (the "relevant" drive) can be energized by a different biological deficit (the "irrelevant" drive). The prototypical experiment utilizing this methodology was conducted by Webb (1949). Webb trained rats to make a simple instrumental response to attain food while the animals were under 22 hours of food deprivation. The animals then were tested under varying degrees of water deprivation while satiated with food. Table 3-1 shows that resistance to extinction of the response instrumental to the attainment of food is a function of the amount of water deprivation during testing (Groups I–IV), although extinction is slowest when non-reward is introduced under the conditions present during initial learning (Group V). This type of

TABLE 3–1   MEASURES OBTAINED DURING EXTINCTION

Group	N	Motivating Condition (Hours of Deprivation) Hunger	Thirst	Mean Number of Responses to Extinction
I	18	0	0	2.8
II	18	0	3	5.2
III	18	0	12	5.1
IV	18	0	22	7.2
V	16	22	0	14.2

(Adapted from Webb, 1949, p. 10.)

study, however, has been subject to some criticism, for hunger and thirst are not independent. Thirsty rats do not eat as much as rats that are not thirsty. Thus, the rats on greater water deprivation also may have been hungrier.

Another experimental procedure used to demonstrate that drive is an aggregate of various sources of motivation employs fear or shock in conjunction with a deprivation condition. This general procedure is illustrated in an experiment conducted by Meryman (1952). Meryman investigated whether food deprivation would influence the sound-induced startle response, and whether hunger and fear together produce greater augmentation of startle than either of these motivators acting alone. Some of Meryman's animals learned to fear a stimulus during the training period. Then fearful and non-fearful animals were deprived of food for either an hour or 46 hours. The amplitude of a startle response to a loud noise for the four groups (2 levels of fear × 2 levels of hunger) was tested. The results are presented in Figure 3–4. Figure 3–4 shows that the group both fearful and hungry exhibits

Figure 3–4. Investigation by Meryman (1952) examining startle-response amplitude as a function of fear, no fear, intense hunger, weak hunger, and their combinations.

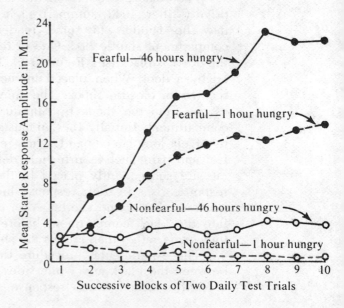

the greatest amplitude of startle, while the non-hungry, non-fearful group manifests the least intensity of response. This is in accordance with the conceptualization of drive as a pooled energy source that multiplies all habits aroused in a stimulus situation.

The experiments concerning the interaction of sex and aggression discussed in Chapter Two also adhere to the general paradigm followed by Webb and Meryman. Either sexual responses are measured while the subject is in a condition of aggressive arousal, or vice versa. As previously indicated, some of this research supports the idea that sex and aggression are overlapping need systems and are mutually facilitative.

Secondary (Learned) Drives

It is evident that humans engage in behaviors that are not energized by the absence of food or water or by the presence of a pain-inducing stimulus. That is, behaviors occur when primary drives are lacking. But given the logic of Hull's conception of motivation, there must exist a drive in these situations that is activating the behavior. Thus, Hull and his associates increasingly emphasized the importance of *learned* or secondary drives. Attempts to account for approach, or appetitive, behavior in terms of learned drives have not been very successful. However, research in the area of avoidance behavior (conditioned fear) illustrates the power of the conception of acquired or learned drives.

Fear as a Learned Drive

The basic procedure in the investigation of fear as an acquired drive (Miller, 1948; summarized in Miller, 1951, and Mowrer, 1960) may be familiar to some readers. Rats are placed in a two-compartment shuttle box. One of the compartments is painted white; the other is black (see Figure 3–5). The two compartments are separated by a door. When placed in the white compartment, the animals receive an electric shock. The construction of the apparatus permits escape from the shock by running through the door into the black compartment. Initially the animals make this escape response with a relatively long latency and, when receiving the shock, exhibit signs of fear and pain, such as urination, defecation, and squealing. When the rats are subsequently placed in the white compartment, the escape response rises in their response hierarchy, and the response latency becomes shorter and shorter. After a number of trials, the animals run into the black compartment before actually being shocked. That is, they *avoid* rather than *escape* the shock.

The experimental procedure then is slightly modified. The door between the black and white sides remains closed when the animals attempt to escape. A new response, such as turning a wheel that opens

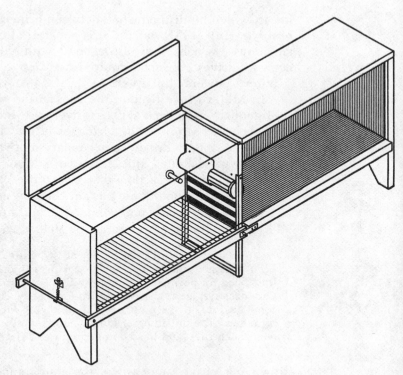

Figure 3–5. The apparatus used by Miller to study the learning of fear. The left compartment is painted white, the right, black. The striped black and white door can be raised so the rat can go from the white into the black compartment, and a shock can be administered through the floor of the white compartment. (From Miller, 1948.)

the door, is required for escape. Further, the shock in the white compartment is not turned on. In this situation the animals again initially exhibit signs of fear when they discover that their previous avenue of escape is no longer available. They then engage in what appear to be random activities. But eventually some of the animals discover the response that enables them to escape. Again, over trials, this response is made with a shorter and shorter latency. (Some of the animals in this situation freeze and do not discover the correct response.)

This experiment had tremendous impact on Hull's conception of motivation. Recall that according to Hull a tissue need acts as a drive and goads the organism into activity. Given no deficits, Hull argued, it would be maladaptive for the organism to continue to expend energy. Yet, in the second phase of Miller's experiment, a new response is learned when the shock is off. In that condition, what motivates the organism or energizes the behavior? There is no damage to any body tissue before the onset of shock. Within the framework of Hull's 1943 conception of behavior, it is impossible to explain the activation of avoidance responses.

Hull corrected this deficit in his 1951 book, *Essentials of Behav-*

ior, in which he distinguished between primary and secondary sources of drive. Hull (1951) stated: "It is a matter of common observation that situations which are associated with drives themselves become ... drives. ... Such acquired associative conditions ... have motivational powers" (pp. 21–22).

In Miller's investigation the cues in the white compartment were contiguously associated with a drive state induced by shock. Therefore, the cues acquired the character of the drive itself. That is, they become secondary drives, or secondary motivators of behavior. Miller and Mowrer labelled this secondary drive fear, or anxiety. It is a learned emotional reaction that is acquired in accordance with the laws of classical conditioning established by Pavlov.

Brown (1961) has contended that many human actions are mediated by learned fear. For example, he states:

> . . . In many instances, if not all, where adult human behavior has been strongly marked by money-seeking responses there appears to be little need for postulating the operation of a learned money-seeking drive. One does not learn to have a drive for money. Instead, one learns to become anxious in the presence of a variety of cues signifying the absence of money. The obtaining of money automatically terminates or drastically alters such cues, and in so doing, produces a decrease in anxiety. (p. 14)

Brown may have emphasized the importance of anxiety in money-seeking behavior because it has proven difficult for stimuli paired with appetitive drives to become secondary drives. This could be because the onset of drives such as hunger and thirst is a relatively slow process. Hull recognized that to become a secondary drive, there must be a rapid change in the primary drive state.

Although the analysis of learned fear seems intuitively reasonable and incontrovertible, in recent years it has come under increasing criticism (see Bolles, 1975b). For example, although it seems reasonable to presume that fear is a response to cues associated with shock, attempts at independent verification of this reaction, such as evidence of an increase in heart rate, have been inconclusive. This is especially important, for, as Bolles (1975b) has noted, one difference between primary and secondary drives is that primary drives are produced by a physiological state. In secondary drives, on the other hand, the physiological state is a response to the conditioned stimulus and is part of the organism's behavior.

An Alteration in the Conception of Action

The investigations of learned fear changed the 1943 Hullian conception of motivation. Sources of drive were no longer limited to tissue deficits. Rather, any internal stimulus could acquire drive properties, if it had sufficient intensity. That is, strong internal stimuli motivate behavior. The conception of drive advocated by Hull in 1951 was:

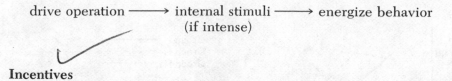

drive operation ⟶ internal stimuli ⟶ energize behavior
                                (if intense)

Incentives

The expansion of Hullian theory to incorporate secondary drives was accompanied by another important conceptual development: the inclusion of the incentive value of the goal, or the properties of the goal object, as a motivator of behavior. The late acknowledgment of the independent role of incentives in motivation was, in part, due to the relatively narrow focus of the early experimental investigators. Researchers employing the Columbia Obstruction Box, for example, rarely manipulated the quantity or the quality of the incentive in the goal box. When they did vary incentives, it was because they believed that the goal object must be appropriate to the drive being manipulated (e.g., food when the animals are hungry and water when they are thirsty). But subsequent investigators, particularly those under the direction of Edward Tolman, became concerned with the behavioral consequences of a *change* in incentives during the course of learning. These investigations led to the emergence of incentive as a determinant of performance.

Latent Learning

The classic experiment involving an incentive change was conducted by Blodgett (1929). In Blodgett's investigation, three groups of rats were trained in a multiple T-maze to approach a reward of food. One group of animals received food at the goal box on every trial. A second group received nothing for two trials, and then food was introduced at the goal box. For a third group of rats, there was no reward for six trials, then food on all subsequent trials. The groups' error scores, which serve as an index of the effectiveness of behavior when running through the maze, are shown in Figure 3–6. It is clear from Figure 3–6 that immediate and disproportionately large drops in errors occur in the performance of the groups first receiving rewards on the third and seventh trials.

Tolman and Honzig (1930) conducted a replication and extension of this experiment. These investigators also employed three groups of animals and a T-maze. One group received a reward on every trial; a second experimental group never received food in the goal box; and for the third group, reward was introduced on the eleventh trial. The findings of this study are shown in Figure 3–7. Again, there is a sudden increment in performance following the introduction of the food incentive.

An experiment by Crespi (1942) also varied the incentive value of the goal. But instead of changing the incentive value from zero to a large amount, Crespi shifted the magnitude of reward during the course of his

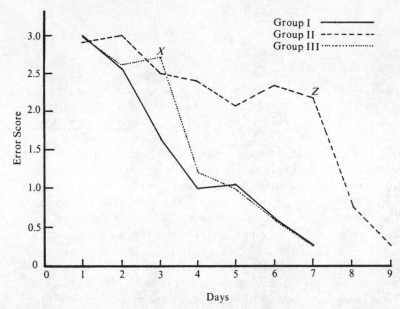

Figure 3–6. The latent learning phenomenon. Group I was given a food reward on every trial. In Group II, the food reward was not introduced until the seventh day (at point *Z*). In Group III, the food reward was introduced the third day (at point *X*). Both Group II and Group III show a substantial decrease in errors after the first rewarded trial. (From Blodgett, 1929, p. 120.)

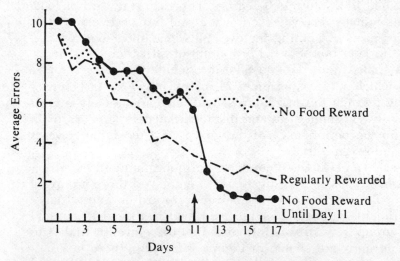

Figure 3–7. Evidence for latent learning in the maze. With no food reward there is some reduction in errors, but not as great a reduction as with regular food reward. Despite the higher scores prior to the introduction of food, the group rewarded only from the eleventh trial immediately begins to do as well as the group that had been regularly rewarded. (After Tolman & Honzig, 1930.)

experiment. One group of animals, after receiving a reward of 256 food pellets, found a reward of only 16 pellets at the goal. On the other hand, a group of rats receiving only one pellet was also shifted to the 16-pellet reward. A third group consistently received 16 pellets.

The data of this investigation, shown in Figure 3–8, again reveal abrupt shifts in the performance levels of the groups. The decreased-reward group displayed immediate declines in performance, while the increased-reward group showed marked performance increments. A particularly interesting aspect of the data is that the decreased-reward group responded below the level of the third group receiving consistent rewards. This has been termed the depression effect and is now well documented in the literature (see Bolles, 1975b). In addition, the increased-reward group responded above the level of the consistent-reward group. This has been termed the elation effect, but it is not a reliable finding.

The results of the studies reviewed above had important implications for Hull's conception of behavior. In these experiments the changes in the level of performance occurred suddenly and dramatically, soon after the introduction or change of the reward. Therefore, it follows that incentive does not influence habit (or at least not only habit), for habits do not vary abruptly, but grow in incremental fashion with each rewarded trial. In addition, within the Hullian framework as presented thus far, it is impossible to account for the performance decrements exhibited in Crespi's experiment when the reward was shifted downward. Drive level had not changed, and habit strength did not decrease, for the response was still being rewarded. Thus, these investigations posed a challenge to Hullian theory.

To account for the data discussed above, Hull (1951) included incentive value as a determinant of performance. His altered conception of behavior specified that motivation is determined by drive, habit, and incentive:

$$\text{Motivation} = \text{Drive} \times \text{Habit} \times \text{Incentive}$$

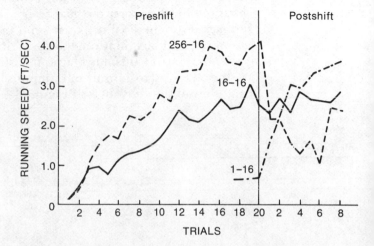

Figure 3–8. Speed of running in a long runway as a function of amount of reinforcement. For the first 19 trials different groups were given 1, 16, or 256 pellets of food (acquisition data for the 1-pellet group are not presented); after trial 20 all subjects were given 16 pellets. (Adapted from Crespi, 1942.)

This expansion in Hull's conception enabled the theory to incorporate the results of the research discussed above. Consider, for example, the findings reported by Crespi. Changing the magnitude of the incentive increases or decreases the strength of motivation. This, theoretically, is expected to change the level of exhibited performance.

Contrasting Drive and Incentive

The equation introduced above shows that drive and incentive multiply habit strength, or activate learned responses. Indeed, it later was suggested by Spence that incentive and drive be added together, inasmuch as they both energize behavior. Why, then, is there a distinction between drive and incentive as motivators of behavior?

The main difference between these two determinants of action is that drive corresponds to a "push," while incentives "pull" the organism (see Bolles, 1975b). The two concepts also are tied to different antecedent conditions. Drive typically is influenced by hours of deprivation, while the incentive value of the goal varies as a function of some property of the goal object, such as its magnitude or taste. Finally, the incentive value of the goal must be learned; the organism is not affected until it "realizes" the value or has knowledge about the goal object. Since incentive value necessitates some learning, the clear distinction between an energizer and a habit that Hull initially maintained had to be discarded when the new conception was introduced.

Incentive, Learning, and Purposive Behavior

The manner in which incentives are learned and function as motivators was clarified by Spence (1956), although in the early 1930's Hull had made similar suggestions. Spence contends that events in the goal box, or the goal responses (R_G), become conditioned to the cues in the goal box. That is, the cues in the goal box come to produce goal responses automatically because of their immediate contiguity with the presentation of the reward. The goal responses include, for example, chewing and salivation. Furthermore, the goal responses produce their own stimulus feedback (S_G). The goal responses and the stimulus feedback that originate in the goal box then generalize to situations that resemble the goal box. Thus, if an organism is placed in a straight runway and fed at a goal box, the pattern of responses and stimulus feedback also will be displayed at the start of the runway (see Figure 3–9).

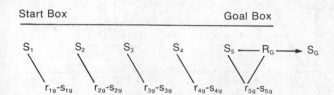

Figure 3–9. Stimulus situation in a straight runway, according to Spence.

The runway goal responses are labelled by Spence as *fractional anticipatory goal responses*. They are "fractional" because the entire goal response is not emitted (e.g., eating behavior is not possible at the start of the alley because food is not yet available). And they are "anticipatory" because the animals appear to be expecting a reward. They lick their lips, salivate, and make chewing motions (see Bindra, 1969, and Bolles, 1975b, for criticisms of this point). Hence, one might infer that the animals are acting in a purposive manner and have foresight of the goal when at the start box. However, Hull and Spence would argue that this mentalistic analysis is incorrect. The stimuli and response associations direct the organism, and incentive and drive produce the energy. Thoughts are not needed to account for behavior.

Spence states that the anticipatory goal response (r_g-s_g) is the mechanism that underlies the incentive construct. The goal responses, by producing their own stimulation, increase the total amount of internal stimuli acting on the organism. Miller's studies of fear as a learned drive resulted in the belief that any strong stimulus would act as a drive. Therefore, because incentives generate an increment in the internal stimulus situation, they have drive properties. Note, then, that the learning of fear and the learning of incentives are determined by the same mechanism — classical conditioning. Thus, Hull's theory was able to incorporate positive and negative motivators (labelled by Mowrer, 1960, as hope and fear) with the same psychological principles.

In the previous pages a very brief overview of drive theory has been presented. Although the theory was not examined in detail, it is evident that it can account for a great deal of the data generated by hungry and thirsty rats running down a straight alleyway or a T-maze for a reward. In the remaining sections of this chapter anxiety, conflict and displacement, frustration and aggression, and social facilitation are examined from the drive theoretical framework. Then a major deficiency of the theory is discussed.

Anxiety

Anxiety is one of the most frequently used psychological terms, permeating the vocabulary of both the professional psychologist and the layperson. In the last chapter it was revealed that Freud considered anxiety an unpleasant affect, as well as a cue or signal to the organism for the activation of defense mechanisms that prevent socially prohibited actions. In a similar manner, Miller and Mowrer describe anxiety as an aversive reaction that is experienced in the presence of cues previously associated with shock. Furthermore, the anxiety reaction instigates behaviors that lead to an escape from a situation that is potentially dangerous. The Miller and Mowrer analysis was guided by Freud's ideas and was part of a broader attempt to translate Freudian concepts into the more scientific and testable scheme formulated by Hullians.

A theoretical analysis more directly integrating anxiety into drive theory is shown in Figure 3–10. Figure 3–10 depicts a conceptual framework for the classical conditioning of aversive events. For example, a neutral cue, such as a tone, is presented prior to the onset of an aversive stimulus, such as a puff of air to the eye. The investigator is then interested in the likelihood of closure of the eyelid given the presentation of the conditioned tone stimulus.

The symbols outside the box in Figure 3–10 signify linkages with the external world that are manipulable by, or are visible to, the experimenter. The terms inside the box are constructs, or intervening variables, that are inferred by the experimenter. It can be seen in Figure 3–10 that habit strength (H) is determined by the number (N) of prior presentations of the conditioned and unconditioned stimuli (tone and air puff). Drive (D), is determined by two factors: the strength of the unconditioned stimulus (S_{ucs}), such as the force of the air puff, and a response on an anxiety scale (R_A). (This scale will soon be described in detail.) In addition, in aversive situations it is assumed that drive is mediated by a persisting, emotional response (r_e). This emotional response is similar to the notion of fear proposed by Miller and Mowrer. That is, the air puff causes the individual to react with a negative emotion, and this affective reaction is presumed to be the mechanism that is responsible for the drive state. Drive and habit, in turn, influence the intensity and the direction of behavior (the eyelid response to the tone), as shown to the right of the box.

One immediate implication of the theory shown in Figure 3–10 is that the reflexive eyelid response to the noxious air puff should vary directly with the manipulated intensity of the stimulus. That is, the greater the aversiveness of the puff, the greater the inferred emotional reaction and magnitude of induced drive. Increased drive augments motivation and the likelihood of the conditioned response (eyelid closure).

Spence (1958b) reports a number of studies demonstrating that the probability of a conditioned eyelid response is a function of the intensity of a puff of air to the eye. Figure 3–11 portrays the results of one such experiment, in which four different intensities of air puff were used. Subjects were given repeated conditioning trials, thus varying habit strength during the course of the experiment. Figure 3–11 reveals that high puff intensity (drive level) and increased trials (habit strength) augment response strength. In addition, the curves representing the various drive levels diverge over trials, supporting the belief that drive and habit relate multiplicatively.

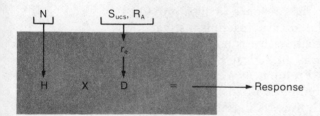

Figure 3–10. Portion of theoretical schema relevant to data for classical conditioning. (Adapted from Spence, 1958, p. 131.)

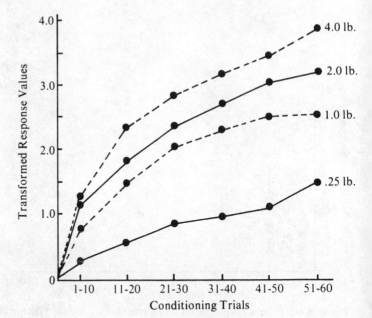

Figure 3–11. Performance during acquisition of eyelid conditioned responses as a function of the intensity of the *UCS* (units in lbs.). (Adapted from Spence, 1958b, p. 78.)

The Manifest Anxiety Scale

In addition to the strength of the aversive stimulus, scores from an anxiety scale also can be used to infer drive level (see Figure 3–10). Spence and his colleagues reasoned that, given the same magnitude of an aversive stimulus, some individuals might act as if it were more intense than other individuals. If these highly reactive persons could be identified, then it would be inferred that they are relatively high in drive and, therefore, should exhibit behaviors consistent with this state. Thus, anxiety can be operationally defined as a response, rather than being exclusively linked with a specified manipulation, such as the strength of an air puff or shock. Note also that the operation of setting two levels of air puff intensity and the operation of setting only one intensity level but identifying two degrees of emotional reactivity are logically equivalent.

To assess the tendency to respond emotionally to an aversive stimulus, Janet Taylor (1953) developed the Manifest Anxiety Scale. The scale consists of fifty keyed items taken from the Minnesota Multiphasic Personality Inventory. The keyed items were agreed upon by four out of five clinicians as being manifestations of high anxiety. Typical items and the anxiety responses are:

    a. I cry easily. (True)
    b. I work under a great deal of tension. (True)

Spence and his colleagues have conducted a number of experiments comparing the performance of subjects classified as high or low in anxiety (drive) in eyelid conditioning situations. A representative experimental result obtained by Spence and Taylor (1951) is shown in Figure 3–12. In

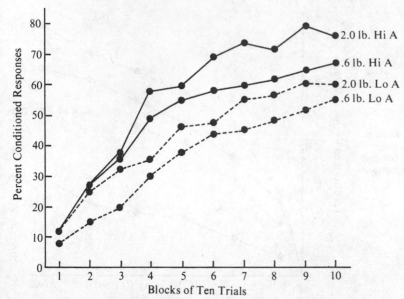

Figure 3–12. Data from Spence and Taylor (1951) showing performance in eyelid conditioning as a function of level of anxiety and intensity of the *UCS*. (Adapted from Spence, 1958a, p. 134.)

this investigation, two levels of puff intensity were combined with two levels of emotional reactivity, yielding four different experimental conditions. Examination of Figure 3–12 shows that within each of the levels of puff intensity, subjects high in anxiety (High A) exhibited more conditioned eyelid responses than subjects low in anxiety (Low A). This adds validity to the contention that the Manifest Anxiety Scale is a measure of drive. In addition, the higher intensity air puff produces faster conditioning than the lower intensity puff, as also was found in the research shown in Figure 3–11. And finally, the divergence of the curves again indicates a multiplicative relationship between drive and habit.

Paired-Associates Learning

Spence and his associates also have applied the Drive × Habit conception to the learning of simple and complex paired-associates. In a paired-associates task, a stimulus, such as a word, is displayed, and the subject must anticipate the response that is paired with it. Spence reasons that a simple list of paired-associates is one in which the correct response is dominant in the person's response hierarchy. That is, the response paired with the stimulus is the most probable response that the individual will give even prior to the learning situation. Spence contends that in this situation an increase in the level of drive will result in faster learning and fewer errors.

The derivation of this hypothesis requires that an increment in drive level increase the absolute difference between the tendencies to emit the correct and incorrect responses to a stimulus. Assume, for example, that a stimulus elicits two responses, one correct (C), the other incorrect (I). Further, assume that the strength of $C = 2$ while the strength of $I = 1$. For a low drive group $(D = 1)$, the difference in the motivation (M) to exhibit the two responses is:

$$M\ (C) = 1 \times 2 = 2$$
$$M\ (I) = 1 \times 1 = 1$$
$$M\ (C - I) = 2 - 1 = 1$$

However, for a high drive group $(D = 2)$, the difference in the motivational strengths would be represented as:

$$M\ (C) = 2 \times 2 = 4$$
$$M\ (I) = 2 \times 1 = 2$$
$$M\ (C - I) = 4 - 2 = 2$$

Thus, the difference between the strengths of motivation between the correct and incorrect responses is greater for persons with high drive. Subjects classified as high in anxiety (drive), therefore, are expected to perform better on this simple task than subjects classified as low in anxiety. This analysis is identical to the one in the conditioning experiments, for in those investigations the eyelid reflex also is dominant in the person's hierarchy of responses. Thus, the more aversive the puff or the higher the anxiety, the greater the aversive conditioning.

The theoretical analysis of performance on a complex task is more difficult and necessitates the use of concepts not yet introduced. Spence reasons that a number of competing responses are aroused by the stimuli of a difficult (complex) task. Some of these responses are below the "threshold" level. The threshold refers to the minimum level of response strength that must be reached before the response can be overtly expressed. The threshold concept, in part, determines the speed of learning on a complex task. Assume a task in which the magnitude of C again is equal to 2. But now assume that there are two competing, incorrect responses, $I_1 = 1$ and $I_2 = 2$. Further, assume that the threshold level is 2; that is, 2 units of motivation are necessary for the response to be overtly expressed. For a weak drive group $(D = 1)$, this situation can be represented as:

$$M\ (C) = 1 \times 2 = 2$$
$$M\ (I_1) = 1 \times 1 = 1$$
$$M\ (I_2) = 1 \times 2 = 2$$
$$M\ (C - I_2) = 2 - 2 = 0$$

Thus, the strength of the motivation to give the incorrect response is equal to that of the motivation to give the correct response. I_1 is not included among the competing responses because the strength of motivation to give that response is one unit below the threshold level.

For a strong drive group ($D = 2$), the situation is conceptualized as:

$$M\ (C) = 2 \times 2 = 4$$
$$M\ (I_1) = 2 \times 1 = 2$$
$$M\ (I_2) = 2 \times 2 = 4$$
$$M[C - (I_1 + I_2)] = 4 - 6 = -2$$

Thus, the combined strengths of the incorrect responses exceed that of the correct response by two units, for both I_1 and I_2 are above the threshold level and have some probability of competing with the correct response. Hence, in this situation, the heightening of drive interfered with performance.

An interaction is therefore expected between drive level and performance at easy and complex tasks. Given an easy task, individuals high in drive are expected to perform better than those low in drive. Conversely, given a difficult (complex) task, persons high in drive are expected to perform worse than those in a low drive group.

Spence and his associates (Spence, Farber, & McFann, 1956; Spence, Taylor, & Ketchel, 1956; Taylor & Chapman, 1955) established the experimental conditions they believed necessary to test the above hypotheses. They employed paired-associates tasks and created easy (noncompetitive) and difficult (competitive) lists by varying the degree of pre-experimental associations between the stimulus-response pairs in the list. In the easy list, the stimulus words tend to elicit the responses prior to list learning. Examples are:

Roving-Nomad
Tranquil-Quiet
Pious-Devout

Because the response members of the pairs are synonyms of the stimulus members, they are high in the repertoire of response associates to the stimulus words. Heightened drive should therefore increase the differences between the motivation associated with the correct and incorrect responses and facilitate learning.

To create a difficult or competitive list of paired-associates, researchers selected the response members of the pairs from words low in the subject's response hierarchy before the task was started. In addition, incorrect responses that are high in the subject's hierarchy were included among other responses in the list. Examples of pairs used to establish competitive lists are:

Tranquil-Placid
Quiet-Double
Serene-Headstrong

The stimulus words in this example are synonyms, and all tend to elicit the response of "placid." Thus, two pairings are created in which an incorrect response has a reasonable probability of being elicited.

The actual experiments are straightforward. Subjects scoring in the upper and lower extremes on the Manifest Anxiety Scale form high and low drive groups. They then are presented the stimulus-response pairs, and must correctly anticipate the response members in the list. The results of this research have been interpreted as supporting the hypothesized interaction predicted by drive theory (see Spence, 1958a).

Some Reservations

As previously indicated, the purpose of this chapter is the presentation of drive theory from the perspective of its proponents; space has not been given to criticisms or shortcomings. Nonetheless, a word of caution regarding the predictions is warranted, for the ease of the derivations may be more apparent than real (see Weiner, 1972). For example, assume that there exists an easy task in which all the incorrect responses are below threshold for a low drive group, but, for a high drive group, some of these responses rise above the threshold. Hence, given this easy task, heightened drive should decrease performance. It is not possible to predict accurately the relative level of performance of high and low drive groups without a complete and exact specification of all the potential responses and their numerical strengths as well as an exact statement about the threshold level. At this time, such precision is not possible.

Conflict

Many types of conflict have been identified, but the one most prevalent in human behavior is labelled an approach-avoidance conflict. This conflict occurs when both hopes and fears are associated with the same action. For example, we like to buy new clothes, but they are expensive; we want to eat a candy bar, but it is fattening; we would like to hit father and be closer to mother, but these actions might be punished.

Observation of approach-avoidance conflicts reveals "ambivalent" behavior. For example, consider a hungry animal in a runway with food at the opposite end and an electrified grid separating it from the food (see Figure 3–1). This illustrates an approach-avoidance conflict, for running down the alleyway will have both beneficial and aversive consequences. In this situation, the animal often approaches the food, turns back from the shock, returns to approach the food, and so on. The behavior oscillates from approach to avoidance, and thus is called ambivalent.

Applying the principles derived from the Drive × Habit conception of motivation, Neal Miller (1944, 1959) was able to describe and predict behavior in approach-avoidance conflicts. His conflict model is among the most cited works in the study of personality and motivation and well illustrates how mechanistic principles derived from the study of infrahumans can aid in the explanation of complex human behavior. We will see, however, that certain aspects of drive theory had to be modified by Miller to account for some of his data.

Miller's Conflict Model

Miller includes six postulates in his analysis of approach-avoidance conflicts. The postulates, and their relation to Hullian theory, are:

Postulate 1:   The tendency to approach a goal is stronger the nearer the subject is to it.

Derivation: It is again useful to consider a hungry rat running down a straight runway to receive a food reward. As the animal traverses the runway, drive level, defined operationally as the number of hours of food deprivation, remains relatively constant. That is, hunger does not greatly change as the animal runs toward the food. However, habit strength does vary as a function of distance from the goal, with approach habit increasing as the goal is approached. (This principle from learning theory will not be examined here and must be accepted on faith.) In Diagram 3–4 values are assigned to both drive and habit to illustrate the strength of motivation as the goal box is approached. Drive level is given a constant value of 2, while habit strength varies from 1 to 5. The diagram indicates that approach motivation increases as the animal approaches the goal. Thus, it should run faster, pull harder, and so on as the goal box is reached.

DIAGRAM 3–4

Strength of the Tendency to Approach a Goal in a Runway

	Start Box				*Goal*
Hunger Drive	2	2	2	2	2
Approach Habit	1	2	3	4	5
Drive × Habit	2	4	6	8	10

Postulate 2:   The tendency to avoid a feared stimulus is stronger the nearer the subject is to it.

Derivation: The reasoning is virtually identical to that already given for Postulate 1.

Postulate 3:   The strength of the avoidance tendency increases more rapidly with nearness to the goal than does the strength of the approach tendency (see Figure 3–13).

Derivation: This is the key postulate in the conflict model, and follows from principles of Drive × Habit theory and the conception of fear as an acquired or learned drive. As already indicated, in an appetitive situation, the level of a drive such as hunger is operationally defined in terms of hours of deprivation. The changes in an animal's appetitive drive during the time it takes to traverse a runway are minimal. On the other hand, in an aversive situation the drive, labelled fear or anxiety, is learned. The degree of fear varies as a function of the similarity between the immediate stimulus situation and the stimuli present at the time the aversive stimulation was received. In a runway it is assumed that the cues in the start box are least similar to the cues in the goal box. Thus, if an animal receives shock at the goal, his fear increases as the goal box is approached. (For example, one exhibits little fear when walking a few

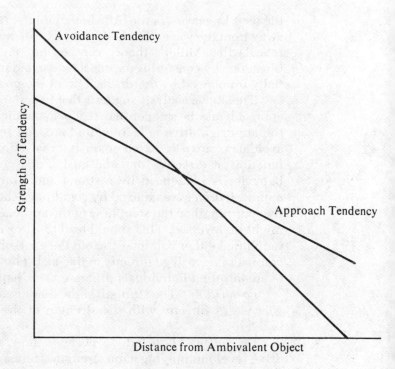

Strength of Tendency

Avoidance Tendency

Approach Tendency

Distance from Ambivalent Object

Figure 3–13. Graphic representation of an approach-avoidance conflict situation. The individual has tendencies to approach and withdraw from an object. The point at which the gradients cross indicates the place of maximal conflict.

feet from the edge of a cliff, but stepping a few paces closer to the edge greatly increases fear.) In addition, the habit strength of avoiding shock also increases as the goal is approached (see Solomon, 1964, for discussion of this point). The avoidance tendency is conceptualized in Diagram 3–5.

DIAGRAM 3–5

Strength of the Tendency to Avoid a Goal in a Runway

	Start Box				Goal
Fear Drive	1	2	3	4	5
Avoidance Habit	1	2	3	4	5
Drive × Habit	1	4	9	16	25

When compared to Diagram 3–4, Diagram 3–5 indicates that the avoidance tendency is steeper than the approach tendency (see Figure 3–13). That is, the change in the strength of the tendencies as a function of the distance from the goal, or the slope of the functions, is greater for the avoidance than the approach tendency. This is because both drive and habit vary with distance in the avoidance situation, while, for approach motivation, only habit strength is affected by distance from the goal. This means that when one is a great distance from the goal, the dominant motivation often is that of approach and attraction. But as the goal is approached, feelings of fear may come to dominate overt expression. The potential bride or groom becoming more and more uncertain as the date of the wedding nears, or the little boy running to the water for a toy and then away from the waves, has been observed on many occasions. Figure 3–13 reveals that Miller's theory can account for such oscillation and ambivalence by construing approach and avoidance motivation as differentially influenced by the distance from the goal.

The above analysis suggests that in certain situations the gradient of approach may be steeper than that of avoidance. This should occur when the approach drive is learned and aroused by external stimuli, but the avoidance drive is based upon internal stimuli that do not vary as a function of distance from the goal. For example, if sexual avoidance behavior is influenced by a strong and fixed super-ego, while sexual approach drives are aroused by cognitions, such as the sight of an attractive partner, then the steepness of the approach and avoidance gradients might be reversed. This should lead to all-or-none behavior. That is, the individual either will totally avoid the goal, or, once beyond the point of ambivalence, will go directly to the goal. This resembles the behavior of overcontrolled individuals discussed in Chapter Two.

Postulate 4:   The strength of the tendencies to approach or avoid the goal varies directly with the strength of the drive on which they are based.

Derivation: This follows because the gradients are determined by drive level multiplying habit strength. Hence, increasing drive, or habit, increases the strength of the motivational tendencies. This postulate suggests that drive is not nondirective, but selective; only the relevant habit is energized by an increment in drive. If drive multiplies habits both relevant and irrelevant to the specific source of drive, as the Drive × Habit conception specifies, then as hunger increases, the strength of both the approach and avoidance tendencies will increase. It would then be impossible to conclude that animals approach closer to a goal given increased hours of food deprivation. This is illustrated in Figure 3–14. In Figure 3–14 both the approach and avoidance tendencies are enhanced by increased food deprivation; there is no change in the distance traversed toward the goal in this particular situation. Thus, Miller does not accept the totally nondirective conception of drive.

Postulate 5:   Below the level of the asymptote of learning, increasing the number of reinforced trials increases the strength of the response tendency that is reinforced.

Derivation: Identical with Postulate 4.

Postulate 6:   When two incompatible response tendencies are in conflict, the stronger one will be expressed.

TESTS OF THE MODEL.   Miller, Brown, and others have conducted a number of experiments to test Miller's conflict model. In one of the original investigations, Brown (1948) developed a technique to measure the strength of the approach and avoidance tendencies in rats. The rats were fitted with a harness device allowing the experimenter to assess how hard they pulled. Animals that had been trained in separate goal boxes either to approach food or to avoid a shock were placed at various distances from the food or shock. As hypothesized, the strength of pull

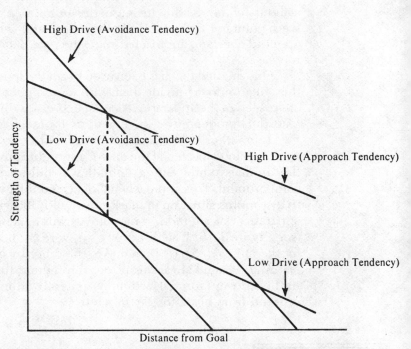

Figure 3–14. Graphic representation of an approach-avoidance conflict situation in which the drive generated by food deprivation also energizes the avoidance habit. The animal does not approach closer to the goal although food deprivation has increased (low-low versus high-high) intersection.

varied directly as a function of distance from the goal. In addition, the distance from the shock compartment influenced the intensity of the pull away from the shock more than the distance from the reward compartment influenced the pull toward the food.

In a subsequent study, animals were trained to receive both food and a shock in the same goal box. Hours of deprivation and the level of shock were varied. The maximum degree of approach to the goal was the dependent variable. The results of this investigation are illustrated in Figure 3–15. The data indicate that for any given level of shock intensity,

Figure 3–15. The joint effects of strength of shock and hunger on the distance animals will traverse toward a goal in a conflict situation. The lower numbers on the graph indicate that the animal approached closer to the goal. Thus, as shock increases and hunger decreases, the animal does not approach as close to the goal. (Adapted from Miller, 1959, p. 212.)

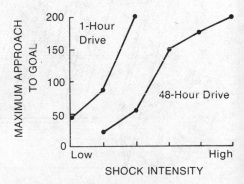

as hours of deprivation increase, the animals approach closer to the goal (zero point in Figure 3–15). On the other hand, when hours of deprivation are held constant, approach toward the goal decreases as shock intensity increases.

One method that has been used to get the animals closer to the goal in this situation is to provide them with some alcoholic beverage before they are placed in the apparatus. Alcohol decreases the amount of experienced fear, thus producing an increment in approach behavior.

In another investigation, Murray and Berkun (1955) trained rats to approach food located at the end of a straight runway. They then shocked the animals while eating until they would no longer enter the goal compartment. This approach-avoidance conflict was aroused in a distinctive stimulus situation (a black runway). Following conflict training, the apparatus was altered and the runway was attached to two other runways (see Figure 3–16). The three runways were connected, and it was possible for the animals to pass from one to the other by going through any of the openings located at various places throughout the alleyway. The stimuli in the runways formed a stimulus generalization continuum: They were ordered from black to gray to white.

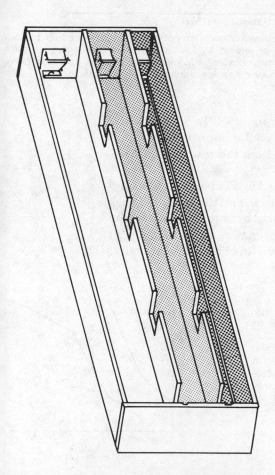

Figure 3–16. White, gray, and black runways, ordered on the basis of stimulus generalization, employed in the study of displacement. Windows in the dividing walls permit the animals to change runways. (From Murray & Berkun, 1955, p. 50.)

After the initial training period, Murray and Berkun expected the animals to approach the food somewhat when replaced in the black alley. At the hypothetical point where the avoidance gradient is stronger than that of the approach gradient, the animals were expected to vacillate and not approach further. It was hypothesized that they would then enter the gray alleyway and would progress farther toward the food. This prediction was based on the assumption that the alteration in the stimulus situation changes the avoidance (fear) drive, but not the approach drive for food. That is, changing the stimuli, like varying the physical distance from the goal, has more of an effect on the avoidance than the approach tendency. Similarly, the animals were again expected to reach a point of equilibrium in the gray alley, and then shift to the white alley. There it was predicted that they would proceed still closer to the goal region. This pattern of behavior was observed by Murray and Berkun.

MILLER'S CONFLICT MODEL AND DISPLACEMENT.   Displacement refers to the observation that objects of behavior change although the desire to attain the original goal has not subsided. As already indicated, Freud contended that there are "vicissitudes of the instincts"; in other words, there are a variety of goals that may satisfy an underlying wish. The most frequently cited example of such displacement activity is in the study of aggression. It is often pointed out that the worker in the family cannot express anger at the boss, and therefore comes home to "take it out" on the unsuspecting mate. In one primitive society, displacement activities are institutionalized. Outside every hut is a dog; when the male of the household is angry, he may punish this unfortunate animal. Freud used a similar but more humorous example to illustrate displacement:

> There was a blacksmith in the village who had committed a capital offense. The Court decided that the crime must be punished; but as the blacksmith was the only one in the village and was indispensable, and as on the other hand there were three tailors living there, one of *them* was hanged instead. (Freud, 1916, pp. 174–175)

Displacement activity, or the shifting of goal objects, has been incorporated into Miller's conflict model. Consider the employee who is angry at the boss, but not directly expressing this hostility. Miller reasons that the aggressive tendency directed toward the supervisor is inhibited by a stronger avoidance tendency. Thus, the person will respond aggressively only to someone similar to the boss (e.g., one's spouse). Aggression is expressed "farther" from the goal because the change in the stimulus situation reduces the avoidance more than the approach drive. This analysis assumes that one's spouse, for example, is similar to the boss along some psychological dimension.

If the horizontal or X axis in Figure 3–13 is altered so that it represents objects, rather than temporal distance, then displacement behavior can be readily illustrated within Miller's conflict model (see Figure 3–17). Figure 3–17 indicates that there is an approach tendency to aggress against the boss, and an inhibitory motivation that functions to prevent direct hostile expression. The individual in this situation would not aggress against the boss, because at that point avoidance or inhibitory mo-

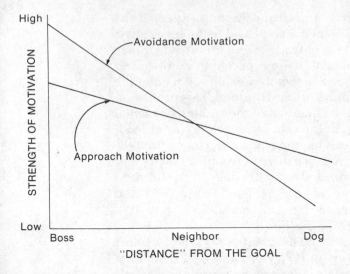

Figure 3-17. Example of the dynamics of displacement.

tivation exceeds approach motivation. The aggression theoretically would be expressed at the point of gradient intersection (the neighbor) or the point at which the approach motivation most exceeds the avoidance motivation (the dog). Thus, the aggressive behavior is "displaced," i.e., directed toward objects that did not provoke the action.

Miller has derived a number of postulates concerning displacement activity from his conflict model. A few of these postulates, along with illustrative examples, are listed here.

1. When the direct response to the original stimulus is prevented by the absence of that stimulus, displaced responses will occur to other similar stimuli, and the strongest displaced response will occur to the most similar stimulus present.

    For example, a girl who is prevented from marrying her sweetheart by his death, and who is completely recovered from her grief and other possibly negative factors, will be expected to prefer the suitor who is most similar to him.

2. When the direct response to the original stimulus is prevented by conflict, the strongest displaced response will occur to stimuli which have an intermediate degree of similarity to the original one.

    Thus a girl who is prevented from marrying her sweetheart by a violent quarrel would be expected to prefer someone not completely similar, but not completely different.

3. If the relative strength of the inhibitory response is increased, the point of strongest displacement, and hence object choice, will shift in the direction of stimuli which are less similar to the original one eliciting the direct response.

    In other words, the more unhappy the girl's experience with her previous sweetheart, the less similar should be her choice of a second love object. (Miller, 1959, pp. 218–219)

In sum, it is evident that principles derived from Hullian drive theory and the study of infrahumans can explain some complex human conflicts and their resolution.

Frustration

"Frustration" has a diversity of meanings for psychologists. Frustration may refer to an independent variable, or experimental manipulation. Often this involves blocking the attainment of a goal, inducing failure, or delivering a personal insult. Performance of the "frustrated" group is then compared to the performance of a "non-frustrated" or control group to assess the effects of the independent manipulation. Frustration also may have reference to a dependent variable, in which case the investigator measures the amount of frustrated behavior. For example, one might examine whether individuals high in anxiety display more frustrated behavior than persons low in anxiety. Finally, frustration frequently pertains to an intervening variable, or a complex process that is inferred from certain observable responses. For example, on the basis of observed aggressive behavior, one might conclude that an individual is frustrated. Many response indicators of frustration have been observed in laboratory situations. These responses include aggression, enhanced goal striving, fixation, and regression. All of these reactions are examined at some place in this book (and perhaps displayed when reading the book).

It also is important to distinguish frustration the product from frustration the process. An analogy with the field of learning makes this distinction clearer. Learning is a product; it refers to a change in the organism as a result of experience. But learning also is a process, or an ongoing activity. In a similar manner, frustration is a product, or a result of an event. But it also is a process, pertaining to a change or a dynamic state within the organism.

Three conceptions of frustration, which are directly linked to drive theory, will now be presented. The drive approach is best able to explain the association between frustration and aggression and the instigating or enhancing properties of frustration.

Frustration and Aggression

The first systematic analysis of frustration and its potential consequences was formulated by the Institute of Human Relations at Yale University. In a manner similar to the analysis of anxiety and conflict, Freudian ideas were borrowed and translated into the terminology of drive theory. Hence, complex phenomena were stated in clear and experimentally testable propositions. The initial insights of the Yale group regarding a relation between frustration and aggression preceded Hull's formal theory of motivation. Nonetheless, it is evident that the ideas regarding frustration are intimately related to Hull's system and to Miller's analysis of conflict and displacement.

Dollard and his Yale colleagues (Dollard, Miller, Doob, Mowrer, & Sears, 1939) postulated a linkage between frustration (defined as a goal response that has been interrupted) and the instigation of aggression (defined as an act that has a goal of injury to another organism). Miller

(1941) describes the hypothesized relation between frustration and aggression as follows:

> The frustration-aggression hypothesis is an attempt to state a relationship believed to be important in many different fields of research. It is intended to suggest to the student of human nature that when he sees aggression he should turn a suspicious eye on possibilities that the organism or group is confronted with frustration; and when he views interference with individual or group habits, he should be on the look-out for, among other things, aggression. This hypothesis is induced from common-sense observation, from clinical case histories, from a few experimental investigations, from sociological studies, and from the results of anthropological field work. The systematic formulation of this hypothesis enables one to call sharp attention to certain common characteristics in a number of observations from all of these historically distinct fields of knowledge and thus to take one modest first step toward the unification of these fields. (p. 337)

This relatively simple formulation generated a great deal of research. Many investigators searched for the conditions that affect the tendency to aggress (see Lawson, 1965; Yates, 1962). More specifically, it was suggested that:

1. The greater the frustration, the greater the instigation to aggression;
2. The stronger the motive or the desire that is frustrated, the more intense is the impulse to aggress; and
3. The greater the number of frustrations, the greater the aggressive tendency.

In addition, Dollard et al. (1939) postulated that expected punishment for aggression will deter hostile responding and result in less direct aggressive expression. Furthermore, it was anticipated that following an aggressive action there would be a reduction in the subsequent tendency to behave aggressively. These hypotheses, which respectively bear upon the notions of displacement and catharsis, were examined earlier in this book and will not be reviewed here. However, it should be noted that frustration, conflict, displacement, and catharsis are interrelated areas of study. Frustration was assumed to arise when a desired goal is blocked. This interruption was thought to produce a tendency to aggress. However, such behavior could be inhibited by a competing avoidance tendency. The competition or conflict between approach and avoidance motivation might then be partially resolved by displacing aggression to a different source. The displaced aggression was believed to serve as a substitute (catharsis) for the original aggressive wish, thereby decreasing the hostile desire. Thus, Hull and his colleagues examined the entire sequence of behavior, from the instigation of action to the offset of motivation.

One of the most noteworthy aspects of the frustration-aggression program of research was that many of the studies were conducted in "real-life" settings, and the theory was applied to social phenomena such as prejudice and scapegoating. For example, in one investigation, Miller and Bugelski (1948) prevented children at a camp from participating in a "bank night" at a local movie theater. This activity was very attractive to the children, and thus, a great amount of frustration was experienced. Both before and after the frustration the campers expressed their attitudes toward two minority groups, Japanese and Mexicans. Following the frustration there was a significant decline in the favorable trait ratings ascribed to these groups. That is, frustration was related to prejudice.

In another study of social aggression, evidence was gathered showing that as the economic depression (and, hence, frustration) continued, the number of lynchings (an index of displaced aggression) also increased. However, the status of this particular relationship remains in doubt.

The frustration-aggression hypothesis is no longer influential in the field of psychology. It is now realized that aggression may be instigated by any number of factors (including frustration), and that there are many consequences of frustration (including aggression). Also, the unitary notion of both frustration and aggression is questioned. There appear to be many kinds of frustration and many kinds of aggression, and they may not substitute for one another or be aggregated. But the frustration-aggression research exemplified the best of the Yale Institute of Human Relations: an interdisciplinary attempt, guided by the behavioristic language of Hull, to explain a wide array of important behaviors.

The Brown-Farber Theory of Frustration

Two subsequent theories derived from Hullian thinking related frustration to generalized drive, rather than linking frustration with one kind of response tendency. The first theory to be presented was formulated by Brown and Farber (1951). These investigators, guided by the work of Dollard et al. (1939), also assumed that frustration results from interference with an ongoing action. The source of the interference may be something that delays response completion, such as a barrier or a competing habit. For example, frustration may be experienced when a flat tire prevents someone from playing in a baseball game, or when competing habits interfere with one another while batting, thus resulting in failure to get a hit. Brown and Farber postulated that frustration has drive properties and that the drive generated by goal thwarting multiplies all the habits aroused in a particular situation.

In one study guided by this conception, Haner and Brown (1955) hypothesized that the amount of frustration produced following goal interference is a function of the strength of motivation to reach the goal. Thus, for example, the more one wants to get to the baseball game, the greater the frustration that results from a flat tire. Following drive theory, Haner and Brown conceive motivation to be equal to Drive × Habit. Thus, they expected that frustration would be positively related to the magnitude of the drive being prevented and the habit strength of the goal response.

Haner and Brown manipulated habit strength in an experimental investigation by employing a task that required subjects to place marbles in holes. Thirty-six holes had to be filled within a given time to complete the activity. The experimenters interrupted the subjects (children) after they had filled 25, 50, 75, 89, or 100 per cent of the holes. Guided by the work of Miller and others, Haner and Brown assumed that the closer the person was to the goal, the greater the strength of approach motivation. In this example, the experimenters assumed that "distance" from the goal, defined as the number of marble completions, theoretically corresponds to the strength of the habit to approach the goal.

Interruption was signaled by a buzzer, followed by the marbles falling to the bottom of the apparatus. The subjects could then push a plunger that turned the buzzer off and allowed them to begin the next trial. The measure of the dependent variable in the experiment, or index of frustration, was the pressure the subjects exerted when pushing the plunger.

The results of the study are shown in Figure 3–18. The data reveal that the intensity of the push response is a function of the distance from the goal at the time of thwarting. Thus, the hypothesis of Haner and Brown is supported. The results apparently demonstrate the nondirective energizing function of a frustration drive. Perhaps the reader can recall a similar reaction in a pinball game following a "just missed" in the previous game.

Well before the Farber-Brown conceptualization, a study relevant to their thinking was conducted by Sears and Sears (1940). These investigators produced frustration in infants by withdrawing the bottle during feeding. They then measured the latency of the crying response. The results of this study are given in Table 3–2. As Table 3–2 shows, the greater the frustration (the less the hunger satisfaction), the faster was the prepotent crying response. This is in accordance with the belief that frustration has drive properties and energizes habits.

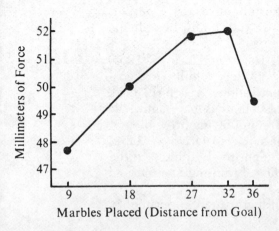

Figure 3–18. The effects of frustration related to five degrees of goal proximity. The dependent variable was the millimeters of force exerted following the interruption of the task. (Adapted from Haner & Brown, 1955, p. 205.)

**TABLE 3-2 LATENCY OF CRYING AS A FUNCTION OF
TIME OF WITHDRAWAL OF BOTTLE**

Oz. Milk Taken Before Withdrawal	Latency of Crying (in seconds)
0.5	5.0
2.5	9.9
4.5	11.5

(From Sears & Sears, 1940, p. 298.)

Amsel's Theory of Frustration

The most systematic theoretical analysis of frustration from the drive theoretical perspective is the work of Amsel and his colleagues (Amsel, 1958, 1967; Amsel and Ward, 1954, 1965). These investigators relate frustration to non-directive drive and build upon the model of Brown and Farber. Amsel and Roussel (1952) define frustration as a state resulting from the non-reinforcement of a response that had been consistently reinforced. That is, if an expectancy of reward is established and the response no longer results in a reward, frustration is experienced. The more one expects a reward, the greater the frustration that occurs when the reward is not given. Frustration is conceived by Amsel as having drive properties. In addition, Amsel postulates that frustration is aversive and that cues similar to those present when frustration is encountered also generate some degree of frustration.

This theory becomes clearer when considering Spence's analysis of the r_g-s_g mechanism that underlies the incentive value of a goal. Recall that, according to Spence, originally neutral cues elicit the expectation of a reward because these or similar cues appear during the time of reward. In a similar manner, Amsel asserts that originally neutral cues paired with frustration become aversive. And cues similar to those appearing when frustration is experienced also become aversive. Therefore, following the failure to attain an expected reward in a straight-runway situation, the animal experiences frustration throughout the runway. Amsel labels the frustration experienced before entering the goal chamber as "anticipatory frustration." Again guided by Spence, Amsel suggests that frustration responses produce their own pattern of stimulus feedback. The increased internal stimulation accounts for the drive properties of frustration.

A demonstration of the drive properties of non-reward was reported by Amsel and Roussel (1952). These experimenters employed an apparatus in which two runways were joined (see Figure 3-19). The goal box in the first runway served as the starting box for the second runway. During the training period the animals were fed in both the first and second goal boxes; in the testing phase, food was withheld in the first goal box. Amsel and Roussel report that following non-reward in the first goal box, the vigor of performance in the second runway increased above the previous level. They contend that this performance increment demon-

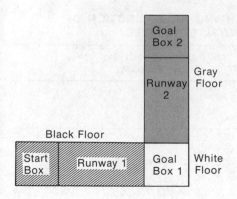

Figure 3–19. Apparatus for the demonstration of the Frustration Effect used by Amsel & Roussel, 1952.

strates the drive effects of frustration. The immediately augmented response strength following non-attainment of an expected reward is termed the Frustration Effect.

Additional research isolated some of the determinants of the Frustration Effect. For example, the energizing effects of frustration increase as a function of the number of rewarded trials (Marzocco, 1951). This logically follows from Amsel's theory, for the greater the number of reinforced trials, the greater the anticipation of the reward, and the greater the amount of experienced frustration when reward does not follow the instrumental response.

Social Facilitation

Many questions of primary interest to social psychologists also have been examined from the perspective of drive theory. Foremost among these is: "What is the effect of the mere presence of other individuals upon the *performance* of the single individual?" (Cottrell, 1972, p. 185). This has been called the study of *social facilitation,* even though it has been demonstrated that other individuals can impede, as well as augment, task performance.

When two or more people act together, the intensity of their individual behavior often increases. Social facilitation among both humans and infrahumans is well documented in the experimental literature. For example, as early as 1897, Triplett observed that bicycle racers seem to ride faster when in direct competition with others. To test this notion, Triplett had riders race either alone (against a clock), with a "pacer," or against another rider. As expected, the presence of a second rider resulted in a faster bicycle speed. Social facilitation also has been reported by other investigators examining performance at a variety of activities, particularly simple motor-learning tasks.

Perhaps surprisingly, the bulk of the research concerning social facilitation has been conducted with infrahumans. For example, socially enhanced eating by chicks is a relatively well substantiated phenomenon: Chicks eat more in the presence of other chicks than when eating alone. Fish and rats also consume more when in the presence of others. In a similar manner, responses such as running, pecking, and nest building are augmented among a variety of infrahumans given the presence of members of their own species (see reviews by Cottrell, 1972; Zajonc, 1965).

Three distinctive paradigms have been identified in the research on social facilitation. The first is the *audience* paradigm, in which one performs in the presence of passive spectators. Secondly, there is a *co-action* paradigm, in which others in the same setting are independently engaged in the identical task as the performer. Finally, there is an *interactive* paradigm, in which numerous individuals are working together on a task. To account for social facilitation, researchers have proposed three major interpretations, which are differentially applicable to the three social paradigms. The interpretations revolve around the concepts of imitation and learning, disinhibition, and drive. The drive theoretical position will be examined first. The other interpretations will then be analyzed to see whether they provide better explanations of social facilitation.

The Drive Theory Interpretation

The drive theory explanation of social facilitation, first proposed by Zajonc (1965), contends that the observer or the co-acting worker induces an irrelevant drive (see Weiss & Miller, 1971). Inasmuch as the presence of others allegedly increases drive level, it follows that performance increments, or social facilitation, should occur on tasks for which the correct or measured response is dominant in habit strength. The increased drive level multiplies habit strength, augmenting the difference between the likelihood of responding with the dominant versus the subordinate response. Hence, performance at simple motor tasks (e.g., eating responses among hungry infrahumans) should be facilitated in social settings. On the other hand, performance at difficult tasks, or during early phases of learning, should be impeded by the presence of others because the incorrect responses dominant in the individual's habit hierarchy are most augmented by the heightened drive. Note that Zajonc's analysis is identical to the one presented earlier in this chapter concerning the relation between level of drive (score on the Manifest Anxiety Scale) and performance on easy and complex paired-associates. A review of the social facilitation literature by Zajonc (1965) revealed a great deal of support for the hypothesized interaction between the task difficulty and the presence or absence of others.

Zajonc and others (e.g., Cottrell, Wack, Sekarak, & Rittle, 1968; Zajonc and Sales, 1966), performed a number of experiments that directly tested the drive interpretation of social facilitation. These experiments either involve "pseudo-recognition" perceptual tasks, word associations, or task performance.

PSEUDO-RECOGNITION.   In an experiment by Cottrell et al. (1968), nonsense words were first presented at unequal frequencies (1, 2, 5, 10, or 25 repetitions). This created disparate levels of habit strength or response potency. These words were then exposed on a tachistoscope for very brief time intervals, and subjects were instructed to report the word they had seen. However, on crucial "pseudo-recognition" trials nothing was exposed. Half the subjects were tested alone, while the rest were tested in front of an audience of two other individuals.

The results of this study are depicted in Figure 3–20. Figure 3–20 shows that subjects responding in front of an audience were significantly more likely to respond with words of high response strength (frequent exposure) than subjects tested alone, and less likely to respond with lower response strength words. These findings are in accord with the hypotheses derived from drive theory. A third condition in the study, labelled "mere presence,"will be discussed later.

Zajonc (1965) offered an interesting implication of this work:

> If one were to draw one practical suggestion from the review of the so-cial-facilitation effects which are summarized in this article, he would advise the student to study all alone, preferably in an isolated cubicle, and to arrange to take his examinations in the company of many other students, on stage, and in the presence of a large audience. The results of his examination would be beyond his wildest expectations, provided, of course, he had learned his material quite thoroughly. (p. 274)

Cottrell (1972) then took issue with the analysis of Zajonc, while still maintaining belief in a drive theory explanation. According to Cottrell, the drive induced by the presence of others is learned rather than

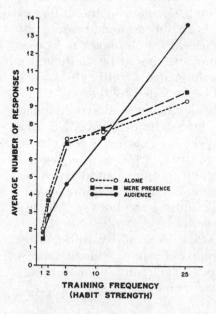

Figure 3–20. Number of responses of different training frequency classes emitted on the pseu-dorecognition trials. (From Cottrell, Wack, Sekarak, & Rittle, 1968, p. 247.)

biologically rooted, and is acquired because the presence of others frequently is paired with reward or punishment. Thus, other people become secondary sources of drive, inducing positive incentive motivation or conditioned fear. Because it has proven exceedingly difficult to establish secondary positive motivators of behavior, Cottrell's theoretical analysis of social facilitation emphasizes the anticipated aversive consequences, or the elicitation of anxiety and fear, in the presence of others. Thus, the "mere presence" of others is not a sufficient explanation of social facilitation, according to Cottrell. Rather, facilitation (or impediment) occurs because others are potential evaluators, and individuals experience apprehension or anxiety in situations in which evaluative judgments about them may be made.

Cottrell et al. (1968) included a crucial experimental condition in their pseudo-recognition experiment to differentiate their position from that of Zajonc. In that condition the subjects were tested in front of an audience of two blindfolded confederates. These experimental stooges supposedly were waiting for a perception experiment and were adapting to darkness. As shown in Figure 3–20, subjects performing in front of a blindfolded audience (the "mere presence" condition) behaved similarly to subjects in the "alone" condition. That is, the "mere presence" of others is not sufficient to induce drive.

While Cottrell (1972) maintains a drive (anxiety) interpretation, it is evident that evaluative apprehension involves cognitive awareness and higher mental processes. Thus, his position is not consistent with the mechanical viewpoint of humans espoused by Hull. Furthermore, the notion of evaluative apprehension is irrelevant to studies of, for example, infrahuman eating and nest building behavior. Thus, Cottrell's position has less generality than the theory proposed by Zajonc.

WORD ASSOCIATIONS.   The study of word associates also offers both positive evidence and difficulties for the drive theory analysis of social facilitation (see Blank, Staff, & Shaver, 1976). In these experiments, the subjects give word associations either in the presence or in the absence of others who are competitors or mere observers (see Matlin & Zajonc, 1968). The word associates can be classified as common or unique on the basis of norms established in the research literature, or by comparison to the total responses that are given in the particular experiment. According to drive theory, the response associates should be more common in the "observer" condition than in the "alone" condition, for common responses are dominant in the subjects' habit hierarchies and augmented by the increased level of drive. Long ago, Allport (1920) and, more recently, Matlin and Zajonc (1968) reported data that apparently support the drive theoretical position.

However, Blank et al. (1976) provide evidence that calls into question the drive theory analysis. In their experiment, subjects were asked to say "the first word you think of" in response to a stimulus word. On one-half of the trials, subjects responded when alone, while on the other half, an observer was present. Response latency and response dominance were measured. In opposition to drive theory predictions, response latencies did not decrease in the presence of an observer. But Blank et al. did find that a measure of response commonness seemed to support the drive theory predictions. However, additional analyses revealed that this was due to the fact that, in the presence of an observer, the subjects gave fewer idiosyncratic responses, rather than increasing their common responses. It appears that subjects avoid giving personal or "strange" responses when someone is watching them. Thus, the data seem best suited to a "social impression" rather than a drive theoretical explanation.

Imitation and Learning Interpretations

The drive interpretation of social facilitation has a number of challengers, for many data seem to contradict drive theoretical predictions or are beyond the "range of convenience" of the theory. That is, the observed behavior often cannot be incorporated within the framework of the drive conception.

One alternative interpretation of social facilitation uses principles derived from the study of imitation. The imitation position is simply that the presence of a co-acting worker provides cues that influence the performer's actions. For example, it has been demonstrated that the co-actors' rate of pecking influences the amount of socially facilitated eating (Tolman, 1967). This finding is consistent with the observation that when a mechanical hen eats only grains of a certain color, the feeding chick is more attracted to that particular grain (Turner, 1964).

The imitation interpretation suggests that if the co-actor is performing below the level of the actor, then performance decrements should occur. This hypothesis assumes that the performer actually copies the actor, rather than just being stimulated by the cues that the actor provides. Such decrements in performance level have been observed among ants that are placed with slower ants (Chen, 1937). The evidence collected by Chen contradicts predictions from drive theory. On the other hand, it also has been reported that the rate of food pecks increases when chicks are fed in the presence of a chick that is placed behind a glass partition without food (Tolman, 1968). In general, the imitation explanation cannot be applied to investigations using the passive audience paradigm.

Another interpretation using principles of learning theory draws upon the belief that experiences in life may teach organisms to respond with greater vigor in group settings. It is known that when infrahumans are fed in groups, there often is food stealing, fighting, and mutual competition for the desired resource. In such settings it is instrumental to eat with greater vigor, for more food will be consumed.

There are numerous investigations supporting the interpretation that learned competitive responses are a necessary condition for social facilitation. For example, it has been demonstrated that prior social experiences in feeding situations influence social facilitation. More specifically, if birds are reared in isolation, feeding in the presence of others does not increase their rate of pecking (see reviews in Cottrell, 1972; Rajecki, Kidd, Wilder, & Jaeger, 1975). Again, however, this interpretation is irrelevant to many studies, such as the Cottrell et al. (1968) pseudo-recognition experiment.

Disinhibition

Still another explanation of social facilitation focuses upon the reduction of avoidance motivation, rather than the onset of anxiety or the augmentation of approach strivings. It has been contended that many infrahumans are frightened during feeding experiments. The presence of others is a signal that reduces fear. The reduction of fear, in turn, facilitates other responses, such as pecking (Rajecki et al., 1975). In support of this interpretation, Rajecki et al. (1975) report that in the presence of other chicks, both dominant and subordinate responses increase during feeding. This contradicts the drive theoretical analysis, which states that the dominant response will replace the subordinate response given heightened drive. Further, Rajecki et al. (1975) also suggest that "animals will consume more in any sort of situation that contains familiar components" (p. 509). Thus, socially reared animals should consume more when placed in social situations. Conversely, the consumption of animals reared alone should be enhanced in isolated conditions. There is much data to support these hypotheses (see Rajecki, et al., 1975).

Summary: Social Facilitation

In sum, it appears that many mechanisms or processes may cause social facilitation or social inhibition. Thus, different experiments seem to require different explanations. This conclusion is not very appealing, for the goal of science is the development of general laws and principles that apply to a variety of observations. But at present no single explanation can account for the majority of the data, and drive theory is not adequate to account for the broad observations of social facilitation. (For a defense of the drive theory view, see Geen & Gange, 1977.)

AROUSAL (ACTIVATION) THEORY

Drive theory specifies two dimensions of behavior: intensity and direction. Drive provides the energy for action and accounts for the intensity of behavior, whereas learning explains the direction that the aroused motivation will take. In this chapter the intensity aspect of behavior has been the focus of attention, for many psychologists equate motivation with the mobilization to act, and issues related to learning are beyond the scope of this book.

There is a body of research in psychology, guided by arousal or activation theory, that concentrates exclusively on the intensity dimension of behavior. Psychologists associated with arousal theory were, in part, responsible for the discovery of the neural mechanisms that apparently mediate the drive state. By identifying the anatomical locus of drive, they provided additional evidence for the validity of this concept and a methodological advancement that promised to quantify precisely the magnitude of drive. Yet, paradoxically, much of the research generated from this viewpoint has contradicted Hull's conception of behavior and played a role in decreasing the number of adherents to this approach. One cause of this decrease was the theory's inability to account for the fact that individuals often strive to increase stimulation. Recall that Freud's conception also contained this flaw. The second shortcoming of Hullian theory, its failure to recognize that individuals think and plan, is elaborated in the subsequent chapters of this book.

The Reticular Formation

A great deal of research in neurophysiology has shown that behavior can be described on a sleeping-waking dimension (see Lindsley, 1957). Furthermore, behavior can vary from alert and attentive to disorganized and without appropriate control (see Figure 3–21). It is possible to monitor the general state of arousal by measuring brain waves with the aid of an electroencephalogram (EEG), as previously discussed in the section on dreams in Chapter Two.

Three anatomical structures have been associated with the sleeping-waking, or coma-disruption, dimension: the cortex, the hypothalamus,

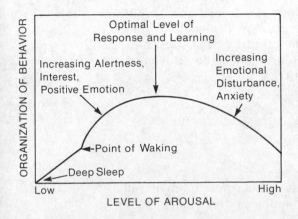

Figure 3–21. Organization of behavior related to the degree of nonspecific arousal. (Adapted from Hebb, 1955, p. 249.)

and the reticular formation. The latter structure, which is an area of the brain that is connected with all the major areas of the cortex, has received the most attention from motivational psychologists.

The initial study relating the reticular formation to arousal was conducted by Moruzzi and Magoun (1949). These investigators electrically stimulated various parts of the brain in cats while the animals were anesthetized. They found that when the reticular formation was stimulated, an EEG was evoked that is similar to that of an awake animal. In support of this finding, lesions of the reticular formation abolish EEG activation (Lindsley, Schreiner, Knowles, & Magoun, 1950). Thus, the reticular formation appears to have a general arousing or alerting function and, in conjunction with other brain structures, such as the hypothalamus, has been considered the intervening mechanism responsible for drive. As stated by Hebb (1955):

> . . . I proposed to you that, whatever you wish to call it, arousal. . . is synonymous with a general drive state, and the conception of drive therefore assumes anatomical and physiological identity. Let me remind you of what we discussed earlier: drive is an energizer, but not a guide; an engine is not a steering gear. These are precisely the specifications of activity in the arousal system. Also, learning is dependent on drive, according to drive theory, and this too is applicable in general terms — no arousal, no learning; and efficient learning is possible only in the waking, alert, responsive animal. (p. 249) [See Figure 3–22A.]

Arousal theorists have isolated many factors that generate arousal, such as the intensity of a stimulus and deprivation in conjunction with the sight of the deprived commodity (Eisman, 1966). They also have identified several factors neglected by drive theorists that contribute to general arousal, such as the complexity, meaningfulness, and novelty of a stimulus. But drive and arousal theorists agree that motivation is essentially a nondirective energization process that results from a variety of drive-inducing antecedents (Ferguson, 1976).

Drive and arousal theorists are not in agreement, however, on two crucial issues:

1. According to arousal theory, individuals prefer and seek out an "optimal level" of stimulation. If stimulation is below the optimal level, individuals will engage in activities that produce increments in arousal; if stimulation is above the optimal level, actions will be initiated to "turn off" that stimulation. In contrast to this position, drive theorists assume that the optimal level of stimulation is at a "zero point," so that behavior is always undertaken to reduce stimulation.
2. According to arousal theory, behavior is curvilinearly related to arousal level (see Figures 3–21 and 3–22B). That is, beyond the optimal level, further increases in arousal produce disorganization and decrements in performance, regardless of the difficulty level of the task. Drive theorists, on the other hand, assume that drive level is linearly related to performance. In situations where the dominant habit is "correct," heightened drive should produce increments in performance; in situations involving many competing responses, heightened drive produces declining performance.

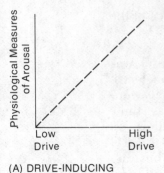

(A) DRIVE-INDUCING
    MANIPULATIONS

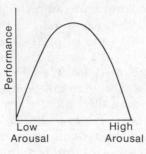

(B) AROUSAL DEFINED BY
    PHYSIOLOGICAL
    MEASURES

Figure 3–22. Arousal related both to drive level and to performance. The right-hand figure reveals there is an "optimal level" of arousal, with greater or lesser arousal resulting in poorer performance. (Adapted from Malmo, 1966.)

The Desire for an Optimal Level of Stimulation

The postulation of an optimal level of stimulus input implies that organisms often are acting to increase external stimulation. As already indicated, many psychologists, including Freud and Hull, conceptualized the person as a stimulus reducer — engaging in aggressive and sexual activities to decrease instinctive pressures, eating to reduce hunger, and so on. But the manifest fact that behaviors instrumental to increasing tension, such as riding a roller coaster or reading a mystery story, are probably more prevalent than activities that reduce tension is now accepted.

The necessity of varied stimulation was dramatically illustrated by Donald Hebb and his colleagues in what is known as the study of "sensory deprivation." In one typical sensory deprivation investigation, the subject lies alone in a white room and wears goggles that permit only homogeneous light (see Heron, 1957). In addition, arms and legs are padded, thus minimizing tactile stimulation. College students placed in this situation reported an inability to think when external inputs were so severely limited. Some also reported hallucinations. Few of the subjects were willing to remain in the setting for more than eight hours, although they were highly paid. The depth of their stimulus-seeking desire was revealed by their repeated requests to listen to the same stock market report, which researchers made available! Of course, we may not really need to conduct controlled experiments to demonstrate the unpleasantness of stimulus deprivation. Any child forced to remain in his or her room or any prisoner reports similar feelings.

Infrahumans as well as humans are seekers of stimulation. Rats will learn to press a light to change their level of visual stimulation; monkeys learn to push a button to receive a puzzle to manipulate. Some of these "intrinsically regulated" motivations are adversely affected by extrinsic incentives, such as a reward of food, that reduce drives. For example, monkeys engage in puzzle manipulations for endless periods of time, pressing a button to receive a puzzle, solving it, and pressing for still another puzzle. If food is given after each puzzle solution, the monkeys will stop pushing the button for the puzzles when the food is later withheld (see Harlow, 1953). That is, the intrinsic attractiveness of the puzzles apparently is no longer sufficient to instigate behavior. The effect of extrinsic motivation on intrinsic interests is examined in detail at a later point in this book (see pp. 257–260).

Spontaneous Alternation

One of the most interesting controversies concerning the desire for varied stimulation involves a phenomenon labelled "spontaneous alternation." In a typical investigation utilizing a T-maze, an organism, such as a rat, is placed in the alleyway and then must turn either right or left at the choice point for a reward. It has been noted that if the rat turns left on trial one, then it is more likely to turn right on trial two, and vice versa. This phenomenon has been called spontaneous alternation, for the organism alters its choice on the two successive experiences. Alternation is not reduced by the receipt of a reward following the initial choice, although the alternation tendency is masked after a few trials because there is repetition of the response that has resulted in a reinforcement (see Dember, 1960).

The Hullians had a simple and parsimonious explanation of alternation. They asserted that after the initial response the muscles connected with the action undergo a temporary state of fatigue. Thus, on the next trial, a different response is made. Of course, this explanation is consistent with their mechanistic conception of action.

On the other hand, psychologists with cognitive orientations postulated a process of stimulus satiation (Glanzer, 1953). That is, there is a reduced responsiveness to a stimulus as a consequence of prior exposure to that stimulus. The stimulus satiation position leads to identical predictions as the response fatigue notion: There should be alternation on successive trials. Furthermore, the greater the time between trials, the less likelihood of alternation, for both fatigue and stimulus satiation decrease over time. This prediction also has been confirmed.

The controversy over fatigue versus satiation is reminiscent of a less sophisticated debate that took place many decades earlier in psychology between mechanists and cognitivists. These two camps debated why it was that moths fly to fire. The mechanists contended that the moths have no choice: The behavior is instinctive and not under volitional control. On the other hand, the cognitivists argued that the moths do it because they are curious!

In an attempt to resolve the alternation question, a critical experiment was devised that permitted a choice between the two explanations (Glanzer, 1953; Montgomery, 1952). A maze was constructed with two

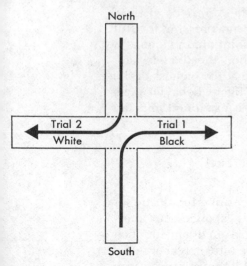

Figure 3–23. Schematic diagram of the stimulus versus response alternation test. If the rat is started from the South on the first trial, it is started from the North on the second. When one starting alley is used, the other is blocked by a gate, as represented by the dotted lines. The arrows indicate the behavior on two successive trials. On the first, the animal turned right, and thereby went into the black arm. On the second trial, the animal also turned right, thereby entering the white arm. Turning responses were repeated, but maze arms were alternated. (From Dember, 1960, p. 345.)

different starting points (see Figure 3–23). One arm of the maze was painted black, while the other arm was white. After an initial trial, the animal was placed in the opposite start box. Thus, if response fatigue had built up, the organism should make a different response on the next trial, which would lead to the same stimulus as in the initial trial. But if stimulus satiation had occurred, then the organism should make the identical muscular response, for this would now expose it to a different stimulus than the one viewed on the previous trial. The results of investigations using this procedure clearly supported the stimulus satiation position. For example, an animal turned right on two successive trials, exposing itself to both the black and white stimuli.

It should be noted, however, that the stimulus satiation explanation, as well as the response fatigue notion, is a "reaction against" theory. It does not propose that organisms are attracted to stimulation in the external environment. Rather, there is a decrease in the attractiveness of some stimulus due to satiation, which makes an alternative stimulus relatively more engaging.

A stimulus-seeking explanation of alternation was then proposed by Dember (1956) and Dember and Earl (1957). These investigators contended that organisms are attracted to novel stimuli and to changes in their environment. To test this hypothesis, Dember (1956) examined the behavior of rats in a Y-shaped maze. One arm of the maze was white, the other black. When the animals were placed in the start box they were delayed before being allowed to enter the arms of the maze. During this delay the white arm was changed to black. Given a stimulus satiation conception, the animals should display no systematic choice preferences because both arms of the maze are identical in color. But if organisms are attracted to change, then they should enter the black arm that previously had been white. The data substantiated this prediction. In a similar experiment, the arms of the Y-maze initially were black and gray and then were both changed to white. In this situation the animals entered the black-to-white arm, which represented the greater change.

A Drive-Theory Explanation of Stimulus Seeking

The data discussed above clearly seem to contradict Hullian principles. However, a theory of stimulus seeking has been formulated by Berlyne that attempts to reconcile the desired increments in stimulation with drive reduction theory. Berlyne is an arousal theorist, but, in the Hullian tradition, he assumes that organisms are always attempting to reduce arousal. Thus, the optimal level of stimulation is at a zero level. This seems antithetical to the notion of stimulus-seeking behavior, but Berlyne is able to integrate these apparently contradictory notions.

Berlyne begins with the assumption that arousal is inversely related to attractiveness (see Figure 3–24a). That is, one desires to be minimally aroused. High arousal is experienced in environments that are too simple and in environments that are too complex (see Figure 3–24b). Hence, given very low stimulus input, as in the sensory deprivation procedure, one experiences heightened arousal, which is manifest in pacing behavior and the lack of integration of thought processes. And given high stimulus complexity, heightened internal arousal is experienced. Therefore, stimuli of intermediate complexity are most desired (see Figure 3–24c). Stimuli at the intermediate level are most attractive because they are least arousing. Although it appears that individuals are seeking stimulation and increases in tension. Berlyne suggests that this behavior in reality is decreasing arousal.

Arousal and Performance

Recall that drive and arousal theorists also disagree on the expected relation between activation level and performance. Drive theorists spec-

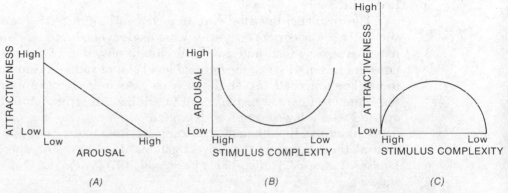

Figure 3–24. Berlyne's theory of curiosity as stimulus-seeking behavior. (From Berlyne, 1959, pp. 319–320.)

ify that drive level is linearly related to performance. Given noncompetitive tasks, such as aversive conditioning or a paired-associates list of synonyms, increases in drive should augment performance. Conversely, given a competitive task, such as a list of paired-associates that includes unpaired synonyms, increases in drive are hypothesized to produce performance decrements. Arousal theorists, on the other hand, specify that for any task there is an optimal level of motivation. As indicated in Figure 3–21, motivation at too high a level produces disorganization and disturbance. Thus, performance is expected to decrease after the optimum level of motivation has been surpassed. Arousal theorists therefore anticipate a curvilinear relation between performance and motivation.

THE YERKES-DODSON LAW.   The curvilinear relationship hypothesized by arousal theorists is complicated by yet another factor: the difficulty level of the task. A very early and oft-cited investigation by Yerkes and Dodson (1908) first called attention to the important interacting affects of task difficulty. Yerkes and Dodson varied the intensity of motivation (shock) given to mice during performance at a visual discrimination task. The correct discrimination enabled the mice to escape from the shock. Yerkes and Dodson reported that given an easy discrimination, the number of correct responses increased as a function of shock intensity. But given a difficult discrimination, performance first increased and then decreased as shock intensity grew in strength.

Thus, although there is assumed to be a curvilinear relation between arousal and performance, performance level is expected to decrease at different intensities of motivation, depending upon the difficulty of the task. In one study directly testing this hypothesis, Broadhurst (1957) detained rats under water for zero to eight seconds before allowing them to enter a Y-maze and escape. One only arm of the maze permitted escape; if the incorrect arm was selected, the animal had to retrace its path under water and enter the correct arm. The arms of the maze differed in brightness, with the brighter arm designated by the experimenter as the correct (escape) choice. Broadhurst then manipulated task difficulty by varying the difference in brightness between the two arms.

The results of this study are depicted in Figure 3–25. Figure 3–25 shows that more correct responses were made when brightness discrimination was easy than under difficult conditions. But, of greater importance for this discussion, the optimal level of motivation was lower given the difficult task rather than the easy task. As indicated in Figure 3–25, the number of correct responses at the difficult discrimination task decreased after a few seconds of detention.

Unfortunately, although the study by Broadhurst is supportive of arousal theory, many other investigations do not confirm the Yerkes-Dodson Law (see Duffy, 1962; Ferguson, 1976). Also, as Duffy (1962) states:

> ... It becomes unhappily apparent that any relationship found between activation and performance can be explained. If the quality of performance

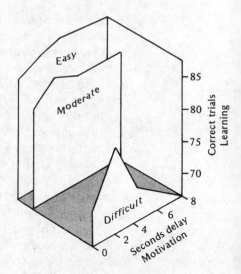

Figure 3–25. A three-dimensional surface showing the relationship between learning scores in a discrimination task and (a) the intensity of the imposed motivation (air deprivation), measured by the number of seconds' delay underwater before release, and (b) the level of difficulty of the task. The overall mean scores are shown. (From Broadhurst, 1957, p. 348.)

increases with an increase in the degree of activation, then the preceding level of activation was too low; if it decreases, then the preceding level of activation was too high. (p. 185)

Hence, although arousal and drive theories do make some differential predictions, a "crucial" experiment supporting one conception rather than the other remains to be conducted.

Summary

In this chapter the drive theoretical approach to motivation was examined. The main theoretical concepts reviewed were drive, learned drive, incentive, and nonspecific energizer. These are the components, or the functions of the components, included in Hull's theory of action. The theory states that behavior is determined by Drive × Habit; with later elaborations, learned drives and incentives came to be included among the determinants of performance.

Four related areas were examined: anxiety, conflict, frustration, and social facilitation. Each of these were interpreted from the perspective of drive theory.

It was indicated that:

1. Anxiety is conceptualized as a nondirective drive. The emotional reaction to a stressor, which is the drive mechanism, is a function of both the aversiveness of that stressor and individual differences in reactions to aversive events. The learning of individuals classified as high in drive is enhanced at easy tasks but inhibited at complex tasks.
2. The study of conflict has been clarified by a model proposed by Miller.

This model postulates that the avoidance gradient, or the change in the strength of avoidance motivation as a function of distance from the goal, is steeper than the approach gradient. This postulate enables the model to account for behavioral ambivalence.

3. There are two drive theories of frustration that can account for the energizing effects of not attaining a goal (Amsel's theory and the Brown-Farber theory).

4. Principles of drive theory can account for some of the data indicating that aggression is one possible consequence of frustration and that following frustration there may be an increase in performance intensity.

5. The drive theoretical approach to social facilitation does not provide an adequate explanation of the majority of the empirical findings. However, some of the observations do fit nicely within the drive theory framework.

The discussion then turned to arousal theory, for arousal is often considered a synonym for the concepts of drive, energy, or activation. Arousal theorists differ from drive theorists in their views on two important issues: 1) Arousal theorists contend that organisms, at times, strive to increase stimulation; and 2) a curvilinear relation between arousal and performance is hypothesized by arousal theorists. It is evident that organisms often do attempt to increase stimulation, as demonstrated in the study of sensory deprivation and spontaneous alternation. These data cast doubts on the philosophical foundations of drive theory, although Berlyne did attempt to account for such observations with a drive framework. The relation between arousal and performance, and how this relation is influenced by task difficulty, remains to be clearly determined.

It is evident that the concept of drive and drive theory have been applied to a wide array of infrahuman and human behavior. Sometimes this application has been quite successful, as in the explanation of the behavior of hungry or thirsty rats running down a maze, or in accounting for complex displacement activities. Conversely, in other domains, drive theory has been relatively unsuccessful.

It appears to this author that the main contribution of drive theory has been the systematic and precise exploration of motivated behavior from an entirely mechanistic position. Drive theorists provided an exemplar for the scientific and experimental study of motivation. They carefully identified the determinants of behavior, created a mathematical model, and then deduced predictions from this model. These predictions were tested in carefully controlled laboratory investigations. This approach sharply contrasts with Freudian psychology, although, as previously indicated, it paradoxically shares much with Freudian theory, including an acceptance of the principles of hedonism, homeostasis, and psychic determinism, and a reliance on energy constructs to provide the motor for action.

Drive theory no longer is the dominant position in psychology, primarily because of its neglect of cognitive processes and its assumption that humans are merely complicated robots. However, it has played, and it continues to play, an important role in furthering our understanding of motivated behavior.

Section II

Expectancy-Value Theories

Chapter Four

KURT LEWIN'S
FIELD THEORY

Introduction

In this section of the book we turn from the mechanistic, drive reduction theories of Freud and Hull to the cognitive, expectancy-value framework advocated by Kurt Lewin, John Atkinson, and Julian Rotter. Lewin is the key transition figure between Sections I and II of this book, for his theory contains many of the tension-reduction notions advocated by Freud and Hull. However, these ideas are incorporated within a more cognitive conception of behavior. Lewin thus provides the bridge from the past to the present. Lewin also was the first psychologist to test experimentally some of Freud's beliefs about psychodynamics and insisted upon the study of complex, everyday behaviors. Yet he built a quasi-mathematical model of behavior that is surprisingly similar to Hull's Drive × Habit theory. In this manner, a step was made to include the divergent goals of Freud and Hull within one framework. Later in this book, we will also learn that Lewin greatly influenced attribution theory, another conception for the study of motivation, and even initiated the "T-group" (group therapy) movement, an essential component of humanistic psychology (see Chapter Nine). The pervasive contributions and influence of Lewin often go unnoticed by psychologists. His theory has had a fate similar to what American economists label as "creeping socialism"—we do not like to admit its presence, but readily accept the benefits that it brings.

The Historical Impact of Gestalt Psychology

Kurt Lewin was a member of the Gestalt school of psychology, which was centered in Berlin in the early 1900's. The founder of the Gestalt movement is believed to have been Max Wertheimer, who first called attention to the "phi phenomenon." Wertheimer noted

KURT LEWIN

(Wide World Photos)

Kurt Lewin was born in Prussia in 1890 and received his doctorate from the University of Berlin in 1914. At Berlin he came under the influence of the Gestalt psychologists, particularly Max Wertheimer, Wolfgang Köhler, and Kurt Koffka. At the time of Hitler's rise to power Lewin was returning to Berlin via Russia after a trip to the United States. He wisely decided that arrival in Germany would be unsafe and returned to settle in the United States. After a brief period at Cornell University, Lewin went to the Child Welfare Station at the University of Iowa (1935–1945). In 1945, he became director of the Research Center for Group Dynamics at the Massachusetts Institute of Technology. Lewin died in 1947 at the age of 56.

Lewin's untimely death of a heart attack was long feared by his colleagues, for his life was one of constant activity. His thoughts encompassed theoretical models of motivation as well as the solution of social problems. His applied interests ranged from the study of adolescence and feeblemindedness to an analysis of national character and food preferences.

Lewin was a warm person who actively worked with his students and colleagues. Students tell stories of Lewin ringing their bell late at night, carrying a bottle of wine, and then discussing psychology until dawn. His students, including Leon Festinger and many others, have dominated the field of social psychology. Lewin strongly identified with America and the American way of life. But he also was a strong supporter of the state of Israel and, prior to his death, was entertaining the idea of settling in the then relatively new Jewish state.

that if two lights are flashed in close temporal and spatial contiguity, there is perceived movement. Of course, we now all know this because of the ever-present movie marquees. To understand perceived motion, one must consider not only the onset of a particular light, but also its relation to the onset of neighboring lights. According to the Gestaltists, the general significance of this finding was that the comprehension of perceptual phenomena is not possible if observations are broken down or analyzed into component parts. Rather, one must deal with the whole, or the total situation as it is perceived by the person. The whole often is different from the mere sum of the parts.

In discussing the total situation, Gestaltists made use of field conceptions originated by physicists. In a given physical field, alteration of any part of that field affects the other parts. A field is organized by all the forces acting upon all the objects within that field.

The Gestaltists applied the notion of fields in their analysis of psychological processes, particularly perception. The perception of an

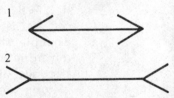

Figure 4–1. The Müller-Lyer illusion. Both lines are about one inch in length. However, Line 2 appears longer than Line 1.

object, they characteristically argued, is determined by the total context in which the object is embedded. This was dramatically illustrated in their demonstration of perceptual illusions, such as the Müller-Lyer illusion (see Figure 4–1). In the Müller-Lyer illusion, two lines of equal length are perceived as being unequal. According to principles of Gestalt psychology, this is caused by the differing fields of forces around the judged lines.

The Gestaltists also expressed an interest in learning, but the type of learning they investigated can be considered a subset of perception and again illustrates the importance of the psychological field and the interrelationships among the parts of the field. In Wolfgang Köhler's book, *The Mentality of Apes* (1925), experiments are reported that demonstrate insight learning in animals. The general procedure in these studies was to place a stick in one corner of an ape's cage and food outside the cage at an opposite corner. The animal could reach the food only if it used the stick as a tool. Köhler reports that the apes were able to perceive the correct solution to the problem and reached the food with the aid of the stick. Köhler contrasted this insight learning with the blind trial-and-error learning exhibited by Thorndike's cats and chicks, which so heavily influenced Hull's theory of behavior.

In Köhler's experiments, learning seems to involve perceptual processes. Although the path to the stick is physically opposite to the path toward food, it must be perceived as lying in the direction of the goal. Thus, the discovery of the correct response in this situation depends upon the way in which the animal organizes the field; the solution to the problem requires the correct perception of the relation between the parts.

The language used by the Gestaltists was adapted by Lewin for the interpretation of motivational phenomena. Terms such as structure of the field, relationship between the parts, subjective perception, reorganization of the field, force, energy, and attraction form the foundation for Lewin's theory. We turn to that theory now.

FIELD THEORY

The conceptual framework advocated by Lewin is called field theory. Field theory starts with the position that behavior is determined by the field as it exists at a moment in time. This approach is *ahistorical,* and is contrasted with a genetic or historical analysis. Assume, for example, that an individual has a compulsion to wash his hands every ten minutes. To explain this behavior, a psychologist advocating the historical approach, such as Freud, would investigate the person's past history, particularly the pattern of child-rearing and the events that occurred during the early stages of development. Ideally, it could then be ascertained how these historical antecedents influence the present action. Lewin, on the other hand, would determine the forces acting on the person in the immediate present. He might represent the individual as avoiding dirt, or the soap as having a positive attraction. The antecedent historical conditions, or the reasons why the individual perceives the situation as he does, would not be essential. What is important is to specify the contemporary or immediate determinants of behavior. The past, as well as the future, is thus incorporated into the present. This ahistorical approach also characterizes Hull's theory, although Hull did not explicitly discuss this aspect of his conception.

A second fundamental position of Lewin already alluded to is that an analysis of behavior must consider the whole situation. As the Gestalt psychologists prior to Lewin emphasized in their study of perceptual events, one must represent the entire field of forces. Each part within a field interacts with the other parts. The use of this principle will become evident as we examine Lewin's concept of the "life space."

The Life Space

Lewin's most basic theoretical statement is that behavior is determined by both the person (P) and the environment (E): $B = f(P,E)$, where f represents some function or relationship. The person and the environment together comprise the life space (see Figure 4–2).

The life space represents *psychological* reality; it depicts the totality of facts that determine behavior at a moment in time. Thus, the life space encompasses the environment as it is perceived by the person. The psychological environment is not identical with the physical environment. To illustrate this point somewhat dramatically, Lewin related the story of a horseback rider lost in a snowstorm. The rider saw a light in the distance and rode directly toward it. Upon

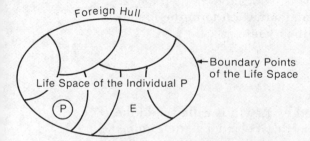

Life Space of the Individual P

Foreign Hull

Boundary Points of the Life Space

Figure 4–2. Representation of a life space. *P* represents the person and *E* represents the psychological environment. (From Lewin, 1936, p. 73.)

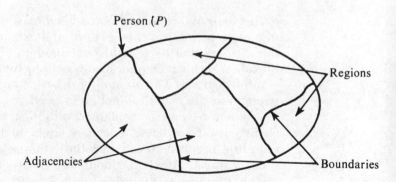

Figure 4–3. Representation of the structural properties of the person. The regions are separated by boundaries, which differ in their permeability. Adjacent regions border one another.

arrival at the destination he was told that he had just crossed a barely frozen lake. This rider's behavior certainly would have been altered if the danger involved in crossing the lake had been a psychological, as well as a physical, reality.

The perceived environment is influenced by many properties of the person, such as needs, values, attitudes, and motives. In a similar manner, the perceived environment influences the person. The sudden appearance of a threatening event, or a physically attractive person, may change the needs or tensions of the individual. According to Lewin, to understand behavior, the person and the environment must be conceived as a constellation. They jointly determine action.

For purposes of discussion, it is convenient to divide Lewin's conceptual scheme into categories that correspond to the person and the environmental components of the life space. Furthermore, both the person and the environment can be described as having structural as well as dynamic properties.

Concepts Related to the Person

STRUCTURAL CONCEPTS.   The person can be thought of either as a point in the life space or as a region. In Figure 4–2 the individual is conceived as an undifferentiated point. In many instances Lewin was concerned primarily with an individual's position or place in the life space, and in these cases it is not convenient to differentiate the person into subparts. But in other situations it is necessary to think of the person as a region in the life space. When conceptualized as a region, the person has structural properties. The structures of greatest importance are the subregions, boundaries, and adjacencies (see Figure 4–3).

The regions within the person are "containers"; they represent "vessels with walls." The walls, or boundaries, of the vessels differ in their permeability; some allow more "leakage" than others. This characteristic of regions is important because it, in part, determines the fate of the tension that is contained within the regions. Tension is the dynamic inner-personal construct.

DYNAMIC CONSTRUCT.   The dynamic construct of tension refers to the state of a region. When a need exists, a region is represented as in a state of tension. For ease of understanding, it often is helpful to think of tension as a fluid contained in the inner-personal regions. (Recall that this metaphor also was used by ethologists in their discussion of instinct.) The amount of this tension varies as a function of the strength or the magnitude of one's needs.

When tension is contained within a region, the region tries to change itself so that it becomes equal in tension to that of the surrounding regions. Recall that the boundaries of the vessels differ in their permeability. If the boundary between two regions is not completely permeable, then some minimal difference in the degree of tension between two regions will be maintained. And if the regions have a common permeable boundary (adjacent regions in Figure 4–3), or if they are in "dynamic communication" (tension from one can flow to the other via an intermediate region), then a need corresponding to one region will become a need in another region. For example, because of the communication between regions, the desire to see movie X may also result in the desire to see movie Y. Adjacent regions thus may be thought of as depicting similar potential needs.

Within the person there are an unspecified number of inner-personal regions that correspond to different needs or intentions. Any time a need or intention arises, a new region is characterized as in a state of tension. Thus, Lewin has a pluralistic conception of needs, as opposed to the Freudian and Hullian notions of a nondirective or pooled source of libido or drive. In the Lewinian system, different regions in tension do not combine to influence all behaviors. Rather, each tense region is associated with a particular goal object or class of objects.

Realization of a goal reduces the level of tension within a region. Goal attainment need not involve the consumption of the desired object. Thinking, remembering, going to a movie, and so on can reduce the level of tension in a region. Note again the difference between the Lewinian and the Freudian or Hullian ideas about goal attainment. For Lewin, needs exist that are not related to bodily functions and survival; this is not true of the Hullian or Freudian theories.

INTEGRATING DYNAMIC AND STRUCTURAL ASPECTS. A need or an intention creates tension in a region of the person. The disequilibrium in tense states between regions causes tension to flow from one region to another. The interchange of tension between the regions depends, in part, on the firmness of the boundaries. If the boundaries are not completely permeable, then a region can remain in a relatively fixed tense state. Tension is postulated to dissipate following goal attainment, which re-establishes equilibrium between the regions.

Concepts Related to the Environment

STRUCTURAL CONCEPTS. The structural characteristics of the environment are identical to those of the person: There are regions, bar-

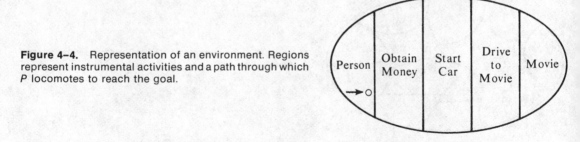

Figure 4–4. Representation of an environment. Regions represent instrumental activities and a path through which P locomotes to reach the goal.

riers, and adjacencies. However, the meanings of the environmental and personal constructs differ. Environmental regions are primarily coordinated with activities. For example, if individual P wishes to attend a movie, then he may have to obtain money from his father, start the car, drive to the movie, and so on (see Figure 4–4). Regions are therefore instrumental actions. But note that the regions also can be considered as "spaces" through which one locomotes to get to the goal.

The number of regions in the life space at any one time is determined by the number of extant psychological differentiations. For each psychological distinction there is a separate region in the life space. The life space may thus change from moment to moment. For example, if the car needed to reach the movie theater fails to start, new regions (such as calling a mechanic) are manifested in the life space.

Regions are surrounded by boundaries that may act as barriers or as impediments to locomotion, just as the boundaries of the inner-personal regions can be impediments to the flowing of tension. The boundaries determine the "space of free movement." Lewin defined the space of free movement as the regions that are accessible to the person. This is limited by what is externally forbidden (environmental constraints) as well as by personal limitations, such as a lack of ability. The space of free movement may be narrow or quite extensive. For example, in a prison, the number of accessible regions is small. In other situations, the space of free movement can be virtually unlimited, yet the individual still may be unable to attain his or her goal. For example, consider the student accepted to many colleges but not the one most desired.

The regions in the life space are represented in what is called a "topological" or, more correctly, a "hodological" space (the Greek stem, "hodos," means "path"). Hodological space is embraced within a nonquantitative, mathematical analysis that does not require certain assumptions about distance. For example, in hodological space, the distance between two points, A and B, is not necessarily equal to the distance from B to A. This might be the case if one feels that the difference between, for example, home and school is greater or less than the distance from school to home. Lewin believed that a hodolob-

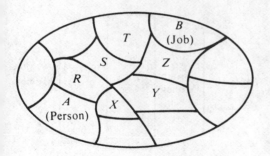

Figure 4–5. Representation of a life space with various paths from *A* to *B*.

ical language makes it possible to take seriously the idea of a psychological space. The concept of psychological space is necessary for many additional reasons. For example, passing an examination or getting married involves psychological movement, although there may be no change in physical location. Psychological direction at times may even be opposite to physical direction, as when one runs toward a burning room in order to escape from the fire, or when Köhler's ape went in the direction of the stick to reach the food.

DIRECTION IN THE LIFE SPACE.   Direction in the life space connotes a relationship between two regions. For example, assume that an individual located in region A wants to locomote in the direction of region B ($d_{A, B}$; see Figure 4–5). The various linkages between regions A and B are considered to be "paths." There might be many paths between any two regions. Figure 4–5 indicates that one path uniting A with B is X, Y, Z: a second path is R, S, T; and still a third path might be X, R, S, T. Recall that the regions in the life space often represent instrumental acts, as well as a "medium" through which one locomotes to reach a goal. Hence, Figure 4–5 could represent an individual in (or doing) A who wants to be in (or to obtain) B (e.g., a new job). To gain this position, the person might either go to school (X, Y, Z) or become an apprentice for the job (R, S, T). Either of these two paths will lead to the desired end state (activity).

TAXONOMY OF DIRECTION.   Lewin provided a relatively simple yet useful taxonomy of the direction of behavior (see Table 4–1). Directions are depicted as either "toward" or "away from" a region, and as either including or not including a region other than the one in which the person is contained. The combination of these two dimensions yields four classes of direction. The "toward" direction may be from a given region (A) to a second region (B), as just discussed, or

TABLE 4–1   LEWINIAN TAXONOMY OF THE DIRECTION OF BEHAVIOR

Number of Regions	Direction of Behavior	
	Toward	*Away From*
One	(*A, A*) Consummatory behavior	(*A, −A*) Escape behavior
Two	(*A, B*) Instrumental behavior	(*B, −A*) Avoidance behavior

from A in the direction of A $(d_{A,A})$. The latter classification portrays situations in which the individual is in a region and wants to remain there.

Direction characterized as "away from" also may or may not have an alternative region specified. One could be in region A, locomoting in a direction away from A $(d_{A,-A})$. For example, administering shock to an infrahuman in a given setting will cause the animal to seek safety, with any no-shock region being an acceptable alternative. Finally, in a fourth type of direction, the individual is in one region, but is going away from a different region. For example, consider a criminal who committed a crime in New York and is now in Chicago, going toward Los Angeles. His direction might be characterized as either away from New York $(d_{A,-B})$ or toward Los Angeles $(d_{A,C})$. But the former designation seems to depict more accurately the dynamics of this situation.

Many of the behaviors discussed in the prior chapters can be incorporated within this classification scheme. Instrumental approach behavior is toward a goal; consummatory behavior reflects the case in which the person wants to remain in the goal region; escape behavior is away from a region; and active avoidance behavior can be depicted as a series of actions leading away from an aversive state, with many of the actions occurring when the individual is no longer in the shocked region. We now turn from these structural considerations to the dynamic environmental constructs.

DYNAMIC ENVIRONMENTAL CONSTRUCTS. There is a relationship between the dynamic properties of the individual and the dynamic properties of the environment. When an inner-personal region is in a state of tension, an appropriate environmental region (object) acquires a valence. Lewin (1935) wrote:

> ... The valence of an object usually derives from the fact that the object is a means to the satisfaction of a need, or has indirectly something to do with the satisfaction of a need. The kind (sign) and the strength of the valence of an object or event thus depends directly upon the momentary condition of the needs of the individual concerned; the valence of environmental objects and the needs of the individual are correlative. (p. 78)

Thus, given a need (and, therefore, a corresponding region in tension), an object that is perceived as one that satisfies the need acquires a property of attraction. For example, if one is hungry, then a steak or some other edible object gains a positive valence. Of course, it is possible that there are needs and regions in tension, but no environmental objects available that are perceived as appropriate to the need. Hence, the existence of a need does not ensure the existence of valences in the environment. However, it is also the case that as the individual becomes hungrier and hungrier, for example, tension increases and there is a tendency to spread to more and more regions. Eventually there may be an object coordinated with these remote personal regions that has the properties necessary to acquire a positive valence — even shoes become perceived as edible given great depri-

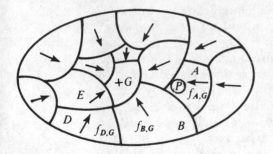

Figure 4–6. A positive central field of forces corresponding to a positive valence. The force has magnitude, represented by the length of the vector, and direction. The point of application is on *P* in the direction of the goal *G*. (Lewin, 1946, p. 933.)

vation. The above discussion implicitly indicates that if an object has a valence, then there must exist a corresponding need. That is, for a steak to be attractive, the individual must have some degree of hunger. In sum, given a valence, there must be a need, but given a need, there may or may not be any valences in the environment.

The amount of valence that an object acquires is directly related to the intensity of the need — a steak is more attractive to one who has not eaten all day than to one without food for only three hours. In addition, the valence of an object depends on its intrinsic properties. For example, a thick, juicy steak will have greater valence than a thin, dried-up piece of meat. Valence, therefore, varies quantitatively as a function of the intensity of the need and the properties of the goal object. Lewin more formally stated this relation as

$$Va(G) = f(t, G)$$

where *Va(G)* represents the valence of the goal, *t* symbolizes tension, and *G* the properties of the goal object.

Valence, however, is not a force; it is not directly coordinated with movement or locomotion. A region with a valence becomes the center of a force field (see Figures 4–6 and 4–7). A force field specifies the magnitude and direction of behavior at all points in the life space. At any given time the person is in one of the regions and, thus, has a specified force acting upon him or her.

In addition to need strength and properties of the goal object, the strength of force is dependent upon one other factor: the relative distance of the person from the goal. Lewin stated that force increases as

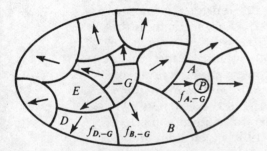

Figure 4–7. A negative central field of forces corresponding to a negative valence. The forces are away from the goal *G*. (Lewin, 1946, p. 933.)

the psychological distance between the person and the goal object decreases. That means, for example, that as we approach a restaurant when hungry, enter the door, and finally see and smell the steak, there is increasing force upon us to reach our goal (eating). Lewin acknowledged that this may not always be true. For instance, at times increased distance actually augments the force towards the goal. Lewin believed this is why far-away countries seem so attractive, as sometimes are mates who play "hard to get." However, these are atypical situations.

Lewin conceptualized the force on the person to reach the goal as follows:

$$\text{force} = f\left[\frac{Va(G)}{e}\right] = \frac{(t, G)}{e}$$

where e symbolizes psychological distance between the person and the goal. The e represents the German "entfernung," or distance.

Given this formula, it is possible to determine the force at every region in the life space. As already intimated, force is conceptualized as a vector: It has a magnitude or amount and a direction. In addition, force has a "point of application." The point of application is the region in which the force manifests itself. Because the individual is located in this region, the point of application is on the person.

When there is a psychological force acting on the person, there is likely to be locomotion in the life space. The force acts on the person in the direction of the desired goal. A goal is a region in the life space. When the goal is attained (the region entered), the tension within the tense inner-personal region dissipates. Because there is no longer any tension within the person, the environmental object loses its valence. This results in a cessation of the force acting on the individual, and goal-seeking behavior is no longer displayed. More specifically, consider a situation in which an individual has not eaten for five hours. Certain objects in the environment then acquire a positive valence. The magnitude of these valences depends upon how hungry the person is and how "good" the food objects are. Because the food acquires a positive valence, a force field is established around them, with all forces acting in their direction. The individual is in one of the regions that contains such a force and, thus, locomotes to attain the goal object. Eating the food reduces hunger and tension. Thus, the remaining food objects no longer are attractive and lose their positive valence. This results in the removal of the force field and the cessation of activity.

Relation to Hullian Theory

It is instructive to note the similarity between the Lewinian statement of the determinants of action and the formula of Hull. For instance, the two positions include similar components in their models: needs of the person (drive D or tension t), properties of the goal object (K or G), and a directional variable (habit H or psychological distance e). However, Lewin's t is specific, G is dependent on the existence of t, and e is a cognitive representation of the environment, reflecting perceived distance.

Because of their conceptual similarity, it was relatively easy for Lewin to explain some phenomena that drive theorists cited in support of the drive conception. In addition, the Lewinian language provides additional insights into the dynamics of the experiments conducted or cited by the Hullians. Consider, for example, investigations employing the Columbia Obstruction Box (see Figure 3–1). To recapitulate briefly, in the experimental paradigm employing the obstruction box, an animal initially is placed in the start box. At the far end of the box is an appropriate incentive. Between the animal and the goal there is an obstacle, such as an electrified grid. In a series of systematic studies, Moss (1924) and other investigators related the amount and type of deprivation to the tendency of the animals to cross the grid. One clear finding was that as hunger increased, the animals crossed the grid with decreased latency. In addition, the properties of the goal objects also influenced behavior, with faster response for more positively valued incentives.

Lewin believed that the obstruction box aids in the measurement of psychological forces (see Figure 4–8). A force to reach the goal (C) is opposed by a force not to enter the shocked region (B). The animal is expected to locomote toward the goal when the force in the start box (A) toward C is greater than the force at B not to enter (−B). That is, locomotion will occur when $f(A,C) > f(B,-B)$. This is the familiar approach-avoidance conflict.

If there is a force from A to C, then the region C must be the center of a field of forces. That is, region C has a positive valence. The animal, therefore, must have an inner-personal region in a state of tension and be aware that an appropriate goal object exists in the environment. To establish this valence, animals are deprived of food (or some other necessary commodity) and are given training (exposure) so that they will discover that food exists in region C.

For one to measure the relative strengths of the approach and avoidance forces, the forces have to be opposed to one another. If the animal could circumvent region B, then a conflict would not occur. The physical environment in which the animals are placed ensures that the forces will act in opposition to one another. Barriers (walls) placed around the regions (runway) limit the space of free movement. The only available path to region C is through region B.

The measure of the strength of the resultant force in the early studies conducted by Moss was often the frequency of grid crossings. If the number of crossings during a given time period is greater in a specified condition (Condition Two) than in a different condition (Condition One), then the force from A to C in Condition Two must be greater than the force from A to C in Condition One. But Lewin

Figure 4-8. Schematic representation of the physical properties of the obstruction box, and the corresponding forces. *P*, the animal, is located in *A*; *G*, the goal, is located in region *C*; *B* is the electrified compartment separating *A* from *C*. There is a force on *P* acting in the direction from *A* to *C* ($f_{A,C}$), and a force acting on *P* in the direction of not entering *B* ($f_{B,-B}$). (Adapted from Lewin, 1938, p. 72.)

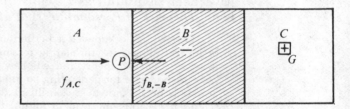

believed that the frequency of crossings generally is not a good dependent variable. If the animal crosses the grid to reach the goal, then the approach force must be greater than the force of avoidance. Why, then, doesn't the animal immediately cross the grid when replaced in the start box? If the animal remains in the start box, then there has been a change in the constellation of forces between the two trials. Lewin said that this "historical" change may have been caused by any of a number of factors, such as chance variation, loss of energy, or increased aversion to B after the initial shock. Because the frequency measure necessitates a "changing constellation of forces," Lewin did not fully accept this motivational index.

Transition to Contemporary Psychology

At the beginning of this chapter it was stated that Lewin provided a bridge between the past and the present in the study of motivation. His connection with the past, that is, with the theories of Freud and Hull, has already been partially documented. It is most evident in his acceptance of the doctrines of hedonism and homeostasis. Individuals are seen as striving to maximize pleasure, and this is accomplished through the reduction of tension. This is precisely the homeostatic conception that characterizes the theories of Freud and Hull. In addition, it is evident throughout the previous pages that Lewin embraced many mechanistic concepts, which certainly is consistent with the thinking of both Freud and Hull.

On the other hand, Lewin is characterized as a "phenomenologist." Behavior is determined by how the world is perceived. This includes the individual's perception of how far away the goal is (psychological distance). Lewin, therefore, is a cognitive theorist—thinking and knowing play essential parts in his conception. This cognitive orientation is consistent with more contemporary approaches to motivation, which he greatly influenced.

EMPIRICAL RESEARCH

We now turn from Lewin's theoretical ideas to some of the research that was initiated by his theory. Few theoretical approaches have been as fruitful as Lewinian field theory. In their well known book, *Theories of Personality,* Hall and Lindzey (1957) assert:

> . . . One widely acknowledged criterion of a "good" theory is the measure of its fruitfulness in stimulating research. In this respect, Lewin's theory is a very "good" theory indeed. Few other theories of personality have been responsible for generating so much experimentation. Lewin himself, although he is known as a brilliant theoretician, was always a working scientist. He took the lead in formulating empirical tests of many of his basic hypotheses, and his great enthusiasm for research has been transmitted to many generations of students in Germany and in the United States. The series of articles in the *Psychologische Forschung* between 1926 and 1930 is one of the most distinguished groups of empirical studies in the psychological literature. Moreover, Lewin's ideas and his genius for devising simple and convincing demonstrations of his theoretical conceptions have acted as catalysts for many psychologists who were never personally associated with him. It is impossible to estimate the number of investigations that bear the imprint of Lewin's influence. Their number is surely legion. Whatever may be the fate of Lewin's theory in the years to come, the body of experimental work instigated by it constitutes an enduring contribution to our knowledge of personality. (pp. 239–40)

The following research topics will be examined here: conflict, frustration, task recall and resumption, substitution, level of aspiration, and psychological ecology. These areas have been selected because they are most germane to Lewin's formal theory and are considered key topics in the understanding of human motivation.

Conflict

At any one moment it is likely that many competing forces are acting upon an individual, impelling the person in different directions. Thus, there are "overlapping force fields" in the life space with which the person must contend. In Lewinian theory this is conceptualized as an individual being within a region that is part of more than one force field (see Figure 4–9). For example, the reader might want to go to a movie, but also wishes to finish reading this thrilling chapter; a child wants to go out and play, but his parents have told him to clean his room; and so on. Certainly the simultaneous existence of multiple wishes and needs is typical in human behavior.

Lewin provided a taxonomy of situations in which more than one force is acting upon the person at a given moment. He defined three types of conflict: approach-approach, approach-avoidance, and avoidance-avoidance. In all such conflict situations, Lewin specified (as did N. Miller) that the person will locomote in the direction of the greatest force.

Approach-Approach Conflicts

In an approach-approach conflict the individual is included in more than one positive force field. For example, a person considers

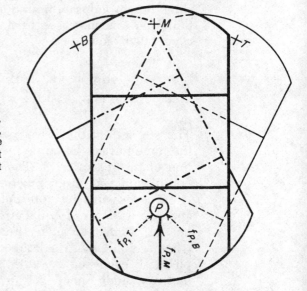

Figure 4–9. Overlapping situations. A child, *P*, wants to go to a movie, $f_{P,M}$; to play with his trains, $f_{P,T}$; and to read a book, $f_{P,B}$. The directions of the forces are different. The direction of the resultant force is eqvivalent to the direction of the dominant (i.e., strongest) force, $f_{P,M}$.

two movies worth seeing; at a restaurant both fish and steak appear good; or a child must choose between spending his allowance on candy or a comic book. Lewin believed that approach-approach conflicts are easily resolvable and, hence, called them unstable situations.

The instability of approach-approach conflicts becomes evident when some simple numerical values are introduced into his model for the determinants of force. Assume, for example, that you are in a cafeteria line. You perceive two pies: apple on the left and cherry on the right. Both pies are equally attractive in physical properties such as size $(G = 4)$, and you are fairly hungry $(t = 3)$. Further, to reach either pie requires the same number of psychological steps. The apple pie requires a left turn and then an arm movement, while the cherry pie requires a right turn and a reaching movement $(e = 2)$. The strengths of the forces involved in this approach-approach conflict therefore are identical:

<table>
<tr><td>Apple pie (left)</td><td>Cherry pie (right)</td></tr>
<tr><td>$\text{Force} = \dfrac{4 \times 3}{2} = 6$</td><td>$\text{Force} = \dfrac{4 \times 3}{2} = 6$</td></tr>
</table>

Hence, the outcome of the action is indeterminate; a momentary equilibrium is established. (Note that it has been assumed that G and t relate multiplicatively; Lewin did not specify this exact mathematical relationship.)

Now suddenly someone in the line behind you becomes rather impatient with the delay and gives you a slight shove. It happens that the shove is toward the right, and you find yourself confronted with the cherry pie. Now the psychological distance from the cherry pie shifts downward, say, from 2 to 1, and the psychological distance from the apple pie increases from 2 to 3. The strengths of the forces are conceptualized as:

Apple pie (left)

$$\text{Force} = \frac{4 \times 3}{3} = 4$$

Cherry pie (right)

$$\text{Force} = \frac{4 \times 3}{1} = 12$$

The strength of the force toward the cherry pie now is greater than the force toward the apple pie. Hence, you will locomote in the direction of the red calories. The conflict is resolved; that is, the conflict equilibrium was only momentary, or unstable.

The example just presented includes only one source of tension and two valences of equal strength. Approach-approach conflicts need not be limited to such situations. Consider the conflict generated when a child has a small amount of money and is deciding whether to purchase candy or a comic book. Assume, for illustrative purposes, that his candy "need" is 10 units, and the jelly beans he plans on buying have a value of 3. Further, he must perform 6 psychologically distinct acts to obtain the candy (dress for the walk, walk three blocks, ask for help to cross the street, and so on). The force moving the child toward the candy has the value of 5 units $[(10 \times 3) \div 6 = 5]$. On the other hand, assume his "need" for the comic book has 2 units of strength, the book has 5 units of valence, and his psychological distance from the book has a value of 2. The forces acting upon him in the direction of the book would also have a value of 5 $[(2 \times 5) \div 2 = 5]$. Equilibrium is thus established; the strengths of the forces acting on the child are equal.

How can this conflict be resolved? Any cognition that changes the relative attractiveness of the two goal objects will create unequal forces. Perhaps seeing a certain TV show will make the comic book more attractive. Or perhaps just vacillating in the decision will make him hungrier, increasing the tension caused by food deprivation, and thus making the force toward the candy greater than the force toward the comic book. Once the forces become unequal, the individual locomotes in the direction of the greater force. This reduces the psychological distance from the object he is approaching and increases the psychological distance from the unselected alternative. The differential shifting of psychological distance further increases the differences in the strength of forces.

In sum, approach-approach conflicts represent situations in which the person is located in overlapping fields of forces generated by positively valued goals. Resolution of the conflict can be achieved if any of the determinants of force (tension, valence, or psychological distance) change. This change can be caused by a new cognition, changes in tension, or any number of other factors. Once an imbalance is created, the individual locomotes toward the goal associated with the greater force. This locomotion further increases the inequality in the magnitude of the forces because the psychological distance from the chosen alternative decreases, while the distance from the unchosen alternative increases.

Avoidance-Avoidance Conflicts

When a person is in overlapping fields of force generated by objects with a negative valence, avoidance-avoidance conflicts are aroused. For example, a child is told he must mow the lawn or do his homework, or a town marshal has gunmen pursuing him from the left and from the right. Lewin specified that avoidance-avoidance conflicts are stable; that is, the opposing forces tend to remain in a state of equilibrium.

A simple mathematical exercise reveals why avoidance-avoidance conflicts tend to remain in a stable state. Consider for a moment the town marshal caught between two gunmen he wishes to avoid. Let us assume that his need for safety is 5 units, and that each gunman is equally despicable ($G = -3$). If the marshal perceives himself as equidistant from the gunmen as they come stalking toward him ($e = 2$), then the forces are as follows:

Gunman on left $\qquad$ Gunman on right

$$\text{Force} = \frac{5(-3)}{2} = -7.5 \qquad \text{Force} = \frac{5(-3)}{2} = -7.5$$

Thus, there are equal and opposite forces to flee both to the left and the right.

Now assume that the marshal suddenly remembers that the gunman on the left is a poor shot or a coward. The new field of forces then might be:

Gunman on left $\qquad$ Gunman on right

$$\text{Force} = \frac{5(-2)}{2} = -5 \qquad \text{Force} = \frac{5(-3)}{2} = -7.5$$

Because the negative valence is now greater away from the right, the marshal proceeds toward the left. In so doing, the psychological distances are altered; the forces might change as follows:

Gunman on left $\qquad$ Gunman on right

$$\text{Force} = \frac{5(-2)}{1} = -10 \qquad \text{Force} = \frac{5(-3)}{3} = -5$$

Now the force to avoid the left gunman is greater than that away from the right gunman. Even though the killer on the left does not appear as aversive, the decrease in psychological distance increases the force to avoid the confrontation. This indicates that the marshal will again shift his direction, this time to the right. In theory, the marshal will continue to oscillate between the two negative alternatives.

Does this mean that it is always impossible to solve avoidance-avoidance conflicts? This clearly is not the case, for humans are indeed placed in many such situations and usually cease their vacillation. A cognitive change might alter the strength of the avoidance forces and help to resolve the conflict. Needs can change, valences can shift in magnitude and even in direction, and psychological distance can be altered. Lewin also indicated that such conflicts are often solved by "leaving the field." This means that a person in such a conflict will frequently follow a path that increases the psychological distance from both alternatives. If the marshal ascended in a helium balloon just before the gunmen arrived, his conflict would be resolved. However, leaving the field can be employed as a method of conflict resolution only if the boundaries around the conflict situation are sufficiently permeable. For example, if a child is told to mow the lawn or do his homework, he apparently is placed in a difficult avoidance-avoidance situation. But if he knows he can escape either task by appealing to his mother or hiding in the attic, then the conflict is readily (if only temporarily) resolved. Lewin indicated that one consequence of establishing behaviors through the use of punishment and negative sanctions is that strong barriers must be erected that keep the person in the situation. And energy must be expended to ensure that these barriers persist.

In sum, avoidance-avoidance conflicts generated by multiple regions of negative valence are not readily resolvable. As one approaches the aversive region, the tendency to avoid that region becomes even stronger. Hence, ambivalent behavior is exhibited; the person vacillates between the various alternatives. For such conflicts to have any degree of permanence, strong boundaries must exist to prevent the person from leaving the field and avoiding all the alternatives.

Approach-Avoidance Conflicts

The third classification of conflicts, approach-avoidance, was discussed in detail in the previous chapter. In such conflicts the same region acquires both positive and negative valence and establishes positive and negative force fields. For example, the reader might want to go to a movie, but does not want to spent the money; she might want to stop reading, but knows that a test is forthcoming. As in all conflict situations, the exhibited behavior is postulated by Lewin to be determined by needs, valences, and psychological distance. In this situation the relative steepness of the approach and avoidance slopes is an important determinant of action.

Approach-avoidance conflicts also are relatively stable. The person is expected to approach the goal, but then avoid it, because of the differential change in the strength of the approach and avoidance tendencies (see the previous chapter). Again, a number of factors can lead to conflict resolution; for example, the positive aspects of the goal may gain in attractiveness, or the person may experience a reduction in the amount of fear.

Empirical Studies of Conflict

Surprisingly few studies have been generated by the Lewinian conflict taxonomy. Probably the most investigated aspect of his classification scheme concerns the relative stability and instability of the various types of conflict. In one prototypical experiment, Arkoff (1957) asked students to decide which of two positive qualities they would rather possess (e.g., would you rather be more intelligent or more attractive?) and which of two negative alternatives they would rather not possess (e.g., would you rather be less intelligent or less attractive?). He then measured the latencies of their responses, or the time necessary to resolve the conflict. Arkoff found, as Lewin had presumed, that the approach-approach conflict situation is less stable, or more easy to resolve, than the avoidance-avoidance conflict. In this study the average time taken to choose an alternative in the positive conflict situation was approximately two minutes, while the latency of the responses in the avoidance-avoidance situation was more than 2.5 minutes. Further, the subjects judged the approach-approach conflict to be easier to resolve than the avoidance-avoidance situation. This appears to be a replicable finding and can be regarded as a "fact."

Frustration and Regression

One interesting scientific game is to compare how various theorists study identical topics. Because the behavior under investigation generally is conceptualized quite differently by the theorists, the experiments conducted and the conclusions reached often are surprisingly unrelated.

A simple examination of the principles of learning introduced in this book illustrates this point. Thorndike believed that reward and punishment are essential for response acquisition. Therefore, his experiments involved responses instrumental to the attainment of a food reward. On the other hand, Pavlov believed contiguity to be the necessary and sufficient condition for learning. Hence, in his experimental paradigm two stimuli were presented in close temporal contiguity. Finally, the Gestaltists contend that organization is an essential characteristic of the learning process. Their experiments on insight learning created situations in which perceptual reorganization apparently was necessary to reach the correct solution. In sum, each theoretical position employed a particular experimental procedure, or reference experiment, that could demonstrate each theorist's own bias. And, quite naturally, the conclusions reached were indeed disparate.

The study of frustration also exemplifies this point. Brown, Farber, and Amsel were trained within the Hullian theoretical framework.

Therefore, in their studies, frustration generally was operationalized by withholding food from a previously rewarded animal. Further, it is not unreasonable to expect that in these investigations the construct of frustration would be related to drive and habits and would be used to explain phenomena such as resistance to extinction. After all, these were the problems with which Hull, Spence, and their cohorts struggled. On the other hand, Lewin was a field theorist with strong interests in personality and child development. His investigations of frustration were directed toward understanding behavior in complex settings and providing insights into the dynamics of development.

In the previous pages it was indicated that Lewin was greatly influenced by Freud and was one of the first investigators to test rigorously some of Freud's fundamental concepts, such as persisting desires, substitution, and regression. Regression refers to a return to an earlier mode of behavior. Freud specified that during the genetic stages of development the individual selects certain "problem solutions" to cope with conflict and stress. These behaviors tend to reduce the amount of the aversive stimulation. During times of later stress, according to Freud, there is a tendency for the person to repeat these earlier modes of behavior, although they might be inadequate or maladaptive given the present situation. A mild regression might be "running home to mother" in difficult times, while a more extreme form of such behavior might involve thumb-sucking all day, as could be exhibited by persons in a severely psychotic state.

Barker, Dembo, and Lewin (1943) considered regression a form of "negative development" (p. 441). Hence, they contended that understanding the laws of development would shed light upon regressive behavior, and vice versa. These investigators reasoned that development could be conceptualized as an increase in the degree of inner-personal differentiation and in the separation of fantasy from reality. Therefore, any state that results in a dedifferentiation of regions and a decrease in the separation of reality from irreality is regressive.

Barker et al. further contended that increasing the level of inner-personal tension could lead to a regressive state, for overriding tension might weaken the boundaries between the regions, causing dedifferentiation. Dedifferentiation indicates that the individual is making fewer psychological distinctions, leading to less sophisticated patterns of behavior.

One manner of increasing tension is to prevent the attainment of a desirable goal. The reader will recall from Chapter Three that goal thwarting is frequently considered to be the operational manipulation that produces frustration. Similarly, frustration, or goal thwarting, was employed by Barker et al. to increase the level of tension and, in turn, to produce regression.

The experiment conducted by Barker et al. to produce regression was relatively straightforward. Children were brought into an experimental room and allowed to play with attractive toys. Then they were separated from the toys by a partition. The children could still see the toys, but were prevented from handling them by the barrier. That is, there was a limitation in their space of free movement. During the separation period the children could play with other objects located in the room. Throughout the "pre-frustration" and "frustration" periods the experimenters measured the "constructiveness of play." Unconstructive play was described as "primitive, simple, and with little structure" (for example, examining toys superficially), while constructive play was described as "imaginative and highly developed" (for example, using toys as part of an elaborate story). Constructiveness of play had been shown to increase as a function of mental age and, thus, could be used to measure regressive tendencies.

The results of the study by Barker, Dembo, and Lewin revealed that the constructiveness of play activities did decrease from the pre-frustration to the frustration period. During the time of frustration the play of the children was more primitive, less elaborate, and so forth. Hence, the investigators concluded that frustration, or tension increment, could lead to regression. (The reader is directed to Lawson, 1965, and Yates, 1962, for further discussion of this research and some methodological criticisms. The main research criticism has been that this study did not include a "no-frustration" control group. Thus, the "regressive" behaviors might be due to fatigue, boredom, or similar factors.)

Task Recall and Task Resumption

The investigations of task recall and task resumption were the first studies in which hypotheses were directly derived from Lewin's conception of motivation. Their importance within the Lewinian system cannot be overemphasized. Lewin (1935) stated:

> . . . All later experimental investigations are built upon this. It was an attempt to break a first path through a primeval forest of facts and assumptions, using concepts the practical utility of which was still wholly untried. (p. 240)

Task Recall

It is said that the idea for the experimental investigation of task recall originated from observations in a restaurant. Lewin noticed that a certain waiter did not write down individuals' orders, yet was able to recall what they had selected when it was time to collect the bill. One day Lewin returned to the restaurant a few moments after he had paid the check and asked the waiter what had been ordered. The waiter no longer retained this information. This led Lewin to believe that there is differential recall of a completed task versus an incomplete task.

Lewin (1951) employed four assumptions, which were implicitly introduced earlier in this chapter, to derive the hypothesis that there would be differential recall of finished and unfinished tasks:

Assumption 1: The intention to reach a certain goal G (to carry out an action leading to G) corresponds to a tension (*t*) in a certain system or region, (S^G) within the person so that $t\ (S^G) > 0$.

Assumption 2: The tension $t\ (S^G)$ is relesed if the goal G is reached:

$$t\ (S^G) = 0 \text{ if } P^cG \text{ [if } P \text{ completes } G]$$

Assumption 3: To a need for G corresponds a force $f_{P,\ G}$ acting upon the person and causing a tendency of locomotion toward G:

$$\text{if } t\ (S^G) > 0 \rightarrow f_{P,\ G} > 0$$

Assumption 3a: A need leads not only to a tendency of actual locomotion towards the goal region but also to thinking about this type of activity; in other words, the force $f_{P,\ G}$ exists not only on the level of doing (reality) but also on the level of thinking (irreality):

$$\text{if } t\ (S^G) > 0 \rightarrow f_{P,\ R} > 0$$

where *R* means recall. (pp. 9–10)

These assumptions logically lead to this derivation concerning differential task recall:

The tendency to recall interrupted activities should be greater than the tendency to recall finished ones. This derivation can be made as follows. We indicate the completed task by *C*, the unfinished one by *U*, and the corresponding systems by S^c and S^u respectively. We can then state:

1. $t\ (S^u) > 0$, according to Assumption 1.
2. $t\ (S^c) = 0$, according to Assumption 2.
3. $f_{P,U} > f_{P,C}$; hence, according to Assumption 3a, on the level of thinking.

In other words: there is a greater tendency spontaneously to recall unfinished tasks than finished tasks. (p. 10)

EMPIRICAL ANALYSIS.   To test this derivation, Lewin and his students (e.g., Marrow, 1938; Zeigarnik, 1927) experimentally manipulated the degree of task completion in a laboratory setting. They then compared the recall of unfinished tasks with the recall of finished tasks. Subjects generally were given 16 or 20 simple puzzles (anagrams, arithmetic problems, and the like) to perform. Half of the tasks were too long to be completed within the allotted time period, while the others were relatively short and could be finished. The experimenter collected all the puzzles and, following an interval of a few minutes, unexpectedly asked the subjects to recall the tasks. Zeigarnik (1927) first demonstrated that there was greater recall of the incomplete tasks than the completed ones. The ratio of incomplete to completed tasks recalled (the Zeigarnik quotient) approached 2:1. The tendency to recall a greater percentage of unfinished tasks became known as the "Zeigarnik effect."

Lewin tested a number of additional derivations from his conception of tense systems, employing differential task recall as the dependent variable. The amount of tension remaining within a tense system had been postulated to be a function of the time the region is in tension and the strength of the boundaries around that region. Therefore, the Zeigarnik quotient was expected to decrease over time and in situations in which the strength of the boundaries between the regions had been weakened. In one study, Zeigarnik found that when task recall was delayed for 24 hours, the Zeigarnik quotient dropped to 1.2:1. Further, tired subjects and individuals subjected to "strong emotional excitation" prior to recall exhibited a greatly decreased Zeigarnik quotient. The operations of fatigue and induced emotion were expected to decrease the firmness of the inner-personal boundaries. In another study, Marrow (1938) demonstrated that subjective, rather than objective, completion influences task recall. He told subjects that interruption meant they were doing well, while allowing them to finish indicated poor performance. Marrow found greater recall of the subjectively incomplete (objectively complete) tasks than subjectively complete (objectively incomplete) tasks.

The general pattern of results confirmed the predictions derived from Lewin's conception of tension and enhanced the validity of the theory. The results were especially supportive of his conception because they did not fit easily into any other theoretical framework.

EMPIRICAL PROBLEMS.   Unfortunately, a contradiction occurred when studies of task recall were conducted in America. Experimenters such as Rosenzweig (1943) and Glixman (1949) obtained results partially opposed to those of the previous investigations. They found greater recall of completed than incompleted tasks in "ego-oriented" or stress situations. To explain these data, Rosenzweig postulated that the incomplete tasks were "repressed." Failure was thought to represent a threat to the self or the ego; not remembering unfinished tasks was anxiety-reducing. For this reason he believed there was relatively greater recall of the successful or completed tasks than the unfinished or failed tasks. (Freud's reaction to this research is shown in Figure 2–3 in his letter to Rosenzweig.)

Subsequent investigators such as Atkinson (1953) attempted to reconcile the contradictory data gathered by Lewin and Rosenzweig by pointing out differences in the subject populations that were tested. However, over the years, many investigators have reported a Zeigarnik effect, many others find "repression," and still others find no difference in recall (see review in Weiner, 1966). Thus, it is not known whether there really is a Zeigarnik effect, and a satisfactory explanation of the conflicting data has not been offered. Since the 1960's there have been very few research investigations in this area, and it is highly unlikely that this empirical issue will be resolved in the near future. Experimental psychologists certainly do not exhibit a Zeigarnik effect, for they are content to move on to new issues, leaving past problems unresolved and forgotten.

Task Resumption

The experimental paradigm used to study task resumption was very similar to the one employed for the investigation of task recall. Subjects, typically children, were given a series of tasks to complete. They were interrupted before they could finish some of these tasks, but given sufficient time for completion of others. The experimenter then removed herself from the experimental room using some pretense — answering a telephone, sharpening a pencil, or performing similar errands. During the intervening time period, the subjects could "spontaneously" resume some of the tasks. At times the tasks remained in the subject's immediate visual field, while on other occasions the tasks were placed out of sight, although they remained available to the subject. In the initial investigation in this area, Ovsiankina (1928) reported a significant tendency for individuals to resume the previously unfinished tasks. This occurred whether the tasks were immediately visible or out of sight.

Further experimentation revealed that the likelihood of resumption is influenced by many factors. These include:

1. The type of activity. Tasks having no definite end state (such as stringing beads) are resumed significantly less often than those that have a definite goal.
2. The point at which the activity is interrupted. In general, the closer the subject is to the goal when the interruption occurs, the greater the likelihood of resumption.
3. The duration of the interruption. As the time between the interruption and the opportunity to resume increases, the tendency to resume the task decreases. This lends support to Lewin's assumption that the amount of tension remaining within a region is, in part, a function of the time that the region is in tension.
4. The attitude and character of the person. According to Lewin (1951), "Children who had the attitude of being examined and of strict obedience showed little resumption owing to the lack of involvement; they were governed mainly by induced forces" (p. 275). That is, there was no intrinsic interest among these children to undertake the activities and, therefore, no region remained in tension. The children performed the task because of an extrinsic source of motivation. As indicated previously, the consequences of intrinsic versus extrinsic motivation are examined in greater depth later.

Since the 1930's there have been extremely few studies of task resumption. It is intuitively reasonable and surely an accepted observation that individuals tend to finish tasks that have been started and do not tend to "resume" completed activities. But the obviousness of an empirical fact does not minimize its theoretical importance. It is obvious that most objects fall; it is also an important empirical fact, and a sophisticated theory was required to explain this datum. Lewinian field theory specifies that unfinished tasks will be resumed. Other theoretical approaches have not focused upon the effects of attaining or not attaining a goal. Hence, the derivation concerning task resumption is unique to Lewinian theory.

More sophisticated questions related to resumption that could further confirm or refute Lewinian theory remain to be raised. For example, some of the data reported by Ovsiankina actually call Lewinian theory into question. Lewin postulated that following the non-attainment of a goal the tension within the inner-personal region associated with the goal persists. Tension is defined operationally as the magnitude of a need; theoretically, it is relatively independent of psychological distance from the goal. Yet Ovsiankina found that resumption is affected by distance from the goal; the closer the goal at the time of interruption, the more likely is resumption. Because resumption is affected by psychological distance, which is a determinant of force and not tension, it is more consistent to postulate that aroused *force* persists following non-attainment of a goal. If only the magnitude of aroused tension persists, then the tendency to resume unfinished tasks should be unrelated to distance from the goal at the time of the interruption. This inference could greatly alter Lewin's theory.

Substitution

As indicated in the discussion of regression, Lewin was strongly influenced by the observations and analyses of Freud. He realized that Freud's insights were not easily put to scientific test and that experimental evidence in support of Freud's conception was indeed sparse. Lewin (1935) wrote:

> . . . Experimental studies of the dynamic laws of the behavior and structure of personality have forced us to consider more and more complicated problems. Instead of investigating the single psychological systems which correspond to simple needs and desires, we have to deal with the interrelationships of these systems, with their differentiation and transformations, and with the different kinds of larger wholes built up from them. These interrelationships and larger wholes are very labile and delicate. Yet one must try to get hold of them experimentally because they are most important for understanding the underlying reality of behavior and personality differences. In doing this we often find facts which Freud first brought to our attention, thereby rendering a great service even though he has not given a clear dynamic theory in regard to them. (p. 180)

The study of substitution provided Lewin the opportunity to examine systematically some of Freud's most important concepts concerning the dynamics of behavior. Freud had postulated that following non-attainment of a goal the tendency to strive for that goal persists. The mechanism responsible for the persisting wish was identified as the "internal stimulus from which there is no flight." You will recall that, according to Freud, this persisting tendency often is inadvertently expressed in dreams, jokes, and slips of the tongue, when the ego is less vigilant or when social rules are more permissive. Lewin incorporated this idea into his theory by including the concept of persisting tense regions.

Within Freudian theory, the object of a desire may change; there are "vicissitudes of the instincts." A forbidden, unfulfilled wish can, for example, become directed toward (attached to) objects that have some similarity to the desired goal. Freud stated that ultimately a libidinal tendency might even be expressed in cultural activities such as painting or composing. As mentioned earlier, in his analyses of Michelangelo and da Vinci he contended that these great artists had strong unfulfilled sexual urges toward their mothers, which were deflected into socially acceptable channels. This defense was labelled by Freud as "sublimation," and typically is included in lists of defense mechanisms, along with repression, perceptual defense, denial, intellectualization, and regression, which have already been discussed.

Lewin (1935) likewise noted that goal objects may change. Substitution, the term Lewin used rather than sublimation, is manifested in many different ways:

> . . . There is, for instance, the man who dreams of a palace and brings a few pieces of marble into his kitchen. There is the man who cannot buy a piano, but who collects piano catalogs. Again, we find the delinquent boy who knows that he will not be allowed to leave his reform school but who asks for a traveling bag as a birthday present. And the little boy who threatens and scolds the larger boy whom he cannot beat on the playground. These and a hundred other examples make us realize how important and far-reaching the problem of substitution is in regard to psychological needs as well as with reference to bodily needs such as hunger and sex. (pp. 180–81)

Experimental Studies

Ovsiankina and Zeigarnik provided the foundation for the experimental investigation of substitution. It was believed that these investigators had demonstrated that tension persists in a region and is reduced with goal attainment. The question asked in the study of substitution is: Can tensions in regions be discharged through some compensatory activity? That is, will there be a decrease in the recall or the resumption of previously interrupted tasks following completion of other activities? If so, then this would be a valid experimental demonstration that one goal has substitute value for another.

The general experimental paradigm used in the study of substitution follows closely the methodology first employed by Ovsiankina. Subjects were given tasks to complete and were interrupted before completion. The experimenter then allowed the subjects to undertake and finish some interpolated activity. Finally, subjects were tested for the spontaneous resumption of the previously unfinished tasks. Resumption, therefore, became the behavioral criterion for the identification of goal substitutes. That is, if the individual resumed the previously unfinished activity, then the interpolated activity did not serve as a substitute goal. But if the originally unfinished activity was not undertaken following the interpolated activity, then the second activity had substitute value.

One of the first experimental studies of substitution was conducted by Lissner (1933). In her experiment, children were interrupted while making a figure from clay. Then, after making a different figure, they were tested for resumption. Lissner identified two factors that influence the substitute value of an activity: its similarity to the first activity and its level of difficulty. The more similar and difficult the interpolated task, the greater its substitute value. In another study, Lissner told the children that the interpolated activity was "completely different" from the one they had just attempted. In that situation the interpolated activity had little substitute value for the original activity. That is, the percentage of task resumption following the activity did not decrease.

Mahler (1933), another of Lewin's students, gave subjects an interpolated activity that could be completed in ways that differed in their proximity to overt behavior (the level of reality). Subjects could think about doing the task, talk through its completion, or actually do it. In general, substitute value varied monotonically with the degree of reality of the action. This implies that daydreams and other such fantasy activity will have little (but *some*) value for the reduction of motivation. Recall that earlier it was indicated that the notion of a catharsis of aggression via fantasy activity has received only weak experimental support.

The experimental attitude of the subject also has been shown to be an important determinant of substitute value (Adler & Kounin, 1939). If the subject's attitude toward a task is concrete, such as "building a house for Mary," then "building a house for a different person" has little substitute value. However, if the task is conceived more abstractly, such as building a house, then an interpolated task of building another house has substitute value.

Lewin (1935) speculated about the psychological characteristics of feeble-minded individuals from their behavior in substitution experiments. Feeble-minded children exhibit great variance in their behavior following completion of an interpolated task. Either they all tend to resume the original activity after the interpolated completion (no substitution), or virtually none of the children resume the original task (complete substitution). Lewin reasoned, therefore, that feeble-minded children have strong boundaries between their inner-personal regions, but fewer regions (differentiations) than normal children (see Figure 4–10). Consequently, two activities are perceived as identical (complete substitution) or as psychologically separate (no substitution). (See Stevenson & Zigler, 1957, and Zigler, 1962, for some objections to this formulation.)

Additional experimental work on substitution was conducted by Henle (1944). Her work concerned the relationship of substitution, valence of the original task, and valence of the interpolated or substitute task. In Henle's studies the subjects first rated the attractiveness of various activities. They then were given a subjectively attractive or unattractive task to complete. Following interruption, an interpolated activity of high or low attractiveness was completed. Again resumption

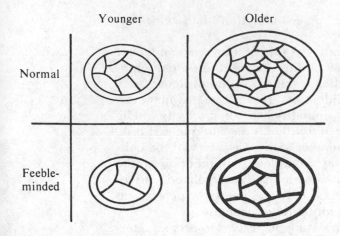

Younger   Older

Normal

Feeble-
minded

Figure 4–10. Representation of the development of normal and feeble-minded individuals. Normal children are assumed to have greater differentiation and weaker boundaries between the inner-personal regions than feeble-minded children. (From Lewin, 1935, p. 210.)

was the behavioral criterion to infer the degree of substitution. Henle found that the greater the valence of the original task, the less the possibility that other tasks can substitute for it. Similarly, the greater the valence of an interpolated activity, the greater is its substitute value.

The studies of Mahler, Lissner, Henle, and others clearly demonstrate that goals can substitute for one another. Further, these studies identified some of the relevant dimensions and determinants of substitution. The data support Lewin's contention that there are interrelationships, or dynamic communications, between psychological systems. That is, needs are not separate psychologically, or, in Lewinian language, tension spreads to neighboring regions. This body of empirical work is again uniquely Lewinian and cannot be readily accounted for within other theoretical systems.

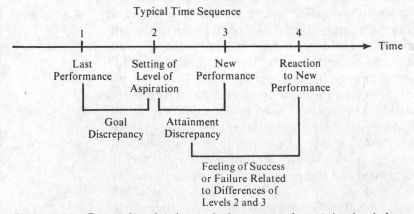

Typical Time Sequence

1   2   3   4

→ Time

Last   Setting of   New   Reaction
Performance   Level of   Performance to New
              Aspiration   Performance

Goal   Attainment
Discrepancy   Discrepancy

Feeling of Success
or Failure Related
to Differences of
Levels 2 and 3

Figure 4–11. Four main points in a typical sequence of events in a level of aspiration situation: Last performance, setting of the level of aspiration for the next performance, new performance, and the psychological reaction to the new performance. (From Lewin, Dembo, Festinger, & Sears, 1944, p. 334.)

Level of Aspiration

One of the most influential series of experiments originating from the Lewinian frame of reference concerns "level of aspiration." Level of aspiration typically is defined as "the level of future performance in a familiar task which an individual, knowing his level of past performance in that task, explicitly undertakes to reach" (Frank, 1935, p. 119). Level of aspiration thus pertains to goal striving and the perceived difficulty of the goals that one wishes to attain. It is aroused when choosing a competitor at an athletic event, when determining the amount of sales that one wants to make in the next month, or when deciding the distance one will walk on a hike. Because many goals (levels of difficulty) are possible in all these situations, level of aspiration involves a choice between various alternatives.

Four temporal boundaries have been distinguished within a level-of-aspiration sequence (see Figure 4–11). For illustrative purposes, assume that an individual is engaged in tossing rings over a peg from some specified distance. The person first becomes familiar with the task and undertakes ten "practice" attempts. During the practice performance the number of successful tosses is counted. In this particular illustration, assume that there was success on six of the ten trials. The individual then specifies an aspiration level for the next series of ten tosses. If this were an experimental situation, this question generally would be phrased as: "How many are you going to try to get over the peg in the next series?" Assume that the individual responds, "Eight." This response, in relation to the level of prior performance, defines the goal discrepancy score. In this case the person is striving for more (+2) than the previous performance; the discrepancy is therefore described as positive. Of course, one could be striving for less than the prior performance, in which case the discrepancy score would be negative. The individual then tosses the rings ten more times. The difference between the number of successes and the stated goal is the attainment discrepancy. If the thrower only gets seven rings over the peg, the discrepancy is −1; the stated goal was not reached. Presumably, affective reactions are related to the goal discrepancy: This individual will probably feel "bad" because the desired level of achievement was not reached.

Empirical Research

Numerous clear empirical findings have emerged from level-of-aspiration research. It has been demonstrated that feelings of success and failure are determined primarily by the attainment or non-attainment of the goal for which one is striving, as opposed to the absolute level of performance. For example, a student with a very high aspiration level might be unhappy when receiving a grade of "B," while an equally bright student with lesser aspirations would be satisfied with this grade. Perception of success and failure involves subjective, rather than objective, levels of attainment. (William James stated that feelings of success or self-esteem are a direct function of actual success and an inverse function of pretensions.) Further, the subsequent aspiration level is, in part, dependent upon the prior attainment discrepancy (subjective success or failure). In most instances, the goal level increases after success and decreases following failure. However, "atypical" reactions are sometimes observed; that is, an aspiration level is lowered after goal attainment or raised after failure. Level of aspiration has been shown to be influenced by individual differences, group standards, and cultural factors. For example, individuals with high ability, or those classified as ambitious, tend to set higher aspiration levels (Hoppe, 1930). In addition, the level that is set tends to be guided by, and conform to, group goals and performance (Festinger, 1942).

Experimentation with level of aspiration also has increased our knowledge about defensive reactions to failure. Failure generally leads to more variable performance and aspirations (Sears, 1942), and is more likely to result in psychological withdrawal from the task. These findings have led some investigators to consider aspiration level more an index of defensiveness than of goal striving.

Resultant Valence Theory

A theoretical analysis guided by the research findings briefly reviewed above was first presented by Escalona (1940) and subsequently elaborated and clarified by Festinger (1942) and Lewin, Dembo, Festinger, and Sears (1944). This analysis, called "resultant valence theory," characterizes level of aspiration as a choice (conflict) situation in which one locomotes toward (chooses) the alternative with the greatest resultant approach force.

Resultant valence theory specifies the determinants of the valence, and force, of the various alternative goals that comprise the possible choices. It is postulated that anticipated success has positive valence and that potential failure has negative valence. Further, the valences of success and failure are assumed to be dependent, in part, upon the difficulty of the task. "The attraction of success seems to increase with the level of difficulty . . . while the negative valence of failure is greater the less difficult the task" (Atkinson, 1964, p. 99).

Given only the specification that choice is a function of valence, and that positive valence is greater for more difficult tasks and negative valence less for more difficult tasks, the greatest force would be in the direction of the most difficult goal. Yet individuals often select tasks of intermediate difficulty or even tasks very easy to perform. Therefore, other determinants of behavior must be influencing aspiration level.

An additional construct postulated by Escalona and Festinger as a determinant of aspiration level is the Lewinian notion of "potency." Potency refers to subjective expectancy or certainty; there is a potency associated with success and a potency linked with failure. A more contemporary view might use the term probability rather than potency. The concept of potency also can be compared to psychological distance; a low potency could be considered an indication of great psychological distance (many steps intervening between the person and his goal), while a high potency could indicate that few instrumental actions are necessary to reach the goal. Lewin, however, did not use the constructs of potency and psychological distance interchangeably. Clearly, one could be many steps from the goal, but each step might have a very high probability of being consummated.

Corresponding to each level of difficulty there is a potency of success (Po_s) and a potency of failure (Po_f). The approach force toward a goal is postulated by Escalona and Festinger to be a function of the valence of success (Va_s) multiplied by the potency of success, while the force away from the goal is postulated to be the negative valence of failure (Va_f) multiplied by the potency of failure. Therefore, the resultant force toward the goal is conceptualized as follows:

$$\text{Resultant force} = (Va_s \times Po_s) - (Va_f \times Po_f)$$

In sum, each alternative can be considered to involve an approach-avoidance conflict between positive and negative forces determined by valences and potencies. Choice involves a comparison of all the available alternatives; the alternative that has the greatest resultant approach force is expected to be selected.

A numerical example adapted from Lewin et al. by Atkinson (1964, p. 101) indicates some of the power of this conception. In the example shown in Table 4–2, the valence of success and the valence of failure are

TABLE 4–2 NUMERICAL ILLUSTRATION OF THE DETERMINANTS OF LEVEL OF ASPIRATION

Levels of Possible Objective	Force to Approach Success $Va_{succ} \times Po_{succ} = fp,_{succ}$[1]			Force to Avoid Failure $Va_{fai} \times Po_{fai} = fp,_{-fai}$[2]			Resultant Force[3]	
Too difficult ↑ 15	10	0	0	0	100	0	0	
14	10	0	0	0	100	0	0	
13	10	0	0	0	100	0	0	
12	10	0	0	0	100	0	0	
11	10	5	50	0	95	0	50	
10	9	10	90	0	90	0	90	Level
9	7	25	175	−1	75	−75	100	of
8	6	40	240	−2	60	−120	120 ← aspiration	
7	5	50	250	−3	50	−150	100	↖ Goal ↙ discrepancy
6	3	60	180	−5	40	−200	−20	Level of
5	2	75	150	−7	25	−175	−25	past
4	1	90	90	−9	10	−90	0	performance
Too easy 3	0	95	0	−10	5	−50	−50	
2	0	100	0	−10	0	0	0	
↓ 1	0	100	0	−10	0	0	0	

[1] Force toward success.
[2] Force away from failure.
[3] Force on the person toward the goal.
(From Atkinson, 1964, p. 101.)

given arbitrary values that increase and decrease respectively with the level of task difficulty. Similarly, the potency of success and failure, which range in value from 0 to 100, vary with objective task difficulty. In the illustration it is assumed that, on the prior task, performance was at level 7. The subsequent choice, that is, the alternative associated with the greatest resultant value, is level 8. Hence, there is a positive goal discrepancy of 1.

It previously was indicated that motivational dispositions also influence level of aspiration. Table 4–3 portrays the situation in which an individual has great anxiety associated with failure. In Table 4–3 the negative valence of failure is double that shown in the prior illustration. The table indicates a surprising result. Although fear of failure increases, the level of aspiration actually rises three steps from past performance. This captures the unrealistic goal striving that is exhibited sometimes by individuals with histories of failure and motivational deficiencies in the area of achievement (see Chapter Five).

Aspiration Level in Social Contexts

The concept of level of aspiration has been modified and used for the analysis of social interaction and interdependence. Thibaut and Kelley (1959) assume that individuals can assess their degree of satisfaction with a relationship, just as one can determine the valence of an achievement-related success or failure. They introduce the concept of

TABLE 4–3 DETERMINANTS OF LEVEL OF ASPIRATION WHEN THE NEGATIVE VALENCE OF FAILURE IS RELATIVELY HIGH

Levels of Possible Objective	Force to Approach Success $Va_{succ} \times Po_{succ} = fp,_{succ}$			Force to Avoid Failure $Va_{fai} \times Po_{fai} = fp,_{-fai}$			Resultant Force	
Too difficult ↑ 15	10	0	0	0	100	0	0	
14	10	0	0	0	100	0	0	
13	10	0	0	0	100	0	0	
12	10	0	0	0	100	0	0	Level
11	10	5	50	0	95	0	50	of
10	9	10	90	0	90	0	90 ← aspiration	
9	7	25	175	−2	75	−150	25	⟍ Goal
8	6	40	240	−4	60	−240	0	discrepancy
7	5	50	250	−6	50	−300	−50	⟋
6	3	60	180	−10	40	−400	−220	⟍ Level of
5	2	75	150	−14	25	−350	−200	past
4	1	90	90	−18	10	−180	−90	performance
Too easy 3	0	95	0	−20	5	−100	−100	
2	0	100	0	−20	0	0	0	
↓ 1	0	100	0	−20	0	0	0	

Note: The values of subjective probability of success and failure are the same as in Table 4–2, but the negative valence of failure is doubled.
(From Atkinson, 1964, p. 102.)

"comparison level" (CL) to define "a neutral point on a scale of satisfaction-dissatisfaction" (Thibaut and Kelley, 1959, p. 81). If the average of "outcomes" from a relationship is above the CL level, the relationship is "rewarding"; however, if the outcome average is below the CL level, the relationship is relatively "punishing." However, even if the relationship is negative, individuals may remain interdependent. The continuation depends, in part, on the alternatives that are available, or the potential satisfactions expected from equivalent relationships or opportunities.

In sum, Thibaut and Kelley (1959) assume a rational person striving to maximize gains, capable of comparing a number of potential satisfiers, and deciding which "goal" (relationship) to pursue. This is clearly a direct extension of the aspiration work into the sphere of interpersonal relations.

Psychological Ecology

Throughout this chapter it has been emphasized that behavior is a function of the life space and that the life space represents psychological, rather than physical, reality. However, Lewin recognized that there are factors that influence behavior, yet reside outside of the life space in the physical world. He included these "nonpsychological" factors in the so-called "foreign hull." The foreign hull was depicted as surrounding (but not part of) the life space (see Figure 4–2). The term "foreign hull" was a tongue-in-cheek reference to Clark Hull, intimating that Hull investigated determinants of behavior that were not part of the individual's psychological reality. According to Lewin (1950),

> Any type of group life occurs in a setting of certain limitations to what is and what is not possible, what might or might not happen. The nonpsychological factors of climate, of communication, of the law of the country or the organization are a frequent part of these "outside limitations." (p. 170)

Lewin was not personally involved in many studies of "nonpsychological" determinants of behavior. However, one pertinent investigation in which he participated attempted to discover the bases of food habits and to find reasons why people eat what they do. One of the main conclusions of this study was that food must pass through many channels or steps before it reaches the table; it must be bought, stored, cooked, and so on. Entering or not entering each of these steps is primarily determined by a "gatekeeper" — a person who controls entry into each channel. In the case of food, the housewife often assumes responsibility for what the family will eat, inasmuch as she controls a great number of channels. In turn, her decisions are determined by cognitive and motivational factors, such as her perceptions of healthy and edible food, her values concerning health as opposed to taste, and the like. For the other members of the family, particularly the children, eating habits are primarily determined by what is placed on the table by the woman of the household. The members of the family generally "like what they eat, rather than eat what they like" (Lewin, 1951, p. 181). Note that in this example the main determinant of eating behavior, the action of the gatekeeper, lies outside of conscious or unconscious awareness of the family. Thus, the significance of the gatekeeper is conceptualized as part of the foreign hull (physical reality) and not part of psychological reality.

T-Data and O-Data

The most extensive contributions to Lewin's conceptualization of so-called nonpsychological factors are the investigations of Roger Barker and his colleagues. Barker (1965) outlines two methods of data collection that are of interest to psychologists. In one procedure the psychologist acts as an "operator." That is, the researcher is directly part of the action, alters the behavior of the organism, and generates the desired data. For example, psychologists ask questions to determine intelligence, place food in a box to stimulate animals to run, erect barriers between children and toys to observe the effects of frustration, and so forth. Barker refers to the data gathered in this manner as "O-data." O-data are the result of typical experimental methodology. The "experimental method" is advantageous because the investigator has some degree of control over the events and can focus upon the variables of primary interest.

A second type of data, referred to as "T-data," is produced without the intervention of the scientist, who is merely a transducer, transferring and translating the observations. That is, the psychologist only receives, codes, and classifies the inputs from the environment. T-data reveal certain facts not ascertainable with O-data. For example, T-data indicate what actually is occurring in the environment. In the study of chemistry, Barker states, it is essential to know what elements really exist, how abundant they are, and where they can be found. Yet psychologists, he says, tend to ignore the description of the real world. The importance of gathering this type of information is well illustrated by Barker. For example, he finds surprisingly few incidents of severe frustration in the lives of most American children. When such frustrations do occur, their effects are often transient. In a second example demonstrating the importance of T-data, Barker notes that in experimental psychology, subjects who do not respond are generally not included in the data analysis. Yet not responding is a characteristic mode of reaction in children. Observing mother-child interactions in a drugstore revealed that children did not respond to nearly one-third of the mothers' inputs!

Behavioral Settings

Behavior in nature, which gives rise to T-data, often occurs in a particular behavioral setting. A behavioral setting has a number of essential properties: It contains physical objects arranged in a special pattern; the behavior exhibited is relatively independent of the particular people located in the setting; the setting may exist unchanged for a great period of time; and the setting generally exists independent of the conscious awareness of the individuals within the setting. For example, the bridge club at the corner is considered a behavioral setting. It has a physical locus and physical properties; the behavior within the club is relatively independent of the particular people; and the club may exist unchanged for a great number of years. Similarly, a baseball field is a behavioral setting. It has physical properties, a certain type of behavior occurs within that setting, and it exists unchanged. In sum, a behavioral setting is visible, involves people, has certain attributes, and greatly influences the behavior that occurs there.

People, of course, are the *sine qua non* of a behavioral setting. They are part of a setting and generally essential to its continuation. The local bridge club would not continue if it had no patrons. Yet the individuals within the setting are, to a great degree, equipotential: a fourth for bridge is a fourth for bridge. Further, each setting has an optimal population requirement. The bridge club should have at least four members present and not more members than table space. Likewise, a game of baseball requires a certain minimum and maximum number of players.

Within these settings a great variety of personal motives are satisfied. The motivations of bridge players can vary from aggression and affiliation to achievement or power. The same is true of the participants in a baseball game. Hence, the unity of the setting is not derived from the unity of the aroused motivations.

The aspect of behavioral settings most thoroughly investigated by Barker and his colleagues has been the psychological effects of the number of people available to function within a setting. Settings have been classified into three categories: undermanned, overmanned, or optimal in number. This characterization has far-reaching consequences for the behaviors of the members in the setting.

Consider, for example, some consequents of participating in a baseball game when your team has only four players instead of the usual nine. The average value of each team member is great, since everyone is needed, and there is less evaluation of individual differences, inasmuch as all the available players are accepted. Further, each person has more obligations; for example, the second baseman must also play first base. This implies that there will be greater variability per person in the displayed behaviors and that more effort will be required than if the setting were optimally manned. In addition, maximum performance is lessened because of the complexity of the task and the augmented demands on each player. Yet more tension is also aroused, more responsibility assumed, and greater insecurity manifested because of the increased demands and abundant number of decisions that must be made. And, of course, there are more incidents of success and failure.

Wicker (1968) summarizes these and other effects as follows:

. . . In undermanned settings, the setting functions are often in jeopardy, and occupants sense the possibility of losing the satisfactions the settings provide. This leads them to invest more time and effort than when occupants are numerous and behavior setting functions are not precarious. Often they take positions of responsibility and engage in a wide range of supportive behaviors. Under pressure to keep activities going, members seek to induce others to participate. Membership requirements are minimized, and attempts are made to bring available personnel to at least the minimal level of performance. Feelings of involvement, success, failure, challenge, responsibility, and insecurity due to dependence upon others are common. (p. 255)

Observations of behaviors in small and large cities, and in average towns in America and England, have supported the observations enumerated in preceding paragraphs. In one series of studies, Barker and his co-workers (see Barker, 1960) found that the typical town in England has fewer behavioral settings and more people available for those settings than a typical small city in America. Therefore, the average person in the American town holds more responsible positions across the diverse settings. According to Barker, because the individual is more important to the survival of the settings in America than in England, different patterns of segregation are exhibited by the two nations. In the typical American town far fewer settings are segregated in terms of age, sex, and social class. These are important considerations in understanding the problems of the aged or in analyzing patterns of juvenile delinquency. Further, because the English village does not really "need" all of its inhabitants, it can afford to send some of its members out of the community. Many children in English towns are educated in boarding schools. This educational practice does not characterize rural America, presumably, in part, because the younger members of the community are needed to maintain the undermanned settings.

Investigations of the effects of population size and behavioral settings also have been conducted in large and small high schools. Generally, small schools are undermanned while large schools have more individuals than are needed for their settings. Wicker (1968) summarizes the results of this research:

. . . Students of small schools, vis-à-vis students of large schools, (a) enter more different kinds of activities, (b) hold more positions of responsibility in activities entered . . . (c) use more dimensions or constructs to describe school activities . . . (d) experience more satisfactions "relating to being challenged, engaging in important actions, to being involved in group activities, and to achieving moral and cultural values" (Barker and Gump, 1964, p. 197), (e) report more internal and external pressures to attend and participate, including feelings of obligation to support the activities. (p. 255)

These differences in the behavioral effects of high schools are not due to size *per se*, but rather to the fact that in the smaller schools more students are placed in positions of responsibility and are needed in the various settings. Thus, students in smaller schools are more likely to be "performers," while students in larger schools are more likely to be "observers."

Summary

Kurt Lewin's theory of motivation developed from the principles of Gestalt psychology. The Gestaltists argued that the perception of an object is influenced by the field of forces surrounding that object and the interrelationships between the forces in the field. In a similar manner, Lewin's theory presumes that behavior occurs within a psychological field and that many interacting forces determine behavior at any one moment.

Lewin's field theory includes structural and dynamic constructs for the person and the environment. The concept of tension integrates the person and environmental constructs. Tension, which results from a need state, is necessary in order for an environmental object to acquire a valence. The creation of a valence also establishes a force field around the valued object. This force acts to locomote the person in the direction of the goal object, with the intensity of the force increasing as the person approaches the desired goal. If the goal is attained, tension is released, thus reducing the valence of the environmental object and, in turn, decreasing the force acting upon the person. The reduction in force leads to a cessation of behavior. Lewin's conception of motivation thus incorporates hedonism and homeostasis. However, unlike other tension reduction theorists, Lewin is a phenomenologist, stressing the perceived, rather than the real, world.

A number of research investigations grew out of Lewin's theory. Among the areas of study are: 1) conflict, with emphasis on the instability (approach-approach conflicts) or the stability (avoidance-avoidance conflicts) of behavior that results from being in a field of overlapping forces; 2) frustration and the relation between lack of goal attainment and regression (dedifferentiation); 3) task recall and resumption, which tested the notion that persisting tense regions will be manifested in the recall and resumption of unfinished tasks; 4) substitution, a concept that captured Freud's idea of an overlap between needs and his belief that some goals derive their value because other more desirable goals are not attainable; 5) level of aspiration, which was explained with resultant valence theory and the concepts of valence and potency of success and failure; and 6) psychological ecology, or the study of factors in the environment, such as behavioral settings, that do not lie within the life space. It is evident that Lewin's theory was a great stimulant for psychological research.

Many similarities and differences between the Freudian, Hullian, and Lewinian schemes have been pointed out. Considering now only Hull and Lewin, it can be seen that both theorists attempted to identify the immediate determinants of action and specified a quasi-mathematical model of behavior. In their models both Hull and Lewin included concepts representing motivational states of the person (drive, tension), the incentive value of the goal (labelled K and G), and a directional or steering variable (habit, psychological distance). But drive theorists primarily gathered their data in experiments with infrahumans, whereas Lewinians were concerned almost exclusively with complex human behavior, at times guided by the insights of Freud. Thus, drive theorists excelled in demonstrating how motivational theorists ought to operate as experimenters, conducting well controlled investigations in the laboratory. On the other hand, the main contribution of the field theorists was pointing out the broader goals of a theory of motivation, which include understanding complex human behavior through an experimentally testable theory that can also explain the simpler behavior of infrahumans.

Chapter Five

ACHIEVEMENT
THEORY

Introduction

The most productive and popular theories of achievement motivation have adhered to the expectancy-value framework. That is, an individual's choice among achievement-related activities, and how hard one works at achievement tasks, is thought to be determined by one's expectancy of success and the value of success. Simply put, what we attempt to accomplish depends upon what we will get and the likelihood of getting it!

In a manner consistent with the aims of drive theory, achievement theorists have sought to predict a limited array of behavior with a reasonable degree of precision. And also consistent with drive theoretical formulations, models of achievement striving employ many mechanistic concepts, such as tendencies and forces. Thus, theories of achievement share features of both the cognitive (expectancy-value) and the mechanistic traditions in the study of motivation. This was also true of the Lewinian conception of behavior, which preceded work in achievement theory and greatly influenced its development.

Historical Antecedents

The starting point for the academic study of achievement motivation must be arbitrarily selected. I will begin with Henry Murray, but in so doing the earlier contributions and influential roles of Freud, Lewin, and Sears are passed over (see Atkinson, 1964; Murray, 1959; Weiner, 1972).

Murray played a dual function in the history of achievement research. On the one hand, he first called attention to a *need* for achievement.

he concepts of drive and need were often used interchange-
closely linked. For example, Hull considered drive the
gical manifestation of a need state. Over time, however, drives
ame identified with states of deprivation, behaviorism, and research
employing infrahuman organisms, while the concept of need became
identified with molar personality theorists and signified more stable
characteristics of individuals.

Murray (1938) devised a taxonomy that included twenty basic human
needs. This taxonomic approach was not unlike some of the earlier,
unsuccessful attempts by McDougall and others to develop lists of instincts. One of these needs, called achievement, was conceived as the desire:

> To accomplish something difficult. To master, manipulate or organize
> physical objects, human beings, or ideas. To do this as rapidly and as
> independently as possible. To overcome obstacles and attain a high standard.
> To excel one's self. To rival and surpass others. To increase self-regard by the
> successful exercise of talent. (p. 164)

These desires, Murray (1938) said, are accompanied by the following actions:

> To make intense, prolonged and repeated efforts to accomplish some-
> thing difficult. To work with singleness of purpose towards a high and distant
> goal. To have the determination to win. To try to do everything well. To be
> stimulated to excel by the presence of others, to enjoy competition. To exert
> will power; to overcome boredom and fatigue. (p. 164)

Murray's second contribution to the study of achievement motivation
was the development of an instrument to assess need states. This measure, called the Thematic Apperception Test (TAT), supposedly revealed
"covert and unconscious complexes" (Murray, 1938, p. 530). The TAT
was almost universally adopted by subsequent investigators to assess
achievement needs.

The next person of historical significance in the study of achievement
motivation was David McClelland. McClelland and his co-workers
(McClelland, Atkinson, Clark & Lowell, 1953) conducted a systematic
study of achievement motivation, using a refinement of the TAT for the
measurement of achievement needs. Two questions considered by
McClelland and pertinent to the legacy left by Murray are worth noting
here: (1) Why was achievement chosen for study, rather than some of the
other needs listed by Murray (e.g., affiliation, aggression)? 2) Why was the
TAT, rather than an objective assessment instrument, used?

Concerning the decision to study achievement needs, McClelland
et al. (1953) stated: "We devoted our attention to the achievement motive, primarily because there seemed to be a set of operations which had
been frequently used in the laboratory for arousing it" (p. 4). That is, instructions could be presented ("this is an intelligence test") that elicited
achievement concerns, and it was possible to manipulate success and
failure in an experimental setting. In addition, McClelland was dissatisfied with the then dominant deficit, or survival, theories of motivation
proposed by Freud and Hull. Their respective convergence upon anxiety

and food deprivation naturally led to "stimulus offset," or *reactive*, theories of behavior. Conversely, an emphasis upon achievement needs readily generates "stimulus onset," or *proactive*, conceptions of motivation. The theory of motivation first formulated by McClelland was influenced by Hebb's work and the notion of an optimal level of stimulation espoused by arousal theorists. Thus, both increases and decreases in stimulation could be accounted for. Finally, the choice to study achievement needs may have been partially dictated by personal, rather than scientific, considerations, such as McClelland's desire to foster social improvements.

As for the second question concerning the selection of Murray's TAT rather than an objective instrument, McClelland indicated that this measure was used because "of our acceptance of the Freudian hypothesis that a good place to look for the effects of motivation is in fantasy" (McClelland et al., 1953, p. 107). Subsequent research indeed provided suggestive evidence that superficial verbal reports of achievement needs are not predictive of achievement-oriented behavior, while fantasy production is a valid index (deCharms et al., 1955; McClelland, 1958; McClelland et al., 1953). But more of measurement later.

There was a bifurcation of achievement research following the publication of *The Achievement Motive* in 1953. McClelland turned from the laboratory to an analysis of economic development and the role of achievement needs in stimulating societal growth. This work culminated in 1961 with the publication of *The Achieving Society*, an awe-inspiring book commanding much attention from various disciplines in the social sciences.

At the same time, John Atkinson, who may be designated as the next figure of historical importance in achievement research, carried on with the experimental study of achievement motivation. The stage of TAT refinement and validation soon gave way to an attempt by Atkinson to construct a theory of achievement motivation. This theory was guided by the prior thoughts of Tolman, decision theorists, and Lewin, and by the level of aspiration model proposed by Festinger and Escalona. Atkinson's achievement model, which first appeared in print in 1957, dominated research in achievement motivation for the next decade and was most fully elucidated in his treatise on motivation (Atkinson, 1964). This theory is the main focus of the present chapter.

The applied and laboratory approaches assumed by McClelland and Atkinson respectively continued over time. However, the "real world" concerns of McClelland shifted from the historical analysis of economic development to behavioral change. A variety of achievement training programs were established that attempted to enhance achievement strivings among the participants (see McClelland & Winter, 1969). Atkinson, on the other hand, became involved in the formulation of a more general theory of behavior, leaning heavily upon mathematical derivations and computer simulation (Atkinson & Birch, 1970; Atkinson & Raynor, 1974).

In addition to these main trends, numerous associated topics have been (and are being) examined. There are attempts to construct new measures of achievement needs; there is a concern with the developmental antecedents that produce dispositions to achieve; attention is being paid to achievement striving among females, with a sudden burst of activity sparked by a hypothesized "fear of success;" a variety of survey research is examining the relations between job satisfaction, success, achievement needs, and a number of demographic variables; and many investigators are studying the perceived causes of success and failure. This latter topic is discussed in the chapter on attribution theory.

The "golden age" for the study of achievement needs, say, 1950 to 1965, is over. But in the face of the fickleness of psychologists, the analysis of achievement concerns has continued without interruption for more than 35 years and is still flourishing. This longevity is in part due to the persistent efforts of some outstanding psychologists, in part to the payoff of the work, and in part to the manifest importance of achievement strivings in this and other cultures.

With this all-too-brief historical introduction out of the way, I will now turn to some of the substantive areas mentioned above. These topics will be examined: 1) how the need for achievement is being measured and some of the controversies surrounding fantasy measurement; 2) the correlates of this personality disposition and issues of motive generality and stability; 3) Atkinson's theory of achievement motivation and its validation in studies of level of aspiration, persistence, and choice; 4) the relationship between achievement needs in a culture and economic progress; 5) the developmental antecedents that produce achievement strivings; 6) training programs designed to enhance achievement strivings; 7) achievement motivation among females; and 8) the influence of the social context on achievement-oriented behavior. The reader is directed to Atkinson, 1964; Atkinson & Feather, 1966; Birney, 1968; Byrne, 1974; Heckhausen, 1967, 1968; and Weiner, 1970, 1972, for other reviews of this huge body of theory and research.

The Measurement of Needs

The Thematic Apperception Test, or TAT, as already indicated, was devised by Henry Murray. In this method of personality assessment an individual writes stories about ambiguous pictures. The content of the story projections is used to infer the personality and areas of conflict of the story teller. Murray (1938) described the TAT as follows:

> The purpose of this procedure is to stimulate literary creativity and thereby evoke fantasies that reveal covert and unconscious complexes.
> The test is based upon the well-recognized fact that when a person interprets an ambiguous social situation he is apt to expose his own personality as much as the phenomenon to which he is attending. Absorbed in his attempt to explain the objective occurrence, he becomes naively unconscious of himself and of the scrutiny of others and, therefore, defensively less vigilant. To one with double hearing, however, he is disclosing certain inner tendencies and cathexes: wishes, fears, and traces of past experiences. Anoth-

er fact which was relied upon in devising the present method is this: that a great deal of written fiction is the conscious or unconscious expression of the author's experiences of fantasies. (Murray shared with his mentor, Jung, a great interest in literature, and was one of the leading interpreters of Melville's *Moby Dick*.)

The original plan was to present subjects with a series of pictures, each of which depicted a dramatic event of some sort, with instructions to interpret the action in each picture and make a plausible guess as to the preceding events and final outcome. It was anticipated that in the performance of this task a subject would necessarily be forced to project some of his own fantasies into the material and thus reveal his more prevailing thematic tendencies. As the subjects who took this test were asked to interpret each picture — that is, to apperceive the plot or dramatic structure exhibited by each picture — we named it the "Thematic Apperception Test." Only by experience did we discover that much more of the personality is revealed if the S is asked to create a dramatic fiction rather than to guess the probable facts. (pp. 530–31)

TAT Procedure

The scoring and administrative procedures developed by Murray were inadequate for use of the TAT as a research tool for the measurement of individual differences in need strength. First, a scheme had to be devised so that individuals would receive scores indicating the *magnitude* of their achievement needs. And second, scoring rules had to be clearly established so there would be "between-judge" agreement, or what is known as inter-rater reliability. When the TAT is used in clinical settings these criteria often are not met.

These difficulties were surmounted by McClelland et al. (1953), and a system was devised so that individuals could receive numerical scores supposedly revealing their levels of achievement concern. Furthermore, high inter-rater agreement ($r \sim .90$) is readily attainable with the scoring system (see Atkinson, 1958a; McClelland et al., 1953).

The general assessment methodology has remained virtually unchanged since its inception. Four to six pictures are shown (see Figure 5–1), typically in a group setting, with the subjects responding to four directing questions (What is happening? What led up to this situation? What is being thought? What will happen?). Four minutes of writing time is allowed for each story, and a total need achievement score is obtained for each person by summing the scores of the individual stories. Some of these procedural decisions were guided by research indicating that after twenty minutes of writing, the TAT protocols do not have predictive validity, and with less time allotted for each story, there is high correlation between word productivity and the need achievement score (see Reitman & Atkinson, 1958; Riccuiti, 1954).

SCORING SYSTEM. The scoring of fantasy protocols is a two-step process. On the basis of the content specified in a scoring manual, researchers first decide whether a story contains achievement-related imagery. Examples of such story imagery include unique accomplishments, such as inventions, or long-term achievement concerns, such as wanting to be a success in life. If the written production does contain such

Figure 5–1.   Picture often used in the TAT assessment of need for achievement.

imagery, the story receives a numerical score of +1, and ten other subcategories are analyzed for particular kinds of achievement-related content. These subcategories include, for example, expressions of affect, instrumental activities, and goal expectations and fears. Each subcategory represented in the story receives a score of +1 (see McClelland et al., 1953). Thus, any given story can receive a total score of +11. However, it has been pointed out that these ten scoring categories add little to the differentiation between the respondents, for a simple 0 or 1 score correlates .90 with the fuller 11-point scoring system (see Entwisle, 1972).

Evaluation of the TAT as a Motive Measure

Three generalizations capture the present beliefs concerning the TAT measurement of achievement needs:

1. The TAT is a rather poor instrument for the assessment of achievement needs.
2. The TAT is the best available instrument for the assessment of achievement needs.
3. Individuals directly involved in achievement research are more influenced by Generalization 2 than Generalization 1; individuals outside the area are more impressed with Generalization 1 than with 2.

SOME SHORTCOMINGS.   Generalization 1 is based on the many evident deficiencies in current TAT procedures. For example, the pictures described by Atkinson (1958a) are used today, although the scenes depicted appear quite antiquated and often evoke laughter. One has no idea how this lack of ecological validity affects achievement imagery and, of course, the reliability and validity of the measure. Further, the choice of which pictures to use from the many that are available remains uncertain. And the question of the "match" between the sex, age, or race of the respondent and the individuals portrayed in the TAT pictures remains unsolved. These are not necessarily damning criticisms, nor even the worst offenses. Rather, they merely point out some of the vast number of unanswered and unexamined questions.

Many of these shortcomings apparently are due to the fact that investigators of need for achievement have concentrated on personality dynamics and motivation rather than on the measurement of personality. Thus, there was a premature halt to the development of the TAT instrument, although theoretical knowledge concerning the laws of achievement motivation continued to grow. Other areas of motivation that include the measurement of individual differences exhibit similar measurement-theory discrepancies. For example, in the Hull-Spence conception of motivation, the Manifest Anxiety Scale used to measure drive is quite primitive when compared to the sophistication of drive theory.

THE CONTROVERSY OVER RELIABILITY.   The issue of reliability has generated more attention and controversy than has the TAT procedure *per se*. The problem raised is simply this: The reported internal consistency (the correlation between the parts of the test, such as the first and second halves) and the test-retest reliability (the correlation of the test with itself on different occasions of testing) are quite low. Entwisle (1972) summarizes data from a number of studies indicating that these reliabilities are around .30. The estimates given by Klinger (1966) are even lower.

Individuals upholding the use of the TAT to measure achievement needs have offered two classes of defense in the face of the reliability figures presented by Entwisle and Klinger. One type of argument questions the soundness of the critics' analyses. For example, it is known that some of the TAT pictures portray scenes related to affiliative or power needs. That is, the test is not "homogeneous" and often is used to assess more than one motive. Little achievement imagery is elicited by pictures highly cued for motives other than achievement. For example, ideas about inventions or thoughts about long-term success are not expressed when the picture scene is one of people eating dinner. Thus, high internal consistency is not possible if the pictures are "cued" to elicit different motivational concerns. Reliabilities of more than .70 have been reported when all the pictures in a TAT administration contain achievement-related scenes (see Haber & Alpert, 1958; McClelland et al., 1953; Morgan, 1953).

Concerning test-retest reliability, it has been found that, despite a very low correlation, the vast majority of the individuals are classified identically on two occasions if a dichotomous (high-low) subject separation is used. That is, if subjects are considered classifiable only as above or below some median point, then the attained reliability is reasonable (see McClelland et al., 1953). It has been thought, therefore, that the measure is not suitable for precise prediction about a particular person (it often is used in such a manner in industrial settings), but is adequate if the researcher is making comparisons between two groups of individuals.

A second type of rejoinder to the Entwisle (1972) and Klinger (1966) criticisms raises fundamental questions concerning the nature of project-ive measurement and "the misleading oversimplification and myths of measurement transmitted in introductory texts on psychological measure-ment" (Atkinson & Birch, 1974, p. 293). The TAT generally is presented as a test of "creative imagination." Thus, subjects may be reluctant to give the same general response on successive occasions. A "saw-toothed" effect has been observed in achievement imagery on the TAT, with the expression of achievement concerns waxing and waning (see McClelland et al., 1953). McClelland et al. (1953) contend:

> The test-retest unreliability of the measure may be due to the change in the subjects produced by the first administration of the test. That is, it is theoretically possible to have a test which will correlate highly with a number of other measures (high "validity") but not with itself on a second administra-tion (low "reliability"). (pp. 193–194)

Imagine, for example, that one hears a joke and responds with a hearty laugh. When the joke is heard for the second time, little laughter might be elicited. The test-retest reliability in this case may not be the proper measure to assess how adequate laughter is as an index of liking. In a similar vein, Atkinson and Raynor (1974) state: "Instead of returning on the second occasion like the constant and unchanging block of metal presumed by traditional test theory borrowed from physics, the subjects might be substantially spoiled for a retest" (p. 9).

The controversial issues sketched above are far from settled. It is evident that some of the critics of the TAT have been overly harsh. But it also is true that the users of the instrument will have to provide better reliability evidence. If it is decided that fantasy behavior is indeed the "best place" to look for motivational differences, then, as Reitman and Atkinson (1958) stated long ago, much more basic methodological re-search is needed.

Alternative Measures

In addition to suspicions concerning reliability, there are practical reasons for replacing the TAT measure of achievement needs. A written protocol requires that the respondent be literate and fairly articulate. Furthermore, writing stories about four to six pictures is extremely wearing and time-consuming. In addition, the TAT responses are particu-larly sensitive to environmental influence. Comparing subjects tested on different occasions or in different settings is likely to lead to false conclu-sions. Finally, scoring the fantasy protocols requires time, as well as train-ing.

But, in spite of the advantages of an objective measurement instrument, in spite of the great demands for a substitute measure, in spite of the reasonably large amount of time devoted to the construction of alternative assessment instruments, and in spite of the controversy surrounding the use of fantasy measures, the TAT has not been supplanted. Entwisle (1972), borrowing from Jensen (1964), speculates that this "amazing phenomenon is a task for future historians of psychology and will probably have to wait upon greater knowledge of the psychology of credulity than we now possess" (Jensen, 1964, p. 75). However, a less psychodynamic explanation is more appropriate: Simple verbal reports concerning one's beliefs about achievement desires (e.g., how much do you want to succeed?) and more complex personality inventories that include achievement-related items have not proven valid (see, for example, de Charms et al., 1955; Hermans, 1970). Some inroads in objective testing have been made (e.g., Hermans, 1970; Mehrabian, 1969), but the research programs and dedication necessary for test development have not accompanied these beginnings. Thus, these tests remain unfulfilled promises.

Personality Measurement and Theory Construction

It is reasonable for the reader to ask why so much space has been devoted to a discussion of the TAT and why there has not been equal discussion of, for example, the Manifest Anxiety scale. The answer to both questions is that achievement theory, in contrast to the conceptions of Freud, Hull, and Lewin, has focused upon the role of individual differences (in achievement needs) in attempting to understand motivational processes.

Both Hull and Lewin did recognize that they had to deal with individual differences. Hull, however, paid relatively little attention to this issue because:

> . . . Behavior theorists have inherited from their empiricist and associationist forebears of previous centuries a bias towards environmentalism. . . . Behavior theorists spend most of their time studying learned behavior and feel that to understand the behavior of higher mammals means, above all, to understand how learning works. . . .
>
> Preoccupation with learning may lead one to disregard innate differences, which must seem the logical starting point to anyone who wishes to throw light on the dissimilarities among human beings. . . .
>
> It is perfectly obvious that human beings are different from one another in some respects but alike in other respects. The question is whether we should first look for statements that apply to all of them or whether we should first try to describe and explain their differences. The behavior theorist feels that research for common principles of human and animal behavior must take precedence. This, he would point out, is how scientific inquiry must proceed. . . . Until we can see what individuals of a class or species have in common, we cannot hope to understand how their dissimilarities have come about or even to find the most fruitful way to describe and classify these dissimilarities. (Berlyne, 1968, pp. 639–641)

In a similar manner, Lewin sought to discover general laws, and the person was usually considered "a mass point of indifferent constitution" (Murray, 1959, p. 29). As Atkinson (1964) pointed out:

> . . . In the theoretical conception and experimental analysis of motivation, Lewinians consider only the momentary and temporary condition of the person, which is represented at $t(S_G)$ [a system in a state of tension]. And in most cases, $t(S_G)$ is assumed to be roughly equivalent for all subjects exposed to the same experimental instructions and arrangements in the course of conducting the experiment. (p. 103)

Achievement theory, on the other hand, is built upon the idea of individual differences, and personality structures are essential determinants of behavior. Atkinson's philosophy is illustrated in the following quotation:

> A most encouraging development in recent experimental analysis of motivation . . . is the use of tests to assess individual differences in the strength of theoretically-relevant motivational dispositions of humans. Here again, the broad implication of Lewinian ideas is apparent. The guiding hypothesis, $B = f(P,E)$, is now represented in a methodological development that may provide a means of bridging the gap between the study of individual differences in personality and the search for basic explanatory principles. [This gap] has so far seriously handicapped both enterprises in psychology's relatively short history. (Atkinson, 1964, p. 271)

The Need for Achievement

Given the importance of personality structure in the study of achievement motivation, it is necessary to review what is known about the personality disposition called "the need to achieve" before turning to achievement theory. Two questions are of special importance:

1. What is the generality (or extensity, or breadth) of the need for achievement?
2. Is this disposition stable, or at least *relatively* enduring?

Unfortunately, these questions have not been answered adequately. It is not known, for example, whether a person who strives for success in a particular occupation also exhibits achievement-type behaviors on the tennis court, in his night school literature class, or in other such situations. In the only study examining this issue, Rosenstein (1952) found that chemistry majors had a significantly higher need achievement score on the TAT than physical education majors when responding to scenes depicting laboratory situations. It certainly seems reasonable to believe that there are circumscribed avenues or outlets of achievement expression for a given individual. That is, similar genotypes or underlying needs may have disparate phenotypic or displayed representations. But this supposition has not been investigated, and the generality (or specificity) of this motive or trait is unknown. The issue of trait generality is discussed in greater detail in the following chapter.

The stability of achievement needs has been the subject of more research than the issue of motive generality. This is perhaps surprising, inasmuch as longitudinal studies are difficult to conduct and require a dedicated masochism. As might be anticipated, research investigations of long-term stability are, therefore, also few in number. The most-cited data concerning motive stability come from what are known as the Fels Institute studies (see Kagan & Moss, 1959; Moss & Kagan, 1961). Kagan and Moss (1959) report low but significant positive correlations ($r = .22$) between TAT scores at ages 8½ and 14½. Birney (1959) found a correlation of a slightly higher magnitude ($r = .29$) given testing over a four-month interval, and Feld (1967) reports correlations of $r = .38$ over a six-year period. In sum, correlations in the magnitude of roughly .25 to .35 are found in studies of long-term achievement stability. This indicates weak, but greater than chance, stability. Clearly, research of this nature is hampered because of the uncertain test-retest reliability of the TAT. It is impossible to determine the consistency of achievement needs, as inferred from fantasy productions, if test-retest reliability for such measures is low.

Given that the essential questions of generality and stability are unanswered, what, then, is known about people who are labelled high in need for achievement, or high in the desire to achieve success? The clearest and most understandable correlates of achievement needs have been derived from the theories of achievement motivation, which are examined in the next section of this chapter, as well as later in the book. For example, the data pertaining to the relationship between achievement needs and task preference will be discussed in detail later. However, it should be noted here that there is suggestive evidence that tasks of intermediate difficulty are more attractive to individuals highly motivated to succeed than to those lower in achievement needs. In a similar vein, individuals high in achievement needs have been characterized as "realistic" and have occupational goals that are congruent with their abilities (Mahone, 1960; Morris, 1966). The desire for intermediate risk may be indicative of a preference for personal feedback or knowledge about oneself. This informational explanation is consistent with the high achiever's reported preference for business occupations, where feedback (profits) is evident (McClelland, 1961, p. 55; Mayer, Walker, & Litwin, 1961). In addition, individuals high in need for achievement apparently are better able to delay gratification (Mischel, 1961) and attain higher grades in school than individuals low in achievement needs, if the grades are instrumental to long-term success (Raynor, 1970). Furthermore, individuals high in achievement needs are conceptualized as "hope" rather than "fear" oriented. It has been suggested, for example, that they bias their probabilities of success upward so their subjective probabilities of success are greater than the objective probabilities (Feather, 1965). Finally, individuals high in achievement needs take personal responsibility for success and generally perceive themselves as high in ability (Kukla, 1972). The self-attribution for success increases their feelings of worth. This helps explain evidence that they volitionally undertake achievement-oriented activities when the opportunity arises (Atkinson, 1953; Green, 1963). In addition, the self-perception of high ability may account, in part, for their high self-concept, as some investigators report (Mukherjee and Sinha, 1970).

There are a host of other reported linkages to achievement needs, although many of the relationships are tenuous or their theoretical meaning is unclear. For example, it has been found that achievement needs are positively correlated with resistance to social influence, preference for particular colors (blue), aesthetic tastes, lowered recognition thresholds for success-related words, selective retention of incomplete tasks, forms of graphic expression (single and S-shaped lines), and high content of serum uric acid (see the reviews cited earlier for references). Although the sampling of associations listed above increases the "relational fertility" of the need for achievement construct, the lasting significance of many of the relationships is questionable because of the absence of clear theoretical relevance of the findings and doubts concerning their replicability.

One final comment about the correlates of need for achievement is appropriate. Entwisle (1972) and others have criticized the TAT measure of need for achievement because of its failure to predict grade point average. That is, individuals high in need for achievement do not attain better grades than other persons. Since the inception of work in this area, investigators have cautioned against attempts to predict overdetermined behaviors, or actions that can be caused by many sources of motivation. In 1953, McClelland et al. stated: "The relationship of need achievement score to college grades . . . is of dubious theoretical significance, since grades in college are affected by many unknown factors" (p. 237). And 20 years later, I essentially repeated that warning:

> Grade point average is an overdetermined motivational index. One may obtain a high grade for any number of reasons, such as to receive a new car from pleased parents or to be deferred from the Army. As the extrinsic sources of motivation to undertake achievement tasks increase, the relative variance accounted for by achievement needs decrease. It therefore should be expected that need for achievement will be only weakly related to GPA. (Weiner, 1972, p. 222)

We now turn from these personality correlates to Atkinson's theory of achievement motivation.

ATKINSON'S THEORY OF ACHIEVEMENT MOTIVATION

In the tradition of Hull and Lewin, Atkinson (1957, 1964) attempted to isolate the determinants of behavior and then specify the mathematical relations between the components of his theory. Thus, he is part of the academic or experimental tradition in the study of motivation. As already intimated, Atkinson differs from other such theorists in his concentration on individual differences. But in spite of this difference in

JOHN W. ATKINSON

(Courtesy of J. W. Atkinson)

John Atkinson first became acquainted with the field of motivation as an undergraduate philosophy major at Wesleyan University. There he participated with David McClelland and others in developing a scoring system for the TAT that would be useful for research purposes. This interest in individual differences persisted throughout his career, and he is most responsible for pointing out the importance of personality structure for the understanding of motivational processes.

Atkinson received his Ph.D. at the University of Michigan and remained at that university for virtually his entire career. His work had a number of rather distinct phases. After the refinement of the TAT, he developed a theory of achievement motivation using an expectancy-value framework. This cognitive theory was introduced at a time when drive theory dominated psychology, and thus came in the face of relatively little support from others in the field. But the history of motivation vindicated his beliefs. He later collaborated with David Birch and others in constructing a general theory of behavior. This theory is currently being revised and expanded. Indeed, change and progress are the most evident characteristics of Atkinson's career.

Atkinson has been one of the most productive psychologists, publishing numerous books and many journal articles. He also is recognized as an outstanding teacher and was responsible for the training of many well known psychologists, including, for example, Norman Feather and Joseph Veroff. (He also was this writer's Ph.D. supervisor!)

emphasis, his conception of behavior is very similar to those proposed by Hull and Lewin. These earlier motivational theorists conceptualized behavior to be a function of a temporary state of the organism (drive or tension), the properties of the goal object (incentive value or valence), and an experiential or learning factor (habit or psychological distance). Atkinson includes a very similar set of individual, environmental, and experiential variables among the immediate determinants of action.

Further, Atkinson's theory of achievement motivation was influenced by Miller's conflict model. Achievement-oriented behavior is viewed by Atkinson as a resultant of a conflict between approach and avoidance tendencies. Associated with every achievement-related action is the possibility of success (with the consequent emotion of pride) and the possibility of failure (with the consequent emotion of shame). The strengths of these anticipated emotions determine whether an individual will approach or avoid achievement-oriented activities. That is, achievement behavior is viewed as the resultant of an emotional conflict between hopes for success and fears of failure.

Hope of Success

The tendency to approach an achievement-related goal (T_S) is conceived as a product of three factors: the need for achievement, also known as the motive for success (M_S); the probability that one will be successful at the task (P_S); and the incentive value of success (I_S). It is postulated that these three components are multiplicatively related:

$$T_S = M_s \times P_s \times I_s$$

THE NEED FOR ACHIEVEMENT.   In the equation of approach motivation, M_S represents a relatively stable or enduring disposition to strive for success. The definition and measurement of this concept, as well as its historical linkage to the work of Murray and McClelland, have already been discussed. Atkinson (1964) defines the need for achievement as a "capacity to experience pride in accomplishment" (p. 214). That is, the achievement need is an affective disposition.

THE PROBABILITY OF SUCCESS.   The probability of success, P_s, refers to a cognitive goal expectancy or the anticipation that an instrumental action will lead to the goal. Atkinson's use of this concept was guided by Tolman's earlier analysis. Tolman contended that when a reward follows a response, response-reward contingencies, or expectancies, are formed. The animal becomes aware that making the same response to the stimulus will be followed by a reward. In discussing his usage of P_s, Atkinson (1964) explains:

> What Tolman originally called the *expectancy of the goal* and conceived as a forward-pointing cognition based on prior experience is represented as the subjective probability of attaining the goal. . . . The two terms *expectancy* and *subjective probability* have been used interchangeably in the theory of achievement motivation which . . . calls attention to the fact that the concept of expectancy . . . serves to represent the associative link between performance of an act and the attainment of the goal. (p. 275)

According to Tolman, expectancy increases as a function of the number of rewarded trials. Further, he states that early and late trials exert special influence on the formation of goal anticipations. Atkinson, however, working with human rather than infrahuman subjects, takes much more liberty in the specification of operations that alter expectancy, or subjective probability. Any information or contrived stimulus situation that influences a subject's beliefs about winning or performing well apparently can be used to define operationally the magnitude of P_s. The most frequently adopted strategy to manipulate P_s is to supply subjects with some normative information about the difficulty of the task they are attempting. For example, the subject might be told: "Our norms indicate that ____ % of the students of your age level and ability are able to solve these puzzles" (see Feather, 1961; Weiner, 1970). Another procedure used to influence P_s is to have subjects compete against varying numbers of others. For examples, Atkinson (1958b) told some of the subjects that they had to perform better than only one other person to win a prize, while others were informed that they were in competition with twenty others. Still a further operation employed to alter P_s is to vary the actual difficulty of a task. For example, many studies of achievement motivation employ a ring-toss game requiring that rings be thrown over a peg. It is generally assumed that the farther one stands from the peg when playing this game, the lower is the subjective expectancy of success. Finally, the altering of reinforcement history also is used to produce varying levels of P_s. In one experiment (Weiner & Rosenbaum, 1965), subjects received puzzle booklets varying in the number of soluble puzzles. The perceived percentage of success at these tasks determined the P_s.

THE INCENTIVE VALUE OF SUCCESS. The third determinant of approach behavior specified by Atkinson is I_s, or the incentive value of success. Guided by the resultant valence theory of Escalona and Festinger, Atkinson postulates that I_s is inversely related to P_s: $I_s = 1 - P_s$. Thus, the incentive value of success increases as P_s decreases. Atkinson contends that the incentive value of an achievement goal is an affect, labelled "pride in accomplishment." It is argued that greater pride is experienced following success at a difficult task than after success at an easy task. For example, little pride should be experienced by the reader when receiving a grade of "A" in an easy course, but much pride would be felt if this grade were earned in a difficult course. In a similar manner, strong positive affect should be experienced when defeating a superior, rather than a poor, athletic team.

Because the incentive value of success is conceived as an affect, it complements the concept of the achievement motive, which is an affective disposition or a capacity to experience pride in achievement. Thus, as in the Lewinian scheme, the final valence of a goal is a function of both the properties of the person (motive strength) and the properties of the goal (task difficulty).

Although the inverse relationship netween I_s and P_s may be considered a postulate within Atkinson's system, it has been the subject of experimental investigation. For example, Litwin (1958; reported in Atkinson & Feather, 1966, and McClelland, 1961) found that the farther one stands from a peg in a ring-toss game, the greater the reward assigned for success (Figure 5–2). In a similar manner, occupations in which the attainment of success is believed to be difficult are accorded greater prestige and salary (I_s) than occupations in which success is believed to be relatively easy (Strodtbeck, McDonald, & Rosen, 1957). Note, however, that in these instances it is not "pride" that is being assessed as the incentive value of success.

Fear of Failure

Achievement-related activities elicit *positive affective anticipations* because of past successful accomplishments and experienced pride, as well as *negative affective anticipations* learned from prior failures and experienced shame. Thus, both a fear of failure and a hope of success are aroused in achievement-related situations.

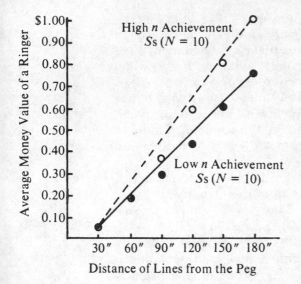

Figure 5–2. Judged mean reward for success at varying distances from the peg. (Reported in McClelland, 1961, p. 236.)

The determinants of fear of failure, or the tendency to avoid achievement tasks, are conceived by Atkinson as analogous to those of the hope of success. It is postulated that the tendency to avoid failure (T_{AF}) is a multiplicative function of the motive to avoid failure (M_{AF}), the probability of failure (P_f), and the incentive value of failure $(-I_f)$:

$$T_{AF} = M_{AF} \times P_f \times (-I_f)$$

THE MOTIVE TO AVOID FAILURE.   Just as M_S is conceived as a capacity to experience pride in accomplishment, M_{AF} is considered a capacity to experience shame given non-attainment of a goal (failure). The conception of an avoidance motive, independent of the approach motive, was introduced well after the TAT assessment studies, and a supporting measurement program was not initiated. Generally, Atkinson and other researchers employ the Mandler-Sarason Test Anxiety Questionnaire, or TAQ (see Mandler & Sarason, 1952), to define operationally the strength of M_{AF}. The TAQ is an objective self-report measure of anxiety. Atkinson therefore employs a projective instrument to assess M_S and an objective self-report measure to assess M_{AF}. This asymmetry is of interest, inasmuch as self-report measures of M_S generally are ineffective and rarely are used by Atkinson and his co-workers (see Atkinson, 1964).

The items on the TAQ pertain only to the anxiety aroused in test-taking situations. Typical items on the TAQ are:

While taking an intelligence test, to what extent do you worry?
Before taking a course examination, to what extent do you perspire?

The questions are answered on rating scales anchored at the extremes (for example, perspire at lot — perspire not at all), and a total score is attained by summing the scores on the 39 test items. Mandler and Sarason (1952) report a correlation of r = .59 between scores on the TAQ and behaviors such as hand and body movements, inappropriate laughter, and talking during an exam. These actions interfere with task performance because the responses are incompatible with, or irrelevant to, exam-taking behavior. Anxiety as measured by the Manifest Anxiety scale and test anxiety assessed by the TAQ correlate from $r = .40$ to $r = .55$.

PROBABILITY AND INCENTIVE VALUE OF FAILURE.   Two environmental factors influence the avoidance of achievement activities: the probability of failure (P_f) and the incentive value of failure $(-I_f)$. It is assumed that the incentive value of failure is a negative affect, "shame." Greater shame is believed to be experienced following failure at an easy task than after failure at a difficult task. Therefore, I_f is conceived as equal to $-(1 - P_f)$. In contrast to the empirical work concerning the determinants of I_s, there have been few successful attempts reported to support the presumed $I_f - P_f$ relationship.

It is further assumed by Atkinson that the probabilities in the model total unity: $P_s + P_f = 1$. Thus, $P_f = 1 - P_s$. It previously was noted that I_s also is equal to $1 - P_s$. Hence, numerically $I_s = P_f$.

Resultant Achievement Motivation

The resultant tendency to approach or avoid an achievement-oriented activity (T_A) is postulated to be a function of the strength of the tendency to approach the task minus the strength of the tendency to avoid the task:

$$T_A = T_S - T_{AF}; \tag{1}$$

or

$$T_A = (M_S \times P_s \times I_s) - (M_{AF} \times P_f \times I_f) \tag{2}$$

It has been indicated that $I_s = 1 - P_s$, $P_f = 1 - P_s$, and that $I_f = P_s$. Simple arithmetic substitution yields:

$$T_A = (M_S - M_{AF}) [P_s \times (1 - P_s)] \tag{3}$$

Inasmuch as M_S and M_{AF} are uncorrelated within the general population, Equation 3 reveals that there are two degrees of freedom among the personal determinants of behavior. However, there is only one degree of freedom among the four environmental determinants of action. Given that P_s is assigned a value, the numerical strengths of I_s, P_f, and I_f are determined. Whether, then, these four variables all can be considered determinants of behavior is a point of theoretical contention.

Further Elaboration of the Model

It is evident from Equation 3 that when $M_S > M_{AF}$, T_A has a positive value. Individuals with this motive constellation, labelled high in resultant achievement motivation, therefore should approach achievement-related activities when given the opportunity. On the other hand, when $M_{AF} > M_S$, T_A has a negative value. Individuals with this motive constellation, labelled low in resultant achievement motivation, should not approach achievement-related activities. Atkinson believes that negative motivation merely indicates what an individual will not do. That is, avoidance motivation is conceptualized as an inhibitory tendency.

It is evident that in our culture the vast majority of individuals engage in some achievement-related actions, such as attending school or working at a job. This apparently contradicts the achievement avoidance behavior expected among individuals in whom $M_{AF} > M_S$. However, achievement-oriented activities are not necessarily initiated to satisfy achievement needs. The sources of motivation may be to avoid punishment, gain power, or satisfy affiliative tendencies. For example, one might study hard at school to impress a potential mate or to win parental favors. This is merely belaboring the self-evident truth that behavior is overdetermined and that many sources of motivation may cause an action.

To capture the overdetermination of achievement behavior, Atkinson specifies that the final tendency to undertake achievement activities is determined by the strength of the resultant achievement-oriented tendency, plus the strengths of all other tendencies elicited in the situation but unrelated (extrinsic) to achievement needs *per se:*

$$\text{Achievement behavior} = T_A + \text{extrinsic motivation} \qquad (4)$$

It is therefore possible for the model to account for achievement-type behavior exhibited by individuals in whom $M_{AF} > M_S$. Such actions are attributed to sources of motivation unrelated to achievement. The strengths of these extrinsic motivations presumably are a function of the magnitudes of other motives, goal expectancies, and incentives.

Combining the Motives

Some readers might reasonably ask: How can one be classified as high or low in the resultant tendency to strive for success? How can the strengths of M_S and M_{AF} be compared, for they are conceived as independent dimensions and assessed with different instruments? The procedure generally followed by Atkinson and other researchers in this area is to assign each individual standard scores, or Z-scores, computed from TAT and TAQ scores using deviations from the means of the population under investigation. By transforming scores on both the TAT and TAQ into Z-scores, it is possible to compare the relative strengths of these motives within any individual. Thus, if an individual scores high on the TAT relative to his comparison group, and low on the TAQ relative to this

TABLE 5–1   RESULTANT ACHIEVEMENT MOTIVATION CLASSIFICATION AS A FUNCTION OF STRENGTH OF THE HOPE OF SUCCESS (GENERALLY ASSESSED WITH THE TAT) AND STRENGTH OF THE FEAR OF FAILURE (GENERALLY ASSESSED WITH THE TAQ)

Hope of Success (Need for Achievement)	Fear of Failure (Anxiety)	Resultant Achievement Motivation
High	Low	High
High	High	Intermediate
Low	Low	Intermediate
Low	High	Low

group, he is classified as high in resultant achievement motivation, or one in whom $M_S > M_{AF}$. One shortcoming of this procedure is that persons scoring high on both measures and those scoring low on both measures are grouped into a common "intermediate" classification (see Table 5–1). It is likely that these two intermediate groups have differentiating characteristics.

Comparison with Hullian and Lewinian Theory

As indicated throughout this chapter, there are important similarities and differences in the approaches to the study of motivation advocated by Atkinson, Hull, and Lewin. Consider first the determinants of action specified by these three theorists (see Table 5–2). Table 5–2 shows that all three postulate that behavior is a function of the properties of the person (motive, drive, or tension), the properties of the goal object (incentive or valence), and an experiential or learning variable (probability of success, habit strength, or psychological distance). However, the property of the person is a stable personality attribute in Atkinson's conception, but a

TABLE 5–2   COMPARISON OF THE DETERMINANTS OF BEHAVIOR INCLUDED IN THE MOTIVATIONAL MODELS OF ATKINSON, HULL, AND LEWIN

Theorist	Construct		
	Person	Environment	Learning
Atkinson	Motive[a] ×	Incentive of success[b] ×	Probability of success
Hull	Drive ×	Incentive ×	Habit
Lewin	Tension,[c]	Valence,[d]	Psychological distance[e]

[a] Represents a stable personality disposition.
[b] Is equal to one minus the probability of success.
[c] Did not specify mathematical relationship between components in theory.
[d] Determined by properties of the goal object, operationally independent of the needs of the person (tension).
[e] The potency of success also is an experiential variable in Lewin's theory.

temporary state of drive or tension in the Hullian and Lewinian theories. Further, in the Hullian and Lewinian conceptions the incentive value of the goal object has an independent operational existence. But for Atkinson, I_s is determined by the value of P_s. (Atkinson, however, does consider achievement to be a special case of a general model in which I_s and P_s are not necessarily related.) Finally, in the Hullian model the learning or associative variable represents a mechanical strengthening of an S-R bond, while for both Atkinson and Lewin the experiential component is conceptualized as cognitive and involves foresight concerning the goal event or the consequences of a response. That is, Atkinson and Lewin contend that mental events (expectancies) intervene between stimulus input and the final response.

The disparities in the conceptions of the learning variable are primarily responsible for the classification of Hullian theory as mechanistic and the conceptions of Atkinson and Lewin as cognitive. Although Atkinson and Lewin are considered cognitive theorists, both also are extremely influenced by physicalistic conceptions and use mechanical concepts. Yet, despite their use of mechanistic terminology, they conceptualize humans as "rational" and able to use mental faculties to aid in reaching desired goals. Thus, Lewin and Atkinson actually represent a transition between mechanistic and cognitive theories.

There are other points of convergence and divergence among the three motivational models. All are hedonistic conceptions. Individuals are believed to act to maximize pleasure and minimize pain. Most theories of motivation link hedonism to homeostatic processes; pleasurable events return the organism to a state of equilibrium. For Hull, as well as for Freud, a state of equilibrium involves no stimulation. All internal stimuli are considered unpleasant and are to be eliminated. Lewin also asserts that motivational processes are derived from homeostatic imbalance. In contrast to the above theorists, Atkinson apparently abandons the concept of homeostasis. It plays no formal role in his theory. Further, because the motivational property associated with the person is a stable trait, rather than a drive or tense state, attainment or non-attainment of a goal cannot dramatically increase or decrease the intrapersonal behavioral determinants.

There are also differences between the actual and stated breadths of the theories under consideration. Although the Hullian conception is formulated as a general behavioral theory, the data cited in support of the conception primarily were generated by hungry rats running down a straight alley. It is only with difficulty and great ingenuity that the theory can explain other behavioral data. Lewin, on the other hand, is more of a general theorist. He attempts to explain the data gathered by Hullians and offers his own research in a variety of areas in support of his theory. In contrast to both Hull and Lewin, Atkinson has limited his theory to the area of achievement-related behavior. Virtually all of the data cited in support of his conception involve success or failure at some achievement activity, or a decision in an achievement-related context. Thus, his conception follows the general trend in psychology to predict and understand more circumscribed domains of behavior. It also is true that Atkinson's model may be considered a general theory of action. But when considered as such, the implicit breadth of the theory is greater than its data base. Whether the model of achievement behavior can also serve as a model for power seeking, affiliative actions, and the like remains to be demonstrated.

Derivations from the Theory and Supporting Evidence

We turn now from the rather abstract analysis of Atkinson's theory to some hypotheses derived from his conception and to empirical studies testing these hypotheses. Two experimental topics will be examined first: level of aspiration and persistence of behavior. Following the format of prior chapters, critical analyses of these bodies of research are not undertaken. Rather, the experiments will serve simply to elucidate the theory. Finally, a third area of investigation, choice behavior, is examined in detail. Task selection has been the main testing ground of Atkinson's theory and currently is being critically examined by many researchers.

Hypotheses in all of these areas of study can be made clear by substituting numerical values for the theory shown in Equation 2, p. 195 (see Table 5–3). In Table 5–3 it is assumed that when $M_S > M_{AF}$, $M_S = 2$ and $M_{AF} = 1$; when $M_S = M_{AF}$, the value assigned to both motives is 1; and when $M_{AF} > M_S$, $M_{AF} = 2$ and $M_S = 1$. The rows in the table indicate the value of the resultant tendency to strive for success as a function of the difficulty (P_s) of the task. In this example, extrinsic motivations are neglected.

It can be seen in Table 5–3 that when $M_S > M_{AF}$, T_A is positive; when $M_S = M_{AF}$, $T_A = 0$; and when $M_{AF} > M_S$, T_A is negative. Thus, the motive scores may be considered relative weights brought to bear upon the environmental sources of motivation. When $M_S > M_{AF}$, greater weight is

TABLE 5–3 STRENGTH OF RESULTANT ACHIEVMENT MOTIVATION RELATED TO TASK DIFFICULTY (PROBABILITY OF SUCCESS) FOR HIGH, INTERMEDIATE, AND LOW ACHIEVING GROUPS

Motive Classification		
High $(M_S > M_{AF})$	Intermediate $(M_S = M_{AF})$	Low $(M_{AF} > M_S)$
M_S P_x I_x M_{AF} P_f I_f	M_S P_x I_x M_{AF} P_f I_f	M_S P_x I_x M_{AF} P_f I_f
$2 \times .1 \times .9 - (1 \times .9 \times .1) = .09$	$1 \times .1 \times .9 - (1 \times .9 \times .1) = 0$	$1 \times .1 \times .9 - (2 \times .9 \times .1) = -.09$
$2 \times .3 \times .7 - (1 \times .7 \times .3) = .21$	$1 \times .3 \times .7 - (1 \times .7 \times .3) = 0$	$1 \times .3 \times .7 - (2 \times .7 \times .3) = -.21$
$2 \times .5 \times .5 - (1 \times .5 \times .5) = .25$	$1 \times .5 \times .5 - (1 \times .5 \times .5) = 0$	$1 \times .5 \times .5 - (2 \times .5 \times .5) = -.25$
$2 \times .7 \times .3 - (1 \times .3 \times .7) = .21$	$1 \times .7 \times .3 - (1 \times .3 \times .7) = 0$	$1 \times .7 \times .3 - (2 \times .3 \times .7) = -.21$
$2 \times .9 \times .1 - (1 \times .1 \times .9) = .09$	$1 \times .9 \times .1 - (1 \times .1 \times .9) = 0$	$1 \times .9 \times .1 - (2 \times .1 \times .9) = -.09$

given to the combination of $P_s \times I_s$ than to $P_f \times -I_f$. On the other hand, when $M_{AF} > M_S$ the negative affect linked with failure is more salient to the individual than is the positive affect associated with success.

More detailed analysis of Table 5–3 yields some rather complex hypotheses. Table 5–3 reveals that achievement motivation varies systematically as a function of the P_s at the task. Among those in whom $M_S > M_{AF}$, motivation is maximum when $P_s = .50$. Further, the strength of motivation decreases symmetrically as P_s increases or decreases from the level of intermediate difficulty. Neither the incentive value of success nor the expectancy of success is greatest at tasks of intermediate difficulty. But the postulation that $I_s = 1 - P_s$ and the specification that I_s and P_s relate multiplicatively mean greatest motivation occurs when P_s, and therefore I_s, are equal to .50.

Turning attention to those in whom $M_{AF} > M_S$, it can be seen that among these individuals motivation is most inhibited at tasks of intermediate difficulty. All achievement tasks are aversive in that they predominantly elicit fear. But tasks that are very easy or very difficult are mildly aversive in comparison to tasks of intermediate difficulty.

Finally, the resultant achievement tendency for individuals in whom positive and negative affective anticipations are equal is 0. Motivation is unaffected by task difficulty. However, the degree of absolute approach-avoidance conflict decreases as task difficulty departs from the intermediate level. At high or low P_s levels, little approach and little avoidance motivation are aroused, while at more intermediate P_s levels, both high approach and high avoidance tendencies are elicited.

Several within- and between-group hypotheses follow from the above analysis. Inasmuch as highly achievement-oriented individuals are most motivated by tasks of intermediate difficulty, they should select such tasks when given the opportunity and should exhibit the greatest intensity of motivation when performing at activities of intermediate difficulty (such as competing against an opponent of equal skill). Conversely, individuals highly fearful of failure are theoretically expected to select easy or difficult tasks (if they must undertake achievement-oriented activities), and should exhibit the greatest intensity of performance at tasks of extreme probabilities (such as competing against an opponent of greater or lesser comparative ability). The derivations concerning task preferences have generated the most research in the achievement area and are responsible for the "risk-preference" label applied to Atkinson's model.

Level of Aspiration

The analysis of task preference described above has been related to the conceptualization of level of aspiration proposed by Escalona and Festinger (which was discussed in the last chapter). Level of aspiration refers to the setting of a performance goal. It can be contended that goal setting necessitates a comparison among a number of possible alternatives differing in P_s level and a selection of one of these alternatives as the subjective goal. For example, when establishing a level of aspiration at a series of arithmetic problems, individuals may believe that the probability of completing 10 problems within the allotted time is .70; 15 problems, .50; 20 problems, .30; and so forth. They then select the level for which they will strive, knowing that easier tasks are more likely to be attained, but that success at easier tasks is less attractive than success at more difficult tasks. Hence, the setting of an aspired level of performance is similar conceptually to a risk-preference, in which selection is made among a number of alternatives differing in difficulty.

An experiment by Moulton (1965) combines a modification of the usual level of aspiration paradigm with achievement theory. Moulton's subjects were first introduced to three tasks that differed in level of difficulty. Task difficulty was manipulated by presenting fraudulent norms indicating that one of the tasks was easy ($P_s = .75$), a second of intermediate difficulty ($P_s = .50$), and a third difficult ($P_s = .25$).

After receiving the normative information, all the subjects were given the task of intermediate difficulty to perform and received either success or failure feedback. The task involved rearranging letters to form a word.

Following the success or failure experience, the subject was asked to select a second task, the choice being between the two remaining tasks that originally had been introduced as easy or difficult. Moulton reasoned that if an individual was successful on the first trial, the "difficult" task would now be perceived as closer to the $P_s = .50$ level than the "easy" task. Success should increase P_s, and the probabilities initially symmetrical around the intermediate level (.25 and .75) would now be, for example, .35 and .85. Thus, the difficult task ($P_s = .35$) is closer to .50, or more intermediate in difficulty, than the easy task.

Given this new asymmetry in probability levels, subjects high in resultant achievement motivation were expected to choose the initially difficult task, and subjects low in resultant achievement motivation were expected to select the easy task. Selection of the easy task following success when $P_s = .50$ was considered an atypical response, for the subject would be lowering the aspiration level following goal attainment.

In a similar manner, it was assumed that P_s decreases following failure. The subjective probabilities may have shifted from .25 and .75 to, for example, .15 and .65. Thus, the task introduced as easy is now more intermediate in difficulty than the task introduced as difficult. Individuals in whom $M_S > M_{AF}$ were expected, therefore, to select the easier task, while those in whom $M_{AF} > M_S$ were expected to make an atypical response by selecting the more difficult task after failure.

The results of this study are shown in Table 5–4. As can be seen, subjects in whom $M_{AF} > M_S$ exhibit more atypical responses than those in the intermediate or high motive groups. Thus Moulton's hypotheses were confirmed, additional support was provided for Atkinson's conception of motivation, and a rapprochement was made between level of aspiration and the study of risk-preference.

TABLE 5–4   TYPE OF SHIFT IN LEVEL OF ASPIRATION AS RELATED TO RESULTANT MOTIVATION

Motive Classification	Resultant Motivation	Type of Shift	
		Atypical	Typical
$M_{AF} > M_S$	Avoidance oriented	11	20
$M_{AF} = M_S$	Ambivalent	3	28
$M_S > M_{AF}$	Approach oriented	1	30

(Adapted from Moulton, 1965, p. 403.)

Persistence of Behavior

Persistence of behavior, along with choice, has been a widely used dependent variable in motivational research. An experiment conducted by Feather (1961), which examined how long an individual would continue to work at an achievement-related task, perhaps best captures the predictive value of Atkinson's theory of achievement motivation.

Feather created a free-choice situation in which subjects were given an achievement-related puzzle to perform. They were instructed that they could work on the task for as long as they desired and could quit whenever they wished to undertake a different puzzle. The task required subjects to trace over all the lines on a complex figure without lifting the pencil from the paper or retracing a line. Although the subjects did not know it, the task was impossible.

Feather introduced false norms to establish a P_s at the task. In one experimental condition the task was presented as quite difficult ("at your age level, approximately 5 per cent of the college students are able to get the solution"). In a second condition the task was introduced as relatively easy ("70 per cent of the college students are able to get the solution"). Feather then examined the number of trials attempted by the subject, or the persistence of behavior, before quitting the task. Persistence was predicted to be a function of the initial P_s at the task and individual differences in the strength of achievement-related needs.

The derivations of Feather's hypotheses are similar to those outlined in the level of aspiration study conducted by Moulton. Table 5–5 shows the strength of motivation toward the achievement tasks in the two experimental conditions for subjects in whom $M_S > M_{AF}$ and for those in whom $M_{AF} > M_S$. Again, for ease of presentation, it is assumed that when $M_S > M_{AF}$, $M_S = 2$ and $M_{AF} = 1$, and vice versa when $M_{AF} > M_S$. In addition, extrinsic motivation is assumed equal to .50, and the decrement of P_s following failure is .10 in the $P_s = .70$ condition and .01 in the $P_s = .05$ condition. The table shows that among subjects in whom $M_S > M_{AF}$, motivation on Trial One is greater when $P_s = .70$ than when $P_s = .05$ (.71 versus .55). Further, following initial failure, motivation rises in the $P_s = .70$ condition, for P_s decreases and moves closer to the level of intermediate difficulty. Assuming that the decrement in P_s remains .10, motivation also should increase after the next failure. On the other hand, motivation immediately decreases following failure in the $P_s = .05$ condition, for P_s moves from the level of intermediate difficulty. Further, motivation continues to decrease given repeated failures. Thus, Feather predicted that persistence, or the number of choices of the activity in progress, would be greater in the $P_s = .70$ than $P_s = .05$ condition among subjects in whom $M_S > M_{AF}$.

The right half of Table 5–5 portrays the hypothetical strength of motivation among subjects in whom $M_{AF} > M_S$. The total motivation for these subjects is positive only because the strength of the assumed extrinsic sources of motivation exceeds the achievement inhibition aroused by the task. When $M_{AF} > M_S$, motivation initially is greater in the $P_s = .05$ than in the $P_s = .70$ condition (.45 versus .29), for .05 is farther from the level of intermediate difficulty than .70. In addition, following failure the motivation in the $P_s = .70$ condition decreases, while it increases in the $P_s = .05$ condition. This is again due to the respective shifting of P_s toward or away from the .50 level. Because repeated failures are experienced, it would be expected that motivation continues to increase in the $P_s = .05$ condition and approaches asymptote (the strength of extrinsic sources) as P_s approaches 0. Hence, Feather predicted that subjects in whom $M_{AF} > M_S$ would persist longer in the $P_s = .05$ than in the $P_s = .70$ condition.

In sum, an interaction was hypothesized between level of resultant achievement needs and task difficulty. Among subjects in whom $M_S > M_{AF}$, greater persistence was predicted in the easy than difficult condition. On the other hand, among subjects in whom $M_{AF} > M_S$, greater persistence was expected at the difficult than at the easy task. The data from the experiment, shown in Table 5–6, confirmed Feather's hypotheses (see Weiner, 1972, for a more detailed analysis of some of the conceptual issues raised by this experiment).

TABLE 5–5 STRENGTH OF MOTIVATION TO UNDERTAKE THE ACTIVITY IN PROGRESS AMONG SUBJECTS HIGH OR LOW IN RESULTANT ACHIEVEMENT MOTIVATION, GIVEN THE TWO EXPERIMENTAL CONDITIONS EMPLOYED BY FEATHER (1961)

Experimental Condition Trial		P_s	Strength of Total Motivation (Achievement plus Extrinsic Motivation) Subject Classification	
			$M_S > M_{AF}$	$M_{AF} > M_S$
$P_s = .70$	1	.70[a]	$2 \times .7 \times .3 - (1 \times .3 \times .7) + .50^c = .71$	$1 \times .7 \times .3 - (2 \times .3 \times .7) + .50 = .29$
	2	.60	$2 \times .6 \times .4 - (1 \times .4 \times .6) + .50 = .74$	$1 \times .6 \times .4 - (2 \times .4 \times .6) + .50 = .26$
	3	.50	$2 \times .5 \times .5 - (1 \times .5 \times .5) + .50 = .75$	$1 \times .5 \times .5 - (2 \times .5 \times .5) + .50 = .25$
$P_s = .05$	1	.05[b]	$2 \times .05 \times .95 - (1 \times .95 \times .05) + .50 = .55$	$1 \times .05 \times .95 - (2 \times .95 \times .05) + .50 = .45$
	2	.04	$2 \times .04 \times .96 - (1 \times .96 \times .04) + .50 = .54$	$1 \times .04 \times .96 - (2 \times .96 \times .04) + .50 = .46$
	3	.03	$2 \times .03 \times .97 - (1 \times .97 \times .03) + .50 = .53$	$1 \times .03 \times .97 - (2 \times .97 \times .03) + .50 = .47$

[a] It is assumed that P_s decreases .10 following failure when the initial $P_s = .70$.
[b] It is assumed that P_s decreases .01 following failure when the initial $P_s = .05$.
[c] Extrinsic motivation is assumed constant and equal to .50.

TABLE 5–6 NUMBER OF SUBJECTS WHO WERE HIGH AND LOW IN PERSISTENCE IN RELATION TO STATED DIFFICULTY OF THE INITIAL TASK AND THE NATURE OF THEIR MOTIVATION

n Achievement	Test Anxiety	Stated Difficulty of Task	Persistence Trials	
			High (Above Median)	*Low (Below Median)*
High	Low	$P_s = .70$ (easy)	6	2
		$P_s = .05$ (difficult)	2	7
Low	High	$P_s = .70$ (easy)	3	6
		$P_s = .05$ (difficult)	6	2

(Adapted from Feather, 1961, p. 558.)

Choice Behavior

As already indicated, choice among achievement tasks varying in difficulty has been the main testing ground of Atkinson's theory of achievement motivation. The general procedure in these studies is illustrated in an experiment by Atkinson and Litwin (1960). In this investigation the subjects attempted to toss rings over a peg. The subjects were allowed to stand at varying distances from the peg and could change positions following each toss. It was assumed by Atkinson and Litwin that a position close to the target corresponds to a high P_s level and that P_s decreases as the distance from the peg increases. Thus, distance from the peg was the observable indicator of choice and of task difficulty.

The subjects were given the TAT and the TAQ and were classified into resultant achievement motivation subgroups. The data on choice from this study are shown in Figure 5–3. Figure 5–3 reveals that intermediate task preference is greatest for the high motive group, least for subjects in whom $M_{AF} > M_S$, and intermediate for subjects either high or low in both motives. Intermediate difficulty in this study was defined either as intermediate physical distance from the peg or the median of the actual distribution of shots. The two measures yielded comparable results.

The data reported by Atkinson and Litwin are typical of most of the findings in the study of risk-preference. Three research questions that guided these studies, and their answers, are:

1. Do individuals high in achievement needs exhibit a preference for tasks of intermediate difficulty? Absolutely yes!
2. Do individuals low in achievement needs exhibit a preference for tasks that are comparatively easy or comparatively difficult? Convincingly not!
3. Do individuals high in achievement needs exhibit a greater preference for tasks of intermediate difficulty than individuals low in

achievement needs? Most likely yes (see review in Meyer, Folkes, & Weiner, 1976).

In sum, all individuals seem to prefer intermediate difficulty, although this preference may be more evident among individuals highly motivated to achieve. These data pose some problems for Atkinson's theory, yet they do tend to support the broad (and often tested) hypothesis that groups classified by the strength of achievement needs will display differential preference for intermediate difficulty tasks.

Atkinson and Feather (1966, pp. 22, 342) acknowledge that individuals classified as highly fearful of failure do not avoid intermediate tasks. They offer two explanations for this finding. On the one hand, they contend that in the populations tested (such as college students) the subjects generally are high in need for achievement. Hence, extreme risks should not be chosen, although differential preference for intermediate difficulty tasks is still expected among groups differing in their level of achievement needs. However, this argument is weakened by the fact that even when high school and grammar school students are subjects, persons low in achievement needs do not avoid intermediate difficulty.

A second argument offered by Atkinson and Feather is that there are sources of motivation in addition to achievement that promote intermediate choice. For example, "unmeasured need for affiliation may function just like need for achievement to overcome resistance to intermediate degree of difficulty" (Atkinson & Feather, 1966, p. 342). Note

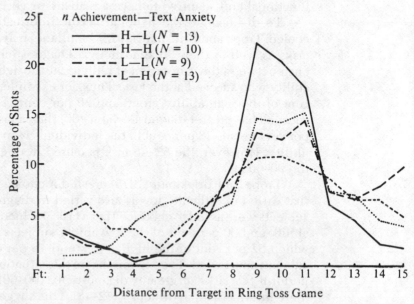

Figure 5–3. Percentage of ring-toss attempts as a function of distance from the peg, with subjects classified according to strength of resultant achievement motivation. (Adapted from Atkinson & Litwin, 1960, p. 55.)

that the arguments proposed by Atkinson and Feather explain the apparently contradictory data within the framework of Atkinson's 1957 theory; the theory is kept totally intact.

AN ALTERNATE EXPLANATION.   Atkinson's prediction of disparate motive-group preferences is based upon the belief that choice among achievement tasks follows the principle of maximization of positive affect for the highly achievement-oriented person and minimization of negative affect for individuals low in achievement needs. That is, anticipatory emotions and hedonic concerns determine what tasks one will attempt to perform.

An alternative interpretation of risk-preference appeals to informational rather than hedonic principles. Research has demonstrated that outcomes at tasks of intermediate difficulty provide performers with the most information about their efforts and capabilities. There are logical reasons why performance at intermediate difficulty tasks provides a maximum of personal information. Selection of easy tasks typically results in success, and that outcome is attributed to the ease of the task (see Weiner and Kukla, 1970). In a similar manner, selection of a very difficult task typically results in failure, and the blame is placed on the characteristics of the task. Thus, selection of easy or difficult tasks generally confirms one's knowledge about the external world. Conversely, tasks of intermediate difficulty are just as likely to produce success as failure. Thus, performance at such tasks provides information about the efforts and abilities of the *person* undertaking the activity. Given this conception, differential risk-preference behavior between groups differing in achievement needs would indicate disparate desires for personal feedback or self-evaluation (see McClelland et al., 1953). Of course, it is quite functional and adaptive to have a realistic or veridical view of oneself.

To disentangle the hedonic versus informational determinants of choice, Trope and Brickman (1975) simultaneously varied the difficulty of tasks as well as their "diagnosticity." Diagnosticity refers to the difference between the proportion of individuals designated as high or low in ability who succeed at the task. Thus, for example, a task at which 90 per cent of the high ability group and 60 per cent of the low ability group succeed has greater diagnostic value (30) than a task accomplished by 52 per cent versus 48 per cent of the individuals respectively high or low in ability. However, the 52–48 task is more intermediate in difficulty than the 90–60 task.

Trope and Brickman (1975) created a choice setting in which tasks that varied in difficulty levels also varied in diagnosticity. For example, subjects were asked to choose either a task at which 90 per cent of the high ability and 60 per cent of the low ability subjects succeeded or a task at which 52 per cent of the high ability and 48 per cent of the low ability subjects succeeded. They report that in this situation the subjects chose to perform the tasks of greater diagnosticity (90–60) rather than the tasks more intermediate in difficulty (52–48). This suggests that the preference for intermediate difficulty reported by so many investigators is attributable to the high diagnostic value of these tasks.

In a replication and extension of this investigation, Trope (1975)

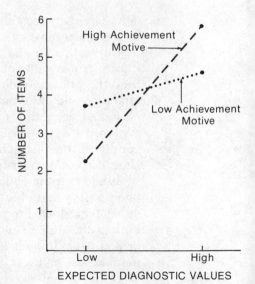

Figure 5-4. Mean number of items chosen from tests varying in expected diagnostic value by subjects varying in achievement motive. (From Trope, 1975, p. 1008.)

again gave subjects a choice between tasks varying in difficulty as well as in diagnosticity. In addition, measures of achievement motivation were taken. The results of this investigation are shown in Figure 5-4. Figure 5-4 reveals that subjects in both motive groups prefer to undertake high rather than low diagnosticity tasks. However, this preference is significantly greater among high achievement-oriented subjects. Thus, the two motive groups apparently differ in their information-seeking desires. Figure 5-5 depicts choice as a function of task difficulty. As can be seen, at all levels of difficulty, tasks of high diagnosticity are preferred. Furthermore, there is no differential preference for tasks of intermediate diffi-

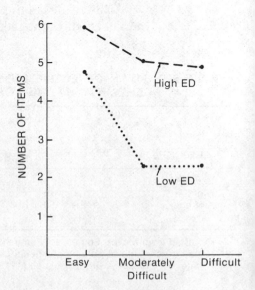

Figure 5-5. Mean number of items chosen from six tests varying in difficulty and expected diagnostic value (ED). (From Trope, 1975, p. 1008.)

culty when diagnosticity is controlled. Indeed, there is a general trend to choose easier tasks.

Investigations by Meyer et al. (1976) demonstrated more directly the informational value of intermediate difficulty choice. Meyer et al. examined the phenomenology of choice behavior by assessing the perceived affective and informational determinants of risk-preference. Subjects classified according to their level of achievement needs expressed a preference among tasks varying in difficulty. In one of the experimental conditions the instructions conveyed that performance at the task chosen should maximize satisfaction, while in a second condition the instructions specified that the choice should maximize the information gained about one's ability and effort expenditure. It was found that the majority of all subjects preferred to undertake tasks of intermediate difficulty and that both positive affect and information gain were perceived to be optimal at or near this difficult level. As already indicated, the finding that intermediate risk taking is displayed by subjects regardless of their magnitude of achievement needs is consistent with a great amount of prior research.

Two additional experiments investigated at what level of task difficulty individuals most desire information about their performance. Police trainees and high school students with disparate self-concepts of their abilities in target shooting and high-jumping respectively were able to receive limited but self-selected performance feedback at a series of shooting or jumping tasks that varied in difficulty. More specifically, in the police study, Meyer et al. (1976) first had policemen rate their general shooting ability prior to a target practice. Targets of varying objective difficulty were then presented, and the policemen rated their subjective probability of success at each of the targets. Finally, the subjects were told they would shoot at each of the targets, but they could learn the results of their performance at only one of these targets. The policemen were allowed to choose the target at which the feedback was desired.

The results of this study are given in Table 5–7, which indicates the target at which the feedback was desired and the subjective likelihood of

TABLE 5–7   MEAN OBJECTIVE DIFFICULTY LEVEL AND SUBJECTIVE CERTAINTY RATING FOR FEEDBACK CHOICE

| | | Target Shooting | |
| | | | |
Ability Group	n	Objective Difficulty	Subjective Certainty
Very high	18	15%[a]	5.22[b]
High	16	39%	6.12
Average	50	47%	5.42
Low	23	75%	6.69

(Adapted from Meyer, Folkes, & Weiner, 1976, p. 420.)
[a]Mean percentage of policemen specified as hitting the target.
[b]Scale: 0 = certainly will not succeed; 11 = certainly will succeed.

success at that target. Among all the policemen, feedback was chosen at the target for which the subjective probability of success was intermediate. Thus, policemen perceiving themselves as poor shots requested feedback at the objectively easy (subjectively intermediate) target, while policemen who perceived themselves as high in shooting ability desired performance information at the objectively difficult (also subjectively intermediate) target. The intermediate ability groups fell between these extremes in their choice behavior.

In sum, the data from choice studies indicate that there is a general tendency to select intermediate difficulty tasks, probably because of their informational (diagnostic) value. However, intermediate preference may be more evident among individuals highly motivated to succeed. These data have great significance for Atkinson's theory. First, although individuals high in achievement needs have been chiefly characterized as "hope" oriented, they perhaps can be better described as information or feedback seekers. The latter identification shifts the emphasis from the affective to the cognitive correlates of the disposition to achieve. Thus, differences in risk-preference between high and low achievement motive groups may be the result of a differential desire for self-evaluation, rather than (or in addition to) disparate emotional anticipations. This analysis of choice completely alters the conceptual foundation of achievement theory. In Chapters Eight and Nine, which deal with attribution theory, this informational approach to motivation is examined more extensively.

The Dynamics of Action

Earlier in this chapter it was indicated that Atkinson and his colleagues, particularly David Birch (Atkinson & Birch, 1970; Birch, Atkinson & Bongort, 1974), are now engaged in the formulation of a more general theory of motivation. This theory, called the "dynamics of action," makes extensive use of mathematical derivations and computer simulation. Hence, it can only be superficially examined in the present context.

Atkinson and Birch (1970) assume that "the behavioral life of an individual is a constant flux of activity" (p. 1). That is, persons are always active, rather than being in or seeking a state of rest, as equilibrium theorists such as Freud and Hull had presumed. Atkinson and Birch therefore contend that the main problem for motivational theorists is to explain and to predict the change from one activity to another, rather than the change from activity to rest or from rest to activity.

Figure 5–6 shows the strength of motivation (or strength of a tendency, T) to undertake each of two activities (A and B) over time. In all cases, one tendency (T_A) initially predominates over another (T_B). However, with the passage of time, the hierarchical ordering of the behavioral tendencies shifts, so that T_B is stronger than T_A. Atkinson and Birch address themselves to the question of what accounts for this change in forces, which theoretically results in the person first performing (choos-

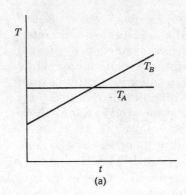

(a)

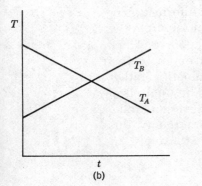

(b)

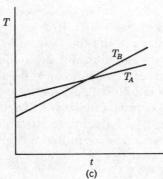

(c)

Figure 5–6. Schematic representation of the five patterns of changes in the strength of tendency of T_A and T_B from time 1 to time 2 that would result in a change from activity A to activity B. (From Atkinson & Birch, 1970, p. 6.)

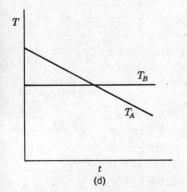

(d)

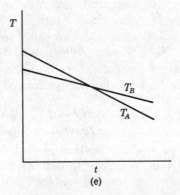

(e)

ing) activity A, and then activity B. Furthermore, they attempt to determine the rate of change from one activity to another.

Included among the instigating forces, or forces that augment behavioral tendencies, are factors as diverse as increasing deprivation or the ringing of a telephone. These examples are conceptually similar, for the instigating stimulus remains, and behavioral tendencies are expected to grow in the face of persisting stimuli associated with rewards. Of course, the sudden appearance and then removal of an external object, such as an attractive member of the opposite sex, also may produce immediate increments in strength of motivation. Actions that decrease motivation include consummatory behavior (goal attainment) or displacement and substitute activities. The latter represent "families" of consummatory behaviors (or, using Lewinian terminology, systems that are in dynamic communication). Atkinson and Birch also discuss inhibitory forces that produce behavioral resistance, such as anticipated punishment.

Even the relatively simple analysis shown in Figure 5–6 leads to some interesting psychological insights. For example, in situation a, T_A is not decreasing in strength. But activity A will cease to be exhibited in behavior, for it gives way to the even stronger activity B. This is likely, however, to be a temporary suppression, and the person is expected to return to activity A once T_B is diminished. On the other hand, in situations b and e, the strength of T_A is decreasing, and activity A would not be likely to reappear at a later date. Situations a, b, and e, therefore, are phenotypically alike, although the underlying or genotypical motivational dynamics are quite disparate and have differential implications for subsequent action.

ACHIEVEMENT MOTIVATION AND ECONOMIC DEVELOPMENT

Numerous sociological and anthropological investigations of achievement motivation have proceeded outside the laboratory. As already indicated, foremost among these was the monumental attempt by McClelland (1961) to relate achievement motivation to economic growth.

McClelland's contentions were guided by findings of Winterbottom (1953) relating need for achievement to child-rearing practices. Winterbottom found that boys relatively high in need for achievement had mothers who retrospectively reported that they expected their sons to be self-reliant and independent at an early age. These mothers believed that their sons should know their way around the city, make their own friends, and the like, at an earlier age than mothers whose sons were low in need for achievement.

McClelland reasoned that the relationship between early independence training and the growth of achievement motivation is pertinent to the linkage postulated by Weber (1904) between the Protestant Reformation and the growth of capitalism. McClelland (1955) noted:

> In the first place, he [Weber] stresses, as others have, that the essence of the Protestant revolt against the Catholic church was a shift from a reliance on an institution to a greater reliance on the self, so far as salvation was concerned. ... As Weber describes it, we have here what seems to be an example of a revolution in ideas which should increase the need for independence training. Certainly Protestant parents, if they were to prepare their children

adequately for increased self-reliance so far as religious matters were concerned, would tend to stress increasingly often and early the necessity for the
child's not depending on adult assistance but seeking his own "salvation."
In the second place, Weber's description of the kind of personality type
which the Protestant Reformation produced is startingly similar to the picture we would draw of a person with high achievement motivation. He notes
that Protestant working girls seemed to work harder and longer, that they
saved their money for long-range goals, that Protestant entrepreneurs seemed
to come to the top more often in the business world despite the initial advantages of wealth many Catholic families had, and so forth. . . .

What then drove him to such prodigious feats of business organization
and development? Weber feels that such a man "gets nothing out of his
wealth for himself, except the irrational sense of having done his job well."
This is exactly how we define the achievement motive. . . . Is it possible that
the Protestant Reformation involves a repetition at a social and historical
level of the linkage that Winterbottom found between independence training and n Achievement among some mothers and their sons in a small town
in Michigan in 1950?

DIAGRAM 5–1

Hypothetical Series of Events Relating Self-Reliance Values with Economic and Technological Development

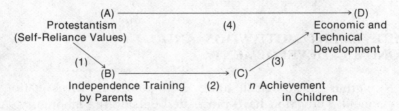

The hypothesis can be diagrammed rather simply [see Diagram 5–1]. In
terms of this diagram Weber was chiefly concerned with the linkage between A and D, with the way in which Protestantism led to a change in the
spirit of capitalism in the direction of a speeded-up, high-pressure, competitive business economy. But the manner in which he describes this relationship strongly suggests that the linkage by which these two events are connected involves steps B and C, namely a change in family socialization practices which in turn increased the number of individuals with high achievement motivation. Thus a full statement of the hypothesis would be that
Protestantism produced an increased stress on independence training which
produced higher achievement motivation which produced more vigorous
entrepreneurial activity and rapid economic development. (pp. 44–46)

The diagram above indicates four relationships McClelland has
examined: (1) Protestantism and early independence training; (2) early
independence training and need for achievement; (3) need for achievement and economic growth; and (4) Protestantism and economic growth.
At this time, the relationship between religious training and child-rearing
practices (1) and the relationship between child-rearing practices and
achievement development (2) remain indeterminate. McClelland cited
evidence available at the time his book was written that Protestant
families expect earlier mastery from their sons than Catholic families,

and that early independence training produces concerns about achievement. Since that time these relationships have been called into question (see the next section of this chapter).

The great bulk of McClelland's personal investigations concern relationships (3) — need for achievement and economic growth — and (4) — Protestantism and economic growth. To investigate the hypothesis that Protestantism is related to economic growth, McClelland (1961) compared the per capita electric power consumption of predominantly Protestant societies with that of Catholic countries. McClelland contended that per capita usage of electricity is the best index of economic growth (rather than, for example, the more widely used index of gross national product) because these data are available, the figures are in comparable units between countries, and modern societies are based upon the use of electrical energy. The findings of this investigation are shown in Table 5–8, which shows the consumption of electricity per capita and the predicted electrical output based on the natural resources of the country. Deviations between the actual and expected consumption are computed and are related to the religious affiliation of the country. The table reveals that the level of economic activity (as measured by McClelland) of Protestant countries exceeds that of Catholic countries.

The crucial question McClelland then attempted to answer was whether the association between Protestantism and economic activity is mediated by achievement needs. He hypothesized that achievement needs precede economic growth and he gathered indicators of these two variables over a wide array of societies and historical periods.

A major problem faced by McClelland and his colleagues was how to assess the level of achievement motivation of a society. Perhaps TAT stories could be collected and scored for a representative sample of the population, or from a sample business entrepreneurs (who, McClelland believes, are most responsible for economic advancement). But this is not possible when examining the achievement motivation of earlier societies. To assess the level of achievement concerns in past generations, McClelland and his colleagues gathered samples of the written products of the society. They then scored the samples for achievement motivation, using the general procedure mentioned earlier in the chapter. Frequently the written material is from children's readers, but folk-tales, speeches of the leaders of the countries, poems and songs, and even the shapes of lines on vases have been used as indicators of achievement motivation.

In a large study of 22 contemporary societies, for example, McClelland compared the difference between the expected and actual gains in electric power consumption per capita between 1929 and 1950 as a function of achievement motivation. Achievement needs were assessed from children's readers published in 1925. The data revealed a dramatically high correlation ($r = .53$) between the achievement score of a society in 1925 and subsequent economic growth.

In a similar manner, achievement needs assessed from children's readers published in 1950 predicted economic growth from 1952 to 1958. Table 5–9 shows the countries in the latter study, the level of achievement

**TABLE 5–8   AVERAGE PER CAPITA CONSUMPTION OF ELECTRIC POWER,
CORRECTED FOR NATURAL RESOURCES, FOR PROTESTANT AND
CATHOLIC COUNTRIES OUTSIDE THE TROPICS OF
CANCER AND CAPRICORN**

Countries	Consumption of Electricity kwh/cap (1950)	Predicted Output kwh/cap	Difference (Predicted– Obtained)	Rank of Difference
Protestant				
Norway	5,310	3,379	1,931	1
Canada	4,120	3,186	964	4
Sweden	2,580	903	1,672	2
United States	2,560	2,328	232	9
Switzerland	2,230	1,253	977	3
New Zealand	1,600	1,526	74	11
Australia	1,160	1,598	– 438	20
United Kingdom	1,115	2,631	–1,566	24
Finland	1,000	652	348	6
Union S. Africa	890	1,430	–540	21
Holland	725	724	1	15
Denmark	500	74	426	5
Average	*1,983*	*1,645*	*338*	*10.1*
Catholic				
Belgium	986	1,959	–973	22
Austria	900	620	280	8
France	790	989	–199	16
Czechoslovakia	730	1,734	–1,004	23
Italy	535	227	308	7
Chile	484	764	–280	18
Poland	375	2,007	–1,632	25
Hungry	304	628	–324	19
Ireland	300	154	146	10
Argentina	255	251	4	14
Spain	225	459	–264	17
Uruguay	165	154	11	18
Portugal	110	82	28	12
Average	*474*	*771*	*–208*	*15.7*

(Adapted from McClelland, 1961, p. 51.)

concerns in 1950, and the deviation from the expected rate of growth. The index of achievement motivation in 1950 did not predict growth rate from 1929 to 1950, but did predict development from 1952 to 1958. Thus, McClelland contends that achievement motivation precedes economic development.

A similar examination was made of the growth and decline of the Greek empire. Level of achievement needs was ascertained by scoring the literary content of leading writers of that era. Three periods of economic growth and decline were identified: 900–475 B.C. (growth), 475–362 B.C. (climax), and 362–100 B.C. (decline). The respective achievement scores in the three periods were 4.74, 2.71, and 1.35. Thus, the

TABLE 5–9 RATE OF GROWTH IN ELECTRICAL OUTPUT (1952–1958) AND NATIONAL n ACHIEVEMENT LEVELS IN 1950

Deviations from Expected Growth Rate in Standard Score Units

	National n Achievement Levels (1950)		Above Expectation	National n Achievement Levels (1950)		Below Expectation
	3.62	Turkey	+1.38			
	2.71	India	+1.12			
	2.38	Australia	+ .42			
	2.33	Israel	+1.18			
	2.33	Spain	+ .01			
High n	2.29	Pakistan	+2.75			
Achievement	2.29	Greece	+1.18	3.38	Argentina	− .56
	2.29	Canada	+ .06	2.71	Lebanon	− .67
	2.24	Bulgaria	+1.37	2.38	France	− .24
	2.24	U.S.A.	+ .47	2.33	U. So. Africa	− .06
	2.14	West Germany	+ .53	2.29	Ireland	− .41
	2.10	U.S.S.R.	+1.62	2.14	Tunisia	−1.87
	2.10	Portugal	+ .76	2.10	Syria	− .25
	1.95	Iraq	+ .29	2.05	New Zealand	− .29
	1.86	Austria	+ .38	1.86	Uruguay	− .75
	1.67	U.K.	+ .17	1.81	Hungary	− .62
	1.57	Mexico	+ .12	1.71	Norway	− .77
	.86	Poland	+1.26	1.62	Sweden	− .64
				1.52	Finland	− .08
Low n				1.48	Netherlands	− .15
Achievement				1.33	Italy	− .57
				1.29	Japan	− .04
				1.20	Switzerland	−1.92
				1.19	Chile	−1.81
				1.05	Denmark	− .89
				.57	Algeria	− .83
				.43	Belgium	−1.65

Correlation of n Achievement level (1950) × deviations from expected growth rate = .43, $p < .01$.

(From McClelland, 1961, p. 100.)

period of climax was preceded by the highest achievement score, and the decrease in economic development followed the decrease in achievement needs.

The reader might now be wondering about the achievement motivation in our culture. Figure 5–7 indicates that achievement needs in America, ascertained from children's readers, increased from 1800 to 1910. Since 1910 the indicators of achievement concerns have steadily decreased. Does this hint that our economy also is going to decline? Figure 5–7 shows that the patent index, one indicator of unique accomplishments, also is falling. The conclusions from this study by de Charms and Moeller (1962) are evident.

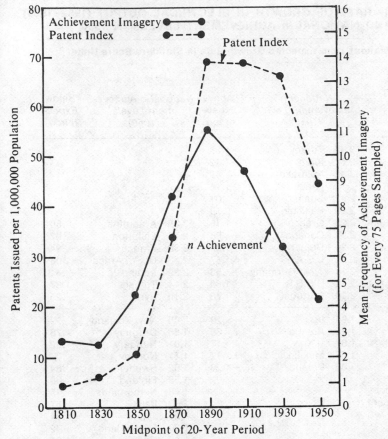

Figure 5–7. Mean frequency of achievement imagery in children's readers and the patent index in the United States, 1800–1950. (Adapted from de Charms and Moeller, 1962, p. 139.)

Developmental Antecedents

The American research tradition in developmental psychology has been to search for the experiential (social) determinants of personality, and has focused upon early parental interactions as the prime influence of later behavior. McClelland (1951) contended that because affective arousal is more intense during infancy, and because the younger child does not make detailed discriminations, "affective associations formed in early childhood are apt to be strong and very resistant to unlearning or forgetting" (p. 257). These caveats dominated the search for the antecedents of achievement needs.

Two early investigations provided the models for the great bulk of subsequent research in this area. In one of the studies that was previously mentioned, Winterbottom (1953; reported in Atkinson, 1958a) obtained TAT achievement scores for a group of boys 8 to 10 years old and also interviewed their mothers to ascertain prior parental attitudes towards independence training. Winterbottom reported that the mothers of sons high in achievement needs expected earlier independence than did the mothers of boys scoring low in need for achievement.

A second influential study, conducted by Rosen and D'Andrade (1959), related the present *behaviors* of parents to the need achievement scores of their sons, rather than relying upon parental retrospective reports. In an experimental setting, children were given tasks to complete, but the parents could interact with the children and come to their aid. Rosen and D'Andrade found that the parents of the highly achievement-oriented sons were more involved in the task, gave more reward and punishment, and had higher expectations than the parents of children scoring low in need for achievement. They therefore contended that achievement training (doing something well) rather than independence training (doing something by oneself) is the important antecedent of the development of achievement needs.

Unfortunately, the high expectations spawned by these influential studies have not been met. Subsequent research produced as many nonconfirmatory as confirmatory results regarding the alleged influence of achievement or independence training on the development of achievement needs (see, for example, Callard, 1964; Chance, 1961). Because of the conflicting data and some additional cross-cultural discrepancies, McClelland (1961) proposed an "optimal level" theory, suggesting that independence training, if too early, would be just as inhibitory on the development of achievement needs as overly protective parental behavior. Again, however, research investigations have failed to yield clear support for this position (see, for example, Bartlett and Smith, 1966; Smith, 1969).

There are enormous complexities within the social learning research studies. For example, the encouragement of achievement and independence is likely to be intertwined with other aspects of child rearing, such as general permissiveness or restrictiveness, beliefs about the child's competence, physical affection and reward giving, general affective climate and warmth in the home, parental expectations, and so on. All of the above, at one time or another, have been found to relate to achievement needs by some investigators, while other investigators have reported no relationship between the variable and achievement needs. Finding unambiguous child-rearing correlates will probably require a conceptual foundation that guides the investigator to particular and specific antecedents. Such theoretical guidelines have been relatively absent in child-rearing research.

There are additional problems in the child-rearing studies. For example, it has been documented that parental practices are responsive to the behavior of the child. Feld (1967) found that during their sons' adolescence the mothers of boys scoring low in achievement needs were particularly concerned about independence. In addition, across the many socialization experiments the subject populations differ in social class, culture, and sex of the child. Behaviors classified as restrictive in one social class may be considered permissive in another. Because there are no pre-established standards for the variable under study, inconclusive results are likely to emerge when heterogeneous samples are used.

In sum, it is intuitively reasonable to believe that what takes place in the home influences the achievement dispositions of the child. But the pertinent research is plagued by a variety of problems, and at present the social antecedents of the need for achievement have not been identified.

Cognitive Development

The cognitive approach to development seeks to identify universal developmental processes, rather than searching for the child-rearing antecedents that produce individual differences. In one exemplary approach, Heckhausen and Roelofsen (1962) contended that the development of achievement-related needs requires that the child be able to "direct the pleasure or the disappointment after success or failure. . . at the self, so that with success the child experiences pleasure about his competence and with failure experiences shame about his incompetence" (p. 378). Thus, Heckhausen and Roelofsen suggested the development of self-attributions is a necessary antecedent to achievement strivings. They also contended that such attributional processes emerge around the age of three.

In another cognitive-developmental study making use of causal attributions, Weiner and Peter (1973) examined evaluative judgments of achievement actions. They had subjects imagine that children in a classroom had been assigned a puzzle to complete. The children were described as high or low in effort expenditure and as high or low in ability. In addition, the puzzles were described as completed or not completed (outcome information). The subjects were presented all eight possible combinations of information (2 levels of effort × 2 levels of ability × 2 levels of outcome). They then were asked to evaluate the hypothetical pupils, with their evaluations ranging from +5 (highest reward) to −5 (greatest punishment). Thus, for example, the subjects rewarded or punished a pupil described as high in effort, low in ability, and successful. The subjects ranged in age from 4 to 18.

Weiner and Peter (1973) report that the relationship between achievement evaluation and effort expenditure is influenced by cognitive growth (see Figure 5–8). Figure 5–8 reveals that reward for positive effort increases with age, while punishment for a lack of effort increases until the age of 12 and then decreases. Overall, effort ascriptions were most influential in determining the evaluations of children ages 10 to 12.

Weiner and Peter (1973) also report that among the younger children achievement evaluation is determined primarily by outcome — success is rewarded while failure is punished (see Figure 5–9). Perceived effort expenditure initially plays only a minor role in the evaluative judgment. However, the differential effects of outcome versus effort information gradually recede, and, among the 10- to 12-year-olds, effort is more influential than outcome in the allocation of reward and punishment.

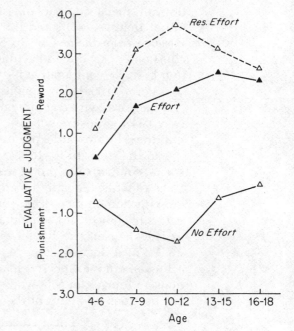

Figure 5–8. Reward for positive achievement effort, punishment for a lack of effort, and the resultant of the reward for effort minus punishment for lack of effort as a function of age. (From Weiner & Peter, 1973, p. 300.)

Among the older subjects, however, the order of importance, or weighting, of these two factors reverses, although effort continues to be an important cue for judgments. In sum, there apparently is a general sequence of development that influences judgments of achievement actions and, perhaps, achievement strivings.

A different cognitive analysis of achievement has been outlined by Veroff (1969). Veroff proposes three stages in the development of achievement strivings: first, an intrapersonal competition, or autonomous, stage in which the child competes with self; second, an interpersonal competi-

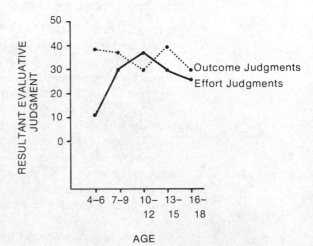

Figure 5–9. Resultant achievement outcome and effort judgments as a function of age. (From Weiner & Peter, 1973, p. 301.)

tion, or social comparison, stage in which competition is with others rather than the self; and third, an integration of the two prior stages. Passage from Stage One to Stage Two typically takes place when the child enters school and acquires the ability to use social norm information to make comparative judgments.

Veroff (1969) also demonstrated that the preference for intermediate risk increases with cognitive maturation. Younger children tend to prefer easy tasks with sure success, but with increasing cognitive maturation, children shift toward a preference for intermediate difficulty. It is tempting to link the ability to use social norm information, and the onset of social comparisons processes, with the desire to select more difficult tasks. That is, the shift toward intermediate difficulty might indicate the growing importance of personal feedback and self-knowledge as motivators of choice, and be mediated by the ability to make self-attributions, as Heckhausen and Roelofsen contended.

A next logical step in the cognitive-developmental analysis of achievement is to specify clearly the implications of achievement evaluations and stages for achievement-related actions and to incorporate these implications into current theoretical frameworks.

Achievement Change

The data reported by McClelland (1961) provide more than suggestive evidence that need achievement is an important factor influencing economic development. Therefore, it would be of utmost importance to determine whether the economic growth of a nation could be accelerated by increasing the achievement motivation of some members of the society. McClelland and Winter (1969) state:

> The book [*The Achieving Society*] ends with the scientist's traditional hope that the knowledge so painstakingly collected will somehow be useful in helping man shape his destiny. At the time it was little more than a pious hope, since it was not at all clear how a developmental specialist or a leader of a new nation could make use of knowledge accumulated about the achievement motive. (pp. 1–2)

Indeed, if achievement-related dispositions are formed during early childhood, and if they are relatively enduring, then attempts to modify an adult's level of achievement needs are fruitless. The only practical way to alter the achievement needs of the members of a society and, as a possible consequence, enhance the economic development of that society, would be to change child-rearing practices and then wait some time to determine whether the changes were effective.

This is a somewhat pessimistic position, rather incompatible with the optimism of American environmentalism. Although McClelland originally accepted the work of Winterbottom (1953), he subsequently disregarded her findings and initiated short-term motivational change programs designed to increase the level of achievement needs of the participants (see McClelland & Winter, 1969).

To increase achievement needs, McClelland and Winter (1969) designed a three- to six-week training course in which the participants become acquainted with the thoughts and actions associated with achievement behavior. They learn to score TATs for achievement motivation, and they are taught the beneficial consequences of intermediate risk-taking and future-time perspective. In addition, the participants undergo a program of self-study in which they describe their life goals, values, self-image, and so forth. The training program assists in the establishment and setting of career goals, as well as suggesting means to assess progress toward these goals. These program "inputs" are in a warm and permissive atmosphere in the company of others, who hopefully will become part of a new reference group. McClelland (1965) describes this as an eclectic method, using all the psychological principles believed to be effective in behavioral change.

At this time the effectiveness of motive change training is uncertain. Positive results with underachievers (Kolb, 1965), school teachers (de Charms, 1972; see pp. 255–256), and businessmen (McClelland & Winter, 1969) have been reported. For example, Kolb (1965) had underachieving boys participate in an achievement change program at a summer camp. The participating students had IQs above 120, but were performing below average in school. The effectiveness of the program, assessed by grade point average, is shown in Figure 5–10. In addition to being classified in the experimental (training) or control group, the students were subdivided according to their socioeconomic class (SES). Figure 5–10 indicates that both participating and nonparticipating students unex-

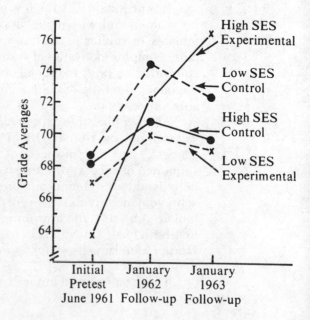

Figure 5–10. School grade averages in pretest and follow-up years as a function of socioeconomic class and participation in the achievement training program. (From Kolb, 1965, p. 789.)

pectedly exhibit GPA increments. However, only the high SES students in the program continued to show academic progress after the first year. Kolb (1965) contends that the values of the subculture of the low SES participants are at variance with the values instilled by the program. These reference group values apparently hinder later development.

However, data that question the effectiveness of change programs also have been reported (see McClelland and Winter, 1969), and the amount of research is small. There certainly is some hope that achievement behavior can be altered, given appropriate intervention techniques. However, much further evidence is needed before this hope can be accepted as truth.

Achievement Needs among Females

McClelland (1958) contended that for an instrument to have validity in assessing motive strength, it must reflect temporary arousal states of the organism. That is, like a thermometer, if the "motive temperature" is turned on, then the instrument should register a high reading. Achievement motive arousal, accomplished via failure induction or "ego-involving" instructions, indeed generates higher TAT need achievement scores than those registered under non-arousal conditions. But this is true only for males; females have not exhibited motive score differences between arousal and neutral conditions. Therefore, it was believed that the TAT motive measure was not valid for females, and females tended to be neglected in achievement research. Of course, some studies did include females and combined the data from both sexes, but an equally large number of research investigations either did not test females or reported systematic data for the male, but not the female, subjects.

It is uncertain why the few motive arousal studies were unsuccessful for women and why males appear to yield more systematic data than females in studies of achievement motivation. Achievement may be a more complex motivational system for females than for males because of cultural inhibitions and social norms that at one time restricted females to the home. But little has been done to substantiate this intuitively reasonable supposition.

Another plausible explanation of the mysterious findings for females was offered by Horner (1968). Horner postulated a motive to "avoid success," or a "fear of success," for females. She suggested that as a consequence of success, the threat of social rejection and fear concerning a perceived lack of femininity are aroused in women. These fears inhibit achievement strivings. To test this notion, Horner (1968) had male and female subjects write four-minute stories to this cue: "At the end of the first-term final, Anne finds herself at the top of her medical school class." Horner found much greater fear-of-success imagery in females' responses than in males'.

These data caused immediate excitement among many psychologists and others. The data meshed with the current feminist movement and were immediately incorporated into courses on the psychology of women. But the generated enthusiasm may have been more a symptom of an extant void and the desire for understanding than a consequence of establishing a scientific truth. Subsequent research has revealed that males exhibit as much fear of success in projective imagery as females (see, for example, Brown, Jennings & Vanik, 1974; Tresemer, 1974). Thus, the findings first reported by Horner are now very much in doubt.

There are some other interesting sex differences reported in the literature on achievement motivation that suggest future research directions. It has been firmly established that females generally have a lower expectancy of success than males (Crandall, 1969). How such a bias is formed and what can be done to alter it are questions for the future.

The Social Context of Achievement

Thus far we have discussed achievement striving as if it were an asocial phenomenon — one individual attempting to accomplish some task. However, achievement strivings typically take place in a social context. Thus, cooperation and competition, group formation, and group goals and performance, to name just a few topics, also deserve attention. In the present chapter two such areas will be examined: group or team formation and some social consequences of achievement strivings.

Group Formation

Many studies of group formation concern coalitions, or individuals banding together for mutual benefit. In research on coalition formation, a dominant paradigm, or method of investigation, has emerged, as well as a clear pattern of data. Specifically, in this paradigm three subjects are assigned disparate strengths of a "resource" that is instrumental to the attainment of a monetary reward. The resource values are represented by the numbers 2, 3, and 4. These resource values multiply the number that is tossed on a die in a simple, luck-determined board game (see Caplow, 1968; Kelley & Arrowood, 1962). The person with the highest value of resources is thus most likely to win. The experimental rules specify that following the assignment of the resources, two of the players must then join together against a third; the resources possessed by the players are additively combined when a coalition forms.

The research investigations indicate that each of the participants generally wishes to coalesce with another player. Both the 4 and 3 resource individuals desire to combine with 2, while the 2 resource player prefers to unite with 3. Thus a 3+2 versus 4 division occurs the majority of the time. A theory formulated by Caplow (1968) suggests that both 3 and 2 believe this partnership maximizes their personal gains by allowing them to vanquish the stronger 4. And neither 3 nor 2 prefers to join with 4, who would be the dominant member of any dyad. Paradoxically, by possessing the greatest resources, 4 often is placed at a disadvantage given this particular setting.

It is intuitively evident, however, that if the motivational determinants of the coalition choice were altered, then the preferred coalition also would change. For example, suppose that the resources possessed by the three participants represented their degree of skill at some craft (again symbolized by the values 2, 3, and 4). Furthermore, assume that individuals want to maximize the quality of their product. In this situation, 3 and 2 may both prefer to be with 4, the most highly skilled individual, whereas 4 is likely to prefer 3 rather than 2. Hence, having the greatest resources would be a benefit in the formation of an alliance. On the other hand, quite different subgroups are likely to form in a work setting that fosters cooperation among all the participants. For example, consider a situation in which three movers are lifting a heavy table, and two must work together at one end. If it is known that damage to the table will result in the forfeiture of all pay, then 3 and 2 may join on one end, opposite 4. Given these circumstances, 4 will probably agree with the subgrouping.

To demonstrate that coalition formation is responsive to motivational influences, an experiment was conducted by Folkes and Weiner (1977) in which the determinants of coalition preferences were manipulated. In one of the experimental conditions the typical paradigm was repeated, with a financial reward (an "extrinsic" motivator) promised to the winner(s) of a luck-determined game. In three other conditions the resources were specified as the abilities of the participants. Because the stated resource was ability, it was presumed that achievement-related sources of motivation would be activated. As already discussed, in achievement contexts individuals prefer to engage in tasks of intermediate difficulty. Hence, in the ability conditions, 3 and 2 should again prefer to be together, but 4 should desire to remain alone. This division results in competition being as equal as possible between all the participants. In two of the ability conditions a high or a low monetary source of motivation was also included. Thus, group formation was presumed to be determined by both intrinsic and extrinsic sources of motivation in these two conditions.

The preferences of the players in the four motivational conditions (one intrinsic-only, two extrinsic-plus-intrinsic, and one extrinsic-only source of motivation) are shown in Figure 5–11. Figure 5–11 indicates that the 2+3 coalition (left side of the figure) is highly preferred by all the members of the triad, given only achievement as the source of motivation (the intrinsic-only condition). However, this coalition is disliked by the high resource player (4), given only extrinsic rewards. The 2+4 coalition is next most preferred, given only achievement as a source of motivation, but is especially disliked by the medium resource player (3), given an extrinsic reward. And the 3+4 coalition is disliked by all the participants, given only intrinsic reward, but is especially disliked by the low resource player (2), given the pure monetary reward condition. In sum, the three

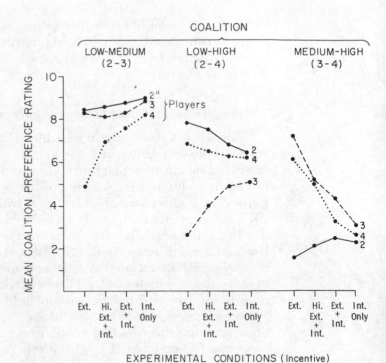

Figure 5–11. Coalition preference ratings as a function of the possessed resources and the motivational condition. "Ext." refers to extrinsic motivators, "Int." to intrinsic ones. (Adapted from Folkes & Weiner, 1977.)
[a]Indicates the desire of player 2 to join with player 3 in the various experimental conditions.

resource players most agree upon the desirability of the various coalitions in the achievement-only motivational condition, with the order of preference progressing away from intermediate difficulty, i.e., 2+3, 2+4, 3+4. There is least agreement in the extrinsic-only motivational condition, for no one wants to be excluded from the team.

In addition, Figure 5–11 shows that the desires of the players are differentially influenced by a change in the characteristics of the game. The low resource player is least affected, since that player always prefers to join with 3. Conversely, the high resource player is greatly affected by the changing motivational conditions, since that player prefers to be alone in the achievement condition (i.e., rates highly the 2+3 coalition) but wants to be with either player 2 or 3 in the monetary conditions.

In sum, given only extrinsic motivation such as money, a 2+3 coalition forms, but the union exists in the face of interpersonal conflict because player 4 is dissatisfied. In contrast, when only intrinsic sources of motivation determine coalition formation, there is agreement among all the players that a 2+3 coalition is best for all.

Given only extrinsic rewards, such as money, the motivational system might be considered "closed," as discussed in the chapter on Freud. That is, there is a fixed amount of incentive, and as the acquisition of that incentive increases for any player, it must decrease for the other player(s).

On the other hand, the intrinsic or achievement motivational systems might be considered "open." The amount of reward is not fixed, and if the incentive gained by one player increases, it need not decrease among the remaining players.

Positive Social Consequences of Success

Success is a positive goal for which most individuals in our culture strive. There are many positive personal consequences of success, such as increased anticipations of future success and feelings of pride and competence. In addition, success has positive social consequences as well. Following goal attainment there is a "warm glow of success" (Isen, 1970) — successful individuals act more benevolently towards others.

In a series of studies demonstrating the "warm glow" phenomenon, Isen and her colleagues (Isen, 1970; Isen, Horn & Rosenhan, 1973) found that people who succeeded were more likely to contribute to a charity and to help someone in need of aid than individuals without a prior success experience. Isen (1970) therefore concluded that there is a "relationship between success and doing nice things" (p. 300). Subsequent investigations revealed that "feeling good" generally produces positive social concerns. For example, it has been reported that individuals finding a coin in a phone booth are more likely later to help others (Isen & Levin, 1972; Levin & Isen, 1975).

The effects of failure on generosity are not entirely clear. It might be anticipated that if success increases positive social behavior, then failure should lead to selfishness and antisocial behaviors. However, it appears that individuals at times attempt to regain their status following failure and want to enhance their public image by acting in a generous manner. But the effects of failure are complex and appear to be dependent upon many factors, such as the public or private context of the situation in which the failed person is placed.

Summary

The experimental study of achievement motivation has its origins in Murray's taxonomy of need systems and his development of a projective instrument, the TAT, to infer an individual's motivational concerns. The TAT was refined by McClelland and his colleagues for use as a research tool to assess the strength of achievement needs. Although this measure has met with some success, and has yet to be supplanted by other instruments, it has many shortcomings. Of particular concern are the low test-retest and internal consistency reliabilities.

The stage of TAT validation gave way to the development of a theory of achievement motivation. This theory was formulated by Atkinson and includes individual differences in achievement needs among the determinants of behavior. The theory specifies that achievement-related behavior is a result of a conflict between a hope of success (approach motivation) and a fear of failure (avoidance motivation). The approach and avoidance tendencies, in turn, are a function of achievement-related needs (need for achievement and anxiety about failure), the expectancy of success and failure, and the incentive value of success and failure. A special assumption of the model is that the incentive value of achievement tasks is determined by the probability of success.

The main derivation of this theory is that individuals high in resultant achievement needs are particularly attracted to tasks of intermediate difficulty, while those low in achievement needs avoid tasks that have a probability of success near .50. Investigations by Moulton, Feather, and Atkinson and Litwin, employing respectively the dependent measures of level of aspiration, persistence, and choice, support the general hypothesis that differential attraction towards tasks of intermediate difficulty is displayed by groups high and low in achievement motivation. However, persons low in achievement needs do not avoid tasks of intermediate difficulty, thus contradicting Atkinson's theory. Rather, they also are attracted to intermediate probability, but less so than individuals high in achievement needs. A general attraction for tasks of intermediate difficulty is displayed in the formation of groups, as well as when a single individual confronts an achievement-related task.

The risk-preference data also have been interpreted from an informational point of view. It has been contended that achievement choice is in part motivated by a desire to discover one's level of competence. Tasks of intermediate difficulty provide the most information about the performer, while easy or difficult tasks merely tend to confirm knowledge about the environment.

Achievement striving also has been studied outside of the laboratory. McClelland has shown that an increase in the level of achievement needs of a society precedes economic development, while decreases in achievement concerns produce subsequent economic decline. Because of the apparent importance of achievement needs for economic progress, there have been attempts to alter achievement motivation. While some promising research findings have been reported, it is still too early to assess the efficacy of these achievement change programs.

The child-rearing antecedents that promote achievement strivings have been examined. Early research findings suggesting that either training a child to do something well or independence training is the cause of high achievement motivation have not been substantiated. More recent investigations have focused upon the cognitive precursors of achievement strivings, and some promising future directions have been uncovered. Finally, the relation between achievement strivings among females and a "fear of success" apparently has not been upheld.

It was suggested previously that drive theorists demonstrated that motivational psychologists could proceed in a scientific and mathematical manner, while Lewin and his colleagues directed attention to the subject matter motivational theorists should investigate. The study of achievement motivation was guided by both these methodological and content concerns. Investigators adopted the procedures and mathematical orientation developed by Hullians, but applied this approach to the study of complex human behaviors observed in "everyday" life. Thus, achievement theory represents the most precise of the "cognitive" motivational models.

Chapter Six

SOCIAL LEARNING THEORY AND PERSONAL RESPONSIBILITY

Introduction

The theories of motivation discussed thus far, particularly those evolving from the observation of human behavior, have stressed the importance of intrapersonal dynamics. Motivators labelled libido, drive, tension, or need activate the organism, with pleasure attained when the goal is reached. Goal attainment often involves the re-establishment of internal equilibrium. Furthermore, there are inhibitors to goal attainment, such as defense mechanisms, barriers in the environment, or fear of failing, that create conflict and frustration. The individual thus is portrayed as in a constant state of battle, attempting to attain happiness in the face of repeated, and often unattainable, internal commands and wishes.

The conceptualizations of Freud and Lewin and, to a lesser extent, Hull and Atkinson often invoke concepts that are not clearly linked with manipulable or measurable observed events. In opposition to these conceptions, a school of psychology developed that stressed situational, rather than intrapersonal, determinants of behavior and relied upon carefully documented principles of learning to explain motivated behavior. This school is called "social learning theory" and encompasses psychologists with rather dissimilar concerns. Nonetheless, all the theorists assume that:

1. The most important determinants of behavior are learned. Genetic and biological factors merely set limits on possible learning experiences.
2. Behavior is situationally specific. That is, "people behave as they do in response to the demands and characteristics of the particular situation that they are in at the moment" (Liebert & Spiegler, 1974, p. 310).

229

3. The essential influences on behavior reside in the external world.
4. A theory of motivation should use few constructs, make a minimum number of inferences, and be guided by experimental data.

Social learning theory is an outgrowth of the behavioristic position associated with John Watson and the neobehaviorism of Hull, Spence, and Dollard and Miller (1950). However, in contrast to classical behaviorism and neobehaviorism, social learning theorists advocate that mental processes and higher-order cognitions influence action (see Diagram 3–3, p. 89). Individuals are believed to learn by means of imitation, attend to appropriate information, discriminate between reinforcing and non-reinforcing environments, develop expectancies concerning the likelihood of goal attainment, and construe the world in subjectively meaningful ways.

In this chapter the theoretical approaches of Bandura and Walters (1963) and Mischel (1968, 1973) are briefly discussed. These psychologists are among the most influential of the social learning theorists. A theory proposed by Julian Rotter (1954) is then examined in detail. In addition to being a major figure in social learning theory, Rotter is an expectancy-value theorist; a review of his conception is, therefore, most appropriate in this section of the book. Rotter also has made fundamental contributions to the study of personal responsiblity. This work is discussed in conjunction with a number of related areas of psychological investigation focusing on personal responsibility. Free will, or perceived freedom, is perhaps the most popular current topic in the field of motivation and thus deserves extensive examination.

Observational Learning

It is evident that individuals learn through observation and imitate the behavior of others. Any number of complex human activities, including, for example, driving a car, hitting a baseball, or making a proper introduction, clearly are facilitated by observing others as they perform these activities. However, such an obvious principle of learning was swept aside when the behavioristic position ruled psychology. Behaviorists, guided by the tenets of operant learning, believed that for learning to occur the organism must make a response, and that response must be followed by a reinforcement. Purely cognitive learning was not part of the psychology of Skinner or other psychologists in the classical behavioristic tradition.

The acquisition of knowledge through the observation of others ("models") was first championed by Bandura and Walters (1963). Because one learns by watching others, the learning is truly a "social" learning. According to Liebert and Spiegler (1974), observational learning involves three stages. First, there must be exposure to a model. However, mere exposure does not ensure learning, for the individual must attend to the actions of the model. Thus, a second stage is proposed in which knowledge of the model's behavior is acquired. Finally, the observations may be accepted or rejected by the individual as a guide to later actions.

What is acquired need not be manifested in action. Thus, social learning theorists distinguish between learning and performance, or knowing and doing. This distinction was articulated much earlier in the history of psychology by Edward Tolman. Tolman was responsible for the study of latent learning, which was discussed previously in Chapter Three. Animals in the latent learning studies apparently "knew" the correct path to the goal region, but only performed that action, or exhibited their knowledge, when food was placed at the goal. Thus, the learning was "latent" or hidden, ready to emerge given the appropriate environmental conditions.

The acquisition-performance distinction, as well as the influence of observational learning on behavior, is illustrated in an oft-cited investigation by Bandura (1965). In Bandura's study, children were first shown a five-minute film that depicted a number of aggressive responses to toys, including hitting a Bobo doll and throwing objects at it. There were three experimental conditions. In one condition a child model in the film was rewarded for this behavior by an adult. In a second condition the child in the movie was punished for the aggressive responses. And in a third experimental condition the film was shown without any final adult reinforcement.

After viewing a version of the film, the children were placed in an experimental room that contained the toys depicted in the movie. They then were secretly observed, and their behavior was recorded. The data revealed that the children viewing the rewarded model were most likely to repeat his behavior, whereas the children viewing the punished model were least likely to exhibit the portrayed behavior. The modeling behavior of the children in the no-reinforcement condition fell between these groups. Subsequently, it also was demonstrated that the children in the three conditions could equally well reproduce the model's behavior when requested to do so by the experimenter. Hence, acquisition of new knowledge did not necessarily influence action, but the model's behavior was imitated by the observers when appropriate reinforcement was present. It appears that perceived rewards and punishments of a model influence performance, but not observational learning.

Researchers in the field of observational learning also distinguish between live and symbolic models. Live models are viewed directly, while symbolic models appear indirectly, through media such as radio, television, movies, or newspapers. The importance of this distinction has been documented in the study of delay of gratification. Recall that, according to Freud, delay is an ego-function and thus is determined by intrapsychic factors. Mischel (1968) contrasts this position with that of the social learning theorists:

> . . . According to the psychoanalytic theory of delay behavior, aroused impulses press for immediate discharge of tension through overt

motoric activity. . . . The psychoanalytic approach . . . leads one to seek determinants of delay behavior in such hypothetical internal events as ego organizations and energy-binding ideations. In contrast, social behavior theory . . . views manipulable social-stimulus events as the critical determinants of self-controlling behavior. (p. 153)

One of the "manipulable social-stimulus events" that Mischel has examined is the role of a model. In another oft-cited experiment, Bandura and Mischel (1965) first identified children who were willing to delay reward, and others who sought immediate gratification. These children then observed a model displaying behavior inconsistent with their own delay preferences. For example, the high delay children observed a model choosing cheaper, plastic chess figures without delay rather than waiting for a more attractive chess set that would be given in one week. In one condition the model was "live," while in a second treatment condition the model's responses were read rather than actually observed.

Both immediately after the model's performance and one month later, delay of gratification again was assessed. Figure 6-1, which depicts only the responses of the high delay children, indicates that their preference for immediate, less valuable rewards increased dramatically, particularly in the "live" condition. Furthermore, the influence of the model remained effective at the one-month retest period and at a related choice task (the "generalization" condition). Conversely, the children exhibiting low delay behavior displayed an increase in delay choice.

In addition to observational learning, there are other procedures and contingencies that can be established to aid in self-control. For example, one woman who had problems controlling her "cussing" fined

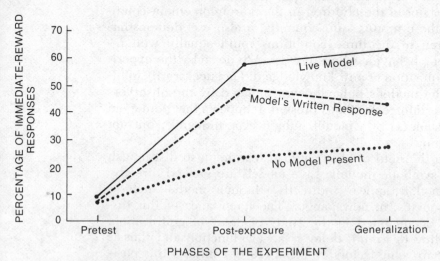

Figure 6-1. Effects of modeling on delay of gratification. Mean percentage of immediate-reward responses by high-delay children on each of three test periods for each of three experimental conditions. (Adapted from Bandura & Mischel, 1965, p. 702.)

herself a dollar every time she swore. This money was immediately put aside for charity. Other control techniques, such as putting a lock on the ice box, have been used to prevent impulsive expression. Even self-instruction or talking to oneself has been used effectively to control motoric discharge ("If I miss this shot, I will not throw my racquet"). In sum, individuals can be social engineers and gain impulse control, and such behavioral changes can be explained without appealing to intrapsychic concepts such as energy-binding hallucinations.

Aggression

The topic of aggression was discussed extensively in the previous chapters of this book. Recall Freud argued that aggression is an instinctive drive that increases in magnitude as a function of the time since it was last expressed. Furthermore, it was contended that aggressive needs could be relieved through displacement activity, and "purged" if one identified with another engaging in an aggressive display. The latter process is called "catharsis."

The so-called catharsis hypothesis leads directly into the question of whether watching television violence, for example, decreases subsequent aggressive needs and behaviors. As already indicated, there is some evidence, although scanty, supporting this position (e.g., Feshbach & Singer, 1971). In contrast to this view, social learning theorists believe that television violence provides models for the viewer to emulate. Hence, exposure to aggression is expected to increase subsequently expressed aggression.

An abundant amount of data supports the position of the observational learning theorists. For example, in one investigation, adult models acted aggressively toward a toy doll while nursery children were watching (Bandura, Ross & Ross, 1961). When the children were left to play freely, they engaged in similar aggressive behaviors, although the boys displayed more imitation of the models than did the girls.

In an investigation more directly related to the impact of television violence, Steuer, Applefield, and Smith (1971) partially controlled the television viewing of children. One-half of the children were instructed to watch a violent program, while other children viewed a non-aggressive show. Observation of the children revealed that those exposed to the television violence became more aggressive toward one another. However, as previously indicated, the effects of watching aggressive programs remain to be unambiguously documented.

Helping Behavior

The study of modeling has been extended to "pro-social," as well as antisocial, behavior. For example, research has shown that children behave more generously toward others if they previously observed a model engaging in unselfish behavior (Liebert & Poulos, 1971).

Some investigations of the effects of modeling on helping behavior have been conducted in field settings. For example, Bryan and Test (1967) examined the influence of a model on aiding a "lady in distress." These investigators stationed a female next to a car with a flat tire. Approximately one-quarter of a mile closer on the same road they placed another car with a flat tire, but this time a young man was helping to fix the flat. Compared to a control condition without a model, a significantly greater number of drivers stopped to offer the second woman assistance.

Discriminativeness of Behavior

At the start of this chapter it was indicated that social learning theory developed in opposition to the Freudian conception of behavior. First, proponents of social learning theory emphasize environmental determinants of behavior (such as the role of models), rather than intrapersonal causes. And secondly, social learning theorists contend that learning is the fundamental concept needed for the explanation of action.

These ideas have important implications for conceptions of personality traits and personality structures and their roles as causes of behavior. According to Freudian theory, a variety of observed actions may be signs of the same underlying dynamic principle. For example, both paranoid acts and an overt sexual approach toward someone of the same sex are indicators of homosexual desires; both artistic products and neurosis are signs of unexpressed sexual wishes; laughter, dreams, and war all may be expressions of aggressive drives; saving money and cleanliness reveal an "anal" personality character; and so on. Social learning theorists such as Mischel (1968, 1973) oppose this viewpoint. Mischel (1976) offers the following counterargument:

> Consider a woman who seems hostile and fiercely independent some of the time but passive, dependent, and feminine on other occasions. What is she really like? Which one of these two patterns reflects the woman that she really is? Is one pattern in the service of the other, or might both be in the service of a third motive? Must she be a really aggressive person with a facade of passivity — or is she a warm, passive-dependent woman with a surface defense of aggressiveness? Social behavior theory suggests that it is possible for her to be *all* of these — a hostile, fiercely independent, passive, dependent, feminine, aggressive, warm person all in one (Mischel, 1969). Of course which of these she is at any particular moment would not be random and capricious; it would depend on discriminative stimuli — who she is with, when, how, and much, much more. But each of these aspects of her self may be a quite genuine and real aspect of her total being . . . .
>
> Seemingly diverse behaviors do not necessarily reflect a uniform underlying motivational pattern. Instead . . . behaviors are relatively discrete and controlled by relatively independent causes and maintaining conditions (p. 86).

Adaptive Functioning

It is clear from the above quotation that social learning theorists do not expect the person to behave consistently across diverse stimulus settings. Consistency of behavior is anticipated only if the same behavior in different environmental settings will lead to the same reinforcement. Thus, for example, if aggression against father is punished, while hostile expressions toward teachers are rewarded, then overt aggression will be displayed in the latter, but not the former, setting.

Individuals, therefore, are conceptualized as highly discriminating, with capacities to identify situations in which particular responses have been rewarded or in which the same responses have been punished. This position may be summarized by the term "behavioral specificity," as opposed to the principle of "behavioral generality" espoused by Freud and trait theorists such as McClelland and Atkinson. According to social learning theorists, the causes of behavior — or why persons behave as they do — depend on the functions of the behavior in a particular setting. Furthermore, the environment in most instances does not automatically or reflexively elicit actions. Rather, persons interpret and construe their social world, or give it meaning. This meaning then provides the instigation to action.

The Trait-Situation Controversy

The opposing beliefs regarding behavioral specificity or generality have given rise to one of the most prominent issues in the contemporary study of personality — the so-called "trait-situation controversy" (Mischel, 1968). As already intimated, Mischel argues that the cross-situational generality of behavior is generally low. For example, individuals honest in one situation (during a school exam) may not be honest in another situation (when given an opportunity to steal). Mischel (1968) has summarized a great deal of information documenting that behavior is, for the most part, situationally specific. He does accept, however, that how one perceives the world, encodes information, or functions intellectually may be quite general (Mischel, 1973).

A number of psychologists have responded to the challenge posed by Mischel and have come to the defense of trait theory and the notion of underlying personality structures. These psychologists accept the belief that there are personality structures that predispose individuals to act in a similar manner across diverse environments. Many of the defenders of the trait position do not question the empirical data gathered by Mischel to document his viewpoint. Rather, they counter with any of the following arguments:

1. Not all individuals act consistently across diverse settings. However, some do! That is, there are individual differences in the generality or specificity of actions. A psychotic person, for example, may

act exactly the same regardless of the environment (Bem & Allen, 1974).

2.   There may be either generality or specificity of behavior, depending on the behavior under consideration and the environments being studied. Thus, the question of generality or specificity is an empirical one, to be decided through research investigations. For example, it has been found that behavior is relatively consistent across settings if these settings arouse ego-involvement or personal stress (Klein & Schoenfeld, 1941). On the other hand, greater specificity is observed when the settings do not promote ego-involvement.

3.   Individuals have preferred "avenues of expression." For example, an individual with high power needs might express such motivations by buying a new car, driving fast, and reading Playboy magazine. On the other hand, a different person may satisfy power motivations by rising in the business or political world and making important decisions. But any given individual typically does not engage in both these types of expression (see Winter, 1973).

4.   Consistency of behavior may be masked because of insufficient differentiations among individuals and the environmental settings. For example, there apparently may be little consistency in the behavior of individuals across two learning environments. However, if these learning environments are classified in terms of difficulty, and the individuals are classified according to their level of anxiety, it will be observed that highly anxious individuals behave in one manner given a certain type of environment, while those low in anxiety behave in a different way. This is a "moderator variable" approach, or one that expects individual differences to interact with environmental variables to account for behavior (see Alker, 1972; Bowers, 1973). That is, behavior is expected to be a function of both the person and the environment. This position, when carried to its extreme, is not inconsistent with Mischel's argument concerning the specificity of behavior.

5.   A distinction must be made between a "phenotype," or the observed behavior, and a "genotype," or the underlying reason for that behavior. Thus, for example, an individual smoking a pipe in one setting and biting his nails in another may be exhibiting different phenotypic behaviors, but they both might reflect the same underlying genotype (see Allport, 1966). In addition, it may be that behavior is consistent if one looks at small units of displayed action. For example, individuals are quite consistent over time and across settings in the size of their figure drawings when asked to draw some object (Wallach & Leggett, 1972).

In sum, the trait-situation controversy is far from resolved. Social learning theorists have raised this issue by calling attention to: a) the necessity of taking the environment into account when predicting action, and b) the importance of cognitive capacities of individuals to differentiate between situations. Thus, these theorists have presented an alternative to the biological and intrapersonal approach of Freud. In so doing, they have helped to redress some imbalances in the study of motivated behavior.

ROTTER'S SOCIAL LEARNING THEORY

Social learning theory as formulated by Bandura and Walters, Mischel, and others surely does not belong in a book section headed "Expectancy-Value Theories," and seems quite out of place following the presentation of Lewin's and Atkinson's theories. However, as previously indicated, the social learning approach has distinct, albeit overlapping, referents in psychology. One social learning theory that is appropriately identified as an expectancy-value conception of behavior is the product of Julian Rotter and his many students. Although Rotter's theory has not had the impact of psychoanalytic, drive, or

JULIAN ROTTER

(Courtesy of J. B. Rotter)

Julian Rotter received his undergraduate education at Brooklyn College, his master's degree at the University of Iowa, and his doctoral diploma at Indiana University in 1941. Each of these settings left an important impact on his theory. In New York he attended a series of seminars given by the then aging Alfred Adler. Adler's teachings convinced Rotter of the importance of considering the perceived social context of behavior, rather than concentrating solely on the intrapersonal determinants of action (see Mosher, 1968). At Iowa and Indiana he was influenced by the Hull-Spence behavioral theory and the ideas of Skinner

concerning the significance of reinforcement (and, thus, the situation) in determining the direction of behavior. In addition, Rotter's theory was greatly shaped by Edward Tolman, who championed the concept of "expectancy" in psychology.

Some years after his graduate training, Rotter became chairman of the program in clinical psychology at Ohio State University. For many years Ohio State was one of the largest clinical psychology training centers in the United States, and the department included three famous clinicians: George Kelly, Carl Rogers, and Rotter. (The ideas of Kelly and Rogers are examined in detail in a later section of this book.) Approximately 15 of Rotter's ex-students are now chairpersons of clinical psychology programs in the United States and Canada, attesting to his impact on psychology. Rotter subsequently moved to the University of Connecticut, where he remains active today (1978).

As already intimated, Rotter is perhaps best known for his development of a locus of control scale. The popularity of this work took even him by surprise. Alluding to the widespread use of this scale, Rotter once confided: "I was walking in the woods, lit my pipe and threw away the match, and when I looked behind me there was a forest fire."

field conceptions of behavior, various by-products or branches of his work, such as the analysis of locus of control, have become exceedingly popular among contemporary psychologists. Indeed, a monograph published by Rotter (1966) on the topic of locus of control was the third most cited publication between 1965 and 1975 among psychologists publishing in the so-called "soft" areas (clinical, personality, and social psychology). (An article by Janet Taylor in 1953 describing the Manifest Anxiety Scale was the most referenced paper in the 1965–75 decade among the "soft" psychologists.) It is reasonable to conclude that the number of times a published paper is referenced by other psychologists indicates the importance or influence of that particular work.

General Theoretical Orientation

Rotter's social learning theory primarily is concerned with the choices that individuals make when confronted with a number of possible alternative ways of behaving (Phares, 1976). To explain choice, or the direction of behavior, Rotter (1954) attempts to integrate the two major approaches in American psychology: the S→R or reinforcement position, as exemplified primarily by Skinner and, to a lesser extent, by Hull, and the cognitive or field position advocated by Tolman and Lewin.

Rotter stresses *learned* social behavior, giving relatively little attention to the unlearned, biological determinants of action focused upon by Freud. For this reason, Rotter is categorized in the tradition of Dollard and Miller, Bandura and Walters, and other social learning theorists. Because learning (the strengthening and weakening of expectancies, or beliefs about reinforcements) is so central to Rotter's theory, the psychological situation also becomes of paramount importance, inasmuch as expectancies are elicited in particular situational contexts. However, Rotter also assumes that on the basis of a variety of learning experiences, general belief systems develop that influence behavior in any specific situation. These general beliefs, such as interpersonal trust or the conviction that one has control over one's fate, are similar to what are typically meant by traits, or personality characteristics. Rotter's social learning theory, therefore, emphasizes the general (trait) and the specific (situational) determinants of action, with both being the product of learning experiences. Hence, in a manner similar to Lewin, Rotter contends that "the unit of investigation for the study of personality is the interaction of the individual and his meaningful environment" (Rotter, 1954, p. 85).

Basic Concepts

There are four basic concepts in Rotter's theory: behavior potential, expectancy, reinforcement value, and the psychological situation.

These are linked with more general concepts (need potential, freedom of movement, and need value) and provide the foundation for still other constructs, including generalized expectancy and minimal goal level. Rotter's basic motivational statement is that the potential of any behavior is determined by the expectancy that the behavior will lead to a reinforcement and by the reinforcing value of the goal:

Behavior potential = f(expectancy of reward and reward value of the goal)

This approach is similar to that advocated by Hull, Lewin, and Atkinson in that an attempt is made to identify the immediate determinants of behavior, and the formulated model "explains" why persons behave as they do.

Behavior Potential

Behavior potential is the likelihood for any given behavior to occur "as calculated in relation to any single reinforcement or set of reinforcements" (Rotter, 1972, p. 12). For example, at a party a man might desire to meet a person of the opposite sex. To do this, he might walk up and introduce himself, wait for an opportunity to be introduced, or promote a meeting by taking part in an activity or game that involves mutual interaction. Each of these actions has a particular potential or likelihood for a specific individual, given the party setting. Behavior potential is a relative concept, for it involves a comparison among many possible behaviors. Furthermore, "behavior" is used in its broadest sense and includes cognitive activity, such as further planning or even invoking a psychological defense. It also includes both molecular and molar overt actions, such as smiling or engaging in one of the relatively complex sequences listed above to meet another person.

Expectancy

Expectancy is perhaps the key concept in Rotter's theory. It is defined as the "probability held by the individual that a particular reinforcement will occur as a function of a specific behavior on his part in a specific situation" (Rotter, 1954, p. 107). Rotter considers expectancy to be a subjective probability: It may or may not be identical with the true or objective likelihood of reaching one's goal. For example, the person at the party might believe that if he introduces himself, he will be considered "impolite" or "forward." This will minimize the subjective likelihood of establishing a friendship (the reinforcer). However, such a conviction may be objectively quite false. Theoretically, expectancies can be measured on a scale that ranges from zero (no likelihood of reward) to one (reward is certain to follow).

The concept of expectancy as used by Rotter has much in common with the prior usage of the term by Edward Tolman (1932), the Lewinian concept of potency, and Atkinson's concept of subjective probability. Rotter contends that in the study of motivation often behavioral predictions are made entirely on the basis of the assumed needs or traits of the person, while the likelihood of goal attainment given an action is ignored. Rotter and Hochreich (1975) state:

> . . . Simply knowing how much an individual wants to reach a certain goal is not sufficient information for predicting his behavior. A student may want very badly to finish school and qualify himself for a well-paying job. But if his past experiences have led him to believe that no amount of studying will result in passing grades — if his expectancy for success in this situation is low — he is unlikely to study, despite his strong desire to graduate. A fellow student may share the same strong goals, and as a result of a different set of past experiences in school, have a high expectancy that studying will lead to academic success. In this instance, one could safely predict that the second student would be likely to study in order to obtain his goals. As you can see, the goals in these two cases are identical, but the expectancies differ, and as a result, the behavior of the two students is likely to differ. (p. 95)

GENERALIZED EXPECTANCY.   It is assumed that beliefs about reinforcements are determined, in part, by one's past history in the specific situation under consideration. However, it is evident that reinforcement expectancies are influenced not only by the prior behavior-outcome experiences in the same situation, but also by experiences in similar circumstances. For example, a person's beliefs about making a friend at a party will be influenced by prior experiences at parties and by the outcome of friendship attempts made in a wide variety of social settings; that is, expectancies generalize from similar behavior-reinforcement sequences. More formally, Rotter proposes that:

$$E_{S1} = f(E_{S1} + GE)$$

The formula conveys that the expectancy of reinforcement in Situation 1 (E_{S1}) is determined on the basis of expectancies in that particular situation, as well as by generalized expectancies (GE) from similar situations. The more novel a situation, the greater the importance of generalized expectancies in determining immediate beliefs. On the other hand, given a great deal of experience in a specific situation, generalized expectancies may have little significance in influencing behavior. Phares (1976) illustrates these statements with the following example:

> . . . Suppose a college student who has never taken any work in chemistry is asked to state her expectancy for receiving an "A" on her first quiz in the course. Her statement might be determined by her overall experience in those science-related courses that she regards as similar. That is, she has no specific expectancies based on prior chemistry experience. However, if that same question were posed at the end of the chemistry course, her answer would be based almost entirely on her specific

experience with chemistry quizzes and hardly at all on expectancies generalized from related courses. (pp. 16–17)

Reinforcement Value

Reinforcement value refers to "the degree of preference for any reinforcement . . . if the possibility of their occurring were all equal" (Rotter, 1954, p. 107). Thus, reinforcement value, like behavioral potential, is a relative or comparative term. Furthermore, some reinforcements gain in value because of their association or relevance to other reinforcements. For example, receiving an "A" in a course is desired in and of itself, but the value of this grade may be enhanced if it is also perceived as aiding the person in being admitted to graduate school.

The reinforcement value of a goal is clearly linked with the needs of an individual. As Lewin previously noted, an object does not acquire a valence, or reinforcement value, unless the person is in a state of need and is desirous of the object. Rotter has contended that most human needs are learned. He suggests six very broad need categories: recognition-status, dominance, independence, protection-dependency, love and affection, and physical comfort. These needs supposedly influence most of the learned, psychological behaviors because of their role in determining perceived reinforcement.

MINIMAL GOAL LEVEL. The concept of a minimal goal level already was implied in the discussion of level of aspiration and the concept of comparison level. According to Rotter, behavioral outcomes can be ordered on a scale ranging from strongly positive to strongly negative reinforcement. The point at which this ordering changes from negative to positive can be considered the minimal goal level. An objectively positive outcome might have a negative value for an individual because that outcome is below the minimal goal level. Furthermore, as indicated in the discussion of level of aspiration, the same outcome might have a positive value for one individual and a negative value for another. For example, the grade of "C" has different values for a person who desires to be admitted to graduate school as opposed to an individual who merely wants to pass the course.

The Psychological Situation

Throughout the prior discussion the importance of the individual's situational context has been stressed. Rotter and Hochreich (1975) state: "Because of its basic learning theory assumptions, [social learning theory] emphasizes that a person learns through past experiences that some satisfactions are more likely to be obtained in certain situations than in others" (p. 98). The situation discussed by Rotter is the psychological situation, or the subjective meaning of the environment. Behavior takes place in this environment and, thus, the social context of behavior must be described in order to understand and predict action.

The Determinants of Action

With this discussion in mind the motivational model formulated by Rotter may be specified in greater detail. His basic formula is:

$$BP_{x, s_1, r_a} = f(E_{x, r_a s_1} + RV_{a, s_1})$$

This formula states that: "The potential for behavior x to occur in Situation 1 in relation to the reinforcement a is a function of the expectancy of the occurrence of reinforcement a following behavior x in Situation 1, and the value of reinforcement a in Situation 1" (Rotter, Chance, & Phares, 1972, p. 14). This formula includes the notion that the expectancy of a reinforcement is a composite of both specific and generalized expectancies, and that the value of a reinforcement is determined by its own reinforcement properties as well as its relation to other potential reinforcers.

Rotter also suggests a more general formula that conveys the same meaning, but is less situation specific. That formula is:

$$N.P. = f(F.M. + N.V.)$$

This reads: "The potentiality of occurrence of a set of behaviors that lead to the satisfaction of some need (need potential) is a function of the expectancies that these behaviors will lead to these reinforcements (freedom of movement) and the strength or value of these reinforcements (need value)" (Rotter, 1954, p. 110).

Relation between the Constructs

Expectancy and reinforcement value have been presented as independent constructs. Expectancy is assumed to be, in part, determined by the number of reinforced experiences relative to total experiences, whereas value is related to the properties of the goal object and one's needs. It is evident, therefore, that Hull's concept of habit (H), Lewin's notion of potency (P_o), and Atkinson's use of probability (P_s) resemble expectancy, while Hull's incentive (K), Lewin's concept of valence (Va) and Atkinson's incentive of success (I_s) are similar to what Rotter means by the "value" of the goal.

However, Rotter also notes (as did Atkinson) that the expectancy and value constructs are not entirely independent. Rotter, Chance, and Phares (1972) suggest that if one fails to attain a goal, then the "reinforcement itself may become associated with the unpleasantness of failure and diminish in value" (p. 19). Conversely, it is often true that difficult goals have high values. For example, it is more rewarding to defeat a good athletic competitor than a poor one, or to complete a difficult, rather than easy, puzzle. That is, high expectancy at times is associated with low value, and vice versa.

LOW EXPECTANCY AND HIGH VALUE. According to social learning theory, one cause of personal difficulties is to experience a low expectancy of success for a highly valued goal. For example, one might want to go to college, but perceive oneself to be low in ability, or might desire to date a person who does not reciprocate the warm feelings. In these situations individuals may learn to avoid the punishment of failure by using maladaptive defenses, such as withdrawal into a fantasy world. The psychological withdrawal decreases subsequent chances of success even further because the chosen behavior is not constructive.

DEVIANT BEHAVIOR. The effects of a discrepancy between expectancy and value also have been analyzed at a social level. Merton (1957) has pointed out that in American society materialistic success is a goal for all individuals. This goal is realized when one has a home, one or two automobiles, and other indicators of a high income. On the other hand, many members of our society have only limited access to what is called the "opportunity structure," or the means to achieve such goals. These means include a high education, influential friends, appropriate manners of behavior, and so on. A discrepancy between values and expectancies, Merton argues, causes individuals to adopt deviant or illegitimate means to attain success. Jessor, Graves, Hanson, and Jessor (1968) report some evidence in support of Merton's ideas. They found that persons with the lowest access to the opportunity structure are most likely to engage in deviant behavior, such as drinking and crime.

Implications for Psychotherapy

Social learning theory was originally formulated by Rotter (1954) to supply a new language for clinical psychologists. Some of the implications of social learning theory for the understanding of psychopathology and psychotherapeutic techniques already have been alluded to in the discussion of the adverse effects of a discrepancy between expectancy and reward value. Social learning theory states that maladjustment represents a learning problem; the goals of psychotherapy are to lessen the occurrence of undesirable actions and to increase the occurrence of desirable actions through new learning (Katkovsky, 1968). Two questions are of special importance to the therapist when considering what the patient should unlearn and learn: 1) What does the client expect? 2) What does the client value?

Expectation and Maladjustment

Low expectancies are one source of personal problems. Expectancy may be low for any number of reasons. On the one hand, the individual may not have learned the necessary skills or appropriate goal-directed behaviors. In this case the therapist may actively suggest new and more instrumental behaviors. The therapist is therefore a teacher. and helps the client to develop competencies. Contrasting this approach with more traditional analytic theory, Rotter and Hochreich (1975) state:

> . . . This emphasis on the acquisition of new and more effective be- haviors distinguishes the social learning theory approach from other kinds of psychotherapy which are based on the assumption that once a person is free from internal conflict and understands himself better, he will auto- matically be able to find healthier ways of achieving his goals. Insight into one's problems may be very useful but does not always lead to actual changes in a person's behavior. (p. 107)

Expectancies also may be low because of erroneous generaliza- tions. For example, a person's self-image during an unattractive ado- lescent period may persist into adulthood when it is no longer suit- able, or an individual who does poorly in school might also expect to do poorly in non-academic settings, even though different skills are involved in these two areas. In these cases the therapist must help the client discriminate between situations and make more adaptive dif- ferentiations. The therapist might also suggest a change in environ- ments so the client can escape the cues that promote low expectan- cies. Thus, for example, the therapist might advise a new job, a different college, or an altered set of acquaintances.

Value and Adjustment

Values also play an important role in problems of maladjustment. For example, the individual may place too great an importance upon a particular goal. This could lead to perceptual-cognitive distortions, such as interpreting all situations as relevant to this particular need (e.g., the paranoid patient who perceives the clanging of the radiator as a signal that someone is watching him). The therapist can aid the patient in altering goals or selecting more appropriate targets of ac- tion. In a similar manner, one's minimal goal level may be set too high, thus promoting dissatisfaction. Or alternately, the person may have several highly valued needs and goals that are incompatible. For example, an individual with both high independence and protection needs may find that the same behavior positively reinforces one need but is a negative reinforcer for the other.

In sum, social learning theory suggests an eclectic approach to psychotherapy. The theory stresses:

> . . . the development of problem-solving skills on the part of the pa- tient, such as looking for alternative ways of reaching goals, analyzing the consequences of behavior, and trying to analyze how situations differ from one another. The goal of therapy is not only to help the person solve his immediate problems, but to provide him with skills which will be useful to him in meeting life's difficulties in the future. (Rotter and Hochreich, 1975, p. 109)

Representative Research

It should come as no surprise to the reader that the research gen- erated by Rotter's social learning theory primarily concerns the measurement of expectancy and value and the effects of these factors on a wide variety of behaviors and personal adjustment. In this section of the chapter a few characteristic research studies examining the antecedents and consequences of expectancy of reinforcement are reported to acquaint the readers with the research methods and the goals of Rotter's approach.

Expectancy Generalization

Crandall (1955) developed a projective method of assessing expectancy of success and then examined the effects of failure on the generalization of expectancies. Subjects made up stories in response to nine different TAT-type pictures. The pictures depicted three need areas: recognition for physical skill, recognition for academic skill, and love and affection from the opposite sex. On the basis of stories about these pictures, Crandall inferred the subjective expectancy of satisfaction of these needs.

The subjects in an experimental group then were given a failure experience at a physical coordination task, while subjects in a control group received no such experience. Following the failure (or neutral control activity), subjects made up stories to a second set of pictures.

The results of this investigation are shown in Figure 6–2. Figure 6–2 indicates that there is a lowering of expectancy in the experimental group, relative to the control group. This is in accordance with the

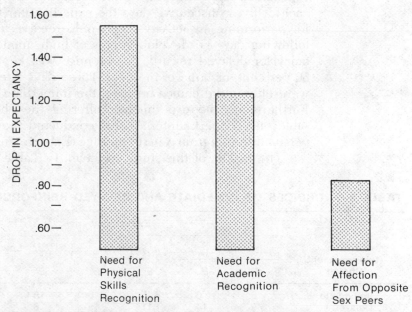

Figure 6–2. Difference in the amounts of lowering of expectancy in Crandall's experimental subjects compared to his control subjects. (From Rotter, 1954, p. 122, based on data reported in Crandall, 1955.)

supposition that expectancies are determined by behavioral-outcome histories. Furthermore, the decrement in expectancy of success depends upon the similarity between the need that was frustrated and the need-related area that was depicted in the pictures. Nonetheless, expectancies did generalize from one need area to another, i.e., failure in a skill-related area even lowered expectancies for academic recognition and physical affection.

Expectancy and Delay of Gratification

Because of the apparently close association between the important topic of ego-control and delay of gratification, delay behavior has been the subject of study from many perspectives. In an earlier chapter, some of the delay investigations conducted by Mischel, and their relation to Freudian psychology, were examined. In addition, delay studies that demonstrated the effectiveness of live and symbolic models in altering delay choice were introduced in the earlier section of this chapter on observational learning. Delay of gratification also has been investigated from the theoretical position espoused by Rotter. The research shows the value of Rotter's theoretical position in the understanding of ego-control.

Guided by social learning theory, Mahrer (1956) demonstrated that delay behavior is, in part, determined by the expectation of reinforcement following the delay interval. Children 7 to 9 years old were offered a choice between a smaller immediate reward and a more attractive delayed reward. Prior to the choice dilemma, three levels of expectancy were induced for the receipt of the promised reward. On each of five consecutive days the experimenter told the children that for performing an activity they would receive a small balloon on the following day. To develop groups of high, moderate, and low expectancy for delayed reward, this promise was kept either 100 per cent, 50 per cent, or none of the time. Three days later these same subjects were offered the choice between the immediate and delayed rewards. Furthermore, the experimenter offering the choices was either the same one (Experimenter A) that conducted the training session or a person differing from A in sex and age (Experimenter B).

The results of this study are given in Table 6–1. The table shows

TABLE 6-1   CHOICES OF IMMEDIATE AND DELAYED REINFORCEMENT

| Reinforcement Choice | Expectancy | | | | | |
| | High | | Moderate | | Low | |
	E_A	E_B	E_A	E_B	E_A	E_B
Immediate	6*	6	15	5	18	7
Delayed	19	14	11	15	6	15

*Number of subjects
(Adapted from Mahrer, 1956, p. 104.)

that the groups of subjects tested by Experimenter B (E_B) all exhibited the same delay behavior, regardless of prior training. On the other hand, responses to Experimenter A (E_A) were consistent with the expectancies based on the prior experiences. Thus, in this setting the expectancies did not generalize, for the highly different experimenters created disparate social situations and served as cues for different expectancies. In sum, prior training influences the choice of delayed reinforcements, and one of the important cues for the expectancy of delayed reinforcement is the social agent responsible for the reinforcer.

Expectancy and Drinking Behavior

Recall Merton (1957) suggested that discrepancies between expectancy and value are one cause of deviant behavior. Jessor, Carman, and Grossman (1968), guided by Merton's ideas, proposed that in a college population two goals are of special importance: academic achievement and social affection. Failure at these goals should lower expectations, which, in part, might cause deviant behavior such as the drinking of alcoholic beverages. Consumption of alcohol not only produces an avoidance of both prior failures, but also might enhance possible satisfactions of other goals, such as dominance and independence, which could partially compensate for failure in the other domains.

To test these ideas, Jessor, Carman, and Grossman (1968) assessed expectancies of need satisfaction in academic achievement and peer affection by means of a questionnaire in which subjects indicated the likelihood that, for example, they would be "in the top half of their class" or would "have many friends in different groups." In addition, three aspects of drinking behavior were assessed: amount of alcoholic intake, frequency of drunkenness, and reported drinking-related complications (e.g., accidents, loss of job, and so on). The results of the investigation supported the hypothesis that drinking is related to low expectancy of success, and were particularly predictive of the drinking behavior of women.

In this experiment the function that alcohol was perceived to serve also was examined. Individuals with low expectancy of success reported that drinking offered a physical relief and was an escape from personal shortcomings, thus further supporting the predictions derived from Merton and social learning theory. These data again were more clear for the female participants.

PERSONAL RESPONSIBILITY

Locus of Control

Social learning theory assumes that "man is a categorizing animal" (Rotter et al., 1972, p. 39), and that individuals subsume diverse situations within the same class or category. These categories represent the underlying, shared properties of situations. One such category or dimension of situations concerns whether a potential reinforcer can be attained through one's own action, or follows from luck or other uncontrollable, external factors. That is, situations can be grouped according to the perceived cause of a reinforcement.

Beliefs concerning personal responsibility for a reward have been postulated to constitute a personality dimension. That is, it is anticipated that some persons perceive greater internal (or external) control over potential reinforcers across a variety of situations than do others. Individual differences in what is called "locus of control" have been the subject of hundreds of research investigations.

Definition

Rotter (1966) defines locus of control as follows:

> When a reinforcement is perceived by the subject as . . . not being entirely contingent upon his action, then, in our culture, it is typically perceived as the result of luck, chance, fate, as under the control of powerful others, or as unpredictable because of the great complexity of the forces surrounding him. When the event is interpreted in this way by an individual, we have labeled this a belief in *external control*. If the person perceives that the event is contingent upon his own behavior or his own relatively permanent characteristics, we have termed this a belief in *internal control*. (p. 1)

Locus of control thus refers to the belief that a response will, or will not, influence the attainment of a reinforcement. Therefore, locus of control is conceived as one determinant of the expectancy of success. However, locus of control is not an expectancy concerning a particular type of reinforcement. Rather, it is considered a "problem-solving" generalized expectancy, addressing the issue of whether behaviors are perceived as instrumental to goal attainment, regardless of the specific nature of the goal or reinforcer. Perceived locus of control is believed to influence the specific goal expectancy in any given situation, with the extent of the influence in part dependent upon the novelty and the ambiguity of the setting, as well as the degree of reinforcement that the individual has directly experienced in that setting.

Skill versus Chance

A series of systematic investigations was undertaken by Rotter and his colleagues to demonstrate that perceptions of control as internal or external influence expectancy of success. These studies compared expectancy of success in situations that were perceived as skill-determined (internal control) or chance-determined (external control). The intuitive rationale guiding these investigations was described by Rotter, Seeman, and Liverant (1962) as follows:

> It is a matter of common sense that most individuals who would find a $5 bill on a given street would not return and walk up and down the

street many times to find more $5 bills, because they consider the event that occurred to be a matter of chance. On the other hand, should someone take up ping pong and be told that he plays an excellent game for someone just learning, he is quite likely to increase the number of times he plays ping-pong. In the first case, the reinforcement appears to be a matter of chance, controlled in some way by people or forces outside the individual, and in the second instance, the reinforcement appears to be dependent on some characteristic or quality of the person, which he can label as a skill. In the latter case, the reinforcement, in a sense, is understood as occurring because of his own behavior (p. 474).

The first of the skill versus chance experiments was conducted by Phares (1957). Phares contended that in skill situations, success and failure indicate to the individual that he "can" or "cannot" perform the task. Hence, Phares hypothesized that in skill situations there would be relatively large increments in the perceived likelihood of future success after a success experience, and large decrements in expectancy after a failure. On the other hand, in situations determined by chance, success and failure are beyond the control of the individual. Therefore, expectancies should change little following success or failure. Phares also suggested that in chance-related tasks there occasionally would be increments in expectancy of success after a failure, and decrements following a success, inasmuch as the direction of luck might be anticipated to change by the subject (these are atypical expectancy shifts).

To test these hypotheses, researchers gave subjects a task that was ambiguous with respect to the objective determinants of success and failure. In one condition the outcome was described as determined by skill, while in a second condition performance was said to be entirely a matter of luck. Prior to each trial the subjects indicated how many of ten chips they would be willing to bet on their next performance. Expectancy of success was inferred from the magnitude of the reported bet. Subjects in both the skill and the chance conditions received the same relatively random reinforcement schedule on 13 test trials.

Phares found that his hypotheses generally were confirmed. In the skill condition there were more typical expectancy shifts, and the shifts were of greater magnitude, than in the chance condition. For example, following success, subjects in the skill condition were more likely to increase their bet on the next trial, and by a greater amount, than subjects in the chance condition. On the other hand, there were more atypical shifts in the chance condition. The atypical shifts often are known as the "gambler's fallacy." This refers to a perceived dependence imposed on independent outcomes, i.e., a loss is expected to be followed by a win, and vice versa.

James and Rotter (1958) extended the Phares study to include different reinforcement schedules, as well as differences in chance and skill instructions. Subjects participating in an "ESP" experiment were asked to identify whether an "X" or an "O" was flashed during a tachistoscopic exposure. In fact, nothing was shown, and the experimenters manipulated the feedback to the subjects during the pseudo-

TABLE 6-2   TRIALS TO EXTINCTION

Group	Trials	Standard Deviation
(100% chance)	15.55	9.86
(50% chance)	29.05	9.41
(100% skill)	22.90	4.84
(50% skill)	19.75	7.27

(From James & Rotter, 1958, p. 401.)

identification trials. Subjects in a 100 per cent reinforcement condition were first given continuous reinforcement, followed by an extinction (no reinforcement) series. In a 50 per cent reinforcement condition, subjects were told they were correct on a random series of one-half of the trials and then also underwent an extinction series. Luck and skill task perceptions were manipulated by telling half the subjects, "there is evidence that some people are considerably skilled at this," while others were told, "scientists have shown so far that this is entirely a matter of luck" (James & Rotter, 1958, p. 359). Prior to each trial the subjects estimated their probability of success on a 10–point scale. The dependent variable, resistance to extinction, was inferred from the stated probability of success. It was assumed that extinction would occur (i.e., the subjects would discontinue responding) when the probability of success was rated .10 or less on three consecutive trials.

The trials to extinction for the four experimental groups (two levels of reinforcement × two levels of instruction) are shown in Table 6–2. The table indicates that extinction is faster in the 100 per cent than in the 50 per cent condition given chance instructions. This finding replicates the general pattern of results in extinction studies that employ infrahumans as subjects. On the other hand, given skill instructions, extinction is faster in the 50 per cent than in the 100 per cent reinforcement condition. This result is a reversal of the oft-cited "partial reinforcement effect."

In sum, the general implication of the research reviewed above is that perceived locus of control (skill or chance orientation) is a determinant of expectancy of success. Given this empirical support, Rotter and his colleagues turned their attention to the study of individual differences in perceived causality.

Individual Differences in Perceived Control

As indicated above, the data collected by Rotter and his associates demonstrate that chance and skill environments differentially affect behavior. The question then raised by this research group was whether, in identical environments, some individuals would act as if

the task were more influenced by chance (or skill) than others. If so, then individual differences would be a determinant of generalized expectancies, and thus would influence the subjective probability of goal attainment and subsequent behavior.

Lefcourt (1976) cites a passage from an interview reported in Oscar Lewis's (1961) classic book on the Mexican culture to illustrate the thoughts of a person who would be labelled as having an external locus of control:

> To me, one's destiny is controlled by a mysterious hand that moves all things. Only for the select, do things turn out as planned; to those of us who are born to be tamale eaters, heaven sends only tamales. We plan and plan and some little thing happens to wash it all away. Like once, I decided to try and save and I said to Paula, "Old girl, put away this money so that some day we'll have a little pile." When we had ninety pesos laid away, pum! my father got sick and I had to give all to him for doctors and medicine. It was the only time I had helped him and the only time I had tried to save! I said to Paula, "There you are! Why should we save if someone gets sick and we have to spend it all!" Sometimes I even think that savings bring on illness! That's why I firmly believe that some of us are born to be poor. (Lewis, 1961, p. 171)

It is worth noting that many research efforts in the field of motivation first demonstrate the importance of environmental influences on behavior, and then examine whether individuals will differ in their relations to these environments. For example, in Chapter Three, it was revealed that individuals condition faster when the intensity of an aversive stimulus (a puff of air to the eye) is increased. Then the Manifest Anxiety scale was developed to determine whether, given the same puff intensity, some individuals would react as if it were more intense than others. If so, then these persons would be identified as high in general level of drive (emotional reactivity). Likewise, in achievement research, it was first demonstrated that arousal conditions produce more achievement-related imagery on the TAT than neutral conditions. Then researchers investigated the hypothesis that, under neutral conditions, some individuals are more aroused to achieve than others. In a similar manner, the locus of control research first examined expectancy shifts under skill versus chance conditions. Researchers in this area then ascertained whether, given the same setting, some individuals would react as if that environment were more chance- (or skill-) determined than other persons.

ASSESSMENT PROCEDURE. Individual differences in the tendency to perceive events as being internally or externally controlled are assessed with a 29-item self-report inventory. The test, called the internal-external control scale (I-E scale), has a forced-choice format with an internal belief pitted against an external belief. The items on the scale are classifiable into six general subcategories on the basis of the types of needs that are portrayed and the characteristics of the described goals. The six categories are: academic recognition, social recognition, love and affection, dominance, social-political beliefs, and life philosophy. Some sample items, and their keyed responses (underscored letters represent externality choices), are:

1. a. Many of the unhappy things in people's lives are partly due to bad luck.
    b. People's misfortunes result from the mistakes they make.
2. a. The idea that teachers are unfair to students is nonsense.
    b. Most students don't realize the extent to which grades are influenced by accidental happenings.

It is evident that the questions on the scale are very broad. As Rotter (1975) indicates: " [The scale] was developed not as an instrument . . . to allow for a very high prediction of some specific situation, such as achievement or political behavior, but rather to allow for a low degree of prediction of behavior across a wide range of potential situations" (p. 62). That is, typically the situational cues in a setting most influence the perceived expectancy of a reinforcement. However, generalized beliefs about control also are presumed to affect the expectancy of success to some extent, with this influence displayed across a wide array of environments.

VALIDITY.   It is reasonable to anticipate that the validation of the scale would involve resistance to extinction and expectancy shifts. But this has not been the case. The few published studies that relate I-E scores to resistance to extinction have failed to find significant results (see, for example, Battle & Rotter, 1963). In addition, the expected greater frequency and magnitude of typical shifts, which have been clearly shown to distinguish chance from skill situations, have not been differentially exhibited by subjects high or low on the I-E scale.

As a general rule, the closer the test-taking situation to the situation in which behavioral data are gathered, the more likely that the test will be "validated." Responses to a measure that includes, for example, questions about happiness in life bear little immediate relevance to investigations of expectancy shifts. Thus, it is not surprising that the I-E scale has not successfully predicted expectancy change. This is not to say that internality-externality is or is not a trait, or a personality dimension having some trans-situational predictive power. Rather, there is too great a gap between the I-E test items (predictor variable) and expectancy changes on some laboratory task, such as guessing an "X" or an "O" on a tachistoscope. This sentiment is in accord with the analysis of Rotter and his associates, who might contend that the situational cues in the skill or chance settings override any differences in behavior that could be generated by personality dispositions, or generalized expectancies.

Phares (1976) states that:

> The best single indicator of the validity of the I-E scale would undoubtedly be evidence showing that internals are more active, alert, or directive in attempting to control and manipulate their environment than are externals. Since locus of control refers to expectancies for control over one's surroundings, a higher level of coping activity would be anticipated from internals. (p. 60)

There is evidence in support of these hypotheses. In one series of studies, Seeman and Evans (1962) and Seeman (1963) reported respectively on the information seeking and the retention of personally relevant information among individuals confined in institutions. Seeman and Evans (1962) found that among hospitalized tuberculosis patients, individuals classified as internals knew more about their illness and asked doctors more questions than patients who were external in locus of control. Seeman (1963) reported that prisoners who were internals retained more information pertinent to parole than did externals. In sum, among both patients and prisoners the behavior displayed by those high in internal control was instrumental to improving their life situation. On the other hand, it appears that among those low in generalized expectancy for personal control, the acquiring of information was seen as less likely to serve any useful function.

Other investigators have studied the differential cognitive activity of internals and externals. For example, Wolk and DuCette (1974) presented subjects with protocols to be scanned for errors. It was found that internals were better at incidental learning (remembering the material that had been scanned) and in finding errors. In general, social learning theorists in this area have contended that "the cognitive functioning of internals should enhance their personal effectiveness as compared to externals. And it apparently does." (Phares, 1976, p. 65).

Locus of Control Research

There is a paradox in the research concerned with perceptions of control. Many studies that manipulate perceived control (e.g., by means of instructions) have focused attention upon the expectancy of success or expectancy shifts. As already indicated, reliable empirical findings that appear to support social learning theory were generated. But the experimental manipulation studies have systematically examined little else. On the other hand, investigations that assess locus of control, rather than manipulating it, have probed almost everything. However, clearly reliable and interpretable findings have emerged in just a few areas, primarily related to information seeking and information utilization, as outlined above. The great bulk of this voluminous literature falls well beyond the network of social learning theory, for many investigators have merely correlated scores on the I-E scale with anything in sight! Thus, there is an imbalance between studies manipulating chance and skill orientations and those that measure individual differences in the perceptions of these environments.

There is a rapidly growing literature originating outside of social learning that manipulates perceptions of control, but examines a number of psychological reactions and states in addition to (or instead of) expectancy shifts. These investigations, and their supporting theories, are the topic of the remainder of this chapter. The theme of personal responsibility and perceived causality will be discussed again in detail later in the book.

Personal Causation

A distinction made by de Charms (1968) between "origin" and "pawn" is similar to Rotter's differentiation of internal and external control. De Charms (1968) states:

> We shall use the terms "Origin" and "Pawn" as shorthand terms to connote the distinction between forced and free. An Origin is a person who perceives his behavior as determined by his own choosing; a Pawn is a person who perceives his behavior as determined by external forces beyond his control... Feeling like an Origin has strong effects on behavior as compared to feeling like a Pawn. The distinction is continuous, not discrete — a person feels *more* like an Origin under some circumstances and *more* like a Pawn under others.
>
> The personal aspect is more important motivationally than objective facts. If the person feels he is an Origin, that is more important in predicting his behavior than any objective indications of coercion. Conversely, if he considers himself a Pawn, his behavior will be strongly influenced, despite any objective evidence that he is free. An Origin has a strong feeling of personal causation, a feeling that the locus for causation of effects in his environment lies within himself. The feedback that reinforces this feeling comes from changes in his environment that are attributed to personal behavior. This is the crux of the concept of personal causation and it is a powerful motivational force directing future behavior. A Pawn has a feeling that causal forces beyond his control, or personal forces residing in others, or in the physical environment, determine his behavior. This constitutes a strong feeling of powerlessness or ineffectiveness. (pp. 273–274)

De Charms associates the concept of origin with intrinsically motivated behavior (own forces), freedom of movement, and the perception of situations as challenging. Conversely, the concept of pawn is linked with extrinsically motivated behavior (induced forces), restriction of movement, and the perception of situations as threatening. Furthermore, the origin-pawn classification also is associated with a good-bad value dimension. De Charms (1976) states:

> Man at his best must be *active*, not *reactive*; he must strive rather than submit as a puppet. Man must author his own behavior, rather than have it dictated by authority. Man is not a pawn to the dictates of others; at his best man is the origin of his actions. (p. 5)

Thus, the origin-pawn dimension goes far beyond the already broad confines of locus of control.

Experiments have been conducted manipulating situational factors that influence the feeling of being an origin or a pawn. The general approach in these experiments is to induce "freedom" in one experimental condition and constraint in a comparison condition. In one experiment, for example, children were given a task of building models (Kuperman, 1967; reported in de Charms, 1968). In the pawn condition the subjects were told exactly what to do; in the origin condition they proceeded in any manner they desired. Subsequent questionnaire data revealed that origins enjoyed the task more and were more interested in continuing the activity than were the pawns. However, significant differences were not observed in the behaviors of children in the two condtions.

Origin Training

Training programs have been developed by de Charms designed to increase achievement accomplishments. This approach to achievement change is somewhat different theoretically from that advocated by McClelland and Winter, for de Charms focuses upon the training of personal causation. The goals of this program are to instill teachers with the belief that they are origins. De Charms (1976) notes:

> In the practical world of the school, the problem is to create conditions that will stimulate commitment and responsible choice felt to be originating from within the individual.
>
> The conditions that promote commitment, internal choice and responsibility within a person, i.e., the conditions that encourage feeling and acting like an Origin, have four basic elements. The person should be encouraged to consider carefully his basic motives (self-study) in a warm atmosphere of acceptance by others in the group. The setting should help him to translate his motives into realistic short- and long-range goals (internal goal settings) and to plan realistic and concrete action to attain the goals (planning and goal-directed behavior). Finally, the setting should help him learn to accept responsibility for selected goals as well as for the success and failure of his attempts to reach them (personal responsibility). (p. 6)

These goals are similar to ones outlined by McClelland and Winter (1969), and, therefore, the achievement and origin-training programs have much in common.

De Charms (1976) reported on a large-scale, four-year program of origin training with black teachers in inner-city schools. During the school year the teachers met regularly with researchers and participated in exercises designed to promote realistic goal setting, achievement concerns, and feelings of personal causation. In addition, the teachers were trained to treat their pupils as origins.

The effectiveness of the training was then assessed by examining the interaction of the teachers and their pupils in the classroom. The effects of origin training on the personal experience and the behavior of the school children were also examined.

The results of this research are complex but generally support de Charms' hypotheses. The origin-trained and non-trained teachers and their pupils differed in a number of respects. According to de Charms, the training led teachers to be more accepting of their pupils. In addition, a TAT showed that origin scores increased when the pupils were treated as origins, while scores did not increase if such experience was withheld, and did not continue to rise if the treatment was not maintained (see Figure 6–3).

In sum, the concept of origin-pawn is similar to the notion of internal-external locus of control. In contrast to Rotter's conception of control, however, the work with personal causation has followed the clinical rather than the experimental approach to motivation. That is,

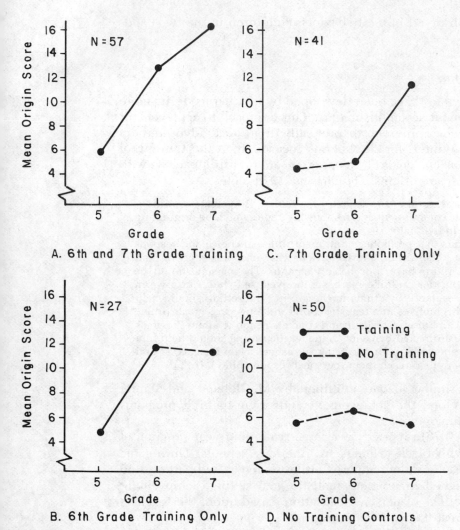

Figure 6–3. Mean origin score before and after motivational training. (Adapted from de Charms, 1976, p. 137.)

rather than specifying the determinants of behavior, de Charms has taken one construct and examined an array of behavior to which it might be applied. This approach has been fruitful and has sparked interesting ideas that have practical application. But the pertinent research is not extensive, and a supporting body of empirical investigations needs to be undertaken.

Intrinsic versus Extrinsic Motivation

Perhaps the most well documented finding in the psychological literature is that pairing a behavior with a reward increases the likelihood that the behavior subsequently will be repeated. This principle of reinforcement was first articulated by Thorndike and later was elaborated in Skinnerian behaviorism. The reinforcement principle also is consistent with the conceptions of behavior discussed in this book. For example, according to Hullian theory, reward reduces a drive, thus augmenting the habit strength of that response and increasing the likelihood that the response will be emitted when the organism is placed in an appropriate stimulus situation. In a similar manner, reward can be construed as increasing the subjective expectancy of goal attainment, which again augments the probability that the organism will engage in the rewarded behavior on future occasions. It certainly makes sense to repeat actions that previously led to desired goals, and theories of motivation are primarily based on the pleasure-pain principle, which is related to the postulated consequences of a reinforcement.

However, there are data that call into question the all-powerful reward principle. For example, Atkinson's theory of achievement motivation and the empirical findings concerning the consequences of success and failure clearly demonstrate that persons desire intermediate risk. Hence, success (a reward) at an easy task should not augment the probability of undertaking that task again. For example, if one defeats a poor tennis player without expending effort, or receives an "A" in a "snap" course, then there is likely to be little desire to compete against that tennis player or to retake the course, even though the prior behavior was "rewarded."

Consistent with the data questioning the positive effects of reward, there is a growing literature documenting that children with initial interest in a task (intrinsic motivation) lose some of that interest when an external reward (extrinsic motivation) is promised for performing that task (Deci, 1975). Stated somewhat differently, when a goal becomes construed as only a means to an end, then that goal loses some of its value (Kruglanski, 1975).

This body of knowledge generally is identified under the heading of "intrinsic versus extrinsic motivation" or "the undermining effects of extrinsic motivation on intrinsic interest." This literature has been influenced by the cognitive evaluation theory of Deci (1975) and is closely related to the distinction made by Rotter and de Charms between internal (origin, intrinsic motivation) and external (pawn, extrinsic motivation) sources of control.

Cognitive Evaluation Theory

The initial proposition of cognitive evaluation theory as proposed by Deci (1975) is:

One process by which intrinsic motivation can be affected is a change in the perceived locus of causality from internal to external. This will cause a decrease in intrinsic motivation, and will occur, under certain circumstances, when someone receives extrinsic rewards for engaging in intrinsically motivated activities." (p. 139)

A fable reported by Ausubel (1948) illustrates this principle:

In a little Southern town where the Klan was riding again, a Jewish tailor had the temerity to open his little shop on the main street. To drive him out of the town the Kleagle of the Klan sent a gang of little ragamuffins to annoy him. Day after day they stood at the entrance of his shop. "Jew! Jew!" they hooted at him. The situation looked serious for the tailor. He took the matter so much to heart that he began to brood and spent sleepless nights over it. Finally out of desperation he evolved a plan.

The following day, when the little hoodlums came to jeer at him, he came to the door and said to them, "From today on any boy who calls me "Jew" will get a dime from me." Then he put his hand in his pocket and gave each boy a dime.

Delighted with their booty, the boys came back the following day and began to shrill, "Jew! Jew!" The tailor came out smiling. He put his hand in his pocket and gave each of the boys a nickel, saying, "A dime is too much — I can only afford a nickel today." The boys went away satisfied because, after all, a nickel was money, too.

However, when they returned the next day to hoot at him, the tailor gave them only a penny each.

"Why do we get only a penny today?" they yelled.

"That's all I can afford."

"But two days ago you gave us a dime, and yesterday we got a nickel. It's not fair, mister."

"Take it or leave it, That's all you're going to get!"

"Do you think we're going to call you "Jew" for one lousy penny?"

"So don't!"

And they didn't. (Ausbel, 1948)

Note that in this story an intrinsically motivated activity (harassing the tailor) became motivated by an external reward (money), and then lost its value. An experiment by Lepper, Greene, and Nisbett (1973) demonstrated this phenomenon in the laboratory. In their study, nursery school children interested in a drawing task were selected as the subjects. The children were asked to perform the task, but under one of three experimental conditions. In an *expected reward* condition the subjects were told beforehand that they would receive a "good player certificate" if they played with the experimental materials. In an *unexpected reward* condition the subjects received the same reward, but they had no knowledge that they were going to receive the certificate until the drawing activity was completed. Finally, in a *control* condition the reward was neither expected nor received.

One or two weeks later the children were given the opportunity to perform the drawing task again during one of their regular classroom hours. The subjects were free to engage in the drawing activity or in other games that also were available. No rewards were mentioned, and the teachers did not encourage play with any particular material. To assess the dependent variable (time spent with the drawing task), researchers secretly observed the children in their free-time activities through a one-way mirror. The data revealed that the children in the expected reward condition exhibited less interest in the task during their free-time period than did the children in the other two conditions. Hence, not only did the expected reward alter subsequent behavior, but the behavior of the rewarded subjects was different from comparable subjects who unexpectedly received the same reward (see Condry, 1977).

Several pertinent questions related to this study immediately come to mind. For example, would extrinsic reward be effective in increasing intrinsic interest among individuals who at first were uninterested in the activity? Would interest be undermined if repeated rewards, rather than only one, were offered, or if a reward other than a "certificate" was given? Is quality of performance, as well as subsequent interest, affected by the source of motivation to perform the activity? What if the reward is given only when the performance is of high quality?

Many of these questions have been examined (see Condry, 1977; Deci, 1975), and some answers have been offered. However, much remains unknown. One useful distinction growing from this work regards the controlling versus the informational aspects of a reward and helps to answer the question raised above regarding the effect of reward for high quality performance. Deci (1975) states:

> Every reward (including feedback) has two aspects, a controlling aspect and an informational aspect which provides the recipient with information about his competence and self-determination... If the controlling aspect is more salient, it will initiate [a] change in perceived locus of causality... If the informational aspect is more salient, [a] change in feelings of competence and self-determination will be initiated. (p. 142)

Research has strongly suggested that contingent rewards indicating that the individual is competent at a task often enhance, rather than undermine, motivation. Hence, for example, a medal for the best performer, which is a sign of superiority, would not be expected to undermine interest.

The "undermining" effect of extrinsic reward appears to be a robust and a powerful phenomenon. The implications of such a finding for the practices of teachers in the classroom, behavior modification procedures, and even for business management are staggering (see Deci, 1975). Thus, in addition to ascertaining the conditions under which such undermining will occur, conceptual frameworks must be developed that can explain the inhibitory effects of external reward. Hopefully, such theoretical networks will be as rich as the theories that account for the positive motivational effects of external reinforcement.

A number of different theoretical explanations of undermining have been offered, although none is able to account for all of the reported data (see Deci, 1975). The most prevalent explanation derives from self-perception theory (Bem, 1972). The self-perception theory proposed by Bem states that individuals infer their personal attitudes and motivations after observing their own behavior. Thus, for example, if individuals performed tasks without external reward, the performers could logically infer that they were intrinsically interested in the tasks. But this conclusion does not follow given an external reward, in which case the individuals could infer that they worked for the reward. Bem's conception is associated with a "radical behaviorism" that asserts thoughts are merely epiphenomena that do not influence action (see Diagram 3–2). Rather, wishes, desires, attitudes, and the like are inferred following action. One must question, however, whether children actually can engage in such complex, post-behavioral inferential processes.

Among the other theoretical explanations of undermining is the suggestion that external reward results in a narrowing of the focus of attention, thus restricting appreciation of the positive or less obvious aspects of a task. However, an experiment contradicting this notion demonstrated that an experimenter's retrospective statement that a reward had been offered for performance, when in reality it had not (the children were being "tricked"), also undermined intrinsic interest (Kruglanski, Alon, & Lewis, 1972). In the study by Kruglanski et al. (1972) unexpected reward caused decrements in behavior, in contrast to the reports of Lepper et al. (1973).

Another interesting theoretical implication of this area of study pertains to the conception of intrinsic and extrinsic motivation provided by Atkinson. According to Atkinson, these two sources of motivation combine to determine the total amount of motivation to undertake an activity. However, the findings of Lepper et al., for example, suggest that intrinsic and extrinsic motivations mutually influence one another, at times in harmful ways. Thus, theorists studying motivation also will have to deal with the interactions between the determinants of action, therefore complicating their task even further.

Perceived Freedom

While the word "freedom" has positive connotations for psychologists when they are in the role of citizens, it often has negative implications when they act in the role of experimentalists. This is because freedom implies the converse of determinism. Freedom is associated with words such as self-determination, or spontaneity, or uncontrolled. On the other hand, many psychologists advocate that behavior is determined. That is, for any given action there are specified antecedents, and in any given situation it can be argued that the displayed behavior "must" have been emitted.

Freud, Hull, and Skinner, opposite in so many respects, agree on the point that behavior is determined. In *Beyond Freedom and Dignity* (1971), Skinner contends that we must give up the illusion of freedom and admit that behaviors are under the control of positive reinforcement. Our knowledge of behavioral engineering can then be used to control human behavior for the betterment of society. But, Skinner states, people refuse to give up the illusion of freedom and the false belief that we are autonomous actors, possessing free will and deserving credit for our actions. If society is to survive, Skinner argues, this conviction must be replaced with the acceptance of external control. In a similar manner, Freud advocated psychic determinism, or the idea that all actions are caused, even slips of the tongue and dreams.

It is possible that action is determined, yet individuals may hold the belief that they have free will. That is, objective causation and subjective freedom are not mutually exclusive. Furthermore, if individuals believe that they have free will, and this influences their action, then even the determinists must accept the existence of this subjective state!

Freedom and Choice

Freedom has been inversely linked with externally imposed constraints upon choice. These constraints may be obvious, such as the limitations on the space of free movement discussed by Lewin (e.g, prisons, rejections, and so on). However, often limitations on freedom of choice are not obvious. For example, Steiner (1970) has proposed that in choice situations, the greater the similarity in the attractiveness of the alternatives, the greater the decision freedom of the actor. For example, assume that a prospective college student can choose between entering two schools. The schools are identical in all respects but cost — one university charges $4,000, while at the other school tuition is $1,000. In this case the person would most likely choose the less expensive college, and it might be argued that there was little freedom of choice, for the properties of the two schools (costs) dictated the decision. That is, the choice was externally controlled, or externally imposed. On the other hand, if the schools are identical in all major aspects, including cost, then there is great freedom of choice. According to this argument, if individuals were asked to judge how much freedom was experienced, they should indicate greater freedom in the latter situation.

One implication of the analysis by Steiner (1970) is that when external forces are strong, perceived freedom is low. Thus, experienced freedom will be minimal, for example, during a job interview or while studying in the library. In these instances the environmental forces dictate a particular kind of decision regarding one's behavior. Because the behavior is "forced" by the environment, one generally cannot learn a great deal about the individuals from observing their actions in those environments. However, in certain instances, persons in those situations will exhibit out-of-role behavior, such as talking in the library or interacting in a hostile manner with the interviewer. In these examples, observers will be quite likely to label the individuals involved as "talkative" or "aggressive" (see Jones, Davis, & Gergen, 1961).

Steiner also has contended that personal freedom varies with the expected value of the alternatives. He labels this "outcome freedom" and states that the greater the positive consequences of the choices, the greater the freedom that is experienced. Thus, for example, a choice between two high-paying jobs should create a greater feeling of freedom than a choice between two lower-paying jobs (assuming these alternatives are equal in all other respects).

Psychological Reactance

Fights for political freedom have occurred throughout history. They often involve acts of extreme heroism and dramatically illustrate the motivational effects of a loss of freedom. In a similar manner, we may be engaged daily in battles to preserve our psychological freedom. There are many common occurrences in which psychological freedom is diminished. Confining a child to his or her room, being forced to accept a decision, hearing a message that one prefers not to listen to, being pressured by others, the imposition of censorship, and even being unable to enroll in a class of one's choice, are some abstract and concrete examples that involve a loss of freedom.

According to Brehm (1966, 1972), when a person's freedom to engage in a behavior is threatened or taken away, the motivation to perform that behavior, and therefore to reinstate freedom, increases. Brehm (1972) states:

> A person is motivationally aroused any time he thinks one of his freedoms has been threatened or eliminated. This motivational arousal, called "psychological reactance" (Brehm, 1966), moves a person to try to restore his freedoms. (p. 1)

Many investigations have demonstrated the motivational effects of psychological reactance. In the majority of these research studies, individuals find themselves unable to engage in behaviors that they thought were originally available. For example, an alternative is eliminated, or an expected message is censored. The experimenter then typically measures the perceived attractiveness of the available and the unavailable options. It is believed that a change in the desirability of the alternatives so that the unavailable alternative gains in attractiveness is one manifestation of an attempt to restore freedom.

In one of the first such experiments, Hammock and Brehm (1966) asked children to rank order the desirability of nine different candy bars. As a reward for this task, some children were told that they would have a *choice* between two candy bars, while others in a control condition were told that they would be *given* one of two different kinds of candy bars. The children were then shown their third and fourth ranked candies, and all were *given* the more attractive of the two. Thus, reactance was created in the decision condition because the children told that they would have a free choice were denied this opportunity. Following the giving of the candy (but before it was eaten), the experimenter had the children re-rate their candy preferences.

If the hypotheses about reactance and perceived attractiveness (attitude) are correct, the preference for the denied ("eliminated") alterna-

TABLE 6–3   MEAN CHANGES IN RANKING OF THE FORCED AND
ELIMINATED CANDY BARS

Conditions	N	Choice Alternative		
		Forced (Rank 3)	Eliminated (Rank 4)	Total Reactance
Experimental	13	−1.23*	.23	1.46
Control	14	.00	−.43	−.43

*A minus indicates a decrease in attractiveness.
(From Hammock & Brehm, 1966, p. 550.)

tive should increase in the choice condition. The data from this investigation are shown in Table 6–3. The findings indicate that the ranking of the eliminated alternative did increase in the experimental or reactance condition. But even more dramatic was the decrease in the attractiveness of the candy bar that the children were forced to take. A second study in which the children were given the less preferred of their choices essentially replicated these findings.

More recently, Mazis (1975) was able to test reactance theory in a real-life situation. In Miami, Florida, an anti-pollution law was imposed that prohibited the use of cleaning materials that contained phosphate. This greatly limited the products that were available to the shoppers. Thus, reactance theory suggested that the buyers should have an increased desire for the banned products, and their positive opinions about these products should be enhanced. To test this idea, Mazis compared attitudes in Miami with those in Tampa, Florida, where the anti-pollution law was not in effect.

Mazis (1975) had subjects (housewives with at least one child living at home) rate the effectiveness of the various detergents they had used during the six months prior to the survey. Table 6–4 shows that the

TABLE 6–4   MEANS FOR EFFECTIVENESS RATINGS OF
PHOSPHATE DETERGENTS

Characteristic	Miami (n = 76)	Tampa (n = 45)
Whiteness	8.68*	8.27
Freshness	8.77	7.87
Cleans in cold water	8.52	7.47
Brightness	8.31	7.84
Stain removal	8.00	6.96
Pours easily	9.45	9.07
Gentleness	8.81	8.71

*Based on an 11-point scale with 11 labelled "absolutely perfect" and 1 labelled "poor."
(Adapted from Mazis, 1975, p. 656.)

ratings of the phosphate detergents were significantly higher in Miami, where the products were unavailable, than in Tampa.

Mazis was able to test additional hypotheses in his field study. Some of the banned products returned to the marketplace without phosphates, but others did not. Thus, the attitudes of individuals who switched products could be compared with those of persons who still used the same brand of detergent. These comparisons revealed that individuals who switched brands rated the effectiveness of their new product lower than those who had not switched. Indeed, the main reactance effect was not that the desirability of phosphate detergent increased, but rather that there was a strong negative attitude toward the quality of the alternative.

Learned Helplessness

The previous section concerning reactance reviewed some studies demonstrating that there are psychological consequences of a loss of freedom and the inability to control one's life. These consequences often may be quite harmful. Two experimental investigations employing rats as subjects dramatically illustrated some of these adverse effects. The procedures used and the consequences observed were so injurious in these experiments that lower organisms had to be the experimental subjects.

In one of these investigations, Mowrer and Viek (1948) gave hungry rats the opportunity to eat food 10 seconds prior to the onset of a shock. For one-half of the animals, the shock could be terminated by a jump into the air. This response was readily learned by the rats. The second group of rats could not terminate the shock through their own actions. Rather, each was paired with a "controlling" rat and received the same amount of shock that the "partner" had received before the partner jumped to terminate the shock.

The experimenters measured the eating behavior of the two groups to examine the effects of the helplessness experience. It was known from prior experimental research that fear inhibits eating. The data revealed that the non-controlling, or "helpless," rats were inhibited in their eating, whereas the consummatory behavior of the controlling rats was not greatly affected. Thus, rats that could terminate shock through their own actions apparently were less fearful, even though the two groups experienced an identical amount of shock.

In the course of subsequent research, Richter (1958) observed many cases of "sudden death" among rats during experimentation. For example, in a study of swimming endurance many unexplained drownings occurred after the rats swam for only a short period of time. Richter (1958) speculated that:

> The situation of these rats is not one that can be resolved by either fight or flight — it is rather one of hopelessness: being restrained in the hand or in the swimming jar with no chance of escape is a situation against which

the rat has no defense. Actually, such a reaction of apparent hopelessness is shown by some wild rats very soon after being grasped in the hand and prevented from moving. They seem literally to give up. (pp. 308–309)

Thus, it again was inferred that a loss of control has adverse effects on the well-being of the organism (see Lefcourt, 1973).

Learned Helplessness and Depression

Perhaps the most systematic and influential analysis of the loss of control is that by Seligman (1975) and his colleagues. The majority of their research investigations have been conducted with infrahumans, although humans are now being increasingly used as research subjects.

Seligman (1975) contends that organisms are helpless when their actions do not influence outcomes. Seligman's analysis of the antecedents of helplessness is depicted in Figure 6–4. In the figure the horizontal axis shows the probability of a reinforcement when a response is made, $p(RF/R)$. The vertical axis shows the probability of the reward, given no reponse, $p(RF/\overline{R})$. According to Seligman, if $p(RF/R) = p(RF/\overline{R})$ (the diagonal line in Figure 6–4), that is, if the response does not increase the likelihood of receiving a reinforcement, then the conditions for helplessness have been established. For example, assume that a baby goes to sleep after crying for one hour. The harried parents try to shorten this aversive period by rocking, or feeding, or even playing music to the baby. Despite all actions, however, the baby still falls to sleep after one hour of crying. Thus, the reinforcer (the offset of crying and the onset of sleep) is independent of the behavior of the mother and father. The parents, therefore, are helpless in this situation. (However, as will be seen, there is some ambiguity as to whether helplessness refers to the reinforcement contingencies or to the reactions of the organism. These are not perfectly correlated.)

To study helplessness in the laboratory, researchers first adminis-

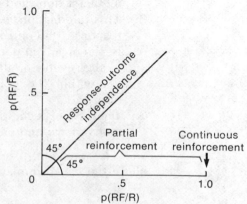

Figure 6–4. Portrayal of the antecedents of learned helplessness. (Adapted from Seligman, 1975, p. 17.)

tered inescapable shock to dogs for a period of time. The dogs were in a harness-type device, and the shock was administered to one of their back legs. Then, these animals, as well as other dogs not given inescapable training, were placed in the shuttle boxes used by Miller in the study of fear. In this situation a conditioned stimulus came on, signalling to the animals that shock would follow. However, unlike in the harness procedure, the shock could be terminated by crossing a barrier in the middle of the shuttle box that separated the "safe" from the "unsafe" compartments.

Seligman and his colleagues (e.g., Seligman and Maier, 1967) observed that many of the dogs given prior inescapable aversive training did not attempt to terminate the shock in the shuttle box. Rather, they passively accepted their supposed fate; they appeared to have "learned helplessness." This behavior contrasted markedly with the actions of dogs not exposed to the prior shock treatment. The untrained dogs engaged in a variety of behaviors until the escape response was learned. Similar differences in behavior have been reported in experiments using inescapable training on a variety of other infrahumans, including fish, rats, and cats.

It must be added, however, that not all animals exposed to inescapable shock exhibit helplessness, and deficits are displayed on some subsequent tasks but not on others. Furthermore, in some cases helplessness is exhibited if testing immediately follows training, while a waiting period erases the helplessness effect. And finally, there is some question as to whether the animals are unable to learn the new responses or are motivationally depressed and, therefore, do not engage in activities that might lead to new learning (see Levis, 1976). Hence, the distinction between learned helplessness as a training condition and learned helplessness as a response pattern or reaction to the conditions is important to make.

To explain the observations of learned helplessness, Seligman (1975) initially proposed a three-stage theory. The theory asserts:

1. Information is gained about the contingency between outcome and responding. In the case of helplessness training, this information reveals that there is no contingency or association between instrumental actions and reward.
2. This information results in the development of the expectation that responses and outcomes will remain independent in the future. That is, the organism perceives or believes that there is nothing it can do to alter events or alleviate its plight. (Note that the theory therefore fits within the general framework of expectancy-value formulations.)
3. The low expectation causes deficits in future learning as well as motivational and emotional disturbances.

This program of research more recently has been expanded to include the use of human subjects. In one research investigation, Hiroto and Seligman (1975) demonstrated the phenomenon of learned helplessness in humans. Subjects were exposed to either an escapable or an inescapable aversive tone. The subjects then were given a "finger shuttle box" task in which they could escape the noise by moving their hands. Hiroto and Seligman report that in this situation the individuals exposed to the prior inescapable tone performed poorly, compared to groups without prior training or with escapable noise training. Hiroto and Seligman also found that failure at solving a discrimination problem (response-outcome independence at a cognitive task) caused decrements in subsequent anagram-solving behavior. Again, however, these findings are not unambiguous, for it is well known from research on achievement strivings that failure often enhances, rather than retards, subsequent learning and performance.

Finally, the research of Seligman and others called attention to a parallel between helplessness learning in the laboratory and human depression. Table 6–5 lists some of the similarities between these two phenomena. It certainly does appear fruitful to think of some kinds of depression as akin to learned helplessness. Seligman's model, originally derived from laboratory work with animals, therefore may aid in the understanding of complex human problems. More recently, an attributional analysis of learned helplessness has been proposed and will be examined in the following chapter.

TABLE 6–5 SUMMARY OF FEATURES COMMON TO LEARNED HELPLESSNESS AND DEPRESSION

	Learned Helplessness	Depression
Symptoms	Passivity	Passivity
	Difficulty learning that responses produce relief	Negative cognitive set
	Dissipates in time	Time course
	Lack of aggression	Introjected hostility
	Weight loss, appetite loss, social and sexual deficits	Weight loss, appetite loss, social and sexual deficits
	Ulcers and stress	Ulcers (?) and stress
		Feelings of helplessness
Cause	Learning that responding and reinforcement are independent	Belief that responding is useless
Cure	Directive therapy: forced exposure to responses that produce reinforcement	Recovery of belief that responding produces reinforcement
	Electroconvulsive shock	Electroconvulsive shock
	Time	Time
Prevention	Immunization by mastery over reinforcement	(?)

(Adapted from Seligman, 1975, p. 106.)

Learned Helplessness and Reactance

It appears that learned helplessness theory and reactance theory generate antithetical predictions about responses to uncontrollable events. Reactance theory states that if one loses control, attempts are made to restore that control. That is, one is motivated to regain freedom and choice. On the other hand, helplessness research suggests that motivation is impaired when control is lost. Organisms are expected to become passive, rather than active, following experiences with uncontrollable events.

Wortman and Brehm (1975) have attempted a rapprochement of these two conceptions. They contend that the theories are not contradictory, but rather represent part of a temporal sequence of psychological reactivity. They state:

> Using the theoretical constructs of expectation of control and importance, we believe that it is possible to integrate the helplessness and reactance models into a single theoretical statement. If a person expects to be able to control or influence outcomes that are of some importance to him, finding those outcomes to be uncontrollable should arouse psychological reactance. Thus, among individuals who initially expect control, the first few trials of helplessness training should act as a threat to their freedom. They should experience increased motivation to exert control, and improved performance should occur. The more important the uncontrollable outcome, the more reactance should be experienced. But despite his increased motivation to do so, the individual comes to learn through extended helplessness training that he cannot control the outcome. When a person becomes convinced that he cannot control his outcomes, he will stop trying.
>
> Reactance will precede helplessness for individuals who originally expect control... Importance is not a variable in Seligman's (1975) model. It is our contention, however, that the importance of the outcome plays a crucial role in the determination of helplessness. A person simply will not be noticeably depressed or bothered by the noncontingency of responses and outcomes if the outcomes are trivial. The impossibility of influencing extremely important outcomes, such as the behavior of a loved one or professional recognition, might plausibly be very upsetting and capable of causing a state of depression. Thus, we hypothesize that when a person becomes convinced that he cannot control an outcome, the state of helplessness is directly proportional to the importance of the outcome that he was trying to influence.
>
> Figure [6–5] summarizes the hypothesized relationships between expectation of control over the outcome, importance of the outcome, and amount of helplessness training or experience with lack of control in the determination of a person's motivation to exert control. At point a, we are assuming that the individual expects to have control over the outcome. If so, moderate amounts of helplessness training will lead to psychological reactance, and increased attempts to maintain control. For this reason, individuals who have undergone just a small amount of helplessness training should be more motivated to exert control, and show better performance, than those who have had no helplessness training. The more important the outcome, the more reactance should be experienced. Of course, a person's expectation of control should decline as he experiences more and more helplessness training. Point b represents the point at which the person has no expectation of control—either because he has learned from helplessness training that control is impossible, or for other reasons. . . . As Fig. [6–5]

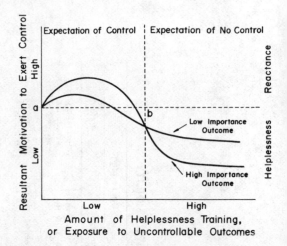

Figure 6–5. The model integrating reactance and helplessness. (From Wortman & Brehm, 1975, p. 309.)

indicates, individuals who do not expect control (see point *b*) will not exhibit reactance regardless of the importance of the outcome. Experience with lack of control will quickly result in helplessness. The more important the outcome, the greater the amount of helplessness that will be experienced. (Wortman & Brehm, 1975, pp. 307–309)

Wortman and Brehm (1975) also review a large amount of research that appears to support their idea that small amounts of helplessness training are facilitative, while large amounts produce passivity (see Roth & Kubal, 1975).

Personal Responsibility: An Integration

Six overlapping areas of research have been examined briefly in this section of the chapter. These research topics are labelled locus of control, personal causation, intrinsic-extrinsic motivation, perceived freedom, reactance, and learned helplessness (see Table 6–6). It is evident that these topics of study have much in common. First of all, they all are concerned with the allocation of responsibility along an internal (self) versus external (environmental) dimension. Thus, the concepts of internality, origin, intrinsic motivation, perceived freedom, and controllability are linked, as are the concepts of externality, pawn, extrinsic motivation, low perceived freedom, and uncontrollability.

Investigations of these concepts have focused on both the antecedents that lead to these particular feelings and the consequences or effects of these states. Among the antecedent conditions (and this is not including all of the possibilities discussed by the pertinent theorists) are the skill or luck involved in the task, the structure of the situation, the amount of external reward offered, the equivalence of the alternatives, the barriers in the world, and the contingency between the response and the outcome (see Table 6–6). These prior conditions affect the amount of information search, expectancy shifts, personal experience of being an

TABLE 6-6 APPROACHES TO THE STUDY OF PERSONAL RESPONSIBILITY

Concept	Theorist	Antecedents		Consequences	
		Internal	External	Internal	External
Locus of Control (Internal-External)	Rotter (1966)	skill task	chance task	information seeking; typical shift in expectancy	information avoidance; atypical shift
Personal Causation (Origin-Pawn)	de Charms (1968)	"correctly" structured setting	overly structured setting	origin feeling; realistic	pawn feeling; unrealistic
Intrinsic-Extrinsic Motivation	Deci (1975)	low external reward; intrinsic motivation	high external reward	continued motivation	lack of continued motivation
Perceived Freedom	Steiner (1970)	equivalent alternatives	unequivalent alternatives	perceived choice freedom	little perceived choice freedom
Reactance	Brehm (1966)	no barriers	barriers	state of equilibrium	attitude shift; motivated to restore equilibrium
Learned Helplessness	Seligman (1975)	response-outcome dependence	response-outcome independence	normal functioning	learning, motivational, and cognitive deficits

origin or a pawn, realism of goal setting, degree of continuing motivation, perceived freedom of choice, attitudes, and the functioning of the organism. Again the reader is reminded that the implications discussed by Rotter, de Charms, Deci, Steiner, Brehm, and Seligman extend far beyond this already enormous range of behaviors and psychological states and processes. It is little wonder, then, that this research has attracted so much attention; at this time, personal responsibility is perhaps the most popular topic in the fields of motivation, personality, and social psychology.

It also is evident from Table 6–6 that personal responsibility has evaluative associations: Internality is "good" and externality is "bad." More specifically, as shown in Table 6–6, internality is supposed to produce openness to information, proper expectancy shifts, the feeling of being an origin, realism, continued motivation, perceived freedom, and normal functioning, while externality produces an avoidance of information, inappropriate expectancy change, the feeling of being a pawn, lack of realism, poor continuing motivation, little perceived freedom of choice, attempts to restore freedom, and deficits in learning, motivation, and cognition. It should be recognized, however, that thinking of some of these consequences as "bad" is a value judgment. For example, given a Marxist orientation, one might contend that giving up personal freedom to the group is a higher goal for which we must strive. That is, the positive consequences of a loss of control may be underestimated if the voluntary giving up of control promotes the greatest good for the greatest number. It certainty is true that the social context of research influences the scientific process; the research on perceived freedom has a distinctly American origin and flavor.

Summary

Social learning theory provides an alternative to the intrapsychic and often scientifically inadequate formulations of psychoanalytic theory. In contrast to those analytic formulations, social learning theorists assert that the important determinants of behavior are learned and that perceptions of the actions of others (models) influence the learning process. In addition, it is believed that the external situation plays a key role in guiding action; behaviors are expected to vary across discriminatively different stimulus situations. These beliefs have resulted in what is known as the trait-situation controversy, presently one of the most debated issues in the field of personality.

Julian Rotter has formulated an expectancy-value theory of behavior from the perspective of social learning. He postulates that behavior potential is determined by the expectancy of goal attainment and the value of the goal or reinforcer. Expectancy, in turn, is believed to be a product of the prior reinforcement history in a specific stimulus situation and a generalized belief about reinforcers learned from behaviors in similar situations. Although expectancy and value are independent, the interrelationships between these constructs greatly affect personal adjustment. A low expectancy of success coupled with a highly valued goal is particularly likely to generate behavioral problems.

One area of research that developed from Rotter's conception of behavior concerns locus of control. Rewards can be perceived as the result of personal ability or effort, as in skill-related tasks, or controlled by external factors, as in chance tasks. Perceptions of environments as skill- or chance-determined influence shifts of expectancy following success and failure. In addition, there are individual differences in the perception of environments as personally or externally controlled. Research investigations have suggested that persons classified as internal in locus of control display more information seeking and make better use of this information than individuals classified as external in locus of control.

In addition to the study of locus of control that grew from Rotter's theory, several other current research areas involve perceived responsibility and personal freedom. These areas are known under the headings of personal causation (origin versus pawn experiences), intrinsic versus extrinsic motivation, perceived freedom, reactance, and learned helplessness. Studies have identified some of the antecedent conditions that influence these beliefs and states, and some of the psychological consequences of beliefs concerning personal control and freedom. Of especial interest is the suggestion that perceived loss of control may be one of the precursors of depression. The study of perceived responsibility presently is the most active research area within the fields of personality, motivation, and social psychology.

In the previous chapters, I indicated the fruitfulness of psychoanalytic theory, the precision of Hullian theory, the real-world concerns of Lewinian theory, and the combination of these values in achievement theory. Social learning theorists advocate a more careful use of concepts, thus bringing more restraint into motivation research. They also have demonstrated the importance of environmental, rather than intrapsychic, determinants of action. In so doing, more balance has been brought to the generally accepted belief that behavior is a function of both the person and the environment. And by initiating the study of personal control, social learning theorists have identified a major psychological issue. It is of interest to note that while concerning themselves with psychology as a science, advocates of social learning theory have prompted a major philosophical debate: the meaning of free will.

Section III

Mastery and Growth Theories

Chapter Seven

ATTRIBUTION
THEORY

Introduction

It is evident that most motivational psychologists have accepted the belief that behavior is in service of the pleasure-pain principle. That is, organisms seek to maximize pleasurable stimulation and to minimize painful experience. This should come as no surprise for, as Freud (1922) noted: "The impressions that underly the hypothesis of the pleasure principle are so obvious that they cannot be overlooked" (p. 1). Freud often is considered the staunchest advocate of the hedonistic position, although both the drive and the expectancy-value theorists also assume that pleasure seeking and pain avoidance are the "springs of action."

Freud, however, did consider a second "motive force," akin to what we now know as mastery behavior, or competence seeking. Recall that the chapter on psychoanalytic theory mentioned that some behaviors, such as traumatic dreams, games of disappearance (peek-a-boo), and transference (the patient acting as if the analyst were a parental figure), are engaged in even though they apparently do not increase pleasure. Freud therefore concluded:

> We shall be forced to admit that ... the whole ground is not covered by the operation of the familiar motive forces [the pleasure principle]. Enough is left unexplained to justify the hypothesis of a compulsion to repeat — something that seems more primitive, more elementary, more instinctual than the pleasure principle which it overrides. (Freud, 1922, p. 17)

Freud then went on to suggest that this compulsion to repeat or return was part of the functioning of the death instinct. But Freud also considered an alternate explanation. Concerning disappearance games, he stated:

> ... One gets an impression that the child turned his experience into a game from another motive. At the outset he was in a *passive* situation — he was overpowered by the experience; but, by repeating it, unpleasurable though it was, as a game, he took on an *active* part. These efforts might be put down to an

275

instinct for mastery that was acting independently of whether the memory was in itself pleasurable or not. (Freud, 1922, p. 10)

Freud also applied the principle of mastery to explain transference and traumatic dreams. On the subject of traumatic dreams, he suggested:

> But it is not in the service of that principle [pleasure] that the dreams of patients suffering from traumatic neuroses lead them back with such regularity to the situation in which the trauma occurred. We may assume, rather, that dreams are here helping to carry out another task, which must be accomplished before the dominance of the pleasure principle can even begin. These dreams are endeavoring to master the stimulus retrospectively. (Freud, 1922, p. 26)

In sum, Freud recognized two fundamental principles of action, or motive forces: 1) hedonism (pleasure-pain), and 2) understanding the environment and oneself. Pleasure-pain has been the principle guiding the field of motivation, and it seems reasonable to expect that it will not be supplanted as a source of action. But in recent years it is increasingly being supplemented by mastery and information-gain notions. Similar ideas were suggested for the explanation of intermediate risk taking in achievement-related contexts (see Chapter Five).

The mastery, or understanding, position today finds its most conspicuous expression among psychologists identified with attribution theory. For example, Harold H. Kelley (1967), one of the leading psychologists in this area, assumes that humans are motivated to "attain a cognitive mastery of the causal structure of [the] environment" (p. 193). One wants to know why an event has occurred—to what source, motive, or state it may be ascribed. Fritz Heider (1958), the acknowledged "founder" of attribution theory, explains:

> The causal structure of the environment, both as the scientist describes it and as the naive person apprehends it, is such that we are usually in contact only with what may be called the offshoots or manifestations of underlying core-processes or core-structures. For example, if I find sand on my desk, I shall want to find out the underlying reason for this circumstance. I make this inquiry not because of idle curiosity, but because only if I refer this relatively insignificant offshoot event to an underlying core event will I attain a stable environment and have the possibility of controlling it. Should I find that the sand comes from a crack in the ceiling and that this crack appeared because of the weakness in one of the walls, then I have reached the layer of understanding conditions which is of vital importance for me. The sand on my desk is merely a symptom, a manifestation that remains ambiguous until it becomes anchored to dispositional properties—cracks and stresses in this case. . . . The search for relatively enduring aspects of our world, the dispositional properties in nature, may carry us quite far from the immediate facts or they may end hardly a step from them. That is, there exists a hierarchy of cognitive awarenesses which begins with the more stimulus-bound recognition of "facts," and gradually goes deeper into the underlying causes of these facts. . . . Man is usually not content simply to register the observables that surround him; he needs to refer them as far as possible to the invariances of his environment. . . . The underlying causes of events, especially the motives of other persons, are the invariances of the environment that are relevant to him; they give meaning to what he experiences and it is these meanings that are recorded in his life space, and are precipitated as the reality of the environment to which he then reacts. (pp. 80–81)

As already suggested in the prior quotes from Freud, the portrayal of humans as information seekers is not unique to attribution theorists. Festinger's theory of social comparison, for example, includes the fundamental proposition that:

> . . . there exists, in the human organism, a drive to evaluate his opinions and his abilities. . . . A person's cognition (his opinions and beliefs) about the situation in which he exists and his appraisals of what he is capable of doing (his evaluation of his abilities) will together have bearing on his behavior. The holding of incorrect opinions and/or inaccurate appraisals of one's abilities can be punishing and even fatal in many situations. (Festinger, 1954, p. 117)

It might be contended that understanding the self and the environment promotes survival, and, in either the short or the long run, is pleasurable. This is implied in the quotation taken from Festinger (1954). Thus, mastery striving would be subsumed within the pleasure principle. However, it also can be argued that the desire for understanding is independent of hedonic concerns and, in the event that the knowledge is unpleasant, information seeking is manifested in spite of a conflicting pleasure principle. That appears to be Freud's contention and is the belief espoused by attribution theorists.

In addition to the acceptance of a mastery principle, a second characteristic of attribution theory that differentiates it from the conceptions discussed thus far is its purely cognitive approach to human motivation. Thus, before presenting the attributional approach in any detail, I will discuss briefly some of the history and basic assumptions of cognitive psychology. After that, I will examine attribution theory and the antecedents that influence the attribution process. This will be followed by some criticisms of the attributional approach, and then by extensions of attribution theory to explain cognitive dissonance, emotions, and selected aspects of infrahuman behavior.

HISTORICAL BACKGROUND AND GUIDELINES OF THE COGNITIVE APPROACH

Cognitive psychology is concerned with how incoming sensory stimulation is "transformed, reduced, elaborated, recovered, and used" (Neisser, 1966, p. 4). Stimuli, as conceived by cognitive theorists, do not goad the organism or initiate mechanistic chains of thought. Rather, the stimuli are viewed as a source of information. It is frequently contended that the processed information is integrated into a "belief" that gives "meaning" to the external, physical environment.

The study of mental processes, which often had been unfruitful, became buried in the psychological avalanche produced by Watson and subsequent behaviorists such as Skinner and neobehaviorists such as Hull. This was partly fostered by the misconception that only the study of behavior (overt responses) could answer the functionalists' question of how an organism adapts to its environment. During the past 30 years, the associationistic grip on psychology has gradually weakened, and is no longer in evidence. The issue raised by contemporary psychologists is not whether cognitions affect behavior, but how and under what conditions will this influence be manifested.

The current acceptance of the study of mediational processes is the result of a multiplicity of factors. Perhaps the main reason for the growth of a cognitive psychology was the inability of the mechanists to explain many behaviors. But Heider (1958) further points out that the wide use of projective testing, the interest in perception by experimental psychologists, and the regard for person perception expressed by social psychologists provided the impetus and climate for the study of higher mental processes. In addition, the advent of information theory and computer models lent scientific respectability to the examination of mental events. These mathematical approaches promised to give more precision and operational anchoring to the often vague terminology associated with the study of the mind. Finally, contemporary cognitive theorists have incorporated the methodological advances and sophistication of behaviorists into their investigations.

Cognitive Theories of Behavior

Baldwin (1969) describes a cognitive theory of behavior in the following manner:

> A cognitive theory of behavior assumes that the first stage in the chain of events initiated by the stimulus situation and resulting in the behavioral act is the construction of a cognitive representation of the distal environment. The later events in the chain are instigated, modified and guided by this cognitive representation. The cognitive representation thus acts as the effective environment which arouses motives and emotions, and guides overt behavior toward its target or goal. (p. 326)

The analysis of behavior therefore requires two distinct steps (see Diagram 7–1). First, there is a cognitive representation (schema) of the perceived stimuli. Second, there is a specification of how the cognition influences the final behavioral response. That is, environmental stimulation is related to mediational interpretations, and behavior is undertaken "because it seemed to me" (Neisser, 1966, p. 4).

DIAGRAM 7–1

Model of a Cognitive Theory of Behavior

Antecedent Stimuli———→Mediating Cognitive Event———→Behavior

Thus, it is apparent that a cognitive theory of action must contain at least the rudiments of a theory of thought to fulfill the first of the two steps outlined above. Of the theories examined thus far, Hull's conception was entirely mechanistic, with no concern about, or acceptance of, mental events. The conceptions of Freud and the expectancy value theorists made use of both mechanistic (energy, tension, force) and cognitive (ego, life space, expectancy) concepts, but without a detailed analysis of mental processes. The primary cognitive component in the expectancy-value theories of Lewin, Atkinson, and Rotter captures experience or learning, and is embodied in the terms psychological distance, subjective probability, and expectancy of goal attainment. But, as Festinger (1957b) noted:

> Certainly, if a person is motivated toward some end, the specific actions in which he engages, will, in part, be determined by his cognition about his environment and about the paths that will lead to the end he desires. But this states only one aspect of the relation between action and cognition. (p. 128)

The theories of motivation presented thus far in the book have ignored these other "aspect[s] of the relation between action and cognition," and have not attempted to construct a theory of thought. They have failed to consider, for example, information scanning and selection, information combination and storage, and perceptions of causality, to name just a few of the higher processes relevant to action. The concern of theorists such as Lewis and Atkinson with other cognitive functions, such as memory organization and fantasy, are peripheral to their formal systems of behavior and are not systematically integrated into their conceptions.

One can only speculate on why theorists such as Lewin, Atkinson, and Rotter have not been more concerned with cognitive processes and the relationship between thought and action. Atkinson, for one, was heavily influenced by Freud's argument that the major determinants of behavior are unconscious. He believed that individuals cannot even accurately report their general level of achievement needs. But it also is true that the major motivational theorists with relatively cognitive orientations were more directly interested in action than in thought. Attribution theorists, if anything, have reversed this order of interest, and have been more concerned with causal inferences than with the behavioral consequences of these inferences. I will now turn to attribution theory and the problem of causal inference.

GENERAL ATTRIBUTIONAL APPROACH

There is no unified body of knowledge that neatly fits into one specific attribution theory; there are many types of attribution theorists and theories. Nevertheless, there are some central problems that guide the thoughts of all investigators in this field (e.g., Heider, 1958; Jones, Kanouse, Kelley, Nisbett, Valins, and Weiner, 1972; Kelley, 1967; Weiner, 1974). Attribution theorists are concerned with perceptions of causality, or the perceived reasons for a particular event's occurrence. Three general programs of research have emerged from the analysis of perceived causality. First, the perceived causes of behavior have been specified, with particular consideration given to a distinction between internal or personal causality and external or environmental causality, as reviewed in the last chapter. Second, general laws have been developed that relate antecedent information and cognitive structures to causal inferences. And third, causal inferences have been associated with various indexes of observed behavior. For example, assume that one's toes are stepped on while riding the subway. Attribution theorists are likely to ask: a) What are the perceived causes of this event (e.g., an intentional aggressive act, an accident, a result of standing too near the door)? b) What information influenced this causal inference (e.g., the clenched fist of the aggressor, the observation that other people's toes are being stepped on, the observation that only people standing near the door were stepped on)? and c) What are the consequences of the causal ascription (e.g., hitting the aggressor, deriding the public transportation system, moving away from the door)?

It should be noted that the perception of causality is an ascription imposed by the perceiver; causes *per se* are not directly observable. You can only infer, for example, that an individual stepped on your toes because "he is aggressive" or because "it was an accident." Hume (1739) argued that causality is not an inherent property of sensory events. To use Hume's example, one can see that upon impact of ball A, ball B moves. One might then conclude that A caused B to change location; that is, one can attribute the moving of B to the impact of A. But one does not "observe" causes. Hume (and later Kant, 1781) contended that causes are constructed by the perceiver because they render the environment more meaningful.

The prevalence of causal constructions was dramatically illustrated in experiments reported by Heider and Simmel (1944) and Michotte (1946). In the Michotte experiments, a red and a black disc (A and B) were presented as moving on a screen. Object A approached and "bumped" B. If B immediately moved, then individuals had the "causal impression" that the withdrawal was due to A. Michotte labelled this the "Launching effect." Perception of the Launching Effect is greatly influenced by the interval between the arrival of A and the departure of B. Figure 7–1 shows that if the interval between A's arrival and B's departure was shorter than 75 milliseconds, a "direct launching" interpretation was given by the subjects. "Delayed launching" was the most probable interpretation if the delay interval approximated 100 milliseconds. If the delay time was longer than 200 milliseconds, subjects did not perceive that A caused B to move. Michotte also noted that if B moves together with A after impact, B was believed to be "carried along" or "joined" with A. He labelled this the "Entraining Effect."

The Heider and Simmel (1944) experimental paradigm was similar to that of Michotte, although they employed three moving figures rather than two. The figures were a large triangle, a small triangle, and a circle. The stimulus configuration was more complex than that employed by Michotte, and interpersonal dramas unfolded from the movements. For example, impacts were interpreted as fights, joint movements generated themes of "belonging," and so forth. Heider and Simmel noted the "great importance which causal interpretation plays in the organization of events" (p. 251). This organization is largely determined by motives that were attributed to the figures. Perceived self-induced actions lead to different interpretations than behaviors perceived as induced by others.

The experiments of Heider and Simmel (1944) and Michotte (1946) blur the distinction between perception of physical objects and perception of persons. Objects were perceived as "people" with motives, emotions, and so forth. Well before these experiments, Hume had reasoned that all perceptions of causation are constructs; he did not differentiate between causal analyses of physical and psychological events.

Heider's Naive Attributional Theory

Heider considers his work an "investigation of common-sense psychology" (1958, p. 79) inasmuch as he is concerned with how the "common man" thinks about causality. The language he employs and many of the basic concepts in attribution theory are taken from common vernacular. Words such as "give," "take," "try," "can," and "may" are the foundation of Heider's conceptual analysis. Heider

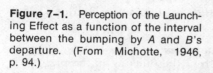

Figure 7-1. Perception of the Launching Effect as a function of the interval between the bumping by A and B's departure. (From Michotte, 1946, p. 94.)

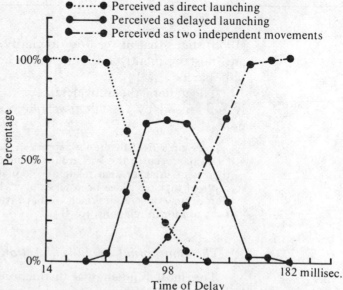

FRITZ HEIDER

(K. G. Heider)

The attributional approach to psychology received its impetus from the writings of Fritz Heider. Heider was born in Austria in 1896 and received his Ph.D. from the University of Graz in 1920. It is interesting to note that Heider's dissertation advisor was Professor Meinong. Meinong had written his dissertation under the direction of Professor Brentano, who is closely identified with the pleasure-pain principle of motivation.

After completing his dissertation, Heider moved to Berlin, where he came under the influence of the Gestalt psychologists, particularly Kurt Lewin and Max Wertheimer. In 1930 Heider went to the school for the deaf at Smith College for what was supposed to be a year-long visit. However, there he met another psychologist, Grace Moore (Heider), and established residency in the United States after their marriage. In the late 1940's Heider left Smith College for the University of Kansas, where he continues to be active today (1978).

Heider's insights into interpersonal relations and common-sense psychology were relatively neglected by psychologists until publication of his book. *The Psychology of Interpersonal Relations* (1958). Heider is responsible for two seminal contributions to psychology: balance theory, which gave rise to theories of cognitive organization, and the study of attribution processes.

Heider's writings are sparked with warmth and wit. He is perhaps unique among academic psychologists in drawing heavily on works of literature for his scientific insights. He exemplifies the scholar-humanist-scientist ideal.

(1958) states that his goal is "to clarify some of the basic concepts that are most frequently encountered in an analysis of naive descriptions of behavior" (p. 14).

The general theoretical framework employed by Heider was strongly influenced by Gestalt psychology and Kurt Lewin. Heider (1958) notes:

> Lewin's field-theoretical approach known as topology (Lewin, 1936, 1938) has been in the background of much of the thinking in the present theory of interpersonal relations. Though not many of the specific concepts of topology have been taken over, they have helped in the construction of new ones with which we have tried to represent some of the basic facts of human relations. (p. 4)

The Conceptual Analysis of Action

The most fundamental distinction made by Heider (1958) is that behavior depends upon factors within the person and factors within the environment. This is manifestly similar to the Lewinian statement that behavior is a function of the person and the environment: $B = f(P,E)$. However, Heider is referring to the perceived causes of behavior and not to the determinants of force actually acting upon the person or influencing an outcome (although he frequently slips into usage of "motivation" rather than "perceived motivation"). The science of motivation and the ethnoscience of motivation (the science of the layman) may yield quite diverse laws. That is, the "true" laws of behavior and the perceived causes of action may not be identical (although they should be interrelated).

A simple example taken from Heider clarifies the person-environment differentiation. Assume that one is rowing across a lake on a windy day. The final outcome (reaching the other side) may be perceived as the result of factors within the person (ability, effort, fatigue) and factors in the environment (wind, waves). Whether the opposite shore is reached depends on a combination of these sources of causation. In a similar manner, success on a test could be perceived as resulting from personal factors (ability, the amount of time spent studying) or factors in the environment (an easy test, grading policy). Heider believes that the internal and external forces combine additively to determine behavior. In the rowing example, either the wind or personal factors such as ability may be sufficient to produce the desired consequence. If the effective environmental forces are zero, then the outcome is dependent only upon personal causal factors. In a similar manner, "without personal intervention ... the wind (could) carry the boat to the shore" (Heider, 1958, p. 82).

The distinction between personal and environmental causes of behavior is implicit in all the theories discussed in this book. Hull, for example, postulated that behavior is, in part, determined by independent drive (person) and incentive (environment) factors. Thus, instrumental action to attain food might be undertaken because the person is hungry (push) or because the goal object is especially attractive (pull). Lewin also specified that the valence of the goal is a function of needs of the person and properties of the goal object. And according to Atkinson's theory of achievement motivation, individuals differing in resultant achievement motivation (personal factor) differentially work to achieve success at tasks varying in difficulty (environmental factor). In sum, both the person and the environment influence action. But Heider, as opposed to Hull, Lewin, and Atkinson, stresses the consequences of differential ascriptions to internal versus external factors.

Consequences of Internal versus External Attributions

One quality that differentiates external and internal determinants of behavior is that only sources of action attributed to the person (internal) can be considered "intentional." This has important implications in the field of interpersonal relations and is examined in the following chapter. More important in the present context, differential allocation of causality between the two factors also results in disparate affective experiences, future expectations, and behaviors. For example, if the rower in the example perceived that reaching the other side was due to the aid of the wind, he might row only on windy days or not attempt to cross the lake again. In a similar manner, if success at a test is attributed to personal factors, such as ability, rather than task ease, the person might expect to do well in other classes, feel more pride, enroll in more difficult courses, raise her occupational aspirations, or study less hard.

The behavioral consequences of person versus environment attribution is discussed at length by Heider (1958):

> Our judgment of a situation and its possible future development may depend greatly on whether we attribute the psychological phenomenon to the subject or to the object. If a person enjoys an object it may be because the object is very enjoyable or it may be because of very personal reasons located in him.
>
> If the former, any person who has commerce with the object will find it satisfying. This is a judgment about the value of the object and refers to a more invariant disposition of the object. Once this judgment is made, a host of expectations that guide our actions are possible. If I want to make a person happy, I will present him with the object, for instance. If I want to annoy him, I may prevent him from obtaining it. Believing that the object is desirable, I may attempt to make someone envious by flaunting it. I may welcome identification as its creator in order to be admired or liked. I myself will attempt to interact with the object again, the interaction taking various forms depending on further conditions. I may try to have physical contact with the object or I may talk about it or think about it. It will be recorded in my belief-value matrix as something I like. . . .
>
> If p believes that the source of enjoyment is located in O [another person] and not in the object, however, very different expectations arise. They depend upon the presumed facts about O implied by the enjoyment. . . .
>
> Attribution to the person . . . could mean that O is easily satisfied, that he is a peculiar person, that he has sophisticated taste, that he is like me, etc. These "facts" implied by the enjoyment of O are personality traits, the dispositional properties upon which expectations are based. Thus, if I attribute O's enjoyment to his sophistication, then I may expect him to enjoy a different but equally artistic object, to dislike something that is trite, to enjoy the company of a connoisseur, etc. In each of these expectations, it is the object or situation that varies, but the dispositional property of the person remains the same.
>
> If we correctly analyze the raw data . . . we know much more about the event itself and about future occurrences. A highly general statement that can be made is: If we know that our present enjoyment is . . . attributed to our own personality, then at most we can expect only persons who have a similar personality to enjoy it. . . .
>
> It is our opinion . . . from the point of view of the psychological meaning of action (motion) it may make all the difference whether A moves and B is still or vice versa, whether Mohammed goes to the mountain or the mountain moves to him. (pp. 147–151)

The analysis by Heider, therefore, can be incorporated within the general context of the study of perceived responsibility and freedom, as summarized in Table 6–6. However, Heider has extended the consequences of perceived causality even beyond the broad range of Rotter, de Charms, and others.

Formal Analysis

Heider has postulated that the outcome of an action is a function of the effective personal force and the effective environmental force:

outcome = f(effective personal force, effective environmental force)

The effective personal force, in turn, is allocated to two factors: power and motivation. Power often refers to ability, although other relatively stable personal attributes (e.g., strength) also determine power. Motivation refers to the direction of a person's behavior (intention) and to how hard one tries (exertion). Thus:

outcome = f(trying, power, effective environment)

Heider believes that trying and power are related multiplicatively. Neither ability without exertion, nor exertion without ability, is able to overcome environmental obstacles. If either of the two factors has a strength of zero, then the effective personal force also is zero.

Heider (1958, p. 84) regroups the three perceived determinants of action so that power (ability) and the effective environment are integrated (see Diagram 7–2). Diagram 7–2 indicates that the relation of power to environmental factors determines whether a goal "can" be attained. For example, one's intelligence in relation to the difficulty of a test determines whether one "can" pass the test. In a similar manner, physical strength in relation to the width of the lake, wind resistance, and so forth determines whether one "can" or "cannot" row to the opposite shore. But whether "can" is exhibited in action depends on motivation, or "try." Heider (1958) summarizes:

> Relating the roles of "can" and "try" in the action outcome to the effective forces of the person and of the environment, we can state the following: When we say, "He can do it, but fails only because he does not try sufficiently" then we mean that the effective personal force is smaller than the restraining environmental force only because the exertion is not great enough; with greater exertion he would succeed. (p. 86)

DIAGRAM 7–2

Perceived Determinants of Action, with Power Grouped Either with Personal Forces or with the Effective Environment

Personal Forces———Effective Environment
Outcome = f(trying, power, effective environment)
Try————Can

Inasmuch as the effective personal force is determined by both power (ability) and exertion, the greater one's ability, the less the effort needed to overcome environmental obstacles (considered here as the difficulty of a task):

$$\text{exertion} = f(\text{difficulty/power})$$

This means that where different people have the same power, the minimum exertion needed to succeed in a task will vary with the difficulty. It also follows that if the task is held constant, the person who has less power or ability will have to exert himself more to succeed. The greatest exertion will be needed when the person has little power and the task is difficult. (Heider, 1958, p. 111)

Simple mathematical transposition also yields:

$$\text{power} = f(\text{difficulty/exertion})$$

Heider (1958) continues:

Thus, if two people exert themselves to the same degree, the one who solves the more difficult task has greater power. The one who has to exert himself more to solve a task of given difficulty has the lesser power. And the greatest power or ability will be shown by the person who solves a difficult task with little exertion. This, by the way, is the theoretical basis for including timed problems in tests of intelligence. The person who can solve a problem quickly does so with less exertion than the one who takes considerably longer and therefore should be given added credit toward his total intelligence score. (p. 111)

ATTRIBUTION OF "CAN" TO THE PERSON OR THE ENVIRONMENT.   The preceding discussion indicated that *can* or *cannot* may be ascribed to the person or to the environment. For example, holding exertion constant, one may ascribe success at a task to high ability or to the ease of the task. In a similar manner, failure can be attributed to a lack of ability or to the difficulty of the task.

In one investigation bearing upon this point, Weiner and Kukla (1970, Exp. VI) gave subjects information concerning the outcome of an achievement task (success or failure). They also included social norm information revealing the percentage of others successfully completing the task (99, 95, 90, 70, 50, 30, 10, 5, 1). The subjects then rated whether the outcome in the 18 conditions (two levels of outcome × nine levels of social norms) was attributable to the hypothetical person who attempted the task. Ascriptions were indicated on a rating scale anchored at the extremes (outcome due/not due to the person).

The results of this investigation are shown in Figure 7–2. It is evident from the figure that the greater the consistency between outcome and the performance of others, the less the attribution to the person (or the greater the inferred attribution to task difficulty). That is, if one succeeds when most others do likewise, or fails when most others fail, the outcomes are ascribed to an easy or hard task respec-

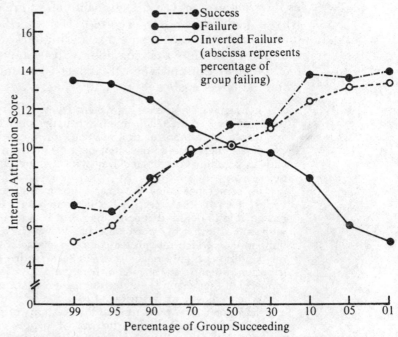

Figure 7-2. Mean internal attribution score for success and failure outcomes as a function of task difficulty. (From Weiner & Kukla, 1970, p. 18.)

tively. But if one succeeds when others fail, or fails when others succeed, the outcomes are attributed to the person. Social norms are, therefore, one source of information that allow an individual or an observer to determine whether "can" or "cannot" is attributable to the person or the environment.

The attribution of "can" to the person or to the environment is of utmost functional significance. As discussed earlier, if success at a task such as passing a course is ascribed to task ease, the individuals might enroll only in other courses given by that teacher, not exert themselves for the next exam, and so forth. On the other hand, if success is ascribed to high ability, they might expect to do well in all other courses, raise their levels of aspiration, and the like.

Figure 7-2 reveals that social norms are an important source of information in determining causality. The most systematic and influential analysis of the determinants of causal inferences has been undertaken by Harold Kelley. This chapter focuses on the analysis of causal antecedents, including those outlined by Kelley, while the following chapter stresses the consequences of causal ascriptions.

Causal Antecedents

Attribution theorists have been particularly concerned with how causal attributions are reached — the information used or the processes or structures activated that enable one to reach an ascription about why a particular event occurred. Heider (1958), guided by Mill's method of inquiry, contends that attributions are reached according to the following rule: "that condition will be held responsible for an effect which is present when the effect is present and which is absent when the effect is absent" (p. 152). Thus,

> . . . if I always experience enjoyment when I interact with an object, and something other than enjoyment when the object is removed (longing, annoyance, or a more neutral reaction, for instance) then I will consider the object the cause of the enjoyment. The effect, enjoyment, is seen to vary in a highly coordinated way with the presence and absence of the object. . . .
>
> If I sometimes enjoy the object and sometimes do not, then the effect varies, not with the object, but with something within me. I may or may not be able to define that something, but I know that the effect has to do with some fluctuating personal state. It may be my mood, my state of hunger, etc., which though temporary in character, are often detectable as the conditions highly related to the effect. Notice that in this type of attribution, a temporary state and therefore a more or less nondispositional property of the person is singled out as the source of the pleasure. . . .
>
> When enjoyment is attributed to a dispositional property of the person, additional data pertaining to the reactions of other people are necessary. Concretely, if I observe that not all people enjoy the object, then I may attribute the effect to individual differences. . . . That is to say, the effect, enjoyment in this case, depends upon who the person is. With o enjoyment is present, with q it is absent. We sometimes, then, speak about differences in taste. The important point is that the presence and absence of the enjoyment is not correlated with the presence and absence of the object, but rather with the presence and absence of different people. Therefore o is felt to enjoy x, and q to be dissatisfied with x, because of the kind of person each is. (pp. 152–53)

Kelley (1967) has systematized the factors that result in causal attributions to either person or environmental factors. He also assumes that covariation is the foundation of the attribution process and likens the ascription of causality to the more formal statistical procedures employed by scientists. Assume, he writes, that an individual enjoys a movie. The question then raised is whether the enjoyment, or "raw data," is attributed to the person (for example, she is easily pleased) or to the perceived properties of the entity (it is a good movie). Kelley (1967) reasons that the responsible factor may be determined by examining the covariation of the effect and causal factors over "a) entities (movies), b) persons (other viewers of the movie), c) time (the same person on repeated exposures), and d) modalities of interaction with the entity (different ways of viewing the movie)" (p. 194). Attribution of the enjoyment to the entity (movie) rather than to the person or self is most likely if the individual responds differentially to movies, if the response to this movie is consistent over time and modalities, and if the response agrees with the social consensus of others. Thus, the probability of attribution to the movie is maximized when the individual enjoys only that movie (high distinctiveness), when she enjoys it on repeated occasions and over different modalities (high consistency) and when all others also like the movie (high consensus). On the other hand, if the individual likes all movies, that is, her response to the entity is not distinctive, if her enjoyment of the movie varies (low consistency), and if no one else likes this particular picture (low consensus), then we would ascribe the enjoyment to temporary or stable attributes of the viewer, or perhaps to the circumstance at the time of viewing.

McArthur (1972) tested some of Kelley's speculations regarding the antecedents of causal ascriptions. She gave subjects information concerning the consensus, distinctiveness, and consistency of a behavior. Each bit of information indicated that the behavior was characterized as either high or low on these three antecedent dimensions. Subjects were informed, for example, that "John laughs at the comedian."

> Consensus information took the form:
> a. Almost everyone who hears the comedian laughs at him. (high consensus)
> or b. Hardly anyone who hears the comedian laughs at him. (low consensus)
> Distinctiveness information took the form:
> a. John does not laugh at almost any other comedian. (high distinctiveness)
> or b. John also laughs at almost every other comedian. (low distinctiveness)
> Consistency information took the form:
> a. In the past John has almost always laughed at the same comedian. (high consistency)
> or b. In the past John has almost never laughed at the same comedian. (low consistency) (McArthur, 1972, p. 174)

The subjects were required to assign causality for the event to one of four alternatives:

> a. Something about the person (John) probably caused him to make Response X (laugh) to Stimulus X (the comedian).
> b. Something about Stimulus X probably caused the person to make Response X to it.
> c. Something about the particular circumstances probably caused the person to make Response X to Stimulus X.
> d. Some combination of a, b, and c above probably caused the person to make Response X to Stimulus X. (McArthur, 1972, p. 175)

Note, therefore, that in addition to the familiar internal and external causes, a third alternative of circumstance was introduced. McArthur also included four verb categories — emotion (e.g., is afraid of the dog), accomplishment (e.g., succeeded at a task), opinion (e.g., thinks the teacher is unfair), and action (e.g., contributes a large sum of money). However, these and other complexities of her experiment will not be discussed here.

In general, McArthur's findings confirmed Kelley's suppositions. For example, person attributions were most prevalent given low consensus, low distinctiveness, and highly consistent behavior (see Figure 7–3). Hence, laughter at the comedian was ascribed to John when

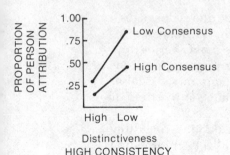

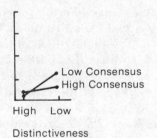

Figure 7–3. Proportion of total attributions made to the person as a function of consensus, distinctiveness, and consistency information. (Adapted from McArthur, 1972, p. 178.)

no one else laughs at this comedian, when John laughs at other comedians, and when he laughs at this comedian on other occasions. On the other hand, attributions to the stimulus, or environmental entity, were generated when the behavior was high in consensus, distinctiveness, and consistency (all people laugh at this comedian, John only laughs at this comedian, and he laughs at this comedian on other occasions). Finally, circumstance ascriptions were generated with highly distinctive behavior that was low in consistency (John only laughs at this comedian, but does not laugh at him on other occasions).

Orvis, Cunningham, and Kelley (1975) replicated these findings and more systematically examined the antecedents of causal ascriptions. These investigators contend that there are particular patterns of evidence associated with ascriptions to the person, stimulus, and circumstances (see Table 7–1). Examination of the columns of Table 7–1 reveals that each causal ascription is uniquely linked with a particular bit of information. Thus, high consensus (everyone laughs at the comedian) should tend to elicit stimulus attributions; low distinctiveness (John laughs at all comedians) should tend to elicit person attributions; and low consistency (John does not laugh on other occasions) is expected to elicit circumstance attributions. Orvis et al. gave subjects either one, two, or three bits of information, and had them make person, stimulus, or circumstance attributions for an action. When only one bit of information was given to the subjects, the following patterns emerged: High consensus yielded stimulus attributions among 70 per cent of the respondents; given low distinctiveness, 94 per cent of the respondents implicated the person; and low consistency resulted in

TABLE 7–1   INFORMATION PATTERNS FOR THE THREE ATTRIBUTIONS

	Information Pattern		
Attribution	Consensus	Distinctiveness	Consistency
Stimulus	High	High	High
Person	Low	Low	High
Circumstance	Low	High	Low

(From Orvis, Cunningham, & Kelley, 1975, p. 607.)

more than half of the subjects making circumstance inferences. In addition, the three patterns of information shown in Table 7–1 also led to respective person, stimulus, and circumstance inferences, but not with any greater frequency than subjects given only the one uniquely associated cue.

Causal Schemata

The investigation by Orvis et al. (1975) revealed that even in the absence of complete information, individuals are able to use partial evidence to reach logical causal inferences. Indeed, in the typical situation all the information needed to perform a complete covariation analysis is not available. In these instances, Kelley (1972) suggests that causal schemata, or general rules that relate causes and effects, are elicited. These rules, which are built up from prior experiences, are activated by appropriate environmental cues and enable the person to transcend situations in which the available information is limited.

One such rule, or schema, suggested by Kelley (1972) relates causal inferences to the magnitude of an event. Kelley hypothesizes that extreme or atypical events elicit "multiple necessary" causal rules, whereas mild or typical events elicit "multiple sufficient" causal rules. To explain what is meant by necessary and sufficient causality, consider a simple situation in which two causes (X and Y) are associated with an effect (Z). For example, eating or not eating (the observed effects) may be associated with the presence or absence of hunger and/or the presence or absence of attractive food (the perceived causes of eating or not eating). An individual may believe that the presence of either hunger *or* attractive food will produce eating behavior. This *disjunctive* set of causal relations, coded linguistically as an "or" relationship, is referred to as a multiple sufficient causal schema. Each cause in and of itself is capable of producing the effect. On the other hand, the person may believe that both hunger *and* the availability of desirable food are required to produce eating behavior. This *conjunctive* set of causal relations, coded as an "and" relationship, is referred to as a multiple necessary causal schema. Both causes are needed to produce the effect (see Kelley, 1972).

The significance of causal schemata is that they permit the individual to predict effects from the presence or absence of certain causes. Furthermore, given an effect, they generate inferences about the underlying causes. For example, if an individual observes someone eating, a multiple necessary schema would lead to the deduction that the person was hungry *and* that the food was attractive. This inference obviously has functional significance.

Necessary schemata and sufficient schemata generate different attributions and beliefs about the world (see Table 7–2). As already indicated, if the attributor knows that Z has occurred, a multiple sufficient schema allows him to infer that either X or Y was present.

Further, if it is known that X was present when Z occurred, there should be uncertainty about the presence of Y, provided that X and Y are independent. As shown in Table 7–2, Z occurs given X regardless of the presence or absence of Y. Thus, for example, if a person eats when hungry, we should be uncertain about the attractiveness of the food, given a sufficient schema relating eating behavior and the presence of hunger. On the other hand, if a multiple necessary schema is used, the occurrence of Z in the presence of X provides unequivocal evidence for the presence of Y. As depicted in Table 7–2, with a necessary schema, Z occurs only when both X and Y occur. Thus, if a necessary schema is used, we infer that the food is attractive when eating behavior is observed.

To test the supposition that extreme or atypical events elicit multiple causality, whereas mild or typical events elicit sufficient causality, Cunningham and Kelley (1975) gave subjects examples of both of these types of situations (e.g., "a theater critic wrote a rather favorable review of a new play" versus "a theater critic . . . described it as one of the best plays of the decade"). The subjects then had to determine whether the described event was due to something about the play and/or something about the writer. As predicted, multiple sufficient causality was more likely to be inferred given extreme events (although there were types of events for which this was not the case).

Lest the reader think that this experiment does not capture "real life" situations, Cunningham and Kelley offer the following examples of situations where we must make similar decisions or causal inferences:

When a person reads in a sports page account of a football game that the defensive guard knocked the opposing quarterback unconscious, he

TABLE 7–2 MULTIPLE SUFFICIENT AND MULTIPLE NECESSARY CAUSAL SCHEMATA SHOWING THE PRESENCE OR ABSENCE OF TWO CAUSES (X AND Y) AND THE PRESENCE OF AN EFFECT (Z)

Multiple Sufficient Schema

		Absent	Present
Cause Y	Present	Z	Z
	Absent	—	Z

Cause X

Multiple Necessary Schema

		Absent	Present
Cause Y	Present	—	Z
	Absent	—	—

Cause X

(From Kun & Weiner, 1973, p. 199.)

may wonder what to make of the event. Does it say something about the guard's skill, size, and aggressiveness, or does it reflect more on the ineptitude and fragility of the quarterback? Similar questions about the causes of the event may occur to the reader when he learns that the local mayor enthusiastically endorses an unknown upstate politician in the senatorial race, that a movie director is madly in love with the ingenue, or that a business man is extremely critical of the director of a particular government agency. (Cunningham & Kelley, 1975, p. 74)

Discounting

Given a multiple sufficient schema, individuals may discount or disregard the extent to which a second cause has contributed to an effect. For example, in the previous chapter it was suggested that individuals who were offered a reward to undertake an intrinsically interesting task may come to believe that they performed the task only for that reward. That is, their intrinsic interest is discounted. "Undermining" then may be explained by the use of a particular causal schema.

Another example of discounting has been demonstrated in a study of surveillance (Strickland, 1958). In Strickland's experiment, a subject was assigned to be a supervisor over two (fictitious) students supposedly performing a task. The supervisor had the power to observe and punish one of the workers more than the other. The supervisor was given feedback that the two workers exhibited identical satisfactory performance, and punishment was not administered. The causal determinants of the subordinates' performances were then indicated by the supervisor. In addition, a subsequent task was performed in which the supervisor was free to monitor the performance of either worker. Trust was inferred from the relative amount of time spent observing the two subordinates and from self-reports obtained in a questionnaire.

The results of the study indicated that the supervisor ascribed the performance of the more monitored worker to the external threat of punishment, verbalized less trust in him, and monitored him more on the subsequent task. Thus, the worker's role as a cause was discounted in this context.

Power over another, even if not used, often results in attributions of successful outcomes to the power source. Attributions of confidence and trust to another person apparently are not made unless there has been an opportunity to exhibit positive performance under non-power conditions. The power situation inherent in the student-teacher relationship may foster a similar attributional error in which the principle of discounting plays a major role.

The Actor-Observer Perspective

Throughout the discussion of attribution theory it has been indicated that a distinction between dispositional factors and situational factors is especially important, inasmuch as attributions to either the subject or object pole have quite disparate consequences. It has been demonstrated that specific cues, such as consensus, consistency, and distinctiveness information, influence whether ascriptions are to the person or the environment. In addition, it has been contended that there are systematic differences in attributions as a function of the perspective of the attributor. More specifically, Jones and Nisbett (1972) have stated that "there is a pervasive tendency for actors to attribute their actions to situational requirements, whereas observers tend to attribute the same actions to stable personal dispositions" (p. 2). Statements such as "I hit him because he provoked me" and "you hit him because you are an aggressive person" exemplify the antici-pated actor-situation and observer-person inferential biases.

Jones and Nisbett (1972) offered a number of plausible reasons for these biases. They contend that actors have knowledge about how they acted across diverse situations. Their variance in behavior across different settings diverts them from making dispositional attributions about their own actions. (Note that this explanation assumes that indi-viduals indeed behave differently in disparate environmental settings, as Mischel and other social learning theorists have contended.) On the other hand, the absence of distinctiveness information may bias ob-servers toward a dispositional attribution. Secondly, Jones and Nisbett suggest that actors focus their attention upon the environment, but ob-servers concentrate on the actors and their behavior. Hence, actors will perceive the environment as salient, while observers perceive the per-son as prominent. In sum, actors and observers base their inferences on disparate information and, hence, may reach incongruous judgments.

If attention or focus is responsible for attributional biases, then it should be possible to alter these biases by manipulating relative self-awareness. A number of research investigations apparently have dem-onstrated that altering perspective does change causal ascriptions. For example, Duval and Wicklund (1973) had subjects read several scen-arios, such as:

> Imagine that you have selected and purchased a race horse. You enter the horse in a major race and hire a good jockey to ride him. The horse wins first place. To what degree did your actions cause the victory and to what degree did the actions of the jockey cause the victory?
> Imagine that a friend of yours wants to get you a date. You tell her what characteristics you like in a date and she selects one of her friends. You go out with him and have a very good time. To what degree did your actions cause the successful date and to what degree did the actions of your friend cause the successful date? (p. 26)

Half the subjects read these stories under normal conditions; the rest read the passage while in front of a conspicuous mirror. The presence of the mirror was expected to alter the focus of awareness to oneself and thus bias the attribution toward the self. In accordance with the reasoning of Jones and Nisbett, individuals in the "mirror" condition made relatively more self attributions, while subjects in the control condition gave more situation (e.g., the friend) ascriptions. On the basis of these data and related findings, Duval and Wicklund (1972, 1973) suggest that in all instances the locus of causality is determined by the focus of attention.

In a related investigation, Storms (1973) suggested that if observers were provided with the perspective of an actor, and if actors were provided with a view of their behavior from the perspective of an observer, then these re-orientations should weaken or reverse the hypothesized actor-observer biases. To test these ideas, Storms videotaped a brief get-acquainted conversation between two strangers (actors). Two other subjects (observers) merely watched the conversation. In one of the experimental conditions the actors and the observers were then shown tapes of the conversation with the same orientation they had at the time of the act. In a second condition, the actors saw themselves on videotape, while the observers watched a videotape of the conversation from the perspective of the actor. The subjects then were asked, among other questions, to what extent personal characteristics or the situation influenced their friendliness, talkativeness, nervousness, and dominance. As Storms hypothesized, the actors viewing themselves from the orientation of the observer became relatively more dispositional in their attributions, while observers seeing the perspective of the actor became more situational.

However, in spite of these confirmatory findings, the status of the actor-observer hypothesis remains uncertain (see Monson and Snyder, 1977). Part of the problem is that self and environmental attributions are not always clearly one or the other. For example, if female X states that she dates male Y because he is sensitive, does that indicate a situational attribution, or that she likes sensitive people, a trait attribution? This confounding is made even sharper if we consider the "freedom" of behavior (internality) among the different species. In general, the higher the species, the greater the variability in behavior within a particular situation. An instinctive pattern of behavior is one that once initiated, remains invariant despite changes in the situation. Does this indicate that the lower the species, the greater the internality (person attribution), and the higher the species, the more the behavior is externally controlled? Or does it reveal that higher organisms are sensitive to their environments and that this sensitivity is a characteristic of self-determined behavior? The latter seems to be a more plausible interpretation.

In addition to this confounding, reversals in the actor-observer biases also have been found (see review in Monson and Snyder, 1977). In achievement-related contexts, for example, actors typically ascribe success and failure to ability and/or effort, which are personal factors. In sum, although the actor-observer hypothesis has attracted as much (or more) attention than any single supposition in attribution theory, relatively little is known as yet about the effects of perspective on attributional biasing.

The Rational Person

The prior discussion of informational antecedents and causal schemata portrayed humans as scientists and rational decision makers — taking data from the world, performing covariation analyses or imposing pre-existent rules, and reaching logical causal inferences. Differences in inference making between individuals, when evident, were ascribed, in part, to disparities in focus of attention, which again can be considered evidence concerning the information-processing tendencies and capabilities of humans.

The conception of humans as rational has been called into question by (at least) three sources of evidence. First, it has been contended that there are motivated errors in judgment. That is, ascriptions are biased because often they have hedonic consequences. Second, there is a growing array of data demonstrating that humans are poor information processors — they have limited informational capabilities, use incorrect rules, make judgments given insufficient evidence, and so forth. And third, it has been contended that many actions are not mediated by complex cognitions or causal inferences. Rather, behaviors often are automatically elicited by environmental stimuli.

Hedonic Biases

A large amount of research on hedonic biasing has been conducted in achievement-related contexts. In one experimental demonstration of a "motivated" attributional error (Johnson, Feigenbaum, & Weiby, 1964), teachers conveyed arithmetical concepts to two fictitious "students." The feedback to the teachers was manipulated. Performance of one of the pupils remained high over trials, while the performance of the second student was portrayed either as repeatedly low (L-L) or as ascending from low to high (L-H). Following performance feedback, attributions for the success and failure of the students were ascertained. The data indicated that the teachers primarily attributed the performance of students in the L-L condition externally to the pupils (low ability and/or low effort). On the other hand, in the L-H condition the teachers ascribed the performance to themselves.

Beckman (1970) reports a similar finding. In her experiment, teachers also conveyed mathematical concepts to two fictitious students. However, Beckman included a descending performance conditon (H-L) in her study and examined the causal judgments of uninvolved "observers" as well as those of the participating teachers. The attributions for the pupils' performances in the H-L and L-H conditions are shown in Table 7–3. The table reveals that the participating teachers were more likely to attribute the ascending rather than the descending performance to themselves. On the other hand, the observers stated that the teachers were more responsible for the H-L than L-H performance! These findings, although provocative, have been questioned because in other investigations such attributional biases by

TABLE 7–3   TEACHING SKILLS AS A PERCEIVED CAUSAL FACTOR IN STUDENT PERFORMANCE

Experimental Condition (Pattern of Performance)	Teachers		Observers	
	Yes	No	Yes	No
Low-High	13*	4	2	10
High-Low	7	12	7	8

*Number of subjects employing teaching ability as a perceived cause.
(From Beckman, 1970, p. 79.)

teachers have not been displayed (see Beckman, 1973; Ross, Bierbrauer & Polly, 1974).

Perhaps the clearest finding of what appears to be a motivated error in attribution is that individuals are prone to accept credit for success while placing the blame for failure on an external cause (see review in Miller and Ross, 1975). However, even this finding, if correct, can be explained without recourse to motivational concepts. Success may be a more typical outcome than is failure. Hence, failure is high in distinctiveness and low in consistency, which leads to external (task difficulty) or circumstantial inferences, whereas success, which is low in distinctiveness and high in consistency, is ascribed to the person.

There are other errors in causal ascriptions that seem to be indicative of ego-defensive or ego-enhancing tendencies, but instead may be the result of ignorance or misuse of information. For example, Kelley (1967) notes that during periods of inflation, business gains may be ascribed by a businessman to his acumen rather than to the favorable economic circumstances. This error is fostered by the tendency for rewarded responses to be repeated. The repetition of the response-reward sequence provides evidence of covariation and results in a causal inference of self responsibility. On the other hand, during a depression, it is likely that unfavorable economic conditions are blamed for decreasing profits. Regardless of the individual's actions, business declines. Thus, there is no covariation of response with outcome, and the consequences are apt to be externally ascribed. But note that the ascription of success to the self and of failure to the environment is not attributable to a motivational bias to enhance the self. The same explanation can account for the findings of teacher biases in attribution.

In general, it has proven quite difficult to demonstrate unambiguously self-serving biases in the attribution of causality (see Miller and Ross, 1975). However, in the face of the overwhelming evidence that behavior is a function of both the id and the ego (wishes and reality), it seems impossible that motivated inferential errors do not exist. And everyday observations often reveal instances of mass personal delusion! Thus, the current failure to demonstrate strong and pervasive hedonic biases must be attributable to the experimental paradigms that thus far have been used, particularly their relatively weak manipulations. For example, success or failure at some relatively meaningless laboratory task is unlikely to produce strong causal biasing.

In one of the more involving experiments that demonstrated a hedonic bias, Pepitone (1950) led subjects to believe that their ideas about athletics could be instrumental to the attainment of desirable athletic tickets. Three judges (stooges) questioned the subject, and varied in their expressions of approval and apparent power to make the ticket-granting decision. The data revealed that the subjects rated the judges expressing approval of their ideas as more powerful in making the final decision than relatively disapproving judges.

In sum, the rational approach of attribution theorists has not been contradicted by the large number of studies searching for self-serving attributional biases. At the same time, such biases are bound to exist and have been demonstrated. The conception of a rational or logical human proposed by most attribution theorists was not meant to imply that we are not affected by unfulfilled wishes, a desire to protect self-esteem, and so on. Rather, the general belief is that persons typically behave in a rational manner, and logical thinking may explain a great deal, but not all, of causal inference making.

The Boundaries of Rationality

The prior discussion suggested that some so-called motivated errors might be due to inadequacies in cognitive processes such as information search and integration. There is a growing literature demonstrating that because of cognitive limitations humans indeed are poor decision makers (see Tversky and Kahneman, 1974). Herbert Simon, one of the leading decision theorists, has stated:

> The capacity of the human mind for formulating and solving complex problems is very small compared with the size of the problems whose solution is required for objectively rational behavior in the real world —or even for a reasonable approximation to such objective rationality. (Simon, 1957, p. 198)

Inasmuch as reaching a causal attribution can also be considered a complex decision problem, it should be anticipated that humans will be imperfect attributors. Hence, the capabilities of the attributor appear to fall short of the conception of rationality put forth by attribution theorists. In the following pages some of these cognitive deficiencies are reviewed and related to the attribution process.

THE "FALSE CONSENSUS" EFFECT. One source of attributional bias uncovered by Ross, Greene, and House (1977) has been called the "false consensus" effect. This effect refers to the tendency to perceive one's own behavior as "common and appropriate to existing circumstances, while viewing alternate responses as uncommon, deviant, and inappropriate" (Ross et al., 1977, p. 280). Since one's own responses are perceived as common (high consensus), they will tend to be ascribed to factors in the situation. On the other hand, responses of others that differ from one's own responses are perceived as uncommon (low consensus) and will tend to be ascribed to the person. The false consensus effect, therefore, can explain the hypothesized actor-observer attributional bias.

To demonstrate such inaccurate beliefs about consensus, Ross et al. (1977) presented subjects with a number of scenarios, such as:

> As you are leaving your neighborhood supermarket a man in a business suit asks you whether you like shopping in that store. You reply quite honestly that you do like shopping there and indicate that in addition to being close to your home the supermarket seems to have very good meats and produce at reasonably low prices. The man then reveals that a videotape crew filmed your comments and asks you to sign a release allowing them to use the unedited film for a TV commercial that the supermarket chain is preparing. (p. 281)

This story was followed by two queries:

a.   What per cent of your peers do you estimate would sign the release?____%
b.   What per cent would refuse to sign it?____% (Total should be 100%)

After responding to this questionnaire, the subjects were asked which of the two options they personally would choose. They also completed personality scales concerning persons who would choose option a, and identical scales concerning persons who would choose option b.

The data very clearly revealed that behavioral choice was associated with the perception of behavioral consensus. For example, individuals who personally would sign the release also believed that others would sign, while non-signers expected others not to sign. In addition, the trait ratings indicated that stronger personality inferences were made about individuals who would choose the response that differed from one's personal choice.

In a related experiment, subjects were asked to describe some of their preferences and perceived traits. They were then asked to rate "college students in general" on these same categories. The results supported the social consensus hypothesis, for persons perceived their own traits and preferences as consistent with others.

PERCEPTIONS OF RANDOMNESS AND ILLUSIONS OF CONTROL AT CHANCE TASKS.   It clearly is important to distinguish chance from skill situations. Any effort invested in instrumental responding in a chance situation is "wasted," whereas misperception of a skill task as one of chance could result in a failure to expend the appropriate effort needed for goal attainment. Yet investigators have demonstrated that individuals often misperceive chance and skill tasks. For example, randomness of outcome is one characteristic of a chance task. But individuals do not recognize randomness when they see it and cannot produce random patterns when asked (Bakan, 1960; Cohen and Hansel, 1956). A random sequence constructed by "naive" persons has too many alternations. For example, in a series of coin tosses, subjects expect alternate or double alternate head (H) and tail (T) sequences, such as HTHTHT or HHT and TTH, while the frequencies of sequences such as HHHTTT are underestimated.

In addition, chance events often are misperceived as skill determined, as if the outcomes at a chance-determined task were under personal control. The reader has probably observed gamblers at slot machines or dice games acting as if they were personally "responsible" for hitting the jackpot or throwing a seven. Some of the determinants of such illusions of control have been identified and include the availability of choice, familiarity with the situation, active involvement, and competition (Langer, 1975).

For example, competition typically is associated with skill-related tasks, such as tennis or bridge. Hence, the introduction of competition into a luck setting could give the illusion that the game is skill determined. To test this notion, Langer had subjects compete against another person in a card selection game. The person choosing the higher card from the deck, which is entirely luck-determined, was the winner. In one experimental condition the subject competed against a person acting in a confident manner (actually a confederate), while in a second condition the confederate "appeared rather shy, behaved awkwardly, had a nervous twitch, and was dressed in a sportcoat that was too small for him" (Langer, 1975, p. 314).

The subjects were allowed to wager up to 25 cents on each of four bets. The amount of the bet was assumed to be an index of expectancy of success. Inasmuch as the task was entirely one of chance, the characteristics of the competitor should not have altered the perceptions of winning. However, the data revealed that the subjects wagered more when competing against the "schnook."

In other demonstrations of fallacious reasoning reported by Langer (1975), persons were less willing to sell a lottery ticket when they selected the number than when merely being given a ticket. Thus, the introduction of choice or preference seemed to create the illusion of control. In addition, individuals were less willing to sell a lottery ticket if it contained familiar letters rather than unfamiliar symbols. On the bases of these data and the personal responsibility literature, Langer (1975) concluded that there is a motivation to control events and that this desire is responsible for creating the illusion of control. Furthermore, she reasoned that the greater the similarity between chance and skill situations in terms of their stimulus properties, the more likely that this illusion will be manifested.

Related findings have been reported by Wortman (1975). Wortman hypothesized that individuals are likely to believe that chance events can be controlled if they can initiate the outcome and have foreknowledge of what result is desired.

To test these hypotheses, Wortman (1975) showed subjects two consumer items. The subjects were told that they would be receiving one of these items on the basis of a chance drawing. Two marbles were then placed in a can and represented the two consumer objects.

For one-third of the subjects the experimenter selected the marble, although the subjects were told beforehand what marble represented each consumer item. Another one-third of the subjects selected their own marble, also knowing what prize it represented. Finally, in a third condition, the subjects chose their own marble but without knowledge of its paired prize. Wortman found that subjects who "caused" their own outcome by selecting the marble, and also knew what each marble represented, perceived that they had more control over the outcome and thought they were more personally responsible for the result. Thus, here again it can be seen that an objective chance event is subjectively perceived as under personal control, given certain environmental conditions.

ILLUSORY CORRELATIONS.   Recall that both Heider and Kelley contend that covariation is the foundation of the attribution process. A covariation or a correlation between two variables means that knowledge of one variable enables prediction about the second variable. Research has shown that correlations often are misjudged because of deficiencies in the cognitive system.

Two sources of error have been uncovered in the study of correlations. Chapman and Chapman (1969) demonstrated that prior expectations about the relation between two variables can lead to the perception of a correlation that does not exist. Chapman and Chapman presented subjects with information concerning several hypothetical mental patients. The information was a drawing by a particular patient and that patient's hospital diagnosis. Later the subjects estimated the frequency with which diagnostic categories (such as paranoia) had been accompanied by a specific type of drawing. In making these judgments, the subjects overestimated the covariation or association between certain of the variables. The Chapmans label this an "illusory correlation," for subjects perceived what they expected to find (e.g., a correlation between paranoia and "suspicious eyes" drawings). The Chapmans point out that clinical diagnosticians may be victims of some of the same type of errors.

A second source of error in judgments of correlations is that individuals do not make equal use of all the information that they have. Smedslund (1963) and Jenkins and Ward (1965) have demonstrated that associative beliefs primarily are based on instances of the joint positive occurrences of the judged variables. Slovic (1972) illustrates this principle with the following example:

> A woman asked Abigail Van Buren the following question: "Why do so many people say that marijuana is harmless? Our daughter began using it in January. She went on to mescaline in March, and was in a mental hospital in July." (Slovic, 1972, p. 7)

This woman erred in basing her belief about a covariation between marijuana use and mental illness on only one case. But in addition, this example also illustrates an instance in which positive values of both variables under consideration were in evidence. Instances in which

persons using marijuana did not become mentally ill, or in which individuals not using marijuana did become mentally ill, were ignored.

IMPLICATIONS FOR ATTRIBUTION THEORY.   There are a number of
demonstrations that persons are not optimal users of information. They
perceive false consensus, they confound skill and chance situations, and
they misperceive covariation. But these are only some of the cognitive
deficits; many other examples could have been presented (see Tversky &
Kahneman, 1974). Clearly, attribution theorists must take these shortcomings into account. Perhaps individuals should not be portrayed as rational,
but rather as perceiving themselves as rational, or as trying to act in a
rational manner. Inasmuch as attribution theorists embrace phenomenology, or the world as perceived by the actor, such an alteration would not
violate the basic tenets of attribution theory.

The Role of Cognitions

The attributional viewpoint, which is closely aligned with cognitive
psychology, assumes that thoughts guide behavior. However, it is not
known, for example, when and how often individuals actually make
causal attributions, or impose "rules" to direct their actions. Many psychologists are now suggesting that the prevalence of attributions — and
their functional significance — is much less than that presumed by attribution theorists.

One critique of the rationalistic approach centers on the concept of
"scripts" (Abelson, 1976). A script is considered a "linked chain of
vignettes stored as a unit". . . (Abelson, 1976, p. 34). With experience, one
comes to expect or anticipate an entire script when just exposed to part of
it. Thus, one does not have to process cognitively all the information that
is given in a situation. This reduces "cognitive strain."

Langer and her colleagues (Langer, 1978; Langer, Blank, & Chanowitz, 1978) have provided direct support for this "nonthinking" hypothesis by demonstrating the mindlessness of certain social interactions. In
one of these investigations, a person about to use a copying machine was
approached by someone who asked to use the machine first. This request
was made in one of three ways:

1. *Request Only:* Excuse me, I have 5 (20) pages. May I use the Xerox machine?
2. *Placebic Information:* Excuse me, I have 5 (20) pages. May I use the Xerox machine
   because I have to make copies?
3. *Real Information:* Excuse me, I have 5 (20) pages. May I use the Xerox machine
   because I'm in a rush? (Langer et al. 1978, p. 635)

Langer (1978) explains:

> Condition 2 is called placebic information because the reason offered is
> entirely redundant with the request. What else would one do with a copying
> machine except make copies of something? Thus, if subjects were processing
> the information communicated by the experimenter, then the rate of compli-
> ance for subjects in the request-only condition and in the placebic information
> condition should be the same since the same information is conveyed, and
> both may be different from Condition 3 since here additional information is

**TABLE 7–4   THE PROPORTION OF SUBJECTS WHO AGREED TO
LET THE EXPERIMENTER USE THE COPIER**

		Reason		
		No Info	Placebic Info	Real Info
Favor	Small	.60	.93	.94
	Big	.24	.24	.42

(From Langer, Blank, & Chanowitz, 1978, p. 637.)

given. If, on the other hand, people are only processing a minimal amount of information and are responding to a script that goes something like "favor X + reason Y→ comply," then the rate of compliance should be the same for the placebic and real information conditions and different from the request-only group. (p. 48)

However, Langer goes on to quality this prediction by stating that if the favor requested was important or "effortful," then the subjects would process the entire communication.

The results of this study are shown in Table 7–4 and support Langer's hypotheses. It indeed appears that in the "small favor" condition people proceed rather mindlessly. Langer, therefore, contends that there may be more noncognitively generated behavior than attribution theorists, and other cognitive psychologists, have recognized in their conceptions.

Thus far I have analyzed some of the antecedents of causal ascriptions and the rationality or veridicality of these ascriptions. I will now briefly discuss three other research areas from the attributional perspective: cognitive dissonance, emotion, and selected animal behaviors. In the following chapter achievement strivings are examined in detail from an attributional perspective.

Cognitive Dissonance

It is generally acknowledged that "the problem of cognitive dynamics is *the* social psychological problem of the decade" (Zajonc, 1968, p. 338). "Cognitive dynamics" refers to the tendency toward change brought about when cognitions are in conflict; that is, when they are inconsistent or "do not fit." In the last 20 years a number of theories of cognitive consistency have been formulated. These theories, although labelled differently (they are variously called balance, congruity, or dissonance), "all have in common the notion that the person tends to behave in ways that minimize the internal inconsistency among his inter-personal relations, among his intrapersonal cognitions, and among his beliefs, feelings, and action" (McGuire, 1966, p. 1).

The best known of the consistency approaches is the theory of cognitive dissonance. Dissonance theory is concerned with the motivational effects of the relationships between cognitive elements. The elements in dissonance theory refer to "beliefs" or "knowledge." These elements may be unrelated to one another, or can be related in a consonant or dissonant manner. According to Festinger (1957), two cognitions are postulated to be in a state of dissonance if "the obverse of one element would follow from the other" (p. 13). For example, the knowledge that one smokes and that smoking causes cancer are dissonant cognitions. Similarly, of one decides to buy a car knowing that the brand has a bad reputation, and the car is indeed a "lemon," then the cognitions do not fit. If one believes smoking causes cancer or perceives that a car brand is poor, then it follows that one should not smoke or buy that make of car. Festinger postulates that dissonance is a motivating state, producing behaviors that reduce dissonance by altering the discrepant parts.

The way in which the "discrepant parts" are reduced will depend, in part, on the resistance to change of the relevant cognitions. Opinions and beliefs are clearly easier to alter than an actual prior behavior (Wicklund and Brehm, 1976). However, for example, if the individual continues to believe that he has purchased a "lemon," then dissonance reduction may be more easily accomplished by coming to believe that the purchase was a mistake and selling the car, rather than convincing oneself that the automobile is really not that bad.

The proposed magnitude of dissonance is a function of the proportion of dissonant to consonant cognitions. Thus, for example, if the car was cheaply purchased, and other cars also require much repair, then the dissonance of the car purchase is lessened. In addition, dissonance is determined by the importance of the cognitions under consideration. It is manifestly more disturbing to discover that the car one purchased is a lemon than to find that one bought a relatively poor article of clothing. According to Wicklund and Brehm (1976), the formula for the magnitude of aroused dissonance is:

$$\frac{\text{dissonant cognitions} \times \text{importance of cognitions}}{\text{consonant cognitions} \times \text{importance of cognitions}}$$

The rather straightforward principles outlined by Festinger have led to a number of interesting observations of "real life" behavior. For example, Festinger (1957) notes that one way of reducing the dissonance created by smoking when it is believed that smoking causes cancer is to persuade oneself that the latter cognition is false. (Of course, another way to reduce this dissonance is to discontinue smoking, but that often cannot be accomplished.) In one government survey study, individuals classified according to the strength of their smoking habits were asked whether they thought that the alleged link between smoking and cancer had been sufficiently proven. The respondents were categorized into four groups on the basis of their smoking habits: non-smokers and light, medium, and heavy smokers. The number of respondents reporting that they did not think that the evidence was conclusive totaled 55 per cent of the non-smoking group and 68, 75, and 86 per cent respectively for light, medium, and heavy smokers. Apparently, when cognitions are not in harmony, processes are instigated to help bring cognitive structures into consonance.

Attaining social support for one's beliefs is another method employed to reduce the dissonance between cognitions. In the book *When Prophecy Fails*, Festinger, Riecken, and Schachter (1956) report on the behavior of a group of cultists who predicted the world was about to come to an end. When their expectation was not confirmed, they dramatically increased their proselytizing behavior. In so doing, they apparently could bolster their own belief systems and reduce the dissonance created between their beliefs and the cognitions of the events in the real world. There is not a great deal of data supporting the idea of proselytizing after a belief has been invalidated. But McGuire (1966) notes, "This notion would explain some historical occurrences of more than a little importance that have puzzled many. It is an appealing proposition that deserves to be true" (p. 18).

Although some evidence gathered in field studies supports predictions from dissonance theory, by far the vast majority of the investigations have been conducted in laboratory settings, under controlled experimental conditions. Many of the studies involve engaging subjects in a behavior that normally would be avoided. The negative aspects of the action are dissonant with the knowledge that the behavior was performed. These are known as "forced compliance" or "insufficient justification" studies.

Forced Compliance

The research studies included within the forced-compliance paradigm often examine the effects of public actions that are discrepant with the private opinion of the actor. Further, the actions are performed for relatively small rewards. It is hypothesized that in such situations forces are aroused that act upon the individual to justify the prior action.

This hypothesis was first tested in a classic (and controversial) study by Festinger and Carlsmith (1959). In that study, subjects participated in an extremely boring "psychological experiment." The subjects were then requested to tell future participants that the experiment was interesting and fun. For this task, half the subjects were offered $20 and the rest were offered $1. Afterwards, the experimenters asked the subjects to rate how interesting the experiment actually had been. The results indicated that the subjects in the $1 condition rated the objectively boring experiment as more interesting than subjects in the $20 condition. That is, the smaller reward produced greater liking of the experiment than the larger one. Festinger and Carlsmith (1959) argued that behavior contrary to one's beliefs is not very dissonant when there is a strong external inducement (a large reward) to commit the action, for the external reward creates a consonant cognition. However, if the reward is small, then the discrepant behavior is seen as not sufficiently justified and much dissonance is created. In the Festinger and Carlsmith experiment this dissonance apparently initiated processes that modified the cognitions (attitudes) concerning the intrinsic value of the experiment.

The insufficient justification paradigm was later extended to the study of punished actions. Aronson and Carlsmith (1963) reason that:

> . . . If a person is induced to cease the performance of a desired act by the threat of punishment, his cognition that the act is desirable is dissonant with his cognition that he is not performing it. A threat of severe punishment, in and of itself, provides ample cognitions consonant with ceasing the action. If a person ceases to perform a desired action in the face of a mild threat, however, he lacks these consonant cognitions and, therefore, must seek additional justification for not performing the desired act. One method of justification is to convince himself that the desired act is no longer desirable. Thus, if a person is induced to cease performing a desired action by a threat of punishment, the milder the threat the greater will be his tendency to derogate the action. (pp. 584–5)

To test this hypothesis, Aronson and Carlsmith (1963) prevented children from playing with attractive toys, using either a mild or severe threat. Both before the threat and after a period of not playing with the toys, the attractiveness ratings of the toys were ascertained. Table 7–5 indicates that the relative attractiveness of the toys was greater in the severe than in the mild threat condition, supporting the prediction of Aronson and Carlsmith.

The general advice offered by Festinger (1957) for both rewarding and punishing situations is: "If one wanted to obtain private changes in addition to public compliance, the best way to do this would be to offer just enough reward or punishment to elicit overt compliance" (p. 95). This proposition contradicts the reinforcement approach to attitude change, which states that opinions vary monotonically as a function of their perceived reward value, and inversely as a function of their perceived aversive consequences. Thus, a lively debate has ensued between dissonance and reinforcement theorists, for it appears to be the case that both dissonance and reinforcement affect attitudes, and in opposing directions (see Wicklund and Brehm, 1976, for a discussion of this issue).

Traditional Motivational Research

The theory of cognitive dissonance has given rise to a great deal of research concerned with "traditional" motivational questions. Dissonance is treated as a drive, with the same conceptual status as hunger,

TABLE 7–5   CHANGE IN ATTRACTIVENESS OF FORBIDDEN TOY

Strength of Threat	Rating		
	Increase	Same	Decrease
Mild	4	10	8
Severe	14	8	0

(From Aronson & Carlsmith, 1963, p. 586.)

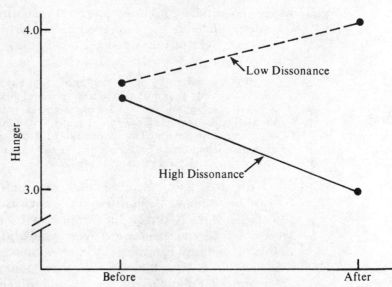

Figure 7–4. Mean self-ratings of hunger for selected subjects, before and after the dissonance manipulation. (From Brehm, 1962, p. 62.)

thirst, and other physiological states of deprivation. Like other drives, dissonance is postulated to energize and direct behavior, and its offset is reinforcing. Festinger (1957) states: "Successful reduction of dissonance is rewarding in the same sense that eating is rewarding" (p. 70). Further, like other deprivation states, dissonance is aversive, and the theoretical optimal state is one of zero dissonance.

HUNGER-THIRST.   Investigations demonstrating the motivational consequences of dissonance employ some variation of the public compliance-insufficient justification paradigm first introduced by Festinger and Carlsmith (1959). Brehm (1962) reports a series of studies in which feelings of hunger and thirst, as well as actual water consumption, were assessed following an insufficient justification procedure. In one of these investigations, subjects were asked to refrain from eating breakfast and lunch, under the guise of examining the effects of deprivation on intellectual and motor functioning. Prior to the expected task performance the subjects rated their degree of hunger. After completion of the required tasks the subjects were asked to undergo continued deprivation and to return later for additional testing. In the low dissonance condition $5 was offered as a reward for further participation, while in the high dissonance condition no additional incentive was offered. Thus, conditions of sufficient and insufficient justification were established. After a volitional commitment to continue deprivation, hunger ratings again were obtained. Figure 7–4 shows the result for subjects equal in their initial hunger ratings. The figure indicates that low dissonance subjects perceive themselves as hungrier after the commitment, while high dissonance subjects report feeling less hungry. Presumably, in the high dissonance condition continued deprivation is justified by altering the cognition related to the perceived discomfort of hunger.

In the light of these and related findings, Brehm (1962) concluded:

> It is only what the organism "knows" about its motivational state that affects learning, performance, perception, and so on. Noncognitive components of motivation, such as the physiological state of the organism, could then affect behaviors like learning only to the extent that they affected the cognitive components. That is, a state of deprivation, short of killing the organism, would have to have cognitive representation in order to have any kind of psychological effect at all. (p. 75)

PAIN AND FEAR.   Experimental paradigms similar to those reported by Brehm also have demonstrated the cognitive control of pain. In one illustrative study (Grinker, 1967; reported in Zimbardo, 1969b), subjects were given 20 trials of classical aversive eyelid conditioning. Recall that in this procedure a conditional stimulus, such as a tone, is paired with an aversive puff of air to the eye, and subsequent responses to the stimulus are measured. Following the 20 trials, the subjects were told that on future trials the air puff would be more intense. Earlier studies had demonstrated that this stress warning increases classical aversive conditioning.

To create high and low dissonance conditions, different degrees of verbal justification and choice were given for participating in the experiment, although all subjects did agree to participate. A control group was given neither choice nor justification.

Figure 7–5 shows that in this investigation the change in response strength from the pre- to the post-dissonance trials is an inverse function of the degree of aroused dissonance. Because of the increased stress, conditioning increased for all groups of subjects. However, it appears that

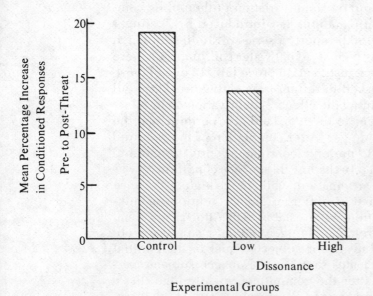

Figure 7–5. Mean percentage increase of conditioned responses from trials 11–20 to trials 21–30 (pre- and post-threat) for control and dissonance groups. (From Grinker, 1967; reported in Zimbardo, 1969, p. 130.)

dissonance suppresses the fear response, and conditioning, by inducing subjects to *think* that the puff is not very intense. That is, choosing to participate in an aversive experiment with minimal justification seems to decrease the emotionality that is caused by the unpleasant air puff and this, in turn, retards eyelid conditioning.

Resistance to Extinction

One further area of dissonance research deserving mention concerns resistance to extinction. This work has important implications within general experimental psychology and is pertinent to a discussion in the next chapter.

The insufficient justification paradigm used by Festinger and Carlsmith and others is created by having the extrinsic rewards for "forced" behavior not congruent with the significance of the action. This analysis has been extended to situations in which the subject performs instrumental responses that are somewhat aversive and the intrinsic value of the reward is not sufficient given the "output" of the subjects. It is postulated that in such situations dissonance is aroused and can be reduced if the reward or incentive value of the goal is perceived as greater than it really "is." In the first demonstration of this principle Aronson and Mills (1959) had females volunteer to join a group discussion concerning sex. Half of the volunteers first participated in a lengthy and embarrassing "initiation" that included the repeating of "dirty" words (high dissonance). A second group was given an easy initiation procedure (low dissonance). The girls then listened to a rather boring group discussion about sex. Aronson and Mills (1959) found that the subjects in the high dissonance condition rated the discussion more interesting, liked the participating girls more, and so forth than did subjects in the low dissonance condition. In sum, the cognition "I have experienced pain to attain an unattractive object" is dissonant; dissonance is reduced by perceiving the attained object as attractive.

Lawrence and Festinger (1962) applied this analysis to experimental procedures that apparently arouse dissonance in research on infrahumans. Included among these dissonance-creating procedures is the requirement of effortful responses to obtain a reward. These are situations that infrahumans (and humans) would avoid, if possible. Thus, responses under these conditions are dissonance arousing relative to conditions in which there is an "easy" response. Again, the dissonance may be reduced by perceiving "extra" rewards in the goal situation and thus experiencing a resulting increase in the attractiveness of the goal object.

In one experiment demonstrating the effects of effort on performance, rats were required to traverse inclines differing in steepness to receive a food reward. The group expending the greater effort took longer to extinguish, and ran faster during the extinction period, than the group expending less effort during the learning period (see Table 7–6). Subsequent experiments conducted by Lawrence and Festinger demonstrated that effort results in greater resistance to extinction regardless of the

TABLE 7-6 AVERAGE RUNNING TIME DURING EXTINCTION (IN SECONDS) FOR DIFFERENT EFFORT CONDITIONS

	Effort Condition	
	25° Incline (N = 31)	50° Incline (N = 31)
Last day of acquisition	1.8	2.0
First day of extinction	7.1	3.8
Second day of extinction	26.1	16.4
Third day of extinction	37.2	31.0

(From Lawrence & Festinger, 1962, p. 43.)

reward schedule and that with minimal effort the absence of reward still increases resistance to extinction.

Cognitive Dissonance: An Attributional Perspective

Attributional language has been employed to explain cognitive dissonance phenomena. Consider, for example, the insufficient justification paradigm of Festinger and Carlsmith (1959). Some subjects in that experiment were offered a large monetary reward to comply with a request to praise an experiment publicly. The positive evaluation of the experiment was contradictory to their private opinions. These subjects maintained their private unfavorable opinion of the experiment following the compliance. On the other hand, subjects given only a small reward for compliance altered their private opinions so they were more consistent with their public behavior. It is assumed that the attitude change resulting from the insufficient justification brought the cognitive elements into greater consonance.

Attribution language leads to the interpretation that in the Festinger and Carlsmith experiment the subjects in the large reward condition attribute their behavior to external factors (the reward). Conversely, subjects in the small reward condition cannot ascribe their actions to the external situation. Therefore, they attribute their compliance to internal determinants, such as an altered belief system.

The attributional approach to dissonance-reducing behavior rests heavily on the theoretical analysis of Bem (1967, 1972). As indicated previously, in his theory of self-perception, Bem suggests that individuals infer their internal states from their behavior, just as they would when making judgments about other people. According to this line of reasoning, in the cognitive dissonance paradigm an individual perceives that he acted given insufficient external justification, and on the basis of this action infers that the act must have intrinsic merit. The subject is therefore making an attributional "error" in explaining the past behavior.

Hence, a key problem in dissonance experiments is first to elicit the behavior despite insufficient justification. As Kelley (1967) points out, the subjects have only the "illusion of freedom" in the insufficient justification paradigm, for virtually all comply with the experimenter's request, although the situation is presented as one of free choice. Kelley (1967) reasons:

> The successful experiment is one in which strong situational demands, entirely sufficient to produce total or near-total compliance, are successfully camouflaged by a network of cues as to self-determination. From an attribution point of view, the situation surrounding the behavior is misleading. . . . When the subject in the low-incentive condition reviews his recent behavior it does not occur to him to attribute it to the situation [monetary reward] . . . In the high-incentive condition, the salient fact of the large payment suggests to him a[n] . . . attribution for his behavior. (p. 229).

The general explanation of dissonance phenomena by attributional theorists is that the less the extrinsic forces are consistent with behavior, and the less able the subject is to identify external reasons for his action, the more likely the action will be attributed to internal factors, such as the intrinsic value of the action.

Nisbett and Valins (1971) have extended this analysis to situations in which the intrinsic reward is consonant with the performed act. They reason that the greater the extrinsic reward for behavior consonant with one's true beliefs, the less the likelihood that the behavior will then be ascribed to internal factors (the belief). Thus, being paid to state a belief consistent with one's true feelings might result in a *weakening* of that belief. Nisbett and Valins review a number of studies supporting this general supposition. For example, it has been found that subjects paid a relatively large sum of money to read a speech consistent with their private opinion (overly sufficient justification) are later more likely to be dissuaded from that opinion than subjects paid only a small amount of money to read a speech conveying their beliefs (Kiesler & Sakumura, 1966). Note this is virtually the same analysis used by Deci (1975) to explain the undermining effects of extrinsic reward.

Nisbett and Valins (1971) conclude that the attributional (informational) approach to explain dissonance-type phenomena has more generality than the Festinger-guided motivational explanation. When the behavior in question is insufficiently justified, the dissonance theorist can argue that this knowledge is painful and that attitude change is a motivated behavior rather than a less dynamic, inferential process. But Nisbett and Valins contend that if the behavior is justified, the situation is not dissonant and dissonance theory cannot make predictions about attitude change. An information-processing approach, however, can explain the shift in attitudes given overly-sufficient justification.

AROUSAL AND ATTRIBUTION: A RAPPROCHEMENT. In a series of investigations, Cooper, Zanna, and their associates have tested the contrasting attributional (cognitive) and arousal (drive) interpretations of

dissonance phenomena. Zanna and Cooper (1976) review this controversy in the following manner:

> This is a tale of two theories. On the one hand, there is cognitive
> dissonance; on the other, there is attribution. Dissonance theory sees man as
> aroused by inconsistencies among his cognitions. As in the classical arousal
> theories of experimental psychology (Hull, 1943), man is viewed as motivated
> to rid himself of the drive-like, uncomfortable tension that accompanies
> perceived inconsistency. Attribution models, on the other hand, see man as in
> a constant process of making sense out of his environment. In such models,
> man is viewed as a scientist, using attributional rules to infer causality in an
> otherwise chaotic world of social stimuli.
>
> At first, the two approaches had no difficulty in peaceful coexistence.
> Attributional models (for example, Heider, 1958; Jones & Davis, 1965) concen-
> trated on how we make sense of the actions of others, while dissonance theory
> was concerned with the somewhat unusual ways that we go about putting our
> own cognitive houses in order. A virtual state of war, however, broke out
> between the two theories when it was proposed by theorists who later became
> recognized as attribution proponents that the rules that had been developed
> for understanding the environment could be redirected at oneself (Bem, 1965,
> 1972). If we considered ourselves to be observers of our own actions and
> applied the rules to ourselves, then many of the effects that had been thought
> of as deriving from the drive-like process of cognitive dissonance could be
> explained using the nonmotivational, nonarousal, non-drive-like model of
> attribution. Proponents of each model set out on fascinating forays to credit
> and discredit the other point of view (for example, Jones, Linder, Kiesler,
> Zanna, & Brehm, 1968; Bem, 1968). (p. 199)

Zanna and Cooper then go on to demonstrate that attributional
concepts actually can be used to demonstrate that arousal is a necessary
antecedent for dissonance-type phenomena. College students were asked
to write an essay on banning speakers from campus, which was contrary to
their beliefs. In one condition, the attitude-discrepant opinion was written under forced (no choice) conditions, whereas in a second condition
the illusion of free choice was created. According to Festinger's conception and subsequent modifications of his theory, when attitude-
discrepant behavior is freely engaged in, dissonance is aroused. Hence,
there should be attitude change in order to bring the cognitions into
greater consonance. On the other hand, when the behavior is forced,
dissonance is not aroused because the discrepant behavior is consistent
with external demands. Attitude shifts, therefore, should not be displayed.

Prior to the counter-attitudinal essay, some of the subjects in this
experiment received a placebo pill under a ruse that need not be discussed here. Half of these subjects were told that the pill would make
them tense, while the others were told that it would produce a state of
relaxation. At the end of the experiment, the subject's attitudes toward
banning speakers were assessed. Zanna and Cooper (1976) explain:

> If dissonance is truly a state of arousal and if attitude change following
> induced compliance is based upon the reduction of that arousal, then it
> follows that misattribution of the arousal to an external agent should reduce
> the need for attitude change. . . .
>
> A similar logic led us to predict that if subjects believed they should feel

TABLE 7–7   MEAN OF SUBJECTS' OPINIONS TOWARD BANNING SPEAKERS ON CAMPUS

Decision Freedom	Potential Side Effect of the Drug		
	Arousal	*No Drug*	*Relaxation*
Choice	3.40	9.10	13.40
No choice	3.50	4.50	4.70

Note: Cell $n = 10$. The larger the mean, the more agreement with the attitude-discrepant essay.
(Adapted from Zanna & Cooper, 1976, p. 204.)

sedated by a drug, yet still felt arousal after writing the counter-attitudinal essay, they should be motivated to alter their attitudes even more than subjects who had no such explanation. (p. 202)

The results of this investigation are shown in Table 7–7. The table reveals that in a "no drug" control condition a typical dissonance effect is displayed — attitudes toward banning speakers, which is generally unpopular among students, were higher when subjects felt that they freely chose to write the attitude-discrepant essay. However, given the pill as the perceived source of arousal, the dissonance effect was eliminated. And when the subjects expected to be in a state of relaxation, even a larger dissonance effect was displayed, as though subjects inferred that they must have been very upset by their inconsistent behavior.

Subsequent research reported by these investigators supports the position that arousal is necessary for a dissonance effect and attitude change. This, of course, is in opposition to the information-processing explanations of Bem and Kelley. In one investigation a tranquilizer or amphetamine was administered to the subjects prior to their writing a counter-attitudinal opinion. In the tranquilizer condition a dissonance effect was not displayed, while in the amphetamine condition attitude change was augmented.

On the basis of these findings and other research, Zanna and Cooper (1976) conclude:

The essential question is, what shall we take self-attribution in counter-attitudinal advocacy situations to mean? If it is taken to mean that people engage in a process of deducing their opinions without the experience of an internal tension state, the data presented here cast serious doubt on that view. . . . All that our research has been intended to demonstrate is that aversive arousal accompanies cognitive inconsistency. It does not indicate that people never engage in attributional processes nor that, in some situations, attributional rules will not lead to accurate predictions regarding attitudinal outcomes. Indeed, our reliance on attributional processes to make the predictions that we have presented indicates that self-attributional phenomena are alive and well.

And so, a truce is proposed that will enable us to go beyond the simple conflict between the motivation-free, information-processing perspective of attribution theory and the motivational perspective of dissonance theory. By sharpening the areas of applicability of the two approaches, we may be able to arrive at a more precise understanding of each. (pp. 215–216)

Emotions

The word "emotion" comes from the Latin stem *"emovere"* (to move). Young (1943), as noted by Cofer and Appley (1964), concisely described how the term "emotion" found its way into the field of psychology:

> . . . Originally the word meant a moving out of one place into another, in the sense of a migration. Thus: "The divers emotions of that people (the Turks)" (1603). "Some accidental emotion . . . of the Center of Gravity" (1695). The word came to mean a moving, stirring, agitation, perturbation, and was so used in a strictly physical sense. Thus: "Thunder . . . caused so great an Emotion in the air" (1708). "The saters continuing in the caverns . . . caused the emotion or earthquake" (1758). This physical meaning was transferred to political and social agitation, the word coming to mean *tumult*, popular disturbance. Thus: "There were . . . great stirres and emocions in Lombardye" (1579). "Accounts of public Emotions, occasioned by the Want of Corn" (1709). Finally the word came to be used to designate any agitated, vehement, or excited mental state of the individual. Thus: "The joy of gratification is properly called an emotion" (1762). (p. 25)

The study of emotions is obviously of central importance to the field of motivation. Indeed, it has been proposed that affects are the chief movers of behavior, as in the doctrine of hedonism, and even that drive does not generate action without the "amplification" of affects. Tomkins (1970) illustrates the interaction of drive and affect with the following anecdote:

> Consider anoxic deprivation. Almost any interference with normal breathing will immediately arouse the most desperate gasping for breath. Is there any motivational claim more urgent than the demand of one who is drowning or choking to death for want of air? Yet it is not simply the imperious demand for oxygen that we observe under such circumstances. We are also observing the rapidly mounting panic ordinarily recruited whenever the air supply is suddenly jeopardized. The panic amplifies the drive signal, and it is the combination of drive signal and panic which we have mistakenly identified as the drive signal. We have only to change the rate of anoxic deprivation to change the nature of the recruited affect which accompanies the anoxic drive signal. Thus, in the Second World War, those pilots who refused to wear their oxygen masks at 30,000 feet suffered a more gradual anoxic deprivation. They did not panic for want of oxygen. They became euphoric. It was the affect of enjoyment which the more slowly developing anoxic signal recruited. Some of these men, therefore, met their deaths with smiles on their lips. (p. 101–102)

History of the Study of Emotions

Plutchik (1970) outlined three major traditions that have influenced the study of emotions:

1. The Darwinian tradition. This position stresses the innate basis of emotional expression. Facial characteristics that generalize across a variety of species and relate to behavioral expression have been identified (e.g., the bearing of fangs by wolves and the sneering of humans are innate indicators of rage and anger).

2. The Freudian tradition. As indicated in Chapter Two, the Freudian viewpoint emphasizes the unconscious determinants of affect, as well as affects such as guilt and anxiety.
3. The "sequence" tradition. This refers to a concern with the temporal relation between bodily expression and emotional feeling. Many psychologists argue that emotions give rise to bodily change and activity, while others, such as William James, have contended that the experience of emotion is a consequence of particular bodily processes or visceral reactions (see the earlier discussion of the Body-Mind problem and Diagram 3–2). The sequence issue has generated a number of experimental studies of emotion and is most pertinent to a conception of emotion proposed by attribution theorists.

The Sequential Controversy

William James (1884) and Carl Lange were responsible for first raising the sequential issue. James and Lange stated that when a reaction to an emotional stimulus involves a bodily or visceral structure, the reaction is perceived as an emotional feeling. Thus, the James-Lange theory pertains to the basis of emotional experience and suggests that "peripheral somatic and visceral responses . . . [are] necessary to add an emotional quality to the perception of an event" (Buck, 1976, p. 43). As Buck (1976) explains:

> . . . Thus, we do not cry because we are sorry. We see something that makes us cry, and our feeling of the crying is the sorrow. We see a bear, tremble, and run, and our feeling of the trembling and running is fear. (p. 42)

There is intuitive evidence supporting the James-Lange theory. For example, as James (1890) stated:

> . . . Can one fancy the state of rage and picture no ebullition in the chest, no flushing of the face, no dilation of the nostrils, no clenching of the teeth, no impulse to vigorous action. . . . The more closely I scrutinize my states, the more persuaded I become that whatever moods, affections, and passions I have are in very truth constituted by, and made up of, those bodily changes which we ordinarily call their expression or consequence. (p. 452; from Levanthal, 1974)

One interesting implication of this position pointed out by Levanthal (1974) is that if we behave in a manner that differs from our feelings, our feelings will change. Many common songs, such as "Whistle a happy tune when you are afraid," also echo this sentiment.

The James-Lange theory that emotional states result from perceived differences in bodily activity was severely criticized by a number of scientists, particularly Walter Cannon (1927). Cannon noted that:

1. Total separation of the viscera from the central nervous system does not alter emotional behavior.
2. The same visceral changes occur in very different emotional states and in non-emotional states.
3. Visceral changes are too slow to be a source of emotional feeling.

4.   Artificial induction of the visceral changes typical of strong emotions does not produce those emotions.

These points are accepted as valid (see Mandler, 1975), although there is some evidence that, as James suggested, visceral activation is necessary for emotional experience. For example, it has been reported that among patients with injuries that block visceral stimulation, little emotion is experienced (Hohmann, 1966; also see Mandler, 1975). On the other hand, clinical reports (see Dana, 1921) also document cases in which individuals have suffered complete loss of bodily sensations, yet still exhibit a complete range of emotions.

Cannon also reported that different emotions are not characterized by different patterns of internal activity. That is, there is not an identity between physiological states and psychological (emotional) reactions. Such a correspondence is strongly implied by the James-Lange theory of emotions. Cannon contended that all emotional reactions are character-ized by a gross discharge of the sympathetic nervous system. For example, during both rage and fear cats exhibit similar reactions, such as increased heart rate and deep respiration. Cannon thus proposed a "mass action" theory of emotion. Furthermore, emotions were believed to mobilize action and therefore they preceded, rather than followed, instrumental behavior.

The Arousal Theory of Emotions

Cannon's theory resulted in the study of just a few underlying dimensions along which emotions could be described. The dimension of intensity received the most attention. It was thought that intensity could be assessed by monitoring the activity of the reticular activating system. Thus, the physiological indicator of arousal also became the indicator for the emotions!

It was initially believed that too high an activation level resulted in over-excitement, whereas too low a level produced depression. Further-more, the intensity of arousal influences the direction (approach or withdrawal) of behavior, as previously revealed in the study of stimulus seeking. And also as previously indicated (see Figure 3–21), emotion could lead to either behavioral organization or disorganization, depend-ing upon the intensity of the emotion. Schlosberg (1954) illustrates this point with the following vignette:

> [A sleeping man] . . . is near the zero level of activation. His cerebral cortex is relatively inactive . . . The muscles are relaxed . . . As a result of this general condition, he doesn't respond to ordinary stimuli; he is uncon-scious.
> Now let the alarm clock ring. It is a strong stimulus, and breaks through the high threshold. Gross muscular responses occur, and feed back impulses into the central nervous system. There is also autonomic discharge, and the resulting responses of muscle and gland lead to more feedback, . . . The individual is awake and responsive to stimulation . . .
> Let us assume that our hero has reached an optimum level of activation by 10:00 A.M. He is alert, and responds efficiently to his environment. But now

he finds that a book he needs is missing from his shelf. This frustration produces an increment in level of activation, perhaps not high enough at first to be dignified by the name of anger. But as he continues to search for the book the level of activation builds up until he is "blind with rage." . . . He probably wouldn't find the book now if it were under his nose. (pp. 82–3)

Schachter's Two-Factor Attributional Theory of Emotions

The arousal theory of emotions was beset by two severe problems. First, arousal level could not be unambiguously determined. Changes in heart rate, for example, may or may not be accompanied by changes in electrical skin conductance, muscular tension, and brain wave patterns. And, more importantly, it is evident that arousal is not a sufficient explanation of experienced emotions. Given the same level of arousal, there are different emotional reactions. For example, high arousal might be accompanied by the experience of intense hate, intense love, excitement, or bewilderment. Arousal theory did not provide the conceptual tools to distinguish between the emotions.

Schachter (1964) and Schachter and Singer (1962) supplemented arousal theory with attributional concepts so that it would be able to differentiate between emotions. They proposed that emotions are a function of two factors: level of arousal and cognitions about the arousing situation. The cognitive factors provide the "steering" or directionality for emotional expression by labelling (ascribing the cause for) the experienced arousal and thus guiding the appropriate emotional experience.

In real-life situations the cues that arouse the organism also provide the information necessary for understanding the event. For example, the appearance of a birthday cake may raise arousal and is a stimulus for positive affect; the sight of a gun is likely to produce physiological activation and is a cue for fear. However, in laboratory settings, Schachter and his colleagues were able to manipulate arousal and cognitive factors independently and apparently demonstrated their joint effects on emotional expression.

In the first of a series of studies, Schachter and Singer (1962) injected epinephrine into subjects under the guise of studying "how vitamin supplements affect the visual skills" (p. 382). Epinephrine is an activating agent that often produces autonomic arousal and symptoms such as heart palpitation and a general "high" feeling. Some subjects were informed about the effects of the drugs and thus could appropriately label the source of their feelings. Other subjects were either uninformed or misinformed about the drug effects, while control subjects were injected with a placebo. The subjects then waited for their "visual test" in the presence of a stooge subject. The stooge either acted in a very euphoric manner, playing with various objects, or feigned anger at some personal inquiries that were part of a questionnaire administered during the waiting period. During this time interval the behaviors of the subjects were observed and rated for euphoria or anger. The subjects also answered a questionnaire pertaining to their present feeling state.

The main findings of this experiment were that uninformed epi-nephrine-injected subjects (aroused, but "unlabelled") were relatively angrier in the anger-inducing situation and relatively more euphoric in the social situation cued for euphoria than subjects in the control condi-tion. Thus, emotion is a function of arousal level, and individuals in an aroused state may experience disparate emotions as a function of the social (cognitive) situation in which they find themselves. In sum, Schachter and Singer demonstrated that level of arousal and cognitive processes, when manipulated independently, and contiguously rather than simultaneously, determine the direction and magnitude of experi-enced emotion.

In a subsequent experiment, Schachter and Wheeler (1962) repli-cated the effects of arousal level on emotional expression. Subjects were injected with either epinephrine, a placebo, or chlorpromazine, a sympa-thetic blocking agent that dampens arousal. Subjects then viewed a short comedy film. During the film their expressions of amusement were observed. As expected, the level of expressed amusement varied mono-tonically as a function of the induced level of physiological arousal, with greatest expression in the epinephrine condition and least in the chlor-promazine condition. However, it also must be noted that although expressed amusement varied as predicted, there was no difference in the subjects' evaluations of the movies.

In sum, Schachter's theory suggests that emotional experience re-sults from the following sequence:

a. There is a bodily reaction (arousal);
b. The individual becomes aware of this reaction;
c. There is a need to seek a reason or explanation of the reaction;
d. An external cue is identified, and the internal reaction is labelled. This labelling provides the quality of the emotional feeling.

Criticisms of Schachter's Two-Factor Theory of Emotions

The study by Schachter and Singer (and the general theoretical formulation of Schachter) has proven astonishingly heuristic and contrib-uted to a growing resurgence in the experimental study of emotions. Yet this work has also been criticized because of both methodological and theoretical shortcomings. Concerning the specific methodology used by Schachter and Singer (1962), it has been noted that some subjects were discarded from the data analysis; the euphoria and anger ratings were combined into one index; many individuals do not respond to epineph-rine with arousal; and pulse rate, a relatively poor index, was used as the indicator of arousal (see, for example, Plutchik and Ax, 1967). More importantly, however, some serious theoretical criticisms also have been voiced.

THE AROUSAL-EMOTION SEQUENCE.   Schachter contends that the perception of an external event, or the administration of a drug, produces arousal. The social situation then provides the cues to interpret the arousal and thus label its origin. But work by investigators such as

Lazarus, as discussed in Chapter Two, strongly suggests that arousal is influenced by cognitive factors. More specifically, how one interprets a stressful situation influences the amount of fear that is generated. Hence, arousal and cognitions interact and mutually influence one another. It is presently not known whether arousal precedes, accompanies, or follows an emotional experience.

THE NECESSITY OF AROUSAL. Schachter's two-factor theory of emotion also has been called into question by a number of experiments conducted by Valins and his colleagues. These studies suggest that cognitions are sufficient to produce emotional behavior without arousal.

To demonstrate that the *energizing* effects of arousal do not influence emotional expression, Valins presented fraudulent information to subjects revealing that they were in a state of arousal. He then investigated the effects of the false evidence on the intensity of emotional expression. Thus, the cue or informational function of internal states was manipulated, while the actual level of arousal remained constant. This reverses the procedure used by Schachter and Wheeler (1962) in which the level of arousal was manipulated while the external stimulus situation remained constant.

In the first of his experiments, Valins (1966) manipulated the extent to which male subjects perceived that their hearts reacted to the perception of a slide of a semi-nude female. Subjects were allowed to overhear bogus "monitored heart-rate" information, although they were instructed to "try to ignore the heart sounds" (p. 402). For the experimental subjects, half of the slides were associated with a change in heart rate (either acceleration or deceleration). Subjects in a control group also heard the heart-beat sounds, but were told that they were meaningless noise. Following the viewing of the stimuli, the subjects rated the attractiveness of the nudes and selected some photographs of the viewed slides to take home as a reward for their participation.

The results of the study revealed that in the experimental group the nudes associated with a perceived change in heart rate were judged as more attractive and their pictures were more likely to be chosen to take home than were pictures of the nudes not linked with this bogus information. The sound *per se* did not affect the emotional ratings of subjects in the control group. Valins (1966) therefore concluded:

> . . . The results are exactly what one would have expected had heart-rate changes and veridical feelings of palpitation been pharmacologically induced to some slides but not to others. The mechanism operating to produce these effects is presumably the same regardless of the veridicality of the feedback. Internal events are a source of cognitive information and . . . when an emotional explanation is prepotent, they will label their reactions accordingly. (pp. 406, 407)

Valins also notes that when subjects are exposed to the fraudulent heart-rate "they seemed to actively persuade themselves that [the nude] was attractive. They report looking at the slide more closely and it is evident that they attempt to justify the feedback" (p. 407). In subsequent investigations of this "hypothesis testing" interpretation of the data,

Valins (1974) found that a debriefing about the nature of the experiment did not alter the subjects' post-treatment opinions about the nudes. Thus, subjects apparently were not just passively listening to the heart-rate information that was presented. Further, Barefoot and Straub (1971) found that the attractiveness ratings of the stimuli associated with the false arousal information increase when subjects are allowed more time for viewing. It appears that during this time interval they look more closely at the stimuli and find evidence to support their perceived feeling state. In general, these effects are stronger given heart-beat acceleration than deceleration, for deceleration is an ambiguous signal (see Liebhart, 1976).

In sum, Valins and his co-workers have shown that arousal *per se* is not a necessary antecedent of emotional feelings, but the arousal cues are a source of information that individuals use to judge their feeling state (for example, "my heart is pounding, I must be angry or euphoric"; I feel high, I must think this movie is funny"; and so on). Cognitions appear to be sufficient condition for an emotional response.

There is one important condition that must be met before Valin's position can be accepted. It must be the case that *perception* of bogus heart rate information does not lead to an *actual* change in heart rate. If this were true, then Schachter's theory would be supported rather than contradicted! The possible relationship between perceived and real arousal is yet to be clearly determined, although Goldstein, Fink, and Mettee (1972) found that perceived physiological arousal produces actual arousal.

Emotions and Misattribution

Guided by the misattribution paradigm introduced by Schachter and Singer (1962), subsequent studies also examined the effects of causal ascriptions on reported feelings and behavior. Many of the studies aroused fear by informing subjects they were about to receive a series of electric shocks. Then an external agent, such as a pill or a loud noise, was introduced. Reactions to these agents were described as similar to the symptoms experienced when frightened. Thus, the subjects could attribute their fear reactions to the non-shock external sources. The misattribution of the fear symptoms was expected to result in a reduction of the fear itself.

An experiment by Nisbett and Schachter (1966) closely conforms to the experimental paradigm outlined above. Subjects in that experiment were given a placebo after being told that they were about to receive a series of electric shocks. All of the subjects were informed that the placebo had side effects. In one condition the side effects were described as tremors, shaky hands, pounding heart, a feeling of "butterflies" in the stomach, and so on. That is, the side effects were identical with fear-arousal symptoms. In a second condition the side effects were described as itching, headache, and other reactions unrelated to fear symptoms.

Subjects were then given a series of shocks that progressively increased in intensity. The dependent variables included the point at which pain was first experienced and the intensity at which the shock was reported unendurable. The data revealed that, within the range of shock at which the subjects reasonably could attribute their arousal symptoms to the two possible causal sources, the individuals in the pill-attribution condition reported that they first experienced pain at a higher level of intensity, and had a higher tolerance level, than subjects who apparently attributed their arousal reactions to the fear of shock.

In a subsequent study, Ross, Rodin, and Zimbardo (1969) employed a modification of the procedure introduced by Nisbett and Schachter. Subjects again were led to expect electric shocks. A loud noise was then presented during the experiment. For half of the subjects the noise was described as producing the fear-related symptoms listed earlier, while for the remaining subjects the reactions to the noise were described as unrelated to the fear response. Ross et al. employed a behavioral dependent variable to infer the effects of causal misattribution, rather than relying on self-reports of pain, as had Nisbett and Schachter. Subjects were allowed to work on either of two tasks; success at one of the tasks was instrumental to shock avoidance, while success at the other task was expected to result in a monetary reward. It was assumed that a subject's perseverance on the "shock-puzzle," while ignoring the reward puzzle, would provide behavioral data to test the hypothesis that attribution of arousal symptoms to the noise lessens fear.

The data reported by Ross et al. supported the general hypothesis. The most dramatic of the findings are illustrated in Figure 7–6, which

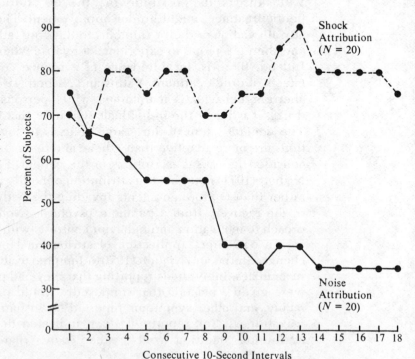

Figure 7–6. The percentage of subjects in the shock attribution and noise misattribution conditions working to solve the shock-avoidance puzzle over time. (From Ross, Rodin, & Zimbardo, 1969, p. 286.)

shows the percentage of subjects who worked on the shock-avoidance puzzle over time. It is evident that subjects who attribute their naturally occurring arousal to fear maintain a high rate of behavior instrumental to shock avoidance. On the other hand, subjects who are led to misattribute their fear symptoms to the loud noise display decreasing shock-avoidance behavior.

Davison and Valins (1969) altered this procedure so the subjects received shock under identical attributional belief systems. In their experiment, Davison and Valins first determined the subjects' pain thresholds. Then a placebo, described as a "fast-acting drug," was administered, and a new pain threshold was ascertained. During the new determination the shocks were reduced in intensity so it appeared that the subjects were able to endure more pain. Half of the subjects then were told that the administered drug was in fact a placebo. The "undrugged" subjects therefore could not attribute their "improved" shock tolerance to the drug. The performance during the second threshold testing thus could be self-attributed. In the final stage of the experiment a third pain threshold was determined. The data revealed that subjects in the "undrugged" condition tolerated more pain than the "drugged" subjects. Davison and Valins suggest that debriefed subjects re-evaluate their prior behavior on the basis of their actions. That is, the subjects could conclude: "If I tolerated more shock, then I must not be afraid of shock, or perhaps shocks are not as painful as I thought."

One interesting aspect of the theoretical analyses and supporting data in the studies by Ross et al. and by Davison and Valins is the immediate relevance of this work to psychotherapy. For example, Davison and Valins discuss the possibility that the use of drugs during psychotherapeutic treatment might hinder improvement. The patients can attribute any alleviation of their symptoms to the drug rather than to themselves, and then are prone to experience a relapse when the drug is withheld. Indeed, there is an abundance of evidence concerning the transient effects of drug treatment. Valins and Nisbett (1971) also point out that if aberrant behavior is maintained while persons are under prescribed drugs, it is likely the individuals will infer that they are getting worse. The general intent of these arguments is to suggest that some attributions are more adaptive than others, and that existent treatments should consider the causal ascriptions of the patient. For example, Valins and Nisbett (1971) note that the attribution of bodily pain to somatic sources, rather than to "foreign agents invading the body," could be a key step in the recovery from a paranoid psychosis. Note how this rational approach to motivation and behavior contrasts with Freudian assumptions.

In one direct application of attributional principles to behavioral change, Storms and Nisbett (1970) attempted to alter the sleep behavior of insomniacs. Individuals reporting that they had problems going to sleep were given a placebo that supposedly would produce alertness, mind racing, and other symptoms reported by insomniacs during periods of wakefulness. Self-reports of sleep indicated that subjects in this pill-attribution condition went to sleep *sooner* than subjects unable to attribute their wakefulness to the pill. Conversely, subjects given a placebo "relaxation" pill reported that they took longer to fall alseep. There is, however, some question about the reliability of these findings.

Storms and Nisbett reason that during periods of wakefulness the insomniac introspects about his neuroticism, inferred from his inability to sleep. These thoughts of self-inadequacy further interfere with sleep. Attribution of the wakefulness to the pill breaks the postulated wakefulness-introspection-wakefulness cycle, enabling the insomniac to sleep.

A similar application of attributional principles to dysfunctional behavior is offered by Storms and McCaul (1976). They suggest that:

> (a) Attribution of an unwanted, dysfunctional behavior to the self leads to an increased emotional state (which loosely can be called "anxiety") and (b) this anxiety may serve to increase the frequency or intensity of the dysfunctional behavior. (p. 44)

Hence, self-attribution is believed to increase emotionality and cause further behavioral problems. In support of these propositions, Storms and McCaul report that self-attribution of speech disfluencies exacerbates subsequent stammering, whereas ascription of such disfluencies to the difficulties of being an experimental subject results in no subsequent speech problems. The relation of locus of causality to affective reactions is examined in further detail in the following chapter.

Attribution in Animal Experimentation

Some experiments that have been conducted with infrahuman subjects can be interpreted from an attributional framework. Of course, the question immediately raised is whether infrahumans make ascriptions and differentiate the self from external factors. In discussing the cognitive capacities of infrahuman organisms (rats), Festinger (1961) states:

> All that is meant by cognition is knowledge or information. It seems to me that one can assume that an organism has cognitions or information if one can observe some behavioral difference under different stimulus conditions. If the organism changes his behavior when the environment changes, then obviously he uses information about the environment and, equally obviously, can be said to have cognitions.
>
> Now for the question of whether or not rats reduce dissonance as humans do. . . . I suspect that the rat is a rather stupid organism and does not reduce dissonance nearly as effectively as the human being does. I suspect that the mechanisms available to the rat for dissonance reduction are very limited and that the amount of dissonance which gets effectively reduced is relatively small. Still, I suspect that they *do* reduce dissonance. At any rate, if we find that the theory of dissonance can make valid predictions for rat behavior, this will be evidence that they do, indeed, reduce dissonance. (p. 4)

A simple taxonomy aids in the selection of animal investigations pertinent to attribution theory. The proposed taxonomy includes two dimensions: the subjective (perceived) and the objective (veridical) origins of causality. A combination of these two dimensions yields four experimental classifications, as shown in Table 7–8.

TABLE 7-8   TAXONOMY OF EXPERIMENTAL PARADIGMS (INFRAHUMAN SUBJECTS) PERTINENT TO ATTRIBUTION THEORY

		Subjective (Perceived) Causality	
		Self	*Environment (External Agent)*
Objective (Veridical) Causality	*Self*	(I) Simple instrumental learning	(II) Instrumental escape learning following classical aversive conditioning (learned helplessness)
	Environment (External Agent)	(III) Reward following experimenter-established time interval (superstitious behavior)	(IV) Simple classical conditioning

Following Heider and Kelley, assume that causation is inferred from a systematic covariation of antecedents and consequents. If an effect occurs given one set of antecedents and does not occur when those antecedents are absent, it is assumed that the effect is perceived as caused by those particular antecedents. For example, if food always follows a lever press and does not appear when the lever is not pressed, it is postulated that the responding organism will ascribe the presence of food to the instrumental lever press. Thus, a simple instrumental-learning paradigm is classified within quadrant I in Table 7–8: The outcome objectively is controlled by the organism, and causation is perceived as due to personal factors.

Now consider quadrant IV. Inasmuch as outcomes are externally controlled, any response the animal makes should not covary with an effect. The effect sometimes occurs in the presence of a particular response, sometimes in the absence of that response, and at other times in the presence of differing responses. This apparently corresponds to the classical conditioning paradigm. In a classical conditioning procedure the reward or punishment, or the presentation of unconditioned stimulus, is independent of the organism's response, and is so perceived.

The remaining two quadrants in Table 7–8 represent situations in which attributional errors are made. Quadrant III includes experimental paradigms that induce the outcome to be perceived as caused by the self, when, in fact, the outcomes are under environmental control. Beliefs labelled *"superstitious"* can be described as attributional errors, and are included in quadrant III. The experimental paradigm resulting in such misattribution generally involves the presentation of food to a hungry animal following some experimentally determined time interval. Prior to the reception of the food the animal happens to be engaging in some response, and errs in ascribing the appearance of the reward to his behavior. Subsequently, this "superstitious" response is repeated.

In sum, because a response has inadvertently preceded a reinforcement, the animal makes the false (but not unreasonable) inference that the reward was *caused* by the response. This attributional error receives repeated confirmation, for repetition of the behavior is at times accompanied by reception of the reward. But rather than calling this superstitious behavior, it may be better understood as an honest error in information processing and inference making. The animal apparently weights the response-reward covariation more heavily than the information gained during response-nonreward sequences. What is needed to correct this false causal inference is information that the reward will also appear in the absence of the "superstitious" response. The animal may then discover that the reward is not contingent upon any self-generated behavior.

An animal placed on a partial reinforcement schedule, or a schedule in which one of every given number of responses is rewarded, is acting rationally when making instrumental responses. Yet an animal engaging in virtually the same behavior, given a different experimental procedure, is considered superstitious. In both instances the animals are responding in the absence of a one-to-one correspondence between each single response and a reward; the information available to the organisms regarding response-reward contingencies is virtually identical in the two situations. But in the superstitious-behavior paradigm further evidence is available that would reveal to the organism that the inference is incorrect. To attain this evidence the perceived instrumental response must cease. But hungry animals are not likely to stop trying to get food. In the superstition paradigm, reward would continue if the perceived "instrumental" response was withheld, while in the truly instrumental paradigm the reward would cease.

A reverse attributional error is shown in quadrant II: There is attribution of an outcome to external agents when the outcome is, or may by, self-determined. Thus, for example, in the investigation by Zanna and Cooper, "tension" was ascribed to a pill, when in reality it was self-generated. In a similar manner, in studies of learned helplessness, dogs first trained with a classical aversive conditioning procedure do not display performance gains over trials in a subsequent instrumental avoidance learning situation. Indeed, the majority of the previously conditioned animals never learn the escape response. Apparently, the dogs are making attributional errors; they are generalizing their prior conclusions about the inescapability of shock and making the incorrect inference that in this new situation, shock termination is independent of their personal behavior.

Summary

In this chapter the attributional approach to behavior was introduced. Attribution theory is a more cognitive, or mental, analysis than the other theories of behavior discussed in this book. The underlying assumption of this conceptual approach is that humans are motivated to attain a causal picture of the world. That is, they want to know "why" an event has occurred.

The acknowledged "founder" of the attributional view is Fritz Heider. According to Heider, causal attributions can be dichotomized into person (ability, try) or environmental factors. Thus, for example, crossing a lake in a row boat might be ascribed to high rowing ability, much exertion, and/or the force of the wind. These are among the most fundamental differentiations within attribution theory because disparate causal ascriptions to ability, effort and environmental factors have far-reaching behavioral implications.

In part because of these consequences, it is essential for individuals to reach veridical causal decisions. Kelley has been most insightful in describing the rational attribution process. According to Kelley, the attribution process is akin to a scientific procedure in which covariation is examined across situations, persons, time, and modalities. There is much evidence to support this rational processing conception. In addition, in the absence of complete covariation information, persons use causal rules, or schemata, to account for events. Two such schemata, necessary and sufficient, are elicited respectively in extreme and usual situations. In addition, given the presence of a sufficient cause, individuals often "discount" the influence of another cause.

Although there is much evidence to support the conception of a rational, information-processing individual, there also is a growing belief that humans are less logical than assumed by attribution theorists. Individuals bias perceived causation to enhance self-esteem (although perhaps less than one might imagine); they believe that others would make the same decisions they do, and therefore, they often tend to perceive the behavior of nonconforming others as "trait" caused; and they misperceive chance events as skill determined. Likewise, covariation inferences are based on only a small portion of the available data, particularly those from positively confirming cases, and less of the information in social interactions may be processed by participants than is apparent to a naive viewer.

Finally, attribution theory clarifies our understanding of dissonance phenomena, emotions, and animal behavior. In all of these cases the key process involves attribution of an event (e.g., reading a speech inconsistent with one's own attitudes, reacting with fear symptoms, pressing a lever for food) to oneself as opposed to a situational factor.

Attribution theory is not conceived as a panacea for the solution of all the problems in the study of motivation. Nor is it held to be the only possible cognitive approach to behavior. Rather, the emphasis on causal cognitions is a reasonable direction for the formulation of a general theory in which thoughts are systematically related to action. The specification of the relation between action and knowing is the goal of a cognitive theory of behavior. In the next chapter, I will examine the extent to which causal inferences influence expectations, affect, and goal-directed behaviors.

Chapter Eight

AN ATTRIBUTIONAL THEORY OF BEHAVIOR

Introduction

In this chapter an attributional theory of motivation is presented. This theory adheres to the expectancy-value framework adopted by Lewin, Atkinson, and Rotter and highlights the effects of attributions on the expectancy of goal attainment, affective responses, and interpersonal evaluation. Thus, although the attributional approach to motivation is contained with Section III of this book (mastery and growth theories), it also could have been included in Section II with other expectancy-value conceptions.

The attributional approach to motivation will be reviewed first in the context of achievement strivings, for investigations that manipulated success and failure provided the initial empirical foundation for this conceptual analysis. I will examine the topics of cue utilization, causal schemata, and other attributional antecedents, such as reinforcement schedules, to ascertain whether the analyses in the last chapter also are applicable to the achievement domain. Then the effects of causal ascriptions on expectancy, affect, and evaluation are examined. This discussion embraces diverse topics, including skill and chance settings, self-concept maintenance, reinforcement schedules, other- versus self-evaluation, and behavioral change programs. Lastly, I present additional areas of psychological research that document the range of the attributional approach, including parole decisions, loneliness and affiliation, mastery, hyperactivity, and depression.

The Perceived Causes of Success and Failure

Attribution theorists assume that individuals utilize a number of ascriptions both to postdict (interpret) and to predict the outcome of an achievement-related event. The attributional analysis of achievement strivings began with a compilation of these perceived causes.

Recall that Heider (1958) postulated that outcomes at achievement-related activities are a function of both internal and external (environmental) factors. Internal causes, in turn, are dichotomized into "power" (such as ability) and "try." Thus, the causes of success and failure specified by Heider are ability, effort, and characteristics of the environment, such as the ease or difficulty of a task. Heider also acknowledged that in certain situations luck is perceived as the determinant of success or failure.

In an empirical investigation examining the perceived causes of success and failure, Frieze (1976b) asked subjects to assume that:

> You received a very high score on (or failed) an exam.
> You won (or lost) the game.

The subjects were instructed to state why these events might occur. The most common attributions, as anticipated by Heider, were ability and immediate effort expenditure. Among other causal ascriptions that Frieze identified were task ease or difficulty, luck, other people, mood, and long-term effort.

Of course, there are additional perceived causes of success and failure, such as fatigue, illness, or drugs, as well as causes that are unique to specific situations. In a cross-cultural survey it was reported that even patience (in Greece and Japan) and tact and unity (in India) are perceived causes of success (Triandis, 1972). But in our culture, and within the confines of academic, occupational, and athletic accomplishment, it has been clearly documented that ability and effort typically are believed to be the dominant causes of success and failure, and task ease or difficulty often is perceived among other causes of achievement outcomes.

If the four causes specified by Heider are accepted as most salient in a particular situation, then task outcome (O) would be perceived as a function of ability (A), effort (E), task difficulty (T) and luck (L):

$$O = f(A, E, T, L)$$

That is, in attempting to explain the prior success or failure at an achievement-related event, the individual would assess her level of ability, the amount of effort that was expended, the difficulty of the task, and the magnitude and direction of experienced luck. It is assumed that rather general values are assigned to these elements and that the task outcome is differentially ascribed to the causal sources. In a similar manner, future expectations of success and failure would be based upon one's perceived level of ability in relation to the perceived difficulty of the task (labelled by Heider as "can"), as well as an estimation of intended effort and anticipated luck.

The mathematical relationships between the causal factors have not been specified. The components could, for example, combine either conjunctively or disjunctively, as suggested in the analysis of causal schemata. Thus, for example, in a skill situation that excluded the possibility of a luck ascription, it is conceivable that an individual would believe two of the remaining three proposed determinants of a positive outcome (high ability, high effort, an easy task) must be present for goal attainment. That is, given a task perceived as difficult, both ability and effort are needed for success, and given a task perceived as easy (TE), either ability or effort must be present for goal attainment. The relation of success (S) to the presence or absence of perceived causes would then be symbolized as:

$$S \rightarrow (A \wedge E) \vee (A \wedge TE) \vee (TE \wedge E)$$

Given the above analysis, any two causal determinants can compensate for the absence of the third causal factor. Of course, the additional possibility of luck or other factors as causes of success greatly complicates matters. Thus, at this time it is somewhat premature to specify the quantitative properties of causes, although this problem will be touched upon in subsequent discussions.

CAUSAL ANTECEDENTS

To reach causal inferences, that is, to decide why one succeeds or fails, requires that various sources of information be utilized and combined. Some of this information will originate from the current situation, while other evidence is gleaned from memories of past events. Inferences about causality for success and failure often are quite complex. Consider, for example, the difficulty a coach faces in determining why his team lost a key game, or the problems of a student in deciding why she was able to get a high grade in one course while doing so poorly in a second. In the following discussion, inferences about the self are not differentiated from inferences about others, although factors such as hedonic bias and knowledge about intentionality and past behavior may play a more central role in self- than in other-perception.

ABILITY ANTECEDENTS. Ability inferences primarily are determined by information about the past. Repeated success or failure, in part, indicates whether an individual "can" or "cannot." Hence, consistency is an important cue for ability inferences. For example, high grades often are accepted as evidence that a person is "smart"; winning games are the proof of a "good" team; and so on. Outcome information, particularly when considered in conjunction with social norms, is used to infer ability level (see Frieze & Weiner, 1971;

Weiner & Kukla, 1970). If, for example, someone succeeds at a task that all others fail, the person is likely to be perceived as very able (see Figure 7–2).

In addition to past history and social norms, two cues that appear to influence ability inferences are the pattern of performance and the maximum performance level. Given identical overall mean performance scores, persons exhibiting descending performance levels frequently are judged as more able than persons displaying random or ascending performance (Jones, Rock, Shaver, Goethals, & Ward, 1968). That is, there is a "primacy effect" in ability inferences. Further, it has been reported that given identical overall performance, individuals exhibiting a peak performance are judged as more able than those not displaying such a peak (Rosenbaum, 1971). Performance highs seem to indicate a person's underlying capabilities. Figure 8–1 portrays disparate levels of three cues discussed here (past success history, pattern of performance, and peak performance) and indicates their relative effects on ability judgments.

EFFORT ANTECEDENTS. It might be anticipated that one "knows" how hard one has tried, and that proprioceptive feedback or introspective knowledge provides sufficient information to reach conclusions about effort expenditure. But this often is not the case. For example, individuals use performance (outcome) information to infer how hard they tried. Subjects in experiments by Weiner and Kukla (1970) and Kukla (1972) anticipated whether 0 or 1 was going to be the next digit in a number series. The series actually was random, although subjects believed that "solutions" could be discerned. Following performance feedback, the subjects rated their effort expenditure. It was found that successful individuals perceived that they tried harder than unsuccessful individuals, even though the outcome was entirely a matter of chance. There is little reason to believe that lucky guessers in fact expend more energy than unlucky guessers, and there is no clear evidence demonstrating that motivation is increased more

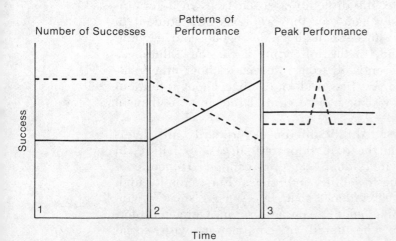

Figure 8–1. Three informational cues that influence ability inferences. In all cases the broken line indicates higher perceptions of ability.

by success than by failure. A similar finding is reported by Jenkins and Ward (1965). One attributional explanation of this misperception is that in one's life effort and outcome covary. Therefore, given a positive outcome, one infers the presence of effort, while given a negative outcome, one infers the absence of effort.

Pattern of performance also is a cue for effort attributions. In one of the experiments conducted by Jones et al. (1968), subjects received ascending, descending, or random patterns of success. These outcomes influenced self-perceptions of effort expenditure. Subjects in the ascending condition believed that they tried significantly harder than subjects in the other conditions. Again the outcome was entirely under experimental control and was independent of actual effort.

It also is probable that external indicators of exertion, such as muscular tension, perspiration, persistence of behavior, and the like, prompt effort attributions. In addition, perhaps covariation of performance with the incentive value of the goal will result in causal ascriptions to effort. In general, if a task is perceived as skill determined, and the environment is constant, variations in performance are likely to be ascribed to changes in motivation (effort expenditure).

TASK ANTECEDENTS.   Subjective task difficulty is, in part, a function of the perceived performance of others at the task. If many others succeed, then the task is "easy;" if few succeed, then it is "difficult." Hence, consensus information is a key cue in inferring difficulty. It is apparent that objective characteristics of the task, such as length, complexity, and novelty, also influence initial judgments of task difficulty. But this information is likely to receive relatively little weight in relation to outcome data. If everyone correctly performs a task, it is of little importance that it "appears" to be difficult.

Perhaps task characteristics are most important in judgments of outcomes at clearly difficult activities. For example, failure in climbing a mountain is likely to be attributed by observers to task difficulty, even though most of the highly selective individuals attempting the task succeed. It is quite possible, however, that a climber who fails will attribute the outcome to himself, judging difficulty not on the basis of task characteristics or norms over the whole population, but rather on the basis of the performance of others in his reference group.

LUCK ANTECEDENTS.   In psychological experiments luck ascriptions usually are induced by specific instructions; subjects merely are informed that the outcome at a task is due to chance (for example, see Phares, 1957, and Chapter Six). But generally, the most salient cue for luck attributions is the structure of a task. Flipping a coin, drawing a playing card from a shuffled deck, or guessing where the ball will drop in a roulette wheel logically results in luck ascriptions for success and failure. The more valid information for luck ascriptions, however, is the pattern of outcomes. Independence and randomness of outcome indicate that luck is the causal determinant (although, as discussed previously, there often is misunderstanding of randomness and misperception of a chance task as skill-determined). If a coin re-

TABLE 8–1   SOME CUES UTILIZED FOR INFERENCES CONCERNING THE CAUSES OF SUCCESS AND FAILURE

Causes	Cues
Ability	Number of successes, percentage of successes, pattern of success, maximal performance, task difficulty.
Effort	Outcome, pattern of performance, perceived muscular tension, sweating, persistance at the task, covariation of performance with incentive value of the goal.
Task Difficulty	Objective task characteristics, social norms.
Luck	Objective task characteristics, independence of outcomes, randomness of outcomes, uniqueness of event.

peatedly turns up heads, or a card player consistently draws aces, luck will no longer be perceived as the sole causal determinant, despite the task structure.

Unique events also give rise to luck attributions. For example, finding money on the street or experiencing failure after a series of successes often results in luck attributions (Feather, 1969; Feather & Simon, 1971). Finally, it is said that "luck is responsible for the success of your enemies." In one study bearing upon this point, Mann (1974) asked spectators at a football game why the winning team had been victorious. When the game was close, 93 per cent of the supporters of the winning team ascribed the success to superior play. However, 50 per cent of the supporters of the losing team attributed its defeat to bad luck (while another 10 per cent blamed poor officiating!).

OVERVIEW.   Table 8–1 summarizes some of the information used to infer causality in achievement-related contexts. These are only a small subset of the cues believed to be used, and the list would be further expanded if the discussion had not been limited to ability, effort, task difficulty, and luck. However, the cues summarized in Table 8–1 are likely to be salient in many achievement-related situations.

Investigations of Cue Utilization

Experiments have been conducted to determine whether individuals can use and combine information from some of the diverse sources listed above and reach reliable conclusions about the causes of success and failure. In one investigation (Frieze & Weiner, 1971), the subjects were given information that specified the percentage of success a hypothetical person experienced at a task (100, 50, or 0), the percentage of success this person encountered at similar tasks (100, 50, 0), and the percentage of others successful at the particular task (100, 50, 0). These three sources of information were selected because they roughly correspond to the attributional criteria specified by Kelley (1967), namely, consistency of behavior and social consensus. The nature of the task was left unknown. Further, the subjects were told that the individual attempted the task again and either succeeded or failed.

For example, the subjects were informed that an individual who succeeded on 100 per cent of past trials at the task and 50 per cent of past
trials at similar tasks attempted the task again and succeeded. They
also were informed that none of the other individuals was able to succeed at the task. The subjects then ascribed the causes of the immedi-

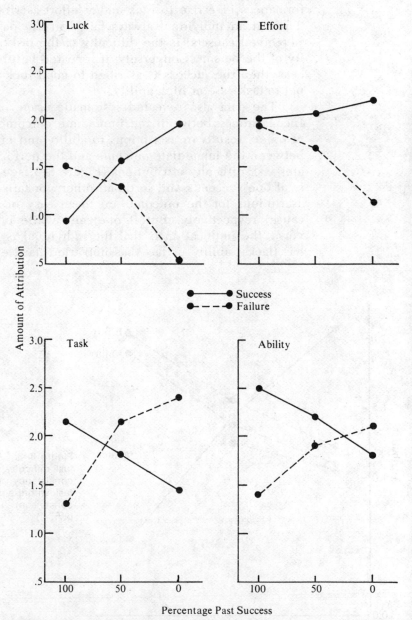

Figure 8-2. Attributions to luck, effort, task, and ability as a function of the
consistency of the immediate outcome with past performance at the task.
(Adapted from Frieze & Weiner, 1971, p. 60.)

ate success to ability, effort, task difficulty, and luck. Ratings could range from 0 (not a cause) to 3 (very much a cause).

The data revealed that all of the information supplied was used to reach causal judgments. Considering, for example, the cue of prior performance at the task, it was found that consistency of the present outcome with prior performance results in attributions to ability and/or task difficulty, while discrepancies between the past and present performances give rise to luck and/or effort ascriptions (see Figure 8–2). Thus, if an individual always failed in the past, and fails again, the perceived cause(s) is the difficulty of the task and/or the lack of ability of the person. Conversely, if repeated failure is followed by a success, then the success is ascribed to good luck and/or extra effort, but not to task ease or high ability.

The data also revealed systematic usage of the social norm cue. Inconsistency between the immediate outcome and the performance of others results in ascriptions to ability and effort, while consistency between the immediate outcome and the performance of others generates task difficulty attributions (Figure 8–3; see also Figure 7–2). That is, if one succeeds and so do all others, or fails when others fail, then ascriptions for the outcome are to an easy or hard task (an external cause) respectively. But if one fails while others succeed, or vice versa, the implication is that the individual is responsible. Either he has (lacks) ability or has (has not) tried hard enough. These data are

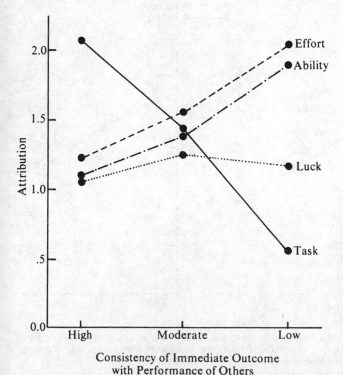

Figure 8–3. Attributions to ability, effort, task difficulty, and luck as a function of the consistency of immediate outcome at the task with the performance of others (social consensus). (From Frieze & Weiner, 1971, p. 594.)

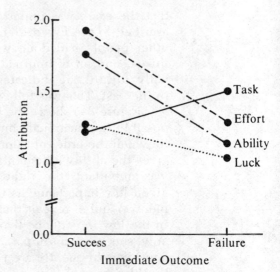

Figure 8-4. Attributions to ability, effort, task difficulty, and luck as a function of success or failure at the task. (From Frieze & Weiner, 1971, p. 596.)

consistent with the prior findings of McArthur (1972) and Orvis et al. (1975), which were presented in the prior chapter.

Finally, considering outcome information, the data revealed that success tends to be ascribed to internal factors (ability and effort) while failure is ascribed to the difficulty of the task (see Figure 8–4). These findings suggest ego-enhancing and ego-defensive attributional tendencies.

Information Preference

In addition to being able to use multiple cues to reach causal inferences, individuals also have preferred informational cues that are weighted most heavily in their judgments. In one study demonstrating such preferences, Frieze (1976a) asked subjects to judge why a person succeeded at an exam. The subjects received information about the importance (I) of the exam, the social norms (N) regarding the performance of others, and the prior performance (P) of the actor. In one experimental condition the subjects first received the importance information, followed by the norms and prior performance cues (order INP). In a second experimental condition the order of information was PIN. That is, the past history cue was presented first, followed by the importance and social consensus information. Following the reception of each cue, the subjects ascribed the reported success to ability, effort, task difficulty, luck, and mood.

More specifically, a subject was told that a student succeeded and that the exam was important (or unimportant). The success was then ascribed to the five designated causes. The subject was then told that other people had done well (or poorly). Following the reception of this second bit of information, causal judgments were again made. Finally, a third cue indicated that the person had done well (or poorly) in the past. This was followed by a final causal judgment.

Figure 8–5 shows the attributions of success to *ability* in the eight possible informational combinations. The figure depicts the condition in which the order of information was INP. The left half of Figure 8–5 gives the ability judgments when the first cue conveyed that the exam was important; the right half of the figure portrays the ascriptions given low importance as the first bit of information. Comparing judgments A and A′ reveals that ascription of success to high ability is greater in the low importance than in the high importance condition. Presumably, success at an important task will be ascribed to high effort. Ability and effort frequently are perceived as compensatory. Thus, the greater the likelihood that a cue will elicit high effort ascriptions, the less the likelihood that ascriptions also will be made to high ability.

The second cue given to the subjects pertained to the social norms associated with success. Low norms convey that most others have failed; high norms indicate that most others have succeeded at the exam. Given either high or low importance information, knowledge that others have failed (B_1 and B'_1) increases the ascription of success to high

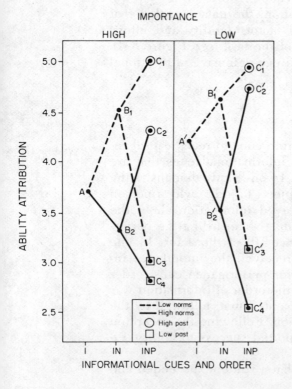

Figure 8–5. Ability attributions after success as a function of the order and type of information. Subjects first receive the importance cue, followed by normative information, and then the past history cue. (From Frieze, 1973, p. 97.)

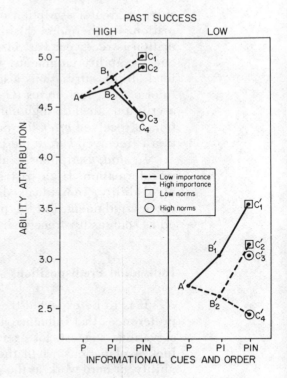

Figure 8–6. Ability attributions after success as a function of the order and type of information. Subjects first receive the past history cue, followed by the importance information, and then the social norm cue. (From Frieze, 1973, p. 97.)

ability. Thus, as already indicated, performance inconsistent with social norms elicits internal ascriptions. Further, comparing point B_1 with B'_1 (high importance, low norms versus low importance, low norms) and point B_2 with B'_2 (high importance, high norms versus low importance, high norms) reveals that the judgments *within* levels of norms but *between* levels of importance are virtually identical. Thus, the importance cue no longer differentially affects ability ascriptions, and is superceded by the normative information.

The third cue received by the subjects pertained to the prior success and failure experiences of the actor. The judgments indicate that attributions for success to ability are higher when one has done well (C_1, C_2, C'_1, C'_2) rather than poorly (C_3, C_4, C'_3, C'_4) in the past. Even though the social norms for success may be high, suggesting that the task is easy (B_2 and B'_2), attributions for success are made to ability given that a person has succeeded in the past (C_2 and C'_2). Thus, it can again be observed that new information supercedes the prior knowledge as the basis for causal judgments.

Figure 8–6 shows the ability judgments when the order of information presentation is PIN, rather than INP. That is, the past history cue is received first. The left half of Figure 8–6 illustrates the ability judgments given high past success; the right half of the figure shows the judgments in the low past success condition. The difference between the A and the A' ascriptions, respectively in the left and right half of Figure 8–6, shows clearly that high P information results in greater ascription of success to high ability than low P information. Furthermore, this disparity is not greatly altered as new information is received. Past history, therefore, again is the most dominant cue for ability judgments. However, Figure 8–6 does reveal that the final ability attributions also are somewhat influenced by social norm information; low norms (C_1, C_2, C'_1, and C'_2) produce greater ability ascriptions than do high norms (C_3, C_4, C'_3, and C'_4). Thus, if information is received *after* the preferred source, then it is used; if information is received *before* the preferred source, then it is discounted.

In sum, ascriptions to ability primarily are a function of past history information. High past success produces ascriptions of success to high ability. Individuals do use whatever information they have to reach a judgment. But the preferred past history cue is heavily weighted as soon as it is received.

Individual Predispositions

It is to be expected that there are individual differences in causal preferences that influence attributional decision making. Everyday observations suggest, for example, that some individuals readily invoke luck explanations when they interpret events, while others perceive ability, or hard work, as the primary determinant of achievement-related success.

There has been extensive work investigating achievement needs and gender that apparently demonstrates the effects of predispositions on causal ascriptions. Although some of these investigations have yielded promising results (see optimistic statements in Weiner, 1972), the prior enthusiasm must now be tempered, inasmuch as many other investigations either fail to replicate prior findings or report contradictory data. In the following pages two studies yielding positive evidence of causal biases on attributions are presented. These investigations are reported to illustrate the types of experiments that have been conducted and to convey the data that have been anticipated.

Achievement Needs

A study by Kukla (1972) was briefly alluded to earlier in the discussion of causal antecedents. Kukla had subjects guess whether the next digit in a series would be 0 or 1. The sequence of numbers was randomly arranged, although the subjects were led to believe that there was a systematic progression within the series. Entirely because of chance, some subjects succeeded while others failed in correctly anticipating the numbers. Subjects then made attributions for their performance.

The mean attributions to ability and effort as a function of individual differences in achievement needs are depicted in Figure 8–7. Figure 8–7 reveals that, given a success, persons high in achievement

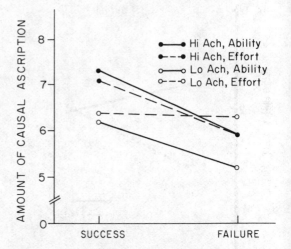

Figure 8–7. Causal ascriptions to ability and effort following success and failure for subjects classified as high or low in achievement needs. (Based on data from Kukla, 1972.)

motivation were more likely to perceive high ability and high effort as the responsible factors than were persons low in achievement needs. On the other hand, given a failure, individuals high in achievement needs were more likely to ascribe the outcome to a lack of effort than were persons low in achievement needs. The latter perceived failure as caused by a lack of ability.

In sum, the motive groups differed in their relative *internality* for success, with individuals high in achievement needs assuming more personal responsibility for favorable outcomes than persons low in achievement needs. Furthermore, the *stability* and *controllability* of the perceived causes for failure differed. (These concepts will be discussed in detail later in this chapter.) That is, individuals high in achievement needs implicated a cause for failure (insufficient effort) that can be altered, while persons low in achievement needs ascribed causality to a relatively fixed and uncontrollable factor (ability).

Figure 8–7 also shows that persons high in achievement needs perceive themselves to be relatively high in ability and believe that effort and outcome covary. Perceived effort-outcome covariation, or the belief that performance depends on how hard one has tried, does not characterize the attributional pattern of persons low in achievement needs. The behavioral consequences of these disparate causal cognitions are discussed at length later in this chapter.

Gender

There is suggestive evidence that the achievement outcomes of males and females are perceived by observers as caused by different factors. In addition, males and females may differ in their self-perceptions concerning causality. In a study of other-perception, Deaux and Emswiller (1974) had observer subjects evaluate the reasons for successful male and female performance at a visual discrimi-

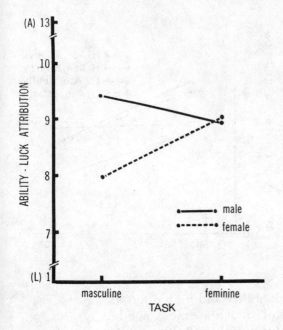

Figure 8–8. Ability minus luck attributions as a function of sex-linked characteristics of the task and the sex of the performer. (From Deaux & Emswiller, 1974, p. 82.)

nation task. Some of the to-be-discriminated objects were household articles (e.g., a mop), while others were "male-oriented" (e.g., tools). The performance of both the males and the females was presented as better than average. The observer subjects then rated the causes of the good performance on a scale ranging from ability on one end to luck at the other.

The results of this study are depicted in Figure 8–8. Figure 8–8 shows that the success of males in discriminating "male" objects is attributed more to their ability (and less to luck) than that of females given the masculine items. On the other hand, attributional differences were not displayed in judgments concerning successful discrimination of household items. Similar results have been reported when males and females judge their own performances (Deaux & Farris, 1977).

Causal Schemata

The preceding discussion reviewed evidence demonstrating that individuals use particular cues to reach causal inferences and that the cues are combined in a systematic and "rational" manner. Furthermore, individual differences in achievement needs and gender may produce causal biases, or attributional preferences. In addition, research has demonstrated that in achievement-related contexts causal schemata also influence the judgment process. Recall that a causal schema is a relatively permanent structure that refers to the beliefs a person holds about the relationship between an observed event (an effect) and the perceived causes of that event (Kelley, 1972).

Two distinct schemata have been identified: multiple sufficient schemata and multiple necessary schemata. Multiple sufficient schemata are employed to account for common events, while unusual or extreme events elicit multiple necessary schemata to explain their occurrence (Cunningham et al., 1975; Kelley, 1972). In achievement-related contexts, success at an easy task and failure at a difficult task are usual events, while success at a difficult task and failure at an easy task are unusual events. In accordance with Kelley's conception, it is therefore expected that success at an easy task will be perceived as the result of ability or effort, and that failure at a difficult task will be attributed to the absence of ability or effort. On the other hand, success at a difficult task should be perceived as caused by the presence of ability and effort, and failure at an easy task should be perceived as caused by the absence of both ability and effort.

To demonstrate the effects of causal schemata on causal inferences, Kun and Weiner (1973) created situations to elicit necessary or sufficient causal schemata. More specifically, subjects were provided information regarding success and failure at tasks varying in difficulty. After receiving the outcome and task difficulty information, the subjects were informed about the presence or absence of one cause (ability or effort). They then had to decide whether the complementary cause (effort or ability) was present or absent. For example, the subjects were told that an individual performed excellently on an exam, and that 90 per cent of the other students also performed excellently (an easy task). Furthermore, the pupil was described as high in ability. The subjects then judged whether the pupil also tried hard. Judgments were made on a scale ranging from "definitely tried hard" to "definitely did not try."

Figure 8–9 shows the judgments in this experiment. There were three levels of task difficulty (success by 90, 50, or 10 per cent of other students), two levels of outcome (success or failure), and information regarding ability or effort. The given cause was characterized as present or absent. As already indicated, the subjects had to judge the presence or the absence of the other cause. For success outcomes, the reported causes were high ability or high effort, while for failure outcomes, ability and effort were always described as low.

Figure 8–9 shows that when told of success at the most difficult task and the presence of ability (or effort), subjects indicated that effort (or ability) was also present. Thus, a multiple necessary schema is used. Conversely, given success at the easiest task, subjects infer that the complementary cause was absent. Turning to the failure condition, given failure at the most difficult task and low ability (or low effort), subjects expressed the belief that low effort (or low ability) was not a cause. And given failure at the easiest task, there is a slight tendency to infer the presence of both low ability and low effort.

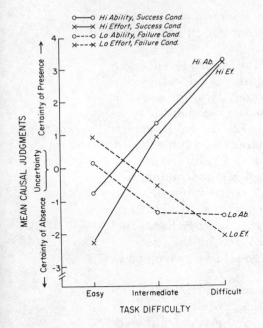

Figure 8–9. Mean certainty judgments of ability or effort given information concerning the complementary cause (effort or ability), task outcome, and the difficulty of the task. The labels indicate the cause being judged. (From Kun & Weiner, 1973, p. 203.)

In sum, when performance outcomes are uncommon, attributions tend to include multiple causes; when performance outcomes are common, attributions are made to only one cause. Thus, causal schemata elicited in achievement-related contexts by information concerning the commonness of an event influence the attribution process and perceptions of causality.

Figure 8–9 also shows that over an extended range of task difficulty levels, both ability and effort are believed to be necessary to attain success. This is evident in the figure because both the intermediate- and difficult-task judgments are above the uncertainty point in the success condition, indicating the presence of the complementary causal factor. On the other hand, over an extended range of task difficulty levels, either low ability or low effort is believed to be sufficient to produce a failure. As shown in Figure 8–9, both the intermediate and the difficult task causal judgments are below the uncertainty point, indicating the absence of the complementary causal factor. One is reminded of the saying that a chain is only as strong as its weakest link; i.e., all components must be strong for "success," and the absence of strength in any of the subparts is sufficient for "failure." It therefore appears that the attributions for success and failure might be governed by somewhat different psychological rules.

Schedules of Reinforcement

An individual working at an achievement-related activity typically undergoes a series of successes and failures. The person may at first experience repeated failure, then attain partial success, and finally have repeated success. This ascending pattern of performance often indicates a growth of skill. The reverse pattern also is possible. For example, the valedictorian of a grammar school class might score in the top 10 per cent of her high school class, the top 25 per cent of college seniors, below the median of her colleagues in graduate school, and then fail at an academic job. This is a descending pattern of success that unfortunately has counterparts in real-life situations.

There is a vast literature in psychology examining the effects of reinforcement schedules and patterns on a variety of indexes of motivation. Here I will consider only how such schedules of reward might affect perceptions of causality; later in the chapter the effects of these causal perceptions on behavior will be examined.

Partial versus 100 Per Cent Schedules

The percentage of reinforced trials during a training or learning period has been one of the most examined variables in psychology. A typical study employs infrahuman subjects and contrasts the effects of a random partial reward schedule (50 per cent reward) versus repeated (100 per cent) reward. It previously was contended that variability or randomness in a series of outcomes elicits luck attributions. Hence, following this logic, a 50 per cent random reward schedule also should generate attributions of success and failure (reward and nonreward) to chance. That is, a random schedule of reinforcement during the training period of an experiment using infrahumans is conceptually similar to telling a human subject that the outcome of the task, or the reception of the reward, is determined by luck. Of course, imputing luck attributions to lower organisms such as rats may be unrealistic, given their cognitive capacities. But infrahumans do process information and learn. Thus, they perhaps make some primitive attributions for causality. Clearly, before accepting or rejecting attributional processes among infrahumans, the intellectual and symbolizing limits of lower organisms must be determined.

On the other hand, repeated success at a task (100 per cent reward) indicates that there is a contingency between the responses that the organism is making and the reception of the reward. Hence, the organism should conclude that it is "responsible" or is personally causing the onset of the reward. Furthermore, inasmuch as the percentage of reward is one indicator of ability, individuals given a 100 per cent reward schedule should infer that they have high ability at the task (or that the task is easy).

Ratio versus Interval Schedules

Reinforcement schedules frequently are designated as either ratio or interval. In a fixed ratio schedule the reinforcement follows a certain number of responses. Because rewards covary with responses, organisms should make internal attributions (ability and/or effort) for the reward. On the other hand, in a fixed interval schedule the reinforcement is presented following the first response after an established time period. Given this schedule, the reinforcements are externally controlled. There are no behaviors that an organism can make that will increase the frequency of the reward; the organism is learning that nothing it does matters. This is conceptually similar to learned helplessness training (see Chapter Six). Hence, attributions for any reward should be ascribed to external sources, such as time or luck.

Other Antecedents

There are, of course, many other categories of antecedents that influence causal ascriptions. For example, communications from others certainly will be an important contribution to attributional knowledge. Someone stating that "you certainly are smart" or "you really were lucky" is likely to influence one's attributions for success. In addition, stereotypes can influence attributions for the behaviors of others ("they really are lazy"), just as one's general self-concept might in-

TABLE 8–2   THE ATTRIBUTION PROCESS FOR SUCCESS AND FAILURE

Antecedents	Causal Categories
Specific Cues	
Past outcome history	
Social norms	
Performance peak	
Pattern of performance	
Persistence of behavior	
Task characteristics	
Randomness of outcome	
Incentive × performance covariation	Ability
	Effort
Causal Schemata	Task Difficulty
	Luck
Necessary schema	Mood
Sufficient schema	Fatigue
	Illness
Individual Predispositions	Other People
Achievement-related needs	
Gender	
Reinforcement Schedules	
100% versus 50%	
Ratio versus interval	
Others	
Communication from others	
Stereotypes	

fluence self-perceptions of causality at a particular task. In sum, there are many, many determinants that influence the attribution process (see Table 8–2).

CAUSAL DIMENSIONS

It already has been indicated that there are numerous possible perceived causes of success and failure. Indeed, this list may be infinite, given the idiosyncratic explanations plausible for any given event. For example, failure at a school exam might be ascribed to copying from the wrong person, the heat or noise in the room, studying the wrong material, or a fight with one's mate, just to name some atypical causes. Because of this diversity, it is essential to create a classification scheme or a taxonomy of causes, and in so doing delineate their similarities and differences and identify their underlying properties.

The theoretical analyses of Rotter (1966) and Heider (1958) are available to serve as initial guides in this endeavor. Rotter and his colleagues proposed a one-dimensional classification scheme of perceptions of causality. Causes were either within (internal) or outside of (external to) the person. In a similar manner, Heider, as well as deCharms, Deci, and others, articulated an internal-external classification of causes. Rotter labelled this dimension "locus of control," rather than "locus of causality." It is not clear whether control and causal concepts should be distinguished. Fontaine (1972) suggested that control refers to forward-looking (predictive) processes, whereas perceptions of causality refer to backward-looking (postdictive) judgments. In this chapter, locus of control is considered to be a causal belief, and the internal-external dimension is referred to as the "locus of causality."

The causes listed in Table 8–2 can readily be classified as internal or external to the individual. Ability, effort, mood, fatigue, and illness are personal causes, whereas task difficulty, luck, and other people are external sources of causality. Of course, the placement of a cause within this dimension is not invariant over time or between people. For example, luck may be perceived as an internal factor ("I am a lucky person") or as an external cause (a "chance" event). Inasmuch as attribution theory deals with phenomenal causality, such personal interpretations must be taken into account. That is, the taxonomic placement of a cause depends upon the subjective meaning of that cause to the individual. However, despite possible individual variation, there is general agreement on the classification of causes as internal or external.

There are other dimensions of causality, or properties of causes, in addition to locus, although they have not received as much attention as the internal-external classification. Heider (1958) distinguished dispositional and relatively fixed characteristics such as ability from fluctuating factors such as effort and luck. Hence, a second dimension of causality characterizes causes on continuum from stable (invariant) to unstable (variant). Ability, the difficulty of a task, and the bias of others are likely to be perceived as relatively fixed, while luck, effort, mood, fatigue, and illness are more unstable — luck implies random variability; effort may be augmented or decreased from one episode to the next; and mood, fatigue, and illness are conceived as temporary states. Here again, the perceived properties of the causes may vary. For example, a "lucky" person may perceive luck as quite enduring; illness can be correctly or incorrectly perceived as a permanent state; and so forth. In addition, experimenters can alter causal characteristics. For example, Valle and Frieze (1976) portrayed task difficulty as unstable by anchoring this concept to assigned sales territory, which could be shifted for any salesperson.

Table 8–3 classifies causes into the locus and stability dimensions. The table reveals that ability is an internal, stable cause; effort, mood, fatigue, and illness are internal but unstable; task difficulty is external and stable; and luck is both external and unstable. However, it must be remembered that any of these causes, at times, can be classified differently. There even are fluctuations in ability level ("today I played very well"), and effort can be a temporary exertion or the manifestation of a trait of industriousness.

A third dimension of causality, which was identified by Heider and later incorporated into the achievement domain by Rosenbaum (1972), has been labelled "intentionality." Here this dimension will be more appropriately called "controllability" (see Litman-Adizes, 1978). Causes such as effort are likely to be perceived as controllable, whereas ability, the difficulty of a task, mood, and illness are not subject to volitional control. This dimension is not clearly distinct from the locus and stability dimensions of causality. For example, if a cause is both internal and stable, such as ability, then it must be uncontrollable. However, some causes, such as mood and fatigue, are internal and unstable but not under volitional control, whereas effort is likewise internal and unstable, but controllable. Hence, it seems reasonable to distinguish this third dimension of causality.

Table 8–4 subsumes the causes discussed thus far within the locus, stability, and controllability dimensions. Table 8–4 indicates, for example, that both ability and effort can be perceived as stable or

TABLE 8–3   A TWO-DIMENSIONAL CLASSIFICATION SCHEME FOR THE PERCEIVED DETERMINANTS OF ACHIEVEMENT BEHAVIOR

| Stability | Locus of Control | |
	Internal	External
Stable	Ability	Task difficulty
Unstable	Effort, mood, fatigue, illness	Luck

TABLE 8–4   A THREE-DIMENSIONAL TAXONOMY OF THE PERCEIVED CAUSES OF SUCCESS AND FAILURE

	Controllable		Uncontrollable	
	Stable	*Unstable*	*Stable*	*Unstable*
Internal	Stable effort of self	Unstable effort of self	Ability of self	Fatigue, mood, and fluctuations in skill of self
External	Stable effort of others	Unstable effort of others	Ability of others, task difficulty	Fatigue, mood, and fluctuations in skill of others, luck

(Adapted from Rosenbaum, 1972, p. 21.)

unstable (there are temporary fluctuations in ability as well as in effort). Further, external factors, such as other people, may affect one's achievements. From the perspective of the actor, all external causes may be uncontrollable. However, Table 8–4 assumes that even external causes are controllable. Finally, Table 8–4 indicates that to distinguish ability from effort on the grounds that one is stable but the other is not (see Table 8–3) is insufficient, for this distinction neglects the essential fact that ability is not subject to volitional control, while effort is considered to be controllable.

Other dimensions of causality that identify the general properties of causes are likely to emerge with further analysis. Of particular importance is a differentiation between the concepts of controllability and intentionality. An individual might state, for example, "I intend not to drink, but I can't seem to control my behavior." Furthermore, negligence involves an unintentional action that is perceived by others as controllable. Finally, intentionality, but not controllability, implies desire or want. The above points suggest that intentionality differs from controllability. However, the differentiation between intentionality and controllability is difficult to support with any surety.

The dimensions are "second order" concepts (Schütz, 1967, p. 59); they are concepts used by attribution theorists to organize the causal concepts of the layman. The distinction between lay concepts and scientific concepts is important to bear in mind. The starting point for attribution theory was the language of the layman—words such as "can" and "try." But order is imposed on this language by using scientific terms, such as "locus of causality," that might not be in the vocabulary of the layman. Heider (1958) recognized the distinction between a naive psychology and a scientific psychology. He stated:

There is no a priori reason why the causal description [scientific language] should be the same as the phenomenal description [naive language], though, of course, the former should adequately account for the latter. (p. 22)

TABLE 8–5   CAUSES FOR THE SUCCESS AND FAILURE CONDITIONS

Success Condition

Pat did well on the exam because . . .

1. Pat studied the appropriate material for the exam.
2. Pat felt fine emotionally that day, was in a good mood.
3. Pat cares about grades and doing well in school.
4. Pat has a lot of self-confidence on exams.
5. the questions were clearly worded and fair.
6. Pat knew the material.
7. the course was easy.
8. Pat was calm, didn't get nervous during the exam.
9. Pat always studies hard for exams.
10. Pat was motivated to do well on this exam.
11. the exam was easy (everyone got a good grade).
12. the teacher just asked the "right" questions.
13. Pat had time to finish the exam.
14. Pat has a lot of ability in this subject.
15. Pat is industrious, a hard worker.
16. Pat had enough time to study for the exam.
17. the teacher did a good job of preparing the class.
18. Pat studied hard for this exam.

Failure Condition

Pat did poorly on the exam because . . .

1. Pat didn't study the appropriate material for the exam.
2. Pat felt bad emotionally that day, was in a bad mood.
3. Pat doesn't care about grades or doing well in school.
4. Pat doesn't have a lot of self-confidence on exams.
5. the questions were not clearly worded and were unfair.
6. Pat didn't know the material.
7. the course is hard.
8. Pat got nervous during the exam, "blanked out."
9. Pat never studies hard for exams.
10. Pat wasn't motivated to do well on this exam.
11. the exam was hard (everyone got a poor grade).
12. the teacher just asked the "wrong" questions.
13. Pat didn't have time to finish the exam.
14. Pat doesn't have much ability in this subject.
15. Pat is lazy, not a hard worker.
16. Pat didn't have enough time to study for the exam.
17. the teacher did a bad job of preparing the class.
18. Pat didn't study hard for this exam.

(From Passer, 1977.)

The dimensions of locus, stability, controllability, and intentionality were derived from the intuitions of investigators such as Rotter, Heider, and Rosenbaum. They are scientific concepts to help explain the psychology of the layman, although some of the concepts (e.g., intentionality) also appear in the lay vocabulary. A number of investigators presently are employing techniques such as factor analysis or multidimensional scaling to discover whether the dimensions generated by the logical analysis also will emerge with empirical methods. Of course, the two endeavors need not yield parallel results. For example, a layperson may not spontaneously recognize that mood and effort are alike in that both are unstable; thus, a stability dimension will not emerge in a multidimensional scaling procedure. But a scientist may find it useful to classify these concepts similarly because they lead to identical behavioral predictions.

In one empirical study of the dimensions of achievement-related causes, Passer (1977) had male and female subjects rate the similarity of the causes of either success or failure in an academic (test) situation (see Table 8–5). Eighteen causes of either success or failure were presented in all possible pairs to the subjects. The similarity judgments that were made then provided the input for a multidimensional scaling procedure. This method of analysis is akin to a cluster or factor analysis and suggests the number of underlying dimensions of the judgments.

One of the scaling solutions from the study, based on the failure judgments made by the male subjects, is depicted in Figure 8–10. Figure 8–10 reveals that two dimensions of causality were evident in the analysis: 1) an internal-external (locus) dimension, anchored at the internal end with causes such as bad mood and no self-confidence and at the external end with causes such as bad teacher and hard exam;

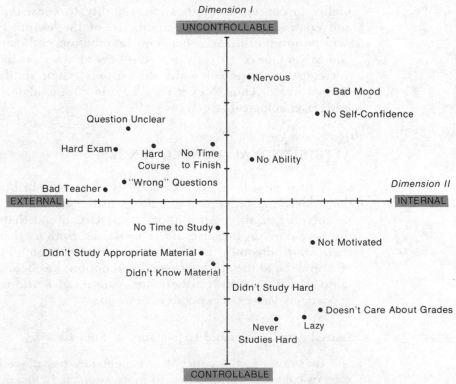

Figure 8–10. Two-dimensional solution for causal structure. (Adapted from Passer, 1977, p. 113.)

and 2) an uncontrollable-controllable dimension, anchored at the uncontrollable end with causes such as nervousness and bad mood and at the controllable end with "never studies hard" and "lazy." The findings reported by Passer were similar for both the males and females in both the success and failure scaling solutions.

The proposed third dimension of causality, stability, was not displayed. For this dimension to emerge, it would be necessary for the temporal characteristics of the situation to be made salient to the subjects. For example, if the subjects were to rate the similarity of the causes of success or failure in the context of selecting a teammate for a game to be played at some future date, then the concept of causal stability might be activated, and stability would be revealed as a dimension of causality. Thoughts of the future were not made salient in the situation selected by Passer. Nevertheless, Passer's results are encouraging in that two of the assumed dimensions of causality were manifested, and unknown dimensions that had not been part of the logical analysis were not displayed.

Even more recently, Meyer (1978) had subjects rate nine perceived causes of success and failure at an exam. These ratings were based on cues regarding the importance of the exam, the consistency of exam outcome with prior performance, and social norms regarding the performance of others at the exam. A factor analysis revealed three factors: locus, stability, and controllability. Furthermore, locus related highly to consensus information, stability to consistency information, and controllability to the importance of the exam. Therefore, there may be unique linkages between information and causal dimensions. One advantage of Meyer's procedure over Passer's is that subjects need not consciously perceive the dimensions when similarity judgments are not made. Thus, Meyer may have more adequately tapped underlying psychological structures.

ATTRIBUTIONAL CONSEQUENCES

I turn now from the antecedents of causal attributions, and from the underlying properties of causes, to the behavioral implications of perceived causality. Attribution theorists contend that people behave the way they do because of the causal ascriptions that they make for their prior outcomes. Thus, attribution theory, which initially provided an approach to the study of social perception, has been used to explain motivated behavior. Furthermore, causal attributions are linked to expectancy-value conceptions of behavior.

Causal Attributions and Expectancy of Success

Inasmuch as the concept of expectancy has played such a central role in cognitive approaches to motivation, it is disappointing that its operational linkages and specified antecedents have remained so vague. The first systematic analysis of the determinants of expectancies was undertaken by Tolman (1932). On the basis of research with infrahumans, Tolman posited that expectancies of reward are determined by learning capacities and environmental variables. The environmental variables believed to be most important were the frequency and the recency of reward for a particular behavior.

Surprisingly, the inferred determinants of expectancy and expectancy shifts deduced from research with humans are even less satisfying. Investigators in the level of aspiration and achievement domains, in which the concept of expectancy plays such a central role, have not systematically examined the antecedents of the subjective probability of success. And the only determinants of expectancy shifts that have been identified are success and failure: following success, expectancy generally rises, while after failure it typically falls (these are called "typical" shifts).

Social learning theorists have fared little better in their analyses of expectancy. Expectancies rather vaguely were considered to be a function of both specific and general reinforcement histories (see Chapter Six). Rotter and his colleagues did demonstrate, however, that expectancy shifts do differ between skill (internal locus of control) and chance (external control) settings. Following successful accomplishment in a skill-related situation, expectancy rises to a greater extent than it does after success in a chance-related setting. In a similar manner, decrements in expectancy after failure are greater given skill, rather than chance, determinants of performance.

Guided in part by these data, research in the attributional domain has proven that causal ascriptions for past performance are an important determinant of goal expectancies. For example, failure that is ascribed to low ability or to the difficulty of a task decreases the expectation of future success more than failure that is ascribed to bad luck or a lack of effort. In a similar manner, success ascribed to good luck or extra exertion results in lesser increments in the subjective expectancy of future success at that task than does success ascribed to high ability or to the ease of the task. More generally, it has been determined that expectancy shifts after success and failure are dependent upon the perceived stability of the cause of the prior outcome: ascription of an outcome to stable factors (such as ability and task difficulty) produces greater typical shifts in expectancy than do ascriptions to unstable causes (such as effort and luck). Stated somewhat differently, if one attains success (or failure), and if the conditions or causes of that outcome are expected to remain unchanged, then success (or failure) will be anticipated with an increased degree of certainty. But if the conditions or causes are perceived as subject to change, then there is some doubt that the prior outcome will be repeated.

A summary of the relations between expectancy shifts and causal ascriptions is shown in Figure 8–11. The figure, which includes only the causes of ability, effort, task difficulty, and luck, indicates that the

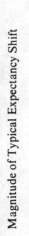

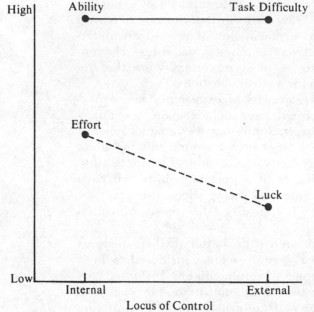

Figure 8–11. Magnitude of expectancy change (increase after success and decrease after failure) as a function of causal ascriptions for an outcome.

differential shifting of expectancies as a function of the stability of the attributions occurs given both internal (ability or effort) and external (task difficulty or luck) causal attributions. However, as shown in Figure 8–11, attributions to effort produce greater typical shifts than do attributions to luck. This is because effort is more likely to be perceived as stable than is luck, particularly given a successful outcome, for the intent to succeed is likely to remain relatively constant.

Empirical Evidence

A large number of research investigations and logical extensions of the reported empirical findings provided the basis for Figure 8–11 (see Fontaine, 1974; McMahan, 1973; Meyer, 1970; Ostrove, 1978; Pancer and Eiser, 1975; Rosenbaum, 1972; Valle, 1974; Valle and Frieze, 1976; and Weiner, Nierenberg, & Goldstein, 1976). The initial investigation in this area was conducted by Meyer (1970; reported, in part, in Weiner, Heckhausen, Meyer, & Cook, 1972). In Meyer's experiment male high school students experienced five repeated failures at a digit-symbol substitution task. Following each trial the subjects attributed their failure to low ability, insufficient effort, task difficulty, or bad luck. In addition, they estimated their probability of successfully completing the next trial. The attributions were in percentage figures and were required to total 100 per cent. Therefore, the causal ascriptions were not independent of one another.

The relationships between the causal ascriptions and expectancy of success are shown in Figures 8–12 and 8–13. Figure 8–12 compares

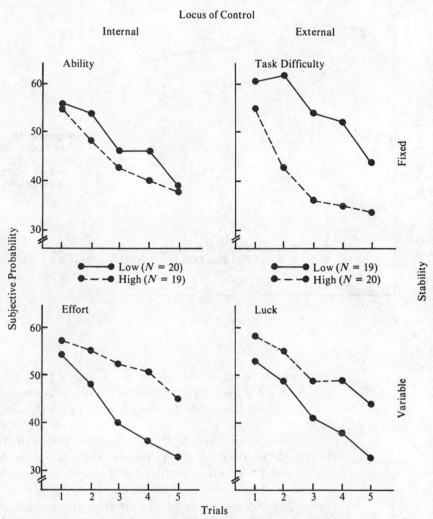

Figure 8–12. Expectancy of success as a function of above- or below-median ascription to the four causal elements. High ascription indicates lack of ability, a difficult task, lack of effort, and bad luck. (Adapted from Meyer, 1970.)

the expectancy shifts given high (above the median) versus low (below the median) attributions to the individual causes, while Figure 8–13 portrays expectancy changes given high or low attributions to the combined stable causes. The figures reveal that expectancy decrements following failure are most evident when ascriptions to low ability and task difficulty are high and when attributions to lack of effort and bad luck are low.

McMahan (1973) replicated these findings, also using a correlational approach in which the subjects reported both their causal ascriptions and the expectancy of success. However, in his investigation,

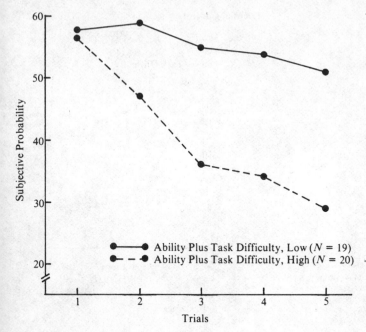

Figure 8–13. Subjective probabilities given repeated failure for groups high or low in ascription to stable factors (lack of ability plus task difficulty). (Adapted from Meyer, 1970.)

attributions were assessed by means of a paired-comparison method ("Which of these two causes was more responsible for your outcome?"), and the subjects ranged from approximately 11 to 20 years of age.

Subsequent investigations by Fontaine (1974) and Rosenbaum (1972) departed from the paradigm introduced by Meyer (1970). Fontaine and Rosenbaum manipulated causal attributions for success and failure and then assessed the subjective expectancy of success. Hence, their designs are considered experimental rather than correlational in that the subjects were randomly assigned to causal attribution conditions.

Rosenbaum told his subjects that a supervisor and a subordinate were working together on an unspecified project. One group of subjects was informed that the outcome of the project was a success; a second group was told that the outcome was a failure. The cause was specified as the stable or unstable ability or effort of either the supervisor or the subordinate (see Table 8–6). After receiving the outcome and causal attribution information, the subjects indicated their expectancies concerning the outcome of the next project undertaken by the supervisor and the subordinate.

The results of this study are depicted in Figure 8–14. The figure reveals a significant effect for outcome: Expectancies of future success are higher after success than after a failure. Of more importance in the present context, expectancies are highest when success is ascribed to stable causes and are lowest when failure is attributed to stable causes. This is true whether ability or effort of the supervisor or the

TABLE 8–6   EIGHT DESCRIPTIONS OF PROJECT OUTCOMES VARYING ACCORDING TO THE NATURE OF THE OUTCOME, THE STABILITY OF THE CAUSE AND THE INTENTIONALITY OF THE CAUSE

	Success	
	The project was of high quality because . . .	
	Intentional	*Unintentional*
Stable	Your subordinate (supervisor) is the kind of person who usually tries hard to produce high quality projects.	Your subordinate (supervisor) is the kind of person who usually has the ability to produce high quality projects.
Unstable	Your subordinate's (supervisor's) effort to produce a high quality project was higher on that occasion than it usually is.	Your subordinate's (supervisor's) ability to produce a high quality project was higher on that occasion than it usually is.
	Failure	
	The project was of low quality because . . .	
Stable	Your subordinate (supervisor) is the kind of person who usually doesn't try hard to produce high quality projects.	Your subordinate (supervisor) is the kind of person who usually doesn't have the ability to produce high quality projects.
Unstable	Your subordinate's (supervisor's) effort to produce a high quality project was lower on that occasion than it usually is.	Your subordinate's (supervisor's) ability to produce a high quality project was lower on that occasion than it usually is.

(Adapted from Rosenbaum, 1972, p. 71.)

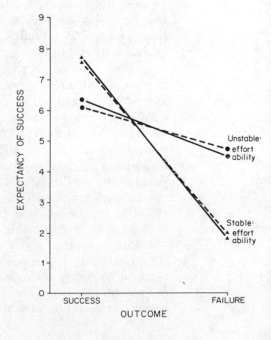

Figure 8–14. The effect of the stability causal dimension upon expectancy of success following success and failure. The causes of success are high ability or high effort; the causes of failure are low ability or low effort. (From Rosenbaum, 1972, p. 83).

subordinate is the given cause. Thus, the results of Meyer and McMahan were replicated when the causes were manipulated, rather than inferred from the subjects' responses.

A Re-Examination of Locus of Control

The research from the locus of control literature concerning expectancy shifts that is most germane to the attributional analysis has been conducted by Rotter and his colleagues. As previously discussed (see Chapter Six), Rotter·(1966) contends that typical expectancy shifts will be maximized when reinforcements are perceived as internally controlled (skill situations), and minimized when reinforcements are perceived as externally controlled (chance situations). This position clearly contrasts with the attributional analysis. Both the social learning and the attributional positions agree that causal ascriptions influence expectancy; however, social learning theorists relate expectancy change to the locus dimension of causality, whereas attribution theorists associate expectancy change with the stability dimension.

A number of investigations apparently have confirmed the hypothesized relations between locus of control and expectancy shifts. In one of the initial demonstrations, Phares (1957) led subjects to believe that their performances at a discrimination task were influenced by either skill or chance. Success and failure were then induced, and the subjective probability of success was inferred from betting behavior. As predicted by the locus of control analysis, the magnitude of the expectancy increments and decrements was greater in the skill than in the chance condition.

In addition, other researchers have shown that in games of chance, atypical shifts (decrements in the expectancy of success following a success and increments after a failure) frequently are made (e.g., Jarvik, 1951; Phares, 1957; Skinner, 1942). Such shifts have been labelled the "gambler's fallacy," referring to the misconception that in games of chance events are not perceived as independent and the same outcome is believed unlikely to recur on successive occasions (the "negative recency" effect). Furthermore, in chance tasks the conviction that the future outcome will differ from the prior results increases as a function of the number of consecutive occurrences of the past event (Jarvik, 1951; Lepley, 1963). This finding is in marked opposition to data in skill situations, for with increasing success (or failure) at a skill-related task, there is increasing certainty that success (or failure) again will be experienced. That is, a "positive recency" effect is displayed (see for example, Diggory, Riley, & Blumenfeld, 1960; Zajonc & Brickman, 1969).

The data cited above apparently support the locus of control position. But Table 8–3 reveals that skill (ability) and chance (luck) perceptions of causality differ not only in locus of control, but also in their degree of stability. One's skill is relatively stable, while luck is perceived as variable. Hence, comparisons of expectancy shifts between tasks that elicit either skill or chance perceptions of responsibility confound two dimensions of causality. This makes it impossible to determine whether the differential expectancy shifts that have been observed in skill settings versus chance settings are to be attributed to differences in locus of control, as the social learning theorists have reasoned, or to disparate beliefs about stability, as the attributionists have argued.

Note, therefore, that there is no disagreement concerning the validity of the data; differential typical and atypical shifts in expectancies given games of skill versus chance cannot be questioned. Rather, there is disagreement concerning the explanation or conceptual analysis of these empirical facts. It is rather rare in the field of motivation to find unequivocal empirical evidence and two theories that are commensurate with respect to the data. That is, the two theories can be directly compared, and one can be judged as "better" than the other with respect to a specific prediction.

The research by Fontaine (1972) McMahan (1973), Meyer (1970), and Rosenbaum (1972) did separate the locus of control from the stability dimension of causality, and it was reported that expectancy shifts were unrelated to an internal-external classification, but were related to the stable-unstable distinction. In addition, an investigation by Weiner, Nierenberg, & Goldstein (1976) directly pitted the locus of control analysis against the causal stability explanation. Weiner et al. (1976) gave subjects either zero, one, two, three, four, or five success experiences at a block-design task. In contrast to the study by Meyer (1970), different subjects were placed in the various experimental conditions. Following the success trial(s) subjects indicated their expectancy of success and causal ascriptions.

Expectancy of future success was determined by having subjects indicate "how many of the next ten similar designs he believed that he would successfully complete" (Weiner et al., 1976, p. 61). To assess perceptions of causality, researchers had subjects mark four rating scales that were identical with respect to either the stability or locus of control dimensional anchors, but differed along the alternate dimension. For example, one attribution question was, "Did you succeed on this task because you are always good at these kinds of tasks or because you tried especially hard on this particular task?" "Always good" and "tried hard," the anchors on this scale, are identical on the locus of causality dimension (internal), but they differ in perceived stability, with ability a stable attribute and effort an unstable cause. In a similar manner, judgments were made between "lucky" and "tried hard" (unstable causes differing in locus of causality), "these tasks are always easy" and "lucky" (external causes differing in stability), and "always good" and "always easy" (stable causes differing in locus). Thus, the judgments were made *within* a single causal dimension. This permitted a direct test of the locus versus stability interpretations of expectancy change.

Expectancy estimates were examined separately for each of the

causal judgments. Figure 8–15 shows the relation between causal stability and the expectancy judgments within internal control (ability versus effort ascriptions), while Figure 8–16 depicts this relation within
the external locus of causality (task difficulty versus luck ascriptions).
The figures show that given both the internal and the external causes,
expectancy increments are positively associated with the stability of the
ascription. It also can be observed that this relation is exhibited in all
of the ten independent comparisons. Comparing locus of causality differences within either the stable or the unstable ascriptions revealed
that the disparate causal locus groups did not differ in expectancy of
success.

In sum, the research data clearly support the attributional conception and contradict the predictions from social learning theory. The
stability of causal ascriptions, and not their locus, is related to shifts in
expectancy of success. These findings have a number of implications
for the study of locus of control. First, locus of control refers to a causal belief and represents one particular dimension associated with the
encoding of the causal structure of one's world. Thus, internal-external
locus of control should perhaps be dislodged from the conceptual
foundation of social learning theory and expectancy of reinforcement,
which it does not predict, and be placed within a broader cognitive
framework.

Further, it is evident that there are dimensions of causality in addition to locus. The concentration of research upon any single causal

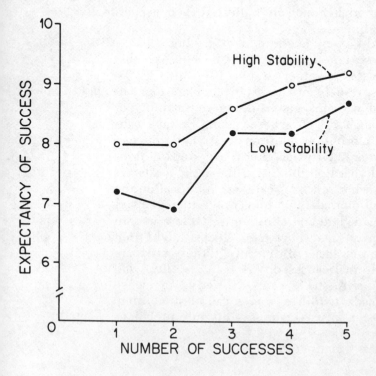

Figure 8–15. Mean expectancy of
success as a function of the number
of successes for subjects classified
according to stability ascription,
within internal locus of control (ability versus effort attribution). (From
Weiner, Nierenberg, & Goldstein,
1976, p. 63.)

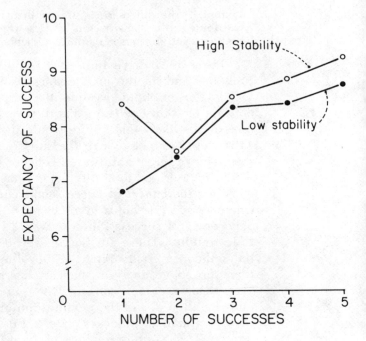

Figure 8-16. Mean expectancy of success as a function of the number of successes for subjects classified according to stability ascription, within external locus of control (task difficulty versus luck attribution). (From Weiner, Nierenberg, & Goldstein, 1976, p. 63.)

dimension, to the exclusion of other dimensions, constrains both empirical and theoretical growth.

Finally, there are a wide array of internal determinants of behavior in addition to skill, and an equally far-reaching variety of external determinants of behavior in addition to luck. There are important differences between, for example, ability and effort, or luck and powerful others, although these dissimilarities have not been distinguished in locus of control theory and research. These distinctions will have to be taken into consideratrion in future investigations and theorizing.

FORMAL ANALYSIS AND SELF-CONCEPT MAINTENANCE. McMahan (1973) and Valle and Frieze (1976) have developed more formal models of expectancy shifts based upon the concept of causal stability. Valle and Frieze postulate that predictions of expectancies (P) are a function of the initial expectancy (E) plus the degree to which outcomes (O) are attributed to stable causes (S):

$$P = f(E + O\,[f(S)])$$

Valle and Frieze (1976) also note that the perceived causes of success or failure are related to the initial expectation of success. As discussed previously, it has been clearly documented that unexpected success or failure leads to unstable attributions, particularly luck (Feather, 1969; Feather & Simon, 1971; Frieze & Weiner, 1971). Hence, Valle and Frieze (1976) conclude:

There is some value for difference between the initial expectations and the actual outcome that will maximally change a person's predictions for the

> future. If the difference is greater than this point, the outcome will be attributed to unstable factors to such a great extent that it will have less influence on the person's future predictions. (p. 581)

These ideas have important implications for attributional change programs and for the maintenance of one's self-concept (see Weiner, 1974). For example, assume that an individual with a high self-concept of ability believes that there is a high probability of success at a task. It is likely that failure would then be ascribed to luck. Such an ascription may not reduce the subsequent expectancy of success and maintains a high ability self-concept. On the other hand, success would be ascribed to ability, which increases both the subsequent expectancy (certainty) of success and confirms one's self-concept. The converse analysis holds given a low self-concept of ability and a low expectancy of success: Success would be ascribed to luck and failure to low ability. These attributions result in the maintenance of the initial self-concept (see Fitch, 1970; Gilmore & Minton, 1974). In addition, the above analysis suggests that in change programs involving expectancies or self-concept, the perceived causes of performance must be altered, and the modification of self-perception would have to involve a gradual process (Valle & Frieze, 1976). (See Ickes and Layden, 1978, for a fuller analysis of the relation between self-esteem and attributions.)

In one research investigation guided by this line of reasoning, Ames, Ames, and Garrison (1977) had children of high or low social status in the classroom attribute causality for positive and negative interpersonal outcomes. For example, the children were given situations such as:

a. Suppose you meet a new student at school and you become friends quickly; or
b. Imagine you ask someone to play with you after school, but he says he cannot play.

The children then attributed causality for each situation either to an internal, external, or mutual cause. The data revealed that given negative interpersonal outcomes, the children of high social status made greater use of external causal ascriptions, while given positive interpersonal outcomes, they tended to make more internal attributions than the low social status pupils.

Attribution, Causal Stability, and Resistance to Extinction

The attributional framework developed here is generalizable to another psychological problem — experimental extinction. Experimental extinction is often defined as the cessation of a previously instrumental response following the permanent withholding of the reward. It is presumed that when a response is perceived as no longer instrumental to goal attainment, the organism will cease to make that response. Thus, any attribution that maximizes the expectation that the response will not be followed by the goal should produce relatively fast extinction. On the other hand, any attribution that minimizes goal expectancy decrements after non-reward should retard extinction.

Furthermore, as has been stated frequently in this chapter, the stability or instability of the perceived causal factors influences the expectancy that the behavioral outcome of an action will change or remain relatively unchanged on subsequent occasions. It is therefore suggested that resistance to extinction is a function of attributions to the causal dimension of stability during the period of nonreinforcement. More specifically, ascriptions of nonreinforcement during the extinction period to bad luck or a lack of effort are hypothesized to retard expectancy decrements and result in slower extinction than attributions of non-attainment of a goal to high task difficulty or lack of ability.

It has been well documented that resistance to extinction is augmented in infrahuman research when a 50 per cent random schedule of reward is given. It also has been demonstrated that variability in a series of outcomes elicits luck attributions (Weiner et al., 1971). Hence, it is suggested that random partial reinforcement schedules increase resistance to extinction because they elicit unstable causal attributions. In a similar manner, chance (rather than skill) instructions also increase resistance to extinction (Phares, 1957).

A second and related notion is that information that generates lack of effort ascriptions for failure also should result in response maintenance in the face of nonreinforcement. There are data in the experimental literature that may be interpreted as supporting this hypothesis. For example, Lawrence and Festinger (1962), marshaling evidence to support their cognitive dissonance explanation of extinction, report that resistance to extinction is positively related to the effortfulness of a response. Response-reward contingencies linked with heightened exertion take longer to extinguish than responses requiring little effort (see Chapter Seven).

Lawrence and Festinger contend that the increased dissonance following non-reward results in more positive perceptions of the value of the goal object. However, if this were correct, the animals should prefer a goal region associated with high effort. This apparently is not the case, for a preference for the most easily attained goal has been relatively well documented in studies using hunger motivation (see Tolman, 1925). Thus, a different explanation is called for.

Attribution theory suggests that non-attainment of a reward during the extinction period in the Lawrence and Festinger investigations is ascribed to insufficient effort by animals in the high exertion condition. The great exertion required to attain the reward functions to increase the salience of effort as the cause of goal attainment. Thus, the expectancy of reward following non-attainment of the goal should be relatively unchanged, and extinction is prolonged. With repeated non-reward, however, the ascription shifts from effort to ability and/or task difficulty, expectancy decreases, and extinction occurs.

Another theory of extinction postulates that non-reward following a series of rewarded trials elicits frustration (Amsel, 1958). Extinction occurs because the anticipation of frustration eventually results in the withholding of the approach response. In a study by Amsel and Roussel (1952) that frequently is cited in support of Amsel's frustration theory, a 100 per cent reward schedule was instituted during initial learning. Following the first few non-rewarded trials, performance intensity increased, presumably demonstrating the energizing properties of frustration (see Chapter Three).

The attributional analysis advocated here also may be applied to these data. It has been demonstrated that non-reward following repeated reinforcement is ascribed to bad luck, lack of effort, or both (see Figure 8–2). Hence, the enhanced response strength following non-reward may be considered evidence that the animal has made an attribution to these unstable elements and that this inference results in increments in subsequent performance. Continued non-reward, however, will shift the attribution to stable elements and result in experimental extinction.

In sum, it is suggested that the relations among reward schedules, character (effortfulness) of the response, and resistance to extinction are mediated by perceptions of causality, which, in turn, influence the expectancy of success:

$$
\begin{array}{l}
\text{reinforcement schedule;} \quad \xrightarrow{\text{(observation)}} \text{resistance to extinction} \\
\text{effortfulness of the response} \\
\qquad \searrow \qquad\qquad\qquad\qquad\qquad\qquad\qquad \nearrow \\
\text{causal attributions for} \longrightarrow \text{stability of the} \longrightarrow \text{expectancy of future} \\
\text{reward and non-reward} \qquad\quad \text{attribution} \qquad\quad \text{goal attainment} \\
\underbrace{\hspace{9cm}} \\
\text{(inference)}
\end{array}
$$

Causal Ascriptions and Affective Reactions

Cognitive theories of motivation generally maintain that the intensity of aroused motivation is determined jointly by the expectation that the response will lead to the goal and the attractiveness of the goal object. The greater the perceived likelihood of goal attainment and the greater the incentive value of the goal, the more intense is the presumed degree of positive motivation. It has been shown that goal expectations are markedly influenced by the stability of the perceived causes of success and failure. What, then, is the relationship between causal ascriptions and the incentive value or the affective consequences of goal attainment?

Causal attributions, in part, determine affective reactions to success and failure. For example, one is not likely to experience pride in success, or feelings of competence, when receiving an "A" from a teacher who gives only that grade, or when defeating a tennis player who always loses. In these instances the causes of success are external to the actor (task ease). On the other hand, an "A" from a teacher who gives few high grades or a victory over a highly rated tennis player following a great deal of practice generates great positive affect. In these instances the causes of success are likely to be perceived as high ability, great effort expenditure, or both (see Figures 7–2 and 8–3). The current movement in industry stressing that the worker be given personal credit for the product is another example that is guided by an intuitively perceived relation between causal ascriptions and affect. In sum, it is reasonable to hypothesize that there is an association between causal ascriptions for achievement outcomes and our feelings about these accomplishments.

There are two distinct areas of experimentation supporting the position that perceived causality influences emotional reactivity. One body of research has examined fear reactions, utilizing a misattribution paradigm that was discussed in the last chapter. To briefly recapitulate, the prototype misattribution experiment was conducted by Schachter and Singer (1962). These investigators augmented internal arousal by giving subjects epinephrine, an activating agent. When the true cause of the internal arousal was unknown by the subjects, increased affect apparently was exhibited in social situations eliciting anger or euphoria. Thus, nonveridical internal ascriptions for arousal magnified emotionality. Nisbett and Schachter (1966) then reversed the misattribution procedure introduced by Schachter and Singer. In the investigation by Nisbett and Schachter, subjects incorrectly inferred that their emotional state during a shock experiment was caused by a drug. Attribution of fear symptoms (e.g., rapid heart rate, shaky hands) to the drug, rather than to one's natural reactions to an impending shock, reduced fear. Ross, Rodin, and Zimbardo (1969) replicated this finding, using a loud noise rather than a pill as the misattribution agent. And finally, Storms and Nisbett (1970) provided suggestive evidence that when insomniacs ascribe wakefulness to a placebo pill, emotionality decreases and sleep is facilitated.

In sum, manipulation of the perceived reasons for internal arousal, fear symptoms, or wakefulness alters emotional reactions. Nonveridical ascription of arousal to oneself increases affective expression, while incorrect external attributions of fear symptoms or wakefulness dampen emotional responses.

A second area of research examining the effects of perceived causality upon affect is directly relevant to achievement-related motivation. In these studies success and failure and the perceived causes of achievement outcomes are experimentally manipulated. Various affects, such as experienced pride or shame, are then assessed and related to the causal perceptions.

One of the initial experiments using the methodology outlined above was conducted by Feather (1967). Feather induced success or failure at matching tasks of varying perceived difficulty and had subjects report the "attractiveness" of success and the "repulsiveness" of failure. In addition, the outcome of the matching task was described as determined by either skill or luck.

Figure 8–17 shows these ratings as a function of the perceived difficulty of the task and the chance versus skill instructions. Feather found that when success and failure were ascribed to skill rather than luck, there were higher ratings of attractiveness for success and repulsion for failure. In addition, Figure 8–17 shows that task difficulty also influenced the rated affects. Success at difficult tasks and failure at easy tasks were rated as most attractive and most repulsive respectively. Recall that Atkinson postulated that the incentive values of success (pride, or I_s) and failure (shame, or I_f) are inversely related to the probabilities of success (P_s) and failure (P_f) at a task; i.e., $I_s = 1 - P_s$ and $I_f = 1 - P_f$. More specifically, one experiences greatest pride when succeeding at a difficult task and greatest shame following failure at an easy task. These postulates are consistent with the data portrayed in Figure 8–17.

From an attributional perspective, success at a difficult task and failure at an easy task produce internal attributions, or the perception of self-responsibility (see Figures 7–2 and 8–3). This is because the outcomes are at variance with the social norms. Hence, Figure 8–17 also documents that ascriptions of causality to self or others, as inferred from task difficulty information, influence affective reactions.

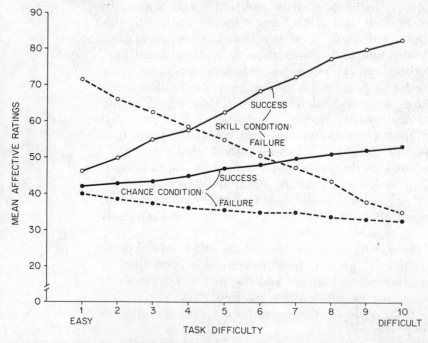

Figure 8–17. Mean attractiveness of success and repulsiveness of failure as a function of chance versus skill attributions and the difficulty of the task. High scores indicate greater positive affect for success and greater negative affect for failure. The reader should compare the two success and the two failure functions. (From Feather, 1967, pp. 379–380.)

In sum, Feather manipulated internal versus external causality perceptions by means of skill or chance instructions and by including both task difficulty and outcome information. In conditions of highest self-attribution (success at a difficult, skill-related task and failure at an easy, skill-related task), the affective ratings are most augmented.

AFFECTIVE RANGE IN ACHIEVEMENT CONTEXTS. As discussed in Chapter Five, prior conceptions of achievement motivation (Atkinson, 1964; McClelland et al., 1953) linked achievement concerns with one particular affective dimension, labelled pride-shame (which could have been an essential part of what Feather's subjects interpreted as attractiveness and repulsiveness). Yet there is neither experimental nor anecdotal evidence supporting the belief that the affect one experiences in a "pure" achievement setting is pride or shame. It is equally reasonable to propose that following success or failure one experiences feelings of confidence (lack of confidence), safety (fear), contentment (agitation), or gratitude (vindictiveness). In addition, all of these affects, including pride and shame, might be experienced in contexts unrelated to achievement (e.g., pride may be sensed after winning an election, which is defined by Veroff, 1957, and others as a power concern; one may feel shame in a situation eliciting moral concerns; and so on). A series of investigations was initiated by Weiner, Russell, and Lerman (1978) to determine the emotional reactions in achievement-relating settings and to relate these specific feelings to the perceived causes of success and failure.

In one study, researchers compiled a dictionary list of nearly 250 potential affective reactions to success and failure in an academic context. Next, ascriptions for achievement outcomes that accounted for the majority of free-response attributions in prior investigations were selected (see Frieze, 1976b). Weiner et al. (1978) then merely gave a cause for success or failure within a brief story format, randomly listed the affective reactions that had been found, and asked subjects to report the affective intensity that would be experienced in the story situation. Responses were made on a rating scale anchored at the extremes.

This procedure is fraught with danger. First of all, it was assumed that individuals would project their own emotional experiences, or those observed in others, upon the characters in the stories. Second, it was assumed that the affective labels reflect the "real" experiences of the subjects. Finally, it was assumed that repression and suppression, memory distortion, response sets, experimenter demands and individual differences in affective labelling and in the subjective meaning of these labels would not render the results meaningless. In sum, there obviously are many limitations to this study; it is hoped that other methodologies will evolve that permit better "royal roads" (or even dirty alleys) to inner experience. The best defense of the methodology that was employed is the systematic, significant, and heuristic findings that emerged.

There were three general findings of interest. First, there was a set of "outcome-dependent, attributionally independent" affects that represented general positive or negative reactions to success and failure, regardless of the "why" of the outcome. For example, given success, the affects "pleased," "happy," "satisfied," "good," and so on were reported as equally experienced, regardless of the attribution for the positive outcome. In a similar manner, given failure, there were several outcome-dependent, attribution-independent affects, such as "uncheerful," "displeasure," and "upset."

But, for both success and failure, there were many affects discriminably related to specific attributions (see Table 8–7). Table 8–7 shows the causal attributions for success and failure that were linked with specific distinguishing affects. The table shows many associations that intuition will readily verify: Success due to perceived ability leads to feelings of confidence and competence; gratitude is experienced if we attribute success to others; luck ascriptions generate feelings of surprise; and so on. One unexpected finding in the table is that stable and unstable effort ascriptions generated opposite degrees of arousal: Short-term, intense effort led to activation (affects such as "delirious" and "zestful"), while long-term, persistent effort led to calmness and relaxation after success. Table 8–7 also shows that the failure-related affects of incompetence, guilt, resignation, and vindictiveness follow from different perceived reasons for failure. It is of interest to note that at times the identical causal attribution for success and failure yields opposing reactions (competence versus incompetence given ability attributions, gratitude versus vindictiveness given attributions to others); at times the same affect accompanies both positive and negative outcomes due to a particular ascription (surprise given a luck attribution); and given still other ascriptions, such as high or low effort,

TABLE 8–7   ATTRIBUTIONS AND DOMINANT DISCRIMINATING AFFECTS FOR SUCCESS AND FAILURE

Attribution	Affect
Success	
Ability	Confidence (competence)
Unstable effort	Activation, augmentation
Stable effort	Relaxation
Own personality	Self-enhancement
Other's effort and personality	Gratitude
Luck	Surprise
Failure	
Ability	Incompetence
Unstable effort; stable effort	Guilt (shame)
Personality; intrinsic motivation	Resignation
Other's efforts; other's motivation and personality	Aggression
Luck	Surprise

the affects that accompany success are unrelated to the failure-tied affects.

Subsequent research in which subjects freely reported their emotional feelings in particular situations that were characterized by specific causal ascriptions replicated many of the findings shown in Table 8–7. In addition, when given a list of discriminating affects, subjects can identify the causal attribution for success or failure (Weiner, Russell, & Lerman, in press).

The data presented thus far have a number of implications for the study of achievement motivation, the general field of emotions, and the attributional theory of motivation that has been discussed in this chapter. Regarding achievement motivation, it is evident that a wide array of emotions are reported in achievement-related contexts. There is good reason not to subscribe to the belief espoused by Atkinson (1964) and McClelland et al. (1953) that pride and shame are the emotions that characterize the achievement system. Indeed, whether achievement strivings are linked most closely with any particular affective reaction remains to be discovered.

Concerning the general study of emotions, research at present is greatly influenced by the two-factor theory proposed by Schachter (1964) and Schachter and Singer (1962). These investigators have argued that arousal is a necessary antecedent for an emotional experience and that the labelling of arousal guides the appropriate emotional experience (see Chapter Seven). However, the data shown in Table 8–7 suggest that whether success, for example, is followed by activation or calmness depends, in part, on the perception of the cause of success. In a similar manner, data reported by Lazarus (1966, 1968) strongly indicate that arousal itself is a product of cognitive factors. More specifically, Lazarus reports that how one interprets a stressful situation influences the amount of fear (arousal) that is generated (see pp. 76–78).

As previously indicated, it presently is not known whether arousal precedes, accompanies, or follows an emotional experience, or if all of the above may be true given disparate situations (also see Plutchik, 1977). The empirical findings reported by Schachter and Singer (1962). may indeed be valid, yet there may be other instances in which arousal is not a necessary condition for emotional experience. One implication of the preliminary data shown in Table 8–7 is that cognitions are *necessary and sufficient* causes of emotion. Feeling confident because of perceived high ability, or feeling grateful because of an ascription to the help of others, does not appear to require a prior state of arousal that the individual must seek to interpret. A change in the conception of emotions so that it follows a historical sequence of *Drive → Drive and cognition → Cognition only* is reminiscent of other historical progressions in the field of motivation. Many motivational theorists have come to believe that the drive concept is a "way station" in psychological explanation (see Atkinson, 1964; Bolles, 1975b; Weiner, 1972); this may also be the case in the study of emotions.

The position that cognitions are sufficient determinants of affect is consistent with the theoretical ideas of Valins (1966). As indicated in the prior chapter, Valins has suggested that arousal is merely another source of information used to elicit appropriate emotional reactions. But there is evidence questioning the conclusion of his investigations (Goldstein, Fink, & Mettee, 1972), and the issues remain unsettled.

Finally, in regards to the attribution theory presented here, it is evident that particular affective reactions are associated with particular causes. Some of these affects, such as feelings of competence and in-competence, are likely to have important implications for achievement strivings, while other affects, such as anger or gratitude, will provide directionality for other behavioral expressions and may not influence achievement expression.

Thus far, the discussion suggests that affects are tied to achievement-related outcomes or directly to attributions, without the causal dimensions serving any affective function. However, this is not the case. Additional analyses of these data suggested that causal dimen-sions play an essential role in affective life. Given internal attributions for success (ability, effort, personality), subjects reported the affects of "pride," "competence," "confident," and "satisfied" more frequently than when external attributions were given. Internal ascriptions for failure generated "guilt," "regret," "aimless," and "humble." In sum, particular affects clustered within the internal causes for both success and failure. Conversely, anger and thankfulness were most often dis-played given external ascriptions.

It therefore appears that in achievement situations there are (at least) three sources of affect. First, there are emotions tied directly to the outcome. One feels "good" given success and "bad" given failure, regardless of the reason for the outcome. These probably are the ini-tial and strongest reactions. Second, accompanying these general feel-ings are more distinct emotions, such as gratitude or hostility when success or failure is due to others; surprise when the outcome is due to luck; and so on. Third, the affects that are associated with self-esteem, such as competence, pride and shame, are mediated by self-ascriptions. Many emotional reactions are common to ascriptions of either ability or effort, the two dominant internal attributions. It there-fore may be that the central self-esteem emotions that facilitate or im-pede subsequent achievement performance are dimensionally linked, involving self-attribution.

STABILITY AND AFFECT. In addition to the locus-affect linkage, there also is a relation between causal stability and emotions. Weiner et al. (1978) found that the affects of depression, apathy, and resigna-tion were reported primarily when attributions for failure were internal and stable (lack of ability, lack of typical effort, personality deficit) This suggests that only those attributions conveying that events will not change in the future beget feelings of helplessness, giving up, and depression. Hence, the dimensions of locus and stability relate to dif-ferent sets of emotions. Furthermore, the dimension-tied affects are likely to have greater longevity than the outcome- or attribution-linked emotions.

In another research investigation supporting a stability-emotion union, Arkin and Maruyama (1979) assessed students' attributions for their success or failure in a college class. In addition, anxiety associated with school performance was measured. It was found that among successful students the stability of their attributions was negatively correlated with anxiety. That is, when success is ascribed to stable causes, students report relatively little anxiety. On the other hand, among the unsuccessful students, attributional stability and anxiety correlated positively; most fear was reported when failure was perceived as likely to recur in the future.

The Cognition-Emotion Sequence in Achievement Contexts

The preceding discussion suggests that in achievement-related contexts (and, in particular, school settings) the actor progresses through something like the following cognition-emotion scenarios:

a. "I just received a 'D' in the exam. That is a very low grade." (This generates feelings of being frustrated and upset.) "I received this grade because I just am not smart enough" (followed by feelings of incompetence and lack of confidence). "There really is something lacking in me, and it is permanent" (followed by low self-esteem or lack of worth and hopelessness).

b. "I just received an 'A' on the exam. That is a very high grade" (generating happiness and satisfaction). "I received this grade because I worked very hard during the entire school year" (producing contentment and relaxation). "I really do have some positive qualities, and will continue to have them in the future" (followed by high self-esteem and feelings of self-worth, as well as optimism for the future).

Controllability and Reactions toward Others

Attribution theory as formulated by Heider (1958) and Kelley (1967) primarily concerns person-perception, or inferences about the intentions and dispositions of others. But thus far in this chapter the main concern has been with self-perception. Conversely, the following examination of the dimension of control focuses on inferences about others, and how beliefs about another's responsibility for success and failure influence an actor's reactions toward the person.

Determinants of Evaluation

A number of investigations have examined the association between affective reactions toward others (liking and disliking or administered reward and punishment) and causal attributions. In contexts other than achievement such studies have been especially prevalent in the area of aggressive retaliation. For example, in one early experiment by Mallick and McCandless (1966), frustration was induced by having a stooge prevent subjects from completing tasks, thereby causing the subjects to lose a monetary reward. In one experimental condition it was explained that the frustrator was "sleepy and upset." Subjects given this interpretation were less likely to aggress against the stooge than others not provided with a reasonable explanation of the stooge's behavior. In a conceptually similar investigation, Nickel (1974) used the aggressive shock paradigm introduced in Chapter Two (see pp. 43, 47). Subjects first received a low or high intensity shock from a confederate subject as a "motivator" during an ESP task. The roles of the subject and the confederate were then reversed, and the subject could shock the confederate at the same task. In one experimental condition the confederate indicated he was confused about the magnitude of shock that he delivered; when a small shock was given, he revealed that a large shock was intended, and vice versa. In a control condition nothing was said. It was found that the subjects administered more retaliatory shock when large punishment was intended, regardless of the actual amount of shock that was received. That is, attribution of the prior shock to the confederate's intent to punish maximized apparent dislike and aggression.

More pertinent to the focus of the present chapter was a series of studies in the achievement domain that directly manipulated ability, effort, and task difficulty information. In an experiment devised by Lanzetta and Hannah (1969), subjects acted as "trainers" with the power to reward or punish others during performance at a discrimination task. The reward could be either of two amounts of monetary payment, the punishment either of two intensities of shock. Prior to the training period the trainer was given false information indicating that his "pupil" possessed high or low ability. The trainer also was informed that the discrimination task was either easy or difficult.

The data concerning the trainer behavior revealed that the money allotted for correct responses at the discrimination task did not differ between the experimental conditions, for high reward invariably was given for success. But greater punishment was administered for failure at the easy task than at the difficult one. Furthermore, at the difficult task, competent pupils were punished more than those perceived as incompetent. Pupils high in ability who failed an easy task thus received the greatest amount of punishment (see Figure 8–18).

Lanzetta and Hannah (1969) suggest that in the latter condition failure is ascribed to a lack of effort. Thus, most punishment is administered when an individual can succeed, but fails because of an inferred absence of trying. Failure ascribed to this particular causal pattern is "reacted to more negatively ... [and] motivate[s] behavior that might effect a change in the responsible factors" (p. 251).

One shortcoming of the methodology used by Lanzetta and Hannah is that effort ascriptions must be inferred without any empirical confirmation. In a number of subsequent experiments, information was pro-

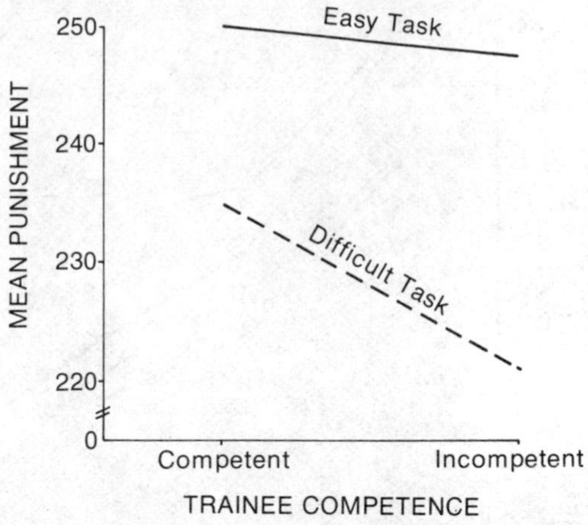

Figure 8–18. Mean punitiveness of reinforcement as a function of trainee competence and the difficulty of the task. High scores indicate greater punishment. (From Lanzetta & Hannah, 1969, p. 250.)

vided both about the ability of the pupils and about their effort expenditures (see Eswara, 1972; Kaplan & Swant, 1973; Rest, Nierenberg, Weiner & Heckhausen, 1973; Weiner & Kukla, 1970; and Zander, Fuller, & Armstrong, 1972). In the experimental paradigm under consideration, subjects are asked to pretend that they are teachers and must provide "evaluative feedback" to their grade school pupils. The pupils have just taken an exam and received one of five possible outcomes: excellent, fair, borderline, failure, and clear failure. In addition, the pupils are described in terms of ability (high or low) and effort expenditure (high or low). Each subject evaluates all twenty possible experimental combinations (five levels of outcome × two levels of ability × two levels of effort). Thus, for example, one pupil is characterized as high in ability, low in effort, and as having a borderline performance. Evaluation frequently is indicated by giving each pupil a score from + 5 (highest reward) to − 5 (highest punishment).

The results of a representative experiment (Weiner & Kukla, 1970) are depicted in Figure 8–19. The figure reveals that good exam performance is rewarded while poor performance is punished. This is an application of the *merit* rule of fairness: Greater reward and less punishment are given to pupils who do better work. But causal attributions also affect evaluation. First of all, high effort results in a more positive evaluation than does low effort at all outcome levels. And, to our initial surprise, low ability produces higher evaluation than does high ability. The latter finding is due to the particular constellation of information provided in this experiment. Low ability coupled with both high effort and success is especially rewarded. For example, the handicapped person who completes a marathon race or the retarded child who persists to complete a task elicits great social approval. On the other hand, high ability coupled with low effort and failure is maximally punished. For example, the gifted athlete who refuses to practice and performs poorly or the bright "dropout" generates great social disapproval. Because low ability coupled with high effort and success is so rewarded, while high

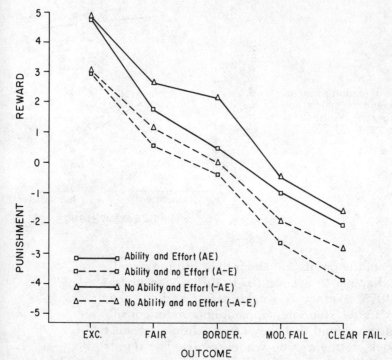

Figure 8–19. Evaluation as a function of pupil outcome, effort, and ability. (From Weiner & Kukla, 1970, p. 3.)

ability linked with low effort and failure is so punished, lack of ability emerges as a beneficial attribute in this achievement context.

One interesting extrapolation from these findings has been noted by Gold (1975). Gold suggests that if one highly rewards another for success at an easy task, the rewarded individual might infer that he or she is perceived as having low ability. That is, reward for success and the building of a positive self-concept may at times be negatively related (assuming, of course, that the communication is accepted). Consider, for example, your own reaction toward being highly praised for good performance at a very simple task! The general implication of this discussion is that self-concept, in part, depends upon the perceived attributions made by others.

The general pattern of results shown in Figure 8–19 has been replicated in different cultures (America, India, and Switzerland), different social situations (group and individual tasks), and different levels of task difficulty (easy, medium, and difficult). There can be no doubt that effort ascriptions have a profound influence on affective (evaluative) reactions towards others. High effort always is evaluated more positively than low effort. However, in not all instances has it been found that a lack of ability enhances evaluative ratings.

COGNITIVE MATURITY.   Figure 8–19 shows the evaluations made by *adult* subjects. It is reasonable to anticipate that the judgments of children will differ in some important respects from those of adults. It has been found, for example, that in the moral domain children primarily (but not exclusively) use outcome information to determine their judgments, while adults most heavily weight information about intent to decide moral evaluation. If this pattern, in part, characterizes achievement judgments, then among the younger children effort and perceptions of control will have little influence on achievement evaluation.

To ascertain whether achievement judgments vary with age, the experiment previously described was administered to children and young adults, ranging from 4 to 18 years old (Weiner & Peter, 1973). Some of the pertinent results of this investigation are depicted in Figures 8–20 and 8–21. Figure 8–20 reveals that the use of effort information changes with age. Reward for positive effort increases with maturity, while punishment for a lack of effort increases until the age of 12 and then decreases. Thus, the resultant efforts curve (reward for effort minus punishment for a lack of effort) indicates that effort ascriptions are most important among children 10 to 12 years old.

Figure 8–21 depicts the evaluative effects of effort and outcome as a function of the age of the subjects. The figure indicates that among younger children evaluation primarily is determined by outcome — success is rewarded while failure is punished. Perceived effort initially plays only a minor role in determining judgments. However, the differential effects of outcome versus effort gradually recede, and among children 10 to 12 effort is a more influential evaluative determinant than is outcome. Among the older subjects, however, the order of importance of

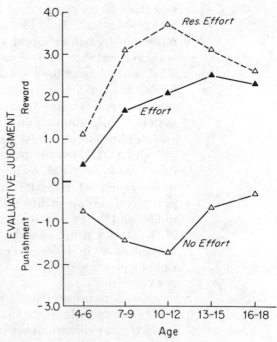

Figure 8–20. Reward for positive achievement effort, punishment for a lack of effort, and the resultant of reward for effort minus punishment for a lack of effort, as a function of age. (From Weiner & Peter, 1973, p. 300.)

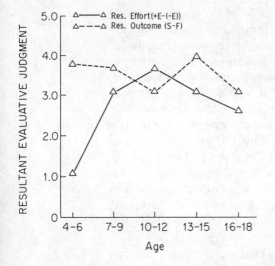

Figure 8-21. Resultant outcome (reward for success minus punishment for failure) and resultant effort judgments as a function of age. (From Weiner & Peter, 1973, p. 301.)

these two factors again is reversed, although effort does remain an important judgmental dimension. Ability had only a minor influence upon reward and punishment and will not be discussed here.

In addition to achievement evaluation, Weiner and Peter (1973) also required evaluative judgments in a moral context (helping a lost child find the way home). The achievement and moral judgments are shown together in Figure 8-22. Comparison of the moral and the achievement data indicates that subjective factors (intent or effort) become more important in moral than in achievement evaluation. On the other hand, objective factors (outcome) become more heavily weighted in achievement judgment. In addition, achievement evaluations are generally more positive than moral evaluations. This is because success in an achievement activity is rewarded more than success for a moral action, while punishment for a negative moral intent is greater than punishment for a lack of achievement-directed effort (see Figure 8-23). Thus, achievement, relative to morality, is more an outcome-oriented reward system, while among adults, morality, relative to achievement, is more an intent-oriented punishment system.

CULTURAL INFLUENCES. Thus far it has been revealed that feelings toward (evaluations of) another are determined by a diversity of factors, such as the merit (success) of the action, the causal ascription and perceived responsibility for the outcome, the cognitive maturity of the judge, and the evaluative schema (moral or achievement) that the action elicits. In addition, causal ascriptions are differentially used for evaluative purposes in different cultures. Specific culture-based learning experiences produce differences in values that are evidenced in interpersonal evaluations.

To determine whether cultural learning experiences influence achievement judgments, Salili, Maehr, and Gillmore (1976) administered the previously described experiment to 291 Iranian children and

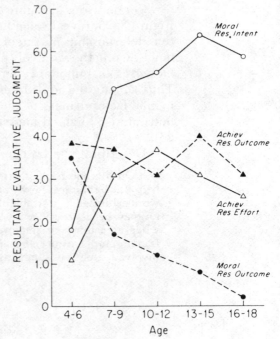

Figure 8–22. Resultant of the outcome and subjective intent judgments for the achievement and the moral situations as a function of age. (From Weiner & Peter, 1973, p. 307.)

young adults. Again the teacher-pupil situation was described, with some slight procedural modifications to accommodate cultural differences.

Figure 8–24 shows that among the Iranian students the use of effort information changes with maturity. The ratings for positive effort steadily increase, while ratings for a lack of effort decrease from the first to the second age group and then remain relatively constant. Thus, the resultant effort curve reveals that effort, and perceived controllability, becomes more important as a determinant of evaluation with increasing cognitive maturity. The outcome effect did not significantly change with age; for all subjects, positive outcomes are rewarded more than negative outcomes (see Figure 8–25).

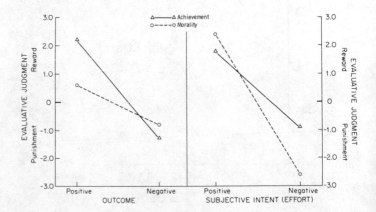

Figure 8–23. Judgments in the achievement and moral conditions as a function of outcome (left side) and subjective intent (right side). (From Weiner & Peter, 1973, p. 304.)

Comparisons of Figure 8–20 with Figure 8–24, and Figure 8–21 with Figure 8–25, reveal some fundamental differences between the evaluative determinants of Americans and Iranians. Effort *decreases* in importance among the relatively older American subjects, while it consistently *increases* in importance among the Iranians (Figures 8–20 and 8–24). Thus, among the adult Iranian subjects, effort is a more important judgmental factor than is outcome, while among the American adult subjects, outcome is weighted more than is effort (Figure 8–21 versus Figure 8–25).

Describing the Iranian culture, Salili et al. (1976) state:

> On the one hand, the most achievement-oriented American could not help but be impressed with the continued, methodical, and persistent hard work exhibited by a sizable share of the Iranian citizenry. On the other hand, he may be distressed with the lack of care for product or outcome. Thus, when a customer or employer complains about the quality of *outcome*, the Iranian employee or merchant is likely to emphasize the hard work (effort) involved. One may summarize the differences by suggesting that in the U.S.

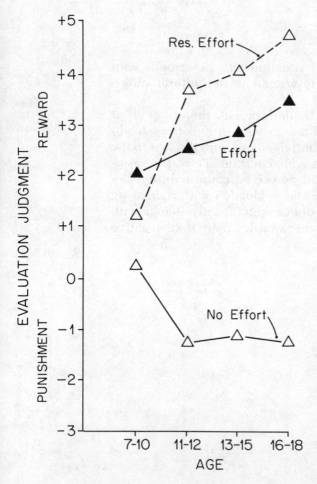

Figure 8–24. Reward for positive achievement effort, punishment for a lack of effort, and the resultant of the reward minus the punishment, as a function of the age of Iranian students. (From Salili, Maehr, & Gilmore, 1976, p. 331.)

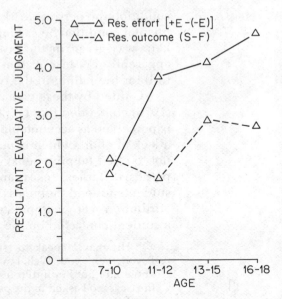

Figure 8–25. Resultant outcome (reward for success minus punishment for failure) and resultant effort judgments as a function of age of Iranian students. (Data from Salili, Maehr, & Gilmore, 1976.)

it is not sufficient merely to try. You must also produce — you are judged by your product. (p. 336)

They then go on to speculate:

> . . . The findings with U.S. and Iranian subjects suggest that a major difference in achievement in the two societies does exist. Moreover, it may be that this is representative of a more general pattern. Thus the dual effort and outcome orientation (U.S. subjects) might be characteristic of societies in which status is more typically accorded as the result of achievement (producing an outcome or product), whereas the effort orientation is more characteristic of societies in which status is *ascribed* and where, consequently, there is less interest in whether trying gets one anywhere. (pp. 336–337)

Helping Behavior

The prior discussion indicated that perceived controllability (attribution to effort expenditure) is one of the essential determinants of how others are evaluated. In addition, it has been well documented that perceived controllability influences helping behavior and whether we like others. The examination of helping has clearly shown that the decision to help another, in part, depends upon the perceived cause of the other's needy state. For example, Berkowitz (1969) found that help for a fellow subject was more likely when the need was the result of an error on the part of the experimenter, rather than the subject's own fault. That is, an external perception of causation was more likely to elicit help than perceived internal causation (also see Schopler & Matthews, 1965). In addition, within the internal causal dimension, ability ascriptions elicit greater help than effort ascriptions. For example, Piliavin, Rodin, and Piliavin (1969) staged an "accident" in a New York subway. A man collapsed on the floor in the presence of a number of onlookers. In one condition the person clearly had been drinking, while in a second experimental condition he carried a cane. The data clearly revealed that more help was given in the "cane" than the "drunk" condition. This was apparently because of the disparities in perceived responsibility (control) for the falling in the two conditions.

Guided by these data as well as their own research, Ickes and Kidd (1976) contended that helping is least likely when the needy individual is perceived as accountable for his or her own plight. Thus, ascriptions to a lack of effort, which is perceived as subject to volitional control, tend not to elicit helping behavior. In a field experiment confirming this hypothesis, Barnes, Ickes, and Kidd (1977) examined the willingness of students to lend their class notes to another student. Two dimensions of attribution were manipulated — stability and control. More specifically, a student contacted on the phone heard the following plea:

> Hi, may I speak to (subject's name)? (Subject)? You're taking Intro Psych, aren't you? Well, I'm (Tony Freeman/Julie Pearson). I don't think you know me, but I'm in (Professor)'s section, too. I don't know anyone else in the class, so I asked in the psych office for the class roster and got your name off of it. I hate to bother you, but I really need some help before the final.
>
> I just don't seem to have the (ability/motivation) to take good notes; I really (try to/can) take good notes, but (sometimes I just can't do it/I just can't ever do it/sometimes I just don't try/I just don't ever try), so the notes I have (sometimes aren't/are never) very good to study for an exam with.

He was then asked if he would lend his notes, and for how long the notes could be kept.

The findings from this study are shown in Table 8–8. The data reveal that requests for notes due to a lack of trying were least likely to be answered. Again, effort appears to be the pivotal attribution in help-related situations because it is perceived as under volitional control; the person who does not try is perceived as not deserving of aid. In addition, helping is influenced by the stability of the perceived cause of the need. If the cause of dependency is perceived as unstable, the potential helper may question the degree to which help is really required. Table 8–8

TABLE 8–8   MEAN NUMBER OF HELPING REQUESTS AGREED TO

Perceived Stability of Other's Outcome	Perceived Controllability of Other's Outcome		
	Lack of Ability (uncontrollable)	Lack of Effort (controllable)	$\overline{X} =$
Stable	4.27*	3.48	3.88
Unstable	3.50	2.75	3.13
$\overline{X} =$	3.90	3.12	

*High number indicates greater help.
(Adapted from Barnes, Ickes, & Kidd, 1977.)

shows that help was most likely to be given when the perceived cause of not having the class notes was a stable factor.

Sentiments

Investigations linking liking to perceptions of controllability primarily have been conducted in the area of loneliness (see Peplau, Russell, & Heim, in press). Michela, Peplau, and Weeks (1978) found that persons lonely for reasons thought to be controllable (e.g., does not try to make friends) are liked less than individuals lonely for uncontrollable reasons (e.g., no opportunity to meet people). In addition, when a lonely person puts forth effort to make friends, that person is liked and elicits sympathy (Wimer & Peplau, 1978). In contrast, if it is believed that the lonely individual is responsible for his or her plight, then sympathy is not forthcoming, and respondents indicate they would avoid such persons. I assume that this pattern of results will also be evident in achievement-related contexts. Surely a teacher will not particularly like a student who does not try, and failure perceived as due to lack of effort does not elicit sympathy.

Overview: Controllability and Reaction to Others

Attributions of positive and negative events to controllable factors, such as effort expenditure or a desire to help or harm, maximize reward and punishment toward these individuals. Although the relation between attributions to effort and evaluation is modified by the age and culture of the evaluator and the specific action under consideration, the generality of this association is nevertheless upheld. In addition, attributions to control greatly influence the likelihood of helping another in need, as well as our sentiments towards others.

Summary: Causal Inferences

A variety of sources of information are used to reach causal inferences in achievement-related contexts. The perceived causes of success and failure primarily are ability and effort, but also include a small number of other salient factors such as home environment and teacher, and a countless host of idiosyncratic factors. These causes can be comprised within three primary dimensions of causality: stability, locus, and control. The three main dimensions are linked respectively to expectancy changes, esteem-related affects, and interpersonal judgments (decisions about helping, evaluation, and sentiments). In addition, there are secondary linkages between the causal dimensions and psychological effects: Stability relates to depression-type affects and control is associated with particular feeling states and behaviors (see Chapter Six). It will now be contended that causal attributions, through their influence on both expectancy and affect, influence achievement-related actions.

BEHAVIORAL CONSEQUENCES

It has been stated repeatedly in this book that cognitive theories of motivation specify that performance is a function of the expectancy that the response will lead to the goal and the affective consequences of goal attainment. It has been established that causal ascriptions influence both goal expectations and emotional experience. It therefore follows that causal ascriptions also should influence a variety of behaviors.

Some of the behavioral implications of causal ascriptions already have been discussed. For example, the effects of reward schedules and response effortfulness on resistance to extinction, and the continuation of instrumental behavior following failure to attain a reward, may be mediated by perceptions of causality. In the next section of this chapter various indicators of achievement strivings are examined from the attributional perspective. Three facets of behavior — what one selects (choice), the intensity of performance, and how long one engages in an activity (persistence) — are considered the main indexes of motivated behavior (Atkinson, 1964). Hence, these variables are selected for examination.

Choice

The attributional interpretation of choice behavior was presented in the chapter on achievement motivation (see Chapter Five). In that chapter, the Atkinsonian and attributional conceptions were contrasted on the issue of risk preference. Atkinson's model leads to the prediction that individuals highly motivated to succeed will select tasks of intermediate difficulty, while persons low in achievement motivation prefer to undertake tasks that are very easy or very difficult. These disparate preferences theoretically maximize positive affect for the person highly motivated to achieve and minimize negative affect for the individual low in achievement needs.

Attribution theorists, on the other hand, assume that humans are rational, information-gathering beings, seeking to understand the causal structure of the world (Heider, 1958). It has been contended that because of these information-striving tendencies there is a general desire to undertake tasks of intermediate difficulty. This is because performance at easy or difficult tasks yields relatively little information about one's ability and effort expenditure. Behavior consistent with social norms, which is the typical experience at such tasks, leads to situational or environmental causal inferences (Frieze & Weiner, 1971; Kelley,

1967; Weiner & Kukla, 1970). Conversely, over a series of occasions a great deal of information about the self is gained given the selection of intermediate difficulty tasks. Inasmuch as some of the individuals undertaking these tasks succeed while others fail, the causal attribution for success or failure is to the person. That is, there is person-outcome, rather than task-outcome, covariation.

The investigations of Meyer et al. (1976), Trope (1975), and Trope and Brickman (1975) have supported the attributional viewpoint. The studies of Trope (1975) and Trope and Brickman (1975) are especially persuasive. Recall that these investigators gave subjects a choice between tasks that varied in difficulty as well as in "diagnosticity." Diagnosticity was operationally defined as the difference in the percentages of success at a given task for individuals high in ability versus those low in ability. The data indicate that individuals prefer to undertake tasks of high diagnosticity, relatively independent of the objective task difficulty level. That is, self-knowledge (ability feedback) was demonstrated to be a crucial determinant of risk-preference.

Intensity and Persistence of Behavior

The study of the intensity and the persistence of behavior has been guided by three basic assumptions:

1. Behavior is mediated by both expectancies of success and the anticipated emotional reactions to these outcomes.
2. Expectancies are influenced by attributions to the stability dimension of causality. Any causal ascription for failure to unstable causes, such as insufficient effort or bad luck, will augment intensity and persistence more than ascriptions of failure to low ability or task difficulty. Effort attributions for failure seem especially facilitative because effort is subject to volitional control.
3. Affects also are influenced by perceived causality. In achievement domains, feelings of adequacy-inadequacy (competence-incompetence) are particularly important determinants of action. Hence, attributions of failure to low ability are especially detrimental to future performance, compared to ascriptions to bad luck, lack of effort, and so on.

The analysis of the effects of causal ascriptions for success is not as evident as it is for failure. For example, it is not known whether ascriptions of success to high ability or high effort are most facilitative. Although ability ascriptions promote feelings of self-efficacy, effort ascriptions give rise to the feeling of volitional control and perhaps activation. To date, the research studies have concentrated almost exclusively on the motivational effects of failure, which, in part, is responsible for the lack of knowledge concerning the effects of ascriptions for success.

One of the initial investigations (Meyer, 1970) of the influence of causal attributions on intensity of performance in failure situations already has been discussed. In Meyer's experiment, subjects attempting a digit-symbol substitution task received five consecutive failures. After each outcome the failure was attributed to low ability, lack of effort, task difficulty, and/or bad luck. Then expectancy of success was stated for the next trial. Meyer induced failure by interrupting subjects when they had completed approximately 75 per cent of the digit-symbol task. The time taken to reach that degree of task completion (intensity of performance) also was assessed.

Figure 8–26 shows the relationship between the difference in performance on Trial One minus Trial Two and the causal attributions for failure following the initial trial. Attributions to bad luck and lack of effort, the unstable elements, related positively to performance increments. If the subject believed that he had failed because he did not try hard enough, or because of bad luck, he then worked with greater intensity on the next occasion. On the other hand, attributions to the stable elements (low ability and task difficulty) were negatively associated with performance change. If the subject thought that he could not perform the task because of low ability or high task difficulty, he generally disengaged from behavior (effort expenditure) instrumental to goal attainment. The correlation between increments in performance and attribution to the combined stable elements was $r = -.43$. That is,

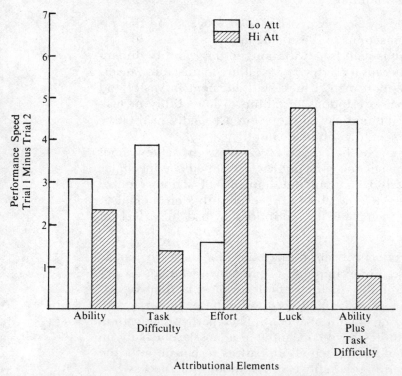

Figure 8–26. Intensity of performance in seconds (Trial 1 minus Trial 2) as a function of attribution to the four causal elements and to the combined stable factors. High numbers indicate greater improvement in speed. (Adapted from W. Meyer, 1970.)

the greater the increment between Trial Two and Trial One, the less the attribution of failure to stable elements.

ATTRIBUTIONAL CHANGE.   The studies best demonstrating the relation of causal ascriptions to the intensity and the persistence of behavior in achievement contexts have been part of therapeutic attempts to increase achievement strivings. Clearly, if causal attributions, in part, determine behavior, then it logically follows that a change in attributions should produce a change in action. The simple belief that alterations in thought are necessary and/or sufficient to give rise to behavioral change has been advocated by many clinical psychologists (e.g., Ellis, 1974; Kelly, 1955). Even within the behavioristic camp there is now a strong movement contending that internal speech can be used to control overt behavior (see Meichenbaum & Cameron, 1974).

Two distinct programs of research are pertinent to the efficacy of attributional training procedures. The first program of research emanates from broad-gauged achievement change programs (de Charms, 1972; McClelland & Winter, 1969; see pp. 220–222; 255–256). These training programs make use of a variety of techniques thought to be effective in altering behavior, including persuasion, reinforcement, and group and individual therapy (see McClelland, 1965). They also teach the importance of self-responsibility or internal control. Because the notion of internal control or personal causation is introduced, the programs are quite relevant to attributional approaches. However, the contribution of attributional training cannot be assessed, for the entire program is multifaceted.

The second research strategy, which is directly relevant to the theory advocated here, is to train subjects *not* to attribute failure to low ability. Ascription of failure to a lack of ability seems to be particularly devastating. As indicated so many times, ability is a stable, internal, uncontrollable cause. Thus, when failure is ascribed to low ability, there is no "hope" for future success. Furthermore, ability ascriptions generate feelings of inadequacy, which are also believed to interfere with goal strivings. Indeed, perhaps the feelings of inadequacy are elicited by the realization that future success cannot be attained.

To replace ability ascriptions for failure, investigators often attempt to train the subjects to ascribe failure to a lack of effort. Since effort is unstable and under volitional control, ascription to insufficient effort should maintain "hope" and thus be an adaptive construal in certain situations. However, it also is adaptive, at times, to ascribe failure to environmental factors, such as "unfair" barriers, and in so doing minimize feelings of low self-esteem. A similar point has been made by Lao (1970) and Sanger and Alker (1972), who report that external attributions among blacks and females are positively related to attempts to alter their environments.

In an investigation that provided a foundation for attributional change studies, Dweck and Reppucci (1973) examined the effects of attributional biases in situations of repeated failure. Subjects received 30 trials of continual failure at a block design task in a distinctive stimulus situation. Two soluble problems were then presented, and the time taken to solve these problems was assessed. In addition, the subjects were administered the Intellectual Achievement Responsibility (IAR) scale (Crandall, Katkovsky, & Crandall, 1965). This scale consists of 34 forced-choice items describing positive and negative achievement experiences (e.g., success or failure at an exam). The forced choice responses pit an external cause (e.g., someone helped you) against an internal cause. The internal causes either pertain to one's level of ability (e.g., you play well), or to the amount of effort expended (e.g., you tried hard).

The subjects who exhibited poor performance on the two soluble test trials were labelled as "helpless," while those who performed relatively well were designated as "persistent." Table 8–9 shows the IAR scores of the helpless and the persistent male and female subjects. The table reveals that individuals classified as persistent make more internal ascriptions for both success (+) and failure (−) than do the helpless subjects. A more detailed analysis of the internal scores indicates that there is little difference between the helpless and the persistent subjects in their ability ascriptions. However, both male and female subjects who do well after a series of prior failures have a greater tendency to ascribe success to high effort, and failure to low effort, than do subjects who perform poorly after the failure series. That is, a bias to attribute outcomes to effort is associated with the maintenance of instrumental responding in the face of failure.

Following this correlational finding, Dweck (1975) attempted to change the behavior of children characterized by "expectation of failure and deterioration of performance in the face of failure" (p. 676). To accomplish this change, researchers imposed an experimental treatment in which some of these children (selected by the school psychologist, a teacher, and the principal) received 80 per cent success and 20 per cent failure experiences at a series of training tasks. The failure trials were accompanied by an attribution to a lack of effort: "You got only --------- right. That means you should have tried harder" (Dweck, 1975, p. 679).

TABLE 8–9 MEAN INTERNAL RESPONSIBILITY SCORES FOR ITEMS WITH POSITIVE (I +) AND NEGATIVE (I−) OUTCOMES AND ABILITY (a) AND EFFORT (e) STEMS FOR HELPLESS AND PERSISTENT FEMALES AND MALES

Subject	I+	I+(a)	I+(e)	I−	I−(a)	I−(e)
Female						
Helpless	13.0	6.2	6.8	10.7	4.8	5.9
Persistent	14.7	6.4	8.3	13.1	5.1	8.0
Male						
Helpless	12.2	5.6	6.6	10.9	4.0	6.9
Persistent	14.6	6.5	8.1	13.7	4.6	9.1

Note: N = 10 in all cases.
(From Dweck & Reppucci 1973, p. 115.)

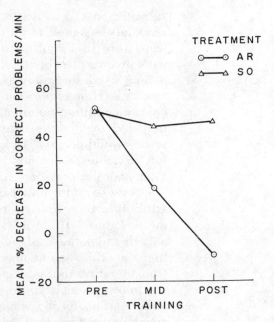

Figure 8–27. Mean percentage decrease in correct problems per minute at pre-training, mid-training, and post-training for the attribution retraining (AR) and the success only (SO) treatments. (From Dweck, 1975, p. 682.)

This treatment was compared to one in which subjects received 100 per cent success training without attributional information.

During the test phase of this experiment the effects of failure on performance were assessed. Dweck (1975) reports that only subjects in the attributional training condition handled failure better and exhibited improved intensity of performance relative to pre-training behavior (see Figure 8–27). In addition, only these pupils displayed increments in their general tendency to ascribe failure to a lack of effort.

Unfortunately, Dweck's procedure was somewhat faulty in that attributional training was confounded with reinforcement schedule. That is, the two treatment groups differed not only in the presence or absence of attributional information, but also in the percentage of success experiences. Subsequently, Chapin and Dyck (1976) replicated Dweck's finding, unconfounding these variables. Furthermore, they used persistence of behavior, rather than intensity, as the dependent variable.

In the study by Chapin and Dyck (1976), subjects with learning difficulties received partial reinforcement training, either accompanied by effort attributions on both success and failure trials or else not paired with attributional information. The effectiveness of the training was determined by assessing persistence of behavior at a difficult reading test. Again it was found that attributional training facilitated achievement strivings (increased persistence) (see also Andrews & Debus, 1978).

One additional experiment illustrates how the various associations specified by attribution theorists influence intensity of performance. Attributions for failure among individuals differing in achievement needs were experimentally manipulated by Weiner and Sierad (1975). Subjects were given four trials of repeated failure at a digit-symbol substitution task. Prior to the failure, one-half of the subjects were randomly assigned to a drug-attribution condition; the remaining subjects were in a control condition. The subjects in the drug condition were given a placebo pill that allegedly interfered with hand-eye coordination, a skill described as needed for good performance at the substitution task. Hence, personal failure could be ascribed to the drug. In the control condition no attempt was made to alter attributions. It was anticipated that in the control condition subjects high in achievement needs would perceive lack of effort as the cause of failure, while subjects low in achievement needs would perceive low ability as the cause of their poor performance (see Figure 8–7).

Now consider how expectancy-value theory, when combined with attribution theory, leads to predictions in this rather complex experiment. Table 8–10 outlines the temporal sequence of mediating events and the hypothesized behavioral consequences for subjects low and high in achievement needs in the control and in the pill conditions. Consider first the subjects low in achievement needs. Their bias to attribute personal failure to low ability is altered by the experimental manipulation, for in the experimental condition failure is ascribed to the action of the drug. Both low ability and the drug effects are perceived as stable within the time period of the experiment. Thus, failure should be expected to continue and the expectancy of success is assumed to be equally low in both conditions. But the pill is an external agent, while ability is an internal cause. Following Table 8–7, greater self-esteem should be maintained in the experimental than in the control condition. That is, one should feel more competent when failing because of an experimenter-induced drug state than when failing because of low ability. On the basis of expectancy-value theory, it was hypothesized that subjects low in achievement needs would therefore perform better in the experimental than in the control condition. The pill attribution decreases the aversive consequences of failure and thereby increases the motivation to perform the task.

Now consider the subjects high in achievement needs. Their bias to ascribe failure to a lack of effort also is altered by the experimental manipulation, which produces a drug attribution. The effects of the drug are perceived as stable within the time limit of the experiment, while effort is modifiable. Thus, the expectancy of future success is lower in the experimental than in the control condition. Effort can be augmented, but the detrimental effects of the drug cannot be changed. In addition, the drug is an external agent, while effort expenditure is under personal control. Thus, less guilt or shame for failure should be experienced in the drug condition.

In sum, expectancy of success is lower in the pill condition than in the control condition, but the aversive consequences of failure are lessened by the attribution to the drug. It is therefore difficult to specify the relative performance effects of the pill ascription. One of the determinants of behavior (expectancy) altered by the experimental manipulation functions to *decrease* performance, while the second determinant of

**TABLE 8–10   THE ATTRIBUTIONAL SEQUENCE AND HYPOTHESIZED
BEHAVIOR CONSEQUENCES FOR SUBJECTS HIGH AND LOW IN
ACHIEVEMENT NEEDS IN THE CONTROL AND
EXPERIMENTAL (PILL) CONDITIONS**

	Achievement Motivation Group			
	Low	*Low*	*High*	*High*
Condition	Control	Experimental	Control	Experimental
Failure Attribution	Low Ability	Drug	Low Effort	Drug
Expectancy of Success	Low	Low	High	Low
Negative Affect (low self-esteem or shame)	High	Low	High	Low
Performance	Low	High	High*	Low

*Indicates performance relative to same-motive subjects in the alternate condition.

behavior (affect) is changed in a direction that might *increase* performance. What is needed to predict the performance effects of the pill attribution is knowledge about the relative importance, or the weighting, of the expectancy and affective determinants of behavior, and more knowledge about the performance consequences of feelings such as shame and guilt.

In an earlier publication (Weiner, 1970), I speculated that individuals high in achievement motivation are "realistic" (p. 103). More specifically, it was suggested at that time that individuals highly motivated to succeed weight environmental information and future probabilities of success more heavily than the prior affective consequences of their actions. If this is the case, then the inhibition of performance produced by the low expectancy of future success in the pill condition should outweigh any increase in achievement strivings arising from the decreased negative affect. Thus, the performance of individuals high in achievement needs should be lower in the pill than in the control condition. In sum, it was anticipated that the pill attributions would enhance the performance of individuals low in achievement needs, but would decrease the performance of persons high in achievement needs.

The combined results of two identical experiments are shown in Figure 8–28. The index of motivation is the improvement in the speed of performance (number of digit substitutions per unit of time) over trials, relative to pretest performance. Looking first at the results in the control condition, the data indicate that individuals high in achievement needs improve more than subjects low in achievement needs. On the other hand, in the experimental condition, persons low in achievement needs exhibit greater improvement in their speed of performance than subjects in the high motive group. These confirmations of the hypotheses provide strong support for the attributional analysis of achievement strivings.

Achievement Strivings Reconsidered

It is evident that Atkinson's approach to achievement strivings and the attributional analysis contrast in a number of ways. Consider first the definition of achievement needs. Atkinson defines the achievement motive as a "capacity for experiencing pride in accomplishment" (1964, p. 214). Further, the affective anticipations of success (hope) and of failure (fear), which are emotional reactions elicited by appropriate achievement cues, theoretically determine whether an achievement-related goal is approached or avoided. On the other hand, the attributional model suggests that the achievement motive be defined as a "capacity for perceiving success as caused by internal factors and failure by unstable factors." Hence, esteem-related affects, such as competence and pride, are experienced in success by high motive individuals because of their particular mediating beliefs about causality. Thus, the achievement motive is a cognitive, rather than affective, disposition. It has been contended in this chapter that affect follows cognitive appraisal.

It appears that two fundamentally different conceptions of motivation are represented by the two achievement models. On the one hand, Atkinson's initial conception of achievement motivation may be portrayed as:

$$\text{Stimulus} \longrightarrow \begin{array}{c} \text{Emotional} \\ \text{anticipation} \\ \text{(hopes}-\text{fears)} \end{array} \longrightarrow \text{Instrumental response}$$

Conversely, the theoretical structure of the attributional model is:

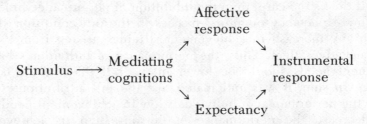

One implication of the position that the achievement motive be viewed as a cognitive disposition is the possibility that achievement motivation can be aroused by inducing appropriate causal ascriptions. In one test of this hypothesis, Breit (1969) had subjects compose essays in which success was attributed either to oneself or to external factors. Subjects in the internal success condition subsequently exhibited behavior associated with high achievement needs to a greater extent than subjects in the external success ascription condition.

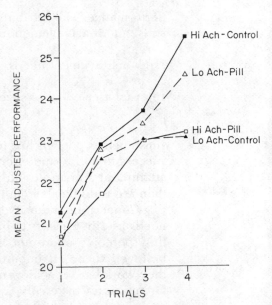

Figure 8–28. Mean increments in performance speed (number of digit-symbol substitutions) relative to pre-test performance on four test trials as a function of the level of achievement needs (high versus low) and the experimental condition (pill versus control). (From Weiner and Sierad, 1975, p. 419.)

Using the language of attribution theory, it is also possible to rein-terpret the data cited by Atkinson as supporting his conception. Accord-ing to Atkinson (1964), persons high in achievement needs initiate achievement activities, work with heightened intensity at those tasks, and persist in the face of failure. On the other hand, persons low in achievement needs avoid undertaking achievement tasks, work with relatively little intensity, and quit when they are failing (although it was indicated in Chapter Five that the alleged relations between achieve-ment needs and various aspects of behavior have not been definitively proven).

How might these presumably contrasting actions be explained with-in the theoretical framework of attribution theory? Recall that individuals differing in achievement needs may have disparate perceptions of causality for success and failure. It has been suggested that persons high in achievement needs ascribe success to high ability and high effort, and failure to a lack of effort. On the other hand, persons low in achieve-ment needs display no clear attributional preferences for success and ascribe failure to low ability (see Figure 8–7).

Now consider the hypothesis that individuals highly motivated to achieve success are more likely to undertake achievement activities than persons low in achievement needs. Guided by the vast amount of re-search in learning theory, attribution theorists believe that free choice behavior, or the decision to undertake achievement tasks, is, in part, determined by prior reinforcement history. On past occasions in which success has been attained, persons high in achievement needs ascribed the outcome to internal factors (ability and effort). Hence, they experi-enced feelings of competence, which is a "reward" for achievement performance. This attributional predilection increases the probability of subsequent achievement-related behavior:

High achievement needs   Achievement choice
         ↘   ↗
Internal ascription for success ⟶ Pride in accomplishment, feelings of
                                              competence

Inasmuch as persons low in achievement needs are less likely to ascribe success to ability and effort, they experience modulated reward for goal attainment and are less likely to initiate achievement-related activities than are individuals high in achievement needs.

Concerning intensity of performance, persons high in achievement needs ascribe success to high effort and failure to a lack of effort. Thus, they perceive effort-outcome covariation; that is, effort expenditure is believed to be an important determinant of performance. Therefore, they work hard at achievement tasks, for effort is perceived as necessary for success. Conversely, among persons low in achievement needs, the perceived level of effort expenditure is little influenced by success and failure (see Figure 8–7). It appears that these individuals do not perceive effort-outcome covariation or the efficacy of effort. Thus, they display relatively little intensity at achievement-related tasks.

It also appears that all individuals work with greatest intensity at tasks of intermediate difficulty (although Atkinson expects this only among persons high in achievement needs). An attributional analysis of the relationship between task difficulty and intensity of performance is based upon perceptions of effort as a determinant of outcome. It is suggested that task difficulty is a cue that gives rise to differential beliefs about the efficacy of effort. At an easy task, effort may be perceived as unnecessary for success, while at a very difficult task, effort may seem a "waste of energy." Thus, effort may be considered most important at tasks of intermediate difficulty.

To examine the perceived relationship between effort and task difficulty, Weiner, Heckhausen, Meyer, and Cook (1972) asked subjects to evaluate the "importance of effort as a determinant of outcome" (not differentiating success from failure outcomes) in five tasks that varied according to the percentage of others succeeding at the task (10 per cent, 30 per cent, 50 per cent, 70 per cent, and 90 per cent). Later in this experiment, the subjects also were asked at what task it would be most functional to expend effort. On both questions the subjects rank-ordered the five alternatives differing in task difficulty.

The results of this investigation are shown in Figure 8–29. Effort is judged the most important determinant of outcome at tasks of intermediate difficulty, and it is believed that the best performance strategy is to try hard at tasks of intermediate difficulty. The remaining conditions are relatively symmetrical around the intermediate level.

Finally, persons high in achievement concerns ascribe failure to a lack of effort. Effort is variable and under personal control, so it may be

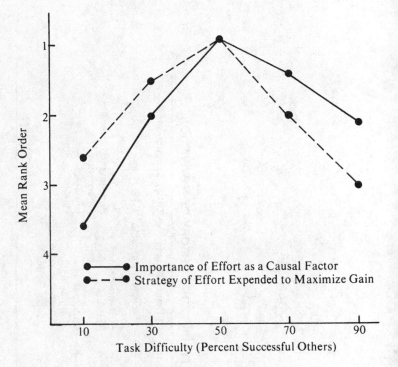

Figure 8–29. Perceived importance of effort as a causal determinant of achievement outcome, and beliefs concerning the functional value of effort, as a function of task difficulty. (From Weiner, Heckhausen, Meyer, & Cook, 1972, p. 246.)

augmented on future occasions. This attributional bias results in the maintenance of "hope" and the continuation of goal striving following failure. On the other hand, persons low in achievement needs ascribe failure to a lack of ability. Ability is perceived as stable and not subject to volitional control. In most domains it does not fluctuate from moment to moment. In addition, persons low in achievement needs feel incompetent when failing. Hence, they quit in the face of failure.

In sum, an attributional analysis of Atkinson's conception suggests that individual differences in achievement motivation, as well as cues such as task difficulty, influence mediating cognitions concerning the causes of behavioral outcomes. These causal inferences then influence subsequent achievement behavior. More specifically, if the data cited by Atkinson are accepted, then the preceding discussion indicates:

A. Individuals high in resultant achievement motivation:

1. Approach achievement-related activities (mediated by the attribution of success to high ability and effort, thus producing heightened "reward" for accomplishment).
2. Persist in the face of failure (mediated by the ascription of failure to a lack of effort, which is presumed to be modifiable).
3. Select tasks of intermediate difficulty (mediated by the perception that tasks of intermediate difficulty yield the most self-evaluative feedback).
4. Perform with relatively great vigor (mediated by the belief that outcome is determined by effort).

TABLE 8-11   PARTIAL REPRESENTATION OF AN ATTRIBUTIONAL THEORY OF MOTIVATION

Antecedent Conditions →	Perceived Causes →	Causal Dimensions →	Primary Effects →	Other Consequences
Specific information Causal schemata Individual differences Reinforcement schedules Other	Ability	Stability	Expectancy change	Performance intensity Persistence Choice Others
	Effort (typical and immediate)	Locus	Esteem-related affects	
	Others (students, family, teacher)	Control	Interpersonal judgments; intrapersonal feeling states	
	Motivation (atten- tion, interest)			

B.   Individuals low in resultant achievement motivation:

1.   Do not approach achievement-related activities (mediated by the relative attribution of success to external rather than internal factors and the exclusion of effort as a causal factor, thus resulting in modulated reward for goal attainment).
2.   Quit in the face of failure (mediated by the belief that failure is caused by a lack of ability, which presumably is uncontrollable and unchangeable).
3.   Select easy or difficult tasks (because such tasks yield minimal self-evaluative feedback).
4.   Perform with relatively little vigor (mediated by the belief that outcome is comparatively independent of effort).

Theoretical Overview

A summary of the attributional theory of motivation is shown in Table 8–11. The table indicates that persons utilize a number of cues, predilections, and rules to reach inferences about the causes of success and failure (for greater detail, see Table 8–2). The most salient causal inferences are ability and effort, but many other factors are also influential. These causes share three main properties: stability (unstable versus stable), locus (internal versus external) and controllability (controllable versus uncontrollable). Two of the dimensions, stability and locus, relate respectively to expectancy change and to esteem-related affects, while perceived control relates to interpersonal evaluations and feeling states. The dimensions of causality determine a wide range of behaviors.

THEORETICAL RANGE

At the outset of this chapter it was suggested that achievement settings merely provided the research sites for the initial development of an attributional theory of behavior, and that a more general conceptual scheme is being developed. In this section these statements will be documented by showing the range of phenomena to which the attributional approach is applicable. In addition, the theory outlined in Table 8–11 provides the guidelines for a general method of psychological analysis.

Parole Decisions

A parole decision is a complex judgment in which causal attributions play a major role. Figure 8–30 depicts the parole decision process as conceptualized by Carroll and Payne (1976, 1977). The figure indicates that the decision maker is provided with a variety of information about the criminal, the crime, and other pertinent facts. This information is combined and synthesized, yielding attributions about the cause of the crime. The causal attributions, in turn, influence judgments about deserved punishment and risk, which are believed to be the basis for the final parole decision.

Carroll and Payne (1976), after reviewing an array of literature, contend that the parole decision process is:

> . . . based on a simple two-part model. In the first part, the primary concern of the decision maker is to make the punishment fit the crime. . . . At the second part . . . the primary concern . . . is with parole risk, i.e., the probability that the person being considered for release will again violate the laws of society. (p. 15)

According to Figure 8–30, crimes that are ascribed to internal and/or intentional factors (e.g., personality characteristics, evil intents) should result in harsher personal evaluation (punishment) than crimes attributed to external and/or unintentional causes (e.g., economic conditions, bad friends). This is not surprising, for we know that the law distinguishes between murder and manslaughter, and the subjective determinants of moral judgment have been well documented by Piaget, Kohlberg, and others. In addition, the risk associated with parole should depend upon the stability of the perceived cause of the original crime. If, for example, the crime is attributed to some fixed personality trait, the decision maker is likely to expect that the prisoner will again commit crimes after parole. On the other hand, if the cause of the crime has been altered (e.g., economic conditions have improved, bad friends have left, rehabilitation was successful), the criminal will be perceived as a good parole risk.

It follows then that a criminal is least likely to be paroled if the cause of the crime is perceived as internal and/or intentional and stable ("he is a bad seed with evil intents"). Conversely, parole is most likely to be granted when the crime is perceived as caused by external and/or unintentional and unstable factors (e.g., prior economic conditions). The

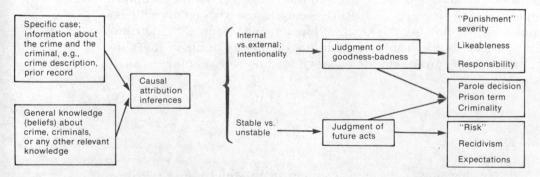

Figure 8–30. Attributional analysis of perceptions of crime and criminals. (From Carroll & Payne, 1977.)

remaining causal combinations should fall between these extremes in predicting parole likelihood. Carroll and Payne have furnished support for these hypotheses, examining professional parole decision makers and the judgments of college students when given simulated criminal cases. Carroll and Payne find that perceptions of the locus, stability, and intentionality of causes significantly relate to indexes such as perceived responsibility for the crime, likelihood of recidivism, likability, length of prison term, and the purpose of a prison sentence.

More specifically, in one experiment, college students were given eight possible causes of a crime. The causes represented the attributional dimensions of internality, stability, and intentionality (which is more appropriate in this moral context than is controllability). For example, an internal, stable, and intentional cause was illustrated by the following case:

Mr. Green is a 25-year-old male convicted of second-degree murder. He was in a bar having a drink and talking to the victim when they began to argue, push and punch each other. He pulled out a gun and shot the victim several times; the victim was pronounced dead on arrival at the hospital. Mr. Green surrendered himself to police called by the bartender.

He has no previous record of convictions.

Interviews indicated that he had thought about this situation for some time and had developed several plans.

On the other hand, an external, stable, and unintentional cause was described as follows:

Mr. Green is a 25-year-old male convicted of second-degree murder. He was in a bar having a drink and talking to the victim when they began to argue, push and punch each other. He pulled out a gun and shot the victim several times; the victim was pronounced dead on arrival at the hospital. Mr. Green surrendered himself to police called by the bartender.

He has no previous record of convictions.

Interviews indicated that he could not find a good job because his skill had been replaced by mechanization. The circumstances around the crime had been acting on him for some time.

Table 8–12 shows the causal manipulation for all eight crime conditions.

The subjects then indicated the prison term that they felt should be imposed. Carroll and Payne (1977) report:

Averaging across eight crimes, crimes with internal causes were given an average prison term of 7.8 years, crimes with external causes were given an average of 4.4 years. Crimes with stable causes were given an average term of 7.1 years compared to 5.1 years for unstable causes. The effects of these dimensions were additive, such that the internal-stable causal information led to an average of 9.1 year sentence against the 3.6 years for external-unstable causes.

These results, however, were not as clear-cut when professional parole decision makers were used as the judges. The professionals have access to special knowledge that influences their decision making. For example, they know that murderers tend not to recommit murder when they are released. Hence, such information, which is not shared by the general population, enters into their decision process.

TABLE 8–12   CAUSE MANIPULATIONS

	Stable	Unstable
Intentional		
Internal	Interviews indicated that he had thought about this situation for some time and had developed several plans.	Interviews indicated that he had made a momentary decision to do it and had deliberately ignored the consequences.
External	Interviews indicated that he had been under constant intense pressure from his elderly mother and his family to do things for them, make more money, and give up his free time.	Interviews indicated that his wife had told him without warning that she had decided to divorce him.
Unintentional		
Internal	Interviews indicated that he has an aggressive nature and exhibits many hostile feelings toward society in general. He has difficulty following social rules.	Interviews indicated that he was in a depressed mood, had been drinking, and was overcome by impulse.
External	Interviews indicated that he could not find a good job because his skill had been replaced by mechanization. The circumstances around the crime had been acting on him for some time.	Interviews indicated that he had been temporarily laid off work due to economic situations. At the time of the act, circumstances seemed to come together to make it happen.

(From Carroll & Payne, 1977, p. 201.)

In sum, according to Carroll and Payne, the parole decision procedure is conceptually identical to the perceived sequence of events in the achievement domain: antecedent information is processed; a causal judgment is reached; the cause is placed within the locus, stability, and intentionality dimensions; and this influences evaluation and expectancy, which are among the main determinants of the parole decision.

Affiliation and Loneliness

It has been suggested that in our culture two sources of motivation are most dominant: achievement and social recognition (or, in Freud's more general terms, *Arbeit und Liebe*). Hence, affiliative motivation is a natural area to turn toward in the development of a general theory of behavior.

An attributional analysis of affiliative motivation guided by the theory shown in Table 8–11 conceives of loneliness as a social failure (Gordon, 1976; Stein & Bailey, 1973). Hanusa (1975) and Heim (1975) examined the perceived causes of social success and failure and found them to be similar to the causes of achievement success and failure. The most dominant of the perceived causes of loneliness expressed by college students are external circumstances (e.g., "I was in a situation where it was difficult to make friends") and lack of effort in pursuit of friendships (see Peplau, Russell, & Heim, in press).

Michela and Peplau (1977) used scaling procedures to discover the dimensions of the causes of social failure. Thirteen causes of social failure were paired with one another and rated in terms of perceived similarity. These data provided the input for a multidimensional scaling procedure. A three-dimensional scaling solution was obtained, with the dimensions labelled: 1) locus (anchored with internal causes of "physically unattractive" and "too shy" versus external causes of "impersonal situations" and "no opportunities"); 2) stability (anchored by stable causes of "unpleasant personality" and "physically unattractive" versus unstable causes of "no opportunities" and "doesn't try hard"); and 3) controllability or intentionality (anchored by controllable causes of "doesn't try hard enough" and "doesn't know what to do" versus uncontrollable or unintentional causes of "physically unattractive" and "others have their own groups"). On the basis of these data Michela and Peplau (1977) conclude:

> The overall picture . . . seems to support rather well the applicability of Weiner's dimensional model of attributions for performance to the social failure of loneliness. Intuitive and empirical procedures for labelling dimensions converged on identification of dimensions very similar to Weiner's. This finding is all the more dramatic due to the divergent methodologies used in previous research on academic achievement compared to this study. Weiner's model was originally developed by a *deductive* process of reasoning from characteristics of specific causes to postulating general dimensions, and then empirically testing predictions dictated by the model. But the present study used an *inductive* process from the outset, namely, multidimensional scaling, to derive dimensions empirically. (p. 4).

The question that remains is whether the causes and attributional dimensions in the affiliative domain relate to affect, expectancy, and evaluation in the same manner as in the achievement domain. Intuitively, that appears to be the case. For example, social failure ascribed to internal factors such as "physically unattractive" or "unpleasant personality" (which are akin to low ability in the achievement domain) should result in greater negative affect and loss of self-esteem (feelings of incompetence and a lack of confidence) than attributions to external causes such as "lack of opportunities" or "others have their own groups." Furthermore, one can reasonably hypothesize that unstable causes of social failure will result in a higher expectancy of future affiliative success than attributions to stable causes. In support of this line of reasoning, Folkes (1978) found that rejection in a romantic relationship because of perceived internal reasons leads to "hurt feelings," and that stable reasons ("she did not like my personality") result in a lower expectancy of establishing a relationship with the rejector than rejections for perceived unstable reasons (e.g., a prior commitment). Older individuals in particular attribute feelings of loneliness to stable causes and express the belief that nothing can alleviate this situation (see Peplau et al., in press). Furthermore, stable and internal causes strongly relate to feelings of despair. Both affect and expectancy, in turn, are likely to influence a variety of instrumental actions related to affiliation.

In addition to having a profound effect on personal behavior, attributions influence relations with others. An attributional analysis of the control dimension suggests:

> . . . People will be more sympathetic to the lonely when they are the victims of circumstance, and have exerted effort to overcome their loneliness. The person who is responsible for his or her loneliness "deserves" to suffer, and is less likely to receive sympathy or be seen as a likable person." (Peplau et al., in press)

In support of this general hypothesis, Peplau et al. report data from an investigation in which students were asked to imagine a person who was lonely because of any one of thirteen common causes (e.g., shyness, no opportunities). The students then indicated their reaction to the person. It was found that ratings of likability strongly related to the controllability dimension of causality, but not to causal stability or locus. Persons perceived as personally responsible for their problem were least liked.

In sum, the few published empirical investigations of affiliation and loneliness report the same general pattern of data obtained in the achievement domain. It appears that the attributional approach fits these two common sources of behavior equally well.

Mastery Behavior

The labels "mastery" and "competence" are prominent among the writings of psychologists (e.g., Nissen, 1954; White, 1959). Competence is often used to connote:

> . . . fitness or ability, and the suggested synonyms [of] capability, capacity, efficiency, proficiency, and skill. It is therefore a suitable word to describe such things as grasping and exploring, crawling and walking, attention and perception, language and thinking, manipulating and changing the surroundings, all of which promote an effective — a competent — interaction with the environment. . . . The behavior that leads to the building up of effective grasping, handling and letting go of objects, to take one example, is not random behavior produced by a general overflow of energy. It is directed, selective, and persistent, and it is continued not because it serves primary drives, which indeed it cannot serve until it is almost perfected, but because it satisfies an intrinsic need to deal with the environment. (White, 1959, pp. 317–318)

As already indicated, attribution theorists also embrace the postulate that humans are striving for understanding and mastery.

In spite of the popularity of the terms "mastery" and "competence" in accounting for human action, they rarely have been the subject of direct experimentation and examination. An investigation by Nuttin (1973) is one of the few that demonstrates what he calls "causality pleasure." Nuttin distinguishes causality pleasure, or the positive affect that is gained when one causes an event, from stimulus pleasure, which is the pleasure associated with the event *per se*. Nuttin placed five-year-olds in an experimental room containing two "machines." The machines each had colored lights and movable handles. For one machine (A), the onset of the lights was preprogrammed by the experimenter. On the other hand, the lights in the alternate machine (B) went on or off when the handle was moved beyond a certain point. Thus, although both machines stimulated the viewer perceptually, the children were the producers, or the causes, of the stimulation only with machine B.

The subjects in this experiment were free to spend their time with either machine. The experimenters then recorded various indexes of preference, such as the time spent with each machine and verbal reports of liking. Both observational and self-report data revealed that the children strongly preferred machine B over machine A.

From the theoretical perspective shown in Table 8–11, the experiment by Nuttin illustrates a temporal sequence involving the use of covariation information, inferences concerning causality, positive affect, and some behavioral consequences of affective states. That is, on the basis of the observed covariation between their own actions and the onset of the light in machine B, the children inferred that they were personally responsible for the stimulation from that machine. Self-attribution for the outcome to ability and/or effort, or the perception of personal control, augments certain positive affects, such as feelings of competence, and the enhanced positive affect increases the likelihood of engaging in the action again.

This analysis is applicable to another developmental study that has not been thought of as involving mastery-type behaviors. Watson (1966, 1967) demonstrated that infants as young as eight weeks old can learn an instrumental response to increase stimulation. In Watson's study, children were placed in a crib with a mobile above their head. By turning their head to the right an electrical apparatus in their pillow was activated that caused the mobile to move. For other children the mobile merely was moved by the experimenter. Watson then measured the frequency of head-turning responses. Representative data (from Watson & Ramey,

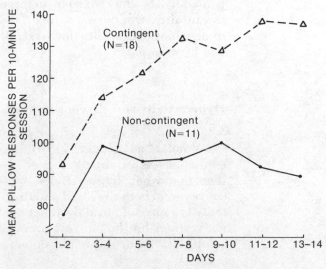

Figure 8–31. Pillow responses across two weeks for the two groups. (Adapted from J. Watson & Ramey, 1972, p. 222.)

1972) clearly reveal that children in the personal causality condition learn the "correct" response, for their head turning increases over time, while the head turning of the children unable to control the movement of the mobile remains relatively constant (see Figure 8–31). The stimulation must therefore be "rewarding," for it increases appropriate responding. But of greater importance in the present context was that infants in the instrumental response condition apparently displayed more positive affect (smiling, cooing) than children in the condition in which the mobile movement was controlled by the experimenter. This again suggests a temporal sequence of: response-outcome covariation — perceived self-causation (ability and/or effort) — positive affects such as feelings of competence — increased choice behavior. That is, the enhanced positive affect and the subsequent performance of the instrumental response are mediated by perceptions of self-responsibility.

The underlying premise of this interpretation of Watson's study is that affect and choice can be used to infer cognitive processes (perceptions of causality). It may be far-fetched to infer that eight-week-olds have the cognitive capacities to make causal inferences. However, it may also be that a differentiation between the self and the environment has developed by that age, and that primitive inferences involving proprioceptive feedback information can be drawn. If this interpretation has any validity, then Watson has perhaps identified the existence of achievement-like behaviors and attempts at mastery among very young infants.

It is intuitively reasonable to suggest that the locus of causality dimension will develop relatively early in the growth cycle. The growing child must learn to differentiate the self from the rest of the world. Next the child is likely to learn how to act on the environment and must come to understand the predictability of events. This would involve the development of the concept of stability. Finally, one must learn how to evaluate others and to understand abstract principles of justice, including concepts of goodness, badness, and "ought." This would be accompanied by the emergence of an intentionality (controllability) dimension of causality. Of course, at this time the sequential development of the dimensions of causality (locus, stability, and then intentionality) is merely a hypothesis.

Hyperactivity and Psychostimulants

Whalen and Henker (1976) have outlined an attributional analysis of the effects of drug treatment for hyperactive children. They contend that when hyperactivity is combatted with a drug, the belief is conveyed to both the child and the parents that the cause of the hyperactivity is a physiological dysfunction. Hence, the involved individuals are not responsible for, or in control of, the maladaptive behavior that is exhibited. Because this physiological deficit is perceived as an uncontrollable cause, neither the child nor the parents need feel guilty or blame themselves for the aberrant behavior. That is, the shift in perceived causality minimizes self-blame and negative evaluations. This appears to be a beneficial and an unanticipated side effect of the treatment technique.

On the other hand, Whalen and Henker (1976) also state that "the reputed physiological dysfunctions used to explain the failure of the hyperactive child are frequently viewed as stable and relatively unresponsive to behavioral change effects" (p. 1123). Thus, the perception of fixed causation "leads to demoralization about problem solutions . . . and interferes with effective coping" (p. 1124).

In sum, again there is an analysis of a psychological phenomenon from the perspective shown in Table 8–11. Individuals utilize information (treatment technique) to infer causation about an event (hyperactivity). The perceived cause (a genetic deficit) minimizes negative affect (a beneficial effect) but also reduces the perceived likelihood of recovery (a harmful effect). These two factors, in turn, influence the long-range consequences of the treatment (negatively, according to Whalen and Henker, inasmuch as expectancy is assumed to be a more potent determinant of long-term behavioral change than affect).

Learned Helplessness and Depression

A theoretical framework proposed to explain "learned helplessness" (see Chapter Six) suggests that: 1) An objective noncontingency between responding and outcome 2) produces an expectation that outcomes are uncontrollable, which is 3) sufficient to generate cognitive (e.g., negative beliefs about oneself), emotional (e.g., sadness), and motivational (e.g., passivity) consequences, or a syndrome resembling depression.

Objective Noncontingency

Perhaps because the notion of learned helplessness is rooted in learning theory and animal psychology, it has been postulated that this state originates when there has been a prior *objective* noncontingency between actions and outcomes. An objective noncontingency, of course, is readily established in an experimental setting.

Attribution theory, on the other hand, is concerned with phenomenal causality. Two scientists, for example, one with a history of accomplishment (objective contingency between actions and outcomes) and the other with a history of failure (objective noncontingency) may feel equally unworthy and exhibit depressive symptoms, the former because of the distorted belief that his or her actions have not led to success. That is, both scientists are "depressed," although in one case the symptoms were preceded only by subjective noncontingency, whereas in the second instance they were preceded by objective and subjective noncontingency.

In sum, the stipulation of objectivity in the antecedent conditions specified by Seligman and his colleagues appears to be unnecessary. The expectancy-value approach to motivation discussed in this chapter is phenomenological and ahistorical — what matters is the contemporary evaluation of the physical and the social world, regardless of the veridicality or the source of one's beliefs. Indeed, an organism first trained in a classical aversive conditioning situation and exhibiting helplessness in a subsequent operant setting because of the prior noncontingency training is responding to the subjective, rather than the objective, stimuli in the new context. Thus, the learned helplessness formulation already has a phenomenological flavor.

Causal Attributions

Given a perceived noncontingency between actions and outcomes, the attributional approach suggests that the next phase in the development of depression involves a "why" question, such as, Why am I not able to succeed in my work? or Why am I unable to establish social or emotional relationships? This step initially was neglected in the learned helplessness literature, again perhaps because the bulk of this research has used infrahuman subjects. However, recent restatements of this work recognize the importance of causal attributions (see Abramson, Seligman, & Teasdale, 1978; Miller & Norman, 1979). There are, of course, a myriad of answers to such "why" questions. In the perspective outlined in this chapter, the three porperties (dimensional placements) of the causal ascriptions are of particular importance.

CAUSAL STABILITY.   It has been contended by Seligman and his colleagues that beliefs about prior noncontingency carry over to future contingent contexts. For example, given a noncontingent aversive outcome (shock or failure), the expectancy of these events persists over time. For this to be the case, the actor must ascribe the prior outcome, or lack of control, to stable causes. Only if a cause is perceived to be invariant over time (e.g., inability, unattractiveness), is there likely to be expectancy generalization on future occasions.

HELPLESSNESS VERSUS HOPELESSNESS.   Seligman and his associates have specified that learned helplessness involves a low expectancy generalized on the basis of prior noncontingent responding in an aversive setting. However, the more accurate designation for a low expectancy of goal attainment is learned *hopelessness*. Clearly one may be helpless (probabilities of reward are not increased by personal responding) without being hopeless. Positive anticipations may be sustained by the knowledge that someone else is going to help or by ascribing the current noncontingency to unstable causes. If one assumes that a low expectancy of goal attainment is the key antecedent of depression, then hopelessness, rather than helplessness, is the appropriate concept to stress. Helplessness would then be a necessary, rather than a sufficient, antecedent of depression.

CAUSALITY AND AFFECTIVE REACTIONS. Depression is considered an affective, rather than a cognitive, disorder. As previously indicated, perceived causality is believed to be important in determining affective reactions to success and failure. For example, attributions for failure to causes such as low ability or lack of effort maximize feelings of inadequacy, low self-esteem, and shame.

A number of investigations have demonstrated the differential influences of causal ascriptions upon behavioral manifestations of depression. These differences supposedly arise because the different ascriptions have disparate influences on affect. For example, Klein, Fencil-Morse, and Seligman (1976) demonstrated that performance deficits normally exhibited by depressives are alleviated when prior lack of control (failure) can be ascribed to external causes. More specifically, depressive subjects who were informed that the task they were attempting was exceedingly difficult did not exhibit impairment in performance following failure. This suggests that an attribution for failure to task difficulty did not generate feelings of low self-esteem and thus did not adversely influence later performance. On the basis of these data Klein et al. (1976) concluded that "the learned helplessness model of depression needs an extra construct concerning attribution of helplessness to personal failure" (p. 515).

In sum, the study of Klein et al. (1976) seems to indicate that a low expectancy of success is not sufficient to generate learned helplessness and depression. Rather, low expectancy must be accompanied by self-attributions for prior failure, and associated affects such as blame, guilt, incompetence, and lowered self-esteem (see also Beck, 1967, 1974, 1976; Lichtenberg, 1957). Hence, given this analysis, the necessary precondition for learned helplessness is ascription of prior response-outcome independence to stable *and* internal causes. Miller and Seligman (1975) also presented some data supporting this hypothesis. They noted that two of their subjects in a learned helplessness condition who became angry at the experimenter (ascription of non-control to an external source) reported little depression and performed well at a subsequent task.

The notion that depression is a consequence of internal, stable ascriptions also is in accord with the phenomenology of depression expressed by college students. Weiner et al. (1978) found that motivational indicators of depression such as apathy and resignation were expected to emerge only when a hypothetical person made stable and internal ascriptions for failure (i.e., attribution for failure to lack of ability, low intrinsic motivation, or personality deficits).

However, in contrast to the above conclusion, it also is evident that in some situations depression does occur given external ascriptions for uncontrollable "failures." For example, catastrophic natural events, the death of a significant other, and placement in a prisoner-of-war camp, all of which are uncontrollable and aversive, often promote depression. Abramson et al. label this "universal depression." Furthermore, these events typically are explained with external ascriptions, such as bad luck, God's will, or evil others. This would seem to indicate that depression can occur as a consequence of hopelessness and the affect generated by an external causal ascription. Affects associated with external causality include, for example, aggression and anger (ascription to evil others), and bewilderment and feelings of being stunned (attribution to bad luck). Furthermore, negative affects are produced by non-attainment of a desired goal, independent of any particular causal attribution. Such affects include being upset, displeased, and unhappy (see Weiner et al., 1978).

If the arguments in the preceding paragraph are accepted, then it appears that depression may or may not be accompanied by self-attributions. However, depression must be accompanied by expectations of non-attainment of desired goals (hopelessness) and negative affects, which may be generated either by internal or external ascriptions, or by the negative outcome of an event.

To summarize, it has been suggested that expectancy and affect, which are often mediated by causal attributions, are essential determinants of what has been called learned helplessness (depression). It is further suggested that there are disparate genotypes for a general class, or a phenotype, labelled depression. The genotypic categories include: 1) low expectation of goal attainment (hopelessness) accompanied by internal attributions (e.g., lack of ability) and their linked affects (e.g., low self-esteem); 2) hopelessness accompanied by external ascriptions (e.g., others) and their linked affects (e.g., anger); 3) hopelessness accompanied by general negative affects that arise from non-attainment of a goal and are not attributionally mediated (e.g., upset).

Finally, to add even further complexities, causal attributions are not fixed over time. There are likely to be primary and secondary appraisals of events, as Lazarus (1966) and others have contended. This might be evidenced, for example, when an initial reaction of self-blame for failure and lowered self-esteem changes to blaming others and displaying aggression and anger. Such a sequence is reminiscent of the "vicissitudes of the instincts" championed by Freud and is consistent with his contention that aggression may be redirected inwardly or outwardly. From an attributional perspective, such fluctuations in affect are indicators of cognitive (attributional) change or distortion, and could be an important aspect of the depressive disorder.

Summary

A number of causes are used to explain success or failure in achievement-related contexts. The primary perceived causes of achievement-related outcomes are ability and effort, but the difficulty of the task, luck, mood, and help or hindrance from others are included among the other possible explanations of success and failure. Causes are inferred on the basis of several factors, including specific informational cues (e.g., past success history, social norms, pattern of performance), causal preferences, rules that relate causes to effects (causal schemata), reinforcement history, and communications from others.

The causes of success and failure have been classified within three dimensions, labelled locus of causality (internal versus external), stability (stable versus unstable), and controllability (controllable vs. uncontrollable). The causal dimension of stability relates to expectancy changes after success and failure. Relatively enduring causes indicate that the past outcome will be repeated again in the future, whereas variable causes signify that the future may differ from the past. Thus, typical expectancy shifts are greater in games of skill, while atypical shifts are more prevalent given games of chance. In earlier work, social learning theorists erred in attributing expectancy shifts to the locus, rather than to the stability, dimension of causality. The relation between causal stability and expectancy shifts also may be responsible for the augmented resistance to extinction that is displayed given partial random reinforcement schedules and a highly effortful response.

The dimension of controllability relates to the evaluation of others. Success because of high expenditure of effort, and failure due to a lack of trying elicit particularly heightened reward and punishment. This apparently is because effort is perceived as being subject to volitional control.

In addition to influencing interpersonal evaluation, attributions also affect personal reactions to success and failure. Particular causal attributions are associated with specific emotional reactions. For example, success because of ability promotes feelings of competence; helpful others elicit gratitude; and luck generates surprise. For failure, causal ascriptions to a lack of ability promote feelings of incompetence; others who are perceived as hindering goal attainment elicit aggression; lack of effort gives rise to feelings of shame and guilt; and so on. In addition, the locus dimension of causality relates to esteem-related affects. The affective consequence of internal versus external attributions appears to be the main functional significance of the perceived locus of causality.

Finally, expectancy and affect, both of which are mediated by causal attributions, influence the choice, intensity, and persistence of behavior. Attributions of failure to a lack of ability are particularly debilitating, perhaps because ability is a stable cause that also generates feelings of incompetence. On the other hand, causal attributions of failure to a lack of effort seem to enhance performance. The implications of causal ascriptions highlight some of the disparities between the attributional and the Atkinsonian approaches to achievement strivings, even though both follow the expectancy-value tradition in the study of motivation and personality.

In addition to its explanatory value in the achievement domain, the attributional theory of behavior reviewed in this chapter is applicable to a wide range of psychological phenomena:

1. Parole decisions are based, in part, on recidivism risk and the punishment "deserved" by the criminal. These factors, in turn, are influenced by the perceived stability, locus, and/or intentionality of the crime.

2. Helping behavior is, in part, a function of the perceived reasons the individual is in need of aid. Unstable and controllable causes (lack of trying) typically do not elicit helping behavior.

3. The perceived causes of loneliness influence how one feels about oneself and the expectation of future affiliative relationships, as well as how one reacts to a lonely person.

4. Mastery behavior involves the perception of effort-outcome covariation, or the perceived responsibility for the manipulation and change of one's environment. Mastery strivings might be exhibited by children as young as eight weeks old.

5. Drug treatments for hyperactivity may retard a permanent cure because the treatment information conveys that the cause is stable (a genetic deficit). However, drug prescriptions also intimate that neither the child nor the parents are responsible for the disruptive behavior, thus reducing negative evaluations from others and feelings of guilt.

6. Learned helplessness and depression may be produced by a low expectancy of future success in conjunction with an affect that is linked either with internal causes, external causes, or the aversive outcome. It is suggested that disparate genotypes characterize the depressive disorder.

The extensive literature concerning achievement strivings, as well as the many problem areas that fall outside of the success-failure domain, suggests that a general conception of motivation and a method of psychological analysis are evolving from attributional language. Laws of person-perception and laws of motivation may have a common foundation, thereby bringing two distinct areas of psychology under one rubric.

Chapter Nine

HUMANISTIC THEORY AND PERSONAL CONSTRUCTS

Introduction

It often is contended that prior to the 1960's there were two main movements in psychology: psychoanalytic and behavioristic. Sociologists of science suggest that the development of both these theoretical perspectives was greatly influenced by cultural factors. Psychoanalytic theory originated in the supposedly repressive society of Vienna around the beginning of the twentieth century. This social milieu, in part, may have accounted for the psychoanalytic emphasis upon repression, conflict, and neurosis. On the other hand, behaviorism was spawned in turn-of-the-century America. It embraced Darwin's concern with adaptation and function, as well as the belief that behavior is completely modifiable. Sociologists of science point out that this latter assumption was consistent with the optimistic psychological climate in America at that time.

Around 1960, a so-called "third force" in psychology came into existence. This third force, humanistic psychology, focused not only on what the person is, but also on what the person has the potential to become. Humanism emerged at a time when many individuals were questioning traditional values, including the striving for success and achievement. And controversy about issues such as pollution of the environment raised questions about the quality and the richness of life. Emphasis upon existential problems naturally gave rise to a more humanistic psychology. Thus, three major theoretical positions in psychology, each having the status of a "movement," appear to be intimately linked with the social and cultural factors of their times.

Because of its current popularity and unique approach to motivation, the humanistic conception of action is examined briefly in this chapter. However, although worthy of discussion, in my opinion humanistic theory has not greatly advanced our knowledge of human motivation. Hence, a full chapter devoted to this conception is not warranted. There is, however, pertinent material to complement a discussion of humanism: The ideas of George Kelly concerning the construal of oneself and of others have much in common with humanistic theory because of their mutual allegiance to phenomenology and their interest in how perceivers (actors) make sense out of the world and themselves. Kelly's theory also is subsumed within a literature entitled "implicit psychology." Implicit psychology is concerned with the perceived laws of behavior held by the "naive" observer, and therefore provides a bridge to the attributional conceptions just presented.

HUMANISTIC THEORY

The social precursors of humanistic psychology mentioned in the introduction were in evidence when the Association of Humanistic Psychology was founded in 1962. Four interrelated principles were adopted by the humanists to guide their pursuits:

1. The experiencing person is of primary interest. Humanistic psychology begins with the study of individuals in real-life circumstances. Humans are subjects, rather than mere objects, of study. Psychological research, the humanists contend, cannot be modeled after early physics, in which the objects of study are "out there." The person must be examined and described in terms of personal consciousness, which includes subjective experience and how the individual perceives and values himself or herself. The basic question that humanists grapple with is, Who am I? Individuals, as travelers in life, must determine where they are and where they wish to go. Humanists follow a holistic approach in which experiences are not broken down into component parts like "single frames within a film;" instead, the entirety of life is considered. This is consistent with the position of Gestalt psychologists.

2. Human choice, creativity, and self-actualization are the preferred topics of investigation. Humanists argue that the study of psychologically crippled people has led to a crippled psychology, while the study of lower organisms has yielded an incomplete psychology devoid of consciousness. The humanists believe that psychologists should study wholesome and healthy individuals, persons who are creative and fully functioning. People have a need to push forward in life, to develop their potentialities and capabilities. These self-actualizing tendencies are of particular significance.

3. Meaningfulness must precede objectivity in the selection of research problems. Psychological research, according to the humanists, has centered on methods rather than on problems. Often research topics are selected chiefly because objective and convenient methods are available. But research projects should be undertaken because they are significant and pertain to human issues, even if the methods available are weak. Research cannot be value-free; psychologists must study the important issues of people's lives.

4. Ultimate value is placed on the dignity of the person. Above all, humans are accepted as unique and noble. Psychologists must understand people, rather than predict or control their behavior. Individuals are believed to have a higher nature with a need for meaningful work, responsibility, and an opportunity for creative expression.

Among the prominent spokesmen for humanistic psychology are Gordon Allport, Abraham Maslow, and Carl Rogers. The viewpoints of Maslow and Rogers are briefly examined in the following pages. Although these theorists are not in complete agreement, and each has unique theoretical ideas not adopted by the other, their conceptions have enough in common to be presented together. Often, however, I will identify which of the two theorists is responsible for a particular contribution.

Motivational Principles

According to Rogers and Maslow, the core tendency of a person is to actualize individual potential. There is an internal, biological pressure to develop fully the capacities and the talents that have been inherited; the central motivation of the individual is to grow and to enhance the basic self.

The acceptance of an actualization tendency is an axiom of humanistic psychology — it is not subject to proof or disproof. Maslow and others have "demonstrated" the validity of this principle by studying certain individuals whom they believe best display the qualities of the optimum person. Maslow (1971) has contended:

If we want to answer the question of how tall the human species can grow, then obviously it is well to pick out the ones who already are tallest and study them. If we want to know how fast a human being can run, then it is no use to average out the speed of a "good sample" of the population; it is far better to collect Olympic gold medal winners and see how well they can do. If we want to know the possibilities for spiritual growth, or moral development in human beings, then I maintain that we can learn most by studying our most moral, ethical, or saintly people. (p. 7) [Maslow identified Ruth Benedict and Max Wertheimer as two of these "saintly people."]

There are many dangers in following this scientific procedure. For example, it is possible for one to select for study the "worst" people

CARL ROGERS

ABRAHAM MASLOW

Carl Rogers was born in 1902 near Chicago, Illinois. Two early patterns of experience affected the course of his schooling and career. First, there was a strong fundamentalist atmosphere in his home, with emphasis on the Protestant ethic as a way of life. Second, when he was 12 his family moved to a farm, where he developed a strong interest in the science of agriculture. When Rogers first entered college, he chose to major in agriculture, but he later switched to theology to prepare for the ministry. However, he became increasingly liberal, or humanistic, in his religious views, and this eventually influenced his decision to seek a Ph.D. in clinical psychology. His doctorate was from the Teachers College of Columbia University.

Rogers' career spiraled upward as he moved from the Rochester Child Guidance Center to Ohio State University (with Kelly and Rotter), the University of Chicago, the University of Wisconsin, and finally to the Center for the Study of the Person near San Diego, California. He first became well known as the founder of client-centered therapy, a treatment technique in which the therapist focuses on the subjective experience (frame of reference) of the client. Later, Rogers became recognized as one of the central figures in humanistic psychology. He has led, and continues to lead, an extremely active and productive life, publishing many books and articles for both practicing psychologists and for the general public.

Abraham Maslow was born in 1908 in Brooklyn, New York, and died in 1970. Maslow studied at Cornell University and then at the University of Wisconsin. He was first drawn to behaviorism, and his Ph.D. at Wisconsin concerned primate sexuality and dominance. The dissertation was supervised by another prominent psychologist, Harry Harlow. But Maslow slowly left the restrictions of behaviorism and, after the birth of his child, remarked that "anyone who ... [observes] a baby could not be a behaviorist."

Maslow then began reading psychoanalytic and Gestalt theory, and conducted extended discussions with the wave of European social scientists leaving Nazi Germany. These intellectual experiences resulted in his gravitation toward the humanistic perspective. He totally embraced the humanistic philosophy, devoting himself to the betterment of social and individual life. Maslow spent much of his academic career at Brandeis University near Boston, but just prior to his death had moved to California and was attempting to formulate a general philosophy of politics and ethics guided by humanistic principles.

and hold with equal conviction the belief that the basic tendencies of humans are for self- and other-destruction. Furthermore, the examination of extremes to demonstrate or discover a general principle can be misleading. Following this procedure, one might discover that the basic function of aspirin is to harm individuals, for ingestion of 200 aspirins (an extreme) results in death!

Actualizing Principle: Antecedents

In the field of motivation one typically attempts to specify the antecedents of a particular motivational state (ranging, for example, from food deprivation to restriction of choice), and then the consequences or behavioral manifestations of the inferred motivational state (ranging from resistance to extinction to changing attitudes). Considering antecedents, both Rogers and Maslow assume that actualization striving is akin to an instinct in that it is innate, or genetically given. But the locus of the assumed actualizing tendency is unclear. Maddi (1976) notes that:

> Rogers . . . is thinking in terms of some sort of genetic blueprint, to which form and substance is added as life progresses. But the precise outlines of the blueprint are a mystery. Does it have to do with such biological considerations as the size and tonus of the muscles, the excellence of brain structures and organization, and the rapidity of metabolic functioning? Does it have to do with more psychological considerations such as needs to master or be imaginative or gregarious? Rogers gives virtually no guidance. Another kind of question that goes unanswered is whether — and if so, how — there are differences among people in inherent potentialities. (p. 83)

Rather than focusing upon the source or strength of the actualizing tendency, Rogers and Maslow have given attention to what might stand in the way of, or inhibit, this basic human motivation. Rogers (1959) has been particularly concerned with blockage of the tendency toward *self*-actualization, which is one component of the more general actualizing tendency.

Rogers (1959, p. 200) defines the self as the "organized . . . gestalt . . . of the 'I' or 'me'." One's self-concept is socially learned, as are the needs for positive regard and positive self-regard. If an individual is totally accepted by others (unconditional positive regard), then positive self-regard emerges. But if actions rather than the total person are evaluated, and if some actions are judged positively and others negatively (conditional positive regard), then *conditions of worth* develop. The person experiences "do" or "do not" as necessary in order to feel appreciated and accepted. A condition of worth, in turn, leads to defensive functioning or the closing off of experiences. This generates discrepancies between the objective and the subjective world, producing anxiety and threat. Thus, incongruence, which is one consequence of social practices that produce conditions of worth, prevents self-actualization.

In sum, self-actualization can be facilitated or impeded by appropriate interactions and feedback from others. Full acceptance by others leads to acceptance of the self and congruence, and promotes self-actualization. Note, therefore, that in opposition to Freud's beliefs, Rogers argues that defenses do not help adaptation and successful functioning in life. Rather, they interfere with satisfactions by causing the experience of incongruities. Furthermore, society is not necessarily restrictive; the social environment can enhance mental health. And finally, in the humanistic system beliefs about oneself and attitudes towards others are positively related: If we feel good about others, we also feel positively about ourselves, while negative opinions about others are related to negative self-evaluation. Conversely, in the Freudian system there is a fixed amount of libidinal energy; aggression expressed against others theoretically reduces self-aggression, and vice versa.

MASLOW'S NEED HIERARCHY. Rather than postulating just one source of motivation, Maslow acknowledges a multiplicity of need systems. The hierarchical ordering of the needs is another factor that might prevent the emergence of self-actualization goals.

More specifically, Maslow delineated five basic classes or categories of needs, which he defined as physiological, safety, love, esteem, and actualization (see Table 9–1). Arkes and Garske (1977) point out that these needs have common characteristics, such as:

1. Failure to gratify the need results in a related form of dysfunction or disturbance. For example, lack of vitamins can produce malnutrition, lack of love can produce depression, and so on.
2. Restoration of the gratification remedies the dysfunction.
3. In a free choice situation, the gratification of one basic need will be preferred over the gratification of others. For example, Maslow (1943) states:

> If all the needs are unsatisfied, and the organism is then dominated by physiological needs, all other needs may become simply non-existent or pushed into the background. It is then fair to characterize the whole organism as saying simply that it is hungry, for consciousness is almost completely preempted by hunger. . . . The urge to write poetry, the desire to acquire an automobile, the interest in American history . . . are . . . forgotten or become of secondary importance. (p. 372)

Table 9–1 shows the hierarchy of needs postulated by Maslow, conditions of deficiency and fulfillment, and a commonplace example of such fulfillment. As already intimated, there is a prepotency of needs, with the lower needs, which are physiologically based, having the greater strength, and the higher needs, which are psychologically based, being relatively weaker. Hence, the lower needs must be satisfied before the higher ones can seek fulfillment. Schultz (1976) lists a number of other distinctions between the higher and the lower needs:

1. The higher needs appeared later in the evolutionary development of mankind. All living things need food and water, but only humans have a need to self-actualize and to know and understand. Therefore, the higher the need the more distinctly human it is.

TABLE 9–1   NEED HIERARCHY AND LEVELS OF PERSONALITY FUNCTIONING

Need Hierarchy	Condition of Deficiency	Fulfillment	Illustration
Physiological	Hunger, thirst Sexual frustration Tension Fatigue Illness Lack of proper shelter	Relaxation Release from tension Experiences of pleasure from senses Experiences of pleasure from senses Physical well-being Comfort	Feeling satisfied after a good meal
Safety	Insecurity Yearning Sense of loss Fear Obsession Compulsion	Security Comfort Balance Poise Calm Tranquility	Being secure in a full-time job
Love	Self-consciousness Feeling of being unwanted Feeling of worthlessness Emptiness Loneliness Isolation Incompleteness	Free expression of emotions Sense of wholeness Sense of warmth Renewed sense of life and strength Sense of growing together Sense of growing together Sense of growing together	Experiencing total acceptance in a love relationship
Esteem	Feeling of incompetence Negativism Feeling of inferiority	Confidence Sense of mastery Positive self-regard Self-respect Self-extension	Receiving an award for an outstanding performance on some project
Self-Actualization	Alienation Metapathologies Absence of meaning in life Boredom Routine living Limited activities	Healthy curiosity Peak experiences Realization of potentials Work which is pleasurable and embodies values Creative living	Experiencing a profound insight

(From DiCaprio, 1974, p. 411.)

2. Higher needs appear later in the development of an individual. Self-actualization, for example, may not appear until midlife, while the infant has physiological and safety needs.
3. Higher needs are less necessary for sheer survival, hence their gratification can be postponed longer. Failure to satisfy a higher need does not produce as much of an immediate emergency or a crisis reaction as failure to satisfy a lower need.
4. While they are less necessary for survival, the higher needs nevertheless contribute to survival and growth. Higher-level need satisfaction produces better health, longer life, and a generally enhanced biological efficiency. For this reason, the higher needs are also called *growth needs*.
5. Higher-need satisfaction is productive or beneficial not only biologically but psychologically as well, because it produces deeper happiness, peace of mind, and fullness in one's inner life.
6. Higher-need gratification involves more preconditions and greater complexity than lower-need satisfaction. The search for self-actualization, for example, has the precondition that all the other needs have first been satisfied and involves more complicated and sophisticated behavior and goals than, say, the search for food.
7. Higher-need gratification requires better external conditions (social, economic, and political) than lower-need gratification. For example, greater freedom of expression and opportunity are required for self-actualization than for safety. (pp. 221–222)

D-VALUES VERSUS B-VALUES. This listing indicates that lower and higher needs are in some respects qualitatively distinct. Maslow characterizes the lower needs as deficit (D) values: attainment of their desired goal produces tension reduction and returns the organism to a state of equilibrium. Freud and Hull were exclusively concerned with D-values.

On the other hand, Maslow also postulates that there are being (B) values. B-values are associated with growth motivation, increased tension, and expanded horizons. Among the B-values identified by Maslow are wholeness, perfection, justice, beauty, uniqueness, creativity, and truth. One experiences tension from the need to create, or to produce beauty, but this tension, Maslow asserts, is associated with positive rather than negative affects.

Consequences of Self-Actualization

It has been indicated that humanists assume self-actualization to be an inborn tendency that can be impeded by certain social experiences or by the existence of unfulfilled needs and may be facilitated by appropriate environmental supports. What, then, are the consequences or the behavioral manifestations of the psychological movement toward self-actualization? Rogers (1963) describes the expression of the actualizing tendency with the following illustration:

During a vacation weekend some months ago I was standing on a headland overlooking one of the rugged coves which dot the coastline of northern California. Several large rock outcroppings were at the mouth of the cove, and these received the full force of the great Pacific combers which, beating upon them, broke into mountains of spray before surging into the cliff-lined shore. As I watched the waves breaking over these large rocks in the distance, I noticed with surprise what appeared to be tiny palm trees on the rocks, no more than two or three feet high, taking the pounding of the breakers. Through my binoculars I saw that these were some type of seaweed, with a slender "trunk" topped off with a head of leaves. As one examined a specimen in the interval between the waves it seemed clear that this fragile, erect, top-heavy plant would be utterly crushed and broken by the next breaker. When the wave crunched down upon it, the trunk bent almost flat, the leaves were whipped into a single line by the torrent of water, yet the moment the wave had passed, here was the plant again, erect, tough, resilient. It seemed incredible that it was able to take this incessant pounding hour after hour, day after night, week after week, perhaps, for all I know, year after year, and all the time nourishing itself, extending its domain, reproducing itself; in short, maintaining and enhancing itself in this position which, in our shorthand, we call growth. Here in this palmlike seaweed was the tenacity of life, the forward thrust of life, the ability to push into an incredibly hostile environment and not only hold its own, but to adapt, develop, become itself. (p. 1)

Rogers lists a number of traits or characteristics of self-actualizing (fully functioning) individuals. They include such positive qualities as being self-aware, creative, spontaneous, open to experience, self-accepting, and so on. Adjectives such as happy and satisfied are less appropriate in describing the lives of these individuals, Maslow contends, than are such words as challenging, exciting, and meaningful. Maslow adds to the list of characteristics of self-actualizing individuals social interest, democratic character structure, and the ability to have "peak" experiences in which one feels excellence or perfection.

Empirical Research: Self-Concept

Given the vagueness of humanistic theory, and its identification with ideals and values rather than with science, it should not be surprising that this conception has generated little research and few testable hypotheses. Rather, humanistic thinking primarily has called attention to neglected areas of human motivation that indeed are in need of thought and research.

Perhaps the area of concern most central to humanists is the "self." Constructs such as self-concept and self-esteem are of great importance to the field of motivation. It is evident that individuals experience themselves as separate from the environment and believe that they are the "same" over time. These characteristics, in part, define what is meant by a self-concept. In addition, Hilgard (1949) has even suggested that one's inferred self is responsible for the continuity of particular motivational patterns throughout life.

In the last 30 years there have been, according to McGuire and Padawer-Singer (1976), "a good thousand (if not a thousand good)" investigations of the self (see Wylie, 1961, 1974). Unfortunately, this research has had relatively little yield. Wylie (1968) states:

> Considering the importance assigned to the self-concept in accounting for . . . a wide variety of behavior, it is amazing to be able to find so few statements saying anything definite or potentially operational about the relationship of the self-concept to behavior. (p. 751)

In the following pages I provide an overview of research on the self and examine a few selected research investigations on self-concept and self-esteem. I also will describe research with infrahumans suggesting that self-awareness may not be confined to human beings. The discussion stresses the antecedents of self-awareness and self-esteem, rather than with the consequences of differential self-perception.

Categories of Research

Wylie (1961, 1968) has suggested that research on the self-concept can be grouped, in part, into the following categories:

1. Descriptive studies of the development of the self-concept.

2. Studies of specific variables presumed to influence self-concept development, such as:

   a. Interactions with parents, peers, or other significant social figures.
   b. Gender identity and bodily characteristics.
   c. Prior success and failure.

3. Studies relating self-concept to behaviors, such as performance during experimentally induced success and failure, level of aspiration, personal adjustment, and so on.

Many of these investigations have been guided by the view that the self is a trait of the person. Thus, one's self-concept is assumed to have generalizability across situations and to be relatively enduring over time. But the research data suggest that the self-concept has much specificity; I may, for example, consider myself a failure in social contexts but a success at academic subjects. Or even more specifically, I may perceive myself positively at spelling but negatively at math. Thus, feelings of inferiority and superiority will depend on the specific situation, and particularly the social context (see Webster & Sobieszek, 1974). Furthermore, many of the research investigations have attempted to construct measures of the self-concept. However, these instruments typically are divorced from theoretical considerations, are not heuristic, and have little validity, particularly outside of the situations in which they are used.

Included among the research accepting the idea of a general self-concept was a series of investigations examining the efficacy of client-centered psychotherapy (Rogers & Dymond, 1954). Rogers and Dymond were, in part, concerned with changes during the course of therapy in the client's own discrepancy between self-concept and ideal self. The ideal self refers to the person an individual would like to be, possessing certain positive attributes and free of certain negative characteristics.

One of the most frequently used instruments to assess both self-concept and the ideal self is the Q-sort (Stephenson, 1953). In the Q-sort, the person is presented with a large number of statements, such as:

> I am satisfied with myself.
> I have warm emotional relationships with others.
> I have few values and standards of my own.
> I don't trust my emotions.

These descriptive statements are written on separate cards. The test taker then sorts these cards into categories from "least like me" to "most like me." Typically there are from nine to eleven categories, and each category is assigned a number of points from, say, one to eleven. The respondent is required to place a certain number of cards in each category. Often a normal distribution is imposed by the experimenter, so that the subject must place 2, 4, 8, 11, 16, 18, 16, 11, 8, 4, or 2 cards respectively in each of the eleven categories. This procedure permits specific percepts about the self, as well as the ideal self, to be quantified.

It is then possible to compare numerically the sorts for the self and the ideal self. The difference between the two sorts is called the "self-ideal discrepancy." Lack of correlation, or a negative correlation, reveals feelings of low self-esteem and personal worth, and is one index of maladjustment. By administering the self and the ideal Q-sorts at various times during the course of psychotherapy, the effectiveness of the therapy can be examined.

In one oft-cited investigation guided by these ideas, Butler and Haigh (1954), as part of the Rogers and Dymond project, reported that the self-ideal correlation of individuals seeking psychotherapy averaged $-.01$. However, following therapy this correlation increased to .58, while that of a control group did not change. This finding provides evidence for the effectiveness of client-centered therapy, gives the Q-sort assessment instrument some validity, and illustrates one research endeavor guided by a concern with the self and acceptance of a highly general self-concept.

Determinants of Self-Concept

McGuire and Padawer-Singer (1976) identified some of the situational and personal determinants of one's self-concept, including:

1. Situational demands (e.g., the self-perceptions that are evoked by questions about oneself in a job interview differ from those evoked in a conversation with a new acquaintance).
2. Stimulus intensity (e.g., gross characteristics, such as hair color, are more likely to be part of the self-concept than more subtle characteristics, such as eyebrow shape).

3. Availability (e.g., people are more likely to think of themselves in terms of recent activities than earlier ones).
4. Momentary needs (e.g., current unfulfilled desires are likely to be incorporated into the immediate self-concept).
5. Enduring values (e.g., a long-term religious affiliation is likely to be part of one's self-concept).
6. Past reinforcement history (e.g., what has determined rewards and punishments in the past is likely to be salient in a self-description).

McGuire and Padawer-Singer (1976) contend that in addition to the above factors, an especially important determinant of self-concept is distinctiveness. They state: "We notice any aspect (or dimension) of ourselves to the extent that our characteristic on that dimension is peculiar to our social milieu" (p. 744). Perceived uniqueness is believed to be essential to one's self-perception because:

> the person in a complex stimulus field focuses on points of maximum information, so that one selectively notices the aspects of the object that are most peculiar. . . . Each person is his or her most complex stimulus object . . . hence . . . personal distinctiveness is noticed in one's spontaneous self-concept. (McGuire & Padawer-Singer, 1976, p. 744)

To test these ideas, McGuire and Padawer-Singer asked children in sixth grade to "tell us about yourself." They also collected descriptive information about the children, including physical appearance (e.g., height, weight, hair color, and eye color), demographic characteristics (e.g., birth date and birthplace), and family composition. This information enabled the experimenters to determine the areas of uniqueness for each participant (e.g., whether one's weight or eye color was part of the modal group or was distinctive among members of the class).

The categories of the children's self-descriptions are shown in Table 9–2. The table indicates that self-description frequently involves hobbies, family and friends, attitudes, and teachers. It is of interest to note that pets were mentioned by 22 per cent of the children, although fewer than half of the pupils actually had pets. Thus, "if a child has a pet, she or he is more likely to mention that pet than to mention all other family members combined" (McGuire & Padawer-Singer, 1976, p. 748). Self-evaluation responses (e.g., "I am smart" or "I cry easily") composed only a minimal part of the self-concept. This is especially instructional because, as McGuire and Padawer-Singer (1976) and Wylie (1961) point out, the great majority of the self-concept investigations focus on self-evaluation.

The descriptive statements given by the child (there was an average of about ten statements per child) supported the distinctiveness hypothesis. For example, 70 per cent of the children were born in the city of their present school. Of these, only six per cent mentioned their birthplaces as part of their self-descriptions. But 23 per cent of those born in a different city mentioned their birthplaces. Even more

TABLE 9-2 CATEGORIZATION OF SIXTH GRADERS' RESPONSES TO "TELL US ABOUT YOURSELF"

Category	% of Children	Category	% of Children
Own activities		School (excluding teachers)	71
Hobbies, amusements	48	Miscellaneous	5
Sports	43	Demographic	
Daily schedule	43	Age, birthdate	25
Places lived	5	Name	19
Skills	8	Residence	16
TV	10	Birthplace	11
Books	6	Health	11
Jobs	3	Sex	10
Miscellaneous experiences	6	Race, ethnic	5
Significant others		Religion	3
Family	38	Self-evaluation	
Friends	43	Moral	20
Pets	22	Physical	15
Teachers	16	Intellectual	10
Public figures	0	Emotional	2
Attitudes		Physical characteristics	
Likes and dislikes	52	Hair color	13
Vocational	18	Weight	11
Hopes and desires	12	Height	10
		Eye color	11

(Adapted from McGuire & Padawer-Singer, 1976, p. 748.)

dramatically, 44 per cent of the foreign-born pupils included birthplace in their responses. Similar data are reported for hair color, eye color, and weight.

This research and the reported data seem especially relevant at this time in light of integration attempts involving only a small number of minority students. According to the research of McGuire and Padawer-Singer, for these children race should become an even more integral part of the self-concept.

Do Infrahumans Have a Self-Concept?

An exceedingly interesting question is whether self-awareness, or a self-concept, is an exclusively human characteristic not shared by other species. Research with what is called mirror-image stimulation has provided a tentative answer to this question (see Gallup, 1970, 1975).

For almost any infrahuman, a view of its own image in a mirror functions as a social stimulus. That is, the infrahuman responds as if in the presence of another animal of the same species. Frequently this response is one of aggression, although social facilitation and even egg-laying have been elicited by mirror images. In addition, the mirror reflection is often more effective in eliciting and maintaining certain responses than is a live companion.

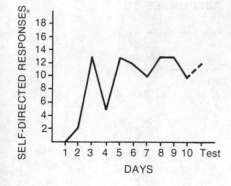

Figure 9–1. Total number of time-sampled responses directed toward the self through the mirror reflection over days. (From Gallup, 1975, p. 323.)

Many humans also do not recognize themselves in the mirror. Children, for example, apparently do not recognize their own reflection until they are about 20 months old (Amsterdam, 1972). In a similar manner, retardates and individuals with congenital but just corrected visual defects exhibit other-directed responses to mirrors. Thus, the ability to recognize the self seems to require experience as well as the capacity to learn.

Gallup (1970) exposed chimpanzees to a full-length mirror for ten consecutive days in a small cage. It was observed that over this period of time the number of self-directed responses increased (see Figure 9–1). These behaviors included grooming parts of the body while watching the results, guiding fingers in the mirror, and picking at teeth with the aid of the mirror. Describing one chimp, Gallup (1975) states:

> Marge used the mirror to play with and inspect the bottom of her feet; she also looked at herself upside down in the mirror while suspended by her feet from the top of the cage; . . . she was also observed to stuff celery leaves up her nose using the mirror for purposes of visually guiding the stems into each nostril. (p. 324).

Then researchers devised a further test of self-recognition. The chimps were anesthetized and marks were placed over their eyebrows and behind their ears, areas the chimps could not directly observe.

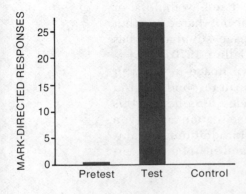

Figure 9–2. Number of mark-directed responses made by experimental animals before being exposed to a mirror and by experimental and control animals during the test of self-recognition. (From Gallup, 1975, p. 326.)

The mirror was temporarily removed from the room, and base-line data regarding their attempts to touch these areas were recorded. Figure 9–2 shows the number of touch attempts both before and after the reintroduction of the mirror. The data clearly suggest that chimps do recognize themselves, or are self-aware, for their attempts to touch the marks increased when they viewed themselves. Citing further evidence for this argument, Gallup notes chimps that had no prior experience with the mirror (the control group in Figure 9–2) did not direct behavior to these marks when first exposed to the mirror. That is, the other chimps must have remembered "what they looked like," and responded to the marks because there were changes in their appearance. Gallup (1975) therefore concluded:

> To the extent that self-recognition implies the existence of a self-concept, the data on chimpanzees would seem to qualify as one of the first experimental demonstrations of a self-concept in a nonhuman form. (p. 330)

Gallup also reports that self-recognition characterizes only chimpanzees among the infrahumans; monkeys and other species exhibit no such recognition.

These findings are even more intriguing because Gallup, McClure, Hill, and Bundy (1971) found that self-recognition is influenced by early experience. Animals reared in isolation do not exhibit the marking effect, whereas animals reared in the wild do (see Figure 9–3).

Many sociologists have proposed a "looking-glass" concept of self, in which self-concept arises out of social interaction with others. Perhaps the social environment provides information about the self, or facilitates an individual's awareness of the self as a distinct entity. I am not sure that sociologists would anticipate that their contentions apply to social interactions among non-verbal species, but their conception does fit nicely with the data shown in Figure 9–3.

Figure 9–3. Number of times any marked portion of the skin was touched by wild-born and isolate chimpanzees during a thirty-minute pretest without the mirror and a thirty-minute test. (From Gallup, 1975, p. 333.)

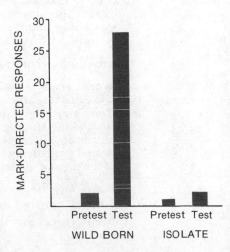

Self-Esteem

It was indicated previously that much of the literature concerning self-concept involves self-esteem. However, self-concept clearly is more than just self-esteem: Self-concept embraces bodily awareness, social roles and self-presentation, enduring values, and the numerous other factors pointed out by McGuire and Padawer-Singer (1976). Self-esteem denotes individuals' evaluations or judgments of themselves. Hence, it is one component of the self-concept and logically appears to be most closely linked with the general affective state, psychological disorders, and perhaps personal adjustment. This justifies somewhat the tendency of the self-concept research to stress evaluative factors.

Self-esteem, just as the more general notion of self-concept, has been shown to fluctuate as a function of the situation confronting the individual. Morse and Gergen (1970) contend that:

> It . . . seems clear that people are often concerned with their personal attractiveness and general value as human beings. They may frequently compare themselves with others in their immediate environment (and in the mass media) to judge their own personal worth. Thus, for example, to find oneself disheveled when those around are tastefully dressed may be humiliating. Or, for the typical student to discover that he has obtained the highest score in his class may boost his self-esteem. (p. 148)

In support of this line of reasoning, it has been reported that high school students from minority groups have lower self-esteem when they live in ethnically mixed, as opposed to homogeneous, neighborhoods (Rosenberg, 1965).

To test these ideas in a controlled laboratory setting, Morse and Gergen (1970) had individuals encounter another person as they were applying for a job. For one-half of the subjects the person observed appeared to be highly desirable:

> He wore a dark suit and appeared well-groomed and self-confident. After he had been seated, he immediately opened an attaché case, pulled out several sharpened pencils, and began to work on his [application] forms diligently. The subject could see that he also had a statistics book, a slide rule, and a copy of a college philosophy text in his case. (Morse & Gergen, 1970, p. 150)

On the other hand, the person encountered by the rest of the subjects

> wore a smelly sweatshirt, ripped trousers, no socks, and seemed somewhat dazed by the whole procedure. He placed his worm paperback edition of The Carpetbaggers on the table in front of him, and after staring aimlessly around the office for a few seconds, began searching for a pencil, which he finally found on the table. Once he began filling out the application, he would periodically stop, scratch his head, and glance around the office as if looking for guidance. (Morse & Gergen, 1970, p. 150)

Among the forms to be completed was a modified version of an inventory created by Coopersmith (1967) that often is used in self-esteem research. The inventory that was used included statements such as "I can make up my mind without too much trouble" and "I'm proud of my work at college so far." Answers to these items were made on simple rating scales. Similar forms of this inventory were filled out both before (pretest) and after (posttest) the arrival of the other person. The data revealed that in the presence of "Mr. Clean" self-esteem dropped nearly four points from the pretest to the posttest, whereas after subjects encountered "Mr. Dirty," self-esteem increased on the scale by almost the same amount.

In sum, self-esteem and, therefore, self-concept are influenced by the social milieu and the social comparison processes that are elicited in a situation. Individuals evaluate themselves relative to others, thus producing fluctuations in feelings of personal worth.

There are, of course, additional sources of influence on self-esteem. For example, it has been demonstrated that physical attractiveness and self-esteem are positively related for females but not for males (Mathes & Kahn, 1975). Furthermore, sex-role identification appears to be linked with self-esteem. In studying early adolescent males, Connell and Johnson (1970) found that high sex-role identification was associated with high self-esteem, while low sex-role identification was related to low self-esteem. (It must be remembered that this was a correlational study and did not demonstrate that identification is a cause of self-esteem). On the other hand, Connell and Johnson (1970) also report that among early adolescent females, role identification and self-esteem are unrelated. In sum, there appear to be meaningful differences in the determinants of self-esteem among males and females.

PERSONAL CONSTRUCT THEORY

As we have seen, humanistic psychologists are particularly concerned with how individuals feel about and perceive themselves, i.e., one's perceived personal value or worth, the dimensions along which the self is known, and the antecedents and the consequences of various self-definitions. Similarly, personal construct theory deals with how the individual organizes the perceived world, that is, the manner in which events are construed or interpreted. Thus, as is true of humanism, personal construct theory is part of the phenomenological approach in psychology. However, in contrast to humanistic theory, thought rather than feeling is stressed, and affect is simply considered one of the consequences of particular thought processes.

Principle of Motivation

George Kelly, the originator of personal construct theory, rejected the notion of motivational constructs. He believed that individuals are continuously active and that the concept of motivation "can appear only as a redundancy" (Kelly, 1958, p. 50). To clarify this position, Kelly stated:

> Suppose we began by assuming that the fundamental thing about life is that it goes on. It isn't that something *makes* you go on; the going on *is the thing itself*. It isn't that motives *make* a man come alert and do things; his alertness is an aspect of his very being. (Kelly, 1962, p. 85)

It would therefore seem inappropriate to examine personal construct theory in this book. However, Kelly equated the concept of motivation exclusively with an energizing or an activating function and the associated constructs of libido, drive and tension. If the field of motivation is broadened to include the more general question of "why organisms behave as they do," it is quite evident that Kelly's conception contains a clear statement about motivation. The underlying goal of the individual, Kelly contended, is to predict and to control the events that are experienced. Hence, Kelly can be included among the mastery theorists. In addition, his ideas are very similar to those of Heider and other attributionists. For example, Kelly assumed that behavior is completely determined by the preceding thought processes, or the manner in which experience is understood (see Diagram 3–3). However, because of his concern with personal adjustment, his association with clinical psychology, and other similarities that will be pointed out, I arbitrarily have chosen to introduce Kelly's work within the same chapter as humanistic psychology, rather than in the earlier chapters that dealt with the more limited topic of perceived causality.

There is, however, a paradox in the contrast between Kelly and the more traditional motivational theorists. By stating that the individual construes the environment in order to predict and to control, Kelly implied that individuals categorize the world "to minimize the disruptive surprises that it can wreak on us" (Bruner, 1956, p. 356). Bruner's insight points out a similarity between personal construct theory and the earlier stimulus reduction conceptions that appear to be antithetical to the Kellian system.

Scientific Behavior as a Model for Human Behavior

It is puzzling that while psychologists try to explain the behavior of their clients, or people in general, the theories they have formulated cannot account for their own scientific activity. For example, if persons are impelled by sexual and aggressive instincts, and if all behavior is directed toward the reduction of these primary urges, as the Freudians argue, then what motivated Freud to formulate his theory of personality? Freud did contend that higher intellectual activities, such as scientific pursuits, are derivatives of instinctual drives and are in service of these basic drives. However, this analysis is far from convincing. In a similar manner, if humans are mere robots, as the behaviorists such as Hull and Skinner would have us believe, then how did the new ideas formulated by Hull and Skinner originate? Furthermore, why should these psychologists even read scientific reports, if only the *behavior* of organisms is reliable and worthy of consideration? In sum, Freudian and Hullian theory, which dominated psychology for so many years, cannot account for the scientific behavior of Freud and Hull.

Kelly's theory of personal constructs can explain scientific endeavors, for Kelly considered the average person an intuitive scientist, having the goal of predicting and understanding behavior. To accomplish this aim, the naive person formulates hypotheses about the world and the self, collects data that confirm or disconfirm these hypotheses, and then alters personal theories to account for the new data. Hence, the average person operates in the same manner as the professional scientist, although professional scientists may be more accurate and more self-conscious in their attempts to achieve cognitive clarity and understanding.

For example, assume that a woman (Nancy) believes that a man (John) has strong negative feelings toward her. When Nancy meets John at a party, she anticipates that he will ignore her, make an insulting remark, or embarrass her in front of friends. However, assume that to the surprise of Nancy, John acts in a friendly manner and seems happy to see her. Assume also that this unanticipated behavior is repeatedly experienced by Nancy so that, in attributional language, John's friendliness at the party cannot be ascribed to a temporary mood state or to the immediate social pressure. On the basis of the new data, Nancy should reformulate her hypothesis and perceive that John likes her. The new construction more accurately predicts behavior and allows her to anticipate correctly the interactions with John.

In discussing his conception of the person as a seeker of truth, Kelly (1955) asserted:

> It is customary to say that *the scientist's ultimate aim is to predict and to control.* This is a summary statement that psychologists frequently like to quote in characterizing their own aspirations. Yet, curiously enough, psychologists rarely credit the human subjects in their experiments with having similar aspirations. It is as though the psychologist were saying to himself, "I, being a *psychologist,* and therefore a *scientist,* am performing this experiment in order to improve the prediction and control of certain human phenomena; but my subject, being merely a human organism, is obviously propelled by inexorable drives welling up within him, or else he is in gluttonous pursuit of sustenance and shelter." (p. 5)

Many other psychologists implicitly accept the conception of the individual as an intuitive scientist. Of great concern to experimental psychologists is the possibility that the subject will infer what the experimenter is trying to prove and then will consciously or unconsciously comply with the hypothesis (Orne, 1962). The "demand characteristics" of the experiment, therefore, must be carefully controlled or concealed in many psychological investigations, particularly in the field of motivation. But the very existence of such controls implies that the subjects search for meaning in their environment, formulate hypotheses, and act on the basis of these belief systems. Of course the subject might perceive the experimenter as a nasty or an intrusive person and then try to "ruin" the experiment by disproving the experimenter's hypothesis. This behavior also is in service of the subject's goal and is based on a personal belief system, as well as on inferences about the purpose of the investigation.

Bannister and Fransella (1971), commenting on the "human as scientist" formulation, note:

> One of the effects of this is to make the model man of personal construct theory look recognizably like you: that is, unless you are the very modest kind of man who can see himself as the stimulus-jerked puppet of learning theory, the primitive infant of psychoanalytic theory, or the perambulating telephone exchange of information theory. If you do not recognize yourself at any point in personal construct theory, you have discovered a major defect in it and are entitled to be suspicious of its claims. (p. 16)

An interesting similarity between humanistic theory and personal construct theory arises as a consequence of the "human as scientist" model. Both the psychologist and the client ("subject") are now equal parts of a dyad. That is, the psychologist is not "higher" than the "naive" person and the person is not a mere "lower object" of study. Rather, as Bannister and Fransella (1971) suggest:

> Construct theory sees each man as trying to make sense out of himself and his world. It sees psychology as a meta-discipline, an attempt to make sense out of the ways in which men make sense out of their worlds. This not only puts the psychologist in the same interpretive business as his so-called subject — it makes them partners in the business, for on no other basis can one man understand another. (p. 42)

Note, then, that similar to the attribution theorists, Kelly proposed an ultrarational image of humans. To understand a person's thoughts is to understand the person. Bruner (1956) speculates that this theory of personality was, in part, a product of the particular clinical experiences that Kelly encountered. For many years Kelly was a counselor of college students. Rather than patients with hysterical paralyses or bizarre dreams, "the young men and women of Professor Kelly's clinical examples are worried about their dates, their studies, and even their conformity" (Bruner, 1956, p. 357). Hence, Kelley spent relatively little time considering the unconscious, deep-seated urges, or even defenses. As with the other conceptions presented in this book, his ideas are therefore able to account well for some aspects of behavior, but cannot begin to explain other phenomena (see the final chapter in this book for an elaboration of this point).

Philosophical Position: Constructive Alternativism

Kelly labelled his basic philosophical assumption *constructive alternativism*, or "epistimological responsibility" (Kelly, 1966, p. 31). Meaning, Kelly asserted, is not inherent in an event, but depends upon how the person construes or interprets that event. He stated:

> The events we face today are subject to as great a variety of construction as our wits enable us to contrive . . . All our present perceptions are open to

question and reconsideration . . . . The most obvious occurrences of everyday life might appear utterly transformed if we were inventive enough to
construe them differently. (Kelly, 1966, p. 28)

Thus, there is no "reality;" reality depends on the eyes of the
beholder. Hence, some of Kelly's ideas are closely associated with the
psychoanalytic notion that needs, values, and similar factors influence
"reality."

Because meaning is subject to change, Kelly reasoned that individuals are personally responsible (i.e., *able* to respond) for their own future.
Nature does not dictate one's life; or, as Kelly contended, "no one needs
to be the victim of his biography." This position again links personal
construct theory with humanistic thinking by placing change processes
within the grasp and capability of the individual. Credit for a successful
life and blame for an unsuccessful life are attributed directly to the actor.
One might say that Kelly construed responsibility and coping, or "psychological initiative," along an internal-external dimension and perceived that one is (or can be) an "origin" rather than a "pawn."

Formal Theory

Kelly's formal theory consists of one fundamental postulate and
eleven corollaries. I will briefly examine the postulate and some of the
corollaries, selecting those that shed the most light on his conception of
behavior.

Fundamental Postulate. *A person's processes are psychologically
channelized by the ways in which he anticipates events.* By this Kelly
meant that an individual's *life* (conduct) is guided by how the world is
construed. Furthermore, the predictive power of the construal is demonstrated or proven by how much sense has been made out of the world,
i.e., the accuracy with which one is able to predict future events. Kelly
(1966) asserted that: "Confirmation or disconfirmation of one's predictions are accorded greater psychological significance than rewards, punishments, or . . . drive reduction" (p. 38).

Individual Corollary. *Persons differ from each other in their construction of events.* Since individuals perceive the same objective stimulus situation in a different manner, it follows that their behaviors also
will differ. Furthermore, because no two constructions are exactly alike,
each person is unique. This is in accord with the position of humanists
such as Allport and Maslow.

Dichotomy Corollary. *A person's construction system is composed
of a finite number of dichotomous constructs.* Kelly asserted that all
constructs are bipolar, or dichotomous. Hence, if we perceive an individual as honest and sincere, we implicitly deny that the individual is dishonest and insincere. A construct, therefore, also involves a contrast.

Range Corollary. *A construct is convenient for the anticipation of a
finite range of events only.* A given construction is not appropriate for all
events. For example, the construct tall-short may be appropriate for the

anticipation of play on a basketball court, but is likely to be quite irrelevant in predicting an individual's honesty. Kelly distinguished between the "range of convenience" and the "focus of convenience" of a construct. The range of convenience indicates the breadth of different phenomena to which a construct may be applied. The focus of convenience refers to the area in which the construct is maximally useful. Thus, the focus involves those events for which the construct was developed.

The range and focus notions frequently are employed by scientists when describing and evaluating psychological theories. Freudians, for example, argue that the range of convenience of their theory includes war, wit, and neurosis; such generalizability is a positive attribute of a theory. But perhaps the focus of convenience of the Freudian model is intrapersonal conflict. A similar description of the range and focus of convenience of all the theories presented in this book could be made and would prove useful for purposes of comparison and evaluation (see the following chapter).

Experience Corollary.   A person's construction system varies as he successfully construes the replication of events. Since a construct is akin to a hypothesis, the confirmation or disconfirmation of a hypothesis may result in the changing of constructs. Kelly suggests that confirmation may lead to as much future change as disconfirmation because confirmation prompts the exploration of new experiences, which expose the person to situations that require the alteration of the present construct system.

Psychotherapy, in Kelly's perspective, is a process in which one's construct system is altered with the aid of a therapist. The therapist first must discover how the client is perceiving the world and then assist the client in reorganizing the old system and in finding new constructs that are more functional. The therapist might help the client design and implement "experiments" that test particular hypotheses. For example, if an individual perceives a parent or a spouse as "aggressive" or "dominating," special behaviors might be suggested to test whether this perception is "valid," i.e., aids in the anticipation of events. Role playing and modeling frequently are used to help alter construct systems. The therapist might suggest, for example, that the client act as if the parent or the spouse were not aggressive or not dominant in order to test an alternative hypothesis. (Earlier in his life Kelly taught drama, and that may in part account for his selection of role playing as a technique for altering construct systems.)

In one social experiment involving the change of constructs, the subjects were teachers who believed that their students were not learning because the children were "lazy" (Kelly, 1958). Experimenters suggested that the teachers give the children nothing to do in the classroom and see what happens. Of course, the pupils would not sit without activity. On the basis of this contradictory evidence, the teachers began to consider the school environment and their own inadequacy as causes of poor learning, rather than blaming the problems entirely on the children.

The Role Construct Repertory (Rep) Test

Kelly devised a particularly ingenious testing instrument to ascertain an individual's personal construct system. The test reflects Kelly's belief that the psychologist should not impose constructs on the test taker as, for example, is the case in tests of internal-external locus of control. This particular construal or dimension of thought may be irrelevant to the test taker. Rather, the respondents should be allowed to display the constructs that they naturally use to give meaning to the world.

In the Role Construct Repertory (Rep) Test, the test taker first lists the names of individuals who play or have played certain roles in his or her life, such as mother, father, rejecting person, threatening person, and so on. On the standard Rep Test grid, shown in Figure 9–4, the three circles in each row designate three roles to be considered together. For each triad the subject determines the construct, such as cold-warm or dominant-submissive, that links two individuals in the triad and differentiates them from the third member. This procedure clearly is guided by Kelly's belief in the bipolarity of constructs. The construct selected is assumed to represent a dimension along which significant people in the respondent's life are ordered, or compared. Row 1 of the grid, for

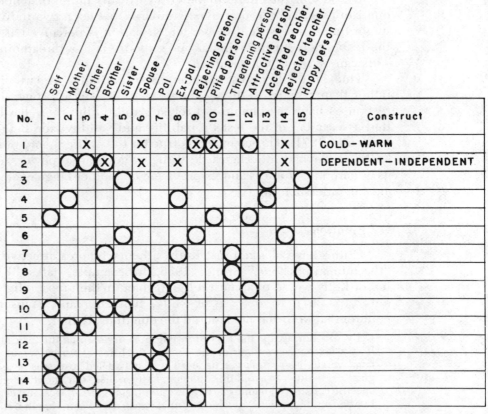

Figure 9–4. Simplified grid form of Rep Test.

example, indicates that a respondent perceives the individuals identified as rejecting and pitied to be cold and the attractive person to be warm. The respondent then judges the remaining 12 people as having or not having the quality (coldness) of the two linked individuals in the triad, and places an X in the box if that particular characteristic is possessed. Figure 9–4 shows that father, spouse, and rejected teacher are perceived as cold. The respondent completes the remaining 14 rows in this manner, selecting a construct for each triad.

Using sophisticated but not difficult mathematical techniques akin to factor analysis, the tester can reduce the constructs chosen to just a few basic ones that represent the respondent's typical way of perceiving and classifying others. Even without training, however, the reader can ascertain which constructs vary together and thus are not distinct. For example, if the reader reports that men are cold and women are warm, and uses male-female to distinguish members of another triad, then we know that warm-cold also could have been selected as the construct to differentiate the second triad. That is, male and coldness, and female and warmth, are not used as separate constructs. If all the constructs in a grid are highly interrelated, then the respondent may experience anxiety because the construct sytem is too narrow to accommodate new situations.

By viewing the circles in the grid vertically rather than horizontally, one can ascertain the perceived similarity between two individuals. It might be of interest to discover which parent is perceived as most like the respondent, or how similar one's spouse is to a threatening person. This can be readily determined.

Thus far the Rep Test has been used sparingly, primarily in clinical rather than research settings. Some reliability studies suggest that grid responses have reasonable test-retest stability, but there has been limited assessment of the test's reliability and validity (see Bannister and Fransella, 1971). This comment is true for the entire theory proposed by Kelly. It has had little heuristic value or generative power, in spite of its apparent usefulness and its provision of another language for psychological understanding.

Emotions

Critics have charged that Kelly's theory ignores affective states, or "the human passions." Bruner (1956), for example, states: "I wish Professor Kelly would treat most religious men in their most religious moments" (p. 357). In defense of Kelly, Bannister and Fransella (1971) counter that Kelly has not ignored the emotions. Rather,

> Kelly did not accept the cognition-emotion division as intrinsically valid. It is a jargon descendant of the ancient dualities of *reason* versus *passion*, *mind* versus *body*, *flesh* versus *spirit* which had led to dualistic psychologies. . . . In order to avoid this dualism, Kelly focuses our attention on certain specific constructs, namely *anxiety, hostility, guilt, threat, fear,* and *aggression*, but defines them all as "awareness" that construct systems are in transitional states. (pp. 34–35)

Anxiety, according to Kelly, occurs when one's construct system provides no means for dealing with an experience. Bannister and Fransella (1971) elaborate this as follows:

> We become anxious when we can only partially construe the events which we encounter and too many of their implications are obscure. Sex for the chaste, adulthood for the adolescent, books for the illiterate, power for the humble and death for nearly all of us tend to provoke anxiety. It is the *unknown* aspect of things that go bump in the night that give them their potency. (p. 35)

In a similar manner, interacting with a person whom we cannot understand often gives rise to vague feelings of uneasiness. And even greater anxiety is experienced when starting a new job or confronting a new environment. If anxiety reactions are frequent and severe, the range of constructs must be broadened so that more phenomena can be incorporated. Disconfirmation of a belief also arouses anxiety because it reveals an inadequacy in the construct system. Anxiety, therefore, is not necessarily bad, for this affective experience is one precondition for construct change.

Kelly distinguished between threat and anxiety, although both result from defective, and therefore transitional, conceptual systems. *Threat* is experienced when a fundamental change is about to occur in one's construct system. For example, threat is experienced "when our major beliefs about the nature of our personal, social, and practical situation are invalidated and the world around us appears to become chaotic" (Bannister & Fransella, 1971, p. 37). Thus, for example, questioning the purpose of life is threatening, for it is likely to lead to basic conceptual changes. In a similar manner, a deeply involving extramarital affair may alter one's conception of what it is to be a parent or a spouse, and thus may engender a threat. Psychotherapists have to be aware of the possibility that they may be viewed as threatening inasmuch as they are perceived as agents of construct change.

Finally, in Kelly's system *guilt* results from a discrepancy between one's ideal self and one's actions. Thus, "if you find yourself doing, in important respects, those things you would not have expected to do if you are the kind of person you always thought you were, then you suffer from guilt" (Bannister & Fransella, 1971, p. 36). It therefore follows that if you value dishonesty, and see yourself as dishonest, then honest actions should produce feelings of guilt!

Summary: Kelly's Theory

Kelly asserted that humans are intuitive scientists, construing the world in idiosyncratic ways to give it meaning. Meaning is the interpretation of events with dichotomous constructs; it enables one to predict (anticipate) the future. Construct systems are not immutable; individuals are able to produce alternate constructs, and they are personally responsible for their own well-being. Finally, certain emotions, such as anxiety, threat, and guilt, are products of construct systems that are inadequate and undergoing change.

Kelly's conception is unlike other clinically derived theories and provides an alternate language for understanding (construing) human action. It has not generated a great deal for research (the reader will note that no research studies are cited in this discussion), but it has given rise to new and valuable insights and to a novel method of measurement. I anticipate that in the future this theory will be elaborated and made more precise so that it leads to testable hypotheses and research investigations.

IMPLICIT PSYCHOLOGY

Psychologists are becoming increasingly interested in a distinction between *science* and *ethnoscience*, i.e., the reasons people behave as they do versus the perceived reasons that they behave as they do. (The latter is also known positively as "folk wisdom" and negatively as "bubba psychology;" see Wegner and Vallacher, 1977). It is evident that individuals have ideas, and often elaborate theories, about what people are like and what motivates them. Although these theories are "implicit" (Bruner and Tagiuri, 1954), they determine social reality.

Implicit theories of trait or attribute covariation already have received much attention from psychological researchers (see Schneider, 1973). Beliefs such as "fat people are jolly," "people who wear glasses are introverts," and "intelligent people are witty" are examples of such implicit theories of personality. Individuals often are not consciously aware that they hold such theories, and they do not put them systematically to test. But these notions do greatly influence expectations and actions.

The Rep test devised by Kelly represents one attempt to measure implicit theories of person-perception by ascertaining the constructs people employ as well as the perceived interrelationships among these constructs. Indeed, as already indicated, Kelly's entire theory rests upon the presumption that people are naive scientists, formulating idiosyncratic psychological theories. Furthermore, Kelly even contends that, at times, these theories do not "work" and that the individual must be aided in the construction of "better" theories.

In addition to implicit theories of personality and person-perception, there are implicit theories of child psychology, abnormal psychology, psychodynamics, and virtually any other area within psychology. For example, we exhibit our implicit ideas about children in the ways that we communicate with them. As Wegner and Vallacher (1977) state:

> The hostess at a dinner party is not likely to say "Hot, hot!" when she places a steaming dish before a guest, but often makes similar remarks to her five-year-old. She does not say "Look both ways, now" when she sends the guests across the street to their cars, but often will repeat this warning to her child. . . .Many of these wholesome and insipid expressions would be totally inappropriate in adult conversation. (p. 303) (see Gleason, 1973)

In a similar manner, implicit theories of abnormal psychology abound. After the layperson had been introduced to Freudian theory, often through "pop psychology" sources, early childhood experience became perceived as an important cause of adult abnormal behavior. For example, schizophrenia or autism is now attributed to "bad" child-rearing practices, sibling rivalry, Oedipal wishes, and so forth.

Implicit theories of motivation already have been examined in this book, and include Kelly's theory of personal constructs. But the clearest example of such a theory is the attributional work of Heider. Heider intuited that in achievement-related contexts the naive person believes behavior is, in part, determined by ability and effort. Furthermore, these two factors are perceived as multiplicatively related: The absence of either reduces the perceived effective personal force to zero.

The naive psychology of the layperson and the "true" laws of personality, child psychology, abnormal psychology, and motivation may or may not be identical. For example, most laypersons are unaware that certain types of schizophrenia have a strong genetic component and that active schizophrenia among these individuals may be unrelated to early experience such as parent-child interactions. In a similar manner, it may be that in particular achievement-related contexts performance is determined by effort plus luck, or, as Atkinson suggests, unconscious motives × probability of success × the incentive value of success, rather than the naive formulation of ability × effort.

An investigation by Whiteman (1967) illustrates some of the differences between the "science" of defense mechanisms and defenses as perceived (or not perceived) by younger children. Whiteman presented children with a number of scenarios, such as:

> *Displacement theme.* "There was once a little girl named Jane. One day her mother promised that Jane's favorite dessert, ice cream, would be served at supper. But Jane's mother forget to buy the ice cream, and so there wasn't any ice cream for dessert. Jane didn't say anything to her mother about the ice cream. After supper Jane went to play with her dolls and did something she never did before. She spanked her dolls. Why did she spank her dolls? (Whiteman, 1967, pp. 145-146)

Whiteman (1967) reports that a large percentage of the younger children (ages five to six) did not relate the psychological reaction (e.g., spanking the dolls) to the given psychological cause (e.g., ice cream deprivation). Rather, in the displacement theme, the younger children attributed the spanking to, for example, the naughtiness of the doll. In sum, the "science" of defense mechanisms outlined by Freud and subsequent ego psychologists contrasts with the perceived laws of behavior voiced by younger children.

It also is evident, however, that science and ethnoscience overlap and are interactive. One does perceive, for example, that the outcome of a die toss is at least partially, if not wholly, chance-determined. And extensive media coverage has conveyed some of the laws of psychology to the layperson. But it is reasonable to assume that in most instances the naive person is not conversant with the "complete" laws of behavior, particularly, for example, the mathematical relations between the components in a motivational model.

In addition to the "real" laws that influence naive psychology, the perceived laws are likely to affect the "real" determinants of action. For instance, what we believe about children and how we communicate with them influence their comprehension and language acquisition. In some sense the way we communicate with children is a "self-fulfilling prophecy," for the naive belief is influencing the actual capabilities of the child and, hence, the "real" science. In a similar manner, if we perceive ourselves as having free will, then this implicit theory has to be considered among the real determinants of action. That is, assuming that thoughts influence behavior, free will (a typical "naive" belief) and determinism (a typical scientific stance) are not mutually exclusive. Indeed, to make matters even more complex, the so-called "real" laws are imposed by scientists and are themselves only constructions. As Kelly has contended, there is no reality independent of the perceiver.

Summary

Humanistic theory, known as the "third force" in psychology, stresses the subjective experience of the human actor. Humanists such as Rogers and Maslow presume that individuals strive to maximize their inborn potentialities. These self-actualization tendencies may be inhibited because of socializing experiences that promote "conditions of worth" or because of the lack of satisfaction of the lower, and relatively stronger, physiological needs. Maslow contends that the lower needs represent D (deficit) values, whereas the higher needs are B (being) values. Deficit values are satisfied through need reduction, whereas being values are linked with tension increments.

The main areas of empirical research connected with humanism pertain to self-concept and self-esteem. This research has had relatively little pay-off, in part because of the invalid assumption of many researchers that the self-concept is stable and generalizable across situations. Also, self-concept research often involves the construction of individual difference scales that have little validity outside of the particular setting in which they are used. The absence of theoretical advances to guide scale construction is partially responsible for this problem.

Researchers have identified a number of factors that influence self-concept and self-esteem, including distinctive personal characteristics and the perceived characteristics of others. Hence, social comparison processes play an important role in determining one's self-definition. In addition, there is some evidence that self-concept changes during the course of psychotherapy and becomes more closely aligned with the ideal-self. Finally, some infrahumans apparently have a self-concept. Mirror-image studies using chimpanzees have shown that members of this species do recognize themselves in a mirror. Chimps familiar with their mirror images respond to changes in body markings that are visible only in the mirror.

Personal construct theory, which is considered one of a number of "implicit psychologies," is related to humanistic theory because both:

1. Accept the phenomenological approach to psychology.
2. Are concerned with the perception of self and others.
3. Assume that individuals are personally responsible for their fate.
4. Place the subject (client) and the experimenter (therapist) on equal levels.

The primary creator of personal construct theory was George Kelly. Kelly assumed that individuals strive to master and understand their environments. Individuals are construed as naive scientists, testing hypotheses and discarding the ones that do not enable them to anticipate events correctly. Thus, psychology is conceived as a meta-discipline, attempting to make sense out of the way people make sense of their worlds. Kelly also assumed that: 1) individuals perceive the world in dichotomous constructs; 2) there are individual differences in construals; and 3) constructs may change as a result of new experiences. To assess personal constructs, Kelly devised the Rep Test. This is a free response measure that has respondents reveal how certain figures in their lives are similar and different from one another. In addition, according to Kelly, emotions such as anxiety, threat, and guilt are consequences of particular ways of construing the world.

Kelly's theory and humanistic theory have generated few testable hypotheses and little experimental research. But these conceptions have contributed to the study of motivation in many ways. First, they have called attention to problems ignored in the more traditional approaches to motivation, such as striving to self-actualize, the determinants of self-concept and self-esteem, and so on. Second, they have suggested novel theoretical linkages for the understanding of human behavior and generated a new scientific vocabularly that includes such phrases as "unconditional positive regard," "focus of convenience," and "range of convenience." And finally, these approaches have given the "subjects" of study greater prestige and dignity. This has important ethical, as well as methodological, implications for the study of humans, and offers an alternate conception of humans that contrasts with the previously dominant views of Freud and Hull.

The humanistic and personal construct approaches are relatively new; their potentialities remain to be realized and demonstrated. Thus, at present, these approaches must be regarded as guides for future discoveries.

Section IV

Conclusion

Chapter Ten

OVERVIEW AND
CONCLUDING
REMARKS

Often in the final chapter of a book the author integrates, or attempts to integrate, all that went before. A grand scheme is devised, or some sweeping generalizations are offered. Unfortunately, I have no such insights to suggest; there is no grand design, no overall conception, that can bring together under one common framework the wealth of material discussed in the preceding chapters.

In this concluding chapter I would first like to present an overview of the prior chapters. Seven theories of human motivation were considered: psychoanalytic, drive, field, achievement, social learning, attributional, and humanistic. These conceptual frameworks were created to account for quite disparate phenomena. The theories rarely are commensurate; they cannot be easily compared with regard to one or more phenomena so that we can judge one as "better" or "worse" than the others in its ability to predict or explain these phenomena. There are, of course, some exceptions to this statement and instances in which comparisons are possible. For example, attribution theory and social learning theory offer contrasting explanations of expectancy shifts: Attributionists relate expectancy change to causal stability, whereas social learning theorists relate expectancy shifts to causal locus. Similarly, attribution theory and achievement theory offer contrasting explanations of intermediate difficulty choice: Attributionists relate choice to information gain, while achievement theorists specify that the choice of intermediate tasks maximizes resultant pleasure. In another example of theoretical comparison, psychoanalytic and social learning theories anticipate different consequences arising from viewing an aggressive behavior: Psychoanalytic theorists might expect decreases in subsequent aggression (catharsis); social learning theorists would predict increases in displayed aggression (modeling). But these comparisons, and others that I have not repeated here, are relatively rare given the array of phenomena that the conceptual frameworks attempt to explain. Furthermore, the so-called "crucial" experiments that differentiate between the theories typically are not definitive, even for the single phenomenon under consideration (e.g., modeling could be displayed following the viewing of aggressive behavior, yet there still might be catharsis and the reduction of a persisting aggressive drive).

In sum, the theories must stand side-by-side in a horizontal array, rather than vertically in a hierarchical ordering of "goodness." While this state of affairs is not unique to the field of motivation, the coexistence of alternate theoretical conceptions in psychology is perhaps most prevalent in molar areas of study.

The theories that were discussed in the first nine chapters can be compared and contrasted along many dimensions (see Table 10–1). Table 10–1 first lists the major theories presented in the text (subtheories such as dissonance, arousal and helplessness are not included in the table). The persons most closely identified with the theories, and the 20-year spans in which the major contributions were made, are shown in columns 2 and 3. It is evident from the table that there is a chronological separation between the development of psychoanalytic, drive, and field theories and the origin of other conceptions. This difference, in part, accounts for the relative lack of recent progress in the former group of theories. Skipping across to columns 9 and 10, the reader will observe that the "older" theories use energy constructs and rely on the concept of homeostasis: Behavior is undertaken to return the organism to some state of internal equilibrium and to "turn off" the energy. This is accomplished by the reduction of a biological need or, in the case of Lewinian theory, by the reduction of a "quasi-need" that is not rooted in the viscera. But this mechanical and homeostatic conception of behavior has lost favor and is not represented among the more recently formulated conceptions of human action.

Column 4 of Table 10–1 lists some of the main concepts of the theories. Of course, this is not a complete catalogue, but it is a fairly inclusive recounting of the conceptual frameworks. Columns 5 and 6 include some of the phenomena for which the theory is relevant. Again, this is not a complete representation, but it does indicate the goals and the "flavor" of each conception.

The phenomena listed in columns 5 and 6 illustrate why the theories are not commensurate and why it is not possible to declare that one is "better" than the others (although each does have particularly favorable and unfavorable features). Each theory can explain some phenomena with some degree of insight and accuracy, while other phenomena are beyond its "range of convenience." For example, one cannot expect psychoanalytic theory, as encompassing as it is, to account for expectancy shifts at skill and chance tasks, any more than one can expect social learning theory to have much to say about slips of the tongue or the origination of the incest taboo. In a similar manner, achievement theory does not examine the psychological determinants of aggression, and drive theory is irrelevant to the problem of choice between achievement tasks that differ in level of difficulty.

Column 7 in Table 10–1 classifies the theories as mechanistic or cognitive. This distinction was the basis of my earlier book, *Theories of Motivation*. In most instances the theories contain both mechanistic and cognitive concepts. For example, psychoanalytic theory includes assumptions about energy and energy distribution and also conscious and unconscious thought processes. Likewise, Lewinian field theory is phenomenological (the field as construed by the person at a moment in time), yet the phenomenological field has forces that impel the person to action, and the strongest force "wins." In a similar manner, social learning theory makes use of the concept of expectancy, yet is tied to Skinnerian and Hullian versions of stimulus-response learning, and achievement theory includes many mechanistic concepts not discussed here, yet infers need strength from imaginative thought. In sum, both mechanistic principles and mental concepts are used to account for human action.

On the other hand, drive theory is classified as entirely mechanistic, while attribution and humanistic theories are entirely cognitive. As column 11 shows, the two cognitive theories are phenomenologies, as is Lewinian field theory.

Column 8 in the table is guided by a distinction made in the introductory chapter of this book. Some theories have attempted to create quasi-mathematical models of motivated behavior. That is, the determinants of action were identified, and then the mathematical relations between the components of the model were specified. Typically these models have been guided by data derived from laboratory experimentation. The models that have been postulated are shown in simplified forms in parentheses. It should be noted that Lewin and Rotter were less specific about the mathematical relations of the components in their models.

It is evident from column 8 that three of the theories make central use of the concept of goal expectancy. In addition, the attributional conception of motivation presented here also takes the form of an expectancy-value theory. However, there is not an explicit attempt among the attributionists to create a mathematical model of behavior. Conversely, psychoanalytic and humanistic theory grew from clinical observations rather than from controlled laboratory experimentation. Instead of formulating more precise models of action, advocates of these approaches identified and documented the basic principles of behavior through everyday observations, literary anecdotes, and clinical evidence. Attribution theory as formulated by Heider also follows this approach.

Finally, column 12 shows the individual-difference measures that are associated with the theories. Both achievement theory and social learning theory place great reliance on the respective measurement of achievement needs (with the TAT) and locus of control (with the I-E

TABLE 10–1 OVERVIEW OF THEORETICAL PERSPECTIVES

1 Theory	2 Contributors (discussed here)	3 20-Year Span of Main Contributions	4 Main Concepts	5 Empirical Focus
Psychoanalytic	Freud	1900–1920	Id, ego, super-ego, energy, cathexis, instinct, pleasure-pain principle	Neurosis, dreams, slips of the tongue, defenses, incest taboo
Drive	Hull, Spence, Miller	1930–1950	Drive, habit, incentive, anticipatory goal response, drive reduction	Deprivation effects on intensity, latency, and resistance to extinction; aversive conditioning
Field	Lewin	1920–1940	Tension, valence, life space, psychological distance, region, overlapping force fields, force, potency	Recall and resumption of incompleted tasks, substitution, level of aspiration, conflict
Achievement	Atkinson, McClelland	1950–1970	Motive, expectancy, incentive, emotional anticipation, tendency	Risk preference (aspiration level), persistance at achievement tasks
Social Learning	Rotter	1955–1975	Expectancy, generalized expectancy, value, locus of control	Expectancy shifts, expectancy generalization, information seeking and use
Attribution	Heider, Kelley, Weiner	1960–	Cause, causal schemata, causal dimensions, expectancy, affect	Causal inferences, expectancy shift, affective reaction, interpersonal evaluation
Humanistic	Maslow, Rogers	1950–1970	Positive self-regard, conditional regard, unconditional regard	Self-ideal discrepancy, openness to experience, self-actualization

TABLE 10-1 OVERVIEW OF THEORETICAL PERSPECTIVES *(Continued)*

Theory	6 Empirical Range	7 Mechanistic or Cognitive	8 Math Model	9 Basic Principle of Behavior	10 Principle of Homeostasis (use of energy concepts)	11 Phenomenology	12 Related Individual-Difference Measure
Psychoanalytic	De-individuation effects, delay of gratification, authoritarianism, cognitive styles and controls	Mixture	No	Reduce instinctual urges (free energy)	Yes	No	Cognitive styles (cognitive control)
Drive	Paired-associates learning, social facilitation, emotions, aggression, frustration, dissonance-related phenomena, conflict	Mechanistic	Yes $(D \times H)$	Reduce internal stimulation (drive stimuli)	Yes	No	Manifest Anxiety Scale
Field	Frustration, regression, feeble-mindedness	Mixture	Yes $\dfrac{(t,\, G)}{e}$	Bring regions into equilibrium	Yes	Yes	None
Achievement	Task recall, coalition formation, economic development, achievement change	Mixture	Yes $(M \times E \times I)$	Increase positive and reduce negative emotional states	No	No	Thematic Apperception Test
Social Learning	Antisocial behavior, delay of gratification	Mixture	Yes $(E,\, RV)$	Satisfy needs	No	No	Locus of Control (I-E) Scale
Attributional	Dissonance-related phenomena, superstitious behavior, helping, parole decisions, depression	Cognitive	No	Gain information	No	Yes	None
Humanistic		Cognitive	No	Self-actualize, enhance self	No	Yes	Q-sort

scale). This is less true in the case of drive theory, which was merely extended to incorporate individual differences in emotional reactivity. Testing and identification of individual differences are of even lesser importance in psychoanalytic and humanistic theories. In neither of these conceptions are the assessment tests and empirical data from individual difference studies central or necessary to theoretical developments.

Of course, many measures pertinent to the conceptions presented in the book are not included in Table 10–1. For example, the repression-sensitization scale and the authoritarian (F) scale are relevant to the psychoanalytic theory of action, as is the Test Anxiety Questionnaire for achievement theory. And again, it must be emphasized that Table 10–1 includes only some of the dimensions along which the theories can be compared and contrasted. But sufficient information is provided in the table to reveal the idiosyncracies of each conception as well as possible points of overlap and intersection.

A "Complete" Theory and Future Directions

The diversity of constructs and phenomena in Table 10–1 accurately indicates the complexity that a "complete" theory of motivation will have to exhibit. First of all, and quite obviously, such a general theory will need many, many concepts. Years ago Kurt Lewin said:

> Psychology cannot try to explain everything with a single construct, such as association, instinct, or gestalt. A variety of constructs has to be used. (Lewin, 1935, p. 7)

Given the diversity shown in Table 10–1, one can hardly disagree with Lewin's conclusion.

What, then, are the broad observations that one must try to explain with such a complete theory? They are many, including:

1. *Humans are rational.* They can consciously employ coping strategies to handle threat and anxiety (ego psychologists); cognitions are compared to see if they "fit" (Festinger); goal expectancies are calculated, payoff matrixes are roughly formulated, and logical decisions are made (Lewin, Atkinson, Rotter); information is sought and processed, causal inferences are made (Heider, Kelley), and self-insight may be attained (Maslow, Rogers).

2. *Humans are irrational.* Motivations are unconscious, instincts urge for expression, and we defend ourselves in ways unknown to us (Freud); sources of motivation pool together and become undifferentiated (Hull); in times of stress and frustration, distinctions are blurred (Lewin); goal expectancies are biased and humans are impelled toward or away from goals by unknown hopes and fears (Atkinson); overgeneralizations are made when there have been prior unfavorable outcomes and perceived lack of control (Seligman); information is not properly processed, illogical decisions are

reached, and causal inferences are faulty (decision theorists); and there is gross personal delusion (humanists).

3. *There are multiple principles and determinants of action, and often they are apparently contradictory or mutually exclusive.* For example, there is a striving to maximize pleasure and minimize pain (Freud), and a striving to gain information even though that knowledge may be unpleasant (Heider); there is a tendency to reduce stimulation by satisfying needs (Freud, Hull), and a tendency to increase stimulation and create new need systems (Hebb, Berlyne); behavior is reflexive, not mediated by thought processes (Hull, Spence), and behavior is reflective, guided by higher mental processes (Heider); society is restrictive, causing the foregoing of gratifications (Freud), and society is facilitative, providing the means and the opportunities for higher satisfactions (Rogers, Maslow); rewards are motivating (Hull), and repeated rewards lead to boredom and a decrement in intrinsic interest (Atkinson, Deci). Clearly, this listing of opposites could go on and on. Because in any given situation any of the above principles may be operating, the creation of a general theory of motivation is, indeed, a difficult undertaking.

Suggestions for Theory Construction

I would now like to offer a few very general and modest suggestions for the building of a general theory of motivation. These are merely guidelines that reflect the writer's present personal biases.

Where to Start?

There is a controversy among theorists concerning the appropriate data for theory building in psychology. Lewin believed that the psychologist should study the complex phenomena that occur in nature: The existing problems, rather than the availability of "proper" methodology," should guide theory construction. Lewin argued that the purpose of psychology is to explain the events that one observes in everyday life.

In contrast to this position, Spence (1957) contended that the study of motivation should be built upon an understanding of simple standing of simple phenomena such as animal learning and classical conditioning. He stated:

> One must also agree . . . that we objectivists have tended to concentrate our efforts in these simpler areas; not, however . . . because we have any special aversion to the problems of personality and certainly not because we have a preference . . . "for externals rather than internals, for elements rather than patterns, for geneticism, and for a passive or reactive organism rather than for one that is spontaneous and active." The explanation of our interests is, I think, much simpler. . . . We have chosen to investigate simpler phenomena first because we are of the belief that prog-

ress in the formulation of psychological laws and theories will be more rapid in this area than in the case of more complex behavior. We also believe that many of the variables and laws isolated in the study of simpler forms of behavior will be operative in more complex instances, interacting presumably with the additional factors introduced into these more complex situations. If such is the case it would appear to be more efficient in the long run to investigate the simpler phenomena first. (pp. 102-3)

As an alternative to these contradictory strategies, I suggest that we use as our starting point for theory building relatively complex phenomena that can be reproduced with certainty in laboratory experimentation. That is, the phenomena should be complex yet should have the virtues of a conditioning experiment, specifically, the ability to produce base-rate information that is constant between experimental laboratories. For example, considering the attributional perspective, with which I am most familiar:

1. Expectancy shifts differ in games of skill and chance. There is no doubt that expectancies rise more after success and drop more after failure in skill- rather than luck-determined settings, assuming that the situations are accurately perceived by the respondents.
2. Individuals prefer intermediate risk. We prefer a competitor somewhat our equal in skill, and tasks that are of intermediate difficulty; in achievement settings, we form groups that maximize the relative equality of the teams.
3. Attributions of success to, for example, luck versus other people's aid versus skill lead to the affective reactions of surprise, gratitude, or confidence respectively. Given failure, the affects given these three attributions are surprise, vindictiveness, and lack of confidence (feelings of incompetence) respectively.

Because of the reasonable clarity (certainty and replicability) of these experimental results, they can serve as building blocks for understanding related phenomena and more complex problems.

The Environment

Psychologists have worked for many years to create taxonomies of the person, attempting to identify various motives or traits and the basic dimensions of personality. Unfortunately, these attempts have not been very successful. No two lists of personality traits are identical. It perhaps is time to consider taxonomies of the environment rather than (in addition to?) intrapersonal structures. Of special importance, I feel, is a classification of environments in terms of the satisfactions that they potentially provide.

General Laws versus Individual Difference

The reader will recall that Atkinson has been especially eloquent in his plea to relate individual differences to the study of motivational processes. However, in contrast to his position, I believe that at this time we should search for general laws to the relative neglect of individual differences. Given the difficulties of personality measurement, and the situational specificity of behavior, it may be more fruitful to search for general laws than to search for Person × Environment interactions. Of course, the relative disregard of individual differences might be misleading if highly significant Person × Environment interactions of a particular type exist. For example, if individuals high in achievement needs prefer tasks of intermediate difficulty, and if individuals low in achievement needs prefer easy or difficult tasks, and if these motive groups are equally represented in the population, then one would observe no overall task preference. Hence, an important determinant of behavior might go unidentified. However, if both motive groups are attracted to intermediate difficulty, but with differential strengths, then pooling all subjects together would not wash out an observed task preference. Thus far in motivation, interactions between the person and the situation that completely mask main effects are rare. This suggests that we should first concentrate on the discovery of general laws, and then turn to the study of individual differences to refine our generalizations.

Traditional Phenomena

Another current prejudice of mine is that there should be a return to the study of certain basic psychodynamic phenomena, particularly substitution and displacement. Lewin and Freud both pointed out the importance of the interrelationships of need systems, and the fact that attainment of one goal could serve to satisfy other unfulfilled needs. This seems to me to be one of the key problems in the field of motivation, yet it has not been the subject of any systematic investigation since the 1940's.

The Zeitgeist

It has been repeatedly pointed out that there are waves in the study of psychological phenomena and in the acceptance of theories, with one wave rising and falling, giving way to another wave. As indicated above, substitution and displacement were once central areas of inquiry, but that no longer is the case. The same may be said of the Authoritarian personality, the relation of drive level to paired-associates learning, level of aspiration, and so on. Frequently, researchers abandon areas, leaving no permanent contribution to knowledge. At the level of theory, for example, cognitive dissonance dominated social psychology in the 1960's but has now been replaced by an even more dominant attributional approach. Such shifts have resulted in a lack of accumulation of knowledge and the absence of an agreed-upon scientific structure.

There are many logical reasons why investigators do not pursue a particular phenomenon or continue to develop a theoretical framework. First, there are diminishing payoffs for the study of any given problem or theory. Second, there is a multiplicity of other interesting issues and ideas competing for attention. And finally, each investigator wants to establish his or her own reputation in an uncharted area. These are often valid reasons and laudible goals. But I believe that for long-run progress there must be systematic and repeated study of particular phenomena, probably by teams of investigators. As it now stands, the typical research psychologist works alone with various students, having very little communication with other psychologists at the same institution. This does not seem to be a viable procedure for long-run progress.

Methodology

There will have to be methodological advances, particularly in the field of cognitive psychology. We need "cognitive X-rays," or the ability to discern thoughts without intervening in the process. The same may be said about affective experiences. It appears that some theoretical advances will have to wait for better methodological tools. The tools that have gone before range from the Skinner box to dream analysis. Other tools are now needed for the study of consciousness and the study of emotions.

BIBLIOGRAPHY

Abelson, R. A. A script theory of understanding, attitude, and behavior. In J. Carroll & T. Payne (Eds.), *Cognition and social behavior*. Hillsdale, N.J.: Erlbaum Press, 1976.

Abramson, L. Y., Seligman, M. E. P., & Teasdale, J. D. Learned helplessness in humans: Critique and reformulation. *Journal of Abnormal Psychology*, 1978, 87, 49–74.

Adler, D. L., & Kounin, J. S. Some factors operating at the moment of resumption of interrupted tasks. *Journal of Psychology*, 1939, 7, 255–267.

Adorno, T. W., Frenkel-Brunswick, E., Levinson, D. J., & Sanford, R. N. *The authoritarian personality*. New York: Harper, 1950.

Alker, H. A. Is personality situationally specific or intrapsychically consistent? *Journal of Personality*, 1972, 40, 1–16.

Allport, F. H. The influence of the group upon association and thought. *Journal of Experimental Psychology*, 1920, 3, 159–182.

Allport, G. W. Traits revisited. *American Psychologist*, 1966, 21, 1–10.

Ames, R., Ames, C., & Garrison, W. Children's causal ascriptions for positive and negative interpersonal outcomes. *Psychological Reports*, 1977, 41, 595–602.

Amsel, A. The role of frustrative nonreward in noncontinuous reward situations. *Psychological Bulletin*, 1958, 55, 102–119.

Amsel, A. Partial reinforcement. In K. W. Spence & J. A. Taylor (Eds.), *The psychology of learning and motivation* (Vol. 1). New York: Academic Press, 1967.

Amsel, A., & Roussel, J. Motivational properties of frustration: I. Effect on a running response of the addition of frustration to the motivational complex. *Journal of Experimental Psychology*, 1952, 43, 363–368.

Amsel, A., & Ward, J. S. Motivational properties of frustration: II. Frustration drive stimulus and frustration reduction in selective learning. *Journal of Experimental Psychology*, 1954, 48, 37–47.

Amsel, A., & Ward, J. S. Frustration and persistence: Resistance to discrimination following prior experience with the discriminanda. *Psychological Monographs*, 1965, 79 (4, Whole No. 597).

Amsterdam, B. Mirror self-image reactions before age two. *Developmental Psychobiology*, 1972, 5, 297–305.

Andrews, G. R., & Debus, R. L. Persistence and causal perceptions of failure: Modifying cognitive attributions. *Journal of Educational Psychology*, 1978, 70, 154–166.

Arkes, H. R., & Garske, J. P. *Psychological theories of motivation*. Monterey, Calif.: Brooks-Cole, 1977.

Arkin, R. M., & Maruyama, G. M. Attribution, affect, and college exam performance. *Journal of Educational Psychology*, 1979, 71, 85–93.

Arkoff, A. Resolution of approach-approach and avoidance-avoidance conflicts. *Journal of Abnormal and Social Psychology*, 1957, 55, 402–404.

Aronson, E., & Carlsmith, J. M. Effects of severity of threat on the deviation of forbidden behavior. *Journal of Abnormal and Social Psychology*, 1963, 66, 584–588.

Aronson, E., & Mills, J. The effect of severity of initiation on liking for a group. *Journal of Abnormal and Social Psychology*, 1959, 59, 177–181.

Asch, S. E. Studies of independence and conformity: A minority of one against a unanimous majority. *Psychological Monographs*, 1956, 70 (Whole No. 416).

449

Atkinson, J. W. The achievement motive and recall of interrupted and completed tasks. *Journal of Experimental Psychology*, 1953, *46*, 381–390.

Atkinson, J. W. Motivational determinants of risk-taking behavior. *Psychological Review*, 1957, *64*, 359–372.

Atkinson, J. W. (Ed.). *Motives in fantasy, action, and society.* Princeton, N.J.: Van Nostrand, 1958. (a)

Atkinson, J. W. Towards experimental analysis of human motivation in terms of motives, expectancies, and incentives. In J. W. Atkinson (Ed.), *Motives in fantasy, action, and society.* Princeton, N.J.: Van Nostrand, 1958. (b)

Atkinson, J. W. *An introduction to motivation.* Princeton, N.J.: Van Nostrand, 1964.

Atkinson, J. W., & Birch, D. *The dynamics of action.* New York; Wiley, 1970.

Atkinson, J. W., & Birch, D. The dynamics of achievement-oriented activity. In J. W. Atkinson & J. O. Raynor (Eds.), *Motivation and achievement.* Washington, D.C.: V. H. Winston, 1974.

Atkinson, J. W., & Feather, N. T. (Eds.). *A theory of achievement motivation.* New York: Wiley, 1966.

Atkinson, J. W., & Litwin, G. Achievement motive and test anxiety conceived as motive to approach success and motive to avoid failure. *Journal of Abnormal and Social Psychology*, 1960, *60*, 52–63.

Atkinson, J. W., & Raynor, J. O. (Eds.). *Motivation and achievement.* Washington, D.C.: V. H. Winston, 1974.

Ausubel, N. (Ed.). Applied psychology. In *A treasury of Jewish folklore.* New York: Crown, 1948.

Bakan, P. Response tendencies in attempts to generate random binary series. *American Journal of Psychology*, 1960, *73*, 127–131.

Baldwin, A. L. A cognitive theory of socialization. In D. A. Goslin (Ed.), *Handbook of socialization theory and research.* Chicago: Rand McNally, 1969.

Bandura, A. Influence of models' reinforcement contingencies on the acquisition of imitative responses. *Journal of Personality and Social Psychology*, 1965, *1*, 589–595.

Bandura, A. *Social learning theory.* Morristown, N.J.: General Learning Press, 1971.

Bandura, A., & Mischel, W. Modification of self-imposed delay or reward through exposure to live and symbolic models. *Journal of Personality and Social Psychology*, 1965, *2*, 698–705.

Bandura, A., Ross, D., & Ross, S. Transmission of aggression through imitation of aggressive models. *Journal of Abnormal and Social Psychology*, 1961, *63*, 575–582.

Bandura, A., & Walters, R. H. *Social learning and personality development.* New York: Holt, Rinehart, & Winston, 1963.

Bannister, D., & Fransella, F. *Inquiring man.* Baltimore: Penguin Books, 1971.

Barefoot, J. C., & Straub, R. B. Opportunity for information search and the effect of false heart feedback. *Journal of Personality and Social Psychology*, 1971, *17*, 154–157.

Barker, R. G. Ecology and motivation. In M. R. Jones (Ed.), *Nebraska symposium on motivation.* Lincoln: University of Nebraska Press, 1960.

Barker, R. G. Explorations in ecological psychology. *American Psychologist*, 1965, *20*, 1–13.

Barker, R. G., Dembo, T., & Lewin, K. Frustration and regression. In R. G. Barker, J. S. Kounin, & H. F. Wright (Eds.), *Child behavior and development.* New York: McGraw-Hill, 1943.

Barker, R. G., & Gump, P. V. (Eds.). *Big school, small school: High school size and student behavior.* Stanford, Calif.: Stanford University Press, 1964.

Barnes, R. D., Ickes, W. J., & Kidd, R. F. Effects of the perceived intentionality and stability of another's dependency on helping behavior: A field experiment. Unpublished manuscript, University of Wisconsin, 1977.

Baron, R. A. The aggression-inhibiting influence of heightened sexual arousal. *Journal of Personality and Social Psychology*, 1974, *30*, 318–322.

Baron, R. A., & Eggleston, R. J. Performance on the "aggression machine": Motivation to help or harm? *Psychonomic Science*, 1972, *26*, 321–322.

Bartlett, E. W., & Smith, C. P. Child-rearing practices, birth order, and the development of achievement-related motives. *Psychological Reports*, 1966, *19*, 1207–1216.

Battle, E., & Rotter, J. B. Children's feelings of personal control as related to social class and ethnic groups. *Journal of Personality*, 1963, *31*, 482–490.

Beach, F. The descent of instinct. *Psychological Review*, 1955, *62*, 401–410.

Beck, A. T. *Depression: Clinical, experimental, and theoretical aspects.* New York: Harper & Row, 1967.

Beck, A. T. Cognition, affect, and psychopathology. In H. London & R. E. Nisbett (Eds.), *Thought and feeling.* Chicago, Ill.: Aldine, 1974.

Beck, A. T. *Cognitive therapy and the emotional disorders.* New York: International Universities Press, 1976.

Beckman, L. Effects of students' performance on teachers' and observers' attributions of causality. *Journal of Educational Psychology,* 1970, *61,* 76–82.

Beckman, L. Teachers' and observers' perceptions of causality for a child's performance. *Journal of Educational Psychology,* 1973, *65,* 198–204.

Bem, D. J. Self-perception: An alternative interpretation of cognitive dissonance phenomena. *Psychological Review,* 1967, *74,* 183–200.

Bem, D. J. The epistemological status of interpersonal simulations: A reply to Jones, Linder, Kiesler, Zanna, and Brehm. *Journal of Experimental Social Psychology,* 1968, *4,* 270–274.

Bem, D. J. Self perception theory. In L. Berkowitz (Ed.), *Advances in experimental social psychology* (Vol. 6). New York: Academic Press, 1972.

Bem, D. J., & Allen, A. On predicting some of the people some of the time: The search for cross-situational consistencies in behavior. *Psychological Review,* 1974, *81,* 506–520.

Bentham, J. (1779) *An introduction to the principles of morals and legislation.* Oxford: B. Blackwell, 1948.

Berkowitz, L. Resistance to improper dependency relationships. *Journal of Experimental Social Psychology,* 1969, *5,* 283–294.

Berkowitz, L. The contagion of violence. In W. J. Arnold & M. M. Page (Eds.), *Nebraska symposium on motivation.* Lincoln: University of Nebraska Press, 1970.

Berkowitz, L., & LaPage, A. Weapons as aggression-eliciting stimuli. *Journal of Personality and Social Psychology,* 1967, *7,* 202–207.

Berlyne, D. The influence of complexity and novelty in visual figures on orienting responses. *Journal of Experimental Psychology,* 1958, *55,* 289–296.

Berlyne, D. Motivational problems raised by exploratory and epistemic behavior. In S. Koch (Ed.), *Psychology: A study of a science.* New York: McGraw-Hill, 1959.

Berlyne, D. *Conflict, arousal, and curiosity.* New York: McGraw-Hill, 1960.

Berlyne, D. Behavior theory as personality theory. In E. F. Borgatta & W. W. Lambert (Eds.), *Handbook of personality theory and research.* Chicago: Rand McNally, 1968.

Bindra, D. The interrelated mechanisms of reinforcement and motivation, and the nature of their influence on response. In W. J. Arnold & D. Levine (Eds.), *Nebraska symposium on motivation.* Lincoln: University of Nebraska Press, 1969.

Birch, D., Atkinson, J. W., & Bongort, K. Cognitive control of action. In B. Weiner (Ed.), *Cognitive views of human motivation.* New York: Academic Press, 1974.

Birney, R. C. The reliability of the achievement motive. *Journal of Abnormal and Social Psychology,* 1959, *58,* 266–267.

Birney, R. C. Research on the achievement motive. In E. F. Borgatta & W. W. Lambert (Eds.), *Handbook of personality theory and research.* Chicago: Rand McNally, 1968.

Blank, T. O., Staff, I., & Shaver, P. Social facilitation of word associations: Further questions. *Journal of Personality and Social Psychology,* 1976, *34,* 725–733.

Blodgett, H. C. The effect of the introduction of reward upon maze performance of rats. Berkeley: *University of California Publication in Psychology,* 1929, *4,* No. 8, 113–134.

Blum, G. S. *A model of the mind.* New York: Wiley, 1961.

Bolles, R. C. Learning, motivation, and cognition. In W. K. Estes (Ed.), *Handbook of learning and cognitive processes* (Vol. 1). Hillsdale, N.J.: Erlbaum Press, 1975. (a)

Bolles, R. C. *Theory of motivation* (2nd ed.). New York: Harper & Row, 1975. (b)

Bowers, K. Situationism in psychology: An analysis and a critique. *Psychological Review,* 1973, *80,* 307–336.

Breger, L. *From instinct to identity: The development of personality.* Englewood Cliffs, N.J.: Prentice-Hall, 1974.

Brehm, J. W. Motivation effects of cognitive dissonance. In M. R. Jones (Ed.), *Nebraska symposium on motivation.* Lincoln: University of Nebraska Press, 1962.

Brehm, J. W. (Ed.). *A theory of psychological reactance.* New York: Academic Press, 1966.

Brehm, J. W. *Responses to loss of freedom: A theory of psychological reactance.* Morristown, N.J.: General Learning Press, 1972.

Breit, S. Arousal of achievement motivation with causal attributions. *Psychological Reports,* 1969, *25,* 539–542.

Broadhurst, P. L. Emotionality and the Yerkes-Dodson Law. *Journal of Experimental Psychology,* 1957, *54,* 345–352.

Brown, J. S. Gradients of approach and avoidance responses and their relation to level of motivation. *Journal of Comparative and Physiological Psychology*, 1948, *41*, 450–465.

Brown, J. S. Problems presented by the concept of acquired drives. In M. R. Jones (Ed.), *Nebraska symposium on motivation*. Lincoln: Unversity of Nebraska Press, 1953.

Brown, J. S. *The motivation of behavior*. New York: McGraw-Hill, 1961.

Brown, J. S., & Farber, I. E. Emotions conceptualized as intervening variables: With suggestions toward a theory of frustration. *Psychological Bulletin*, 1951, *48*, 465–495.

Brown, M., Jennings, J., & Vanik, V. The motive to avoid success: A further examination. *Journal of Research in Personality*, 1974, *8*, 172–176.

Bruner, J. S. A cognitive theory of personality. *Contemporary Psychology*, 1956, *I*, 355–357.

Bruner, J. S., & Tagiuri, R. The perception of people. In G. Lindzey (Ed.), *Handbook of social psychology*. Cambridge, Mass: Addison-Wesley, 1954.

Bryan, J. H., & Test, M. A. Models and helping: Naturalistic studies in aiding behavior. *Journal of Personality and Social Psychology*, 1967, *6*, 400–407.

Buck, R. *Human motivation and emotion*. New York: Wiley, 1976.

Buck-Morss, S. The Adorno legacy. *Personality and Social Psychology Bulletin*, 1977, *3*, 707–713.

Buss, A. H., Booker, A., & Buss, E. Firing a weapon and aggression. *Journal of Personality and Social Psychology*, 1972, *22*, 296–302.

Butler, J. M., & Haigh, G. V. Changes in the relation between self-concepts and ideal concepts consequent upon client-centered counseling. In C. R. Rogers & R. F. Dymond (Eds.), *Psychotherapy and personality change*. Chicago: University of Chicago Press, 1954.

Byrne, D. Repression-sensitization as a dimension of personality. In B. A. Maher (Ed.), *Progress in experimental personality research* (Vol. #1). New York: Academic Press, 1964.

Byrne, D. *An introduction to personality*. Englewood Cliffs, N.J.: Prentice-Hall, 1966.

Byrne, D. *An introduction to personality* (2nd ed.). Englewood Cliffs, N.J.: Prentice-Hall, 1974.

Byrne, D. Social psychology and the study of sexual behavior. *Personality and Social Psychology Bulletin*, 1977, *3*, 3–30.

Callard, E. *Achievement motive in the four-year-old and its relationship to achievement expectancies of mothers*. Unpublished doctoral dissertation, University of Michigan, 1964.

Campbell, A. Subjective measures of well-being. *American Psychologist*, 1976, *31*, 117–124.

Cannon, W. B. The James-Lange theory of emotion: A critical examination and an alternative theory. *American Journal of Psychology*, 1927, *39*, 106–124.

Cannon, W. B. *The wisdom of the body*. New York: W. W. Norton, 1932.

Caplow, T. C. *Two against one*. Englewood Cliffs, N.J.: Prentice-Hall, 1968.

Carroll, J. S., & Payne, J. W. The psychology of the parole decision process: A joint application of attribution theory and information processing psychology. In J. S. Carroll & J. W. Payne (Eds.), *Cognition and social behavior*. Hillsdale, N.J.: Erlbaum Press, 1976.

Carroll, J. S., & Payne, J. W. Judgments about crime and the criminal: A model and method for investigating parole decision. In B. D. Sales (Ed.), *Prospectives in law and psychology: Vol. 1. The criminal justice system*. New York: Plenum, 1977.

Chance, J. E. Independence training and first graders' achievement. *Journal of Consulting Psychology*, 1961, *25*, 228–238.

Chapin, M., & Dyck, D. G. Persistence in children's reading behavior as a function of N length and attribution retraining. *Journal of Abnormal Psychology*, 1976, *85*, 511–515.

Chapman, L. J., & Chapman, J. P. Illusory correlation as an obstacle to the use of valid psychodiagnostic signs. *Journal of Abnormal Psychology*, 1969, *74*, 271–280.

Chen, S. C. Social modification of the activity of ants in nest-building. *Physiological Zoology*, 1937, *10*, 420–436.

Clemes, S. R. Repression and hypnotic amnesia. *Journal of Abnormal and Social Psychology*, 1964, *69*, 62–69.

Cofer, C. N., & Appley, M. H. *Motivation: Theory and research*. New York: Wiley, 1964.

Cohen, J., & Hansel, C. E. M. *Risk and gambling*. London: Longmans Green, 1956.

Condry, J. Enemies of exploration: Self-initiated versus other-initiated learning. *Journal of Personality and Social Psychology*, 1977, *35*, 459–477.

Connell, D. M., & Johnson, J. E. Relationship between sex-role identification and self-esteem in early adolescents. *Developmental Psychology*, 1970, *3*, 268.

Coopersmith, S. *The antecedents of self-esteem.* San Francisco: W. H. Freeman, 1967.

Cottrell, N. B. Social facilitation. In C. G. McClintock (Ed.), *Experimental social psychology.* New York: Holt, Rinehart, & Winston, 1972.

Cottrell, N. B., Wack, D. L., Sekarak, G. J., & Rittle, R. Social facilitation of dominant responses by the presence of an audience and the mere presence of others. *Journal of Personality and Social Psychology,* 1968, 9, 245–250.

Covington, M. V., & Beery, R. G. *Self-worth and school learning.* New York: Holt, Rinehart, & Winston, 1976.

Crandall, V. C. Sex differences in expectancy of intellectual and academic reinforcement. In C. P. Smith (Ed.), *Achievement-related motives in children.* New York: Russell Sage, 1969.

Crandall, V. C., Katkovsky, W., & Crandall, V. J. Children's beliefs in their own control of reinforcements in intellectual-academic achievement situation. *Child Development,* 1965, 36, 91–109.

Crandall, V. J. An investigation of the specificity of reinforcement of induced frustration. *Journal of Social Psychology,* 1955, 41, 311–318.

Crespi, L. P. Quantitative variation of incentive and performance in the white rat. *American Journal of Psychology,* 1942, 55, 467–517.

Cunningham, J. D., & Kelley, H. H. Causal attributions for interpersonal events of varying magnitude. *Journal of Personality,* 1975, 43, 74–93.

Dana, C. L. The anatomic seat of the emotions: A discussion of the James-Lange theory. *Archives of Neurology and Psychiatry,* 1921, 6, 634–639.

Darwin, C. (1859) *Origin of species.* New York: Modern Library, 1936.

Davison, G. C., & Valins, S. Maintenance of self-attributed and drug-attributed behavior change. *Journal of Personality and Social Psychology,* 1969, 1, 25–33.

Deaux, K., & Emswiller, T. Explanations of successful performance on sex-linked tasks: What's skill for the male is luck for the female. *Journal of Personality and Social Psychology,* 1974, 29, 80–85.

Deaux, K., & Farris, E. Attributing causes for one's own performance: The effects of sex, norms, and outcome. *Journal of Research in Personality,* 1977, 11, 59–72.

de Charms, R. *Personal causation.* New York: Academic Press, 1968.

de Charms, R. Personal causation training in the schools. *Journal of Applied Social Psychology,* 1972, 2, 95–113.

de Charms, R. *Enhancing motivation: Change in the classroom.* New York: Irvington Publishers, 1976.

de Charms, R., & Moeller, G. H. Values expressed in American children's readers: 1800–1950. *Journal of Abnormal and Social Psychology,* 1962, 64, 136–142.

de Charms, R., Morrison, H. W., Reitman, W. R., & McClelland, D. C. Behavioral correlates of directly measured and indirectly measured achievement motivation. In D. C. McClelland (Ed.), *Studies in motivation.* New York: Appleton-Century-Crofts, 1955.

Deci, E. L. *Intrinsic motivation.* New York: Plenum, 1975.

Dember, W. N. Response by the rat to environmental change. *Journal of Comparative and Physiological Psychology,* 1956, 49, 93–95.

Dember, W. N. *The psychology of perception.* New York: Holt, 1960.

Dember, W. N., & Earl, R. W. Analysis of exploratory, manipulatory, and curiosity behavior. *Psychological Review,* 1957, 64, 91–96.

Dement, W. C. The effect of dream deprivation. *Science,* 1960, 131, 1705–1707.

Dement, W. C. An essay on dreams: The role of physiology in understanding their nature. In F. Barron (Ed.), *New directions in psychology* (Vol. 2). New York: Holt, Rinehart, & Winston, 1965.

Dement, W. C., & Kleitman, N. The relation of eye movements during sleep to dream activity: An objective method for the study of dreaming. *Journal of Experimental Psychology,* 1957, 53, 339–346.

DiCaprio, N. S. *Personality theories: Guides to living.* Philadelphia: Saunders, 1974.

Diener, E., Fraser, S. C., Beaman, A. L., & Kelem, R. T. Effects of deindividuation variables on stealing among halloween trick-or-treaters. *Journal of Personality and Social Psychology,* 1976, 33, 178–183.

Diggory, J. C., Riley, E. J., & Blumenfeld, R. Estimated probability of success for a fixed goal. *American Journal of Psychology,* 1960, 73, 41–55.

Dipboye, R. L. Alternative approaches to deindividuation. *Psychological Bulletin,* 1977, 84, 1057–1075.

Dixon, N. F. *Subliminal perception: The nature of a controversy.* London: McGraw-Hill, 1971.

Dollard, J., & Miller, N. E. *Personality and psychotherapy: An analysis in terms of learning, thinking, and culture*. New York: McGraw-Hill, 1950.

Dollard, J., Miller, N. E., Doob, L. W., Mowrer, O. H., & Sears, R. R. *Frustration and aggression*. New Haven, Conn.: Yale University Press, 1939.

Duffy, E. *Activation and behavior*. New York: Wiley, 1962.

Dulany, D. E., Jr. Avoidance learning of perceptual defense and vigilance. *Journal of Abnormal and Social Psychology*, 1957, 55, 333–338.

Duval, S., & Wicklund, R. A. (Eds.). *A theory of objective self awareness*. New York: Academic Press, 1972.

Duval, S., & Wicklund, R. A. Effects of objective self-awareness on attribution of causality. *Journal of Experimental Social Psychology*, 1973, 9, 17–31.

Dweck, C. S. The role of expectations and attributions in the alleviation of learned helplessness. *Journal of Personality and Social Psychology*, 1975, 31, 674–685.

Dweck, C. S., & Reppucci, N. D. Learned helplessness and reinforcement responsibility in children. *Journal of Personality and Social Psychology*, 1973, 25, 109–116.

Eisman, E. Effects of deprivation and consummatory activity on heart rate. *Journal of Comparative and Physiological Psychology*, 1966, 62, 71–75.

Ellis, A. Rational emotive therapy. In A. Burton (Ed.), *Operational theories of personality*. New York: Brunner/Mazel, 1974.

Entwisle, D. R. To dispel fantasies about fantasy-based measures of achievement motivation. *Psychological Bulletin*, 1972, 77, 377–391.

Epstein, R. Authoritarianism, displaced aggression, and social status of the target. *Journal of Personality and Social Psychology*, 1965, 2, 585–589.

Epstein, S., & Fenz, W. D. Steepness of approach and avoidance gradients in humans as a function of experience: Theory and experiment. *Journal of Experimental Psychology*, 1965, 70, 1–12.

Erdelyi, M. H. A new look at the new look: Perceptual defense and vigilance. *Psychological Review*, 1974, 81, 1–25.

Eriksen, C. W. Unconscious processes. In M. R. Jones (Ed.), *Nebraska symposium on motivation*. Lincoln: University of Nebraska Press, 1958.

Eriksen, C. W. Discrimination and learning without awareness: A methodological survey and evaluation. *Psychological Review*, 1960, 67, 279–300.

Escalona, S. K. The effect of success and failure upon the level of aspiration and behavior in manic-depressive psychoses. University of Iowa: *Studies in Child Welfare*, 1940, 16, 199–302.

Eswara, H. S. Administration of reward and punishment in relation to ability, effort, and performance. *Journal of Social Psychology*, 1972, 87, 139–140.

Feather, N. T. The relationship of persistence at a task to expectation of success and achievement-related motives. *Journal of Abnormal and Social Psychology*, 1961, 63, 552–561.

Feather, N. T. The relationship of expectation of success to n Achievement and test anxiety. *Journal of Personality and Social Psychology*, 1965, 1, 118–126.

Feather, N. T. Valence of outcome and expectation of success in relation to task difficulty and perceived locus of control. *Journal of Personality and Social Psychology*, 1967, 7, 372–386.

Feather, N. T. Attribution of responsibility and valence of success and failure in relation to initial confidence and task performance. *Journal of Personality and Social Psychology*, 1969, 13, 129–144.

Feather, N. T., & Simon, J. G. Causal attributions for success and failure in relation to expectations of success based upon selective or manipulative control. *Journal of Personality*, 1971, 39, 527–554.

Feld, S. Longitudinal study of the origins of achievement strivings. *Journal of Personality and Social Psychology*, 1967, 7, 408–414.

Ferguson, E. D. *Motivation: An experimental approach*. New York: Holt, Rinehart, & Winston, 1976.

Feshbach, S. The function of aggression and the regulation of aggressive drive. *Psychological Review*, 1964, 71, 257–272.

Feshbach, S., & Singer, R. D. *Television and aggression*. San Francisco: Jossey-Bass, 1971.

Festinger, L. A theoretical interpretation of shifts in level of aspiration. *Psychological Review*, 1942, 49, 235–250.

Festinger, L. A theory of social comparison processes. *Human Relations*, 1954, 7, 117–140.

Festinger, L. *A theory of cognitive dissonance*. Evanston, Ill.: Row, Peterson, 1957. (a)

Festinger, L. The relation between behavior and cognition. In *Colorado symposium on cognition.* London: Oxford University Press, 1957. (b)

Festinger, L. The psychology of insufficient rewards. *American Psychologist*, 1961, *16*, 1–11.

Festinger, L., & Carlsmith, J. M. Cognitive consequences of forced compliance. *Journal of Abnormal and Social Psychology*, 1959, *58*, 203–210.

Festinger, L., Pepitone, A., & Newcomb, T. Some consequences of deindividuation in a group. *Journal of Abnormal and Social Psychology*, 1952, *47*, 382–389.

Festinger, L., Riecken, H. W., & Schachter, S. *When prophecy fails.* Minneapolis: University of Minnesota Press, 1956.

Fitch, G. Effects of self-esteem, perceived performance, and choice on causal attributions. *Journal of Personality and Social Psychology*, 1970, *16*, 311–315.

Folkes, V. S. *Causal communications in the early stages of affiliative relationships.* Unpublished doctoral dissertation, University of California, Los Angeles, 1978.

Folkes, V. S., & Weiner, B. Motivational determinants of coalition formation. *Journal of Experimental Social Psychology*, 1977, *13*, 536–542.

Fontaine, G. *Some situational determinants of causal attribution.* Unpublished doctoral dissertation, University of Western Australia, Nedlands, Australia, 1972.

Fontaine, G. Social comparison and some determinants of expected personal control and expected performance in a novel situation. *Journal of Personality and Social Psychology*, 1974, *29*, 487–496.

Foulkes, D. *The psychology of sleep.* New York: Scribner, 1966.

Frank, J. D. Individual differences in certain aspects of the level of aspiration. *American Journal of Psychology*, 1935, *47*, 119–128.

Freud, S. (1900) *The interpretation of dreams.* London: Hogarth Press, 1953.

Freud, S. (1901) *The psychopathology of everyday life.* New York: New American Library, 1951.

Freud, S. (1911) Formulations regarding the two principles of mental functioning. In *Collected papers* (Vol. 4). New York: Basic Books, 1959.

Freud, S. (1915) Instincts and their vicissitudes. In *Collected papers* (Vol. 4). London: Hogarth Press and the Institute of Psycho-Analysis, 1948. (a)

Freud, S. (1915) *A general introduction to psychoanalysis.* New York: Washington Square Press, 1934. (b)

Freud, S. (1920) *Beyond the pleasure principle. The standard edition* (Vol. 18). London: Hogarth Press, 1955.

Freud, S. (1926) *The problem of anxiety.* New York: W. W. Norton, 1936.

Freud, S. *Civilization and its discontents.* London: Hogarth Press, 1930.

Freud, S. (1933) *New introductory lectures on psycho-analysis.* New York: W. W. Norton, 1961.

Freud, S. (1935) Letter to an American mother. *American Journal of Psychiatry*, 1951, *107*, 787.

Frieze, I. H. *Studies of information processing and the attributional process.* Unpublished doctoral dissertation, University of California, Los Angeles, 1973.

Frieze, I. H. The role of information processing in making causal attributions for success and failure. In J. S. Carroll & J. W. Payne (Eds.), *Cognition and social behavior.* Hillsdale, N.J.: Erlbaum Press, 1976. (a)

Frieze, I. H. Causal attributions and information seeking to explain success and failure. *Journal of Research in Personality*, 1976, *10*, 293–305. (b)

Frieze, I. H., & Weiner, B. Cue utilization and attributional judgments for success and failure. *Journal of Personality*, 1971, *39*, 591–606.

Frisch, K., von. *The dancing bees.* London: Methuen, 1954.

Gallup, G. G., Jr. Chimpanzees: Self-recognition. *Science*, 1970, *167*, 86–87.

Gallup, G. G., Jr. Towards an operational definition of self-awareness. In R. H. Tuttle (Ed.), *Socioecology and psychology of primates.* The Hague: Mouton, 1975.

Gallup, G. G., Jr., McClure, M. K., Hill, S. D., & Bundy, R. A. Capacity for self-recognition in differentially reared chimpanzees. *The Psychological Record*, 1971, *21*, 69–74.

Gardner, R. W., Holzman, P. S., Klein, G. S., Linton, H., & Spence, D. P. Cognitive control. *Psychological Issues*, 1959, *1*, No. 4.

Geen, R. G., & Gange, J. J. Drive theory of social facilitation: Twelve years of theory and research. *Psychological Bulletin*, 1977, *84*, 1267–1288.

Gilmore, T. M., & Minton, H. L. Internal versus external attribution of task performance as a function of locus of control, initial confidence and success-failure outcome. *Journal of Personality*, 1974, *42*, 159–174.

Glanzer, M. The role of stimulus satiation in spontaneous alternation. *Journal of Experimental Psychology*, 1953, *45*, 387–393.

Gleason, J. B. Code switching in children's language. In T. E. Moore (Ed.), *Cognitive development and the acquisition of language*. New York: Academic Press, 1973.

Glixman, A. F. Recall of completed and incompleted activities under varying degrees of stress. *Journal of Experimental Psychology*, 1949, *39*, 281–295.

Goffman, E. *Asylums*. Garden City, N.Y.: Doubleday, 1961.

Gold, M. *Vocational skill functioning of the severely retarded*. Paper presented at the American Psychological Association Convention, Chicago, September 1975.

Goldstein, D., Fink, D., & Mettee, D. R. Cognition of arousal and actual arousal as determinants of emotion. *Journal of Personality and Social Psychology*, 1972, *21*, 41–51.

Gordon, S. *Lonely in America*. New York: Simon & Schuster, 1976.

Green, D. R. Volunteering and the recall of interrupted tasks. *Journal of Abnormal and Social Psychology*, 1963, *66*, 397–401.

Grinker, J. *The control of classical conditioning by cognitive manipulation*. Unpublished doctoral dissertation, New York University, 1967.

Guhl, A. M. The social order of chickens. *Scientific American*, 1956, *194*, 42–46.

Haber, R. N., & Alpert, R. The role of situation and picture cues in projective measurement of the achievement motive. In J. W. Atkinson (Ed.), *Motives in fantasy, action, and society*. Princeton, N.J.: Van Nostrand, 1958.

Hall, C. S., & Lindzey, G. *Theories of personality*. New York: Wiley, 1957.

Hammock, T., & Brehm, J. W. The attractiveness of choice alternatives when freedom to choose is eliminated by a social agent. *Journal of Personality*, 1966, *34*, 546–554.

Haner, C. F., & Brown, J. S. Clarification of the instigation to action concept in the frustration-aggression hypothesis. *Journal of Abnormal and Social Psychology*, 1955, *51*, 204–206.

Hanusa, B. H. *An extension of Weiner's attribution approach to social situations: Sex differences in social situations*. Paper presented at the Eastern Psychological Association Convention, New York, April 1975.

Harlow, H. F. Motivation as a factor in the acquisition of new responses. In M. R. Jones (Ed.), *Nebraska symposium on motivation*. Lincoln: University of Nebraska Press, 1953.

Hartmann, E. The D-State: A review and discussion of studies on the physiological state concomitant with dreaming. *New England Journal of Medicine*, 1965, *273*, 30–35.

Hartmann, H., Kris, E., & Lowenstein, R. M. Comments on the formation of psychic structure. In R. Eissler, A. Freud, H. Hartmann, S. Lustman, & M. Kris (Eds.), *The psychoanalytic study of the child* (Vol. 2). New York: International Universities Press, 1946.

Hebb, D. O. Drives and the C.N.S. (conceptual nervous system). *Psychological Review*, 1955, *62*, 243–254.

Heckhausen, H. *The anatomy of achievement motivation*. New York: Academic Press, 1967.

Heckhausen, H. Achievement motive research: Current problems and some contributions toward a central theory of motivation. In D. Levine (Ed.), *Nebraska symposium on motivation*. Lincoln: University of Nebraska Press, 1968.

Heckhausen, H., & Roelofsen, I. Anfänge und Entwicklung der Leistungsmotivation: (I) Im Wetteifer des Kleinkindes. *Psychologische Forschung*, 1962, *26*, 313–397.

Heider, F. *The psychology of interpersonal relations*. New York: Wiley, 1958.

Heider, F., & Simmel, M. An experimental study of apparent behavior. *American Journal of Psychology*, 1944, *57*, 243–259.

Heim, M. *Sex diferences in causal attributions for achievement in social tasks*. Paper presented at the Eastern Psychological Association Convention, New York, April 1975.

Henle, M. The influence of valence on substitution. *Journal of Psychology*, 1944, *17*, 11–19.

Hermans, H. J. M. A questionnaire measure of achievement motivation. *Journal of Applied Psychology*, 1970, *54*, 353–363.

Heron, W. The pathology of boredom. *Scientific American*, 1957, *196*, 52–56.

Hess, E. H. Attitude and pupil size. *Scientific American*, 1965, *212*, 46–54.

Hilgard, E. R. Human motives and the concept of the self. *American Psychologist*, 1949, *4*, 374–382.

Hinde, R. A. Energy models of motivation. *Symposium of the Society of Experimental Biology*, 1960, *14*, 199–213.

Hiroto, D. S., & Seligman, M. E. P. Generality of learned helplessness in man. *Journal of Personality and Social Psychology*, 1975, *31*, 311–327.

Hogan, R. *Personality theory*. Englewood Cliffs, N.J.: Prentice-Hall, 1976.

Hohmann, G. W. Some effects of spinal cord lesions on experienced emotional feelings. *Psychophysiology*, 1966, *3*, 143–156.

Holmes, T. H., & Rahe, R. H. The social readjustment rating scale. *Journal of Psychosomatic Research*, 1967, *11*, 213–218.

Holt, E. B. *Animal drive and the learning process, an essay toward radical empiricism* (Vol. 1). New York: Holt, 1931.

Holzman, P. S., & Gardner, R. W. Leveling and repression. *Journal of Abnormal and Social Psychology*, 1959, *59*, 151–155.

Holzman, P. S., & Gardner, R. W. Leveling-sharpening and memory organization. *Journal of Abnormal and Social Psychology*, 1960, *61*, 176–180.

Hoppe, F. Untersuchungen zur Handlungs — und affekt — psychologie. IX. Erfolg und Misserfolg. *Psychologische Forschung*, 1930, *14*, 1–63.

Horner, M. S. *Sex differences in achievement motivation and performance in competitive and non-competitive situations*. Unpublished doctoral dissertation, University of Michigan, 1968.

Howes, D. H., & Solomon, R. L. Visual duration threshold as a function of word-probability. *Journal of Experimental Psychology*, 1951, *41*, 401–410.

Hull, C. L. *Principles of behavior*. New York: Appleton-Century-Crofts, 1943.

Hull, C. L. *Essentials of behavior*. New Haven, Conn.: Yale University Press, 1951.

Hume, D. (1739) *A treatise of human nature*. London: Clarendon Press, 1888.

Ickes, W. J., & Kidd, R. F. An attributional analysis of helping behavior. In J. H. Harvey, W. J. Ickes, & R. F. Kidd (Eds.), *New directions in attribution research* (Vol. 1). Hillsdale, N.J.: Erlbaum Press, 1976.

Ickes, W. J., & Layden, M. A. Attributional styles. In J. H. Harvey, W. J. Ickes, & R. F. Kidd (Eds.), *New directions in attribution research* (Vol. 2). Hillsdale, N.J.: Erlbaum Press, 1978.

Isen, A. M. Success, failure, attention, and reactions to others: The warm glow of success. *Journal of Personality and Social Psychology*, 1970, *15*, 294–301.

Isen, A. M., Horn, N., & Rosenhan, D. L. Effects of success and failure on children's generosity. *Journal of Personality and Social Psychology*, 1973, *27*, 239–247.

Isen, A. M., & Levin, P. F. Effect of feeling good on helping: Cookies and kindness. *Journal of Personality and Social Psychology*, 1972, *21*, 384–388.

Jaffe, Y., Malamuth, N., Feingold, J., & Feshbach, S. Sexual arousal and behavioral aggression. *Journal of Personality and Social Psychology*, 1974, *30*, 759–764.

James, W. What is an emotion? *Mind*, 1884, 9, 188–205.

James, W. (1890) The emotions. In *Principles of Psychology*. New York: Dover Publications, 1950.

James, W., & Rotter, J. B. Partial and 100% reinforcement under chance and skill conditions. *Journal of Experimental Psychology*, 1958, 55, 397–403.

Jarvik, M. E. Negative recency effect in probability learning. *Journal of Experimental Psychology*, 1951, *41*, 291–297.

Jenkins, H. M., & Ward, W. C. Judgment of contingency between responses and outcome. *Psychological Monographs*, 1965, *79* (1, Whole No. 594).

Jensen, A. R. The Rorschach technique: A reevaluation. *Acta Psychologica*, 1964, *22*, 60–77.

Jessor, R., Carman, R. S., & Grossman, P. H. Expectations of need satisfaction and drinking patterns of college students. *Quarterly Journal of Studies in Alcohol*, 1968, *29*, 101–116.

Jessor, R., Graves, T. D., Hanson, R. C., & Jessor, S. L. *Society, personality, and deviant behavior*. New York: Holt, Rinehart, & Winston, 1968.

Johnson, R. N. *Aggression in man and animals*. Philadelphia: Saunders, 1972.

Johnson, T. J., Feigenbaum, R., & Weiby, M. Some determinants and consequences of the teacher's perception of causation. *Journal of Educational Psychology*, 1964, *55*, 237–246.

Jones, E. *The life and work of Sigmund Freud* (Vols. I–III). New York: Basic Books, 1953–1957.

Jones, E. E., & Davis, K. E. From acts to dispositions: The attribution process in person perception. In L. Berkowitz (Ed.), *Advances in experimental social psychology* (Vol. 2). New York: Academic Press, 1965.

Jones, E. E., Davis, K. E., & Gergen, K. J. Role playing variations and their informational value for person perception. *Journal of Abnormal and Social Psychology*, 1961, *63*, 302–310.

Jones, E. E., Kanouse, D. E., Kelley, H. H., Nisbett, R. E., Valins, S., & Weiner, B. (Eds.). *Attribution: Perceiving the causes of behavior*. Morristown, N. J.: General Learning Press, 1972.

Jones, E. E., & Nisbett, R. E. The actor and the observer: Divergent perceptions of the causes of behavior. In E. E. Jones, D. E. Kanouse, H. H. Kelley, R. E. Nisbett, S. Valins, & B. Weiner (Eds.), *Attribution: Perceiving the causes of behavior*. Morristown, N.J.: General Learning Press, 1972.

Jones, E. E., Rock, L., Shaver, K. G., Goethals, G. R., & Ward, L. M. Pattern of performance and ability attribution: An unexpected primacy effect. *Journal of Personality and Social Psychology*, 1968, *10*, 317–340.

Jones, R. A., Linder, D. E., Kiesler, C. A., Zanna, M., & Brehm, J. W. Internal states or external stimuli: Observers' judgments and the dissonance-self perception controversy. *Journal of Experimental Social Psychology*, 1968, *4*, 247–269.

Kagan, J., & Moss, H. A. Stability and validity of achievement fantasy. *Journal of Abnormal and Social Psychology*, 1959, *58*, 357–364.

Kant, I. (1781) *The critique of pure reason*. In R. M. Hutchins (Ed.), *Great books of the Western World* (Vol. 42). Chicago: Encyclopaedia Britannica, 1952.

Kaplan, R. M., & Swant, S. G. Reward characteristics of appraisal of achievement behavior. *Representative Research in Social Psychology*, 1973, *4*, 11–17.

Katkovsky, W. Social learning theory and maladjustment. In L. Gorlow & W. Katkovsky (Eds.), *Readings in the psychology of adjustment* (2nd ed.). New York: McGraw-Hill, 1968.

Kelley, H. H. Attribution theory in social psychology. In D. Levine (Ed.), *Nebraska symposium on motivation*. Lincoln: University of Nebraska Press, 1967.

Kelley, H. H. Causal schemata and the attribution process. In E. E. Jones, D. E. Kanouse, H. H. Kelley, R. E. Nisbett, S. Valins, & B. Weiner (Eds.), *Attribution: Perceiving the causes of behavior*. Morristown, N.J.: General Learning Press, 1972.

Kelley, H. H., & Arrowood, J. A. Coalitions in the triad: Critique and experiment. *Sociometry*, 1962, *23*, 231–244.

Kelly, G. A. *The psychology of personal constructs*. New York: W. W. Norton, 1955.

Kelly, G. A. Man's construction of his alternatives. In G. Lindzey (Ed.), *Assessment of human motives*. New York: Grove Press, 1958.

Kelly, G. A. Europe's matrix of decision. In M. R. Jones (Ed.), *Nebraska symposium on motivation*. Lincoln: University of Nebraska Press, 1962.

Kelly, G. A. *A theory of personality: The psychology of personal constructs*. New York: W. W. Norton, 1963.

Kelly, G. A. (1966) A summary statement of a cognitive-oriented comprehensive theory of behavior. In J. C. Mancuso (Ed.), *Readings for a cognitive theory of personality*. New York: Holt, Rinehart, & Winston, 1970.

Kiesler, C. A., & Sakumura, J. A test of a model for commitment. *Journal of Personality and Social Psychology*, 1966, *3*, 349–353.

Kinsey, A. C., Pomeroy, W. B., & Martin, C. E. *Sexual behavior in the human male*. Philadelphia: Saunders, 1948.

Kinsey, A. C., Pomeroy, W. B., Martin, C. E., & Gebhard, P. H. *Sexual behavior in the human female*. Philadelphia: Saunders, 1953.

Klein, D. C., Fencil-Morse, E., & Seligman, M. E. P. Learned helplessness, depression, and the attribution of failure. *Journal of Personality and Social Psychology*, 1976, *33*, 508–516.

Klein, G. S. Need and regulation. In M. R. Jones (Ed.), *Nebraska symposium on motivation*. Lincoln: University of Nebraska Press, 1954.

Klein, G. S. Freud's two theories of sexuality. In L. Breger (Ed.), *Clinical-cognitive psychology*. Englewood Cliffs, N.J.: Prentice-Hall, 1969.

Klein, G. S., & Schoenfeld, N. The influence of ego-involvement on confidence. *Journal of Abnormal and Social Psychology*, 1941, *36*, 249–258.

Klinger, E. Fantasy need achievement as a motivational construct. *Psychological Bulletin*, 1966, *66*, 291–308.

Köhler, W. *The mentality of apes*. New York: Harcourt & Brace, 1925.

Kolb, D. Achievement motivation training for underachieving high-school boys. *Journal of Personality and Social Psychology*, 1965, *2*, 783–792.

Korman, A. K. *The psychology of motivation*. Englewood Cliffs, N.J.: Prentice-Hall, 1974.

Kruglanski, A. W. The endogenous-exogenous partition in attribution theory. *Psychological Review*, 1975, *82*, 387–406.

Kruglanski, A. W., Alon, S., & Lewis, T. Retrospective misattribution and task enjoyment. *Journal of Experimental Social Psychology*, 1972, *8*, 493–501.

Kukla, A. *Cognitive determinants of achieving behavior*. Unpublished doctoral dissertation, University of California, Los Angeles, 1970.

Kukla, A. Foundations of an attributional theory of performance. *Psychological Review*, 1972, *79*, 454–470.

Kun, A., & Weiner, B. Necessary versus sufficient causal schemata for success and failure. *Journal of Research in Personality*, 1973, *7*, 197–207.

Kuperman, A. *Relations between differential constraints, affect, and the origin-pawn variable*. Unpublished doctoral dissertation, Washington University, St. Louis, 1967.

Laing, R. D. *The divided self: An existential study in sanity and madness*. Baltimore: Penguin Books, 1965.

Langer, E. J. The illusion of control. *Journal of Personality and Social Psychology*, 1975, *32*, 311–328.

Langer, E. J. Rethinking the role of thought in social interaction. In J. H. Harvey, W. J. Ickes, & R. F. Kidd (Eds.), *New directions in attribution research* (Vol. 2). Hillsdale, N.J.: Erlbaum Press, 1978.

Langer, E. J., Blank, A., & Chanowitz, B. The mindlessness of ostensibly thoughtful action: The role of "placebic" information in interpersonal interaction. *Journal of Personality and Social Psychology*, 1978, *36*, 635–642.

Lanzetta, J. T., & Hannah, T. E. Reinforcing behavior of "naive" trainers. *Journal of Personality and Social Psychology*, 1969, *11*, 245–252.

Lao, R. C. Internal-external control and competent and innovative behavior among Negro college students. *Journal of Personality and Social Psychology*, 1970, *14*, 263–270.

Lawrence, D. H., & Festinger, L. *Deterrents and reinforcement*. Stanford, Calif.: Stanford University Press, 1962.

Lawson, R. *Frustration: The development of a scientific concept*. New York: Macmillan, 1965.

Lazarus, R. S. *Psychological stress and the coping process*. New York: McGraw-Hill, 1966.

Lazarus, R. S. Emotions and adaptation: Conceptual and empirical relations. In W. J. Arnold (Ed.), *Nebraska symposium on motivation*. Lincoln: University of Nebraska Press, 1968.

Lazarus, R. S. Cognitive and coping processes in emotion. In B. Weiner (Ed.), *Cognitive views of human motivation*. New York: Academic Press, 1975.

Lazarus, R. S., & Alfert, E. The short-circuiting of threat by experimentally altering cognitive appraisal. *Journal of Abnormal and Social Psychology*, 1964, *69*, 195–205.

Lazarus, R. S., Opton, E. M., Jr., Nomikos, M. S., & Rankin, N. D. The principle of short-circuiting of threat: Further evidence. *Journal of Personality*, 1965, *33*, 622–635.

Lefcourt, H. M. The function of illusions of control and freedom. *American Psychologist*, 1973, *28*, 417–425.

Lefcourt, H. M. *Locus of control*. Hillsdale, N.J.: Erlbaum Press, 1976.

Lehrman, D. S. A critique of Konrad Lorenz's theory of instinctive behavior. *Quarterly Review of Biology*, 1953, *28*, 337–363.

Lepley, W. M. The maturity of the chances: A gambler's fallacy. *Journal of Psychology*, 1963, *56*, 69–72.

Lepper, M. R., Greene, D., & Nisbett, R. E. Undermining children's intrinsic interest with extrinsic reward: A test of the overjustification hypothesis. *Journal of Personality and Social Psychology*, 1973, *28*, 129–137.

Leventhal, H. Emotions: A basic problem for social psychology. In C. Nemeth (Ed.), *Social psychology: Classic and contemporary integrations*. Chicago: Rand McNally, 1974.

Levin, P. F., & Isen, A. M. Further studies on the effect of feeling good on helping. *Sociometry*, 1975, *38*, 141–147.

Levis, D. J. Learned helplessness: A reply and an alternative S-R interpretation. *Journal of Experimental Psychology: General*, 1976, *105*, 47–65.

Lewin, K. *A dynamic theory of personality*. New York: McGraw-Hill, 1935.

Lewin, K. *Principles of topological psychology*. New York: McGraw-Hill, 1936.

Lewin, K. *The conceptual representation and the measurement of psychological forces*. Durham, N.C.: Duke University Press, 1938.

Lewin, K. *Resolving social conflicts*. New York: Harper, 1948.

Lewin, K. *Field theory in social science*. New York: Harper, 1951.

Lewin, K. (1946). Behavior and development as a function of the total situation. In L. Carmichael (Ed.), *Manual of child psychology*. New York: Wiley, 1963.

Lewin, K., Dembo, T., Festinger, L., & Sears, P. S. Level of aspiration. In J. McV. Hunt (Ed.), *Personality and the behavioral disorders* (Vol. 1). New York: Ronald Press, 1944.

Lewis, O. *Children of Sanchez*. New York: Random House, 1961.

Lichtenberg, P. A. A definition and analysis of depression. *Archives of Neurology and Psychiatry*, 1957, 77, 516–527.

Liebert, R. M., Neale, J. M., & Davidson, E. S. *The early window: Effects of television on children and youth*. New York: Pergamon, 1973.

Liebert, R. M., & Poulos, R. W. Eliciting the norm of giving: Effects of modeling and the presence of a witness on children's sharing behavior. *Proceedings of the 79th Annual Convention of the American Psychological Association*, 1971, 6, 345–346.

Liebert, R. M., & Spiegler, M. D. *Personality: Strategies for the study of man*. Homewood, Ill.: Dorsey, 1974.

Liebhart, E. H. Attributing fictitious cardiac responses. *Perceptual and Motor Skills*, 1976, 43, 202.

Lindsley, D. B. Psychophysiology and motivation. In M. R. Jones (Ed.), *Nebraska symposium on motivation*. Lincoln: University of Nebraska Press, 1957.

Lindsley, D. B., Schreiner, L. H., Knowles, W. B., & Magoun, H. W. Behavioral and EEG changes following chronic brainstem lesions in the cat. *Electroencephalography and Clinical Neurophysiology*, 1950, 2, 483–498.

Lindzey, G. Some remarks concerning incest, the incest taboo, and psychoanalytic theory. *American Psychologist*, 1967, 22, 1051–1059.

Lissner, K. Die Entspannung von Bedürfnissen durch Ersatzhandlungen. *Psychologische Forschung*, 1933, 18, 218–250.

Litman-Adizes, T. An attributional model of depression. Unpublished doctoral dissertation, University of California, Los Angeles, 1978.

Litwin, G. H. (1958) Motives and expectancies as determinants of preference for degrees of risk. In J. W. Atkinson & N. T. Feather (Eds.), *A theory of achievement motivation*. New York: Wiley, 1966.

Lorenz, K. The comparative method in studying innate behaviour patterns. *Symposium of the Society of Experimental Biology*, 1950, 4, 221–268.

Lorenz, K. The evolution of behavior. *Scientific American*, 1958, 199, 67–78.

Lorenz, K. *On aggression*. New York: Harcourt, Brace & World, 1966.

Maddi, S. R., *Personality theories: A comparative analysis* (3rd ed.). Homewood, Ill.: Dorsey, 1976.

Mahler, V. Ersatzhandlungen verschiedenen Realitätsgrades. *Psychologische Forschung*, 1933, 18, 26–89.

Mahone, C. H. Fear of failure and unrealistic vocational aspiration. *Journal of Abnormal and Social Psychology*, 1960, 60, 253–261.

Mahrer, A. R. The role of expectancy in delayed reinforcement. *Journal of Experimental Psychology*, 1956, 52, 101–105.

Maier, S. F., Seligman, M. E. P., & Solomon, R. L. Pavlovian fear conditioning and learned helplessness: Effects of escape and avoidance behavior of (a) the CS-UCS contingency and (b) the independence of voluntary responding. In B. A. Campbell & R. M. Church (Eds.), *Punishment and aversive behavior*. New York: Appleton-Century-Crofts, 1969.

Mallick, S. K., & McCandless, B. R. A study of catharsis of aggression. *Journal of Personality and Social Psychology*, 1966, 4, 591–596.

Malmo, R. B. Studies of anxiety: Some clinical origins of the activation concept. In C. D. Spielberger (Ed.), *Anxiety and behavior*. New York: Academic Press, 1966.

Mandler, G. *Mind and emotion*. New York: Wiley, 1975.

Mandler, G., & Sarason, S. B. A study of anxiety and learning. *Journal of Abnormal and Social Psychology*, 1952, 47, 166–173.

Mann, L. On being a sore loser: How fans react to their team's failure. *Australian Journal of Psychology*, 1974, 26, 37–47.

Marler, P. On animal aggression. *American Psychologist*, 1975, 31, 239–246.

Marrow, A. J. Goal tensions and recall: I. *Journal of General Psychology*, 1938, 19, 3–35.

Marzocco, F. N. *Frustration effect as a function of drive level, habit strength and distribution of trials during extinction*. Unpublished doctoral dissertation, State University of Iowa, 1951.

Maslow, A. H. A theory of human motivation. *Psychological Review*, 1943, 50, 370–396.

Maslow, A. H. A theory of metamotivation: The biological rooting of the value-life. *Journal of Humanistic Psychology*, 1967, 7, 93–127.

Maslow, A. H. *The farther reaches of human nature.* New York: Viking Press, 1971.

Masters, W. H., & Johnson, V. E. *Human sexual response.* Boston: Little, Brown, & Co., 1966.

Masters, W. H., & Johnson, V. E. *Human sexual inadequacy.* Boston: Little, Brown, & Co., 1970.

Mathes, E. W., & Kahn, A. Physical attractiveness, happiness, neuroticism, and self-esteem. *Journal of Psychology,* 1975, *90,* 27–30.

Matlin, M. W., & Zajonc, R. B. Social facilitation of word associations. *Journal of Personality and Social Psychology,* 1968, 10, 455–460.

Mayer, H. H., Walker, W. B., & Litwin, G. H. Motive patterns and risk preference associated with entrepreneurship. *Journal of Abnormal and Social Psychology,* 1961, *63,* 570–574.

Mazis, M. B. Antipollution measures and psychological reactance theory: A field experiment. *Journal of Personality and Social Psychology,* 1975, *31,* 654–660.

McArthur, L. A. The how of what and why: Some determinants and consequences of causal attributions. *Journal of Personality and Social Psychology,,* 1972, *22,* 171–193.

McClelland, D. C. *Personality.* New York: William Sloane, 1951.

McClelland, D. C. Some social consequences of achievement motivation. In M. R. Jones (Ed.), *Nebraska symposium on motivation* (Vol. 3). Lincoln: University of Nebraska Press, 1955.

McClelland, D. C. Freud and Hull: Pioneers of scientific psychology. *American Scientist,* 1957, *45,* 101–113.

McClelland, D. C. Methods of measuring human motivation. In J. W. Atkinson (Ed.), *Motives in fantasy, action, and society.* Princeton, N.J.: Van Nostrand, 1958.

McClelland, D. C. *The achieving society.* Princeton, N.J.: Van Nostrand, 1961.

McClelland, D. C. Toward a theory of motive acquisition. *American Psychologist,* 1965, *20,* 321–333.

McClelland, D. C., Atkinson, J. W., Clark, R. W., & Lowell, E. L. *The achievement motive.* New York: Appleton-Century-Crofts, 1953.

McClelland, D. C., & Winter, D. G. *Motivating economic achievement.* New York: The Free Press, 1969.

McDougall, W. *Outline of psychology.* New York: Scribner, 1923.

McGinnies, E. Emotionality and perceptual defense. *Psychological Review,* 1949, *56,* 244–251.

McGuire, W. J. The current status of cognitive consistency theories. In S. Feldman (Ed.), *Cognitive consistency.* New York: Academic Press, 1966.

McGuire, W. J., & Padawer-Singer, A. Trait salience in the spontaneous self-concept. *Journal of Personality and Social Psychology,* 1973, *28,* 108–115.

McMahan, I. D. Relationships between causal attributions and expectancy of success. *Journal of Personality and Social Psychology,* 1973, *28,* 108–115.

Megargee, E. I. Undercontrolled and overcontrolled personality types in extreme antisocial aggression. *Psychological Monographs,* 1966, *80* (Whole No. 611).

Mehrabian, A. Measures of achieving tendency. *Educational and Psychological Measurement,* 1969, *29,* 445–451.

Meichenbaum, D., & Cameron, R. The clinical potential of modifying what clients say to themselves. In M. J. Mahoney & C. E. Thoresen (Eds.), *Self-control: Power to the person.* Monterey, Calif.: Brooks-Cole, 1974.

Merton, R. K. *Social theory and social structure.* Glencoe, Ill.: Free Press, 1957.

Meryman, J. J. *Magnitude of startle response as a function of hunger and fear.* Unpublished master's thesis, University of Iowa, 1952.

Meyer, J. P. *Dimensions of causal attribution for success and failure: A multivariate investigation.* Unpublished doctoral dissertation, University of Western Ontario, 1978.

Meyer, W. U. *Selbstverantwortlichkeit und Leistungsmotivation.* Unpublished doctoral dissertation, Ruhr Universität, Bochum, Germany, 1970.

Meyer, W. U., Folkes, V. S., & Weiner, B. The perceived informational value and affective consequences of choice behavior and intermediate difficulty task selection. *Journal of Research in Personality,* 1976, *10,* 410–423.

Michela, J. L., & Peplau, L. A. *Applying attributional models of achievement to social settings.* Paper presented at the Western Psychological Association Convention, Seattle, April 1977.

Michela, J. L., Peplau, L. A., & Weeks, D. Perceived dimensions and consequences of attributions for loneliness. Unpublished manuscript. University of California, Los Angeles, 1978.

Michotte, A. (1946) *The perception of causality.* New York: Basic Books, 1963.

Milgram, S. Behavioral study of obedience. *Journal of Abnormal and Social Psychology*,, 1963, *67*, 371–378.

Milgram, S. Group pressure and action against a person. *Journal of Abnormal and Social Psychology*, 1964, *69*, 137–143.

Milgram, S. Liberating effects of group pressure. *Journal of Personality and Social Psychology*, 1965, *1*, 127–134.

Milgram, S. *Obedience to authority*. New York: Harper & Row, 1974.

Miller, D. T., & Ross, M. Self-serving biases in the attribution of causality: Fact or fiction? *Psychological Bulletin*, 1975, *82*, 213–225.

Miller, I. W., III, & Norman, W. H. Learned helplessness: A review and attribution-theory model. *Psychological Bulletin*, 1979, *86*, 93–118.

Miller, N. E. The frustration-aggression hypothesis. *Psychological Review*, 1941, *48*, 337–342.

Miller, N. E. Experimental studies of conflict. In J. McV. Hunt (Ed.), *Personality and the behavioral disorders* (Vol. 1). New York: Ronald, 1944.

Miller, N. E. Studies of fear as an acquirable drive: I. Fear as motivation and fear-reduction as reinforcement in the learning of new responses. *Journal of Experimental Psychology*, 1948, *38*, 89–101.

Miller, N. E. Learnable drives and rewards. In S. S. Stevens (Ed.), *Handbook of experimental psychology*. New York: Wiley, 1951.

Miller, N. E. Liberalization of basic S-R concepts: Extensions to conflict behavior, motivation, and social learning. In S. Koch (Ed.), *Psychology: A study of a science* (Vol. 2). New York: McGraw-Hill, 1959.

Miller, N. E., & Bugelski, R. Minor studies of aggression. II. The influence of frustration imposed by the in-group on attitudes expressed toward out-groups. *Journal of Psychology*, 1948, *25*, 437–442.

Miller, W. R., & Seligman, M. E. P. Depression and learned helplessness in man. *Journal of Abnormal Psychology*, 1975, *84*, 228–238.

Mischel, W. Delay of gratification, need for achievement, and acquiescence in another culture. *Journal of Abnormal and Social Psychology*, 1961, *62*, 543–552.

Mischel, W. *Personality and assessment*. New York: Wiley, 1968.

Mischel, W. Continuity and change in personality. *American Psychologist*, 1969, *24*, 1012–1018.

Mischel, W. Toward a cognitive social learning reconceptualization of personality. *Psychological Review*, 1973, *80*, 252–283.

Mischel, W. Cognitive appraisals and transformations in self-control. In B. Weiner (Ed.), *Cognitive views of human motivation*. New York: Academic Press, 1974. (a)

Mischel, W. Processes in delay of gratification. In L. Berkowitz (Ed.), *Advances in experimental social psychology* (Vol. 7). New York: Academic Press, 1974. (b)

Mischel, W. *Introduction to personality* (2nd ed.). New York: Holt, Rinehart, & Winston, 1976.

Mischel, W., & Ebbesen, E. B. Attention in delay of gratification. *Journal of Personality and Social Psychology*, 1970, *16*, 329–337.

Mischel, W., Ebbesen, E. B., & Zeiss, A. Cognitive and attentional mechanisms in delay of gratification. *Journal of Personality and Social Psychology*, 1972, *21*, 204–218.

Monson, T. C., & Snyder, M. Actors, observers, and the attribution process: Toward a reconceptualization. *Journal of Experimental Social Psychology*, 1977, *13*, 89–111.

Monte, C. F. *Beneath the mask*. New York: Praeger, 1977.

Montgomery, K. C. A test of two explanations of spontaneous alternation. *Journal of Comparative and Physiological Psychology*, 1952, *45*, 287–293.

Morgan, C. T. *Physiological psychology*. New York: McGraw-Hill, 1943.

Morgan, H. H. Measuring achievement motivation with "picture interpretation." *Journal of Consulting Psychology*, 1953, *17*, 289–292.

Morin, S. F. Heterosexual bias in psychological research on lesbianism and male homosexuality. *American Psychologist*, 1977, *32*, 629–637.

Morris, J. L. Propensity for risk taking as a determinant of vocational choice: An extension of the theory of achievement motivation. *Journal of Personality and Social Psychology*, 1966, *3*, 328–335.

Morse, S., & Gergen, K. J. Social comparison, self-consistency, and the concept of self. *Journal of Personality and Social Psychology*, 1970, *16*, 148–156.

Moruzzi, G., & Magoun, H. W. Brainstem reticular formation and activation of the EEG. *Electroencephalography and Clinical Neurophysiology*, 1949, *1*, 455–473.

Mosher, D. L. The influence of Adler on Rotter's social learning theory of personality. *Journal of Individual Psychology*, 1968, *24*, 33–45.

Moss, F. A. Study of animal drives. *Journal of Experimental Psychology*, 1924, 7, 165–185.

Moss, H. A., & Kagan, J. Stability of achievement and recognition seeking behaviors from early childhood through adulthood. *Journal of Abnormal and Social Psychology*, 1961, 62, 504–513.

Moulton, R. W. Effects of success and failure on level of aspiration as related to achievement motives. *Journal of Personality and Social Psychology*, 1965, 1, 399–406.

Mowrer, O. H. *Learning theory and behavior*, New York: Wiley, 1960.

Mowrer, O. H., & Viek, P. An experimental analogue of fear from a sense of helplessness. *Journal of Abnormal and Social Psychology*, 1948, 43, 193–200.

Mukherjee, B. N., & Sinha, R. Achievement values and self-ideal discrepancies in college students. *Personality: An International Journal*, 1970, 1, 275–301.

Murray, E. J., & Berkun, M. M. Displacement as a function of conflict. *Journal of Abnormal and Social Psychology*, 1955, 51, 47–56.

Murray, H. A. *Explorations in personality*. New York: Oxford University Press, 1938.

Murray, H. A. Preparations for the scaffold of a comprehensive system. In S. Koch (Ed.), *Psychology: A study of a science* (Vol. 3). New York: McGraw-Hill, 1959.

Neisser, U. *Cognitive psychology*. New York: Appleton-Century-Crofts, 1966.

Newman, J. R. *Stimulus generalization of an instrumental response as a function of drive strength*. Unpublished doctoral dissertation. University of Illinois, 1955.

Nicholls, J. G. Effort is virtuous, but it's better to have ability: Evaluative responses to perceptions of effort and ability. *Journal of Research in Personality*, 1976, 10, 306–315.

Nickel, T. W. The attribution of intention as a critical factor in the relation between frustration and aggression. *Journal of Personality*, 1974, 42, 482–492.

Nisbett, R. E., & Schachter, S. Cognitive manipulation of pain. *Journal of Experimental Social Psychology*, 1966, 2, 227–236.

Nisbett, R. E., & Valins, S. *Perceiving the causes of one's own behavior*. Morristown, N.J.: General Learning Press, 1971.

Nissen, H. W. The nature of drive as innate determinant of behavioral organization. In M. R. Jones (Ed.), *Nebraska symposium on motivation*. Lincoln: University of Nebraska Press, 1954.

Nuttin, J. R. Pleasure and reward in motivation and learning. In D. Berlyne (Ed.), *Pleasure, reward, preference*. New York: Academic Press, 1973.

Orne, M. T. On the social psychology of the psychological experiment. *American Psychologist*, 1962, 17, 776–783.

Orvis, B. R., Cunningham, J. D., & Kelley, H. H. A closer examination of causal inference: The role of consensus, distinctiveness, and consistency information. *Journal of Personality and Social Psychology*, 1975, 32, 605–616.

Ostrove, N. Expectations for success on effort-determined tasks as a function of incentive and performance feedback. *Journal of Personality and Social Psychology*, 1978, 36, 909–916.

Ovsiankina, M. Die Wiederaufnahme unterbrochener Handlungen. *Psychologische Forschung*, 1928, 11, 302–379.

Pancer, S. M., & Eiser, J. R. *Expectations, aspirations, and evaluations as influenced by another's attributions for success and failure*. Paper presented at the meeting of the American Psychological Association, Chicago, September 1975.

Passer, M. W. *Perceiving the causes of success and failure revisited: A multidimensional scaling approach*. Unpublished doctoral dissertation, University of California, Los Angeles, 1977.

Pepitone, A. Motivational effects in social perception. *Human Relations*, 1950, 1, 57–76.

Peplau, L. A., Russell, D., & Heim, M. An attributional analysis of loneliness. In I. H. Frieze, D. Bar-Tal, & J. Carroll (Eds.), *Attribution theory: Applications to social problems*. New York: Jossey-Bass, in press.

Perin, C. T. Behavior potentiality as a joint function of the amount of training and the degree of hunger at the time of extinction. *Journal of Experimental Psychology*, 1942, 30, 93–113.

Phares, E. J. Expectancy changes in skill and chance situations. *Journal of Abnormal and Social Psychology*, 1957, 54, 339–342.

Phares, E. J. A social learning approach to psychopathology. In J. B. Rotter, J. E. Chance, & E. J. Phares (Eds.), *Applications of a social learning theory of personality*. New York: Holt, Rinehart, & Winston, 1972.

Phares, E. J. *Locus of control in personality*. Morristown, N.J.: General Learning Press, 1976.

Piliavin, I. M., Rodin, J., & Piliavin, J. A. Good Samaritanism: An underground phenomenon? *Journal of Personality and Social Psychology*, 1969, *13*, 289–299.

Plutchik, R. Emotions, evolution, and adaptive processes. In M. B. Arnold (Ed.), *Feelings and emotions*. New York: Academic Press, 1970.

Plutchik, R. Cognitions in service of emotions: An evolutionary perspective. In D. K. Candland, J. P. Fell, E. Kenn, A. I. Leshner, R. Plutchik, & R. M. Tarpy (Eds.), *Emotion*. Monterey, Calif.: Brooks-Cole, 1977.

Plutchik, R., & Ax, A. F. A critique of *Determinants of emotional state* by Schachter and Singer (1962). *Psychophysiology*, 1967, *4*, 79–82.

Rajecki, D. W., Kidd, R. F., Wilder, D. A., & Jaeger, J. Social factors in the facilitation of feeding in chickens: Effects of imitation, arousal, or disinhibition? *Journal of Personality and Social Psychology*, 1975, 32, 510–518.

Rapaport, D. *Emotions and memory*. Baltimore: Williams & Wilkins, 1942.

Rapaport, D. The structure of psychoanalytic theory. In S. Koch (Ed.), *Psychology: A study of a science* (Vol. 3). New York: McGraw-Hill, 1959.

Raynor, J. O. Relationships between achievement-related motives, future orientation, and academic performance. *Journal of Personality and Social Psychology*, 1970, *15*, 28–33.

Reitman, W. R., & Atkinson, J. W. Some methodological problems in the use of thematic apperceptive measures of human motives. In J. W. Atkinson (Ed.), *Motives in fantasy, action, and society*. Princeton, N.J.: Van Nostrand, 1958.

Rest, S., Nierenberg, R., Weiner, B., & Heckhausen, H. Further evidence concerning the effects of perceptions of effort and ability on achievement evaluation. *Journal of Personality and Social Psychology*, 1973, 28, 187–191.

Ricciuti, H. N. *The prediction of academic grades with a projective test of achievement motivation: I. Initial validation studies*. Princeton, N.J.: Educational Testing Service, 1954.

Richter, C. P. Animal behavior and internal drives. *Quarterly Review of Biology*, 1927, *2*, 307–343.

Richter, C. P. The phenomenon of unexplained sudden death in animals and man. In W. H. Gant (Ed.), *Physiological basis of psychiatry*. Springfield, Ill.: Charles C Thomas, 1958.

Robertson, D. R. Social control of sex reversal in a coral-reef fish. *Science*, 1972, 77, 1007–1009.

Rogers, C. R. A theory of therapy, personality, and interpersonal relationships, as developed in the client-centered framework. In S. Koch (Ed.), *Psychology: A study of a science* (Vol. 3). New York: McGraw-Hill, 1959.

Rogers, C. R. *On becoming a person*. Boston: Houghton Mifflin, 1961.

Rogers, C. R. Actualizing tendency in relation to "motives" and to consciousness. In M. R. Jones (Ed.), *Nebraska symposium on motivation*. Lincoln: University of Nebraska Press, 1963.

Rogers, C. R., & Dymond, R. F. (Eds.). *Psychotherapy and personality change*. Chicago: University of Chicago Press, 1954.

Rorer, L. G. The great response-style myth. *Psychological Bulletin*, 1965, *63*, 129–156.

Rosen, B., & D'Andrade, R. C. The psychosocial origins of achievement motivation. *Sociometry*, 1959, *22*, 185–218.

Rosenbaum, R. M. The effects of peak performance on estimates of ability. Unpublished manuscript. University of California, Los Angeles, 1971.

Rosenbaum, R. M. *A dimensional analysis of the perceived causes of success and failure*. Unpublished doctoral dissertation. University of California, Los Angeles, 1972.

Rosenberg, M. *Society and the adolescent self-image*. Princeton, N.J.: Princeton University Press, 1965.

Rosenstein, A. *The specificity of the achievement motive and the motivational effects of picture cues*. Unpublished doctoral dissertation, University of Michigan, 1952.

Rosenzweig, S. An experimental study of "repression" with special reference to need-persistive and ego-defensive reactions to frustration. *Journal of Experimental Psychology*, 1943, *32*, 64–74.

Ross, L., Bierbrauer, G., & Polly, S. Attribution of educational outcomes by professional and nonprofessional instructors. *Journal of Personality and Social Psychology*, 1974, *29*, 609–618.

Ross, L., Greene, D., & House, P. The "False Consensus Effect": An egocentric bias in social perception and attribution process. *Journal of Experimental Social Psychology*, 1977, *13*, 279–301.

Ross, L., Rodin, J., & Zimbardo, P. G. Toward an attribution therapy: The reduction of fear through induced cognitive-emotional misattribution. *Journal of Personality and Social Psychology*, 1969, *12*, 279–288.

Roth, S., & Kubal, L. The effects of noncontingent reinforcement on tasks of differing importance: Facilitation and learned helplessness. *Journal of Personality and Social Psychology*, 1975, *32*, 680–691.

Rotter, J. B. *Social learning and clinical psychology*. Englewood Cliffs, N. J.: Prentice-Hall, 1954.

Rotter, J. B. Generalized expectancies for internal versus external control of reinforcement. *Psychological Monographs*, 1966, *80* (1, Whole No. 609).

Rotter, J. B. Some problems and misconceptions related to the construct of internal vs. external control of reinforcement. *Journal of Consulting and Clinical Psychology*, 1975, *43*, 55–67.

Rotter, J. B., Chance, J. E., & Phares, E. J. An introduction to social learning theory. In J. B. Rotter, J. E. Chance, & E. J. Phares (Eds.), *Applications of a social learning theory of personality*. New York: Holt, Rinehart, & Winston, 1972.

Rotter, J. B., & Hochreich, D. J. *Personality*. Glenview, Ill.: Scott Foresman, 1975.

Rotter, J. B., Seeman, M., & Liverant, S. Internal versus external control of reinforcement: A major variable in behavior theory. In N. F. Washburne (Ed.), *Decisions, values, and groups* (Vol. 2). London: Pergamon, 1962.

Rowell, C. H. F. Displacement grooming in the chaffinch. *Animal Behaviour*, 1961, *9*, 38–63.

Salili, F., Maehr, M. L., & Gillmore, G. Achievement and morality: A cross-cultural analysis of causal attribution and evaluation. *Journal of Personality and Social Psychology*, 1976, *33*, 327–337.

Sanford, N. The approach of the authoritarian personality. In J. L. McCary (Ed.), *Psychology of personality: Six modern approaches*. New York: Logos, 1956.

Sanger, S. P., & Alker, H. A. Dimensions of internal-external locus of control and women's liberation. *Journal of Social Issues*, 1972, *28*, 115–130.

Sarbin, T. R. Contextualism: A world view for modern psychology. In J. K. Cole (Ed.), *Nebraska symposium on motivation*. Lincoln: University of Nebraska Press, 1976.

Schachter, S. The interaction of cognitive and physiological determinants of emotional state. In L. Berkowitz (Ed.), *Advances in experimental social psychology* (Vol. 1). New York: Academic Press, 1964.

Schachter, S., & Singer, J. E. Cognitive, social, and physiological determinants of emotional state. *Psychological Review*, 1962, *69*, 379–399.

Schachter, S., & Wheeler, L. Epinephrine, chlorpromazine, and amusement. *Journal of Abnormal and Social Psychology*, 1962, *65*, 121–128.

Schlosberg, H. Three dimensions of emotion. *Psychological Review*, 1954, *61*, 81–88.

Schneider, D. J. Implicit theory: A review. *Psychological Bulletin*, 1973, *79*, 294–309.

Schopler, J., & Matthews, M. The influence of perceived causal locus of partner's dependence on the use of interpersonal power. *Journal of Personality and Social Psychology*, 1965, *2*, 609–612.

Schultz, D. *Theories of personality*. Monterey, Calif.: Brooks-Cole, 1976.

Schütz, A. *Collected papers. I. The problem of social reality*. The Hague: Martinus Nijhoff, 1967.

Sears, R. R. *Success and failure: A study of motility*. New York: McGraw-Hill, 1942.

Sears, R. R., & Sears, P. S. Minor studies of aggression: V. Strength of frustration-reaction as a function of strength of drive. *Journal of Psychology*, 1940, *9*, 297–300.

Seeman, M. Alienation and social learning in a reformatory. *American Journal of Sociology*, 1963, *69*, 270–284.

Seeman, M., & Evans, J. W. Alienation and learning in a hospital setting. *American Sociological Review*, 1962, *27*, 772–783.

Seligman, M. E. P. *Helplessness: On depression, development, and death*. San Francisco: Freeman, 1975.

Seligman, M. E. P., & Maier, S. F. Failure to escape traumatic shock. *Journal of Experimental Psychology*, 1967, *74*, 1–9.

Selye, H. *The stress of life*. New York: McGraw-Hill, 1956.

Service, E. R. *The hunters*. Englewood Cliffs, N. J.: Prentice-Hall, 1966.

Shakow, D., & Rapaport, D. The influence of Freud on American psychology. *Psychological Issues*, 1964, No. 13.

Simon, H. A. *Models of man: Social and national*. New York: Wiley, 1957.

Singer, J. S. *Imagery and daydream methods in psychotherapy and behavior modification*. New York: Academic Press, 1974.

Skinner, B. F. The process involved in the repeated guessing of alternatives. *Journal of Experimental Psychology*, 1942, *30*, 495–503.

Skinner, B. F. *Beyond freedom and dignity*. New York: Alfred A. Knopf, 1971.

Slovic, P. From Shakespeare to Simon: Speculations and some evidence about man's ability to process information. *Research Bulletin of the Oregon Research Institute*, 1972, *12*, No. 2.

Smedslund, J. The concept of correlation in adults. *Scandinavian Journal of Psychology*, 1963, *4*, 165–173.

Smith, C. P. (Ed.). *Achievement-related motives in children*. New York: Russell Sage, 1969.

Solomon, R. L. Punishment. *American Psychologist*, 1964, *19*, 239–253.

Spence, K. W. *Behavior theory and conditioning*. New Haven, Conn.: Yale University Press, 1956.

Spence, K. W. The empirical basis and theoretical structure of psychology. *Philosophy of Science*, 1957, *24*, 97–108.

Spence, K. W. A theory of emotionally based drive (D) and its relation to performance in simple learning situations. *American Psychologist*, 1958, 13, 131–141. (a)

Spence, K. W. Behavior theory and selective learning. In M. R. Jones (Ed.), *Nebraska symposium on motivation*. Lincoln: University of Nebraska Press, 1958. (b).

Spence, K. W., Farber, I. E., & McFann, H. H. The relation of anxiety (drive) level of performance in competitional and non-competitional paired-associates learning. *Journal of Experimental Psychology*, 1956, *52*, 296–305.

Spence, K. W., & Taylor, J. A. Anxiety and strength of the US as a determinant of the amount of eyelid conditioning. *Journal of Experimental Psychology*, 1951, *42*, 183–188.

Spence, K. W., Taylor, J. A., & Ketchel, R. Anxiety (drive) level and degree of competition in paired-associates learning. *Journal of Experimental Psychology*, 1956, *52*, 306–310.

Stein, A. H., & Bailey, M. M. The socialization of achievement motivation in females. *Psychological Bulletin*, 1973, *80*, 345–366.

Steiner, I. D. Perceived freedom. In L. Berkowitz (Ed.), *Advances in experimental social psychology* (Vol. 5). New York: Academic Press, 1970.

Stephenson, W. *The study of behavior*. Chicago: University of Chicago Press, 1953.

Steuer, F. B., Applefield, J. M., & Smith, R. Televised aggression and the interpersonal aggression of preschool children. *Journal of Experimental Child Psychology*, 1971, *11*, 442–447.

Stevenson, H. W., & Zigler, E. Discrimination learning and rigidity in normal and feeble-minded individuals. *Journal of Personality*, 1957, *25*, 699–711.

Storms, M. D. Videotape and the attribution process: Reversing actors' and observers' points of view. *Journal of Personality and Social Psychology*, 1973, 27, 165–175.

Storms, M. D., & McCaul, K. D. Attribution processes and emotional exacerbation of dysfunctional behavior. In J. H. Harvey, W. J. Ickes, & R. F. Kidd (Eds.), *New directions in attribution research* (Vol. 1). Hillsdale, N.J.: Erlbaum Press, 1976.

Storms, M. D., & Nisbett, R. E. Insomnia and the attribution process. *Journal of Personality and Social Psychology*, 1970, *16*, 319–328.

Strickland, L. H. Surveillance and trust. *Journal of Personality*, 1958, *26*, 200–215.

Strodtbeck, F. L., McDonald, M. R., & Rosen, B. Evaluations of occupations: A reflection of Jewish and Italian mobility differences. *American Sociological Review*, 1957, 22, 546–553.

Stroop, J. R. Studies of interference in serial verbal reactions. *Journal of Experimental Psychology*, 1935, *18*, 643–661.

Tadeschi, J. T., Smith, R. B., III, & Brown, R. C., Jr. A reinterpretation of research on aggression. *Psychological Bulletin*,1974, *81*, 540–562.

Taylor, J. A. A personality scale of manifest anxiety. *Journal of Abnormal and Social Psychology*, 1953, *48*, 285–290.

Taylor, J. A., & Chapman, J. P. Anxiety and the learning of paired-associates. *American Journal of Psychology*, 1955, *68*, 671.

Tennen, H., & Eller, S. J. Attributional components of learned helplessness and facilitation. *Journal of Personality and Social Psychology*, 1977, *35*, 265–271.

Thibaut, J. W., & Kelley, H. H. *The social psychology of groups*. New York: Wiley, 1959.

Thorndike, E. L. *Animal intelligence*. New York: Macmillan, 1911.

Tinbergen, N. Derived activities: Their causation, biological significance, and origin and emancipation during evolution. *Quarterly Review of Biology*, 1952, *27*, 1–32.

Tinbergen, N. On war and peace in animals and man. *Science*, 1968, *160*, 1411–1418.

Tinbergen, N., & van Iersel, J. J. A. Displacement reactions in the three-spined stickle-back. *Behaviour*, 1947, *1*, 56–63.

Tolman, C. W. The feeding behavior of domestic chicks as a function of pecking by a surrogate companion. *Behaviour*, 1967, *29*, 57–62.

Tolman, C. W. The varieties of social stimulation in the feeding behaviour of domestic chicks. *Behaviour*, 1968, *30*, 275–286.

Tolman, E. C. Purpose and cognition: The determinants of animal learning. *Psychological Review*, 1925, *32*, 285–297.

Tolman, E. C. *Purposive behavior in animals and men.* New York: Appleton-Century-Crofts, 1932.

Tolman, E. C., & Honzig, C. H. Introduction and renewal of reward, and maze performance in rats. Berkeley: *University of California Publication in Psychology*, 1930, *4*, No. 19, 267.

Tomkins, S. Affect as the primary motivational system. In M. B. Arnold (Ed.), *Feelings and emotions.* New York: Academic Press, 1970.

Tresemer, D. Fear of success: Popular, but unproven. *Psychology Today*, 1974, *7*, 82–85.

Triandis, H. *The analysis of subjective culture.* New York: Wiley-Interscience, 1972.

Triplett, N. The dynamogenic factors in pacemaking and competition. *American Journal of Psychology*, 1897, *9*, 507–533.

Trope, Y. Seeking information about one's own ability as a determinant of choice among tasks. *Journal of Personality and Social Psychology*, 1975, *32*, 1004–1013.

Trope, Y., & Brickman, P. Difficulty and diagnosticity as determinants of choice among tasks. *Journal of Personality and Social Psychology*, 1975, *31*, 918–926.

Turner, E. R. A. Social feeding in birds. *Behaviour*, 1964, *24*, 1–47.

Tversky, A., & Kahneman, D. Judgment under uncertainty: Heuristics and biases. *Science*, 1974, *185*, 1124–1131.

Valins, S. Cognitive effects of false heart-rate feedback. *Journal of Personality and Social Psychology*, 1966, *4*, 400–408.

Valins, S. Persistent effects of information about internal reactions: Ineffectiveness of debriefing. In R. H. London & R. E. Nisbett (Eds.), *Thought and feeling.* Chicago: Aldine, 1974.

Valins, S., & Nisbett, R. E. *Some implications of the attribution processes for the development and treatment of emotional disorders.* Morristown, N.J.: General Learning Press, 1971.

Valle, F. P. *Motivation: Theories and issues.* Monterey, Calif.: Brooks-Cole, 1975.

Valle, V. A. *Attributions of stability as a mediator in the changing of expectations.* Unpublished doctoral dissertation, University of Pittsburgh, 1974.

Valle, V. A., & Frieze, I. H. Stability of causal attributions as a mediator in changing expectations for success. *Journal of Personality and Social Psychology*, 1976, *33*, 579–587.

Veroff, J. Development and validation of a projective measure of power motivation. *Journal of Abnormal and Social Psychology*, 1957, *54*, 1–8.

Veroff, J. Social comparison and the development of achievement motivation. In C. P. Smith (Ed.), *Achievement-related motives in children.* New York: Academic Press, 1976.

Volosinov, V. N. *Freudianism: A Marxist critique.* New York: Academic Press, 1976.

Wallach, M. A., & Leggett, M. I. Testing the hypothesis that a person will be consistent: Stylistic consistency versus situational specificity in the size of children's drawings. *Journal of Personality*, 1972, *40*, 309–330.

Washburn, S. L. Human behavior and the behavior of other animals. *American Psychologist*, 1978, *33*, 405–418.

Watson, J. S. The development and generalization of "contingency awareness" in early infancy: Some hypotheses. *Merrill-Palmer Quarterly*, 1966, *12*, 123–135.

Watson, J. S. Memory and "contingency analysis" in infant learning. *Merrill-Palmer Quarterly*, 1967, *12*, 55–76.

Watson, J. S., & Ramey, C. G. Reactions to response-contingent stimulation in early infancy. *Merrill Palmer Quarterly*, 1972, *18*, 219–228.

Watson, R. Investigation into deindividuation using a cross-cultural survey technique. *Journal of Personality and Social Psychology*, 1973, *25*, 342–345.

Webb, W. B. The motivational aspect of an irrelevant drive in the behavior of the white rat. *Journal of Experimental Psychology*, 1949, *39*, 1–14.

Weber, M. (1904) *The protestant ethic and the spirit of capitalism.* New York: Scribner's Sons, 1958.

Webster, M., Jr., & Sobieszek, B. *Sources of self-evaluation.* New York: Wiley-Interscience, 1974.

Wegner, D. M., & Ballacher, R. R. *Implicit psychology.* New York: Oxford Press, 1977.

Weiner, B. Effects of motivation on the availability and retrieval of memory traces. *Psychological Bulletin*, 1966, *65*, 24–37.

Weiner, B. New conceptions in the study of achievement motivation. In B. A. Maher (Ed.), *Progress in experimental personality research* (Vol. 5). New York: Academic Press, 1970.

Weiner, B. *Theories of motivation: From mechanism to cognition.* Chicago: Rand McNally, 1972.

Weiner, B. (Ed.). *Achievement motivation and attribution theory.* Morristown, N.J.: General Learning Press, 1974.

Weiner, B., Heckhausen, H., Meyer, W. U., & Cook, R. E. Causal ascriptions and achievement behavior: A conceptual analysis of effort and reanalysis of locus of control. *Journal of Personality and Social Psychology*, 1972, *21*, 239–248.

Weiner, B., & Kukla, A. An attributional analysis of achievement motivation. *Journal of Personality and Social Psychology*, 1970, *15*, 1–20.

Weiner, B., Nierenberg, R., & Goldstein, M. Social learning (locus of control) versus attributional (causal stability) interpretations of expectancy of success. *Journal of Personality*, 1976, *44*, 52–68.

Weiner, B., & Peter, N. A cognitive-developmental analysis of achievement and moral judgments. *Developmental Psychology*, 1973, *9*, 290–309.

Weiner, B., & Rosenbaum, R. M. Determinants of choice between achievement and nonachievement-related activities. *Journal of Experimental Research in Personality*, 1965, *1*, 114–122.

Weiner, B., Russell, D., & Lerman, D. Affective consequences of causal ascriptions. In J. H. Harvey, W. J. Ickes, & R. F. Kidd (Eds.), *New directions in attribution research* (Vol. 2). Hillsdale, N.J.: Erlbaum Press, 1978.

Weiner, B., Russell, D., & Lerman, D. The cognition-emotion process in achievement-related contexts. *Journal of Personality and Social Psychology* (in press).

Weiner, B., & Sierad, J. Misattribution for failure and enhancement of achievement strivings. *Journal of Personality and Social Psychology*, 1975, *31*, 415–421.

Weiss, R. F., & Miller, F. G. The drive theory of social facilitation. *Psychological Review*, 1971, *78*, 44–57.

Whalen, C. K., & Henker, B. Psychostimulants and children: A review and analysis. *Psychological Bulletin*, 1976, *83*, 1113–1130.

White, R. W. Motivation reconsidered: The concept of competence. *Psychological Review*, 1959, *66*, 297–333.

Whiteman, M. Children's conceptions of psychological causality. *Child Development*, 1967, *38*, 143–155.

Whiting, J. W. M. Sorcery, sin, and the superego: A cross-cultural study of some mechanisms of social control. In M. R. Jones (Ed.), *Nebraska symposium on motivation*. Lincoln: University of Nebraska Press, 1959.

Wicker, A. M. Undermanning, performances, and students' subjective experiences in behavioral settings of large and small high schools. *Journal of Personality and Social Psychology*, 1968, *10*, 255–261.

Wicklund, R. A., & Brehm, J. W. *Perspectives on cognitive dissonance.* Hillsdale, N.J.: Erlbaum Press, 1976.

Wiggins, J. S., Renner, K. E., Clore, G. L., & Rose, R. J. *The psychology of personality.* Reading, Mass.: Addison-Wesley, 1971.

Williams, S. B. Resistance to extinction as a function of the number of reinforcements. *Journal of Experimental Psychology*, 1938, *23*, 506–522.

Wimer, S. W., & Peplau, L. A. *Determinants of reactions to lonely others.* Paper presented at the Western Psychological Association Convention, San Francisco, April 1978.

Winter, D. G. *The power motive.* New York: Free Press, 1973.

Winterbottom, M. R. *The relation of childhood training in independence to achievement motivation.* Unpublished doctoral dissertation, University of Michigan, 1953.

Wolk, S., & DuCette, J. Intentional performance and incidental learning as a function of personality and task dimensions. *Journal of Personality and Social Psychology*, 1974, *29*, 90–101.

Woodworth, R. S. *Dynamic psychology.* New York: Columbia University Press, 1918.

Wortman, C. B. Some determinants of perceived control. *Journal of Personality and Social Psychology*, 1975, *31*, 282–294.

Wortman, C. B., & Brehm, J. W. Responses to uncontrollable outcomes: An integration of reactance theory and the learned helplessness model. In L. Berkowitz (Ed.), *Advances in experimental social psychology* (Vol. 8). New York: Academic Press, 1975.

Wylie, R. C. *The self concept: A critical survey of pertinent research literature.* Lincoln: University of Nebraska Press, 1961.

Wylie, R. C. The present status of self theory. In E. F. Borgatta & W. W. Lambert (Eds.), *Handbook of personality theory and research.* Chicago: Rand McNally, 1968.

Wylie, R. C. *The self-concept: A review of methodological considerations and measuring instruments* (Vol. 1). Lincoln: University of Nebraska Press, 1974.

Yates, A. B. *Frustration and conflict.* London: Methuen, 1962.

Yerkes, R. M., & Dodson, J. D. The relation of strength of stimulus to rapidity of habit-formation. *Journal of Comparative Neurology and Psychology, 1908, 18,* 459–482.

Young, P. T. *Emotion in man and animal.* New York: Wiley, 1943.

Zajonc, R. B. Social facilitation. *Science,* 1965, *149,* 269–274.

Zajonc, R. B. Cognitive theories in social psychology. In G. Lindzey & E. Aronson (Eds.), *Handbook of social psychology* (Vol. 1, 2nd ed.). Reading, Mass.: Addison Wesley, 1968.

Zajonc, R. B., & Brickman, P. Expectancy and feedback as independent factors in task performance. *Journal of Personality and Social Psychology,* 1969, *11,* 143–156.

Zajonc, R. B., & Sales, S. M. Social facilitation of dominant and subordinate responses. *Journal of Experimental Social Psychology,* 1966, *2,* 160–168.

Zamansky, H. S. An investigation of the psychoanalytic theory of paranoid delusions. *Journal of Personality,* 1958, *26,* 410–425.

Zander, A., Fuller, R., & Armstrong, W. Attributed pride or shame in group and self. *Journal of Personality and Social Psychology,* 1972, *23,* 346–352.

Zanna, M. P., & Cooper, J. Dissonance and the pill: An attribution approach to studying the arousal properties of dissonance. *Journal of Personality and Social Psychology,* 1974, *29,* 703–709.

Zanna, M. P., & Cooper, J. Dissonance and the attribution process. In J. H. Harvey, W. J. Ickes, & R. F. Kidd (Eds.), *New directions in attribution research* (Vol. 1). Hillsdale, N.J.: Erlbaum Press, 1976.

Zeigarnik, B. Über das Behalten von erledigten und unerledigten Handlungen. *Psychologische Forschung,* 1927, *9,* 1–85.

Zeigler, H. P. Displacement activity and motivational theory: A case study in the history of ethology. *Psychological Bulletin,* 1964, *61,* 362–376.

Zigler, E. Rigidity in the feebleminded. In E. P. Trapp & P. Himmelstein (Eds.), *Readings in the exceptional child.* New York: Appleton-Century-Crofts, 1962.

Zigler, E., & Yospe, L. Perceptual defense and the problem of response suppression. *Journal of Personality,* 1960, *28,* 220–239.

Zimbardo, P. G. The human choice: Individuation, reason, and order versus deindividuation, impulse, and chaos. In W. D. Arnold & D. Levine (Eds.), *Nebraska symposium on motivation.* Lincoln: University of Nebraska Press, 1969 (a)

Zimbardo, P. G. *The cognitive control of motivation.* Glenview, Ill.: Scott, Foresman, 1969. (b)

AUTHOR INDEX

SUBJECT INDEX